GUN VIOLENCE IN AMERICA

DISCARD

GUN VIOLENCE IN AMERICA

The Struggle for Control

Alexander DeConde

With a new epilogue

Northeastern University Press
Boston

Northeastern University Press

Library of Congress Cataloging-in-Publication Data

DeConde, Alexander
    Gun violence in America : the struggle for control / Alexander DeConde.
        p. cm.
    Includes bibliographical references and index.
    ISBN 1–55553–486–4 (cloth : alk. paper)—ISBN 1–55553–592–5 (pbk. : alk. paper)
        1. Gun control—United States. 2. Violent crimes—United States. 3. Firearms ownership—United States. 4. United States—Politics and government. I. Title.

HV7436.D43 2001
363.3'3'0973—dc21   00–054821

Designed by Janis Owens

Composed in Electra by Coghill Composition Company in Richmond, Virginia. Printed and bound by The Maple Press Company in York, Pennsylvania. The paper is Sebago Antique, an acid-free sheet.

Manufactured in the United States of America
05 04 03   5 4 3 2 1

Contents

Introduction   3

1   Origins and Precedents   7
2   The Colonial Record   17
3   To the Second Amendment   27
4   Militias, Duels, and Gun Keeping   39
5   A Gun Culture Emerges   53
6   Reconstruction, Cheap Guns, and the Wild West   71
7   The National Rifle Association   89
8   Urban Control Movements   105
9   Gun-Roaring Twenties   119
10 Direct Federal Controls   137
11 Guns Flourish, Opposition Rises   155
12 Control Act of 1968   171
13 Control Groups on the Rise   189
14 Gun Lobby Glory Years   203
15 A Wholly Owned NRA Subsidiary?   219
16 The Struggle Nationalized   235
17 The Brady Act   249
18 School Shootings and Gun Shows   265
19 Clinton v. the NRA   281
20 Summing Up   299

Epilogue   311
Notes   325
Bibliography   357
Index   395

GUN VIOLENCE IN AMERICA

Introduction

E xcept possibly for abortion, no social issue of recent decades has produced more distorted data and contention among Americans than has the struggle to control gun violence. The controversy stems in part from myths entangling the history of gun keeping, one of the most prominent being that Americans have a special intimacy with firearms going back over three hundred years. Believers in this intimate relationship cite comments such as those of a visiting Englishman in 1774 to support it. "There is not a Man born in America that does not Understand the Use of Firearms and that well," he wrote. A gun "is Almost the First thing they Purchase and take to all the New Settlements and in the Cities you can scarcely find a Lad of 12 years that does not go a Gunning."[1]

Other writers perceive such depiction as part of "a long and, in many cases, glorious tradition of gun ownership and gun use." They represent this inheritance as having developed from the customs of a uniquely "gun minded" people who handled firearms "in a very American way."[2]

Conventional theory holds that this attitude toward the possession of firearms began with English colonists. Supposedly they loved guns so much that when they created their own nation and established a second constitution they guarded the right to own guns with fundamental law. That legal protection laid the basis for Americans equating the right to own guns with a rough-and-ready, self-reliant patriotism. "How wonderful to be a nation of gun lovers!" one defender of private gun-keeping explained later as a sentiment of many, where "there is no right more inherent to an American than the right to own a gun."[3]

Available statistics tell us that in exercising this alleged right Americans have used guns, particularly in the twentieth century, "more often to assault, maim, and kill one another" than have most other peoples in the world. In the 1990s, for instance, Americans killed more people with guns in a typical week than did western Europeans in a whole year.[4] This record stands out because peoples in other technologically advanced countries have not had, and do not have, homicide rates connected to shooting as high as those of Americans. Nor have those countries allowed their citizens to possess firearms with a freedom comparable to that tolerated in the United States.[5]

Richard Hofstadter, one of the first historians to assess this heritage, portrayed the United States as "the only nation so attached to the supposed 'right' to bear arms that its laws abet assassins, professional criminals, berserk murderers, and political terrorists at the expense of the orderly population." It is "the most passive of all major countries in the matter of gun control."[6]

Spokespeople for those who cherished shooting immediately disputed these generalizations, countering that firearms in private hands had been and continued to be beneficial to society. They praised the idea of the nation in arms, a conception a number of Athenian, Florentine, Swiss, French, and English thinkers long ago embraced as an antidote to tyranny from above. The many Americans who perceived the arming of a people with their own weapons as a virtue built a folklore about the social value of firearms and embedded that idea in history books and popular literature. This imaginative rendering of the past portrayed pioneers as building the nation with gun in hand. This version of the past carried the message that ownership of guns had been and should continue to be an essential element of American life.

This glorified perspective of civilian gun-keeping had significant social consequences. It offered an appealing reason why private citizens should have easy access to firearms. Various researchers have viewed this exalting negatively, or as an important piece of the puzzle of why Americans have a unique record for tolerating gun violence. The popularity of guns often intimidated those who deplored their lethal use and wished to curb it. Nonetheless, even in the early Republic among those who disliked private gun-keeping a few spoke out. As the country expanded westward, became urbanized and industrialized, and small firearms became increasingly numerous and deadly, critics rose in number and increasingly challenged the alleged virtues of keeping firearms. What values, they asked, did unfettered civilian gun-toting bring to society? How valid was the assumed legal right of enthusiasts to use firearms as they pleased? Gun keepers had their own answers or joined associations that provided answers for them. They funded an effective lobby dedicated to protecting their interests.

Later, the dispersed critics of the gun culture who felt deep concern over its proliferating casualties organized local groups that advocated restraints on the possession of firearms. This citizenry became the nucleus of an amorphous gun-control movement that lobbied for federal, state, and municipal regulation of personal firearms. As the politicking over gun rights intensified, it aroused emotions cutting across divisions of class, ethnicity, race, and religion. Clashes between pro- and antigun advocates produced rancorous debate, or what some writers call the great American gun war. Protagonists battled in print, on radio and television, and in local, state, and national politics to advance their causes. They also generated an extensive literature recognized widely as "tainted by obvious bias."[7]

Even the works of scholars who researched firearms use reflected partisan emotion. As a rule, control advocates wanted to restrict private gun-keeping but not abolish it. Firearms advocates who opposed virtually any form of control argued that regulation would not reduce gun violence. In the words of social critic and historian Garry Wills, an "industrious band of lawyers, historians, and criminologists . . . created a vast outpouring of articles [and books] justifying individual gun ownership on the basis of the Second Amendment." They contended that their version of history created the "Standard Model for interpreting the Second Amendment."[8]

Dedicated control advocates dismissed this gun-keeper version of constitutional history as flimsy or the work of National Rifle Association hacks. But the books and articles of progun lawyers, criminologists, and historians form an important part of the debate over the proper means of stemming gun violence. This struggle to control the private possession of firearms with federal legislation became significant in the twentieth century but it had roots in the more distant past.

A number of fine scholarly articles, such as those of Michael A. Bellesiles, treat the pertinent colonial and nineteenth-century past of gun keeping in depth and have enriched my understanding of the problem. I regret that in my researches I was unable to make full use of his fine, well-documented book, *Arming America* (New York, 2000). It was published shortly after my manuscript went to press. So far, however, only one book, *The Gun in America* (1975), has attempted to cover the whole of what its authors, Lee Kennett and James L. Anderson, called at the time a largely unexplored field of historical inquiry. That pioneering account, which has become an invaluable source for those who enter the field, concentrates on firearms as part of American culture and an important tool in the national experience. Although this history also deals with that experience, it goes beyond the previous work and differs from it. It focuses on gun violence in America and the struggle to control it rather than on the place of the weapon itself in the nation's history.

This synthesis, based on an array of primary sources, such as government documents, and an extensive secondary literature, analyzes the politics of gun keeping, assesses conflicting interpretations in the historiography of firearms in civilian use, and explores controversies over their use. It traces the rise of the gun-control movement, examines the role of federal police power versus states' rights and local police authority in the control struggle, and recounts the clashes between the two most prominent special-interest groups over the proper means of controlling gun violence. It scrutinizes the militia as an institution and popular resistance to conscription because of their connections with gun keeping.

This study also devotes considerable attention to crime and policing because both sides of the control issue have concentrated, and still concentrate, on the criminal aspect of firearms use. Each side interprets felony statistics to support its stance. Furthermore, crime has much to do with the rise of the gun-control movement and has dominated the debate on gun violence. This work views crime as important but only as part of the reason why societies feel the need to contain civilian gun-keeping.

Unlike conventional accounts, this work questions the perspective that gun controls in the United States, as well as in England and elsewhere, "are a relatively new innovation."[9] It demonstrates that from the time firearms became reasonably reliable personal weapons, local authorities attempted with various restraints to keep them out of the hands of the wrong people. It also challenges the assumption that from the beginning Americans have had such an affinity for gun keeping it became an ingrained, even untouchable, element in the nation's culture. This postulate flourishes in conjunction with the wider idea of exceptionalism, or that the United States has a history marked by unusual virtues and successes, among them gun keeping.

This account questions as well the linking of Americans' exceptional use of guns with virtue, noting the considerable data on the downside of gun keeping. Casualties from firearms violence among Americans have always been and remain extraordinarily high.[10] With striking consistency surveys show that 70 percent of the people involved in homicides use guns and that these shooters account for the majority of all killings. Why, therefore, with all its wealth and power, has the United States failed time and again to establish a legal structure that would confine gun violence within bounds at least comparable to those of other advanced democratic countries? What follows addresses that problem.

1
Origins and Precedents

From the time humans fashioned reasonably sophisticated weapons, they have been fascinated by arms. They equated weapons with power. Those who governed arms-bearing communities attempted to control the dissemination of weapons, usually to keep the weapons out of the hands of those they regarded as enemies. Because men customarily kept the weapons, most societies identified them with virility. This male connection continued with changes in weaponry, as after European and Chinese craftsmen in the thirteenth century constructed crude projectiles, or cannons, fired with confined powder.

Around 1338 European artisans—Italian, Netherlander, and French—created combustible weapons light enough for an individual to carry. Europeans called them hand cannons or fire sticks. Although produced as weapons of war, these early firearms proved so cumbersome and dangerous to the shooter that few soldiers could use them. Improvements came slowly. With the development of the matchlock around 1424 European gunmakers fashioned a portable arm-length firearm as well as one designed for one hand that individuals could carry. These guns were awkward because the shooter had to ignite the gunpowder with an ember before he could fire. Even so, Spanish troops armed with the matchlock arquebus replaced the English bowmen as Europe's most powerful infantry.

Another significant change followed approximately in 1433 when Leonardo da Vinci invented the wheel lock, a metal mechanism attached to the gun that with the pull of a trigger supplied a spark for the gunpowder. The early wheel locks were expensive, difficult to maintain, and dangerous to use. In time, though, as their quality improved, they gained recognition as killing tools comparable to, or more efficient than, swords, pikes, or bows with arrows.

Men who gained access to these guns usually transferred to them their fixa-

7

tion with arms. Among the few educated observers of weaponry in the fifteenth century whose views we have, a number described the new firearms as abominable. As the English historian Polydore Virgil put it in 1499, "of all other weapons that were devised to the destruction of man, the gones be most devilische." Old-fashioned soldiers also lamented the killing power of the primitive guns of their time. "Would to God that this unhappy weapon had never been devised," one French warrior, Blaise de Montluc, declared early in the sixteenth century, "and that so many brave and valiant men had never died by the hands of those . . . who would not dare to look in the face of those whom they lay low with their wretched bullets. They are tools invented by the devil to make it easier to kill each other."[1]

Distant contemporaries of this soldier, such as the rulers of Egypt's Mamluk military society, expressed similar sentiment toward existing firearms. "God curse the man who invented them," one chronicler wrote, "and God curse the man who fires on Muslims with them." To their detriment, the Mamluks refused to adopt firearms "because of the unchivalrous and immoral character of the weapon."[2]

Elsewhere, as in France and England, feudal lords strove to control the dissemination of military arms of any kind among civilians because possession of a deadly weapon was presumed to be intent to inflict great bodily harm.[3] We do not possess reliable statistics on how effective these efforts were, but, along with the high cost, they appear to have kept weaponry out of the hands of most of the lower classes. When small firearms acquired reasonable reliability, authorities attempted to impose similar restrictions on their use, seemingly with comparable success. Western rulers could not, however, prevent guns from traveling to distant lands. In the sixteenth century, in the hands of Spanish, Portuguese, French, and English explorers, firearms spread overseas.

During the conquest of the Americas, craftsmen in Europe invented or improved existing models of flintlock muskets, pistols, breech-loading guns, and revolvers. For years, though, these technical improvements found little practical use. The early rifles and carbines that loaded at the breech were more complicated than muzzle-loaders, and they were heavy, liable to burst and injure the shooter, and difficult to keep dry and clean. Most shooters relied on muzzle-loading muskets. Despite the problems of firing and maintaining these firearms, various writers tell us that civilians gained access to some of them and that they became the weapons of choice for "highway and other brigands."[4] For this and other reasons, authorities in societies that produced small arms tried to control their manufacture, or at least to restrict their ownership to the aristocracy.

Already, political thinkers such as Niccolò Machiavelli, writing between 1513 and 1521, deplored efforts to limit possession of arms to professional soldiers whom he regarded as "servants of tyranny." He preferred a "citizen army" made up of soldiers from their own country. "Weapons borne by citizens or subjects, given by laws and well regulated, never do damage," he contended. "On the contrary they are always an advantage" and the best defense against external danger and internal oppression.[5]

Monarchs, though, disliked the idea of an armed citizenry even as protection for the state. In 1541 England's Henry VIII, for one, tried to check the enthusiasm of "divers gentlemen, yeomen, and serving men" for firearms, especially to use for criminal purposes. In a codified form of discriminatory gun control based on class, he limited the free use of firearms to noblemen and to commoners who had an annual income of at least one hundred pounds. Across the Channel on July 16, 1546, Francis I of France "prohibited all men, including the nobility, from carrying firearms under the severe penalty of immediate confiscation of said arms and death by strangulation."[6] Seven years later, England's Edward VI commanded "all persons who shoot guns" to register their names with local justices of the peace.[7]

In 1561 in France, royal officials ordered all Parisians who owned firearms to turn them in to the city hall within twenty-four hours of receiving the notice.[8] In August 1598, Henry IV decreed "the carrying of firearms punishable by death if the violator was not an aristocrat, prison and a fine if he was an aristocrat, and death if the nobleman was a recidivist."[9] Rulers who followed Henry mandated other selective regulations that also carried a death penalty for those who bore firearms without government authorization.

In imposing these restrictions on their subjects, centralizing monarchs acted on the theory that all power in the state must rest with them. They feared that civilians with guns would challenge their authority and that of the state they embodied. Wherever possible, government exercised its power to disarm citizen groups that its leaders considered dangerous to the peace of the realm. Despite the legal constraints placed on the keeping of firearms in both England and France, some civilians managed illegally to possess them.

Europeans also evaded export controls on firearms. For example, in 1543 three Portuguese seafarers brought matchlock muskets to Japan, where these weapons entranced the warrior class. Soon, with Western help, Japanese craftsmen copied the guns, producing by 1556 more than three hundred thousand of them. Students of the problem testify that the quantity of muskets in Japan's armies came to exceed those in any contemporary European country.

Thirty-one years later, Toyotomi Hideyoshi, Japan's major political unifier, "took the first step toward the control of firearms."[10] He disarmed soldier-monks and peasants and, as had European rulers, restricted the bearing of arms to the military aristocracy. He used firearms to defeat Korean and Chinese enemies. In 1598 a Japanese commander, Asano Yoshinaga, boasted, "I have killed a large number of [enemy] soldiers because I have used guns."[11]

Even though firearms had become a feature of Japanese warfare, many aristocrats preferred their swords to the cumbersome matchlocks. Early in the next century, when dictatorial Tokugawa shoguns through force isolated Japan from much of the world, they also ended that country's first experimentation with guns. For the next two and a half centuries, Japan remained cut off from access to the major improvements in the destructive force of firearms.

Meanwhile, efforts in Europe to exercise some form of control over guns expanded in correlation with their availability. French and English princes often relied on militia equipped with firearms to maintain order and fight wars. In England, the obligation of free men, according to income, to serve the realm with their own arms went back to the Anglo-Saxon fyrd and to Henry II's Assize of Arms in 1181, a practice monarchs relied upon especially in emergencies.[12]

With the rise of the nation-state and the increasing use of professional soldiers, monarchs sought to escape this dependency on part-time citizen-soldiers by replacing militias with standing armies loyal to the Crown. As much as monarchs on the continent, English kings desired armies bound to the sovereign, but they developed full-time soldiers, made use of improved firearms, and exerted control over guns, more slowly, for instance, than did French monarchs. By 1630 French gunsmiths had perfected the flintlock musket, but for years it remained too expensive for extensive use. It gained wide acceptance thirty years later when Louis XIV equipped his army with it. Soon, the English Crown and others adopted it in place of the wheel lock.

As a rule, England's monarch and Parliament expended more money on ships than on soldiers and small arms because they valued fleets over armies. Nonetheless, monarchs strove to reduce their reliance on militias because they dreaded having subjects who owned firearms that could be used in crime or against the government. Parliament, on the other hand, wished to retain the militias because it disliked standing armies with a virtual monopoly over the use of firearms, subject only to orders from the Crown. Unless faced with foreign war, Parliament refused to vote funds for a professional military force of substantial size.

At times, English monarchs tried to overcome this restraint on their exercise of power by revamping the militia. Instead of drawing on the population at large to conscript citizen-soldiers, they enrolled a select number of men, usually owners of property who could pay the costs of their arms and equipment. Out of self-interest, these propertied gun-owners usually sided with the Crown to maintain order. The government mustered them frequently and trained them carefully. Even so, when Charles I, in his quarrels with Parliament, tried with various tactics—including the use of select militiamen—to build his own army, he failed. He could not overcome widespread sentiment against a standing army.

In March 1642, over Charles's opposition, Parliament passed the Militia Ordinance, which allowed it to assume critical control over militias without royal consent. Three years later, to win the civil war that had followed, Oliver Cromwell, the pious Protestant general with his New Model Army, created England's first standing army. After Charles's execution in January 1649, the role of the army and control over gun keeping nevertheless remained contentious. With the title of Lord Protector, Cromwell ruled the succeeding Commonwealth virtually as a dictator through the power of his disciplined, professional troops. As students of the problem have noted, "Men of every political persuasion expressed fear and dislike of the New Model Army and the major-generals."[13]

Cromwell viewed most Catholics as enemies of the state who should not have access to guns. In 1655, therefore, he ordered militia officers, acting as constables, to disarm "all Papists who declare against the present Government." Despite this use of force to protect the privileges of the more numerous Protestants, he could never make his army popular even with them. Among others, political philosopher James Harrington called Cromwell "a Usurper" and denounced his army. As an antidote, Harrington latched onto Machiavelli's idea of armed citizens as defenders of liberty and applied it to his utopian vision of a classical republic for England. From this time onward, much of the English citizenry opposed virtually any kind of compulsory military service with its requirement to bear arms.

After Cromwell's death, Charles II continued the practice of promoting selective ownership of firearms. In 1661, with the intent of preventing "any design of Traitorous and factious persons" from forming, he prohibited the importation of firearms or parts for them. In this way the Crown exercised control over the distribution of guns while its military constabulary kept malcontents under surveillance. Overall, the Crown diminished the capacity of the civilian population to take up arms. Its actions, along with the decline of the compulsory militia, contributed to a reduction in personal firearms among commoners who could afford them and in the number of men proficient in their use.[14]

Parliament went along with the Crown's disarming campaign, passing in the next year a second militia act. It empowered militia officers at their discretion "to search for and seize all arms in the custody or possession of any person or persons" who authorities "shall judge dangerous to the peace of the kingdom." Private gun-keepers and other aroused citizens protested this renewed use of select militia as constables. "Although the country was infested by predatory bands," one gun owner grumbled, "a Protestant gentleman could scarcely obtain permission to keep a brace of pistols."[15]

All along, medieval and Renaissance philosophers and other savants marveled at the destructive power of guns and gunpowder. Some praised the weapons as beneficial to humanity. For example, in 1665 a French virtuoso in arts and sciences commented on the place of the firearm in moral thought, military art, and progress in mechanical devices. He stated that "since the gun is without dispute the goodliest part of the Mechanicks, it follows that the gun and its Invention is the goodliest thing of the World."[16] As we have noted, many thinkers disputed such judgment.

England's upper classes, however, valued guns so much that in 1670 their representatives in Parliament enacted another law restricting their ownership. For commoners who desired firearms, legislators raised the required annual income for ownership to 150 pounds, a hefty sum at that time. Meanwhile, the government framed more measures regulating the use of firearms, the most notable being the game act of the following year that Parliament passed unanimously.

The statute followed the long-established practice in England, France, and Italy of upholding the prerogative of the nobility and men of substance to hunt.[17] This class legislation not only sought to keep commoners from destroying game, but also deprived them, whether Protestant or Catholic, of the privilege of owning firearms. It permitted gamekeepers to search their homes for guns and other prohibited weapons. Under this statute, the possession of a firearm indicated an intent to poach. The law provided the gentry with discretionary means to disarm and punish those they regarded as the wrong people and thereby with the power to maintain their kind of law and order. Critics contended that the game laws, in conjunction with other legislation, had as an important goal the disarming of a populace that by hook or crook had acquired firearms.[18] Later, though, the summary seizure of guns became rare.

Confiscation of firearms in Catholic hands continued, especially in autumn 1678, when people panicked following allegations of a "popish plot" to murder the king and massacre Protestants. They turned violently on Catholics. Throughout the country, militiamen acting as vigilantes ransacked Catholic homes in search of firearms. In addition, to keep them out of reach of Catholics and other wrong people, the government rigorously enforced regulations on the production, trade, and ownership of small arms.

Seven years later, after antipapal sentiment to some extent had abated, James II, a Catholic, came to the throne. As had other kings, he disparaged the compulsory militia as inefficient, ill trained, expensive, and of questionable loyalty to the Crown. He neglected it while enlarging the army. He claimed, "there is nothing but a good force of well disciplined troops in constant pay that can defend us from such, as either at home or abroad, are disposed to disturb us."[19]

This strategy alarmed the landed gentry, which regarded the king's armed force, composed predominantly of Protestants but with a large number of Catholic officers, as a standing army they detested. The gentry also feared he would use his troops to destroy the Protestant militias that as a rule they controlled. For this and other reasons, such as the Crown's granting freedom of worship to Catholics, seven eminent Protestant opponents secretly invited William of Orange, the stadtholder of the Netherlands and a staunch Protestant, to invade England. William accepted. In November 1688 when his army landed, both James's army and the militia deserted. In this Glorious Revolution, wherein soldiers used improved flintlock muskets, Parliament dethroned him.

In February of the next year Parliament obliged William, who had become king, and his queen, Mary, to accept a declaration of rights. In December 1689, with slight changes, Parliament gave the declaration statutory force and the king signed it into law as the Bill of Rights. In this final form, the bill forbade the Crown from "keeping a standing army within the kingdom in time of peace, unless it be with consent of parliament." It also granted Protestants the liberty of having firearms "for their defence suitable to their conditions and as allowed by law"—a first-time, nationwide, legal recognition of this privilege.[20]

At least one analyst interpreted the bill as converting a "customary duty into a right" rather than a privilege. She claimed that this right of citizens to be armed on their own for self-defense, resistance, and preservation, as stated by jurist William Blackstone, became part of English common law. As such, government and immigrants brought this right to the colonies in North America. Later the colonists there passed it on to the American nation they formed.[21]

Most other analysts maintain that by restricting the possession of arms to individuals who met qualifications based on class, who owned a stipulated amount of property, and who belonged to the proper religious faith, the Bill of Rights reinforced traditional selective gun control for the benefit of the right people. Shortly after the bill became law, Parliament voted to disarm Catholics, declaring they had no right to possess weapons. It thereby denied gun ownership by law selectively on a collective rather than an individual basis.[22]

At the same time, Parliament, as well as the Crown, recognized the superiority of a trained, paid army over a self-armed but poorly disciplined citizenry. Still, the Protestant legislators continued to praise local militias and to provide for them because they were popular. Furthermore, the militias, whether compulsory or volunteer, proved serviceable to the new government, which feared the Catholics of occupied Ireland. It used the Protestant, English citizen-soldiers against the Irish.

Even more than Catholics in England, those in Ireland rallied around the deposed James II in his bid to regain the throne. On July 1, 1690, William defeated James's army at the battle of the Boyne but the Irish continued a bitter resistance. Five years later, therefore, Ireland's English-dominated Parliament passed an act "for the Better Security of the Government, by Disarming the Papists." It required Ireland's Catholics to surrender all "arms, armour, and munitions" under the threat of severe penalties.[23] Other prohibitions followed.

In the next decade, most European rulers placed restrictions of more or less comparable severity on the wrong kind of people who might seek to possess guns. Monarchs disarmed or abandoned remaining militias and equipped their professional armies with up-to-date firearms. French kings, for instance, created a well-drilled army based on long-term enlistments. As technology improved the lethality and reliability of guns, authorities became more exacting in their efforts to prohibit the lower classes from obtaining them.

At times, governments even tried to disarm nobles, especially troublesome ones, but failed. Bourbon monarchs acted on the principle that would later become commonplace—the state could protect its subjects better than they could defend themselves. The monarchy controlled all parts of the arms industry and imposed regulations that spelled out who could or could not possess firearms.

Neither English theory nor government practice stretched as far as French practice, largely because of the people's continuing dread of standing armies. Englishmen of substance who expressed themselves openly argued, in the words of John Trenchard, that standing armies "are the instruments of Tyranny and their Country's ruin." Such misery, he added, could be avoided "by making the Militia to consist of the same Persons as have the property."[24] This linking of liberty, property, and select militias would have a long life in both England and America.

The English monarchy functioned in line with these principles, especially after 1707 when it extended legislation regulating the possession of firearms. It placed ownership restraints not only on political and religious dissidents but also on the lower classes regardless of faith or politics. For instance, in 1752 aristocrats who loved hunting as sport formed the Society of Noblemen and Gentlemen for the Preservation of Game. It defined sporting privileges, which included shooting, and promoted a tough enforcement of laws designed to protect the pleasures of sportsmen.[25]

In all, with laws directed against poachers and other wrong people, English gun restraints approximated those of France through much of the eighteenth century. Other European states also imposed regulations dictating who could or could not legally bear firearms. For these reasons and because firearms were scarce, costly, and had little value for ordinary people, most Europeans in the eighteenth century did not associate gun keeping with personal liberties or venerate it as part of their heritage.

2
The Colonial Record

C onventional lore tells us that English colonists brought with them to North America an established personal right to possess firearms. Accordingly, along with basic furnishings in their households they included at least one musket. Nearly every colonial, the story goes, "owned his own weapon and equipment," had a gun ready to battle hostile Native American tribes or to keep slaves in line, and was prepared to fend off other dangers, as from criminals.[1] Furthermore, in contrast to aristocrats in the home country who kept firearms mainly for hunting as sport, settlers in the colonies used their guns from the start for utilitarian purposes, such as to kill game and place food on the table.[2] In all, such tradition maintains that the colonial experience made gun keeping in America unique.

As the record shows, part of the traditional depiction is valid. English colonists did bring firearms with them for self-defense as well as for offense against Indians and rival European settlers. They also brought the practice of restricting gun keeping, usually to selected upper-class males. In the first company of 105 English settlers who established Jamestown, Virginia, in May 1607, only the gentlemen among them had the privilege of carrying firearms. Quickly though, in the interest of defense, local authorities came to lift the restrictions on gun ownership and sought to arm all males. So the necessity to use the available small arms for the benefit of all the settlers in times of crisis gives the appearance of freeing English colonists from old-country restrictions. In this way, assumably, in North America men of the right sort who could afford to own guns were able to acquire them as a privilege regardless of their status as measured by birth and class.

To maintain their protective screen, the armed males "banded together in semi-military fashion."[3] Wherever possible, thereafter, as these bands evolved into militias, colonial leaders tried to funnel whatever firearms they had at hand to them. In time settlers formed two kinds of militias that functioned side by side. One operated with compulsory duty for young males and the other functioned with volunteer members. Both militias relied on firearms to help them protect their communities against hostile Indians and other colonists the English regarded as enemies.[4] Thus, the settlers subordinated whatever personal rights they possessed in the matter of gun keeping to the collective welfare of their communities.

Problems over restrictions on gun keeping arose for a number of reasons but notably because of a clash of interests between individuals and the group as expressed in economics. Early on, when Indians became familiar with firearms, they desired them and were willing to pay well for them. So individual colonists with an eye on profit, when they could, traded firearms to Indians for items such as furs. This commerce alarmed authorities because of the harm the weapons, when in the wrong hands, could inflict on the whole settlement. Invariably, colonial lawmakers placed Indians high on their list of the wrong people. Indeed, all the colonial governments, whether Spanish, French, Dutch, or English, forbade the sale of arms and ammunition to Native Americans.

In keeping with this practice, the Virginia House of Burgesses in 1619 enacted legislation prohibiting any settler, on the penalty of being hanged, from selling or giving firearms to Indians. Three years later, following an Indian massacre of whites, colonial officials exercised their regulatory authority by enrolling every able-bodied male between sixteen and fifty in the compulsory militia. Similarly, in 1623 Plymouth colony passed a law requiring freemen or other inhabitants to arm themselves with muskets or other suitable firearms. Thereafter, colonists imported more firearms to try to meet such goals, but trustworthy weapons remained scarce. For example, by about 1630 when Virginia's settlers had reached nearly five thousand, approximately half of them had guns. Not all of these weapons could be used safely, and not all of the men, even in the structured militias, possessed guns. Moreover, many of those who had firearms did not maintain them properly. This negligence prompted the authorities to fine laggards ten shillings.[5]

Despite these difficulties in sustaining a well-prepared citizen military force, colonial governments, as in Massachusetts Bay in March 1631, continued to adopt laws requiring able-bodied men to enroll in militias with their own firearms. If a man did not have a gun or could not afford one, colonial governments at times advanced him the money to buy one. It was "to be repaid by the citizen as soon as possible."[6] Compliance proved troublesome, as for instance three years later in Virginia when militia officers mustered their companies for drill. The officers discovered that despite the colony's law obligating citizen-soldiers to have a firearm in good working order, few of them possessed such a weapon.

That same year the Puritans in Massachusetts established five militia companies, even though like other colonists they chronically experienced a shortage of firearms.[7] In Virginia only 10 percent of the militia had muskets. Primarily the volunteer militia companies in most colonies, which already had become characterized as social clubs for well-to-do, establishment males, had enough guns for their members.[8]

Despite the shortage of firearms, merchants who could obtain guns continued to trade them to Native Americans. In this manner Indians in New England became reasonably well armed with flintlock muskets and carbines.[9] To the south, Dutch authorities in New Netherland became so exasperated with those who provided firearms to Native Americans that in 1638 they prescribed death as the penalty for settlers who participated in this commerce.

Similarly, just three years later, the English Crown decreed that in its American colonies "in trucking or trading with the Indians, no man shall give them for any commodity of theirs, silver or gold, or any weapons of war, either guns or gunpowder, or sword, nor any other Munition, which might come to be used Against ourselves."[10] In 1642 Connecticut banned the sale of firearms or ammunition to Indians and prohibited colonists from repairing guns the Indians already owned. Nonetheless, English authorities regularly supplied the Iroquois, as allies, with guns and ammunition.

One widely accepted reason for warfare between Indian tribes and between them and Netherland settlers in 1643 was the resentment coastal Indians felt against the Dutch for denying them guns while selling them to Mohawks and Mohicans.[11] Later, in response to the warfare with and between the Native Americans, the Netherland government urged each male colonist to enroll in a militia company and required each to have a firearm, stamped as to ownership to prevent its sale to Indians. In May 1647 the home government ordered Governor Peter Stuyvesant to furnish the colonists with guns. Instead, he sold them to Indians for profit, leading his people to view his actions as bordering on treason.[12]

Meanwhile, in 1644 the United Colonies of New England had urged a ban on the sale of firearms and ammunition "either to the French or Dutch or to any other that do commonly trade the same with Indians."[13] The next year the general laws in Massachusetts followed the Connecticut practice by banning the sale and maintenance of firearms for Indians. Regardless, settlers continued to market firearms and ammunition to Native Americans, instructed them in use of the weapons, and hired them as hunters. Moreover, Indians frequently learned from traders and European allies how to maintain and repair their firearms and to make ammunition. White entrepreneurs persisted in this commerce because colonial authorities often lacked the resources to enforce the trading bans they enacted.

This problem could be seen in Virginia in 1657 when the assembly decreed that anyone "selling arms or ammunition to Indians, forfeits his whole estate."[14] The next year the local lawmakers reversed themselves. They ruled that every man "may freely trade for gunns, powder and shott. It derogating nothing from our safety and adding much to our advantage."[15] In the sparring that led to King Philip's War, in May 1674 Sir Edmund Andros, the governor-general of Massachusetts, sought to disarm local Indians and forbade the sale of guns and powder to all Indians but to no avail.

Meanwhile, frayed relations with Native Americans led the Virginia assembly to reverse itself several times in the matter of gun trafficking. In May 1676 it decreed death for anyone caught selling arms and ammunition to Indians, "whether friendly or enemy." Yet, out of "sade experience," the legislators knew that merchants traded arms in violation of the terms in earlier gun laws and assumed they would do so again.[16] Consequently, whereas the new law excluded regular merchandisers from selling firearms and other goods to Indians, it allowed traders to do so if they obtained a permit from the authorities.

A number of individuals who engaged in the trade, such as Nathaniel Bacon Jr., an Henrico County planter, protested. They accused the governor, Sir William Berkeley, of giving permits to his favorites. Shortly thereafter, Bacon assumed leadership of frontiersmen who in May rose against the governor ostensibly because he refused to mobilize them against Indians who allegedly ravaged white settlements. In reality, the whites took to arms more for offensive purposes, mostly because they wished to seize Indian lands they coveted.

Initially, many of the Virginia rebels belonged to volunteer militias, but later Bacon recruited and armed the wrong people, such as white servants and black slaves. Berkeley's supporters denounced the rebels as rabble, banditti, and the scum of the county. On October 26, 1676, Bacon died suddenly of a "Lousey Disease." The rebels continued to fight for a few more months, but the governor's loyalists defeated them. Although the causes of this struggle are complex, in simplified terms it had much to do with who would control firearms and decide when to use them.

This concern applied also to militia in New York, which in May 1689 sided with Jacob Leisler, a trader recently from Germany, when he seized control of the local government in defiance of colonial authorities. English officials had to use regular troops to suppress the rebellion. Aggrieved colonists in North Carolina, Maryland, and Pennsylvania who had guns also took to them against alleged oppressors. In most of these frontier communities when disputes between colonial officers and settlers became heated, the common-folk militias did not hesitate in turning their arms on the authorities. Beginning in 1692, therefore, in the interest of public order the Massachusetts legislature enacted measures for control of firearms that though limited in scope affected much of the populace. The colony prohibited private citizens from carrying guns and other arms in public.

Restrictions of this nature appear to have had little effect on individuals who owned firearms or who continued to sell them to proscribed people such as Indians. As in the seventeenth century, Indians who obtained firearms and maintained them properly became formidable out of proportion to their numbers. They fought white frontiersmen who encroached on their lands and they terrorized enemy tribes. In the South, with firearms supplied by English traders, the Chickasaw "became the scourge of the defenseless western tribes." By the early years of the eighteenth century, Indians had come to consider firearms so valuable and merchandisers found their sale so profitable that guns had become one of the chief commodities in the trade with forest tribes. Available statistics on this commerce show that traders charged thirty times more for a gun than for a hatchet, a hoe, or even a bottle of rum.[17]

As is well known, in all the colonies but especially in those in the South, authorities dealt differently with blacks than with whites. Racial prejudice and fear of slave insurrections motivated legislators to enact selective laws directed against blacks as evident in Virginia in 1648 in An Act Preventing Negroes from Bearing Arms. Even if at times they succeeded in evading such restrictions, the laws that denied them access to guns remained in force throughout the colonial period. In several instances, local authorities even ordered all white men to carry a gun to church because of the establishment's anxiety that slaves would rebel during the gathering for prayer. South Carolina required masters of slaves to keep all firearms safely locked up in their home. Even Quaker Pennsylvania forbade slaves to carry arms without their masters' certificated approval.

In 1712 South Carolina's legislature and in 1723 Virginia's burgesses attempted to close loopholes in their gun statutes directed at the wrong people. Virginia passed "An Act for the better government of Negroes, Mulattoes, and Indians." It prescribed that "no negro, mullatto, or Indian whatsoever . . . shall hereafter presume to keep, or carry any gun, powder, shot, or any club, or other weapon whatsoever, offensive or defensive."[18] Such legislation affected blacks more than it did Native Americans. In much of the South, armed white men formed slave patrols to keep blacks under surveillance—a task that in time became the responsibility of local militias.

Largely for this reason, white colonial establishments, even though usually short of manpower, refused to enroll blacks, enslaved or free, in militias. As an agent to Carolina merchants wrote in 1715, in considering blacks for military service "there must be great caution used, lest our slaves when armed might become our masters." At times of crisis, though, some militia companies enrolled blacks.[19]

Colonial militias had other long-standing problems. The laws requiring the military training of able-bodied white males, ultimately in some six hundred militias in all the colonies, proved impossible to carry out for a variety of reasons but especially because of the high cost of firearms.[20] In consequence, most colonial authorities ceased trying to compel citizens to acquire guns or providing them with guns.

In New England, colonists hired or appointed professional soldiers to protect them. Provincial officials also employed professionals to train their voluntary citizen militias. In time, every colony except Pennsylvania followed these procedures.[21] Although such training of colonial militias proved adequate for constabulary duties, it did not prepare the soldiers for hostilities against well-armed opponents. When ordered to combat duty, as during the Seven Years' War against France and her Indian allies, the militias performed poorly.

Also during this crisis, out of fear provincial authorities tightened old ethnic and religious regulations on gun ownership. Although the colonial demand for such discriminatory controls sprang from circumstances different from those in England, as in applying them against Indians and blacks, colonists usually followed home-country practices of excluding other distrusted people from ownership. In New England, officials of the dominant faith on occasion confiscated the arms of dissenters. They regularly barred Catholics and indentured servants from possessing firearms.

With its large Catholic population, Maryland had escaped such discrimination, but in 1756 its assembly prohibited Catholics from having firearms and confiscated the guns and ammunition they possessed.[22] Massachusetts authorities seized guns from distrusted inhabitants with the intent of preventing social upheavals. In other colonies, too, ruling establishments perceived a connection between access to guns and rebellion. As in England, local authorities wanted only those individuals they regarded as part of the right people—primarily, white Protestant men who owned property—to have firearms as private possessions with unhampered use.

These discriminatory restrictions embedded in local laws remained in force when the war ended in 1763 with the defeat of France. Though effective overall, the restraints did not prevent some guns, usually through discharged veterans, from becoming scattered through several colonies and reaching individuals of the wrong kind. An unknown number of flintlock muskets, such as the smoothbore English "Brown Bess," and other firearms apparently fell into the hands of criminals.

As prosecutions for homicides in Pennsylvania and elsewhere in the colonies indicate, felons did not have ready access to guns and seldom used them in their offenses.[23] Nonetheless, various forms of crime, such as horse thievery by armed outlaw bands, had existed in the colonies for years. Following the war it escalated, or at least appeared to do so, producing in summer 1766 a surge of violence in the backcountry of the Carolinas. At this time gangs brandishing pistols and other guns robbed and killed. Landowners complained of hunters who "range the Country with their horse and Gun without Home or Habitation."[24]

Because these southern frontier communities lacked adequate constables, sheriffs, or courts, these rampaging criminals escaped punishment. So in July and August 1767 a thousand "respectable Back Countrymen" decided to regulate the criminal forays, armed themselves, and attacked outlaw communities. They flogged or killed suspected lawbreakers.[25] When bandit gangs counterattacked with gunfire, the loosely connected "Regulators" organized themselves as a disciplined paramilitary organization whose members swore oaths to support each other. By March 1768 they suppressed what they perceived as the criminal element.

The vigilantes then turned to violence against other improper people—nonpaying debtors, whores, and less-than-desirable members of the lower classes. In March of the following year, when moderates opposed the Regulators and the provincial government provided frontier communities with district courts and sheriffs, the Regulators disbanded. In their use of privately held firearms, they had set three examples. The first indicated that when law and order failed, private gun-keeping seemed justified; the second showed that private guns had become essential tools for vigilantism; and the third demonstrated that vigilantes could and would use the weapons in policing people they deemed undesirable. Popular chroniclers, as well as scholars, would come to regard these practices as characteristically American.[26]

All the while, the few colonial craftsmen capable of making by hand rifles for hunters and well-to-do sport shooters produced them in numbers sufficient to satisfy local needs. Gunsmiths in the area of Lancaster, Pennsylvania, crafted the best known of these firearms, the Kentucky rifle modeled on the Jaeger, a German hunting rifle. It had a four-foot barrel of grooved, soft iron that made it heavy and cumbersome but with better range and accuracy than the smooth-bore muskets of the time.[27] Even though criminals and vigilantes apparently gained access to some of these guns, the locally crafted firearms and the ammunition for them remained too expensive for widespread private ownership. The other guns in circulation, which for almost two centuries had been coming from England, the Netherlands, and other European sources, also remained too costly for widespread private possession. Still, the availability of guns rose along with the growth of the white population and so did the selective restrictions on firearms use.

These restraints on gun keeping, as with folkways and other practices, continued to follow home-country models. As documented by careful historians, colonial attitudes toward matters of militia, toward standing armies, toward dealing with bandit gangs or frontier violence with vigilantes, and toward maintaining public order with constables, sheriffs, and night watchmen in towns all came from England.[28] Scholars disagree, though, on the nature of English precedents in private gun-ownership. They differ on whether or not precedents changed when they reached North America and its special environment.

Those who perceive personal gun-keeping as necessary for the defense of liberty and as a "right" guaranteed to Englishmen in their Bill of Rights, contend that that right served as a model for the colonists. These writers usually regard England's William Blackstone as most influential on this score. He depicted "the right of having arms" as proper for "self preservation, when the sanctions of society and laws are insufficient." He also recognized the right of society to impose "restrictions" on the "offence of *riding* or *going armed*, with dangerous or unusual weapons," calling it "a crime against the public peace."[29]

Other scholars who have studied the firearms question in the colonial era read the evidence differently. They maintain that colonists employed the phrase "to bear arms" to apply to their militias in a military context, one which did not extend to individual use of guns for private purposes. These researchers contend also that the legislatures in the colonies followed, as we have noted, the English practice of selectively containing private ownership by law. In the legal venues of the colonies, hence, rarely did anyone contest government authority over access to firearms.[30]

This interpretation comes mainly from revisionist historians. It runs counter to conventional versions of gun keeping in seventeenth- and eighteenth-century England and North America. Traditionalists claim that much of the populace at this time had plentiful guns because the price of small arms in England, and hence correspondingly in the colonies, dropped sufficiently to allow ordinary citizens to buy them for personal use as well as for militia service.[31]

Revisionists deny that such an abundance of privately held guns existed at this time. They point, in contrast, to the practice of the English aristocracy of perpetuating paucity by raising barriers even to limited possession by the lower classes. The elite establishment's game laws that imposed a property qualification for hunting also had behind them the intent to institute a selective form of gun regulation over the masses. Doubtless, these controls did not always work as desired. Some of the expensive handcrafted firearms reached the hands of common men in England and the colonies often enough to alarm the upper classes. They dreaded "putting such dangerous weapons into the hands of the people at large," but the regulation usually worked as intended.[32]

The widely held abundance theory as applied to colonial North America can be summarized in the words of a prominent historian who described colonial Virginia as "full of guns," that life there "required guns," and that "you needed guns to stay alive." Various other writers express this point of view with different nuances. They portray the colonists who settled along the Atlantic seaboard and then moved inland not only as well armed but also as promptly modifying the crude, handcrafted matchlocks and wheel locks they imported from Europe to suit their special needs. In the overall conventional perspective, these colonists regarded the gun, along with the ax and the plow, as a personal possession and an ever-ready tool in their continuing conquest of what they perceived incorrectly as a thinly populated wilderness.[33]

This view of the colonial past notes properly a considerable reliance of European settlers on firearms but gives those weapons an exaggerated cultural significance. Through the examination of parliamentary debates that touched on the ownership of firearms, on game laws, and on statutes in England and the American colonies, revisionist historians show that as in Europe guns in private hands in North America were rare rather than ubiquitous. Few ordinary settlers could afford to own and maintain firearms because most of them had to be imported and were expensive. This scholarship demonstrates that the right to own firearms in colonial North America, as in England, took second place to the perceived public welfare and hence had been mostly collective and not part of a personal guarantee.[34]

3

To the Second Amendment

When the English colonies' troubles with the mother country escalated, many of the discontented, military-age colonials belonged to local militias, either as draftees or volunteers. The Crown quickly realized it could not count on them to carry out its laws, so it ordered regular troops to Massachusetts. On October 1, 1768, they landed in Boston to take up the policing of the defiant colonists. After the massacre of March 5, 1770, they withdrew. Four years later, following the dissidents' dumping of English tea in Boston Harbor, the troops, commanded by General Thomas Gage who ruled also as governor of Massachusetts, returned to the city as occupiers. Seeing themselves subjected to rule by a standing army and troubled by other discontents, colonists in Massachusetts and then elsewhere turned to rebellion.

Rebel leaders who assembled in the First Continental Congress in September 1774 in Philadelphia also distrusted the established colonial militias, perceiving them as too closely connected with imperial rule. The Congress therefore urged the people to form their own militias composed mostly of right-thinking native whites supposedly not tainted with loyalty to the Crown. Already, though, members of the rebel legislatures had started creating their own militias and had them out hunting for guns. Authorities in London attempted, among other measures, to control firearms that might fall into the hands of the militiamen. In October Parliament imposed an embargo on firearms, parts, and ammunition to the colonists. In Massachusetts it employed the troops already on duty to enforce this legislation.

Volunteer rebel militias resisted the ban. They also began functioning as a kind of prerevolutionary constabulary, which intimidated those with imperial sympathies. One of these militias amassed arms at Concord, Massachusetts. When Gage learned of this arsenal, which was but twenty-one miles from Boston, he decided to act. On the evening of April 18, 1775, he ordered seven hundred troops to confiscate or destroy the firearms and arrest the militia leaders. In the well-known bloody encounters that began the next day at Lexington and then at Concord, some four thousand volunteers in the county militia, known as minutemen, participated in the attacks on the British regulars as they retreated.

Legend holds that these rebels comprising "the armed populace of Massachusetts" and "the people themselves," suddenly mobilized, prevailed because of their spirit and straight shooting. In fact, even though the minutemen belonged to elite units of militia, which were "well-organized, well-equipped, and relatively well trained," they suffered higher casualties than the British regulars.[1] In accounts of the Revolutionary War that followed years later, writers who placed high value on the role of firearms added to the legend. They claimed that rebel patriots who fought to protect their heritage from England depicted as part of it "an ancient and indubitable right" for "individuals to be armed."[2]

Previously when serving the Crown, the citizen-soldiers, regardless of how they had been recruited, had as one of their main duties the maintenance of domestic order. They also had to keep local Indians and blacks in line. The ability of these part-time troops at least to hold their own at Lexington and Concord, along with the North Americans' inherited distrust of standing armies, led rebel leaders to overvalue the shooting prowess of the volunteer militia. As the conflict spread, the newly formed states and the Congress acted realistically to bolster the patriot militias, all of which lacked adequate arms and training. On June 14 Congress created the Continental army based on a soldiery with long-term commitments. The next day it placed that army under the command of George Washington, a colonel in the Virginia militia.

In the following month Congress called on the rebelling colonies to raise uniform militias to fight with the army. The Virginia burgesses, for instance, in July 1775 passed a defense act mandating the state to furnish arms and ammunition to its new militia. It made clear that the guns belonged to the counties that supplied them and not to individuals. Virginia also appropriated twenty-five hundred pounds for the manufacture of firearms at Fredericksburg, an effort that failed.[3] At the same time, the meager domestic production of handcrafted firearms compelled the rebels to import 80 percent of their firearms and 90 percent of their powder from France and Holland. These munitions came slowly. In summer 1776, for instance, a quarter of Washington's troops lacked arms.

Shortly, too, the performance of the rebel citizen-soldiers when they fought England's regulars head-on convinced even strong supporters of their unreliability as a sustained fighting force. Poorly trained, most ordinary militiamen resisted army discipline, served only brief terms, and frequently deserted. Despite his own militia background, Washington complained that hardly a day passed without these amateur warriors shooting friends or in other ways mishandling their guns. He called the citizen-soldiers "dismayed, Intractable, and, Impatient to return" home. Later, he reported a number of times to Congress that "no dependence could be put in a militia." As military historians point out, militias possessed at least one positive feature. They provided "reinforcements and even reluctant draftees" for the Continental army.[4]

While Washington chastised the militias and labored to whip the army into shape, the rebelling provinces established state governments with constitutions that replaced now-invalid colonial charters. Several of the new documents referred to citizens' privilege to possess firearms as a means of countering tyranny from the top. Similar concerns bothered the framers of the Articles of Confederation, which the Continental Congress adopted on November 15, 1777. Most of them distrusted centralized government. They specified that every state "shall always keep up a well regulated and disciplined militia, sufficiently armed and accoutred" to be ready for action but did not include a proviso on any private right to bear arms.[5]

During the controversy over ratification of the Articles, attitudes of revolutionary political leaders toward the efficacy of the militia shifted slightly. Among others, Samuel Adams, a devotee of the New England militia, expressed doubts about citizen-soldiers. "Would any Man in his Senses, who wishes the War may be carried on with Vigor," he wrote, "prefer the temporary and expensive Drafts of Militia, to a permanent and well-appointed Army!"[6] Nonetheless, in March 1781 the states ratified the Articles as the first national constitution with the militia clause intact.

Two years later, following the United States's achievement of an internationally recognized independence, a Congress still fearful of a standing armed force probed what kind of a peacetime military establishment the country would need. As Adams and other patriots knew, the army rather than the militia had proved itself the most crucial force in winning the Revolutionary War. Later, folklore, patriotic histories, and even military chroniclers would exaggerate the skill of both the regulars and the citizen-soldiers with guns. Most of all, they endowed the contribution of the militia with fabled qualities. In addition, romanticizers, especially those who believed the "red blooded" American and his gun were "inseparable," claimed "the rifle brought about the birth of these United States."[7]

Despite Washington's wartime criticisms of citizen-troopers, at this point he appeared to join the chorus of contemporaries who placed high value on the militia. He responded to a query from Congress on the matter of a peacetime armed force with the comment that "the Militia of this Country must be considered as the Palladium of our security, and the first effectual resort in case of hostility." Proponents of gun keeping later would use this phrase to argue that the founding fathers favored private firearms-ownership in militias for personal as well as for community defense. In his full statement, though, Washington did not recommend arms keeping on an individual basis. He explained "from experience" that "the formation and discipline of the Militia of the Continent should be absolutely uniform" as would be the case with an army and not as with variously mustered militias in the states.[8]

Several months later a special congressional committee recommended that each state establish a "well-regulated militia" along with proper arsenals and magazines.[9] Congress accepted some of this advice. Largely for political reasons, though, it chose to rely for defense on state militias with compulsory duty but without enforceable uniformity. In June 1784 it disbanded the Continental army. As a bonus, Congress allowed its veterans to keep their valuable arms. What remained of a national army now consisted of fifty-five men on duty at West Point and twenty-five at Fort Pitt to help guard stores.

Quickly, though, when Congress needed troops to fight Indians who resisted white encroachment on their lands, it called on the states to supply soldiers from their militias for a small army. Two years later, it extended this practice to deal with a domestic upheaval. The trouble began when debt-ridden farmers in western Massachusetts demanded that the state government reduce their taxes and provide them with relief from debts. In September 1786, under the leadership of Daniel Shays, a farmer and veteran of the Continental army, several thousand of them cast aside peaceful protest to rebel with guns, swords, and other weapons. As had the colonial vigilantes in the Carolinas, they called themselves Regulators. Some men in local militia units refused to fight their neighbors—or even joined the rebels—when ordered to suppress the uprising.

The former revolutionaries, who now comprised the new nation's political establishment, showed no patience with citizens' shouldering arms against them. They viewed the public resort to weaponry as anarchy and a threat to legitimate government. Cabinet officer and presidential adviser Alexander Hamilton, for instance, perceived the uprising as demonstrating the need for a regular military force to maintain order. Washington urged the employment of force at once, if necessary. He wanted the government to be "braced" and that "every violation of the constitution be reprehended. If defective, let it be amended, but not suffered to be trampled upon whilst it has an existence."[10]

In the next month, after failure of the Massachusetts militia to suppress the insurrection, Congress authorized the recruiting of a force of some fourteen hundred men ostensibly to battle Indians but actually to suppress the Shay-sites. It used this excuse to create an army because fundamental law did not provide for the use of federal troops to allay domestic unrest. The federal force proved unnecessary because the governor raised an armed force of approximately seven thousand men, many of them Revolutionary War veterans. In February of the following year, in one bloody encounter that citizen army crushed the heart of the uprising and disarmed most rebels. The fighting killed or wounded more than thirty yeomen and killed three troopers.[11] A few defiant Shaysites continued to raid their opponents for several months and then stopped.

This confrontation between the central government and men armed with their own weapons exacerbated dissatisfaction with the Articles of Confederation that had been brewing for some time. As Washington explained, "but the other day we were shedding our blood to obtain the Constitution under which we now live . . . and now we are unsheathing the sword to overturn them! The thing is so unaccountable that I [have] to persuade my self that I am not under the vision of a dream."[12]

So, before the Shays insurrection had petered out, Congress called a convention to revise the Articles. After the delegates met in Philadelphia on May 25, 1787, they moved to construct a new constitution rather than amend the old one. Two weeks later James Madison, a prime mover for change, described the confederation as inherently defective and urged reorganization of the Union on republican principles. As did other Constitution makers, he frequently expressed dread of a permanent army and fondness for militia. He declared that "as the greatest danger to liberty is from large standing armies, it is best to prevent them by an effectual provision for a good Militia." He envisioned this militia as "amounting to near half a million of citizens with arms in their hands."[13]

At the convention, delegates did not discuss small arms as a governmental concern. Instead, they debated armies, militias, and other issues pertaining to centralized power. A number of the delegates tagged as anti-Federalist, such as George Mason of Virginia and Elbridge Gerry of Massachusetts, urged limitations on the federal government's authority over the lives of citizens. These delegates desired specific guarantees of popular liberties as they assumed they existed in the old homeland in the English Bill of Rights.

Mason recommended a listing of such rights in the Constitution, he said, because of "it having been found from Universal experience that the most express declarations and reservations are necessary to protect the just rights and liberty of Mankind from the silent power and ever active conspiracy of those who govern." Eight months later he still desired a declaration that stated "rights not given to the general government were retained by the states."[14] Still later, he urged the enumeration of citizens' rights as a preface to the Constitution because it "would give great quiet to the people."[15] A few political leaders in several states expressed similar sentiment but the convention declined the rights proposals.

The rejection reflected sentiment among the majority delegates known as Federalists. Determined to have a strong constitution unimpaired with too many restraints, they viewed the proposed declaration of rights as redundant, even nauseous. Madison, one of the most articulate Federalist leaders on this matter, expressed their reasoning succinctly. He deemed a bill of rights unnecessary because "it brings more into question the fundamental principle of Republican Government, that the majority who rule in such governments are the safest Guardians both of public good and of private rights."[16]

On both sides of this issue, the men who debated it were well educated, were immersed in ancient history, understood the rise of monarchical power in western Europe, and drew lessons from what they had read. The Federalists' intense desire for a powerful, energetic central government that would replace that of the confederation caused them to temper their distaste for standing armies as used, in their view, by tyrants in ancient Rome and later in England and France.

In a republican government as proposed, Madison contended, the discipline of the militia should be a national concern "and ought to be provided for in the *National* Constitution." Furthermore, even though he regarded a "standing force" as dangerous, he thought that it, too, "may be a necessary provision" in a constitution that would be "fully adequate to the national defence, and the preservation of the Union."[17]

Unlike Madison, a number of other founders, mostly anti-Federalists, wanted to leave national defense solely to the civilian-soldiers. This proposal led still other founders, such as Washington and John Adams, to protest that draftees drawn from militias could not, on their own, withstand veteran troops. In addition, Adams decried the idea that citizens should use arms at individual discretion except in self-defense. Such a right, he wrote, would "demolish every institution and lay the laws prostrate, so that liberty can be enjoyed by no man."[18] In the face of such sentiment, especially among the delegates, the anti-army proponents lost out.

The men in Philadelphia then fleshed out a document that provided for compulsory militias raised by the states, dividing the power over them between the federal government and the states. To promote a degree of uniformity lacking in the local militias, through Article 1, Section 8 they bestowed on Congress the authority to organize and discipline the part-time soldiers. With such training, the militias could be called into service to execute federal laws, suppress insurrections, and repel invasions. While adopting this plan for the use of militias, the delegates reserved to the states the right to train the troops and appoint the officers. The Constitution also endowed Congress with the power to raise and support armies but limited the funding for a federal armed force to two-year appropriations. As with the Articles of Confederation, the proposed constitution said nothing about the right of private citizens to keep arms.

In September, after the delegates had approved the final document, it went to the thirteen states. They called special conventions to ratify it. In the matter of military power, the anti-Federalists who remained firmly opposed to a professional armed force expressed particular concern with the extent of authority over both a national army and the theoretically uniform militia given to the central government. They viewed the militia under federal control as possessing the same evils as a standing army. Typically, one critic asserted, "By far the greater part of the different nations, who have fallen from the glorious state of liberty, owe their ruin to standing armies."[19]

At the Virginia ratifying convention in June 1788, Patrick Henry, who preferred strength in the states rather than in the federal government, objected that the new frame of government "does not leave us the means of defending our rights, or waging war against tyrants." He asked, "Have we the means of resisting disciplined armies when our only defence, the militia is put into the hands of Congress?"[20] In line with this reasoning, Virginia governor Edmund Randolph reported, "with respect to a standing army, there was not a member of the federal convention who did not feel indignation at such an institution."[21]

During other campaigning for ratification, a number of individuals spoke of a right to bear arms for defense of the people and their states, and even for killing game. Others brought up the previously discarded idea of attaching a bill of rights to the Constitution. This persistent concern over rights persuaded

Madison and other Federalists they could no longer ignore the issue. They mulled it over and then promised the worried anti-Federalists that after ratification of the new constitution they would ask the new Congress to modify or amend it to protect various personal freedoms and to restrict federal powers, as in controlling state militias.[22] These Federalist leaders abandoned their opposition to a bill of rights because they deemed the winning of support for the constitution from some of the prorights, promilitia anti-Federalists as crucial to its ratification, which came in August 1788.

On June 8, 1789, three months after the first Congress of the new government had convened, Madison reluctantly carried out what he had pledged. As anti-Federalists had suggested, he had gone ahead with the idea of amendments to the Constitution, helped draft them, and introduced them to Congress. Both houses discussed the proposals but as with the delegates at the Philadelphia convention, few of the legislators debated openly the virtues or drawbacks of personal gun-keeping. When matters related to firearms came up, they related usually to the militia, what its mission should be, and how it connected to liberty for both individuals and society as a whole.

Elbridge Gerry, now serving in the House of Representatives, took the lead in giving voice to these concerns. "What, sir, is the use of a militia?" he asked and answered. "It is to prevent the establishment of a standing army, the bane of liberty. . . . Whenever Governments mean to invade the rights and liberties of the people, they always attempt to destroy the militia, in order to raise an army upon their ruins."[23] As did many of his anti-Federalist colleagues, he perceived the army as the tool of tyranny and the draft militia with its citizen-soldiers as the people's main instrument of defense against oppression.

After discussion of these and other issues, the legislators weighed the proposed amendments and sent twelve of them to the states for approval. There, officials and the involved publics debated the amendments for two and a half years before the necessary three-fourths of the states approved ten of them. On December 15, 1791, the ten became part of the Constitution. Even though these amendments placed restrictions on federal authority but not on state governments, they became known as the Bill of Rights. In theory they benefited the whole citizenry but in practice they served primarily white male Protestants.

The Second Amendment, which stated that "a well regulated militia, being necessary to the security of a free state, the right of the people to keep and bear arms shall not be infringed," in time became a source of intense controversy. It took on the coloring of a riddle because in part, in adopting it, the legislators did not, as has been seen, carry on probing deliberations that clearly revealed their intent. Several members of Congress who argued in the amendment's favor stressed that if Americans learned "the Use of arms," they could withstand "a forighn [sic] foe." Others debated the propriety of compelling the "religiously scrupulous" to bear arms.[24] In the Senate, a majority favored an amendment that would not have allowed "the militia arms," but the proposal failed to obtain a two-thirds majority because it might have deterred citizen resistance to tyranny.[25]

Beyond this information, we know that from both inherited ideology and experience with occupation troops (as with the British in Boston) most rights supporters could not shed their dislike of a regular army. They continued to view it as a more potent instrument of tyranny than were militias. We know, too, that they understood from the colonial and revolutionary experiences the fundamental weaknesses of the compulsory militias—their lack of adequate training and the unwillingness of drafted citizens to bear the costs of firearms and ammunition on their own.

In addition to working out a political compromise on the arms question, the Second Amendment framers appear to have sought an organized militia as specified in Article 1 of the Constitution. They wanted states to regulate their militias with uniform training so the federal government could call them to duty, ready for action, when needed. From this perspective, as in past practice in England and in the colonial era, militia draftees would keep firearms for defense of the nation and to cope with upheaval or tyranny but not primarily for personal use.

Later, academics and others would offer more elaborate interpretations for the need of the Second Amendment. One version of the amendment's origin favored by those who cherish unrestricted access to firearms holds that the drafters followed the Anglo-American legacy on arms keeping. It contends the amendment descended directly from the English Bill of Rights. From it the framers took the concept of "the individual's right to have weapons for his own defence rather than for collective defence."[26] In this view the founders, "in keeping with colonial precedent, broadened the English protection" of the traditional right of citizens to possess firearms by sweeping away limitations. The framers linked this absolute guarantee to the regulated militia with the aim of preventing the federal government from evolving into a military tyranny.[27]

Advocates of arms keeping of this persuasion would argue also that the "militias, at the time of the Framing, were universal in their membership."[28] By extension, therefore, the militia and the arms bearing mentioned in the Second Amendment applied to the entire citizenry. These theorists would repeat this interpretation so often that many Americans would come to believe it as gospel. Yet in England and in the colonial past, as we have seen, militias had often been select, in the sense of being made up of volunteer local gentry, their core constituency. In North America, colonial legislatures had denied gun possession to citizens whom they deemed threats to the stability of the state and granted it as a privilege to the right people, usually law-abiding Protestant males.

In another perspective, the Second Amendment supposedly followed provisions in the bills of rights that Massachusetts, North Carolina, Pennsylvania, and Vermont had adopted during the Revolutionary War. Still another interpretation maintains that the amendment reflected the desires of ardent anti-Federalists who wanted it as a shield against a standing army in peacetime and as a deterrent to Congress from doing away with the state militias.

Along similar lines but with a different twist, those who came to regard unrestricted personal possession of firearms as a danger to society would argue that Madison modeled the amendment on Item 17 in his state's declaration of rights. He sought to limit Congress's authority over the militia with the aim of preventing the central government from disarming state militias and emasculating the South's system of slave control.[29] In theory, Madison thus refashioned the English concept of regulating the privilege of having arms as a restraint on the Crown into one of restraint on Congress.

Other restriction advocates would contend the amendment emanated from the founders' fear of social turmoil and from a concern for preserving order in fractious communities. Prominent Federalists did, indeed, perceive the amendment as a means of regulating the militia, which would help check tumults such as Shays's Rebellion, riots, and slave uprisings. They saw it also as a necessary concession, engineered by Madison, to the constitutional antagonists who disliked powerful, centralized government.[30] Madison included the amendment in the Bill of Rights as part of the Federalists' bargain with anti-Federalists for a strong constitution that balanced federal and state power over militias. His role had much to do with politics and little to do with the right to own scarce small firearms for personal use in self-defense and hunting or other forms of recreation.

When the Bill of Rights became law no well-regulated or uniform militia, national or state, existed. Nor did the existing militias have universal male membership. Organizers usually discriminated as to who could or could not join. In some instances prominent individuals and communities expressed belief in the right to have firearms for self-protection as well as for the common defense. Nine states had bills of rights that contained either a privilege for individuals to bear arms or a provision for a militia. In addition, every state had some form of selective regulation regarding who could or could not possess a gun for personal use. In practice, therefore, most states treated possession selectively and more as a privilege than a right.

In all, the Second Amendment did not change past practice of keeping guns out of the hands of the wrong people. Nor did it catalyze universal male gun ownership in militias. Those Americans who desired and could afford to buy custom-made firearms for personal use continued to possess them with the minor restraints similar to those of the past. They appear to have had little concern about keeping small firearms for militia service or for combating tyranny should it arise. In time, the number of individual gun-keepers would increase. They would assume a "right" to own firearms because that word appeared in fundamental federal law as well as in a number of state constitutions.

Then, as we shall see, various constitutional analysts would begin to disagree with the rights perspective. Those who desired restraints on firearms ownership would argue that when individual citizens did not belong to a militia or reside in a state that explicitly granted the private bearing of arms, citizens had only a privilege to keep them. They would point out that an individual right has meaning only if available equally to all citizens. That equality in gun keeping did not exist in England, in the North American colonies, or in the American nation in its formative years. The differences in constitutional interpretation would set the stage for a struggle between Americans who contended the Second Amendment guarantees a personal right to own guns and those who viewed it as conferring only a collective privilege that government in its responsibility for the public welfare had the authority to curtail.[31]

4
Militias, Duels, and Gun Keeping

I n the Federalist years following adoption of the Bill of Rights, the central government did not deal head-on with the issue of gun keeping but did touch on it indirectly through concern with the army and militias. Wary of still potent antiarmy sentiment, George Washington's administration did not attempt immediately to build a sizable peacetime armed force. Yet, it had responsibility for protecting citizens on the frontiers against Indians who resisted white encroachments on their lands. Neither settlers nor local militias seemed capable on their own of defeating the Native Americans.

Washington, therefore, asked Congress to increase substantially the small national army of less than nine hundred men and officers he had inherited from the defunct confederation. He met stiff opposition from those who argued "the Constitution certainly never contemplated a standing army in time of peace."[1] Only after Indians in the Old Northwest in October 1790 and November 1791 had routed expeditions under generals Josiah Harmar and Arthur St. Clair did Congress deal meaningfully with this intertwined problem of the army, the militia, and firearms. Congress authorized increases in the size of the regular army and tried to overcome the scanty production of small firearms at home. It forbade the export of such arms and permitted foreign guns to enter the country duty free.

Congress also authorized the president to summon state militias for federal duty and to expand the regular army to more than five thousand men. On May 8, 1792, the Uniform Militia Act, designed to promote regularity in the state militias as called for in the Second Amendment, became law. Indirectly, the act also allowed a nominal federal check over who would use firearms. It required "every free, able-bodied, white male citizen" between ages eighteen and forty-five to enroll in a militia with his own weapon and equipment. As had colonial legislation, this statute barred slaves, freed blacks, and Indians from serving.

Later that year Congress attempted to define dual control of the militias by passing the Calling Forth Act outlining how the president could employ state militias for federal duty. The next year Secretary of War Henry Knox assessed the arms and militia situations, expressing hope "that all the cannon, arms, and ammunition" the armed forces needed might be fabricated in the United States, even though the expense "may be greater than if imported."[2] He estimated also that 450,000 men belonged to militias and that about one in five possessed their own firearms. Of the 44,042 muskets the government owned, more than half were damaged, and similarly for its pistols.[3]

To meet an arms shortage and to help maintain the small army as well as the militias when in federal service, the government stepped up the purchase of arms from importers. It also proceeded, as Knox had suggested, to overcome the dependence on foreign sources by going into the arms-making business, using as a model the arsenals of the French government. On April 2, 1794, Congress authorized the building of "three or four arsenals" for the manufacture of weapons, including muskets and pistols.[4] It established the first arsenal at Springfield, Massachusetts, and a second one four years later at Harper's Ferry, Virginia. In May Congress again prohibited the export of arms, this time for a year.

Within two months, Washington's government had need for arms in facing its first test in the use of militia. The crisis began on July 16 when angry farmers in western Pennsylvania rose in arms to block collection of a federal tax on distilled liquor. Supporters of the administration—who had taken the name Federalists—regarded the uprising, as it spread along the frontier well beyond Pennsylvania, a dire threat to the Republic. Nonetheless, the president moved cautiously to suppress these whiskey rebels, as they became known, because he sought assurance from authorities in nearby states that they would provide the troops he required. Four states—Pennsylvania, New Jersey, Maryland, and Virginia—responded positively but encountered trouble in raising manpower for their militias.

Volunteers represented a small number of the enlisted men, so militia officers called for more. Few responded. For instance, the commanding officer of a Maryland militia unit found even his enrolled men unwilling to serve. "I very much fear that we shall find great difficulty to complete the number required," he reported. "I have not heard of a volunteer in the County."[5] In addition, when the authorities resorted to drafting men, they resisted.

The rank and file that emerged from the recruiting effort consisted mainly of draftees or substitutes, the poor, and the flotsam of society. Those who enlisted did so not out of duty but for bounties. Once paid, they deserted at a high rate. The officers, mostly upper-class gentlemen who volunteered for miscellaneous reasons—some personal, some patriotic—showed greater stability. They held the draftees in contempt, denouncing them as having little value as soldiers. Most of the 12,950 nationalized militiamen lacked their own arms so the war department had to provide nearly two-thirds of them with guns.

This army of the Constitution, as it became known, approximated in size the continental troops Washington had led during the Revolution. The rebels, whom Federalists characterized as the enemies of order, numbered around seven thousand. When the federalized troops, headed at first by Washington himself and then by General "Light Horse Harry" Lee, in October marched on the rebel counties, the opposition melted away because it realized that even with a motley army, the central government had guns and power. Although rebel resentment still festered, the president then released the citizen-soldiers from duty. They had performed about as the framers of the Second Amendment assumed a regulated militia would, as a constabulary to maintain law and order for the establishment. Accordingly, ardent Federalists such as Alexander Hamilton praised the government's energy in putting down armed anarchism.

The outcome of the Whiskey Rebellion had a number of ramifications. It demonstrated the determination of the federal government to maintain the Union and its willingness to use its power on the frontier. It revealed again, as in the Shays uprising, the establishment's lack of respect for the idea that dissatisfied citizens could keep firearms and use them against the will of the government even if the insurgents considered the regime tyrannical. In addition, the rebellion exposed the weakness of counting on untrained, compulsory militias as a meaningful national strike force in a crisis while raising the value of select militias as constabularies.

A month after the rebellion's suppression, Knox underscored the defects of the universal militia concept. He reported that fewer than a third of the half million of the nation's militiamen owned arms as the 1792 law required. Since the militia act provided no means for enforcing the self-arming of citizen-soldiers, he recommended creation of "a limited, but select, and efficient corps of militia."[6] Since neither most citizens nor the government could afford arms for the legislated compulsory militia, the federal government did not provide for organized training of militias. Thus, the citizen-arming requirement Congress had legislated never became effective.

Three years after suppression of the whiskey rebels, as President John Adams faced a crisis with France that led to the Quasi-War, national control over firearms for security again became a concern. The arsenals had not yet become fully functional and could not meet anticipated military need. In May 1797 and April 1798, therefore, Congress once more prohibited the export of firearms. It also appropriated eight hundred thousand dollars for the purchase of arms and ammunition and one hundred thousand dollars for work in the armories. The war department contracted with private craftsmen, such as Simeon North and Eli Whitney in Connecticut, for arms. They and the few other gunsmiths available could produce firearms only on a handicraft basis. So the government still had to rely largely on foreign manufacturers for the arms it desired.

Then, in February 1799, new federal taxes for the government's war program aroused a widespread discontent that came to a head in Pennsylvania. German farmers led by John Fries, a Bucks County auctioneer who had commanded a company of militia during the Revolution and in the whiskey uprising, armed themselves with long guns and swords, harassed tax collectors, and rioted. On March 12 Adams proclaimed them rebels who had committed treason. He asked the governor to order militia into the disaffected counties. To assure compliance, Adams sent five hundred army regulars to assist local authorities in hunting down Fries and his followers.

Most accounts indicate that in crushing the farmers and capturing Fries, the soldiers and militia acted with unnecessary brutality. "And now," a Republican opponent of the administration commented, "we see the effects of a standing army in time of peace." Adams later recalled that the public reacted as though the army were "a ferocious wild beast let loose upon the nation to devour it."[7] Again, the federal government had to bolster local militias and again it showed no regard for a personal right to use arms in a challenge to its authority.

Yet a number of America's early jurists linked citizen arms-keeping with liberty. Look for instance at the words, expressed in 1803, of St. George Tucker, often called the American Blackstone. "Wherever standing armies are kept up, and the right of the people to keep and bear arms is, under any colour or pretext whatsoever, prohibited, liberty, if not already annihilated, is on the brink of destruction."[8]

Regardless of such sentiment, the federal government pursued its goal of attaining a reliable source of weapons for its armed forces, for their use in national defense, and for its own security against armed malcontents. It stepped up the effort when, with the invention of percussion powder in 1807, firearms improved in durability and ease of use. The next year Congress began devoting a large portion of the budget for acquiring firearms. It also enacted legislation permitting the federal government to distribute arms and equipment annually to state militias, thereby eliminating the need for citizens in the compulsory militias to pay for their own guns. Some of the militias now took the name National Guard, a term based on the French revolutionary *garde nationale*.

At this time, too, as the nation started industrializing, arms makers began advancing beyond handicraft production. The government encouraged them to do so, often financing experimentation in the armories for the manufacture of solid, easily repaired small arms with uniform, and hopefully interchangeable, parts. Private manufacturers benefited from innovations in the armories as well as from federal financial assistance, usually in the form of long-term contracts and mass purchases of firearms.

The quest for quality in large-scale home production of arms became pressing as clashes with Great Britain over issues such as the impressment of American seamen pointed to possible war. Nonetheless, the government frequently did not take advantage of the innovation it fostered. For example, early in 1811 John H. Hall, a cabinetmaker from Portland, Maine, patented an improved breech-loading rifle based on similar foreign designs. Although the government had use for such a weapon, it moved slowly in adopting it. American soldiers, therefore, did not use breechloaders in the War of 1812. Later, the Hall breechloader, which he demonstrated could be made with interchangeable parts, became popular in a number of volunteer state militias.[9]

As in the Revolutionary War, America's militias performed badly in this second conflict with Britain, and for a number of reasons. Most soldiers of the compulsory militias lacked training in the use of muskets. In addition, state governors refused to abide by the terms of the Uniform Militia Act. They would not allow their militias to serve outside the home state or could not compel them to do so. Citizens avoided militia duty in large numbers. In most states the militia as an institution deteriorated so badly as to be practically useless in war. When the federal government considered conscription, New England opponents such as Daniel Webster perceived the effort as trying to raise "a standing army out of the militia by draft." Later, the antiwar delegates at the Hartford Convention denounced as constitutionally illegal any resort "to forcible drafts, conscriptions, or impressments."[10]

Meanwhile, in an effort to lure recruits, the federal government used bounties, cash, land, or whatever would produce fighting men. These practices initially did not work well because the strategy of rushing a hastily mobilized citizenry into battle against trained troops, which had always been chancy, had become obsolete. For instance, Andrew Jackson, the war's most noted general, had complained in 1812 that the behavior of Ohio and Kentucky militias "has tarnished the reputation of their state" and more than two years later that a detachment of the Kentucky militia "ingloriously fled before the Enemy."[11]

Thereafter, more and more of the nation's leaders questioned reliance on citizen-soldiers for national security against a foreign foe. Postwar militia officers shared this skepticism. They complained frequently of the citizen-soldiers' misuse of the guns provided them. One officer in Virginia reported that "some of the public arms are in the hands of men who are not on the rolls of the Militia; others are transferred from one individual to another as *private property*, and in many instances are carried out of the state."[12]

While in the postwar years the compulsory militia declined, dueling became increasingly distasteful to many Americans. Opponents of dueling organized one of the first movements to agitate for banishing a specific, personal use of firearms.

Colonists had brought dueling from western Europe, where it had developed from the medieval trial by combat. Men of status had long favored swords as weapons for one-on-one combat, but in the seventeenth century pistols supplanted them. Thereafter, gunsmiths competed in producing refinements that increased the firepower of their dueling guns.[13] In Europe, custom required antagonists to have equal social standing. In America, individuals on various levels of the social scale fought duels even though colonial authorities often opposed such combat on religious and moral grounds. Pennsylvania legislators decreed a punishment of jail and hard labor for those who dueled. Benjamin Franklin condemned the duel as a trial wherein a man sets himself up as judge and attempts to be the executioner. Thomas Paine and Thomas Jefferson advocated the death penalty for such combat. Still, during the Revolution dueling gained an enlarged following, particularly among army officers.

In subsequent years planters, lawyers, newspaper editors, saloon keepers, militia and regular army officers, and politicians fought duels as though an affirmation of manhood. Much of the gentry, newspaper and periodical editors, and state dignitaries such as Jefferson Davis of Mississippi opposed the practice.[14] In many communities, antidueling societies tried to counter the ritual. Although restricted to a minority of gun keepers, dueling aroused pro and con passions similar to those that would arise later over gun keeping.

Among states that by law prohibited dueling, some prescribed jail for violators, disqualified them from holding office, or threatened anyone who killed another in a duel with prosecution for murder. Because men of influence upheld such combat as part of a code of honor, the laws did not have much effect. In the South where men regularly went armed, gentlemen had a penchant for the code duello and ostensibly stood "prepared at all times to turn a minor altercation into killing." They often associated dueling with upward social mobility and concepts of manhood.[15] Regardless of law, many office-seekers believed they had to demonstrate their virility and worthiness in combat by gun. Furthermore, in states that forbade duels, legislators often pardoned survivors.[16]

The nation's most noted duel took place in Weehawken, New Jersey, on July 11, 1804, between Vice President Aaron Burr and Alexander Hamilton over an alleged insult. Although Hamilton detested such combat, under pressure he accepted a challenge from Burr, who killed him. Hamilton's death produced a revulsion against dueling throughout the North. Crowds gathered before Burr's home, chanting

> *Oh Burr, Oh Burr, what hast thou done,*
> *Thou hast shooted dead great Hamilton!*
> *You hid behind a bunch of thistle,*
> *And shooted him dead with a great hoss pistol!*[17]

New Jersey authorities charged Burr with murder. In the next year the general assembly of the Presbyterian Church denounced "the unhappy prevalence of Duelling in the United States" and urged its abolition by law. The Reverend Lyman Beecher preached on this theme, condemning dueling as "a great national sin" and "a wide spreading contagion," and the shooters as murderers. He characterized them as comprising a minority whose opinion politicians "deemed of far greater consequence, than the opinion and feelings of the great mass of the people." If the majority used the ballot against produel politicians, he maintained, "the practice of fighting duels will speedily cease."[18]

Neither this advice nor the public uproar ended dueling, even among men of prominence such as Andrew Jackson. He had the reputation of a sharpshooter with a remarkable record of survival in combat on the field of honor. He fought the best known of his duels over a betting debt and a reputed slandering of his wife, Rachel, against Charles Dickinson, a young lawyer and another expert marksman. Locals in Nashville, Tennessee, treated their confrontation as a sporting event, making bets on its outcome. When the two men met in combat on May 30, 1806, Dickinson's bullet struck first, breaking two of Jackson's ribs. Jackson then aimed, misfired, recocked his pistol, aimed again, and killed Dickinson.

Dickinson's friends and others called the shooting a murder—"a brutal, cold-blooded killing." For a time, the affair harmed Jackson, marking him as "a fearful, violent, vengeful man."[19] People in western Tennessee treated him as an outcast. In the long run though, this episode did not, as in Burr's case, destroy Jackson's career, "tarnish his warlike fame among his admirers," or end his willingness to duel.[20] Eleven years later he challenged General Winfield Scott to single combat but that officer declined, saying neither man had need to prove his honor or courage.

In 1835 John Randolph of Virginia, who in the House of Representatives led the opposition to John Quincy Adams's administration, insulted Secretary of State Henry Clay. Even though a decade earlier Clay had renounced the code of honor, he burned with rage and challenged Randolph to a duel. When on May 31 of the next year they exchanged shots, neither man suffered injury. Since each had denounced dueling out of principle, contemporaries as well as historians regarded this contest as ludicrous.

Nonetheless, specialists taught gentlemen the use of dueling pistols, people visited some fields of death as tourist attractions, and others defended the duel as the mark of a vigorous culture. Louis T. Wigfall, a senator from Texas, claimed it improved society because it "engendered courtesy of speech and demeanor . . . and as a preservative of the domestic relations it was without an equal."[21] In 1838 John Lyde Wilson, a former governor of South Carolina, published a pamphlet detailing civilized procedure for dueling, which was reprinted many times.

Europeans described American duelists as barbarous because, in comparison to their own combatants, they shot to kill rather than just to satisfy honor. This ferocity took place mostly in frontier areas where duels often resembled brawls, with contestants substituting revolvers, rifles, or shotguns for pistols. Dubiously, some writers characterized these contests as reflecting values of a developing society where men of status, or those seeking it, used firearms rather than reputedly inadequate laws to settle grievances.

At the same time, Whig political leaders—who assailed lynching, corporal punishment, child and animal abuse, drunkenness, warfare, and various forms of civil violence, legal and illegal—viewed the practice differently.[22] They damned dueling not only as immoral but also as a form of assassination. Their politicking turned public sentiment against the deadly ritual and produced some effective legislation, as in 1838 when the District of Columbia outlawed dueling. Thereafter, most states banned the practice with laws that amounted to a narrow form of gun regulation.

Reliable statistics on how many duels Americans fought, the number of casualties they produced, and how effectively antidueling laws worked, are sparse or nonexistent. Diehards kept dueling alive illicitly for years after most states had outlawed it. This underground shooting galvanized protests from antidueling groups, many of which extended their opposition to other kinds of gun violence with demands for restrictions on gun bearing.

Meanwhile, concerns over national security generated improvements in the manufacture of firearms. By 1820 the disorganized collection of gun craftsmen at the Springfield armory had become transformed into a body of disciplined industrial workers who produced quality weapons.[23] They used techniques that included replacing hand power with machines, the use of single-purpose machine tools, and substituting individually crafted parts with some that were interchangeable. These methods, with emphasis on mechanization, came in time to be known as the American system of manufactures.[24] A decade later, private manufacturers began producing more muskets, rifles, and revolvers than the military needed. Contracts with the government for military weapons declined. To dispose of their surplus small arms, gunmakers turned to the civilian market. The government helped them by encouraging citizens to buy guns. Private possession of firearms, which had risen slowly until the early thirties, began increasing markedly.[25]

This growth corresponded also with the appearance of a new breed of patent-arms makers. They benefited from three decades of government-sponsored technology that allowed them to produce firearms of uniform quality for the public as well as for the military. In a number of industries incipient mass production reduced costs and lowered prices but not much in the manufacture of firearms. Even as arms making became mechanized, the production of small firearms still required individual skill. Gunsmiths who had it commanded high pay. Manufacturers passed on the costs to the enlarging pool of civilian purchasers. Except for excluded groups such as blacks, Americans who could pay the hefty prices for firearms and had the desire and time to learn shooting skills could purchase guns for personal gratification with no discernible hindrance.

In Britain, in contrast, the civilian demand for guns appeared insufficient to warrant capital-intensive, mechanized production. So, rival firearms industry continued to rely on handicraft production. At the same time, the British government followed its old practice of selective gun regulation while seeking to add broader restraints. In 1819, as part of six laws to control internal security,

Parliament had passed the seizure of arms act authorizing justices of the peace to confiscate guns that revolutionaries might use. Twelve years later a member of Parliament introduced a bill that would have affected all citizens. It would have prohibited individuals from carrying a loaded gun in public places, but the bill did not become law. Other European countries also looked closely at forms of gun control. France's Louis Philippe, for example, in May 1834 proscribed private ownership of military firearms with up to two years' imprisonment for violation of the law.

In the United States as population grew and became more diverse, old-line, white Protestants came to dislike the idea of arming strange, immigrant males, such as Irish Catholic youths, in draft militias and training them to shoot. As did their forefathers, the Anglo nativists deplored placing guns in the hands of inappropriate people. They disguised their desire for selective gun regulation by joining those who scorned militia levies as impractical.

Militias that survived, as in New York and Massachusetts, did so by dropping compulsory drafts and relying on volunteers. These reconstituted militias functioned as upper-class social clubs where members who had the time and money could shoot for recreation. In this manner, class-conscious militia leaders had some control over weapons and avoided giving firearms and training to unsuitable people called into service as citizen-soldiers. Most other states and municipalities followed this practice of forming elite militia companies.

Still, authorities continued to pay lip service to the concept of the universal militia. This abstraction, unsupported by warm bodies, could not provide the federal government with a reliable source of soldiers. Increasingly, the government depended on an armed force with a professional core augmented by the select volunteer militias when needed. By 1830 the federal government was furnishing by far most of the muskets and their accoutrements for what remained of the enrolled militias. Few of these citizen-soldiers, or only about 31 percent, used the arms.[26]

The notion of the conscript citizen-soldier remained alive, however, mainly because of the influence of militia officers and politicians wedded to the concept. Justice Joseph Story of the Supreme Court, writing in 1833 in words used by George Washington, exemplified this traditional sentiment. Story stated that "the right of the citizens to keep, and bear arms, has justly been considered the palladium of the liberties of a republic" because it checked the "usurpation and arbitrary power of rulers."[27] Jackson, who knew the failings of the militia firsthand, as president found it politically expedient to cater to that sentiment by speaking of the militia as the bulwark of national defense and praising the patriotism of citizen-soldiers. He also appealed several times to Congress to do something to improve the militia system. In one instance, he said the problem "illustrated the importance of an increase in the rank and file of the Regular Army" because "the defects in our present militia system are every day more apparent."[28]

For this and other reasons, the rationale for a citizen's private gun-bearing as a member of a militia virtually disappeared. In mounting numbers, Americans also continued to acquire firearms for personal reasons, as for sport in shooting matches and hunting. These activities appealed especially to members of the upwardly mobile middle class who, in their eagerness to acquire social status, frequently aped the doings of the mother country's nobility. In Britain, sport shooting had increased in popularity with the upper classes along with improvements in the safety of the flintlock rifle, which had had a tendency to explode. The enthusiasm for shooting became such that some gentlemen "dedicated their lives to the sport."[29]

The snobbery of the ritualized hunt transferred to those Americans who could afford the guns, the horses, and the other expensive accoutrements. New, elite sporting magazines, such as John Stuart Skinner's *American Turf Register and Sporting Magazine* (1829) and William T. Porter's *Spirit of the Times* (1831), fashioned after those in Britain, associated sport shooting with the qualities British nobility allegedly possessed. The writers praised hunting because supposedly it distinguished ordinary men from gentlemen. The journals focused also on male bonding, depicted guns as objects of affection, and advanced the idea that "our rifles and our liberties are synonymous."[30]

The lower classes did not think in these terms. Despite the greater availability of firearms, most ordinary Americans still could not afford rifles. For them, as for commoners in Britain, ownership of firearms still rated as a luxury.[31] Even so, immigrants such as the Irish, whom the elite despised and who served as volunteer firemen in cities, possessed firearms for use in target companies. Formed first around 1830 in New York communities, these companies practiced marksmanship. They differed from the elite target-shooting clubs founded a decade earlier but not just because of class. The new clubs had larger popular followings and devoted themselves more often to musketry practice than did the elite clubs.

German immigrants, also starting in New York, established different shooting clubs, similar to those they had known in their homeland. Members wore uniforms, marched in military style with firearms, practiced marksmanship as recreation, ate heartily, drank beer, and caroused with women. These societies flourished in every eastern coastal city with a significant German population.

The heyday of these shooting clubs coincided with a rising use of guns in crime and other acts of violence. An attempted assassination brought such gun violence to the attention of the whole nation. On January 30, 1835, as Jackson left the chamber of the House of Representatives, Richard Lawrence, a young, unemployed house painter, from a distance of six feet aimed and triggered two pistols, one after the other, at him. Both misfired. "Boiling with rage," the president lunged at Lawrence and tried to club him. In April, a court ruled Lawrence insane and committed him to an asylum. Although upsetting to many Americans, this first attempt to assassinate a president appeared to have little impact on the spread of personal firearms ownership.

The shooting did add to the perception of the United States as an agricultural society with moving frontiers that bred a gun subculture. The federal government contributed to this nurturing with a system of Indian trading posts in frontier areas. With the posts, until 1822 when they closed, it continued the colonial practice of providing Native Americans with guns in exchange for furs and hides.[32] Theoretically, the government supplied the arms so the Indians could hunt game for a livelihood. Also, the system helped it exercise some control over the trafficking in firearms with Indians, which otherwise would have no discernible regulation. In the West as in the East, most Indians used their guns in intertribal warfare rather than for hunting. Indians of the eastern forests had trapped animals for fur, and those living on the Great Plains rarely used guns to hunt buffalo or other large game.[33]

The federal government revived the trading system in 1834 with the Indian Intercourse Act. Under it, persons licensed by the government sold guns and ammunition to Native Americans.[34] These agents tended to place their authority to monitor gun sales well behind their desire to profit from them. Some Plains Indians desired discriminating federal restraints on the arms trading. They wished to prevent firearms from falling into the hands of enemies, such as the Sioux nations. The Sioux in turn did not like to see guns and ammunition supplied to enemy Cheyenne.[35]

On the frontiers, white citizens who could afford firearms continued to have access to them without meaningful restraint. Imaginative chroniclers would write later of these Americans as carrying firearms everywhere—into the fields where they worked, to the marketplace, and even to church. In one prominent portrayal of frontier life, "men lived with rifles in their hands, ready to mount and ride" against murderous Indians. "A man often stood guard with a rifle while another milked the cow or plowed the field. . . . It was as unusual to see a man without a rifle at that time as one without a hat today. And it always had to be loaded and ready." The rifle, this historian maintained, "was the very center of frontier life." The gun was "actually man's best friend, and a boy early learned to use it."[36] In the real life of grubbing for a livelihood, however, mainly westward-moving migrants routinely carried rifles and other guns.

Writers such as James Fenimore Cooper, America's first major novelist, bestowed heroic qualities on frontier folk. They praised Daniel Boone, the legendary hunter and trapper, as an Indian fighter and militia captain. They exalted the pioneer farmer but also frequently "the figure of the hunter" as shooter. They described his attachment to his rifle as "love with a passion almost comparable to his love of a woman."[37]

This view of firearms did not carry over to Americans who had taken to small, easily concealed handguns in increasing numbers. Nor did social critics perceive a need to love guns. Instead, they expressed concern over "the alarming frequency of bloody affrays attended with fatal results" emanating from such hidden gun-toting. As one of them commented, "This cowardly and disgraceful practice, if it is really unconstitutional to restrain by law, ought to be discountenanced by all persons who are actuated by proper feelings of humanity or a just regard for the dictates of religion." He urged control legislation, asserting "the courts and juries may do much, if they will set their faces against it." They could, he maintained, stem the gun violence "without either violating the constitution, or overstepping any legal principle."[38]

These concerns, along with the increase in gun violence, produced the first efforts to place some kind of limits on the freedom of individuals to use firearms beyond those imposed on blacks, Indians, and other minority peoples. Most states enacted legislation prohibiting even proper citizens from carrying concealed weapons on the assumption that they inflicted more harm than did displayed guns.

Disliking this mild prohibition, gun keepers protested. They contended that local authorities could not deprive them of free use of their firearms. As citizens, they had a constitutional right to arm and protect themselves as they saw fit. Whereas some state courts agreed with them, others differed. Most courts accepted the right of states to impose narrow restrictions on gun use that applied to all citizens as well as to maintain the older controls imposed on proscribed people. These state-court decisions held that the Bill of Rights, in the matter of arms keeping, limited only the authority of the federal government.

Only once did a court overturn state legislation that restrained weapons ownership beyond the previous selective limitations. In *Bliss v. Commonwealth*, 12 Ky. (2 Litt) 90 (1822), Kentucky's supreme court ruled that regulation of concealed weapons, in this instance a sword cane, violated the state's militia amendment that granted individuals a right to bear arms. In response, the legislature modified the state constitution to allow such control. Thereafter, court after court ruled in keeping with the logic expressed by Tennessee's high court in *Aymette v. the State*, 21 Tenn. (2 Hum.) 154 (1840)—that the Constitution did not confer the right to keep concealed arms for personal protection.[39]

5
A Gun Culture Emerges

I n the formative years of the Republic, tolerance for gun keeping, when combined with the practical limitations of enforcing state and local firearms
regulations, translated often into casual law enforcement. Where authorities
had public backing and the desire to monitor compliance with restrictions, they
lacked the resources necessary to perform gun supervision duties. Under these
conditions even laws prohibiting proscribed groups from having firearms often
did not work.

In most parts of the country, responsibility for carrying out local ordinances
and maintaining order fell to sheriffs in counties and constables and night
watchmen in cities and towns. In large emergencies, *posse comitatus*, militia
companies, or even vigilantes assumed the task. The official law-keepers were
often volunteers who sometimes received pay or who, as a civic duty, served
without remuneration. Some citizens found the task so distasteful or dangerous
that even when they were desperately needed or faced possible conscription
they evaded the obligation. As protectors of public safety against robberies and
violent crime, these part-time guardians of law had marked deficiencies, such
as being armed usually only with a club.

Sometimes, in special circumstances as in New York in 1801, the policing
agents could carry guns. Faced with frequent jail breaks, authorities there
equipped a special squad of watchmen with firearms to guard the penitentiary
at night.[1] Cities that rose to the west resorted to part-time constabularies, usually without guns. Pittsburgh in 1804 responded to a rash of burglaries with a
temporary patrol, whereas in the next year Cincinnati required all voters to
serve in a night watch it established.[2]

A number of southern communities allowed their law keepers to carry guns
on a regular basis, primarily to keep slave populations in line. In 1805 New Or-

leans initiated a military-style police, called city guards, who wore uniforms, carried firearms, and received wages rather than fees or performed compulsory, unpaid service as in some northern cities. Charleston, Savannah, Mobile, and Richmond adopted similar law enforcement practices. In contrast to northern cities, southern communities hired armed police primarily to keep black slaves under surveillance and to prevent them and other presumed dangerous people from acquiring guns.[3]

Whether north or south, as much else in the United States, law enforcement practices corresponded to those in the mother country. In both countries, urban taxpayers regarded full-time, armed police forces as too expensive and as smacking of standing armies. In New York City in 1811 Charles Christian, a longtime magistrate, advised a change in policing procedure. He described the population as "increasing beyond all precedent" and the city as a place where "depredators merge in mass, and spoliate in secret and safety." That situation, he believed, required "that there should be established, as soon as possible, as complete a system of preventive Police for this city as our laws will admit of."[4]

That did not happen at this time in New York. In Great Britain an apparent spurt in urban crime and other disorders, along with the political skills of Home Secretary Sir Robert Peel, similar concerns brought notable changes in urban law enforcement. In April 1829 in introducing a request for professional law-keeping in London, Peel told the House of Commons, "It is no longer possible to leave all the responsibility in connection with the detection of offenders, or the prevention of crimes, in the hands of the parochial authorities."[5]

Peel's Metropolitan Police Bill, establishing Britain's day-and-night police force responsible directly to the Home Secretary, passed its first reading in Parliament in June. In September, after it became law, newly hired officers replaced the constables and watchmen and started patrolling London's streets. To avoid a backlash from those who regarded the full-time department as a wedge for a standing army, Peel took pains to ensure that the men in it did not look like soldiers. In contrast to the brightly clad men in the military, the new police wore drab, blue uniforms without decoration and wielded mainly clubs. Those with the rank of inspector or above could carry a pistol. Still, the authorities organized the force hierarchically, allowed it to practice military discipline as in parade-ground drill, and for years former soldiers filled its command structure.

A more important feature in the London force was the theory behind its formation. It corresponded to Christian's earlier recommendation for New York. Previously, those entrusted with enforcing law sought to catch violators when they committed a crime and hold them for punishment. Peel's department had instructions to prevent crime or disorder rather than just to catch lawbreakers after the fact. It came into being as the first large department organized on that principle. This prevention mission led to greater day-and-night surveillance of the lives of the citizenry, some of whom grumbled over loss of personal liberty. In all, though, police intrusion into personal privilege amounted to a trade-off. Individuals lost a bit of their freedom of movement while society as a whole gained more security than in the past.

In the United States, most towns and cities continued to rely on part-time sentinels to maintain order and to enforce regulations against public nuisances and dangerous practices such as discharging guns in public places and storing gunpowder. Fear of explosion, fire, and destruction of large sections of cities made the production, storage, and sale of gunpowder one of the first to be policed as a matter of course. Few could defend the private right to sell or store gunpowder in the heart of America's mushrooming cities.[6]

Crime, it seemed, increased in pace with the growth of cities. Concerned citizens became convinced that self-defense with private arms and reliance on part-time protection against assault, robbery, mobs, and riots had proved inadequate. No reliable data supported this assumption because statistics on crime would not be collected until the next century. Later, statistical studies would indicate that over the long run in the nineteenth century urban crime actually decreased. As in the colonial era, impression and anecdote exaggerated the extent of crime and violence.[7] Nonetheless, belief became the basis for people supporting beefed-up police forces.

Municipal leaders turned to the London experience for guidance in urban policing. A number of them began using permanent police departments to provide security for person and property, particularly for the upper classes. At the same time numerous Americans could not shed their fear of police armed with guns. Even those southern cities with established paramilitary police eyed Britain's civilian model because they found their own military types too menacing. For instance, the *Louisiana Advertiser* complained of the New Orleans police's "parading the streets at noon day in all the panoply of war, 'armed to the teeth' [with] . . . [t]he badge of military rule, the sword belt, and the pistol, and . . . the musket and bayonet[.] And for what? To frighten freemen!"[8] In 1836 New Orleans dropped the requirement for police to wear uniforms and carry firearms.

Meanwhile, marked changes in law-breaking and mayhem had led to fresh problems in policing in northern communities. Previously, thieves, street toughs, and rioters had used mainly fists, clubs, and knives in their violence. Now some of them acquired handguns, posing thereby a challenge that law officers who were still armed mainly with clubs had difficulty meeting. This dilemma led many ordinary people who could afford firearms to buy them, sometimes for settling personal disputes but more often for self-defense as during riots. In a riot in New York City in April 1834 guns came into play because of political rivalry over an election. Whigs broke into a state arsenal, passed out rifles to cohorts, and barricaded the building. They defended the assault by contending they had acted as police auxiliaries.[9]

The next year, on a modest scale, Boston became the first northern city to establish a police force on the preventive principle, but it could not stop riots. In Philadelphia in 1834 and 1838 and Cincinnati in 1841 whites fired their guns supposedly to defend the urban establishment but really to keep down non-Anglo immigrants and oppressed blacks. As for the free blacks, even though they were denied open access to firearms by biased control laws, they seized them as best they could and in pitched battles fired back at rampaging whites. Blacks felt compelled to use guns for self-defense because rarely could they count on police for protection. In all, racial animosities, fear of crime, and inadequate police protection made cities a lucrative civilian market for guns regardless of cost.

For an undetermined number of Americans, the spurt in gun violence, along with the inadequacy of the few restrictive state and local laws on private arms-carrying, indicated a need for better firearms regulation. This attitude appeared in literature directed mainly to upper-class readers. In some instances the criticism went beyond crime and riot. It reflected a disdain for those who used guns for pleasure or sport, as in target shooting or hunting.

In 1843 the first book directed to juvenile readers that lavished attention on details of firearms use condemned their indiscriminate private possession. Carrying weapons, it warned, makes men "fierce in spirit, boastful, and revengeful." It compared men with guns to little boys with sticks who were bound to hit each other with them.[10] Though not widespread, such concern over arms keeping received increasing attention. For example, in *State v. Buzzard*, 4 Ark. 18 (1842), the Arkansas Supreme Court ruled that the sole purpose of the Second Amendment was to secure a well-regulated militia. It did not guarantee an "absolute" personal right to arms. Two years later in *State v. Newsom*, 27 N.C. (5 Ired.) 250, 251 (1844), the North Carolina high court held that the Second Amendment did not constrain state legislation controlling firearms, in this instance a law prohibiting free blacks from owning guns without a license.[11]

At this time also, in May 1844 riots that pitted white nativists, Irish immigrants, and local militia against each other swept over parts of Philadelphia. A disdainful, upper-class witness and militia participant, Sidney George Fisher, commented in his diary that boys "scarce able to carry a musket" shot at people and killed several, while women carried weapons to rioters and cheered them. "These are strange things for Philadelphia," Fisher added. "We have never had anything like it before, but now that firearms have been once used & become familiar to the minds of the mob, we may expect to see them employed on all occasions, and our riots in future will assume a more dangerous character."[12]

When the upheaval ended, with at least twenty people dead and well over one hundred injured, citizen posses armed with guns patrolled the city's streets to keep unruly mobs in check. In July mass terror broke out again when nativists attacked a Catholic church. Authorities called in a militia unit that bombarded the church with a cannon. Irish rioters and others fought back with "musketry and cannon." Fortunately for the troops, the rioters, using old and worn-out guns, could not shoot straight. In addition to numerous injuries, two troopers and about twenty rioters died.[13] Despite the deadliness guns in civilian hands brought to urban life, the chief justice of Pennsylvania's supreme court maintained that "a man has a right to keep whatever arms he pleases in his house. . . . *This is a freeman's choice.*"[14]

The recourse to guns in urban riots corresponded with their continuing use during election campaigns. In New York City in October 1844, for instance, emotionally aroused Democrats stored their small arms at party headquarters. Whig journalists then advised the faithful in their party "to go armed to every political meeting or procession which takes place." Promptly, another writer reported, "the gun shops and hardware stores, where firearms are to be found, have had a most extraordinary increase of business."[15]

New York City's violence led to renewed demands for replacement of the part-time law enforcement system with a professional police force as in London but without centralized control as in England. In responding to the pressure for reform, the state legislature authorized a reorganization of the city's law keeping. The next year the city's Common Council supplemented the constabulary with two hundred salaried police, a force too small to patrol the streets effectively. So the following year a newly elected council abolished the constabulary and established a full-time department.[16] Thereafter, policing authority expanded through much of American society.

Since professional police were not numerous and rarely packed guns, even they could not contain large-scale tumults. During these upheavals, municipal authorities usually called on local militia to aid them. When properly trained, select militiamen could suppress rioting because they had firearms and knew how to use them. And use them they did, invariably causing more bloodshed than did rioters. For this reason, among others, civilians detested the class-based militias. Consequently, these feared urban peacekeepers seldom appeared in accounts on the virtues of gun keeping.

During these years also, private manufacturers continued to benefit from improvements in the design of small arms as sponsored in the government arsenals. One entrepreneur, young Samuel Colt, a Yankee from Connecticut, applied the principle of percussion to single-action revolvers and patented the process in Europe and the United States. In 1836 he began manufacturing the new weapons, which had mostly interchangeable parts, in Paterson, New Jersey, but failed to make a profit. Four years later his company collapsed.

At the Springfield armory another gunsmith, Thomas Warner, employed the American system to fashion a musket with an advanced, reliable percussion cap that when struck sharply would explode. When the musket went into production in 1842 as the Springfield caplock, it replaced the flintlock as the infantry's standard shoulder arm. Because it was also the first firearm with fully interchangeable parts produced in large quantities at the two national armories, it marked something of a technical watershed.[17]

These improvements came as the United States and Mexico plunged toward hostilities. James K. Polk had come to the presidency with a faith in the value of the militia based on a misreading of the past. In December 1845 he told Congress the nation must rely mainly on its citizen-soldiers "who will be ever ready . . . to rush with alacrity, at the call of their country." Yet with the declaration of war against Mexico on May 13, 1846, neither the small regular army, deployed and equipped mainly for Indian-fighting, nor the depleted traditional militias could meet the need for trained military shooters. In December, therefore, he asked Congress, "in order to prosecute the war with vigor and success," for prompt authority to increase the regular army.[18]

Polk could not muster troops immediately by recruiting from the compulsory militia because it was vanishing or by enlarging the regular army through conscription because of bitter political opposition to such a course. So he called for volunteers to fight as part of a national force. Congress authorized fifty thousand volunteers, with allotments for each state, to serve either for a year or for the duration of the war. The eligible citizenry responded to the call in overwhelming numbers. In Tennessee, which had a quota of three thousand soldiers, more than thirty thousand volunteered. Thousands of shooting-club members, as well as men in special militias familiar with small arms, joined the new army.

The federal armories lacked the capacity to arm these quickly mobilized troops while trying also to meet demands for ammunition and artillery. The government therefore turned to importers and private gun-makers such as Eliphalet Remington II and Colt, offering them contracts for small arms for which they frequently lobbied. In the previous year the army had purchased 150 Colt pistols and carbines. After the war had started, officers under "Old Rough-and-Ready" Zachary Taylor, the general in command of the army that invaded Mexico overland, asked for more of Colt's patented firearms. So, on January 4, 1847, the secretary of war granted Colt a contract for one thousand revolvers with "parts sufficiently uniform to be interchanged with slight or no refitting."[19] Lacking the time, capital, and production skills necessary to execute those terms on his own, Colt subcontracted with Eli Whitney Jr. With Whitney's help, Colt made his first profit from handguns and then went into business on his own. With government financial assistance, innovative technology, and an amplified American system, other manufacturers also turned out firearms in quantity for the troops and profited.

During the course of the war, Colt learned something else about profit from the making of guns. About 50 percent of his production failed to meet government standards. He sold the rejected revolvers to civilians. They willingly paid a higher price for them than the war department would offer for first-rate weapons. He wrote at the time that "private orders for my pistols are very large" and that he was anxious "to get the government work off as fast as possible" to meet those orders.[20]

The fighters for whom the new arms were intended brought with them problems similar to those of the citizen-soldiers in America's earlier wars. The new recruits usually lacked discipline, defied their officers, plundered civilians, and raped women. As the journal Niles Register commented, "The graceless and lawless spirits, being the most difficult to control, join the ranks and carry with them their lawless propensities, as a matter of course."[21] About six months later General Winfield Scott noted that almost daily reports reached Washington that "the wild volunteers . . . committed, with impunity, all sorts of atrocities on the persons and properties of Mexicans."[22] With undisguised but not always justified bias, the regulars characterized these volunteers as virtually useless as soldiers.

Despite these problems, the president did not change his attitude toward militia and volunteers. After the decisive American victory, he even relied on the myths of wholesale gun-keeping and American uniqueness to praise them. "Our citizen-soldiers are unlike those drawn from the population of any other country," he stated. "They are armed, and have been accustomed from their youth to handle and use firearms, and a large portion of them, especially in the Western and more newly settled states, are expert marksmen."[23]

Also after the war ended, firearms manufacturers benefited from a surge of popular interest in guns. It enabled manufacturers such as Colt, Sharps, Remington, Robbins and Lawrence, Smith & Wesson, and Winchester to improve the quality of their small arms, expand production, and lower prices. Private users who could afford the guns purchased them on an unprecedented scale. One social critic linked the gun-buying spree to the war and crime. He commented that the war gave fresh impetus to lawlessness and caused a drop in the valuing of human life. When the volunteers returned home, he wrote, "crimes of violence and blood visibly increased. The revolver had become a cheaper and handier weapon."[24]

Colt, the prime maker of the revolver, traveled across America and Europe demonstrating it and drumming up sales for his guns. Since his revolvers had little or no value for hunting and in war only officers carried them, they became weapons prized primarily for use in violent close-quarters situations. Shooters valued them because they fired several rounds quickly, overcame the need for shooting skill, and cost less than comparable guns produced by competitors. As Colt's revolver came "within the reach of the poor as well as the rich," it became notably popular on the western frontier.[25] Users there allegedly coined aphorisms such as "Colt found the pistol a single-shooter and left it a six-shooter" or "God created men; Colonel Colt made them equal." In El Paso one gun lover wrote, "I would as soon go out into the street without my pants as without my Colt."[26]

Despite the hyperbole in this comment, it did indicate that handguns, now produced in quantity, had become a more important feature of American life than in the past. The arms industry's mechanized manufacturing contributed to this change. American firms produced weapons that not only replaced reliance of civilians on craft gun-makers but also relieved the United States from dependence on arms made in other countries such as Britain. Much more than Americans, the British remained wedded largely to handcrafted weapons.[27] The American industry, with a secure home market, patented firearms, and machine production, forged ahead to lead the world in the manufacture of guns. In 1851 at the Great Exhibition in London, American firearms won medals for design and quality of construction.

Among the firearms entrepreneurs, Colt stood out as the most successful in designing handguns specifically for civilians. In 1855 he built the largest private armory in the world, allowing him to fill foreign as well as domestic contracts for his weapons. During the Crimean War, for instance, British, Turkish, and Russian officers wore his revolvers, but more for personal reasons than for combat. When he died seven years later, he "had made and sold almost one million guns, a first in the history of American manufacturing."[28]

The easier civilian access to firearms such as Colt's revolver, along with the tradition that individuals could keep them for any purpose they desired without significant restraints, affected state and local regulatory laws. The denial of firearms to people deemed unfit to have them no longer worked as well as legislators intended. As more people acquired guns, the few narrowly focused restraints became increasingly difficult to enforce. Still, the restrictions designed to keep the dangerous classes disarmed operated with more effect than laws aimed directly at gun-toting, upper-class whites. Consequently, state and local officials continued to impose the special controls and some lower courts approved them. In all, the robust firearms industry, middle-class men who hunted or shot for sport, and lower-class males who aped them created, as the scholarship of Michael Bellesiles has shown, "for the first time a gun subculture."[29]

As could be expected in these circumstances, the expansion in the number of civilian gun-keepers also complicated the maintaining of law, order, and public tranquillity in both town and country. Even New York City's professionalized police continued having difficulty dealing with aroused mobs. The city's most troubling postwar upheaval developed out of animosities between Anglophobes and Anglophiles that rabble-rousers such as the writer Edward Z. C. Judson, better known as Ned Buntline, compounded.

At the height of the tension on May 10, 1849, British tragedian William Macready performed at the Astor Place opera house guarded by about two hundred police and three hundred militiamen. Some twenty thousand people gathered outside, rioted, and showered the protectors with bricks and paving stones, injuring fifty volunteer citizen-soldiers. The militia fired warning shots over the rioters' heads but failed to stop them. The troopers then pumped live ammunition into the crowd, killing twenty-two people and wounding many more.[30]

Those who disliked deploying citizen-soldiers as an elite constabulary denounced this use of firearms to cut down unarmed citizens as though a first-time event. Actually, the militia behaved in line with precedents set in England, in the colonies, and in tumults such as the Shays uprising.

Rioters made the policing of cities difficult but so did the activities of popular, raucous, lowbrow, urban clubs associated with volunteer fire-fighting that sponsored shooting at targets as sport. According to a careful estimate, membership in New York target companies in 1850 had come to number ten thousand.[31] Their drinking, gun blasting, and rowdiness on excursions aroused complaints from those who lived near the contest grounds. Later, the city's police commission recommended outlawing the excursions but the targeters had enough political clout to defeat legislation that would have curbed their shooting and prevented them from parading with arms. Municipal authorities tried to cope with the disturbances with ordinances prohibiting individuals from carrying concealed weapons. These laws frequently flopped.

Failure continued also to dog laws requiring service in traditional militias. Evasion had become so widespread that by midcentury most states had abolished such duty, but they maintained their volunteer militias. As in the Astor Place confrontation, these militias suppressed riots and coped with other public tumults as though extensions of police forces. Most small towns had at least one volunteer company whereas large cities had a dozen or more. Because state officials viewed these units as the most reliable military forces available to them, they readily incorporated them into their National Guard establishment to maintain order on a larger scale.

The popular attitude toward police provided another reason why state and local establishments valued volunteer militias. Much of the citizenry still held to the tradition of viewing any large, well-armed constabulary as a potential instrument of tyranny. In most cities those who governed still hesitated to allow the men entrusted with law enforcement to carry guns—at least officially. City fathers who desired decentralized police forces controlled by civilians still objected to uniforms or military attitudes.

Furthermore, despite their desire for order in the cities, upper-class Americans often distrusted and looked down on the police because they were usually recruited from the lower levels of society. The elite viewed more kindly the militia companies filled with middle-class males who usually were better armed than police and kept their guns in better working condition than had compulsory militiamen. Consequently, in the 1850s most police departments outside the South remained small and not yet legally armed with guns. Six cities had uniformed police and only a few had armed constabularies.[32] In large cities, though, authorities stepped up adoption of professional police departments along with full-time fire departments.

As newspapers played up stories on crimes of violence, these hires seemed necessary. In New York City in summer 1852 homicides rose markedly, increasing the citizenry's fear of venturing onto the streets after dark. The next year the mayor reacted by ordering police, who wore only badges to indicate their status, into uniforms. With uniforms, the *Evening Post* editorialized, police were more likely to "watch society, and society will watch them."[33]

Two years later police in St. Louis could not prevent mob violence. Not even militia with firearms could cope with it. So, mainstream citizens made a run on gun stores.[34] Despite such difficulties, most cities continued to professionalize their police departments, as did Philadelphia the next year. The following year New Orleans reuniformed its police and attempted to reduce gun violence by prohibiting its people to carry concealed weapons.

Permanent police departments tended to enhance security for many urbanites, but they also brought problems. Police frequently became instruments of political factions, abused their power, and incurred public disdain. When city fathers believed they would be less brutal if they did not have firearms, officers armed themselves anyway with pocket revolvers. Some municipal authorities turned a blind eye to this practice.

The debate over whether or not police should officially carry guns beyond emergency situations became heated in New York City when gangs of street toughs using revolvers instigated a rash of robberies. A prominent attorney, George Templeton Strong, noted, "An epidemic of crime this winter [1856–7]. . . . Most of my friends are investing in revolvers and carry them about at night, and if I expect to have to do a great deal of late night street-walking of Broadway, I think I should make the like provision; though it's a very bad practice carrying concealed weapons."[35]

In light of this gun violence and because three officers armed only with billy clubs had been recently murdered, the chief of police asked the police commissioners for authority to arm "ten prudent and discreet patrolmen with revolvers." He believed that this firepower might help his small force in dealing with the crime. Critics contended that the mere knowledge of a few police being armed with revolvers "will invest them with much greater terror than they now possess." Moreover, they perceived "the danger of placing deadly weapons in the hands of men who may use them with impunity at their own discretion, is too great to be lightly incurred; and it is only as the choice of a lesser evil that such a measure could be recommended."[36]

Despite denial of the request, some of the police continued to pack guns anyway. The next year, when one of them killed an escaping prisoner, the shooting aroused public concern. Critics called it "a deliberate murder," saying the police did not use pistols "in *self-defence*" but as "substitutes for swift feet and long arms." These social watchdogs pointed out that police had no authority to have pistols or to violate the local law prohibiting anyone from carrying concealed weapons. They remained opposed to the official arming of police with revolvers.[37] Later, to combat the greater evil of crime and disorder, municipal authorities allowed officers to carry their own revolvers while on duty. At the same time, beginning with Baltimore, more cities authorized their police to use firearms in emergencies.

Meanwhile, civilian gun-violence had become a feature of the controversy over slavery and states' rights. Proslavery and antislavery militants forsook logical discussion for the gun, especially in 1856 in "Bleeding Kansas." Foreign travelers noted the arming and the climate of fear. One of them, after visiting Missouri in May, commented that "deeds of violence were almost daily occurrences. The St. Louis papers contained advertisements, by the half-column, of rifles, revolvers, gunpowder, and lead." For example, one ad announced, "SHOT GUNS will be sold cheap for cash."[38]

In this turmoil, those who wanted to keep Kansas from becoming a slave state, such as members of the Massachusetts Emigrant Aid Company, sponsored free-soil settlers and smuggled new breech-loading Sharps single-shot rifles into the territory with them. Henry Ward Beecher and other abolitionists pointed out that Northern free-soil settlers had gone there with weapons in hand to battle proslavery settlers from neighboring Missouri. These slaveholders, often called "Border Ruffians," entered the territory with enough firearms and ammunition to fight a war. The English visitor observed one of them with a hundred pistols.[39] Beecher, who said that at times self-defense is a religious duty, contributed twenty-five rifles and twenty-five Bibles to free-soilers. Many contemporaries then called the Sharps rifles "Beecher's Bibles" and his Plymouth Church in Brooklyn the "Church of the Holy Rifles."[40]

When Senator Andrew P. Butler of South Carolina urged the disarming of the embattled factions, Charles Sumner, the antislavery senator from Massachusetts, protested. In a two-day speech beginning on May 19 that was immediately published as a pamphlet and sold an estimated one million copies, he conjured up the pioneer gun myth. "The rifle has ever been the companion of the pioneer, and, under God, his tutelary protector against the red man and the beast of the forest," he declared. "Never was this efficient weapon more needed in just self-defence, than now in Kansas, and at least one article in our National Constitution must be blotted out, before the complete right to it can in anyway be impeached." Yet, he added, in defiance of the Second Amendment, the "people of Kansas have been arraigned for keeping and bearing arms."[41]

The Republican National Convention also objected to the disarming. It protested that "the dearest Constitutional rights of the people of Kansas have been fraudulently and violently taken from them" and their territory "has been invaded by an armed force." In sum, it stated, "The right of the people to keep and bear arms has been infringed."[42]

Shortly after, the Supreme Court for the first time touched on the gun issue. Unlike the Republican Party and Sumner, it opted for traditional restrictions on gun keeping by the wrong people. In March 1857 in *Dred Scott v. Sanford*, 60 U.S. (19 How.), 393, 417 (1856), Chief Justice Roger B. Taney indicated legislators could deny blacks, slave or free, the right to possess arms just as they had been denied freedom of speech, assembly, and travel. Now the widespread prejudice against armed blacks, whether free or slave, had the sanction of federal law.

As is well known, sectional differences in matters of race and slavery also soon precipitated the great sectional confrontation on secession. In winter 1860–61 as the crisis came to a head, militants in both the North and the South scampered to amass firearms. Elite militias in the Southern states seized federal forts and arsenals, grabbing all the armaments they could. In the North, when in April 1861 the Civil War erupted, the federal government had more guns than the Confederacy and a small regular army but few state militias trained capably in the use of firearms.

At first, at the order of President Abraham Lincoln, the Union relied on volunteers, select militia, and the army to do the fighting. The Confederacy, too, started with an army of volunteers. When they fell short of the number of troops needed, on April 16, 1862, the South began drafting males eighteen to thirty five years old. In the North, when states failed to meet militia quotas, Congress enacted the militia act of July 17, 1862, the country's first national military draft. It subjected all able-bodied men, for a period of nine months, to national military service. The federal government exercised this power over the citizenry under the guise of militia duty because of the experience in the War of 1812 and the continuing public distaste for conscription. When volunteers lagged, Congress passed the enrollment act of March 13, 1863, which allowed holding draftees for longer service. It, too, carried a deceptive title because of fear that a straightforward name would incite popular resistance.[43] Thereafter, the Union fielded armies composed of volunteers, enticed often with bounties, and ranks filled as well as with conscripts and regulars.

As the armies expanded, the federal government could not furnish the troops with all the small arms they needed. Even though the North contained a well-established arms industry, only twelve firms produced revolvers and none made sophisticated breech-loading guns with fully interchangeable parts.[44] Quickly, though, manufacturers interrupted their more lucrative civilian production to meet military demands. Within a year or so, with new plants and expanded old ones, gunmakers delivered most of what the Union forces required, though mostly muzzle-loading, single-shot rifles. The Union government also contracted abroad for firearms and sent agents to scour Europe's armories for guns, often with the purpose of preventing Confederate buyers from obtaining them. The Union imported one million small arms out of the estimated four million it used.

Lacking a substantial arms industry and the means to build one, the Confederate government had greater difficulty obtaining firearms. At the start of hostilities it had to turn away recruits because its armies had insufficient guns. When Confederate forces captured and then evacuated the arsenal at Harper's Ferry, they carried its rifle-making machinery to Richmond, Virginia, and Fayetteville, North Carolina, where workers produced thousands of firearms.

The Confederate government also contracted with foreign producers for arms. Its agents packed them in special vessels designed to run the Union naval blockade. On its own, the South produced no more than seventy thousand shoulder arms but purchased more than two hundred thousand weapons from European makers until the Union blockade shut off that source. Still, as a student of the subject concluded, "rarely was the South in want of small arms."[45]

At the outset of the conflict, as was the practice in most armies at the time, infantry on both sides used smoothbore muskets because muzzle-loading rifles with longer range took too long to load for use in combat. Soon the contestants started replacing the smoothbores with newly developed guns such as one using a concave-based bullet that expanded on firing and thereby took to the rifle grooves. This bullet made clumsy, muzzle-loading rifles more efficient weapons of death.

Large-scale production of repeating breech-loading guns also significantly changed the style of combat. By 1862 most regiments in the Union army had Springfield or Enfield rifles that embodied these features or became equipped with muskets converted to grooved rifles. In the hands of trained shooters, these weapons proved deadly against traditional infantry tactics. The military historian Russell Weigley maintains that as a consequence "the Civil War became the first great war of the rifle, and the rifle dominated the battlefields."[46]

Internally during the hostilities, Lincoln's government impaired civil liberties as with the suspension of habeas corpus in civilian areas. It also used federal authority to curb private arms-keeping in border states under Union control such as Maryland and Missouri that contained large numbers of Confederate sympathizers. There, under its war power, the Union government confiscated firearms in civilian hands. In 1864 the Democratic National Convention, in a tone similar to that of the Republicans eight years earlier, denounced "subversion of the civil by military law in States not in insurrection." It condemned "the interference with and denial of the right of the people to bear arms in their defence."[47]

Earlier, as the armies battled, urban rioting accompanied by the heightened criminal use of guns led more white civilians, North and South, to pack personal firearms. In 1861 a sheriff described New Orleans, for instance, as a hell on earth because of its murders and deadly assaults. When authorities there enforced the ban on public toting of guns, the violence diminished but did not disappear.

Within Union territory, conscription triggered violence. Well-to-do young men evaded the draft by paying a three-hundred-dollar exemption fee or by hiring substitutes. Poor whites who could not afford such costs perceived the draft not only as an unfair, class-based, federal intrusion into their lives but also properly as falling most heavily on them. When local police and federal authorities tried to enforce the conscription act, thousands of workingmen resisted.

In Detroit, the draft, racism, and the shooting and killing of civilians by police set off a riot in March 1863 whose suppression required five or six hundred militiamen and a detachment of federal troops. Two years later the lesson of this riot led the Detroit fathers to create a permanent police force.[48] In July in New York City and Boston, resisters attacked federal draft-enforcement agents. New York police tried at first to contain the rioters with clubs and in several instances turned on them with personal pistols. When a mob pillaged a building where small arms and ammunition were stored, the police fought pitched battles with roving gangs armed with rifles and handguns. Whole companies of the volunteer fire department joined the rioters.

The city's four days of violence, which degenerated into a pogrom against blacks, stopped only after five regiments of federal troops from Gettysburg used their firearms to restore order. The deaths, inflicted by the guns of the military, numbered at least 105, making this civil upheaval the bloodiest of the century.[49]

Other riots followed in Troy and Buffalo, New York; Newark, New Jersey; Philadelphia; Portsmouth, New Hampshire; and elsewhere. The civilian gun violence in these outbreaks aroused anxiety among local authorities. Draft resisters killed ninety-eight federal registrars. The men at the top of the federal government, though, gave low priority to suppressing civilian gun violence because they concentrated on mobilizing resources to win the war. They concerned themselves much more with the military demand for firearms and victory on the battlefields than with mayhem on city streets.

In the North, the war brought renewed prosperity to the arms industry, which continued to make guns for civilians as well as for soldiers. The conflict also acquainted thousands of youths who knew nothing about firearms with their use. This happened even in the South, where shooting skills were supposedly more widespread than in the North. In the South the conflict brought legal freedom to blacks, but to whites it brought defeat and military occupation.

For most Americans the surrender of the Confederate forces under General Robert E. Lee on April 9, 1865, at Appomattox Court House in Virginia to Union General Ulysses S. Grant symbolized the depth of that defeat. It struck John Wilkes Booth, a disillusioned actor and Southern patriot, particularly hard. He blamed Lincoln for the South's suffering. So, five days later at Ford's Theater in Washington, shouting reputedly *"sic semper tyrannis"* (ever thus to tyrants), he discharged the ball of a single-shot derringer into the president's brain as he stood in an unguarded box. Booth believed that with the pistol he had slain despotism and had achieved enduring fame rather than the infamy that became his fate.[50]

Grant, meanwhile, had allowed Confederate officers to retain their side arms. In capitulations elsewhere in the South that followed Appomattox, the federal government did not always demand complete disarmament of the former enemy soldiers. They had to give up their long guns, but some with pistols kept them for personal use. The Union army allowed its own discharged soldiers to take their firearms home. Thus, thousands of men trained in the use of firearms returned to civilian life with their own government-issue guns.

This reentry of weapons into society appeared to cause no immediate concern to most Americans. Regardless of the complexities of the causes and result of the war, they believed the North's heavy manufacture of firearms had contributed to the salvation of the Union. They also evinced a marked change in sentiment toward volunteer soldiers, regulars, and arms keeping for military use. "It is a little singular that the country receives with perfect equanimity, with positive approval, perhaps," the nation's military periodical commented, "the prospect of the establishment of an institution which for nearly eighty years it has opposed and rejected . . . the establishment of a large Standing Army. The Great Rebellion has reversed national opinion on this point, as on so many others."[51]

Nationalists also accepted as permanent the wartime expansion of federal power well beyond what it had been since the founding of the Republic. In addition, nationalists perceived the war's result as a message that the ability to use a gun made a man better than he had been as well as a sturdier patriot able to defend the nation's liberties.[52] Others who were more concerned with the civilian environment came to value guns as necessary tools for social control.

6

Reconstruction, Cheap Guns, and the Wild West

In the post–Civil War years, firearms became more accessible, more lethal, and subject to greater willingness by Americans to use them in homicides than in the past.[1] As one observer commented, "the increase of crimes of blood has been beyond all comparison to that of the years previous to it. The war, in effect, demoralized and changed the habits and sentiments and conduct of thousands of the men who engaged in it on either side." Many, "reckless of life and hardened to the terrors of death," used their guns for personal violence.[2] Crime and disorder rose throughout the nation at an unprecedented rate.[3]

The most striking—and to many the most disturbing—private use of firearms took place in the South not just for petty crime but for purposes of social control. Before his death, Abraham Lincoln had placed in motion a program for reconstruction that included amnesty for most whites who had backed the Confederacy and aid to emancipated blacks designed to make them, in time, citizens. He moved circumspectly because with the return of free black soldiers to the South—men who had been taught "how to fight"—he anticipated problems. If white Southerners oppressed them and sympathetic Northerners supplied them with firearms, he dreaded a possible race war.[4]

Congress had gone along with Lincoln's plan by establishing on March 3, 1865, the temporary Bureau of Refugees, Freedmen and Abandoned Lands. When Andrew Johnson, the vice president and an antislavery Democrat, took over the presidency he indicated he would follow Lincoln's policy. Soon, on May 29 in a proclamation for North Carolina's reconstruction, Johnson revealed the minimum conditions for return of the Southern states to the Union. This plan excluded blacks from suffrage. As it unfolded in greater detail, it infuriated Republicans, who controlled Congress. They considered it too harsh on blacks and too lenient for former Confederates, particularly in light of the behavior of the white Southern establishment.

These Southerners feared that blacks would arm themselves to seek revenge for past abuses. Occasional black rhetoric added fuel to the rumors of insurrection. For example, in summer a Freedmen's Bureau officer told other blacks in South Carolina that "200,000 of our men well drilled in arms and used to warfare" were ready to fight.[5] As we have seen, before the war whites had always relied on force to keep slaves cowed. Now, purportedly, the fear of armed blacks and the loose talk of some blacks reinforced the resolve of the Southern legislatures to vote to keep guns away from the freedmen, to restrict membership in local militias to whites, and to reimpose bonds of control over freed blacks.

Beginning with Mississippi in November, former Confederate states under presidential Reconstruction codified the new restrictions on the behavior, living conditions, and mobility of the former slaves. In all, these Black Codes negated their rights as free human beings. In addition to reflecting the continuing racism throughout the region, the codes expressed the determination of whites who controlled the police forces and the courts to command black labor on their own terms. So, in a region where whites had routinely flaunted guns for racial reasons, local authorities continued their traditional behavior with the added twist of the codes to impose selective firearms control on African Americans. Virtually all of the codes forbade blacks to possess or carry guns.

In December, when with the Thirteenth Amendment the federal government abolished slavery for good, Congress attempted also to block Southern states from enforcing the discriminatory Black Codes. It debated two bills, one to extend the life of the Freedmen's Bureau and the other to grant civil rights to former slaves, including a provision to prevent white state officials from denying them the privilege of possessing firearms. Proponents referred to the arms-keeping clause in the Second Amendment as among the rights African Americans should be able to exercise freely in all states.

As the congressman and editor of the New York *Times*, Henry J. Raymond, implored his colleagues, "Make the [newly freed] colored man a citizen of the United States" with every right under the Constitution, including "a right to defend himself and his wife and children; a right to bear arms."[6] For this and other reasons, opponents in both the House and Senate fought to kill the bills. Southerners objected vehemently to all their provisions but with particular passion to those that would invalidate state and local laws prohibiting African Americans from possessing firearms or ammunition.

Johnson vetoed both pieces of legislation but on June 9, 1866, Congress overruled him by passing the Civil Rights Act. It extended citizenship and other rights enjoyed by whites to African Americans. When the Supreme Court ruled the act unconstitutional, Congress embodied its features in the Fourteenth Amendment, which on June 13 it approved. The issue of civil rights then moved to the states where opponents battled ratification of the amendment. To protect blacks, Congress on July 16 again overturned the president's veto of legislation to enlarge the authority of the Freedmen's Bureau. Among other rights, Congress permitted freed slaves to bear arms. It thus abolished legally the old practice in local laws of imposing restrictions on gun keeping based on race or color.

The determination of African Americans to exercise their newly acquired privileges and rights and to defend them with available firearms played prominently in race riots in Norfolk, Memphis, and New Orleans. A black Louisiana activist summed up this feeling, declaring, "As one of the disenfranchised race, I would say to every colored soldier, 'Bring your gun home.' "[7] In Norfolk on April 16, 1866, when some eight hundred blacks paraded in celebration of the Civil Rights Act, a white man fired a gun into their midst. The blacks broke ranks, charged, and killed him. Then about one hundred armed men in Confederate gray uniforms gathered to assault the black community. Because the small, all-white police force would not protect the blacks, federal troops did so with minor bloodshed.

Riots in Memphis on May 1 spilled much more blood. There, tension between a number of recently discharged black soldiers aware of their new status and the mostly Irish American police erupted into a pogrom against blacks. The violence destroyed property valued at more than one hundred thousand dollars and left nearly forty-six people, mostly black, dead.

Whites planned another clash, this one in New Orleans, to block a redrafted state charter that granted suffrage to blacks. On the morning of July 29, the involved whites rushed into the city's gun shops and bought up their pistols and ammunition. Then these whites hunted and fired on outnumbered and outgunned blacks. Police, made up mostly of former Confederate soldiers, joined the white mob. The carnage stopped only when federal troops arrived more than three hours later. The official report estimated that the violence killed at least thirty-eight blacks while several hundred suffered wounds. Whites incurred few casualties.[8] The riots, the slaughter of blacks, and the violence against them by secret white-supremacist societies such as the Knights of the White Camellia and the Ku Klux Klan contributed to the eviscerating of Johnson's Reconstruction policy.

In the November elections, Radical Republicans won control of Congress and mapped their own Reconstruction program for the South. On March 2, 1867, over Johnson's veto, the radicals framed and passed the first Reconstruction Act, a rider to an army appropriations bill. It took Reconstruction out of the hands of the president, disbanded the Southern state militias, and divided ten former Confederate states into five military districts commanded by federal generals with powers superior to those of the state governments. Regardless of the Second Amendment, the federal government thus disarmed the organized citizen-soldiers of the Southern states being reconstructed. This disarming stood out as one reason why President Johnson considered the act unconstitutional, but it and two supplemental acts became law anyway.[9]

The southern states, meanwhile, had rejected the Fourteenth Amendment. Congress then required them to ratify it and to adopt constitutions consistent with it before they could reenter the Union. Finally, on July 28, 1868, when the requisite number of states had ratified the amendment, it became part of the federal Constitution. Thereafter, cases involving the constitutionality of civil rights laws, state arms laws, and the Second Amendment began reaching the federal courts.

At this time also, Congress restored the power to establish militias to southern states that Republican regimes now controlled. These governments created new volunteer militias, many of them composed of former slaves officered by black veterans of the Union army. White racist groups such as the Klan, made up in part of Confederate veterans, often had more and better firearms than these militias. So Republican governors sometimes acquired guns for the black citizen-soldiers from Northern manufacturers, but the firearms did not always reach their intended destination.

For example, Governor Powell Clayton of Arkansas bought four thousand rifles with ammunition in New York. When the weapons arrived in Memphis in October 1868, the editor of the Democratic newspaper *Avalanche* claimed the guns were "to be placed in the hands of the negroes of Arkansas . . . for the purpose of shooting down inoffensive citizens." Klansmen then seized the weapons, kept some, and destroyed the others. Similarly, in November Florida's governor purchased for his militia two thousand muskets and forty thousand rounds of ammunition. Klansmen alerted by railroad personnel who belonged to the Klan seized the weapons, which were en route to Tallahassee under guard by federal soldiers, and destroyed them.[10] Through this use of extralegal violence, the Klan attempted, and usually succeeded despite the Second Amendment, in keeping firearms out of the hands of blacks it designated as preeminently the wrong people.

This vigilante control of firearms in the southern states had significance for whites, blacks, Republicans, and Democrats for various reasons but notably because guns provided an effective means of gaining and holding political power. During elections, armed conflict often broke out between black, Republican-supported militias and bands of armed whites backed by local Democrats.

In this ambiance, African Americans viewed guns as symbols of freedom as well as instruments with which to defend it. As scholars have often reported, ever apprehensive of a black revolt, "nothing inflamed whites more than Negroes with guns."[11] Southern whites, on the other hand, used guns to kill, to suppress enfranchised blacks, and to try to restore the old order. By far, in most conflicts, the whites prevailed. A federal report for 1868 estimated that just in Louisiana white terrorists killed more than one thousand people, most of them black.[12]

Then, as southern states regained authority to recreate their own militias and power shifted back into the hands of white Democrats, they cleansed what had been Republican militias of their black members. Also, despite the civil rights guarantees in the amended Constitution, white legislators again resorted to broad discrimination and selective gun controls based on race. They imposed rigid permit systems on African Americans for obtaining firearms or empowered local authorities to confiscate arms, virtually at will, from these allegedly unsuitable people as a class.

As in Tennessee, some laws aimed to keep guns out of the hands not only of blacks but also of poor whites. Although phrased as a generalized form of regulation, such as banning the sale of cheap handguns, the laws usually had a carefully targeted discriminatory intent. A more straightforward Mississippi statute forbade blacks to keep or carry firearms of any kind. Regardless of the Second and Fourteenth Amendments, state courts consistently upheld these prejudicial restrictions on who could or could not possess guns.

Federal legislators, primarily from the North, tended to view the selective firearms curbs as part of the larger civil rights issue involving the illegal activities of secret white-supremacist societies. In an effort to resolve the violence problem and uphold the Fourteenth and Fifteenth Amendments, Congress enacted three enforcement laws. The first in May 1870 and the second in February 1871 empowered the president to use federal courts in cases involving voters who had been denied their constitutional rights, authorized him to use military force when deemed necessary, placed congressional elections under federal supervision, and enhanced federal authority in large cities.

Since the white violence in the South hardly paused, in April 1871 Congress passed a third enforcement law, the tougher Ku Klux Klan Act that expanded the Civil Rights Act of 1866. For the first time, the new law made individuals who committed designated crimes subject to prosecution and punishment by federal authorities. If states failed to protect certain civil rights, the federal government could intervene with armed force. "These are momentous changes," *The Nation* commented. "They not only increase the power of the central government, but they arm it with jurisdiction over a class of cases of which it has hitherto never had, and never pretended to have, any jurisdiction whatever."[13]

Democrats warned that with this intrusion of federal police power in the states, local self-government would vanish. Republicans and freed African Americans contended that if the federal government could not protect the rights of all citizens, why have those rights embodied in the Constitution? This simple logic did not prevent Congress, twenty-three years later when Democrats again controlled it and the presidency, from repealing the Force Acts.

Meanwhile, the white Southerners' gun violence, the intimidation, the murder of blacks, and the enforcement of the codes to keep them disarmed had continued. Occasionally, as in Chicot County, Arkansas, on December 15, 1871, organized African Americans struck back. In this instance, members of "colored militia companies" along with blacks from a nearby plantation smashed into the community of Lake Village, "firing off their weapons as they galloped into town, cursing and making threats to avenge the murder" of a black man. Local whites regarded the arming of these militiamen "with pistols and shot-guns" as irresponsible and as producing what many of them had prophesied, "the humiliating oppression of negro supremacy."[14]

More often blacks had to find refuge from rampaging bands of armed whites. A case in point took place in March 1873 when the Radical Republican sheriff of Colfax, the county seat of Grant Parish in Louisiana, deputized blacks to help defend the small town against white Democrats he feared would seize it. Some 150 black farmers and their families camped in and around a brick stable that served as a courthouse. Black veterans and militia officers led them in armed drills and digging trenches. Most defenders were armed with shotguns but about twelve had Enfield rifles. For about three weeks they held off surrounding whites, who carried more rifles and had a small artillery piece. On Easter Sunday, April 13, the whites prevailed. In their assault they slaughtered most of the defenders, many of these blacks as they tried to surrender. Three whites died. This racial carnage ranks as the worst in a single day "in the history of Reconstruction."[15]

The next year in New Orleans when police seized firearms being smuggled to the White League, an antiblack organization committed to opposing the Radical Republican state government, they set off more communal violence. Ignoring the racial animus behind their own arming, whites complained that the police establishment had infringed their constitutional right to bear arms. On September 14, 1874, several thousand well-armed leaguers and supporters clashed with five hundred police and black militia. The leaguers routed their opponents and temporarily seized control of the state government. Twenty-seven people died and 105 nursed injuries.[16]

Up to this time, neither local nor state laws that touched on the assumed private right to keep firearms had engendered litigation sufficiently significant for it to reach the federal courts. Finally, in *United States v. Cruikshank*, 92 U.S. 542 (1876) 1, the Supreme Court heard its first gun case. It concerned William J. Cruikshank, one of the leaders of the white mob in the Colfax massacre. Local authorities indicted him and ninety-five others identified as participants. Among the various charges lodged against these men under the Enforcement Act of 1870, one asserted that they had prevented black citizens from exercising the constitutional right to bear arms as extended to them through the Fourteenth Amendment.

This charge touched on a legal controversy over whether or not the Bill of Rights applied just to the federal government. In the past, most jurists held that it restricted the powers of the federal government but not those of state and local governments.[17] After passage of the Fourteenth Amendment, various attorneys defending blacks focused on its first section, which followed wording in the Fifth Amendment. That section declared no state shall enact laws abridging the privileges or immunities of citizens "without . . . due process of law." They claimed the Fourteenth Amendment, in its capacity of protecting civil liberties in the Bill of Rights against violation by the states, absorbed the Second Amendment. This explication came to be known as the doctrine of incorporation.

In the Cruikshank case, the Court in a majority opinion on March 27 ruled that the bearing of arms for a lawful purpose was not a right granted by the Constitution. The judges thus held that the Bill of Rights limited the powers of the national government, not those of the states. They thus rejected full incorporation of the Bill of Rights into the Fourteenth Amendment, especially as it applied to the bearing of arms.

For gun owners, this ruling would have great significance. It upheld as principle the right of states to legislate firearms controls affecting individuals without
fear of federal sanction. This decision also had a racist slant. It made federal
prosecution of those who committed crimes against blacks, especially in areas
where local authorities would not enforce the law, virtually impossible. Thus,
in denying blacks a Second Amendment privilege, the Court condoned white
vigilantism.

In South Carolina, for instance, Democratic vigilantes had formed rifle
clubs, wore red shirts, and "rode about with rifles and revolvers to frighten
blacks and disrupt Republican meetings."[18] In one of their excursions in the
town of Hamburg they murdered a black militiaman. To protest that killing and
the rifle clubbers' oppression, blacks, on July 17, 1876, held a rally in Charleston. They cautioned "that there are 80,000 black men in this State who can
bear Winchester rifles and know how to use them." They would not "submit
to be shot down by lawless regulators for no crimes committed against society
and law."[19]

This kind of threat, along with Republican actions such as countering white
gun-violence by arming blacks, as we have noted in other brutal episodes, further incensed rather than deterred the Regulators. In September, sixteen members of the rifle clubs gathered in the town of Ellenton, ostensibly to seek out
those responsible for the rape and robbery of a white woman. The search turned
into a racial witch hunt. For three days and nights, gunmen pursued and shot
blacks until United States Army troops stopped the killing. In this massacre,
forty to fifty blacks died but only two or three whites.

All this gunplay, along with roving bands of outlaws, appeared to substantiate
the popular perception of white Southern society as more violent than that to
the North. Noting that Southerners had been shooting and cutting each other
for decades, historians tended to perceive in them a special fondness for guns
associated with a regional culture of violence and machismo that extended
from the colonial era, through Reconstruction, and beyond. Some writers
claimed that in the Reconstruction years, men, even boys of fourteen, carried
handguns everywhere. Seemingly, one maintained, "every trifling dispute was
ended with the pistol."[20] Another chronicler reported, "it became fashionable
and a sign of manhood" to carry guns. "And the more guns there were, the
more they were used."[21]

Whether or not any single area of the country has nurtured more gun violence than any other has long been speculative. A number of researchers indicate that neither the South nor any other region had a special culture of gun

violence.[22] White Southerners did use guns frequently to decide social issues but so did other Americans. The Southerners' flaunting of firearms, though, affected the lives and safety of blacks who according to constitutional theory could now openly acquire their own guns. Despite selective local statutes and court decisions that vitiated African Americans' free access to firearms, they eagerly sought handguns. At times when they acquired them, as we have seen, they used them for defense against vigilante terrorism. Much as did whites, they also employed guns in crime.[23]

In the postbellum North, meanwhile, crime and economic considerations more than racial clashes aggravated concerns over gun violence. During the war, felonies and prison commitments had dropped, but juvenile offenses had increased. Handguns contributed significantly to the escalating severity of the crimes and became a leading means of self-destruction. They came from an industry that during the war had come to produce some of the most sophisticated small arms in the world. When the conflict ended, the government abruptly ceased its arms purchases, leaving the manufacturers with a greater capacity than even mushrooming civilian customers absorbed. The army aggravated the surplus production problem by dumping its excess guns on the civilian market.

To survive, manufacturers such as Colt and Remington cut output, reduced plant space, shaved profits, attempted to create new foreign outlets, and diversified by making other products such as cash registers. They tailored their firearms to meet particular niches in the civilian market, notably for hunters and for civilians who wanted small, inexpensive, and easily concealed handguns. Having largely abandoned craft production for mass production, manufacturers produced these weapons considerably cheaper in real costs than in the past. Americans reacted to the availability by becoming more interested in handguns and by buying them for private use in greater quantity than before the war. They thus reinvigorated the gun culture that the machine production of firearms had started almost two decades earlier.[24]

The mass production of handguns not only increased their use in violent crime but also altered the nature of criminal assaults, murders, and suicides. Investigators of the postwar crime wave reported "the character of crimes had changed. They had become more marked with violence."[25] Ascertainable rates for murders and suicides climbed because anyone could kill easily with a cheap handgun. Previously, social observers tended to view these deaths as acts of deranged individuals. Now, with the pull of a trigger, suicide attempts became more deadly. With guns, murders seemed more calculated, anonymous, impersonal, and less comprehensible than in the past.

Concealed-weapons carriers, many of them former soldiers who in some state prisons made up more than half the inmates, contributed heavily to the civilian gun violence. Instead of assigning at least some blame to them, municipal authorities in eastern seaboard cities placed the onus on the poor and other members of the local underclass. "They rush eagerly into quarrels and fights," a journalist reported, "and at the first opportunity draw their weapons and fire promiscuously about them." This "sudden passion and ready pistols lead to homicides almost innumerable."[26]

At the same time, gun keepers and firearms merchants intent on profit preached the old doctrine that the individual ownership of firearms served society with a cadre of shooters who could defend liberty when imperiled. They ignored the reality of the militias' ineptness in war and their conversion to special-interest constabularies. Army authorities continued to regard them as "almost valueless in a strictly military point of view."[27]

Still, popular lore stressed a need for the theoretically universal militias and the private gun-keeping associated with them. When used as a booster for patriotism, this assumed need for gun keeping seemed harmless. When employed to justify the reality of indiscriminate gun use in paramilitary organizations, it alarmed military men. The editors of the *Army and Navy Journal* commented, "It is never safe for any community to have irregular bodies of armed men patrolling the streets and practicing with firearms."[28]

In the 1870s the mounting sales of specialty sporting arms, derringers, and other pocket pistols at affordable prices boosted the profit margins of the firearms manufacturers. By the end of the decade the production of the small-arms industry, stimulated by demand at home and by that of foreign markets its leaders had cultivated, reached something of a high point.[29] At least fifty companies were producing small revolvers, often with names such as Protector, Little All Right, Tramp's Terror, and Banker's Pal stamped on the barrel.[30]

At this time, too, firearms makers and shooters refurbished the myth of the frontiersman as a Cincinnatus who had put aside his plow, grabbed his flintlock rifle, always at hand, and joined neighbors to battle Indians, French, British, and Mexicans. This legend lived side by side with the popular image of the Wild West symbolized by the gunslinger. As on earlier frontiers, the conventional story goes, law enforcement in the West lagged behind settlement; therefore "a man had to have a gun" not only "for game to feed his family" but also to defend it.[31]

This attitude toward gun toting could be seen in 1849 during the early movement to the far West. In February Congress voted to sell emigrants surplus pistols, rifles, and ammunition at cost so they could arm themselves against Indians. A number of senators, including Thomas Hart Benton of Missouri, objected. They contended the government "ought not to be peddling arms to anybody," but the plan went through and emigrants to California bought and carried with them a remarkable number of firearms.[32]

As one pioneer, William Swain, in May recorded, "All emigrants are armed to the teeth. It is like one continual glorious 4th of July." He described the emigrants as "walking arsenals" and the frequent injuries from accidental shootings. As they reached the coast, most of them threw their rifles away. By August few men carried guns. In California, he reported in April 1850, "instead of going armed as was necessary two or three months ago, we can traverse the mountain trails . . . with no other arms than a good jackknife to cut our raw pork."[33]

Miners in California felt so secure about life and property that few saw the need for their own firearms, at least not to protect themselves from other Americans. They wrote, for example, that "almost any rifle is useless and valueless to a miner." One remarked that settlers "laugh at the man that talks of taking a Pistol with him," and those that have come with their weapons "seem rather ashamed of them."[34]

Despite this sense of security in the gold fields and San Francisco's creation in 1850 of an up-to-date police force, businessmen and property owners exaggerated crime and gun toting in the city. These reputedly "best men in the city" called the police careless or corrupt, armed themselves, brought together a vigilance committee with a membership of seven hundred, and imposed their kind of law and order. In 1856 some of the same people formed another large committee, about six thousand to eight thousand strong. They claimed "all sorts of assaults, robberies, and other crimes were common" and that they were "tired of having [their] people shot down in the streets."[35] So, the well-armed vigilantes organized themselves into a paramilitary force, causing the governor on June 3 to declare the county of San Francisco in a state of insurrection. Nonetheless, the vigilantes imposed their will on the people. As in the past, strong-willed men had used private firearms for their political or economic purposes in defiance of legitimate authority.

Later, on the Western cattle and mining frontiers of the post–Civil War era, more vigilantism and gun violence erupted with some frequency. Popular writers described Wichita, Kansas, in the 1870s as brimming with pistols. Cowboys, many of them combat veterans, reputedly packed guns everywhere, had itchy trigger fingers, fired freely, and defied local control efforts. With the exception of professional hunters, cowboys had the reputation of being the nation's most heavily armed civilians. They also carried their firearms carelessly. More of them died from accidental gun discharges than from murders.[36] As elsewhere, such fatalities created alarm, leading a Denver editor, for instance, to denounce shootings as too frequent, outrageous, and dangerous to innocent parties.[37]

With omnipresent firearms, Westerners allegedly settled personal disputes resulting from affronts, insults, challenges, feuds, crime, or racial animosities on the spot.[38] To cope with this violence, communities usually hired lower-class men as marshals or sheriffs. Even though many of these gunfighters "did not even know the law they were supposed to enforce," at times they acted as judge, jury, and executioner.[39]

Writers for pulp magazines romanticized gunslinging sheriffs, praised them for upholding a kind of order out of a gun barrel, and embellished their activities with myth. Dime novelists depicted other gunslingers such as Jesse and Frank James, who were former Confederate guerrillas and murderers, James Butler "Wild Bill" Hickok, Wyatt Berry Stapp Earp, and William Barclay "Bat" Masterson as men of heroic stature primarily because allegedly they could shoot straight. Mostly, they could not. Earp and Masterson augmented their incomes as gamblers and procurers. As lawmen and gamblers, Earp and John Henry "Doc" Holliday robbed a stagecoach of eighty thousand dollars and murdered the driver and a passenger.[40] Later, debunkers would characterize such peace officers as social misfits whose only claim to fame rested on violence.

On occasion, when serving on the side of law, gunfighters did try selectively to enforce ordinances against the wearing of firearms. When employed as chief of police in Abilene, Kansas, Hickok, the former Union army scout, posted printed notices stating he would enforce the town's ordinance against carrying firearms. The local newspaper editor commented, "There's no bravery in carrying revolvers in a civilized community. Such a practice is well enough and perhaps necessary when among Indians or other barbarians," he added, "but among white people it ought to be discontinued." Even the right people on occasion disregarded the ordinance, as they did weapons restrictions in Dodge City. There two gunmen murdered Masterson at age twenty-six while in "discharge of his duty" in enforcing law and order as marshal. The local newspaper noted, "A frontier life stimulates all the qualities of manhood—the true, the good and the bad."[41]

Chroniclers who perpetuated the image of frontier gunfighters as heroes ignored their bad qualities while embroidering what may have been true. Later, revisionist scholars would challenge these portrayals. Except for special circumstances, they would argue that "the law of the east was the law of the west."[42] Just as settlements on the early eastern or Midwestern frontiers had not been ridden constantly with gun violence, so it was, they pointed out, with farming and religious settlements along the Great Plains frontier.[43] Neither lumberjacks in Michigan, Norwegian farmers in North Dakota, nor German Mennonites in Kansas squared off with Colt 45s to settle disputes over oxen, land, or personal grievances.

As in cities, when crime and Indian warfare on the frontier did increase, so did gun keeping. In some instances, out of fear, teachers and older male pupils brought firearms to school. Out of resistance to legal restraints, gun-toting Confederate veterans moved in large numbers into Texas where in the central area violence seemed unceasing. From 1865 to 1871 sheriffs reported 4,425 crimes and only 588 arrests. That state had the nation's highest homicide rate, attributable to frontier conditions and inadequate policing.[44] Galveston and Houston sought to curb the violence with fines of one hundred dollars for those caught carrying concealed weapons. In July 1870 the Republican state government organized a state police force, about 60 percent white and 40 percent black, to cope with the crime. Most white Texans hated the force because it placed guns legally in the hands of blacks, and disparaged it as a carpetbag army.

The next year the antipathy precipitated a crisis that began in Groesbeck when a black policeman attempted to arrest a white man for carrying illegally concealed weapons. In an exchange of gunfire, the white man died. A mob of several hundred whites rioted and defied the state's Republican administration. The governor declared martial law in two counties. In April the executive committee of the Dallas Democratic Party attacked the Republican administration's conduct. On the issue of guns, it stated, "Every person shall have the right to keep and bear arms in the lawful defense of himself and the state, under such regulations as the legislature may prescribe."[45] Two years later when a Democratic regime came to power, it abolished the state police force. The Texas Rangers, a paramilitary constabulary that earlier had battled mainly Indians and Mexicans and had been admired by much of the public, took over many of the force's duties.

Meanwhile, elsewhere in the West journalists and politicians called for laws prohibiting the carrying of firearms. Abilene and Wichita, Kansas, did so in 1871 and later so did other cattle towns. Court records and newspaper accounts indicate also that the cow towns enforced these laws.[46] They did not, as legend holds, depend on lone marshals for maintaining order. Some had paid law-enforcement departments. For example, Abilene's funding for police for three months at this time amounted to 48 percent of its expenditure.

Writers who perceive greater gun violence in the rural West than in cities seldom cite such control efforts. They point out instead that the single men common in the frontier cattle and mining communities often resorted to all kinds of violence but that their guns provided the principal instruments of violent death. These chroniclers based their views on various sources, some of them compelling, but also on anecdotal accounts such as those of European visitors who commented on what they regarded as the singular gun-toting penchant of Americans. In total, these writers maintain that the frontier practice of carrying weapons virtually assured a high homicide rate and that few westerners obeyed laws prohibiting such toting.[47]

Instances of such defiance of law could be seen in the rough-and-tumble cattle center of Dodge City, Kansas, and the mining communities of Aurora, Nevada, and Bodie, California, in their heydays in the late 1860s through the 1870s. Aurora and Bodie had few robberies, little larceny, and no rapes but a high rate of homicides, attributable largely to drunken brawls involving single males who toted firearms openly or concealed.[48]

In some parts of the West, government contributed to gun violence. Citizens petitioned state governments for guns to fight Indians and frontier lawlessness. Some just wanted free firearms. Regardless, governors supplied most of them with rifles and pistols. Kansas loaned militia companies, sheriffs, and settlers one hundred thousand dollars for firearms. Overall, though, western homicides do not appear to have ranked higher than those in heavily populated eastern cities. Some researchers, using comparative statistics, explained this phenomenon by contending that crime rates rose more in urban than in rural areas.[49]

As in the East, people in the West defended their right to have guns as constitutionally protected as well as proper for hunting game such as buffalo, for killing pests such as coyotes, and for self-defense. In 1875 in the case of *Horbach v. State of Texas*, the court strengthened the self-defense argument in hidden-gun toting. It ruled that if a man fears a violent attack, he can meet it with equal force, in this instance with a shot in the head. Citizens must be allowed to defend themselves.

As had Indians in the East, those in the West relied on firearms to defend themselves against whites but unsuccessfully. Journalists reported that "it is murder throughout the length and breadth of the Indian country. . . . Villains from four quarters of the United States congregate to murder, rob and steal."[50] Members of the five civilized tribes in Oklahoma tried to curb this gun toting with laws similar to those of cities and states. In 1875 the Cherokee Nation revised a thirty-four-year-old statute prohibiting the carrying of deadly weapons by boosting the fine and adding imprisonment for its violation. The next year the Chickasaw Nation forbade the carrying of guns and their discharge in specified public places under penalty of a fine or imprisonment. The Choctaws had similar gun laws but their constitution stated they had the right to bear arms in defense of self and nation.[51]

In the Territory of New Mexico at this time the use of firearms reputedly had become so prevalent that "death by gunfire became the prevailing method of settling a dispute," and "killings occurred so frequently that they came to be accepted as a matter of course."[52] When local enforcement could not cope with the gun violence known as the Lincoln County War, President Rutherford B. Hayes intervened on October 7, 1878, by declaring the county in a state of insurrection. In this conflict William H. Bonney, a youth with a "preoccupation with guns" known as "Billy the Kid," worked as a hired killer and gained notoriety, even fame.[53] In his twenty-one years of life he shot dead eighteen men.

Concurrently, cattle ranchers, too, came to take a stand against private-firearms violence by cowboys, mainly because it injured their pocketbooks. Investors would not risk their money where gunplay disturbed the peace. As one newspaper editor put it to ranchers in convention, "We hope to see the stockmen . . . adopt a resolution to dispense with the services of those cowboys who cannot move, eat, or sleep without being armed to the teeth like a Mexican bandit."[54]

So in 1882 concerned western journalists and ranchers started what a researcher called "the nation's first gun control movement." Texas ranchers declared that "there is no reason for packing pistols in cow camps, on the range or in towns and cities." The surest way for cattlemen to break up the custom "is to have no man in their employment who persists in carrying such dangerous toggery about them." About a month later an editor pronounced gun packing "an evil that should be eradicated from society." When the weapon carrying persisted, a New Mexico editor asked, "What is a six-shooter?" It is, he said, "a weapon made for the purpose of destroying life. It is not a toy or ornament."[55]

The interpretations of available data on frontier gun violence presents a mixed-up picture. In the West plenty of violence existed, as on the ranching frontier in the 1870s, but the popular, and some historical, literature exaggerated the gunfighting, robbery, and feuding. Gunplay on America's changing frontiers varied according to time, circumstance, and place. Even the cowboy's reputation as a shooter is questionable. For instance, the memoir of a cowpuncher who lived on the ranching frontier in Montana, which historians have used widely, labels "this business of gun fights" as "nearly all exaggeration." He "saw a lot of hard work on the range but very little shooting."[56] Bias against gun keeping by the wrong people flourished in the West as well as elsewhere. So did opposition to flagrant gun-toting.

A different kind of bias affected members of the Church of Jesus Christ of Latter-day Saints who settled in the West. Outsiders reacted against Mormons because they favored theocratic government, allegedly maintained a militia or standing army, and practiced plural marriages. Populist hostility drove Mormons out of New York, Ohio, Missouri, and Illinois.

When their prophet, Brigham Young, finally led Mormons to Utah they created Deseret, their own state. When the United States seized the territory from Mexico, problems arose, especially after Mormons in 1852 publicly acknowledged polygyny. They defended it as a religious right under the Constitution's First Amendment. Critics such as Justin S. Morrill, a Republican congressman from Vermont, attacked polygyny as a moral outrage in religious garb. Congress, which had the authority to make laws for governing territories, could therefore ban the practice without violating freedom of religion. He and others in Congress accused the Saints of defying federal laws, as in February 1857 when they ordered Gentiles to leave Deseret and Mormon militias murdered some of them.

In response, President James Buchanan in May declared Mormons in "a state of substantial rebellion." He ordered twenty-five hundred troops to the Utah Territory to enforce federal law. Mormon leaders massed two thousand men of their Nauvoo Legion to resist what they regarded as an invading army.

On September 7, as the federal troops approached, Mormon zealots and Indian allies in Mountain Meadows in southwest Utah slaughtered 120 immigrants, including women and children, headed for California.[57] This massacre enraged Congress and non-Mormons. That winter when Young recognized that the Saints did not have the weapons to sustain a long war, the confrontation ended. Thereafter the federal government asserted a veneer of control over the territory, but Young retained the real power.

In February 1860 Morrill proposed an antipolygamy bill that denounced the "open and defiant license which, under the name of religion and latitudinous interpretation of our Constitution, has been given to this crime in one of our Territories [Utah]."[58] On July 1, 1862, Abraham Lincoln signed the bill into law. Mormons defied it. Because the president would not divert Union soldiers needed elsewhere to enforce the statute, the law remained a dead letter.

Later, in January 1879 in *Reynolds v. the United States*, the Supreme Court affirmed the measure's legality. Polygamists still defied it. So, in March 1881 Congress passed and President Chester A. Arthur approved the Edmunds Act, which declared polygamy a felony. Six years later, the Edmunds-Tucker Act, considered by some scholars as "one of the most farreaching pieces of federal legislation ever passed in peacetime," provided for stronger enforcement of the laws against plural marriage.[59] It gave federal marshals the authority to conduct cohabitation hunts. They jailed more than thirteen hundred Mormon men and a few women for defying the statute.

Finally, in 1890, the government's enforcement program, and its insistence that for Utah to become a state Mormons must give up plural marriages, compelled the church to capitulate. Four years later Utah attained statehood. Diehards continued secretly to practice polygamy. In the campaign against it the federal government exercised a centralized police power with troops and marshals on the theory that the nation's welfare took precedence over individual rights or a minority's wishes. This episode, as with the government's actions on private gun-keeping during the Civil War and during Reconstruction by white-supremacist militias, had significance as a precedent for those who would in the future seek through federal law to control gun violence.

7

The National Rifle Association

A long with a spreading addiction to private gun-keeping, proliferating shooting clubs, a surge in crime, and public acceptance of policing with guns, post–Civil War America gave birth to a special firearms organization. The idea for the club began small in the minds of a number of Union army veterans and National Guard officers. They had been appalled by what they regarded as the poor marksmanship of soldiers with Springfield and Enfield rifles in the war. So, in August 1871 Colonel William C. Church, editor of the *United States Army and Navy Journal*, Captain George W. Wingate of the New York National Guard, and a number of other Guard officers formed the National Rifle Association, modeled after the twelve-year-old British rifle association but with a specifically American goal.

These men aimed to teach marksmanship with new-style rifles to soldiers in the army and National Guard and promote shooting skills, as a patriotic duty, among youths who might become soldiers. In November the association received a charter as a nonprofit organization from the state of New York. With connections to state and federal government, the rifle club quickly achieved the standing of "a semi-official arm of the War Department," a status that helped it obtain financial support from the state treasury.[1]

Prominent military men, including President Ulysses S. Grant, joined the association. Their presence benefited it as did a craze for shooting matches, which at this time swept over much of the country. The organization sponsored competitions with pistols, rifles, and shotguns. In the following decade the fad ended and in 1880 so did the association's state subsidy. New York's governor, Alonzo B. Cornell, saw no need for the organization or the National Guard except "to show itself in parades and ceremonies." He added, "Rifle practice for these men is a waste of money."[2] The rifle association went into eclipse. Enthusiasm for guns among civilians who hunted or engaged in trap-shooting for sport, however, remained strong.

As did other gun enthusiasts, people who bought firearms as tools for sport continued to experience few restraints while enjoying their hobbies. Often, they adopted the values of past arms keepers, as in backing state and local laws that denied racial, ethnic, or religious minorities the privilege of possessing firearms.

At the same time class restraints on gun keeping broke down because even poor whites determined to have a firearm could buy the mass-produced pistols without difficulty. Firms such as the Norwich Pistol Company manufactured pistols made with pot metal or other cheap materials and sold them for a dollar or two. Children in slums of cities such as New York obtained guns and practiced shooting them in alleys, drew on each other, or shot at goats. Fairs and carnivals dangled guns before customers as prizes. Boys won them for selling gadgets.

A religious weekly, for instance, offered a revolver as a premium to its subscribers. Few readers protested. Indeed, of the many who ordered guns five out of seven were clergymen. One man of God commented, "I have found . . . a sport which professional men can undertake that will give them rest, recreation, and be a sport men would want their wives and children to take part in."[3] Some churches constructed shooting ranges within their premises that members of both sexes could use.

The expanding availability of firearms for civilians became evident also in the civil disturbances that rocked cities. Since police could not cope with the turmoil, state officials in 1877 formed the National Guard Association to do so. After that, state militias became known officially as units of the National Guard that functioned mostly as instruments of state authority to maintain domestic order, protect property, and uphold the prevailing class structure. In the eyes of the laboring class, the citizen-soldiers of the Guard, like some of the earlier volunteer militias, had become vehicles of, rather than opponents of, tyranny.

Despite this view, most states expanded their Guard units. Large towns and cities constructed impressive armories but not as in the past to manufacture small arms. Often built like fortresses, these structures served Guard members as places to store firearms and ammunition, meet, drill, socialize, and muster when they were called to deal with social turbulence.

On July 1 of the year of the Guard Association's formation, railroads cut their employees' wages by 10 percent. Workers at the Baltimore and Ohio line launched a strike that spread from Baltimore to West Virginia, to Chicago, and to other cities. Authorities ordered police, sheriffs, and then Guard and federal army units to open the rail lines. Strikers in Pittsburgh stormed an arsenal to obtain firearms. Thousands elsewhere, armed with guns, knives, and whatever weapons they could scrounge, battled the state militias. In breaking the strike, Guard troops shot and killed as many as a hundred workers.

In the wake of riots in Chicago, newspapers reported that "every man who could beg, buy, or borrow a revolver carried it" with total disregard of a local ordinance against concealed weapons.[4] Journalists estimated that one inhabitant in ten packed a pistol. Similar gun-toting prevailed in New York even though at this time the city's aldermen required individuals to obtain permits to carry hidden pistols. This control measure proved meaningless because officials issued permits virtually to all who asked. Local gun regulations elsewhere suffered from similar inadequate enforcement.

Upper-class businessmen and community leaders formed vigilante groups, or Law and Order Leagues, to keep radicals and the dangerous classes at bay. Corporations established their own private police forces, armed them, and trained them. In Pennsylvania "Railroad Police" and "Coal and Iron Police," accountable only to their employers, "armed with handguns and rifles . . . patrolled the state much like an occupying army."[5] In the South, states used National Guard companies far more than did the northern industrial states in aiding civil authorities in quelling riots and "policing racial incidents." Often, too on the plus side, the Guard tried to prevent white mobs from lynching African Americans.[6]

Europe's industrially advanced nations also had to deal with social unrest and at times they, too, did so with troops. Unlike the United States, Western European countries attacked the problem of gun violence associated with populist turmoil on a broad basis with legislation that placed at least some restrictions on the private ownership of firearms. Britain, for example, had two such gun laws, the Game Licences Act of 1860 and the Gun Licences Act of 1870. The first law obliged hunters to purchase a license and the second required almost any gun owner to obtain a license for ten shillings. Although the legislation imposed a restriction on firearms use, the government designed both acts to raise revenue. But this tax had the effect of restricting gun keeping.

Nine years later Germany's government countered a perceived threat from socialist movements by expanding its police power. In areas of strife, it banned even the possession of civilian guns for up to a year. In Belgium and Holland labor disorders also produced restrictions on the private use of firearms.

Americans who concerned themselves with the problem of social control tended to view such police empowerment through the central government as paving the way to despotism. They still connected the right to firearms with the discredited concept of civil militias as guardians against oppression. Such sentiment had always rested on shaky ground but more so now because the character of the militias' offspring, the National Guard, had changed markedly. By law its citizen-soldiers had become subject to call for muster from Washington and increasingly came under more federal regulation. Indeed, after passage of the *posse comitatus* act in June 1878, which terminated the practice of federal marshals using troops as civilians in a posse to chase outlaws, states regularly employed Guard troops as independent military forces to aid in the suppression of civilian disturbances.[7] The Greenback Party called this practice an "insidious scheme to establish an enormous military power under the guise of militia laws."[8]

All the while, even though the homicide rate and crime broadly defined had declined, the use of firearms in crime rose.[9] Gun violence also again made national headlines. On July 2, 1881, Charles J. Guiteau, a rejected, mentally disturbed office-seeker, shot President James A. Garfield at a railroad station in Washington, inflicting wounds that on September 19 killed him. Popular outrage focused on the shooter, who, among other strange explanations, stated he "never had the slightest doubt as to the Divine inspiration of the act, and that it was for the best interest of the American people."[10] For those concerned with curbing gun violence this deed brought up the question of how a deranged person could easily obtain the firearm that made the assassination possible.

Those who worried about gun fatalities also criticized careless sport shooting. About six weeks after the assault on the president, the New York *Times* reported that three Englishmen engaged in target practice in a vacant field killed a little boy. British authorities punished them for manslaughter. The *Times*'s writer cited the episode as "instructive to American 'target shootists.'" He reported also that American "courts continue to take utmost pains to discourage the practice of brandishing pistols or pointing guns, whether loaded or unloaded."[11]

Five years later, the problem of restraining civilian brandishing of firearms rose beyond local courts to reach the Supreme Court for the second time in the matter of *Presser v. Illinois*, 116 U.S. 252, 265 (1886). The litigation revolved around Herman Presser, who headed a German-American paramilitary shooting organization. An Illinois law prohibited drilling and parading in a military style without a license from the governor. When Presser, on horseback, led a parade of four hundred privately armed men in the streets of Chicago state authorities arrested him and a court convicted him for violating the statute. After lower courts upheld his conviction, Presser appealed to the Supreme Court to overturn it, claiming the state had violated his Second Amendment rights.

In rejecting this defense, the high court reaffirmed the Cruikshank decision, holding that the Second Amendment restricted Congress but not the states. The states possessed authority for maintaining the public security, as for example in suppressing armed mobs bent on riot and rapine. Citizens, therefore, had no right to create their own militias or to own weapons for semimilitary purposes. This decision upheld the states' police power in regulating militias, paramilitary groups, and the private possession of firearms. Other states and cities continued enacting laws that restricted gun keeping in small ways. Lower courts usually upheld these restraints but state judges at times also ruled in favor of the gun owners who claimed the constitutional right to possess and shoot firearms freely.

Meanwhile, fearful urbanites regarded crime with firearms as accelerating in pace with multiplying gun sales. This perception led journalists to demand selective firearms regulation more restrictive than in existing local and state laws. They targeted the practice, still legally tolerated in many communities, of individuals carrying concealed small firearms, citing it as a prime contributor to the spread of deadly violence. Other concerned citizens played up the notion that the mail-order distribution of concealable handguns contributed heavily to their availability and hence to robbing and killing. Some social commentators contended that without ready access to cheap guns the criminal classes could not kill with ease.

When criminals carrying mass-produced guns increasingly felled police, many urbanites switched attitudes on arming their professional defenders. This citizenry concluded that without firearms the police could no longer enforce law and order adequately. Local officials then accepted the idea that those charged with maintaining the law and paid by municipal taxes should carry guns not just in emergencies and for self-protection but also openly while on duty as a deterrent to crime. Even though the popular conception of police as corrupt and abusers of authority did not disappear, more city fathers began officially supplying their law enforcers with firearms.

In New Orleans and Nashville, authorities had been equipping their officers with Winchester rifles and revolvers for a decade. In the 1880s, Philadelphia gave its police on night duty the authority to carry pistols, and Boston in 1884 distributed eight hundred Smith & Wesson .38-caliber revolvers to its police who "for the first time" pounded their beats "routinely armed."[12] New York City during this time officially issued its officers firearms. The character of the police also changed. They became more and more representative of the population at large and hence more democratic, though not necessarily less corrupt.

Statistical data on the placing of guns in the hands of police to curb crime do not tell us clearly how effectively the practice worked as a deterrent. It did, however, theoretically nullify what shooters proclaimed as a fundamental principle of personal gun-keeping—the need for self-protection. Society entrusted police forces with firearms as part of a social contract. As its servants, the police—and not private citizens, individually or collectively as in vigilance committees—could use those arms to fight crime and maintain order. As had monarchs in the rising nation-states with their standing armies, city governments promised or implied that with firepower the police could protect the people more effectively than individuals could defend themselves.

In town and country local gun restrictions, accompanied by the improved policing and by employers who took action against gun-toting workers, appeared to have some effect in curbing firearms violence, but it still appeared high.[13] Fragmentary statistics for the 1880s showed a rise in murders and incarcerations but also indicated a drop in most crimes. Under these conditions guns in the hands of sport shooters and thugs rose and armed police become a feature of America's cityscapes.

In Britain, too, public concern over civilian gun violence connected to crime rose and led to calls for restrictions on the carrying of handguns. London's *Saturday Review* editorialized, "It is impossible to regard with indifference . . . repeated proofs that every kind of criminal and roughs who are ready to commit crimes on the very slightest provocation, carry about with them [handguns with] the potentiality of murder." It urged stiff penalties aimed at stopping this "revolvering."[14] Such agitation persuaded government officials to call for new legislation on the carrying of deadly weapons. Before acting, they decided in 1889 to solicit information on practices in other countries on "the carrying of firearms by private persons in populous places."[15]

The investigation revealed a wide range of attitudes. Scandinavian countries had hardly any laws on the use of firearms. Greece, Italy, Portugal, and Spain, however, required permits for individuals to carry any type of firearm. Most countries still linked the right to bear arms with hunting privileges. They restricted the use of guns by vagrants, minors, the mentally retarded, and habitual criminals. Resting usually on established precedent, these laws represented centralized responses to crime, violence, and sedition in increasingly crowded industrializing societies.

In the relatively uncrowded United States, the local control statutes did not block the flow of firearms into private hands. Aided by a protective tariff coupled with aggressive marketing, domestic manufacturers readily outperformed foreign firms in the sale of cheap weapons and ammunition. American companies produced handguns, shotguns, and rifles in the multiples of thousands.

Few Americans attached stigma to those who kept guns, who manufactured them, or who peddled them for private use. Schools and colleges taught shooting and marksmanship. Harvard University's president, Charles W. Eliot, praised target practice as the finest sport available for young men. As did no other, he said, it built character and coordination. Some educators, such as a regent of the University of Wisconsin, dissented. He complained to another that "discipline which savors least of culture or mentality and most of brute passion and wars, is being pushed most persistently and vigorously. To study classics is choice or whim—to train with a gun and know how to shoot is a requirement."[16]

Social critics commented on "the increase of crimes of violence and bloodshed" in the United States as "without parallel in any other of the enlightened nations of the globe." They blamed the violence on the availability of handguns and their easy concealment. "It is noteworthy," one wrote, "that not until the manufacture of revolvers of small size, suitable to easy concealment on the person, was the increase of crimes of violence and bloodshed so alarming." The jump in these crimes, he maintained, "has been in cities and communities in which the practice of carrying concealed weapons is common." Where they are not allowed, "this order of crime is comparatively rare."[17]

Despite such concern, most of the public appeared to approve of private gun-keeping. It even sided with those who advocated shooting as a part of education. At this time Americans purchased 750,000 pistols, 400,000 shotguns, and 500,000 rifles. This consumption led a journalist to comment, "For a quiet, peace loving nation, it is surprising how many firearms are sold in this country every year."[18]

This acceptance of guns influenced their manufacture. In particular, it helped shield producers against those who would target them for regulation. The industry set its own standards for quality and safety, a practice different from that followed in Europe. Most European countries with small-arms industries entrusted public officials with the testing of commercial arms and required manufacturers to pay for the certification. American firms did their own testing.

America's communities with firearms producers within their jurisdiction possessed the authority to compel manufacturers to meet safety standards. Few manufacturing towns enacted such regulatory laws. For instance, in 1892 Alabama, which required an expensive business license for those who sold handguns, passed legislation governing gun manufacture and sales. The law did little to curtail gun violence because, as did other states, Alabama monitored compliance indifferently. Those states that attempted strict supervision of their firearms laws aroused fierce opposition from gun owners.

This resistance to regulation occurred even in instances of criminal behavior by gun wielders, as in 1894 in the case of *Miller v. Texas*, 153 U.S. 535 (1894). In this litigation, a court in Dallas County, Texas, tried, convicted, and sentenced Franklin P. Miller to execution for shooting a police officer to death, one of the several who sought to arrest him for carrying an unlicensed handgun. At the time state law did not require a warrant for such an arrest. Miller appealed his conviction to the Supreme Court, contending that the Texas law "prohibiting the carrying of dangerous weapons" and allowing the arrest of the individual carrier without warrant violated his Second, Fourth, and Fourteenth Amendment rights. Up to this time, courts usually had confined their rulings on these amendments to matters involving blacks' claims to having the same rights enjoyed by whites.[19]

Miller's lawyers challenged this narrow interpretation of the Fourteenth Amendment's due process clause. They argued it had a broader scope, claiming that under it the states had to respect the individual's right to keep and bear arms, or that the Fourteenth Amendment totally incorporated the Second Amendment. In line with the Cruikshank and Presser decisions, the Court rejected this reasoning. It maintained that the Fourteenth Amendment did not shelter the whole Bill of Rights against the states. The Court thus again followed the doctrine of selective incorporation of the Bill of Rights.

Later, in cases involving usually the criminal process and the civil rights of African Americans, federal courts would accept consistently the incorporating concept but also not in full. They would convert the Fourteenth Amendment's due process clause into a second bill of rights most of whose guaranties applied to the states.[20] In particular, they would exclude the right to bear arms and thereby leave intact the power of states, counties, and cities to enact gun-control laws. Gun owners would protest this exclusion, citing limited opinions that were favorable to total incorporation.

Regardless of the Miller ruling and other federal court decisions upholding selective incorporation, attorneys for firearms organizations would continue to argue that "the second amendment should apply to the states by incorporation through the fourteenth amendment."[21] They would also use a refined interpretation of the incorporation concept to contend "the right to bear arms becomes a quintessentially individual right."[22] As a consequence of gun owners' promoting of total incorporation theory as applied to the Second Amendment and of public acceptance of shooters' privileges, the courts' selective acceptance or rejection of the incorporation theory had little or no immediate effect on the struggle to check gun violence.

Unlike the courts, the executive and legislative branches of the federal government skirted the incorporation issue as applied to individual gun-keeping. Washington also did virtually nothing to regulate the private traffic in firearms. It did not act even in areas of international commerce and foreign relations where it possessed authority greater than in domestic matters. Occasionally it tried to block foreign gunrunning, as to Canada during troubles there in the 1830s and to Chile in 1891 during a civil war there where it earned ill will by denying weapons to the rebels who won the war.[23] In such situations the federal government did not accomplish much because it had little authority to act. Not until 1898 did Congress authorize the president to impose, in such instances, embargoes on arms trafficking.

Meanwhile, the popular opposition to utilizing the National Guard in domestic disputes had become more widespread. For instance, in spring 1892 when the Carnegie Steel Corporation, the nation's largest manufacturer, attempted to lower wages at its Homestead, Pennsylvania, plant the unionized workers went on strike. On July 6 when three hundred heavily armed, private Pinkerton guards tried to bring nonunion workers into the plant, the strikers, armed with carbines, rifles, and pistols, battled the guards head-on. Ten people died and scores incurred injuries. The strikers defeated the Pinkertons but the governor intervened with eight thousand state National Guardsmen, broke the strike, and destroyed the Amalgamated Association of Iron and Steel Workers, one of the country's biggest unions.

Samuel Gompers, head of the American Federation of Labor, declared that the militia, instead of operating as an institution to protect the people, had been transformed into an organization to oppress workers. Populists perceived the Guard as "a private army directly under the command of the capitalists."[24] Others denounced it as an instrument to defeat workingmen on strike. They warned workers, "Don't join the militia."[25]

Two years later, in the wake of a financial depression, the Pullman Palace Car Company slashed wages. When the American Railway Union refused to handle Pullman cars, the confrontation escalated into a national railroad strike. The most notable violence erupted in Chicago. Over the opposition of Illinois's governor, President Grover Cleveland ordered federal troops to the city. These troops, along with the courts, local police, and National Guard soldiers, broke the strike. This upheaval climaxed nearly two decades of industrial and social strife marked by widespread gun wielding.

Organized workers came to view the citizen-soldiers, with their willingness to shoot, as enemies much as Englishmen and earlier Americans regarded other standing armed forces. As a writer for the Knights of Labor stated, "The National Guard is a standing army and a menace to liberty. . . . Its promoters, supporters and patrons are the plutocrats, the corporations, syndicates and trusts."[26] This sentiment did not stop the practice of using armed, uniformed, part-time citizen-soldiers against armed or unarmed worker-citizens.

Also in this last decade of the nineteenth century, the frontier, and much of the gun toting associated with it, passed out of existence. Observers concerned with gun violence believed that New Yorkers now packed more pistols than did Texans. In increasing numbers, Americans deplored the carrying of firearms. More and more, law officers in the major cities—New York, Chicago, San Francisco—joined those who saw a direct relationship between perceived rising crime and the carrying of concealed handguns. In Texas, Governor James Stephen Hogg characterized "the practice of carrying concealed deadly weapons" as unmanly and cowardly and as "a fruitful source of crime." He warned that "the mission of the concealed deadly weapon is murder. To check it is the duty of every self-respecting, law abiding man."[27]

Religious leaders and others backed this attitude, urging enforcement of Texas's pistol law with stiff penalties for violators. They argued that "beyond a doubt the practice of carrying concealed weapons is responsible for the widespread epidemic of murder. Every man who carries a revolver, carries it for the purpose of killing other men. There is no escape from this logic. If he didn't expect to kill with it, he would not have it with him." The writer and others urged the legislature to make carrying of concealed weapons punishable by imprisonment in the state penitentiary from one to five years.[28]

Still, much of the public remained captivated with stories of the last frontier's glorified gunslingers. As in the past, in both urban and rural environments that fascination often included firearms. Gun clubs retained their popularity countrywide, and esteem for those who could shoot was evidenced in the many magazine articles, novels, and accounts of hunters and marksmen in various competitions that appeared. Much of this concern with shooting carried over into the martial fervor leading to the eruption in April 1898 of the Spanish-American War.

Five years earlier the army had adopted the best-known firearm used in the war, the Danish .30-caliber Krag-Jorgenson, a repeating rifle, to replace the decade-old, single-shot, breech-loading Springfield. Unlike the Springfield, the Krag carried a box magazine with a five-round capacity and fired smokeless cartridges. Krags required training to be effective, but few of the troops had benefited from target practice and many were still armed with the Springfields. In its arsenals the government accelerated the production of rifles, carbines, ammunition, and other arms and placed large orders for weapons with private arms-makers. Since the war against Spain was brief, these arms did not come into much use in combat.

As for manpower, at the start of the conflict Congress designated state National Guard units as the main source for volunteers to augment the regular army. These hastily mobilized troops lacked training and discipline. As with militia in past wars, nearly half the Guardsmen refused to leave home for any length of time. The regulars, who did much of the fighting in Cuba, regarded them as unfit for soldiering. Later, the volunteers—about two hundred thousand of them—carried most of the burden of battling Filipinos who fought for independence against the American occupation of their country. The quick victory over Spain with the mix of regulars and National Guardsmen overshadowed the Filipino war, enabling the Guard lobby to extol the volunteers' role in it. The hostilities in Cuba and the Philippines contributed to the popularity of shooting.

Gun boosters enjoyed their war-enhanced status but some of them wanted to take steps to perpetuate it. As had officer veterans of the Civil War in their time, those conspicuous in the gun circles expressed dissatisfaction with the marksmanship of soldiers in the Spanish war as well as with those in the conflict still raging in the Philippines. In June 1900, therefore, Albert S. Jones, an officer in the New Jersey National Guard and secretary of the state's rifle association, invited various gun groups to form a national organization for reenergizing efforts to make marksmen of American youths. Prominent politicians such as Theodore Roosevelt, then governor of New York, backed this move.

At the meeting in September to plan for the new firearms society, Wingate, now president of the National Rifle Association (NRA), suggested that his organization could achieve the goal Jones desired. The delegates agreed, backed away from forming the new society, and allowed Wingate, with the help of politicians and the federal government, to embark on a program for bringing new life to the presently frail rifle association. The organization also helped rejuvenate itself by expanding its membership beyond men with military connections. It swept into its ranks many of the gun owners interested primarily in shooting sports.

As for gun-control legislation, it remained segmented in numerous state and local jurisdictions. Individual gun keepers continued often to defy the usual mild restrictions enacted by these entities. Under these conditions, when Leon F. Czolgosz, the twenty-eight-year-old son of Polish immigrants attracted to doctrines of anarchism, shopped for a gun he had no trouble buying an easily concealed short-barreled .32-caliber Iver-Johnson revolver for four dollars. On September 6, 1901, when he attended a reception for William McKinley at the Pan-American Exposition in Buffalo, New York, he covered the gun in the palm of his hand with a handkerchief. When the president reached out to shake hands with him, Czolgosz fired two shots, mortally wounding McKinley. "I killed the President," the shooter said later, "because he was the enemy of the good people—the good working people. I am not sorry for my crime."[29]

A stunned nation demanded revenge against all anarchists. Police quizzed hundreds of them and arrested many. The assassination did not prompt a notable outcry against the sale of lethal weapons to demented persons. Bursts of crime in cities did, however, spur businesspeople to organize against lawbreakers with handguns. In some cities, as in Houston, the effort produced numerous arrests, but lenient juries voted only mild punishment to pistol-packing criminals.[30]

Meanwhile, Roosevelt, well known as an apostle of the strenuous life, rose from the vice presidency to master of the White House. He had loved guns since receiving his first firearm at age fourteen and collected them. He had hunted animals for sport, belonged to the National Rifle Association, and took a macho pride in his marksmanship. He had explained in one instance that he "never made steadier shooting than at the grizzlies" and that he "had grand sport with the elk too." In comparison to "bear killing," he added, "other sport seemed tame."[31] He also kept in close touch with arms manufacturers.[32]

Roosevelt began his presidency as the regulatory zeal of the Progressive era had started rising and moving in a direction affecting firearms use. His personality fit the times even though he denounced as muckrakers journalists who in inexpensive magazines exposed corruption throughout the nation and gave prominence to the Progressive agenda. Progressive politicians as well as sensationalist writers looked closely at poverty, slums, prostitution, crime, unsanitary health conditions, and child labor in cotton mills, mines, and elsewhere. Disliking what they saw, these social crusaders mobilized public outrage to demand "government intervention—municipal, state, and federal—in behalf of the poor, the weak, and the young."[33] They also campaigned to mitigate the abuse of domesticated animals and to regulate the producing and marketing of food and patent medicines.

The humane movement, led by the Society for the Prevention of Cruelty to Animals, mounted an effort that led many states to ban the use of live pigeons or turkeys in competitive rifle shooting. The shooting continued but at clay pigeons or turkeys. Similarly, conservationists facilitated passage of state game laws that brought hunting under limited controls. These state regulations became sufficiently extensive to prompt the Department of Agriculture to publish an annual bulletin listing them.

In addition, as law enforcement became more professional and the nation's military forces formidable, Progressives questioned the need for perpetuating the myth of a citizenry in arms. Roosevelt agreed, primarily because he wished well-trained troops rather than untrustworthy transfers from the National Guard to enter the federal armed forces. In December 1901 he called for change in military legislation, urging action in the matter of "raising volunteer forces." He pointed out, "Our militia law is obsolete and worthless. The organization and armament of the National Guard of the several states, which are treated as militia in the appropriations by the Congress, should be made identical with those provided for the regular forces."[34]

The next year, in line with presidential thinking, Congress considered a bill that, among other provisions, would have created a national board for the promotion of rifle practice. Roosevelt urged passage, explaining he wanted urgently to teach Americans to shoot by encouraging rifle practice among youths, people of all classes, and those in the military services. "The marksmanship of the men," he told Congress, "must receive special attention."[35]

Congress seemed congenial to the shooting program but refused to go along with the administration's proposed reorganization of the National Guard because its well-organized association opposed some of the bill's features. As Secretary of War Elihu Root put it, this lobby had the clout "to defeat any measure" for a reserve system "which did not commend itself to them."[36] So he met with Guard leaders to work out a compromise for reforming and perpetuating the militia as succeeded by state Guard units.

Finally, on January 19, 1903, largely through the politicking of Charles F.

Dick, a congressman, a major general in the Ohio National Guard, and chairman of the House militia committee, Congress passed legislation that replaced the 111-year-old militia law. This measure attempted to clarify the confusing militia concept primarily by retaining the volunteer National Guard but providing for change in its status. By designating the Guard as the organized militia, it gave new life to the armed citizenry myth by stating that able-bodied males between eighteen and forty-five must serve in the armed forces. That requirement applied to what the legislation called the reserve militia.

In addition, the Dick act enhanced federal influence over the Guard through shared funding, partly from the states and partly from Washington. The war department provided Guard units in the states with arms, ammunition, and training. The law also empowered the president to call out the Guard in case of invasion, rebellion, or when he could not execute laws with other forces at his command.

In harmony with this legislation and at the request of the National Rifle Association, Congress encouraged shooting by establishing, as Roosevelt had asked, the National Board for the Promotion of Rifle Practice and appropriating funds for annual marksmanship contests. From the standpoint of the gun community, the legislators had established "the program of the National Rifle Association as the law of the land."[37] In its initial meeting on March 31, 1903, the association's governing board recommended that the government open federal facilities to civilians for rifle practice. Washington obliged.

A few days after the request, Secretary Root undermined the association's major contention that the nation needed a compulsory militia for national defense. Echoing the president's sentiment, he pointed out that the idea of the nation's founders of relying for defense on a militia composed of the entire male population, with each one keeping "in his own home the gun and powder," in practice "never worked." He declared correctly that the militia had become "absolutely a dead letter."[38] Nonetheless, special-interest lobbying again pumped blood into the compulsory citizen-militia concept.

Two years later, in *Salina v. Blakesly*, 72 Kan. 230, 83 (1905), the connection of the militia to civilian gun-owning again came under legal scrutiny. The Kansas Supreme Court held that the constitutional right to bear arms applied only to members of the state militia in their official capacity while in actual service. It thus upheld the theory of the Second Amendment conferring only a collective right to own arms.[39]

That same year a Congress attuned to the popularity of guns and shooting supported in substance the individual theory of gun ownership by showering more favors on the NRA and affiliated clubs. It gave their members the privilege of buying surplus government rifles, ammunition, and other military equipment at cost. This legislation encouraged still unattached gun enthusiasts to join the rifle association, thereby widening its membership. A change in rules also attracted new members. Unofficially, the association had allowed women to shoot in its matches but, ostensibly because of its quasimilitary character, it had barred them from membership. In 1906 it admitted women. By this time the NRA had emerged from a period of decline larger, more diverse, and stronger than in the past.

With the backing of powerful figures in government such as Roosevelt and Root, now secretary of state, the association became a remarkably successful special-interest group. It succeeded in good measure because its objectives reflected the convictions of America's leaders as well as the attitudes of shooters. Root, for instance, believed "that the young men of America shall know how to shoot straight is one of the fundamental requirements of our scheme of national defense."[40] To solidify its relationship with the government with more direct access to policymakers in promoting national legislation favored by its membership, the NRA in 1908 moved its headquarters from New York City to Washington, D.C.

At the same time, in keeping with the nation's status as a world power, Congress passed another militia act that provided for more centralization of the armed forces. It granted the federal government authority to deploy National Guardsmen beyond the limits of the continental United States and to determine, once they were accepted as federal troops, how long they would serve.[41] This law dealt another blow to the concept, still upheld in theory by gun keepers of the rifle association, of an armed local citizenry as a safeguard against a standing army and as protection against internal tyranny.

This minor setback in a matter of ideology did not deter leaders of the NRA from enlarging its interests. James A. Drain, its president, campaigned to widen its base again, this time geographically. Most members still resided on the East Coast. As a means of converting the association to an umbrella organization for hunters, farmers, ranchers, sport shooters, and gun collectors everywhere, he promoted the founding of rifle club branches throughout the country. He also guided the organization into sponsoring nationwide target shooting contests.

In the year of the move to Washington, the association organized the first American Olympic rifle team, which in the international competition captured the gold medal. American shooters in teams also won other competitions on several continents. A pleased Roosevelt asked Congress to appropriate funds for constructing rifle ranges in public schools. With such official support and popular approval, target shooting became a sport practiced year-round and was widely identified with the NRA.

In this manner the rifle brotherhood completed its transformation from a regional, militarist club to the nation's foremost firearms lobby representing an ideologically conservative and an increasingly politically activist constituency. Throughout the process, the NRA took care to preserve its special relationship with the government. For example, as the army had done previously, in 1910 it gave, or sold at bargain prices, surplus rifles and ammunition only to association members or affiliates.

8
Urban Control Movements

As gun keeping in the early twentieth century experienced growth, Progressive reformers became alarmed by a surge of armed robberies and killings in large cities. This violence led students of criminology to turn from dealing mainly with conjectures to a systematic but still limited probing of the connection between the availability of guns for private use and lawlessness. Criminologists gathered opinions on the problem as expressed mostly by newspaper editorials, newly formed citizen groups alarmed by the crime situation, and police records. In New York City in June 1903 police estimated that twenty thousand people regularly carried handguns, about six thousand of them with requisite permits.[1] Even though these numbers come from crude record-keeping, they and other data did indicate that New Yorkers had a lot of pistols.

Various investigators concluded that pistols, which could be had for two dollars, had become so widespread that society should regulate their possession. Some perturbed journalists urged high taxes on the sale of firearms that would make them too costly for most people to own, a system of indirect constraint going back to the Middle Ages. These concerns over mounting gun violence and schemes hatched to counter it opened to fresh scrutiny the constitutional right to bear arms. The court rulings had brought at least aspects of that assumed right into question, but Americans who worried over the blood spilled with guns believed the courts had not gone far enough. These critics of the status quo desired some form of gun control beyond local ordinances and state laws. They accomplished little because at this time nationally they constituted a clear minority. In addition, gun owners and federal legislators stood firmly behind the preindustrial practice of allowing private gun-keeping with only minimum restrictions.

In contrast, publics in Europe's industrially advanced countries increasingly accepted demands for government-imposed gun controls. In Britain following the Boer War and a spurt in civilian gun violence, popular sentiment provided momentum for the Pistols Act of 1903. It prohibited the sale of pistols and revolvers to minors and felons while permitting only persons with a proper license to own a firearm.[2] Although the law struck mostly at the usual wrong people, it placed for the first time an explicit restriction on gun ownership that applied to the whole population.

In the United States, despite the lack of a significant popular gun-control constituency, a number of states continued their efforts to deal with the problem of firearms violence. They, and municipalities too, enacted broader restrictions than in the past on who could use small arms. For instance, in 1906 Massachusetts prohibited private citizens from carrying a loaded pistol without a permit and jurists spoke of guns such as the repeating pistol as a menace meriting regulation.

Texas in May 1907 passed legislation designed to break the gun-carrying habit by requiring all who sold revolvers to pay a tax of 50 percent on their gross earnings. An editorialist in *The Nation* magazine exclaimed, "A law in Texas against pistols? The thing seems incredible." But he approved, writing that "if there is an industry which we should like to see a Government monopoly, it is the manufacture and sale of firearms. They ought to be made the costliest kind of luxury."[3]

The next month a reader commented, "It seems entirely logical that the manufacture of weapons for the destruction of human life, in this boasted age of enlightenment, should be confined wholly to Government agencies, to be used only against foreign enemies or for police purposes at home." He called laws against concealed weapons "merely plucking a few leaves from the evil tree, whereas the true remedy lies in attacking the tree itself." He urged the "total cutting off of the present superabundant supply of deadly weapons." More than anything else, he concluded, it would mitigate the gun-keeping evil, "the greatest in our social system."[4]

The next year a journalist claimed that an Oklahoma law carrying a fine of fifty dollars and three months in jail for anyone pointing a gun at another person was probably the toughest firearms legislation in the nation.[5] Although the state laws and the budding antigun sentiment upset some gun keepers, the antigun agitation had no discernible impact on their behavior. In Texas, dealers evaded that state's tough law by leasing rather than selling handguns to their customers.

In most instances, the local antigun legislation struck as usual at those designated as belonging to the dangerous classes. As part of a larger pattern, this discrimination reflected the changing values of a society transformed by industrialization and by masses of what earlier settlers perceived as strange newcomers. The established, xenophobic, and often gun-owning citizenry accused those whom they called ignorant and quarrelsome immigrants—Jews, Italians, Poles, and Russians—of allegedly lawbreaking propensities for abusing the use of pistols and instigating violence. This stereotyped thinking, similar to that of the pre–Civil War white upper classes toward outsiders and the poor, led authorities in New York City, for instance, to cancel pistol permits in immigrant neighborhoods.

When this narrowly targeted regulation failed discernibly to alleviate crime, considerable sentiment in the city switched to the support of the emerging gun-control movement that would become the most effective in the nation. Newspaper editors, judges, police officials, and others fed up with the rising criminal use of guns demanded effective action to stop it. Their crusade helped shape the local control sentiment while giving it momentum. At the urging of the district attorney, William T. Jerome, the city's board of aldermen in February 1905 adopted a new concealed-weapons ordinance. It continued an already established permit system but greatly increased the penalty for violation of the law to a maximum fine of 250 dollars and prescribed a prison term of up to six months.

Jerome tried to buttress this measure with a similar state statute. Even though this effort garnered substantial support, it failed to produce the desired legislation. The state legislature then enacted its own selective control measure. It prohibited aliens from carrying firearms in any public place. While New York's control advocates continued their campaign, several other states also attempted to deal with the crime problem with mild regulations on gun sales and ownership.

Also, as the National Rifle Association continued to grow in numbers and political influence, a few gun-control advocates began questioning its cozy relationship with government. In particular, they protested the federal promotion of marksmanship through the association. This concern over the encouraging of shooting even spilled into the national council of the newly organized Boy Scouts of America. Its leaders split over whether or not to have a merit badge for marksmanship. In the end, at the cost of losing some longtime supporters, scout leaders sided with the shooting promoters by authorizing a marksman badge.

Despite this victory for the firearms network and despite its impressive power in repulsing attacks, the most determined of the small number of control pro-moters—newspaper editors, law enforcement officials, and judges—persisted in challenging it. George C. Holt, a federal district court judge who had served in New York, declared that "the repeating pistol is the greatest nuisance in mod-ern life."[6] He characterized carrying it as an indefensible, monstrous habit. These critics called for laws that would make pistol carrying a penitentiary of-fense.

These efforts received a boost from an episode of gun violence splashed across headlines in urban newspapers. On August 9, 1910, James Gallagher, an embittered municipal employee, stalked Mayor William J. Gaynor of New York while he attended a crowded celebration aboard a ship berthed at a municipal pier. Gallagher aimed and fired a pistol, and the bullet pierced Gaynor's neck. The mayor recovered but had to undergo a long, painful convalescence. This shooting and other local gun violence led a coroner, using a popular but flawed analogy, to comment, "This city is like a wild Western town. The gun men rule."[7]

Promptly, organized antigun activists and a number of politicians demanded statewide regulatory legislation, mainly, they said, to curb the reckless and ha-bitual use of firearms in the city. Some of these reformers contended the state should lead the nation in breaking the gun community's grip on legislators when they considered proposals affecting the keeping of firearms.

One of the city's most conspicuous control proponents, George P. Lebrun, secretary to the board of coroners and its chief medical examiner, called for severe measures to curtail the sale of firearms. Other prominent civic leaders such as John Wannamaker, merchant; John D. Rockefeller Jr., oil baron; and Arthur Brisbane, journalist, endorsed this program, maintaining that morality and the public welfare required containment of the pistol habit.

When Timothy D. "Big Tim" Sullivan, a Tammany politician with a forceful personality, not only joined this campaign but also positioned himself at its head, it built up steam. He pledged to introduce a bill in the state legislature, drafted by Lebrun, for regulating the purchase, possession, and carrying of fire-arms. On January 5, 1911, soon after the legislature had convened and as more gun violence rocked New York City, Sullivan introduced the bill. He moved at a moment when criminologists had compiled data that pointed to a correlation between the ready availability of pistols and the perceived rise in crime. Lebrun used these findings in a report showing that in the previous year the number of local gun homicides had jumped upward by almost 50 percent. He suggested, as had the researchers, that easy access to the weapons bore some responsibility for the increase in deaths.

With these statistics at hand, a state legislative committee in the following months held hearings on Sullivan's bill. Hardware merchants and spokesmen for small-arms manufacturers opposed it with arguments that would become standard for gun enthusiasts in protesting virtually any kind of control. Dealers cautioned that the measure would merely drive their pistol customers to New Jersey and Connecticut whereas manufacturers contended it would work the greatest hardship not on criminals but on legitimate gun purchasers, however they might be defined. The firearms constituency also warned that crooks would not obey the law. Felons and others prone to crime would steal, buy elsewhere, or make any handgun they needed.

Thoughtful supporters of the bill did not deny the validity of some of these arguments but insisted the legislation would at least help reduce gun violence. Others, such as Sullivan himself, accused opponents of fronting for a gun trust. He pontificated, "If this bill passes, it will do more to carry out the commandment thou shalt not kill and save more souls than all the talk of all the ministers and priests in the state for the next ten years."[8]

Such rhetoric did less for the bill than did its anticrime focus and the progressive ferment of the times. It fell into the enlarging pattern of social regulation closely fought in Congress and the courts that included demands for the eight-hour day, for exclusion of all children from night work and from tasks dangerous to life or limb, and for the regulation of factory health and safety conditions.[9] The New York legislators voted for the Sullivan bill as part of this reform wave. Later, progun writers would discount this reformist agitation to argue incorrectly that the bill passed because "there was no organized opposition in those days to ill-conceived firearms laws."[10] On May 25 the governor signed the measure into law.

The law revised another two-year-old statute on hidden small arms. As we have seen, other municipalities and states had enforced legislation against concealed gun-carrying but the Sullivan law attempted to do more. Unlike previous state and local gun statutes, it regulated not only the carrying and possession of pistols, machine guns, and sawed-off shotguns but also their sale and private possession. These restrictions as well as the law's requirement of a license to keep a concealable gun in one's home or place of business had no precedent in American law. Violation of the statute's provisions was punishable as a felony rather than as a misdemeanor.

In the same year, legislators enacted another law allowing police to search and arrest without warrant anyone suspected of carrying an illegal gun. It and the Sullivan law were tailored to fit the situation in New York City and State. Proponents, though, hoped the statute would serve as a model for other states seeking to control gun violence. When it went into effect in September, it did have national ramifications. Police, legislators, and gun owners in other parts of the country followed its course.

As New York police and the courts proceeded with enforcement of the statute, critics denounced it as despotic, vicious, asinine, as an outrage against the rights of all Americans, and challenged its constitutionality. In two instances courts upheld the validity of the Sullivan law but its effect on gun keeping brought mixed assessments. Lebrun's report on deaths for 1912 appeared to bear out the control advocates' optimism. He assembled statistics showing that suicides with firearms had dropped 40 percent from the previous year, and credited the law for the decline.

Opponents pointed out, however, that homicides by shooting had increased from 108 in 1910, the last pre-Sullivan year, to 113 in 1912. Moreover, even antigun journalists admitted that criminals remained as well armed as ever. This happened in part because, as opponents had prophesied, New Yorkers who wanted guns bought them in neighboring states without undergoing any questioning. For these reasons critics never ceased calling the legislation a failure.[11] Despite the negative data, supporters claimed the law worked well enough, insisting that in the long run it would show more obviously positive results.

Two of the statute's most articulate defenders, Lebrun and William G. McAdoo, a former police commissioner and the city's chief magistrate who superintended the courts, called for similar legislation in New Jersey and Connecticut that would help make gun control more effective in New York as well as elsewhere. McAdoo believed that "if every citizen joined in the movement to do away with pistols and revolvers, this would be a safer land in which to live." Accordingly, he also urged passage of a federal law banning the carrying of concealed guns.[12]

As for the Sullivan law's ripple effect, a number of states or communities across the country did adopt similar legislation, thereby alarming the National Rifle Association. Previously it had concentrated much of its lobbying on gaining goodwill with leaders in the federal government rather than on opposing scattered lawmaking it disliked. Given the prevalence of progun sentiment, local battles against isolated controllers had not seemed necessary. Under Drain's leadership, the association now jumped into local and state control struggles with carefully organized, well-financed battle plans. He denounced all

Sullivan-like legislation, claiming, in words common in the gun fraternity, that "such laws have the effect of arming the bad man and disarming the good one to the injury of the community."[13]

Since the NRA and gun keepers everywhere would repeat this sentiment as though it were gospel, it prevailed nationally. It appeared plausible also because state and local regulation outside the state of New York as usual failed to stop gun violence or to make a real dent in the sale and possession of firearms. Both the old and the new gun-carrying habits of most Americans remained largely untouched. All of these data convinced many in the control movement that for gun regulation to be effective it needed federal as well as state backing.

No support came from the White House. As did Theodore Roosevelt, President William H. Taft, his successor, belonged to the NRA and approved of teaching the young to shoot. Although he did nothing for the domestic regulation of firearms, for about a year he faced what amounted to a gun-control problem in foreign relations. Beginning in 1910, revolution convulsed Mexico. From the start, without legal or other restraints, American dealers and manufacturers sold guns and ammunition to factions on both sides. Taft wanted to regulate this cross-border commerce so it would reflect his policy toward the upheaval but felt he needed more authority than he assumed he had before he could act. Finally, in consultation with members of Congress, he worked out a plan to block this arms trafficking on his terms.

On March 14, 1912, Congress voted legislation empowering the president to forbid American firms from exporting arms to countries where he found they promoted violence. The next day Taft issued a proclamation banning the export of firearms to Mexico.[14] Violation of this law carried a fine of up to ten thousand dollars, imprisonment of up to two years, or both. No punishment of comparable severity applied to sales of guns at home, an action that could be construed as promoting violence. Indeed, the nation's gun enthusiasts still believed as passionately as ever that they had the right to use their weapons against what they would regard as tyrannical government.

Several months later, this right came under public scrutiny in a way that cast a shadow over the three-way race for the presidency. On October 14, while campaigning in Milwaukee on the third-party Bull Moose ticket, Roosevelt became the target of an assassin. John N. Schrank, a disturbed immigrant from Bavaria who appeared incapable of conceptualizing tyranny but who sported a sign that read, "Theodore Roosevelt is a murderer," wounded the former president with a .38-caliber Colt police revolver he had purchased for fourteen dollars. "Friends," Roosevelt announced immediately, "I have been shot but it takes more than that to kill a Bull Moose." Then with a rib fractured by the bullet that lodged in his chest, he spoke for an hour.

Later, in discussing the attempted murder and Schrank himself, Roosevelt explained, "I have not the slightest feeling against him; I have a very strong feeling against the people, who, by their ceaseless and intemperate abuse, excited him to the action, and against the mushy people who would excuse him and all other criminals once the crime has been committed."[15] In this castigation, however, Roosevelt expressed no anger or other emotion against the society that permitted persons such as Schrank to have unconstrained access to guns.

Of course, as gun defenders pointed out, neither police vigilance nor state gun-control laws could have done much to prevent the kind of shooting that injured Roosevelt. Even federal regulation probably could not have stopped it. Nonetheless, an alarmed minority indicated that those in positions of authority should denounce the unfettered sale of guns to the likes of Schrank. Given that the public did not demand meaningful regulation of firearms, those who desired it were convinced that unstable persons would continue to possess guns freely and would be able to attempt more assassinations.

This pessimism toward controls reflected reality. Legislators, jurists, and most Americans still assumed they could not curb gun violence significantly because the Second Amendment barred virtually any kind of federal regulation. Why battle for tight controls, they reasoned, and surely fail? In addition, the Supreme Court still seldom heard cases touching on that amendment. When the Court did consent to consider appeals from states on litigation involving guns, it focused on the broader points of law rather than specifically on claimed constitutional rights.

In the case of *Joseph Patsone v. Commonwealth*, 1915 232 U.S. 138, which in 1914 reached the Supreme Court on appeal, the justices seemed ready to go beyond former restraints. A resident alien originally from Italy, Patsone challenged a state law that forbade a noncitizen to own firearms. He lost but appealed the lower court's decision. He contended Pennsylvania had violated the due process clause of the Fourteenth Amendment with legislation prohibiting unnaturalized foreign-born persons from possessing firearms to hunt. In ruling against him, the high court again upheld the states' police power to control the use of guns, declaring the state had "the right to prohibit the possession of the instruments of killing" but said also the ban did not extend to "weapons such as pistols that may supposed to be needed occasionally for self-defense."[16] In all, while ruling in support of state power to control, the court still refused to take a firm, clear-cut stand on the constitutional issue of private gun-keeping.

All the while, privately owned guns continued to play a significant role in labor violence, as in Las Animas and Huerfano Counties, Colorado. In the summer of 1913 the Colorado Fuel and Iron Company imported men from Baldwin-Felts, a private detective agency, as guards in anticipation of a strike. According to contemporary estimates, the company equipped them with nine thousand or more firearms. In turn the United Mine Workers armed themselves with Remington, Savage, and larger numbers of Winchester rifles. With such armaments, the strike, which began on September 23, quickly turned into a shooting war that police could not control. The next month President Woodrow Wilson attempted to bring the operators and the miners together for a settlement. His effort failed and the private warfare spread to mining camps throughout the area. So, on October 28, the governor ordered National Guard troops into the fray, an intervention that aggravated the strife because the troops functioned as auxiliaries of the mine owners.[17]

The bloodiest encounter occurred on April 20, 1914, when National Guard troops poured machine-gun and rifle fire into a tent camp of striking miners and their families, killing ten people. Eight days later, as Colorado's governor requested, the president ordered federal troops into the strike zone. He took care to explain that he intervened to maintain order and not to force a settlement, which he said "falls strictly within the fields of State power."[18] Within a week the troopers collected three thousand firearms. Before the strike ended, with the company refusing to recognize the United Mine Workers union, fifty-nine people had died in gunfire whereas total casualties were much higher.[19]

This carnage involving civilian gun-toting and indiscriminate use of firearms by poorly trained Guardsmen had little impact on the movement to restrict private gun-keeping, in particular because of the war that in August 1914 had broken out in Europe. Even so, by this time legal scholars on their own had begun reassessing the problem of private gun violence in light of contemporary social circumstances.

As one academician, Lucius Emery, wrote, "The greater deadliness of small firearms," along with alarming increases in homicides and felonious assaults, "are now pressing home" the limitation of the presumed legal guarantee on arms carrying. "Women, young boys, the blind, tramps, persons *non compos mentis* or dissolute in habits," he asserted, "may be prohibited from carrying weapons." Indeed, he believed government could go further. "For the protection of the people," he maintained, it could restrict, even prohibit, the carrying of weapons.[20] This reasoning attracted little attention beyond the legal and academic communities. Concern over the war just about smothered the nascent gun-control movement where Emery's message had greatest meaning.

Initially, after the outbreak of hostilities, national worry over a business depression aggravated by the loss of trade with belligerents pushed aside reform programs such as firearms regulation. When the war took on the character of a stalemate and Allied belligerents began purchasing munitions and other supplies in the United States, depression turned into prosperity. Economic benefits overshadowed the need for reform.

As the conflict dragged on, perhaps a majority of Americans feared possible involvement. To a small group of military officers such as Major General Leonard Wood, a former army chief of staff, and other aggressive men of prominence such as Roosevelt, it also provided an opportunity to energize a static military-preparedness program they had been advocating. Trained in shooting skills, many of these espousers were militarists and civilian gun enthusiasts who identified with the goals of the National Rifle Association.

Tapping the myth of an armed citizenry rising on its own to defend an endangered nation, these men persuaded citizen groups, patriotic organizations, and corporate leaders to back their program. They created clubs where on weekends civilians drilled with privately owned firearms. Since the originators did their marching and shooting at a camp at Plattsburg, New York, journalists and others dubbed a part of the preparedness campaign the Plattsburg Movement.

These upper-class, primarily East Coast, pro-Allied militarists who organized and advanced the movement wanted to prod the nation into war. They also deplored data indicating that 60 percent of the National Guard personnel could not use the army rifle. To remedy this shooting problem, Roosevelt and other preparedness patriots urged universal military training linked to the old concept of the compulsory militia. He praised the "virile strength of manliness which accepts as the ideal the stern, unflinching performance of duty."[21]

Pacifists, a number of organized minorities, and workers' groups opposed the preparedness movement as class based and militarist. President Wilson and other Democrats disliked it mainly because most of its leaders were antiadministration Republicans. Like the Plattsburgers, though, he still had faith in the concept of an armed citizenry. In October 1914 he had stated that in time of peril the nation should not depend on either a standing army or a reserve army "but upon a citizenry trained and accustomed to arms . . . a system by which every citizen who will volunteer for the training may be made familiar with the use of modern arms."[22]

The following January, as though emphasizing his antimilitarist stance, the president stopped the sale of surplus government guns to the NRA and the clubs affiliated with it. Soon, the public mood shifted. A journal of opinion noted in April, "Nothing has become plainer" than the growth of a "widespread belief that we of the United States must get ready to fight somebody."[23] After a diplomatic clash with Germany, when a U-boat on May 7 torpedoed the British passenger liner *Lusitania* off the Irish coast taking 1,100 lives, the president gradually warmed up to the preparedness idea.

As this happened, Wilson's private secretary, Joseph Tumulty, wrote him in August that adoption of a preparedness program would be "the ultimate test of our party's power to govern the nation."[24] Wilson did not switch to a buildup of arms because of this advice alone. On his own that autumn he realized that preparedness had become a nationwide concern and that opposition to it could affect his reelection campaign. In January 1916 he toured the country plugging his own version of preparedness. In addition to political considerations, difficulties in an armed confrontation with Mexico influenced him.

In March in a reaction to Mexican raids on American border towns, Wilson ordered troops under Brigadier General John J. Pershing into Mexico to pursue the raiders. Because all the army regulars were with Pershing or dispersed on the border, two months later, as allowed by law, the president called National Guard units from several states into federal service to supplement the regulars. Many Guardsmen refused to serve or deserted. As in the past, regulars disparaged the citizen-soldiers who served with them, saying in one instance, their behavior "only strengthens my belief the militia is worthless."[25]

That May, in passing the National Defense Act, Congress accepted only part of the president's preparedness plan. The legislators bowed to the power of the National Guard lobby and to the idea that the country needed an army of citizen-soldiers taken from Guard units as though from militias in the past. The defense statute, which became law on June 3, reasserted the principle of a universal military obligation among able-bodied males, expanded the regular army, and divided the source for citizen-soldiers "into three classes, the National Guard, the Naval Militia, and the unorganized Militia."[26] It placed the National Guard units in the states under federal authority subject to call for duty as part of the army. Promptly, on June 18, Wilson exercised his fresh power by summoning one hundred thousand National Guardsmen to seal off the Mexican border.

The legislation also created the Office of the Director of Civilian Marksmanship. Congress appropriated three hundred thousand dollars for the promotion of private shooting, primarily through the National Rifle Association. The gun organization provided a core of young shooters. Nearly half of its eight thousand members under age eighteen participated as Boy Scouts.[27]

At this time, too, the NRA took over an established gun magazine, *Arms and the Man*, changing its name later to *American Rifleman*, which would become the shooter's bible. As for the nascent gun-control movement, even its most determined supporters realized the futility of denouncing firearms ownership when the nation was arming for possible war.

Despite much of the public's esteem for firearms, the general prosperity, the success of the preparedness movement, and sales to belligerents such as Britain and Russia, gunmakers complained of meager profits. Executives of the Winchester company, for instance, grumbled they had "a plant entirely equipped for making small arms and ammunition and an organization completely trained and nothing to do."[28]

After April 6, 1917, when the United States entered the World War, that situation quickly changed. Much as had involvement in previous conflicts, such as the Civil War, the intervention in Europe revitalized the arms industry. The government again became its foremost customer. The army had 100,000 Springfield rifles on hand and possession of armories that could produce 350,000 a year but it projected a need for 4 million rifles. So army procurement turned to the private arms-makers to provide most of them. At the start, though, until home production could catch up to demand, American troops in France had to use French machine guns and automatic rifles. At home, arms manufacturing became part of a wartime economic boom that attracted thousands upon thousands of Americans to well-paying jobs.

On the day after the declaration of war, as had Abraham Lincoln, Wilson openly abandoned the armed-citizen shibboleth, whether through state militias or national volunteering. He asked Congress for national conscription. Despite considerable popular opposition, expressed especially in a deluge of letters and telegrams, the legislators responded with the Selective Service Act. On May 18 he signed it into law.

That legislation authorized volunteer divisions but the president refused to exercise that authority, preferring instead to conscript young men for service but not call them conscripts. "It [the draft] is in no sense a conscription of the unwilling," he announced. "It is rather, selection from a nation which has volunteered in mass."[29] This convoluted explanation represented the opposite of reality. His and other interventionists' lack of faith in the willingness of the masses to learn to use guns and fight without compulsion produced the conscription that ended heavy reliance on volunteerism. Thereafter, to avoid a possible backlash, administration leaders spoke carefully of "selective service" rather than conscription or the draft and referred to draftees with euphemisms such as "selectees" and "servicemen."[30]

Ostensibly to help pay for the costs of the conflict, Congress in 1919 passed a war revenue act. This statute imposed a manufacturer's tax of 10 percent on firearms and ammunition. Some control proponents perceived this first federal assertion of a regulatory power over guns as a means of reducing "the sale of revolvers and pistols."[31] That did not happen, but beginning with this legislation the Treasury Department's responsibility for enforcement of gun laws became a fixed feature of government procedure. In addition, the statute itself set a precedent for further federal involvement in the control struggle.

In contrast to this anemic domestic measure, the federal government from the start of its occupation of the Philippines had decreed stringent gun control for the people of the conquered islands. The Philippine Constabulary, a nationwide organization of military police, enforced the measure. In October 1917 the American regime had gone further, adopting regulations that forbade "any person to possess any firearms," not even air guns, unless licensed and registered.[32] Noting this double standard that placed controls on Filipinos and none on American citizens, island nationalists attributed it to a racist colonialism. Regardless, the gun controls remained in effect in the Philippines for decades.

In the United States when the war ended so did conscription and the trumpeting of the people-in-arms concept it embodied. Politicians who girded for national elections realized that large segments of the public still had no taste for having its sons compelled to use guns in the military. So to avoid possible alienation of voters, legislators in June 1920 passed the National Defense Act, which, unlike in the act of 1916 that it amended, deleted all reference to the draft or selective service. But the new law retained a militia bureau as part of the War Department.[33]

At this time also the prosperity of the arms industry plummeted, largely because, as after the Civil War, it had a huge investment in plants and equipment, many of which now lay idle. The gun manufacturers also had to cope with a sated domestic civilian market because during the war they had not stopped their commercial production of small arms. In addition, they faced competition from the government, which now sold surplus rifles to civilians below cost. Soon, as had previous postwar manufacturers, arms industrialists absorbed their excess plant capacity by diversifying. The Remington and Winchester companies, for instance, manufactured hardware for homes, cutlery, and cash registers. Most firms also continued to turn out guns for the public because they could make them in quantity, sell them cheaply to expand the market, and, despite competition, earn profits. Thus, in the postwar years industrial production, pumped-up sales efforts, government dumping on a scale greater than ever before, and low cost all contributed to placing a gun within the reach of virtually any American who wanted one. Through its tax on firearms and ammunition the federal government as well as the arms manufacturers benefited from these swelling sales of firearms to civilians.

During the hostilities, as during those of the Civil War, crime in the United States, as measured by prison inmates, decreased while juvenile delinquency rose. When the fighting ceased, crime with small arms as well as fatal gunshot accidents started climbing as had been the case in previous postwar eras.[34] Most belligerent countries experienced an escalation in crime. In all of them the plethora of guns became a worry. In the United States, crime and its associated gun violence became so pervasive as to become the focus of worldwide attention. It generated among concerned Americans renewed efforts to limit the open civilian access to firearms.

9
Gun-Roaring Twenties

As in the past, in the United States in the early twenties the responsibility for dealing with crime and gun violence remained with state and municipal authorities. Even though criminal activity now often crossed state lines, the federal government took care not to intrude directly on those responsibilities. In contrast in Great Britain, government moved to combat the surge in gun violence nationally by stiffening the seventeen-year-old pistols act. The proposed legislation aimed "to prevent criminals and persons of that description from being able to have revolvers and to use them."[1]

During the debate in Parliament, opponents raised the traditional arguments, asserting that additional regulation would not reduce crime but would deny law-abiding people a means of personal protection, and would benefit only murderers and other criminals. Rejecting this rationalizing, the House of Commons on June 8 by a vote of 254 to 6 passed the Firearms Act of 1920, Britain's first comprehensive gun-control law. It repealed what remained of the legal privilege of civilians keeping arms. Now anyone wishing to purchase, possess, use, or carry any description of gun or ammunition for it required a special certificate.

The statute entrusted local chiefs of police with the authority to decide who could obtain this document. They could deny a gun to anyone of intemperate habits, of unsound mind, or, for other reasons, deemed unfit to possess a firearm. In addition, the applicant had to convince the officer that he or she had a good reason for requiring a permit. If refused, an English person could appeal to a court to reverse the certificate decision, but an Irish applicant could not.

Although civilian gun violence caused more blood to flow in the United States, it did not arouse similar sentiment for comparable firearm regulation. Shortly, though, desperadoes who mocked law and order with seeming impunity stimulated the revival of the gun-control movement that in much of the nation had lain dormant during the war. Police departments, city dwellers, and others disgusted with well-armed criminals became involved in the cause.

As in previous postwar periods, some analysts connected the crime to "ex-servicemen" and as "directly traceable to their military experience." Others attributed the rise in homicide rates to cheap guns, automobiles, disillusionment, and economic depression.[2] Some of these activists and much of the public blamed it also on the foremost social issue of the time, the effort to prohibit the manufacture and sale of alcoholic beverages for general consumption. The prohibition campaign had culminated on January 29, 1919, when the Eighteenth Amendment became part of the Constitution.

On October 28, over President Woodrow Wilson's veto, Congress approved the enabling legislation, known as the National Prohibition Act or Volstead Act. As the law provided, on January 17 of the next year the ban went into effect. The Treasury Department placed authority for enforcement in the hands of a commissioner of Prohibition within the bureau of internal revenue. Americans of all classes soon violated what subsequently historians and others dubbed the "toothless" law.

This regulation of the liquor traffic, which gave birth to the first nationwide venture in domestic crime-busting, appeared unenforceable for various reasons. For example, within three years twenty-two thousand bootleg cases, far more than the judiciary could handle, clogged the federal courts.[3] In addition, many in the federal, state, and local agencies entrusted with policing the illicit liquor traffic in the trenches succumbed to corruption. The most notable defiers of the law, mainly gangsters lured by huge profits, made a big business of bootlegging liquor. Their gun violence in battles for turf contributed to swelling murder rates.

Despite Prohibition's failures, it at least achieved one of the objectives its framers desired. The consumption of alcohol declined. Prohibition also brought national authority indirectly into an area of domestic policing through agents attached to a special federal Prohibition unit.[4] In this sense the Volstead Act—along with the earlier Ku Klux Klan Acts, laws against polygamy, and the War Revenue Act—enforced with federal agents, contributed to a precedent for possible future federal policing of gun keeping.

Meanwhile, in a number of cities, robbery and murder seemed rampant. In Chicago, after a rash of daylight bank robberies and lethal shootings, public indignation prompted leading citizens to organize a special crime commission of 130 citizens to oversee politicized and often corrupt law enforcement. On

January 1, 1919, it launched a campaign for police, among their other duties, to round up those who violated the city's regulation on the sale of guns and its ban on the carrying of concealed weapons. Organized gun-keepers decried these anticrime measures as dangerous, arguing they really targeted honest, law-abiding gun owners. Despite the objections, Chicago's regulatory effort continued.

On the basis of the concealment charge, police arrested as many as three alleged violators a day but with little apparent effect on the crime rate. Apprehended individuals usually gained freedom at the hands of lenient judges or by promptly posting bail. They easily replaced their confiscated guns by stealing, by purchasing others in nearby towns, or by buying from mail-order houses. Frustrated Chicagoans fumed over the ineffectiveness of even their city's most modest controls. As part of this anger, in summer 1921 a prominent businessman, John R. Thompson, initiated his own crusade against the handgun. In newspaper notices throughout the country, he offered one thousand dollars "to anyone who would give one good reason why the revolver manufacturing industry should be allowed to exist and enjoy the facilities of the mails."[5] Many of the city's leaders applauded his campaign, but gun crime continued.

In one day's criminal activity in January 1922 Chicago experienced two kidnappings, two burglaries, twenty-eight street robberies, and the attempted murder of the president of a music college. Repeated violence of this nature brought the *Tribune*, the city's most outspoken newspaper, into the antihandgun crusade. Although just a few months earlier it had run advertisements for mail-order pistols, the journal attacked the handgun and the gangsters in daily articles and editorials. In one instance, along with its presentation of crime statistics, it announced that "big guns and little guns, blue steel and nickel steel, continued to plunder Chicagoans . . . at the behest of the Crime Camorra." The *Tribune* also solicited a pledge from the head of the Illinois bar to "rid the state of concealable weapons."[6]

In Chicago and elsewhere, other control advocates demanded tougher official action aimed at the source of guns. They wanted to shut down the factories that produced firearms for civilians, an idea that in September the American Bar Association endorsed. Its committee studying the problem found that over 90 percent of the nation's murderers used pistols. Concluding that the various state and local laws prohibiting the carrying of firearms were ineffective, it recommended a countrywide ban on the manufacture and sale of pistols and ammunition except for law officials and under specified controls.[7] Using the slogan

"If nobody had a gun, nobody would need a gun," some control activists even urged disarming the police.

These ideas failed to convert into action. Indeed, in the perception of city dwellers, gun violence hardly faltered. Appalled because city and state regulations appeared inadequate to stop it, leaders of local gun-control movements turned to Washington for help. Federal legislators with large city constituencies responded positively. They introduced bills for various forms of national firearms regulation but with clocklike regularity the measures expired in committees.

An example of such failure can be seen in a bill that had been sponsored since 1915 by Senator John K. Shields, a Tennessee Democrat, that embodied the hope of those who wanted the federal government to banish the pistol from civilian use. Shields aimed at prohibiting the interstate shipment of handguns except for large army and navy pistols. He assumed that with the weapons' manufacturing industry highly concentrated, this measure ultimately would stop the production of other types of commercial guns because they would become unprofitable. The bill did not attract much attention until April 1921 when the Senate Judiciary Committee granted it a brief hearing.

Most of those who testified, such as a representative of the United States Revolver Association, expressed hostility. Railroad officials spoke against the bill because they feared they would suffer by violating it unwittingly. Pistol manufacturers argued that firearms laws should be left to the state legislatures. A Colt company official warned that the proposal could hamper inventiveness in a field vital to national defense. The bill suffered also because of the racist aim of some of its Southern supporters. They wanted to prevent blacks from carrying concealed pistols. "Can not we, the dominant race, upon whom depends the enforcement of the law," Shields asked, "so enforce the law that we will prevent the colored people from preying upon each other?"[8] All the testimony seemed unnecessary because Frank Brandegee of Connecticut blocked any measure that might injure one of his state's important industries. So until 1924 when Tennessee constituents voted Shields out of office, his bill never traveled beyond the committee hearing.

At this point, the control agitation had little tangible effect on the gun problem nationally or locally because, among other reasons, city, state, and other laws often clashed. Chicago, for instance, issued no permits to individuals to carry pistols but a state court order compelled it to honor firearms licenses issued elsewhere in Illinois. Another court ruled the city's strict pistol ordinance invalid because it conflicted with state law. Approximately the same thing happened to Chattanooga, which had enacted a weapons ban more severe than had the state of Tennessee.[9]

In contrast to their more powerful opponents, the scattered proponents of gun regulation who tried to cope with these miscellaneous laws faced constant disappointment. Members of the gun community succeeded much more often in achieving their goals but they, too, did not always pull together for their common cause. Firearms manufacturers saw no reason to defend the sale of cheap pistols made by foreign competitors who distributed them through mail-order firms. Even though marksmen with military interests and sport shooters in growing numbers now belonged to the rifle association, they, too, did not join readily in politicking for the same goals.

Both shooter groups did stand unified in opposing gun controls but the conservative former military officers who dominated the organization were willing to accept minor regulation. The soldier types still gave high priority to training the young in rifle marksmanship for national defense whereas the sportsmen backed shooting for almost any purpose. Through the staffs of sporting magazines, the recreational shooters attacked even modest antigun agitation as harmful to what they perceived as their legitimate interests, and which they identified with the public welfare. The sporting breed preached the old self-defense doctrine but with a slightly different twist. Instead of focusing on combating potential tyranny, they contended that self-armed citizens stood as society's best protection against robbery, murder, and rape.

Although voiced as propaganda from a special-interest group, this perspective appealed to numerous frightened ordinary citizens who dreaded criminals much as the founding fathers had feared tyrants. In small towns, Americans of this persuasion formed armed bands to shield their banks from robbers. In cities, brokers, bankers, and some women, too, bought pistols in record numbers to defend themselves against possible assault. Owners of gun stores reported a record demand for firearms of every kind.[10] The marketing of guns boomed also because authorities in most localities did not place restrictions, or their enforcement, high on their agendas.

This largely unfettered gun keeping, the distaste for controls in most of the country, and the wall of opposition in Washington to federal regulation discouraged but did not crush the few who espoused some kind of government control. Joined by journalists and concerned city dwellers, they launched selective campaigns for regulation similar to that in Chicago. These dedicated regulators experienced some limited success, mainly in the expansion of state and local policing power in matters pertaining to guns.

For example, in 1923 Arkansas required registration of all handguns in the state, and in California legislators passed a law prohibiting felons from possessing a pistol. Shortly thereafter state authorities prosecuted and a court convicted Joseph Camperlingo, a convicted felon, for violating the statute. He appealed, arguing he had a Second Amendment right to have the weapon. On October 1924, in the *People v. Camperlingo*, 69 CA 466 (1924), the appeals court affirmed his conviction. It held that as a function of the state's police power and for the public safety the "right to bear arms may be either regulated or, in proper cases, entirely destroyed."[11]

In that year Atlanta, which had long barred the discharge of firearms within city limits, adopted a stronger measure designed to control possession of handguns.[12] As with other municipal and state firearm cases, this one had no discernible national impact. All the while, those who agitated for some kind of federal gun control continued to bring a number of regulatory measures before Congress, but they, too, went nowhere.

In Detroit, where crime thrived with bootlegging, homicides rose markedly.[13] The police chief perceived mail-order firms as a cause, estimating that they alone supplied bootleggers, dope dealers, and stick-up men with five thousand pistols a year. Guns available by mail, consequently, evoked a widespread popular concern. Organized control proponents then concentrated on one objective that seemed attainable—keeping pistols from the mails. John F. Miller, a congressman from Washington State, introduced the bill that attracted the most support. It called for a ban on the sending of pistols and other small firearms through the federal mail service across state lines to private individuals.

After emerging from committee hearings with a favorable report, the bill went to the floor of Congress where, for the first time, the legislators had an opportunity to debate openly a direct form of gun control. In the House of Representatives Miller denounced the pistol as "the favorite weapon of the assassin," the "pet of the highway man, of the robber, and the thief," and "the handy weapon for suicides."[14] He and his supporters stressed that city people needed the legislation as a tool to curb crime.

Most congressmen, especially those with urban constituencies, agreed with Miller. Those from the rural South and West opposed his bill. The most vocal among them, Thomas Blanton of Texas, said, "I do not believe this bill would stop a single thug or a single bootlegger or a single murderer from carrying firearms unlawfully." Neither federal nor state laws, he contended, would "keep a criminal from having and carrying arms." He and other opponents argued also that the bill would violate the Second Amendment as well as the states' prerog-ative to control guns.[15] Then the bill stalled.

While Congress procrastinated, the crime issue became more pressing. Screaming headlines recounted the violence of gun-toting gangsters who boot-legged, robbed banks, heisted payrolls, often killed, and streaked away in auto-mobiles. Nowhere did mobsters strike with greater frequency or with more publicity than in Chicago. There gangsters such as John Torrio and Roger Touhy reputedly made the city the "headquarters in America for crime and vice."[16] As the kingpin illegal brewer and beer distributor in the northwestern suburbs, Touhy even employed off-duty police. They served as drivers of trucks hauling illegal booze and as guards to protect the product against hijacking or confisca-tion by honest law-enforcement agents.[17]

This corruption alarmed urbanites but the perceived private firearms menace disturbed Americans nationwide. Gun packing had become so prevalent that the attorney general of South Carolina blamed the local high murder rate on "the deplorable custom of carrying pistols, a custom carried to such an extent that our State may be regarded as an armed camp in time of peace." He pointed out that "pistols are carried, not as protection at night on some lonely road, or in some remote part of the country during the day or in some dangerous neighborhood, but at public meetings, on the streets, at social gatherings, even at dances, even at daily labor and following the plow, and . . . also even at church and prayer meeting."[18]

A prominent statistician asserted that "the outstanding fact of our deplor-able murder situation is the large proportion of homicides by means of fire-arms." He added that "nearly every so-called 'Detective Magazine' carries a string of advertisements of cheap revolvers, guaranteed to kill. Mail order houses furnish weapons to anyone, old or young, sane or insane, good or bad, without the least difficulty."[19] A journalist reported that "in the opinion of many the only way to finally stamp out the firearm evil is a Federal law forbid-ding the advertising of pistols in magazines as well as their shipment through the mails." A group of concerned citizens, organized as the American Reclama-tion Society, offered five thousand dollars for "one good reason for the exis-tence of revolvers."[20]

Gradually this kind of pressure led to the removal of advertisements for cheap pistols from most newspapers and magazines. In addition, the larger mail-order houses began restricting their sales. The Sears and Roebuck com-pany stopped selling handguns from its catalog because it wished to protect its good name and maintain public goodwill. Smaller firms, though, continued using the government mail service to deliver their guns.

At this point control proponents benefited from the support of editors of national journals who viewed the pistol toting as ominous and gave it stepped-up coverage. In addition, seventeen states enacted legislation for some kind of regulation of these handguns. Ardent control activists regarded these measures as inadequate. They believed, as a prominent newspaper editorialized, "that any effective regulation prohibiting the traffic in firearms must be imposed by Federal authority."[21]

This agitation had enough public impact to come to the attention of President Calvin Coolidge. He expressed uncertainty about "whether anything could be accomplished in reducing crime," as controllers wanted, "by legislation prohibiting the shipment of arms in interstate commerce." He expressed his own belief in standard gun-keeping phraseology, stating that "such a law would prevent firearms reaching those entitled to them to protect their homes while criminals would have no trouble obtaining them."[22]

The president's thinking corresponded with that of the gun-keeping public. Most gun owners opposed any kind of federal regulation. They resisted as well the spurt of localized firearms restrictions and viewed the social contract with police as inadequate. They continued to contend that firearms in the hands of the citizenry, more than the police establishment, acted as a deterrent to criminal activity. This concept obviously had little effect in curbing mobster violence. Indeed, gangster feuding and killing became more notorious with a new weapon, the submachine gun.

John T. Thompson, a former brigadier general and a lover of guns, had developed the gun as a trench weapon at the end of the First World War. He received a patent for it in 1921 and within a few years it became available to the public. Known as the "Tommy gun," manufacturers advertised it "for use by those on the side of law and order" and as the "antibandit" gun that would stop getaway cars in their tracks.[23] Few law-enforcement officials bought it but mobsters found it a useful tool for their business. It was portable, automatic, and capable, with the press of a finger, of firing bullets at the rate of eight hundred rounds a minute. A journal writer described the submachine gun as "nothing less than a diabolical engine of death . . . the paramount example of peace-time barbarism" that man had devised "to murder his neighbor." With it one bandit could "stand off a whole platoon of policemen."[24]

Chicago gangsters began using the submachine gun against each other in fall 1925 in battles over turf in their bootlegging rackets. One notorious shooting occurred at noon, September 20, 1926, in Chicago's Cicero area. In eleven cars gunmen affiliated with gangster Hymie Weiss converged on the headquarters of Alphonse "Scarface Al" Capone, a rival mobster and bootlegger. They raked the building with "thousands of bullets and slugs from machine guns, pistols, and shotguns" but missed Capone because he was having lunch next door. Three weeks later enemy thugs riddled Weiss.[25] That month an Illinois crime survey revealed that mobsters at this time had murdered 215 of their own kind and police had killed 160 gangsters.[26] Within a year or two, gangsters elsewhere adopted the submachine gun. Most petty criminals, though, still preferred the pistol.

Meanwhile, control proponents rallied around the stymied Miller proposal. In early February 1926 some of them showered Coolidge with form letters from various states maintaining that the easy access to mail-order pistols lured young boys into crime. "Is there, Mr. President, any good reason to hope," they asked, "that Congress will give relief from this unspeakable thing by enacting a law closing the mails to firearms?"[27]

This publicized event appeared to embolden Miller, for shortly after, on February 17, he managed to have another hearing on his bill. Several control proponents favored stronger measures such as the registration of handguns. Thomas L. Rubey, a representative from Missouri, urged a measure that would ban from the mails journals that carried gun advertisements. He saw this as "one way by which we could stop this firearms business."[28] Miller's more modest bill received a favorable hearing and cleared the House several times. Finally it passed in the Senate and on February 8, 1927, became law. This second federal effort to restrict the free traffic in firearms failed to achieve its purpose of ending their purchase by mail order because traders simply shipped their guns via private express. Efforts to widen the ban to cover delivery by such interstate carriers failed.

At the hearings William G. McAdoo had attacked the gun industry for blocking federal controls. Shortly after he expressed his feelings in a popular journal. He damned the pistol as "the curse of America," whether used in crime or by citizens as a deterrent to crime. "The pistol manufacturers, dealers, importers and mail order people are represented in all our capitals, both state and national, by one of the most efficient, best organized and cleverly managed lobbies connected with any other business enterprise," he complained. "They flood the country with specious and easily answered arguments in favor of pistols."[29]

Neither such denouncing nor opposition activism fazed the gun keepers.

They never tired of repeating arguments, such as the outlawing of pistols would not diminish crime but might increase it because thugs would no longer fear that their victims might be armed with a gun. But criminologists maintained that "it is almost suicidal for the average householder to attempt to use a fire-arm against a professional burglar or robber."[30] Regardless, the reasoning of the gun keepers figured in the repeal of firearms registration laws in Arkansas, Michigan, and Virginia, as well as in the American Bar Association's reversal of its opposition to pistol manufacture.

These setbacks for gun-control advocates, the shortcomings of the Miller law, and the failure of efforts to expand it typified the feebleness in the twenties of the movement to obtain significant federal or state gun regulation. Wherever advocates carried their message, they did so against heavy odds. They failed to circumvent the entrenched congressmen from the New England munitions belt who strangled proposed gun measures as they arose while also exerting enough clout to obtain high tariff protection for local small-arms manufacturers. In addition, control-minded legislators could not overcome the opposition from gun enthusiasts representing Western and Southern constituencies or the indifference in the White House and Congress.

The chief executive and the legislators had a number of precedents for the exercise of a federal police power but they did not use them because they understood the political reality of their time. Americans concerned about states' rights and individual rights remained convinced that the central government should not exercise regulatory authority in domestic matters, as in the liquor traffic. This belief worked against most efforts to establish federal controls over gun keeping. States' rights devotees usually coalesced with gun owners and others against attempts to create such a power. The federal record in the enforcement of Prohibition contributed to the distrust of centering firearms control in Washington. If the federal government could not block the landing and distribution of shiploads of rum, journalists and others asked, how could it prevent criminals from obtaining guns, the most easily concealed and vital tools of their trade?

To those committed to the cause of regulatory measures, the distrust of centralized policing and the indifference to cutting down gun violence seemed shameful. Even though nationally, violent crime had been declining, they perceived small firearms and those who used them in crime as having become more formidable than in the past. They assumed further that this new breed of gun wielders had become too powerful or elusive for local police to control. With ready access to telephones, automobiles, gun silencers, sawed-off shotguns, and submachine guns, desperadoes now roamed larger areas faster than in the past, sped across state lines, robbed and killed, and at times outgunned police.

This mayhem persuaded at least one vocal advocate of government action to argue that "the prevention and detection of crime are national rather than local problems" and could be handled more efficiently on a national scale. He pointed out that among the great powers, only the United States "had not realized the necessity for national supervision of the national problem of crime prevention."[51]

Fourteen months later one of the nation's most notorious submachine-gun slaughters, engineered by Al Capone and his ally Jack Guzik, appeared to give a boost to those who desired federal action on crime and guns. On St. Valentine's Day, February 14, 1929, four of Capone's gunmen, two of them dressed as police, lined up seven men of rival George "Bugs" Moran's gang against a wall in a garage on North Clark Street in Chicago and mowed them down. The murderers escaped punishment. The next April the angered crime commission listed twenty-eight mobsters as the city's most dangerous public enemies. Capone emerged as the nation's public enemy number one. Despite public outrage, the city's infamous crime spree, which added to a surge in homicides, continued for several more years, or until the end of Prohibition.[52]

During this binge of gun violence, newspaper editors, activists in the struggling control movement, and federal legislators alarmed by the perceived rise in crime and some by fear of armed communists demanded a countrywide revolution against what they termed hoodlum depredation. In response, in April 1930 a House of Representatives subcommittee held hearings on six bills aimed at restricting interstate commerce in pistols, revolvers, and machine guns. They included one proposal modeled on the prohibition law and another that would have allowed states to prohibit the weapons from crossing state lines.

Hamilton Fish Jr., a New York Republican, introduced a bill "to prevent organized groups that control crime in the larger cities" from securing "machine guns and automatic rifles and [using] them against the public, against the police and even against themselves in their contests for the control of crime." An opponent of the measure, George Huddleston, a Democrat from Alabama, dismissed it because "the Federal Government has nothing to do with the preservation of public order," a power reserved to the states. The bill, he claimed, would serve an "unconstitutional purpose" under the guise of regulating commerce.[33]

Nonetheless, Joe Crail of California introduced the redraft of a bill he had proposed three years earlier. Like many similar proposals, it aimed to ban pistols, revolvers, short-barreled rifles, and machine guns from interstate commerce. He perceived the measure as "absolutely within all legal and constitutional restrictions." He preferred a ban on the importation of firearms but pushed his milder bill because he thought Congress might accept it.

Crail cited his experience with gun control in a Cuba "infested with bandits" during the Spanish-American War as a reason for advancing the bill. Federal authorities who supervised the occupation of Cuba, he said, forbade "the use of rifles and deadly weapons" and offered a bounty in gold to anyone who gave up a firearm. Cubans surrendered their guns "by the thousands and thousands, old flintlocks, of Revolutionary days, muzzle-loading Remingtons of the Civil War period, and new pieces right up to the minute." The government dumped them in the ocean. Placing firearms "out of the reach of the people" and restricting their possession to law-enforcement officers, he maintained, made peace possible on the island.[34]

Despite this argument as an example of an effective exercise of federal power in regulating firearms, control opponents and devotees of states' rights blocked all the gun bills before Congress. They could not, however, stop the debate in the press, in Congress, or even in the executive branch over whether or not the federal government should take action on regulating guns.

This agitation had an impact on President Herbert C. Hoover. Shortly after taking office he announced that he considered law enforcement the "dominant issue before the American people."[35] So on May 20, 1929, he established the eleven-member National Commission on Law Observance and Enforcement, headed by George W. Wickersham, a former attorney general, to study the problem. After eighteen months of investigation, the commission came up with nothing significant for coping with crime and gun violence.

Since crime remained a foremost public concern, Hoover came under pressure to do more than investigate. Perhaps, some citizens thought, he might address the problem directly with federal authority. He resisted, making a point of defending his attachment to the states'-rights philosophy prominent in the thinking of many Americans and especially among gun defenders in Congress. He opposed any plan to cope with gun violence that resembled a blueprint for a national police force. "Every state has ample laws that cover such criminality," he stated. "What is needed is the enforcement of those laws, and not new laws. Any suggestion of increasing Federal criminal laws in general is a reflection on the sovereignty and the standing of state government."[36] Although true that by this time most states and cities imposed special regulations on firearms sales, to call them adequate required broad imagination.

Within six months of Hoover's words, a fresh crime wave struck New York City and other parts of the nation. One notable tragedy in that city involving the submachine gun—the "Baby Massacre"—created a national furor. On July 28, 1931, racketeer Vincent "Mad Dog" Coll tried to rub out a gangland rival by spraying bullets randomly. He killed one child and wounded five others. Despite the public outrage over this and other bloodletting, mobsters continued to take up the Tommy gun.

Finally, numerous citizens, law officers, and legislators condemned it as a firearm so deadly that no reputable person should want or need it. Above all, they wished to keep it out of the hands of criminals. An assistant federal attorney, for instance, asserted that "the next Congress should take immediate steps to pass a law prohibiting both the transportation of firearms in interstate commerce and the importation of guns from abroad except under Federal supervision."[37]

Such sentiment persuaded control advocates that despite the apprehension over federal policing authority, the assumed crime crisis had converted many Americans to their cause. Even with this optimism, with new followers, and with the aggressiveness of its most dedicated members, the gun-control movement remained weak. Nonetheless, its growing visibility along with its few local accomplishments alarmed shooters.

In particular, the control agitation had long disturbed Karl T. Frederick, a onetime Olympic pistol champion and vice president of the National Rifle Association. He detested New York's Sullivan law and other local gun ordinances. So, right after the World War, he and several other members of a competitive handgun shooting club, the United States Revolver Association, formulated a proposal for a modest pistol statute weaker than the Sullivan law. They hoped it would serve as a model for firearms legislation that all states would adopt. This activity for preemptive legislation coincided with the rifle association's continuing expansion, as in its taking on as affiliates two thousand local sportsmen's clubs.

The federal government contributed to the association's continuing growth, primarily through perpetuating its civilian marksmanship program. Its members continued to benefit from the government's requirement that the War Department sell surplus firearms to them at cost. As in the past, thousands of gun devotees joined the association and affiliated clubs to buy these guns at the bargain rate. In total, shooters purchased some two hundred thousand rifles and other weapons released from government arsenals. When the association took over the youth marksmanship program that the Winchester firearms company had sponsored, membership received another boost, particularly among the young. In tandem with its expansion throughout the twenties, the organization beefed up its political clout.

Meanwhile, Frederick and friends completed the framing of their model for a gun law but only three states adopted it. The sponsors then revised their tactics, producing in August 1926 a tentative draft and, in the following July, a revision of what they called the Uniform Firearms Act or at times the Uniform Revolver Act. It dealt only with pistols and revolvers, requiring a buyer to register with a licensed gun dealer and wait forty-eight hours before receiving the weapon. During that time police could examine the application to determine if the purchaser was a drunkard, a convicted criminal, a drug addict, or a minor—all of whom the measure forbade to own handguns. In addition, the act would have directed police to issue permits to assumed respectable citizens who had good reason to carry a gun. Police and other critics objected to the model act as too soft.

The following year the National Crime Commission, an organization of distinguished citizens, wrote its own tougher archetype for a gun law and submitted it to the states. Opposition from gun enthusiasts, notably from the NRA, killed it. Other groups concerned with doing something about firearms regulation while preserving shooting rights then returned their attention to the uniform act. After undergoing further study and slight change, the act in 1930 went back to the states for consideration. In the next few years, only five states and the District of Columbia adopted it, usually with modifications to meet their special needs.

For a time, beginning late in 1931, lobbyists for the NRA and other gun owners appeared to have pulled a coup for the uniform act in New York State. They pressured the legislature to pass the Hanley-Fake firearms bill aimed at replacing the Sullivan law with the act's weaker regulations. Only the governor's veto prevented the bill from becoming law.

The dissatisfaction with the Uniform Firearms Act persuaded the interstate commission on crime to adopt a new, tougher model designated the Uniform Pistol Act. It included stiffer penalties for designated crimes than did the earlier measure, banned possession of a pistol by anyone convicted of a serious crime, not just one of violence, and required a license for anyone purchasing a pistol. Largely because of this last provision, the rifle association opposed this measure. No state adopted it. In all, the uniform idea, even where accepted, failed to produce meaningful control. Furthermore, the states did not or would not enact gun laws within a standard pattern.

During the gun proponents' experiment with possible model legislation, the control promoters won another small victory. Arthur Capper, a former Progressive newspaperman and now a senator from Kansas, introduced a bill, modeled on the uniform act, to regulate firearms in the District of Columbia. It attracted nationwide attention because a gun battle in downtown Washington between police and bootleggers had caught a senator in the crossfire, seriously wounding him. Even so, before becoming law in 1932, the Capper bill had to survive years of extensive hearings.

Rarely before this time had the gun problem attracted broad attention other than in a context of crime. In January it engaged public interest as a social issue. At a White House conference on child health and protection Capper spoke for the National Anti-Weapons Society, on whose advisory board he served. He linked the plight of disadvantaged children with firearms, pointing to "a growing spirit of lawlessness" in the cities with its "ghastly succession of shootings and murders in which children and young people were principal participants." Then he focused on guns. "To sober minds," he said, it had become evident "that the laws of this country . . . made it too easy to get a gun. Firearms dealers were passing weapons and cartridges over the counter to persons who could not be trusted with any deadly weapon. There was practically no regulation of sales."[38]

Shortly after, on March 1, another tragedy that stunned the nation struck the family of Charles A. Lindbergh, the aviation hero, and his wife, the writer Anne Morrow Lindbergh. An unknown individual snatched their twenty-month-old son out of his crib in their home near Hopewell, New Jersey. Either deliberately or accidentally he killed the child and demanded ransom. Initially this crime had little to do with the gun regulation issue but when state authorities asked the president for help in tracking down the kidnapper, the case came to touch on the control issue through the fundamental question of federal police power.

Hoover offered assistance from national agencies but pointed out that the "federal government does not have police authority in such crimes."[39] This stance, similar to his position on national gun management, failed to stem the public outcry for making kidnapping a federal crime. On June 17 Congress enacted legislation, known as the Lindbergh law, that made the transporting of a kidnapped person from one state to another a federal offense with a maximum penalty of life imprisonment. Five days after its passage, the president reluctantly signed it into law. He also approved a companion bill that made the sending of a demand for ransom, or a threat to kidnap, a federal crime. These laws built up more precedent for possible federal legislation to control gun violence.

Seven months later as Hoover campaigned for reelection, he condemned "the gangster life" in the cities and states as a danger "to the whole of our civilization." He also indicated he had not abandoned his opposition to the expansion of federal power in enforcing domestic security, as with gun regulation. He repeated that "the responsibility for the control of crime rests emphatically upon the States and local communities." Shortly thereafter, his attorney general, William D. Mitchell, echoed this sentiment, stating that prosecution for criminal offenses "primarily belong[s] under State law." He told Congress he had striven to discourage any tendency in his office "to grab cases away from the State criminal authorities."[40]

By this time, the large number of Americans disturbed by what they viewed as rampant crime thought that in this matter the federal government should do what the administration disapproved. The contrasting perspectives on the federal role in dealing with crime clashed in the presidential campaign.

The Democratic candidate, Franklin D. Roosevelt, knew guns from personal use, from having served as assistant secretary of the navy on the board for the promotion of rifle practice, and from working closely with the rifle association. For years, he had served also on the executive committee of the National Crime Commission, which studied means of combating crime nationally. As New York's governor, he had supported restrictive state and federal handgun controls, tangled personally with Karl Frederick on gun-control legislation, and defied the NRA.[41]

When Roosevelt vetoed legislation such as the Hanley-Fake bill, he spoke out forcefully. "A great many sportsmen have urged me to approve this legislation," he declared. "It is hard to understand the interest of sportsmen in pistols. I have myself fished and hunted a great deal. I have a deep interest in outdoor sports and in the various associations which foster them, but it is common knowledge, of course, that fishermen never use a pistol and that hunters practically never use a pistol." Even for "theoretical self-protection," he added, "the value of a revolver is very problematical." A New York *Times* editorial concurred under the headline "Another Wise Veto."[42]

Unlike Hoover, Roosevelt considered aspects of gun violence and crime, along with unemployment, national problems that required federal action. He announced that if elected he would back centralized regulation of interstate commerce in handguns that control proponents had been pushing for years.

After winning the election in a landslide, Roosevelt personally experienced

gun violence. When he visited Miami on February 14, 1933, to address a political rally, Giuseppe Zangara, an unemployed bricklayer and anarchist, standing
thirty-five feet from Roosevelt with a .32-caliber revolver he had purchased in
a local pawnshop for eight dollars, fired five shots. He narrowly missed Roosevelt but struck five bystanders, including Chicago's mayor, Anton J. Cermak,
who died a few weeks later from his wound. "I do not hate Mr. Roosevelt personally," Zangara explained while jailed, "I hate all Presidents, no matter from
what country they come, and I hate all officials and everybody who is rich."[43]
Again, an unbalanced individual's shooting spree shocked the nation. It also
strengthened the determination of control groups to move ahead in pursuit of
federal gun legislation.

Judge Uly O. Thompson, who presided over Zangara's trial and sentenced
him to death, summed up much of the controllers' attitude. He pointed out
that the assassinations of presidents "have either been perfected or undertaken
by a man armed with a pistol." Yet, he added, "the people of this country stead-
fastly permit the manufacture, sale and possession of such deadly and useless
weapons. I say 'useless' for this reason: A pistol in the hands of an assassin is
sure death and murder, while a pistol in the hands of . . . the good people of
this country is about the most useless weapon of defense with which you can
arm yourself." He believed Congress should enact legislation for the "confiscation of all firearms that may be carried or concealed about the person."[44]

Although earlier control activists had often expressed similar sentiment, they
had made no tangible impact on either Congress or the public. Now, along with
Roosevelt's own views and the assassination attempt, the agitation of control
advocates helped pave the way for the first serious exertion for federal legislation to regulate directly an aspect of gun keeping.

10

Direct Federal Controls

O n March 4, 1933, Franklin D. Roosevelt entered the White House as the first president with a record of having fought to control gun violence and with a commitment to do something about it on a national scale. As promised during his campaign, he shortly addressed the issue of civilians' largely uncontrolled access to handguns. He made it part of his New Deal program that focused public attention on social issues such as poverty, crime, and the environment, which, as the conventional wisdom assumed, bred much of the nation's gun violence.

To avoid a head-on battle with gun keepers and others who viewed the Second Amendment as untouchable, the president initially favored a uniform gun licensing law patterned on the concept the NRA had previously accepted and that he had backed while on the National Crime Commission. He intended to use federal authority to persuade the states to adopt his plan, which would be stronger than the NRA's defunct Uniform Firearms Act. With this strategy, he believed he could overcome the traditional American fear of a national police force that in the previous year Herbert Hoover and Congress pointedly had opposed.

Roosevelt placed the national gun-regulation campaign in the hands of his attorney general, Homer S. Cummings, an idealistic former state prosecutor in Connecticut, a Democratic Party national chairman, and the man who had nominated him for the party's presidential candidate. Despite protests from the War Department, the president also cut off federal funding for the national rifle practice program.

As empowered, the attorney general approached firearms regulation in keeping with the president's outlook. Cummings criticized existing state and other pistol laws as woefully deficient for the task at hand. Optimistically, he announced in June that the country's law-enforcement agencies were in a "more cooperative mood than at anytime within memory" with Washington. He maintained that the public appeared ready to accept "a measure of federal leadership that would have been deemed impossible only a short while ago."[1] To push ahead with the gun-control and crime campaign headed by the executive branch but carried out by the states and to implement other reforms, the administration reorganized the investigating responsibilities within the Department of Justice.

Years earlier, in 1907, Theodore Roosevelt's attorney general, Charles J. Bonaparte, had complained that a "Department of Justice with no force of permanent police under its control is assuredly not fully equipped for its work."[2] He asked Congress to authorize such a group within the department. Congress refused. Regardless, in July the next year he launched such a force on his own, staffing it with agents who had worked in the department. This agency grew, especially during the World War, and became the Bureau of Investigation. When Franklin Roosevelt came to power, a young attorney, J. Edgar Hoover, headed it.

In conjunction with his anticrime campaign, Roosevelt left Hoover in charge and by executive order in June 1933 reshaped the bureau with England's Scotland Yard as the model. His confidant and political adviser, Louis McHenry Howe, characterized it as "an organized and disciplined army of inspectors, investigators, and Federal agents such as the department . . . never possessed in history."[3] Two years later the bureau would change its name to the Federal Bureau of Investigation (FBI).

With the aid of the bureau and Justice Department staff officers, Cummings prepared a dozen anticrime bills, including one for direct national controls on firearms. Legislators introduced an equal number of gun bills, several of which called for employing the federal government's taxing power to restrict firearms usage. All this activity seemed to indicate, as Cummings believed, that the time was ripe for passage of at least one of the proposed measures designed to end the easy availability of specified guns.

The continuing gangster killings provided another major stimulant for the control movement as, for instance, in the Kansas City massacre.[4] In that city on June 17 Charles A. "Pretty Boy" Floyd and associates attempted to rescue a friend being returned to a federal prison. With a hail of fire from Tommy guns they slaughtered three policemen and a federal agent. Howe placed the onus for this gun brutality on "modern invention." He explained, "Successful holdups, gang killings and profitable kidnappings have been made possible largely by the automobile and the machine gun." He called revolver shootings "an uncertain form of murder" because "in the old days" rival gangs would shoot at each other for hours without causing serious damage. "But the victim of the modern gang is sprayed with a hundred bullets a minute and is certainly marked for death beyond hope."[5]

In addition, in 1934 the popular and congressional emotion against munitions and gun manufacturers, or so-called merchants of death who reputedly sold arms to whomever would pay for them, appeared indirectly to add to the momentum for some kind of centralized control. Investigators charged that the federal government had become a "sales agency for the arms industry."[6] Despite the close connection between the government and the private arms-makers, the critics demanded that it regulate the international gun-trafficking of the American-based munitions companies. Why, others asked, should it not also exercise some control over domestic arms-trading?

This sentiment in the concerned public, along with the president's commitment to eliminate the gun toter as well as the manufacture of specified guns, except for military and police use, energized Cummings. He acted on the assumption that with his war on crime, with the federal taxing power, and with the authority of the Constitution's commerce clause (sec. 8, para. 3) he could succeed with some form of federal gun regulation where others had failed. As part of the program, he entrusted J. Edgar Hoover and his bureau with enforcing the Lindbergh law against kidnappers and racketeers.

At this time also, Congress furthered this federalizing trend by giving the executive branch more control over the armed forces than it had exercised in the past. Congress authorized the War Department to build a national reserve force with no constitutional ties to the Second Amendment. It declared that federally supported organized militia units now constituted "the National Guard of the United States of America," an organized component of the army.[7] Even though this legislation buried even the ghost of the old militia system, gun advocates continued to insist that the militia tradition as stated in the Second Amendment still stood as a symbol of an armed citizenry.

Meanwhile, Cummings's bills, aimed at stepping up the federal government's involvement in investigating and punishing violent gangsters and racketeers, made no discernible progress in Congress. Legislators who focused on the gun proposals kept the bills stranded in committees. William A. King, a Democratic senator from Utah, on March 29 explained one reason for the stalling. "We are assuming," he said, "that the States are wholly impotent to deal with questions which properly arise under their authority. We are challenging the competency of the States to govern their own affairs. We are substituting a Federal criminal code for the criminal codes of the States."[8] He had touched on what the administration desired, in a small way, in the matter of gun violence.

Meanwhile, the escapades of John Dillinger, a former Indiana farm boy who had become the nation's number one gunman, had given the administration's plan a boost. His shooting, particularly in a fourteen-month rampage beginning in January 1934, shook up Congress. In that period he broke out of jail twice in sensational circumstances; robbed at least a dozen banks; supplied friends in the Michigan City, Indiana, prison with guns and managed their escape; raided a police station in Warsaw, Indiana, for guns; and assaulted city halls elsewhere in the Midwest. On April 22 at Little Bohemia, a resort hotel in Wisconsin, his gang engaged federal agents in a roaring gun battle that left a bystander and one agent dead and two others wounded. Dillinger escaped, but on the heels of this crime rampage Roosevelt asked Congress to step up passage of some of the stalled bills that would increase the federal government's police power.

Congress responded by retreating from its commitment to the priority of states in policing matters. Without even taking a record vote, it passed six crime-control acts. They empowered the federal government to punish those who committed specified crimes such as robbing banks with federal deposits and murdering federal agents. One act made it a federal crime to extort money or other valuables by telephone or by any other means subject to interstate regulation. Another measure amended the Lindbergh law to provide the death penalty for those who injured a kidnapped victim. On May 18, in signing the legislation into law, the president announced that he regarded this "an event of the first importance." He added that "federal men are constantly facing machine-gun fire in the pursuit of gangsters" and that he stood squarely behind the Justice Department's efforts "to bring to book every law breaker, big and little."[9]

By providing the federal government with its first comprehensive criminal code, these statutes thrust it directly into areas formerly entrusted only to the states. Initially, the administration took care not to use its new police power, still dreaded by much of the citizenry, too boldly. It did not, for instance, try on its own to eradicate local crime and criminal organizations. In keeping with this attitude, in another statute the following month the federal government encouraged the states to cooperate with each other in dealing with crime.

Nonetheless, Congress had opened the door much wider than it had with the Volstead Act, the Lindbergh law, and any other peacetime legislation to what it designated as federal crimes. It placed responsibility for enforcing the new laws on the FBI. Its aggressive director strained his still-slender authority to conduct nationwide manhunts for criminals such as Dillinger. On July 22 outside a theater in Chicago, FBI agents shot and killed him. Later that year they also killed, as public enemies, Pretty Boy Floyd near East Liverpool, Ohio, and Baby Face Nelson near Niles Center, Illinois. The public hailed the agents, or G-men as they came to be called, as heroes.

G-man movies took the country by storm. In 1935 Hollywood produced seven of them.[10] The popular praise showered on Hoover and his G-men in newspapers and magazines as well as in the movies appeared to make legislative opposition to federal police power wither.[11] A foremost interpreter of the New Deal perceived the federal government as expanding enormously. Not only New Dealers but also many Republicans accepted "almost unquestionably the use of coercion by the state to achieve reforms."[12] Given that national mood, activists such as Cummings perceived correctly that some form of national gun control probably could slip through the door that had been pushed open to federal police power.

The opening, the mood, and the Dillinger escapades prompted House committees to begin hearings on Cummings's bill and other firearms proposals. His measure called for a federal tax to secure nationwide registration of designated firearms, reputedly favored by criminals, as well as a federal license for anyone who manufactured, imported, or dealt with the weapons. It would have required each purchaser to fill out a form provided by the Internal Revenue Service, submit to fingerprinting, and pay a transfer tax such as one dollar for a pistol and two hundred dollars for a machine gun. One version would have asked all pistol owners to register their guns voluntarily within four months.

In testimony before the House Ways and Means Committee in April, the attorney general stressed the need for federal action. The bills before Congress, he said, "are predicated upon the proposition that there has developed in this country a situation which is far beyond the power of control of merely local authorities." He pointed out that at least five hundred thousand lawbreakers were "carrying about with them, or have available at hand, weapons of the most deadly character."[13]

Representatives of the National Rifle Association, which recently had expanded membership tenfold to become the largest and best-organized gun-user's society in the nation, disagreed. Its executive vice president, retired General Milton A. Reckord of the National Guard, told the House legislators that "the association I represent is absolutely favorable to reasonable legislation." They were not, he added, "obstructionists in any way" and wanted "to help you." Yet he opposed the control bill, warning it would deprive rural America of the opportunity to secure weapons it needed for "self-defense and protection" because in small communities "police forces are not adequate." Karl T. Frederick, now the association's president, focused on the states'-rights issue, denouncing the Cummings bill as a crime measure "under the guise of a revenue raising bill" and hence beyond the power of Congress.[14] Seth Gordon, president of the American Game Association, testified that six million sportsmen in the United States stood against the bill.

In the Senate, Royal S. Copeland of New York, a onetime medical-school dean and former state health commissioner, annually over twelve years had introduced gun-control bills that had gone nowhere. Now he offered legislation stronger than what Cummings had proposed. As had numerous predecessors, Copeland chose to deal with the control problem through the authority of the federal government to regulate interstate commerce. Two of his bills would have allowed only manufacturers to ship concealable firearms across state lines and only to licensed dealers. It would, as well, have banned interstate shipment of machine guns. He wished also to mandate the coding of guns and ammunition for ballistic purposes, a procedure useful in criminal investigations.

Both the senator and the attorney general misjudged the resources of the gun devotees. Following the House hearings fifteen small-arms manufacturers, organized in a trade group called the Sporting Arms and Ammunition Manufacturers Association, along with seventy thousand gun dealers concerned over survival during the Depression, put up a solid front of opposition. So did the gun clubs, with the most effective being the rifle association. The NRA increased the scope and efficiency of its political monitoring to oppose head-on the proposed firearms restrictions.

The association's political activism accompanied a deepening cooperation between it and firearms manufacturers and dealers. Officers of the firearms companies, many of whom had been in the military, joined the shooting clubs. They often took over leadership positions, producing, in the case of the NRA, an intimacy that led critics to dub it the unofficial trade organization for the firearms industry. The gunmakers and dealers supported the association for both practical and ideological reasons. Its firearms advocacy and its extolling of gun ownership as a right contributed to sales and profits. Both groups hated the idea of regulation and both praised the nation's gun culture as a fount of patriotism.

The camaraderie of the gun fraternity stood out during the Senate hearings on the control bills. Representatives of shooting clubs, sporting and wildlife organizations, and weapons manufacturers all testified against the proposed legislation. The Colt company's officers spoke for the small-arms producers who feared that high federal license fees on arms sales would destroy their domestic market. Only Colt manufactured the submachine guns prized by gangsters but Frank C. Nichols, its president, defended his industry as though it were unfairly on trial. His company, he said, had conducted an honorable business for nearly one hundred years, employing utmost care in selling its products.

These opponents, acting as a gun lobby headed by the NRA, proved most potent. It mobilized constituents who flooded Congress with letters and telegrams denouncing the proposed legislation. An NRA circular announced, "The issue is clear cut between the Attorney General and his undesirable law on the one side, and the sportsmen of America and all other law-abiding citizens of America on the other side, with the armed criminals of the country on the side lines, rooting for the Attorney General."[15]

When Copeland on May 28 opened commerce committee hearings on several of the firearms bills before the Senate, he, too, felt gun-lobby heat. He immediately clashed with Reckord, whom senators regarded as the nation's most influential opponent of firearms legislation. Abandoning the conciliatory posture he had assumed during the House hearings, Reckord now testified that the proposed bills would not do a bit of good. With other association leaders, he raised the specter of compulsory registration for all firearms and those who owned them. He warned that with the passage of Cummings's bill "every rifle and shotgun owner in the country will find himself paying a special revenue tax and having himself fingerprinted and photographed for a federal 'rogue's gallery' every time he buys or sells a gun of any description."[16]

An incensed Copeland accused Reckord and the gun lobby of misrepresentation. Deliberately and wrongly, the senator complained, they conveyed the impression that the government sought to keep the farmer from using a revolver or shotgun, from leaving a firearm with his wife, or from carrying a pistol in his car.[17] Copeland's protest had little effect. The scare tactics and the lobbying of the gun groups worked well enough to upset the momentum of the control advocates. Both the House and Senate committees reported to Congress amended versions of the bill that omitted pistols from the list of weapons to be registered and taxed.

The attorney general tried to rescue the legislation by drumming up public support. His assistant told a meeting of the General Confederation of Women's Clubs, with two million members across the country, that in emasculating his bill, the rifle association had shown itself more powerful than the Justice Department. For years the confederation had worked for gun control so as to keep deadly weapons out of the hands of children, irresponsible people, and criminals. Its women responded by mounting a letter and telegram campaign to put the deleted pistol feature back into the measure. The effort failed. Even the amended bill faced obstacles. Hatton W. Sumners of Texas, the chairman of the House Judiciary Committee, blocked it because he judged it as violating states' rights.

Roosevelt called Sumners to the White House, where he succeeded in persuading the congressman to release the legislation. On June 26, 1934, just before adjourning, Congress hurriedly passed the bill as the National Firearms Act, and the president signed it into law. This third federal statute dealing with guns attempted more control than had its predecessors. It aimed to block the traffic in weapons most often identified with the gangster activity of the era, such as submachine guns and sawed-off shotguns. It required firearms manufacturers, dealers, and importers to register, keep records, and pay a special tax. Purchasers of the regulated firearms had to be fingerprinted, undergo a background investigation, endure a waiting period of months, and pay a substantial transfer tax. The legislation, however, ignored pistols, revolvers, shotguns, and rifles.[18] Despite the law's limitations, the rifle association still attacked it as an effort to disguise a federal police measure as a revenue bill.

In this instance, the appeal to the traditional fear of a national police establishment failed. It did so partially because on September 19, after a long, intensive search, agents of the existing national force, the Federal Bureau of Investigation, arrested Bruno R. Hauptmann, a German-born carpenter with a criminal record, for kidnapping the Lindbergh baby. The stock of the federal officers, as well as of the attorney general's crusade against crime, again rose. "The time is ripe for action," Cummings announced. "The American people, unless I misread the public temper, demand action."[19]

In this mood, Cummings again pressed ahead with his anticrime program, including a plea for a more comprehensive gun-control statute. As part of this agenda, he invited representatives from local, state, and federal agencies, as well as others from civic and religious groups, to Washington to discuss a possible law-enforcement alliance. Attended by six hundred people, the three-day conference opened on December 10 with greetings from the president. He called on the public to back the attorney general's crusade, stressing "the importance of common action all along the line, starting with crime prevention."[20] He did not, at this time, mention gun control.

However, another speaker, J. Allen Weston, Massachusetts's attorney general and the chairman of the National Crime Commission, did stress firearms regulation. "The American people have been asleep for a quarter of a century so far as an appreciation of the inadequacy of the existing laws regulating the possession of firearms is concerned," he stated. The federal government and the states have failed utterly "to control by the strong arm of the law the possession and use of firearms." Delegates, as from the General Confederation of Women's Clubs, praised Weston's message. In addition, their spokeswoman, Mrs. William D. Sporborg, urged an amendment to the National Firearms Act that would regulate "all deadly firearms, because if we remove firearms we remove a great part of the danger of the gangster."[21]

Neither the conference nor the government generated enough public pressure for the recommended tougher controls, or for a national alliance against crime. Nonetheless, the conference did bring considerable publicity to the issue of controlling gun violence. Furthermore, in the next few years, the firearms law demonstrated a limited effectiveness. Backed by federal and state authorities, it virtually ended the private ownership and casual sale of the easily portable machine guns of the era.

Meantime, as newspapers and magazines gave increasing coverage to the gun-violence issue, a segment of the public expressed a rising concern over children's use of firearms. *Parents' Magazine* even carried a symposium on the question, "Should a Boy Have a Gun?" The affirmative writer advised, "Give the boy a gun" if he has proper supervision because a rifle offers "healthy sport" and "is also a character builder." He praised the NRA "for its fine work in cultivating rifle shooting and gun handling in general among the schoolboys of the nation."[22] The other side believed differently. It condemned even toy guns as harmful because, as did the real weapons, they symbolized gangsterism and war.

Sensitive to such criticism of its products, the small-arms industry responded to pressure from activists, especially from those in the conservation movement, by creating in April 1935 the American Wildlife Institute, which later became the Wildlife Management Institute. They contributed funds to it and other conservation groups such as the National Wildlife Federation. Even though hunters and the arms makers approved of the conservation agenda, as we have seen, they both disliked the idea of the federal government imposing taxes on firearms. Nonetheless, they backed the Federal Aid in Wild Life Restoration Act, better known as the Pittman-Robertson Act. Signed into law on September 2, 1937, it placed a 10-percent tax on ammunition and firearms used in hunting. Those proceeds went to the states for conservation programs.[23] Even though this law amounted to another federal encroachment on gun rights, it

brought benefits to the manufacturers and the NRA by helping retain conservationists as gun supporters. Six months later the rifle association received unusual approval on another level from the president. He praised its "meritorious
work," particularly in its marksmanship program.[24]

Control advocates, though, perceived no merit in the NRA's lobbying. They,
as well as Cummings and Copeland, regarded it as fundamental in efforts to
undo the new federal firearms law. The statute withstood initial assaults, however. In 1937 in *Sonzinsky v. United States* the Supreme Court upheld the law.
Justice Harlan F. Stone commented that Congress could choose how it exercised its taxing authority and could use it to regulate.

Cummings, who favored controls through the taxing power, still viewed a
comprehensive system of national firearms registration as worthwhile. He characterized it as simpler than automobile registration, saying that "no honest
man can object to it. Show me the man who does not want his gun registered
and I will show you a man who should not have a gun."[25] Accordingly, he proposed another bill to extend the provisions of the National Firearms Act to
cover all types of firearms. Because the rifle association opposed it, out of respect for its power he modified the bill to exclude rifles and shotguns, but still
the gun lobby killed it. In addition, Roosevelt soon backed away from overt
personal involvement in the gun-control issue to devote himself to national and
international concerns he regarded as having a higher priority.

Copeland, though, all the while had remained determined to secure additional gun regulation through federal authority over commerce. Wary of the
power of the NRA, he worked closely with it and framed a bill it approved. On
January 3, 1935, he introduced the bill to Congress and hearings followed.
When Frederick of the rifle association testified, he tried to counter the widely
accepted connection between the NRA and the arms industry, insisting that it
did not "represent any commercial interests, either directly or indirectly." Reckord sounded cooperative, saying he was absolutely in favor of the bill because
it focused on the criminal rather than the gun. Copeland responded, "You
ought to be. You had a lot to do with writing it."[26]

Through the Justice Department, the president opposed the bill. Assistant
Attorney General Joseph B. Keenan explained why. The firearms commerce, he
stated, "should have more drastic treatment," and the bill had provisions that
would weaken the National Firearms Act.[27] In a second hearing, a representative of the then politically influential American Legion, acting as part of the
gun community, supported the bill. With thirteen thousand posts across the
country, annually it taught more than 350,000 young boys how to shoot guns.

A representative of the Colt Patented Firearms Company also gave the bill a firm recommendation.[28]

The bill benefited as well from broad public sentiment as expressed in April in the first Gallup poll on gun control. That survey showed that 84 percent of those queried felt that "all owners of pistols and revolvers should be required to register with the Government."[29] In addition, various organizations such as the New York City Federation of Women's Clubs backed the measure.[30]

In tune with such opinion, Congress on June 30 approved Copeland's bill as the Federal Firearms Act of 1938. This veneer of federal regulation required manufacturers, importers, dealers, and others who engaged in interstate or foreign commerce in guns to obtain a federal license and to keep a record of the disposition of their firearms. The license fee was low—only one dollar. The law also barred the shipment of arms to individuals who did not have permits in the states that required them, prohibited convicted felons from receiving interstate arms shipments, and sought to curb the movement of stolen arms or any guns with altered serial numbers.

The NRA accepted the law because it did little regulating, and the association wanted to fend off the more stringent proposals that control advocates were pressing in Congress. The gun fraternity's strategy paid off. The law never really worked because felons and others easily evaded its provisions by lying and because the Treasury Department did not enforce it adequately.

Even if the Treasury had carried out the law to the letter, the law paled in comparison to gun regulation in Europe. In Britain, for instance, critics had long denounced existing firearms controls as too weak. The example of gun crime in the United States and the murder of a London police officer had moved Parliament in 1934 to study the effectiveness of its gun law. The legislators incorporated their investigatory committee's recommendation in the Firearms Amendment Act of 1937. It strengthened existing controls, prohibited the manufacture and sale of machine guns save by military authority, and banned sawed-off shotguns because the act's framers saw no legitimate reason for civilians to own such weapons. British law provided for penalties of up to fourteen years' imprisonment for anyone possessing a gun in criminal activity. In subsequent years, police policies and increases in fees sharply reduced the number of people in Britain holding certificates permitting gun ownership.[31]

The American federal statutes, on the other hand, placed only insignificant restraints on individuals who wanted guns or possessed one of some kind. As a critic noted, the measures amounted to "a symbolic denunciation of firearms in the hands of criminals coupled with an . . . ineffective regulatory scheme that did not inconvenience the American firearms industry or its customers."[32]

Much in American society still stood in the way of practical regulation. The most obvious obstacles—the Second Amendment, the arms industry, and the gun lobby—remained seemingly insurmountable. Elements of popular culture, such as novels, perpetuated the myths of the frontier, the West, and the cowboy, among them Owen Wister's *The Virginian* (1902) and Zane Grey's *Riders of the Purple Sage* (1910). Something new also contributed to the mystiques of the West and guns—the rising influence of filmmakers. They produced movies, immensely popular with children as well as with adults, that celebrated gun violence, among them *Shooting Straight* (1917), *Gun Law* (1919), *Wild Bill Hickok* (1923), *Cimarron* (1931), *Trail of the Lonesome Pine* (1936), and *Jesse James* (1939).[33]

Gangster films, such as *Public Enemy* (1931), *Little Caesar* (1931), *Scarface* (1934), and *The Roaring Twenties* (1939), became the next moneymakers. In most instances, producers simply transferred qualities they had attributed to the frontier outlaw to the gun-packing gangster. The pervasiveness of guns in films and in other forms of popular culture blended with the popularity of shooting.

Despite the gun-control sponsors' inability to overcome these cultural and other hurdles, they took solace in the passage of the federal statutes. While recognizing the legislation's flaws, some of its defenders argued that the laws had a significance beyond their specific features. At the least, it contributed to an environment that could possibly accommodate more federal gun regulation. Optimistic control advocates went further. They perceived public sentiment toward all firearms as shifting away from acceptance of their free use. They cited the growing number of Americans who had begun viewing even the hunter's shotgun and the marksman's rifle as part of a social problem. For the first time, moreover, the executive branch had made an issue of gun violence and had campaigned for national laws to curb it. Most important, the Roosevelt administration had obtained legislative and public acceptance of the legitimacy of a federal role in controlling the use of personal firearms.

Before Roosevelt's time, presidents usually had been gun enthusiasts or had ignored the issue of control. Now, with a chief executive who had initiated a program for regulation of firearms in private hands, as well as with mounting evidence of a shift in public attitude toward favoring curbs on arms keeping, gun devotees reacted with alarm. Militants among them viewed the attack on the pistol and the machine gun in exaggerated terms. They interpreted this limited goal of the controllers as part of an avowed long-term effort to deny all citizens the right to possess firearms of any kind for any purpose. All the while, most states continued imposing regulation in some manner on gun use and the federal courts kept on upholding this localized form of control.

In several cases, as we have seen, the Supreme Court declared the two federal gun laws valid exercises of the government's taxing and commerce powers. But the most important challenge to the National Firearms Act reached the Supreme Court in 1939 in *United States v. Miller*, 307 US 174, 34. This case began five years earlier when federal authorities arrested two men, Jack Miller and Frank Layton, for violating the firearms act by transporting an unregistered short-barreled shotgun from Oklahoma to Arkansas. The men pleaded the statute violated the Second Amendment because it usurped the police power reserved to the states and improperly used the federal taxing power to control firearms. In agreement, a district court in Arkansas quashed the indictment.

Federal attorneys appealed the case to the Supreme Court, which for the first time in 150 years addressed the scope of the Second Amendment. The high court upheld the constitutionality of the firearms act. It ruled that the "obvious purpose" of the Second Amendment was "to assure the continuation and render possible the effectiveness" of the state militia. It did not protect possession of the shotgun because it was not "any part of the ordinary military equipment" and its use could not "contribute to the common defense." Pro- and antigun activists disputed the intent of this decision as it pertained to broader issues of gun keeping.[34] Regardless, by upholding the government's power to regulate the use of a particular firearm the ruling dealt a blow to the gun fraternity's theory of a personal right to bear firearms of almost any kind.

A dip in crime nationwide and events abroad blunted the impact of this ruling on the struggle to control civilian arms. In September, when war broke out in Europe and then spread over much of the world, many Americans feared it would also engulf them. As during the First World War, concerns for preparedness, coupled with an upper-class martial ardor, sidetracked the movement to check domestic gun violence. On May 16, 1940, a few days after the German army had slammed into the Netherlands and Belgium, the president asked Congress for some $900 million in additional military appropriations and authority to call the National Guard into federal service.

Right after the Nazi conquest of the Low Countries and France in June and with Germans poised to invade England, Americans organized various groups to aid the British, among them the American Committee for Defense of British Homes. Evoking the old concept of militia volunteers arming to combat tyranny, it ran advertisements in the American press that pleaded, "Send a Gun to Defend a British Home." The committee solicited civilian pistols, rifles, revolvers, and shotguns.[35] This made good propaganda, but the seven thousand or so guns that reached the British in this manner did not help much because they needed military arms instead. Other pro-Allied groups lobbied for intervention to save Britain.

Administration leaders encouraged such activities while seeking to prepare for possible war. As had Woodrow Wilson in his preparedness program, Roosevelt considered conscription a vital ingredient. Yet he resisted the urging of eastern-establishment interventionists, such as his Anglophile friend Grenville Clark of the Plattsburg movement of the First World War, to call for a draft publicly. The president moved cautiously because much of the public and many in Congress opposed compulsory militia duty. He did not wish to risk conflict with the legislators over conscription. So, he waited until he could dig up enough votes to secure passage for it in Congress.

Private individuals who worked closely with the interventionists, such as Medal of Honor recipient Colonel William J. Donovan, spoke out publicly. He argued that "primitive military skills," such as those acquired in civilian shooting, would not do in modern mechanized war fought with sophisticated weapons. Nor would a voluntary recruiting system work. No matter how distasteful peacetime conscription might be, he contended, Americans must accept it because "if you want to fight, you've got to be strong."[36]

Acting on this principle, on August 27 Roosevelt ordered the National Guard and other army reserve components to active duty for extended training. Now, after the lobby of interventionists backed by men like Clark had softened Congress, the time for further action without mortal political risk seemed ripe. They framed a conscription bill that went before Congress in the guise of necessary preparation for the defense of the Western Hemisphere.

As for Roosevelt, like his former boss Wilson he carefully avoided hot-button words such as "conscription" and "draft" and hence used the euphemism "selective service" from the First World War because he realized that straightforward terms would arouse intense opposition.[37] He did not fool the emotionally aroused opponents, one of whom blurted out wrongly during the debate in the House of Representatives, "American conscription is American fascism."[38] Congress approved the bill with euphemism intact as the Selective Training and Service Act, known also as the Burke-Wadsworth Act.

The record of the battle for and against the nation's first peacetime conscription law shows no effort to resurrect the dead concept of a citizenry in arms eager to combat tyranny, that is, except by the interventionists and Roosevelt. In signing the bill into law on September 16, he called conscription a "muster" thereby evoking the myth "of the farmers of Lexington and Concord taking their flintlock muskets down from above the fireplace."[39]

Both the National Guard and conscription measures restricted the call to service to one year. When that year ended, after bitter opposition from a Congress and a public that wanted its boys home again, the government extended the laws. It drafted young men not as members of state militias but as individuals to be integrated with Guardsmen on a national basis into the regular army.[40]

Also as part of the preparedness agenda, a plan for registering guns in civilian hands through a national census gained considerable support, even among vociferous patriots. It would, Attorney General Robert H. Jackson explained, "be of great importance in the interests of national defense, as it would hamper the possible accumulation of firearms on the part of subversive groups. It is also of outstanding importance in the enforcement of the criminal law." He added that the legislation would not restrict personal liberty any more than did automobile registration.[41]

Even so, the proposal ran afoul of hunting and sporting periodicals and of organized gun-owners who condemned it as an intrusion on a presumed civil right. The *American Rifleman* claimed that England had to plead with America for small arms and ammunition because she had adopted a firearms registration law that created a shortage of such arms. The editorialist warned, "*America's defense requires the rejection of any attempt to impose on Americans the discredited European firearms registration system.*" A month later the editor maintained that Britain's "Firearms Law has resulted in a condition of gun-ignorance and lack of manufacturing facilities which has gravely threatened the life of that nation."[42] In light of this opposition, nothing came of the registration plan.

Shortly, another preparedness proposal aroused similar concern among gun owners. Congress considered a bill authorizing the president, upon payment of adequate compensation, to requisition private property that had military uses. In the debate in the House, the NRA's legislative allies moved to exclude guns. They accepted the concept of granting "certain extraordinary powers to the Executive in the furtherance of the common defense during critical times," but they saw no need "for the requisition of firearms owned and maintained by the people for sport and recreation" that would in their view infringe the Second Amendment. In the Senate, Albert B. Chandler of Kentucky expressed widespread sentiment when he declared, "We have no reason to take the per-

sonal property of individuals which is kept solely for protection of their homes."
So, in passing the Property Requisition Act Congress exempted privately
owned firearms from its purview.[43]

Less than two months later, after the United States on December 7, 1941,
entered the war, the gun became a symbol of the nation's strength, with profi-
ciency in its use a celebrated asset. For example, gun enthusiasts continued to
urge parents to teach their children to shoot as a game or as a sport. "It makes
for clean, straight living," a gun club officer wrote, "for one must live straight,
and think straight to shoot that way" and to become in time of war an asset to
the nation.[44]

At the same time in 1942, two significant gun-control cases, designed to challenge the Federal Firearms Act, reached the federal courts. In *Cases v. United
States*, 131 F. 2d 916 (1st Cir. 1942), a Puerto Rican felon who possessed a gun
and ammunition in violation of the act claimed a constitutional right to have
them. The First Circuit Court of Appeals upheld the 1938 law, commenting
that it curtailed "to some extent the right of individuals to keep and bear
arms." But, the court added, that right "is not conferred upon the people by
the federal constitution."

In *United States v. Tot*, 131 F. 2d 261 (3d Cir. 1942), Frank Tot, another
former felon, this one in New Jersey, appealed his conviction for possessing a
Colt automatic pistol capable of being fitted with a silencer in violation of the
law. He contended the decision breached his Second Amendment rights. The
third circuit court disagreed. In upholding the ruling and the statute, it stated
that in the common law, weapon bearing had never been an absolute right. It
held that the Second Amendment "was not adopted with individual rights in
mind, but as a protection for the States in the maintenance of their militia
organizations against possible encroachments by federal power."[45]

As with the *Miller* and *Cases* rulings, this decision reflected a continuing
trend in the federal courts to interpret the Second Amendment right to bear
arms as collective, not individual. The courts viewed that right, or privilege, as
existing only to the extent necessary to preserve a militia. As we have seen, that
institution had long been an anachronism but it still retained a constituency
with political influence and therefore remained an excuse for individual gun-
ownership.

The irrelevance of the militia issue to gun keeping and the court decisions
favorable to limited regulation could not counter the wartime fervor for bearing
arms and the legislators' disdain for stronger federal gun controls. The conversion of the United States into an arsenal of democracy and then into a belliger-

ent revived what for several years had been a stagnant arms industry. It became the world's foremost producer of big-ticket munitions. To fulfill government contracts for arms, the Remington company expanded by 2,000 percent. Smith & Wesson, which now produced more arms than in its preceding ninety years, developed a manufacturing capacity larger than that of the combined revolver makers of the world. The war absorbed virtually everything the small-arms firms produced. It thereby created a pent-up civilian demand for guns, a demand that in the immediate postwar years would thwart efforts to contain civilian gun violence.

11

Guns Flourish, Opposition Rises

When the Second World War ended, the prestige of the gun fraternity rode high. The nation's leaders lauded the contributions of the arms industry and the shooting clubs to the great victory. Generals Dwight D. Eisenhower and Omar N. Bradley, among those who had led the armies in Europe, praised the work of the National Rifle Association with its marksmanship program as "vital to the proper training of a citizen army."[1]

President Harry S. Truman, a former National Guard officer who had fought in France during the First World War, also lauded the association for its contribution to the war effort. "The tradition of a citizen soldiery," he wrote, "is firmly, and properly, imbedded in our national ideals. Initiative, discipline, and skill in the use of small arms are essentials for the development of the finished citizen soldier." He expressed hope that the NRA would continue its "splendid" small-arms marksmanship program because it "is good for a free America."[2]

This approbation registered well with the gun community eager to keep the marksmanship program going and to resume buying firearms freely on the open market. To meet this latter desire, domestic manufacturers again peddled small arms to civilians on a grand scale. Many of the twelve million men who had received military training brought home a variety of firearms, either as souvenirs or for personal use. They also returned to civilian life with a continuing interest in weaponry that affected the politics of controlling firearms violence. In addition, more than in the past, cheap guns flooded the country from other sources. While the former warring nations dumped a large number of obsolete but still usable firearms into third-world countries, they exported most of them to the United States. With its lax firearms laws, a huge market of well-heeled firearms zealots, a history of having the world's largest market for civilian guns, and pent-up demand, the United States could absorb them. Gun hobbyists view these early cold war years, when one could have a "choice of useable arms at prices beginning at far less than ten dollars," with nostalgia. As one of them explained, "Many recall this as the golden age of choice in arms along with a freedom of essentially unrestricted purchase."[3]

As documented by the Federal Bureau of Investigation, felons and delinquent minors who generated a postwar surge in crime were prominent among the many who had no real trouble in obtaining a large number of these firearms. In 1946 youths under eighteen years of age committed more than five hundred thousand crimes, most of them with guns.[4] Urbanites frightened by street violence, many of whom previously had no affection for guns, rushed to buy them for self-defense because they assumed police protection had failed them. Organizations such as the Committee to Ban Teen-Age Weapons, which attracted several hundred religious, civic, and other leaders and which in 1947, in New York City, evolved into the National Committee for the Control of Weapons, urged stricter gun laws locally and nationally.

Concurrently, the proliferation of guns in private hands along with escalation in crime also disturbed Attorney General Thomas C. Clark, who decided to try to do something about the situation. He asked Alexander Wiley, chairman of the Senate Judiciary Committee, to introduce legislation requiring individuals who possessed firearms to register them and then to record any transfers of ownership. On the floor of the Senate on January 24, 1947, Wiley explained why the federal government needed the requested authority. "At present," he said, "thousands of small arms, principally revolvers and automatic pistols, originally issued to members of the Armed Forces, are in the possession of persons who do not appear to have acquired them legitimately." He added that high military sources confirmed that a "tremendous number" of the small arms were unaccounted for or lost. Law-enforcement officers believed that underworld thugs bought or stole many of them.

This argument not only failed to persuade the legislators to act on the Justice Department's request but also infuriated leaders of the National Rifle Association. They denounced the proposed measure as another attempt "to revive the idea of a Gestapo-type Federal firearms registration law."[5] This hostility, backed by the resources of the gun lobby, as well as the resistance of his colleagues, caused Wiley to withdraw his bill. Later in the year, crime rates, as measured by police arrests, fell.

In the Wiley episode the NRA's muscle flexing, as usual, demonstrated its political potency. As former soldiers and sailors joined in large numbers that power expanded. Their pressure contributed to change. It led the organization's leaders to acknowledge that the demarcations separating hunter, target shooter, and gun collector had become blurred. It also compelled them to cooperate with all kinds of gun owners and to devote more of their attention to shooting as sport, especially to hunting. These shooters now bought most of the firearms. For example, in 1947 the Winchester Repeating Arms Company reported a record production of sporting guns in response to escalating demand.[6]

By the following year new members had contributed to the tripling of the association's size. Still, its leaders retained some of the old-time military orientation. In 1949 the executive council, for instance, consisted of five generals and a colonel. Its house organ, the *American Rifleman*, in comparison to competitors, seemed geared to articles on technical firearms issues of interest primarily to soldiers and other military veterans. Moreover, it refused advertisements for products the editors considered dangerous or shoddy, such as for bazookas and antitank guns. In all, though, to the interested public the association still conveyed a solid red, white, and blue military image.

When the NRA shed its military trappings and its leaders shared power with the countrywide pool of new members, that image also changed. But the association became immensely popular with shooters of the current generation. It also accommodated itself to the rise of nonmilitary gun clubs, which in a few years had nearly doubled in number.[7] In line with the other changes, in 1949 the expanded membership elected its first woman to the executive council, thereby further widening the association's base.

Furthermore, the NRA shifted focus from its traditional concern with the rifle to a more vehement defense of all firearms but particularly of the handgun. In its various guises, this small firearm had acquired far more firepower and accuracy than during the prewar years when Franklin D. Roosevelt had denounced its use. For this reason, leading shooters claimed it as a hunting weapon even though hunters, as always in the past, still relied mostly on long guns. A more important reason why avid shooters resisted proposed restrictions on the handgun was their conviction that the assault on it would curtail their freedom to choose any kind of firearm. Other gun-keepers touted it as useful for self-defense. These justifications for free and private use of the handgun proved contentious because most Americans viewed it as the favored weapon of criminals.

At the same time, large numbers of those who cherished guns for any reason evaded existing local controls of consequence, such as New York's Sullivan law, with impunity. Not even the rampant crime that had followed the immediate postwar years could channel public outrage sufficiently against guns to reinvigorate the control struggle as an issue of pressing national concern. Nor could scattered shooting episodes, as for instance in 1949.

In January, Atlantic City experienced a crime wave in which juvenile delinquents with guns figured prominently. Elsewhere, older shooters rampaged. In April, in daylight on a street on Staten Island, Charles Van Newkirk, an unemployed merchant marine engineer armed with a .38 special target revolver, shot and wounded Ellsworth H. Buck, a former congressman and former president of New York City's board of education. Newkirk said he had "a grievance against Buck." In October Joe Runyan, a farmer in Waterford, Michigan, went berserk. With a shotgun he suddenly shot and wounded nine persons in two taverns and then killed himself. He told one tavern owner, "If a man feels like he is going to die in his old age he might just as well take a few people along with him."[8]

These shootings do not stand out as isolated incidents. Stories of civilian gun violence could be found almost daily in most newspapers. The violence aroused some concern as expressed by sensationalists and popular writers. One of them, in florid rhetoric, claimed that "a pattern of hoodlum crime has emerged with stark clarity: a pattern of lustful, violent psychopathic crime which has burst upon the streets of the nation like a fearsome plague. It does not differ basically from city to city."[9] For much of the public, though, the easy availability of guns that contributed to the more lethal aspects of the country's crime did not seem to matter much.

Even members of Congress expressed more concern over other aspects of crime such as racketeering and corruption in local politics. So, in response to an alleged groundswell of public sentiment to do something about such crime, the Senate on May 10, 1950, established a special committee, headed by Estes Kefauver of Tennessee, to investigate organized crime in interstate commerce. In highly publicized, year-long hearings held in key cities across the country, some of them televised, he focused mainly on gambling and organized crime, or gangs.

Most of the committee's conclusions, such as that Chicago remained the center of criminal activity in the nation, contained few surprises except one. Even though the committee admitted that "crime is largely a local problem," it recommended creation of "an independent Federal Crime Commission in the executive branch of the Government."[10] Seeing the proposal as a step toward a "national-type police force," the attorney general and others opposed it. Hence, nothing came of it.[11] Surprisingly also, the committee's various reports did not refer to criminal or civilian gun violence of any kind.

During the Kefauver hearings, another episode of gun violence splashed across headlines. On November 1, 1950, two zealous Puerto Rican nationalists from New York City, Oscar Collazo and Griselio Torresola, armed with 9mm automatic German guns, shot their way into Blair House, the president's temporary home, with the intent of assassinating Truman. They murdered one Secret Service agent and wounded two but other agents gunned down one intruder fatally and wounded the other before either could reach the president. The survivor, Collazo, explained the assassination attempt as an effort to draw attention to the cause of their homeland's independence. About fifteen minutes after the shooting, Truman traveled to Arlington, Virginia, to deliver a scheduled speech.

As in previous assassinations or attempted assassinations, no pressing public demand for enhanced federal gun regulation followed. Politicians and press pundits expressed much more concern over the political effect, as on imminent congressional elections, than with the gun violence itself.[12] Moreover, unlike in the recent past when social unrest, civil disorder, and crime had sparked activism for some kind of response from state or federal authorities, the public tolerated the civilian mayhem as though a commonplace activity. In these years, the government's emphasis on armaments, the national anticommunist phobia, which gave stimulus to much of the FBI's activities, and the growing militarism may not have contributed to the violence but they did help enhance the popularity of guns.

The prominence of the military in American life could be seen in Truman's behavior. Unlike Wilson in 1920, he had not at the end of the Second World War terminated conscription. Indeed, in one of his first acts as president he requested an extension of the draft before it expired, and Congress obliged. In May 1946 it extended conscription. Immediately Truman sought to use the law to break a railroad strike by drafting the workers. When his attorney general questioned the constitutionality of such action, the president reportedly retorted, "We'll draft them and think about the law later."[13] Congress turned down his request to conscript.

Truman's administration ended the 1940 draft law in March 1947 but soon he contended the peacetime armed forces could not attract sufficient volunteers to maintain a huge standing army. So, despite protests from educators, pacifists, organized labor, and the black community, he again asked for the draft. Congress responded with the Selective Service Act of 1948. This law, along with the Universal Military and Training Service Act of June 1951, contributed to Truman's ability to fight in Korea without a declaration of war. He needed the draft because few citizens or members of organized reserves volunteered to join the army.[14] Even so, students and blacks and other minorities evinced no interest in becoming military shooters. Where they could, they resisted or evaded conscription.

During the Korean War and after, concern with weapons often dominated public discourse on foreign and military policy. In August 1950, for instance, Truman asked Congress to expand and accelerate "military assistance to vital areas in other parts of the world" and sought four billion dollars for armaments. Several months later, he spoke of the United States as the "arsenal for the defense of freedom" and pledged it would provide "weapons to other free nations."[15]

Although the next president, Dwight D. Eisenhower, preferred a large, professional standing army rather than one filled with conscripts, he also asked Congress to continue the draft, and it did. In addition, he enlarged the anticommunist, military aid program, mainly under the Mutual Security Act of 1954 that gave the State Department authority over importing and exporting arms. Like Truman, he believed American arms would strengthen the defenses of what he called the free world. Throughout 1954 he proposed "a defense establishment in which all three of the services [army, navy, and air force] were to remain far larger, stronger, and more effective than ever previously in peacetime."[16] For similar reasons President John F. Kennedy also supported a big armed establishment and supplied firearms to allies or potential allies.

This maintenance of huge armed forces, an army based on conscription, and a program of dispersing weapons abroad as instruments of foreign policy aroused no major popular opposition. Vocal believers in firearms control continued to express concern over the menacing aspect of gun violence in civilian life but neither the executive branch, nor Congress, nor much of the public demanded more national firearms regulation. For a while, when gun violence on March 1, 1954, again erupted in the nation's capital, the apathy appeared to change. Three Puerto Rican nationalist gunmen, firing twenty to twenty-five times at random from the visitors' gallery onto the floor of the House of Representatives, wounded five congressmen, two of them seriously.[17] Capitol police subdued the assailants. Some observers compared the shootings to the actions of communists.

Other concerns that this turmoil generated dissipated quickly. They did so in part because in the cold-war atmosphere most Americans continued to be attracted to what they perceived as the positive aspects of gun keeping. Magazines and other enterprises associated with guns prospered. Gun enthusiasts read mainly the *American Rifleman* and the annual *Gun Digest* along with articles in hunting journals and a column for gun collectors in *Hobbies* magazine. A few years later other gun journals entered the field, found ready readers, and flourished. Books on firearms that formerly had been rare now became profitable to publish. Before the war, gun collecting had been a pastime for an elite; now it mushroomed into a nationwide hobby with an estimated 650,000 gun collectors.

At this time, too, the self-styled gun buff who liked anything that would shoot, from antique derringer to antitank gun, became prominent in the gun fraternity. In addition to buying the magazines, these enthusiasts built a network with avid collectors, shooters, and gun traders. They attended gun shows held all over the country where they displayed, traded, and bought firearms in staggering numbers without significant restraint.

As in the thirties, gun merchants benefited from a nostalgia for the mythical frontier, for self-reliance, and for rugged masculinity. Gun possession flourished in a popular culture that welcomed books, magazines, and films that dealt with firearms violence. Producers revived old Western themes, portraying the gunslinger in films such as those in the Hopalong Cassidy series in which by 1943 the cowboy hero, as portrayed by former romantic actor William Boyd, "had shot his way through fifty-four separate movies."[18] Gun-toting Cassidy also appeared on 152 radio stations and in 155 newspaper comic strips. Other films, such as *The Gunfighter* (1950), *Colt .45* (1950), *High Noon* (1952), *Springfield Rifle* (1952), *Winchester '73* (1953), *Shane* (1953), and *The Gun That Won the West* (1955), depicted guns as symbols of right and weapons of heroes. In 1956 Hollywood completed "eight films with 'gun' in the title," keeping actors busy "learning to shoot."[19]

The new medium of television often followed the same themes. Night and day with the press of a button Americans could now view programs featuring graphic firearms violence. They watched pop action dramas such as reruns of the Hopalong Cassidy films, which appeared on sixty-three television stations. Various other serialized depictions of violence, such as *Gunsmoke*, *Have Gun Will Travel*, *The Rifleman*, and *Wanted Dead or Alive*, highlighted guns in titles and scripts. Television transformed Davy Crockett into a folk hero and played up his Kentucky rifle as the all-American weapon. Replicas of that rifle, along with always popular toy guns of various kinds for boys, became best sellers while the sales of real guns also zoomed.

Journalists, academics, and others increasingly viewed this fascination with firearms and the depiction of gun violence in comic books, movies, and television as a deeply rooted social problem. One of them, in discussing the gunfighter as "a killer by profession," asked, "What sort of society is it in which those who have money can hire a killer? And what kind of people are we, that our strong men find such work to their liking?"[20]

Educators and others pointed out that the gunfighter model admired by adults posed a social problem because children emulated their parents' values. Parents gave boys toy guns, and sometimes real ones, as though to prepare them for violence in the same way they presented dolls to girls to prepare them for motherhood. Although this indoctrinating of children to value guns had always been a part of American culture, more critics than in the past now denounced it as inherently evil. They also condemned the easy availability of firearms as a prime ingredient in teenage crime. Despite a stable national homicide rate, such crime had risen annually since 1948. These statistics prompted concerned legislators to prod the Senate's Judiciary Committee on May 28, 1953, to authorize a subcommittee to investigate juvenile delinquency.[21]

The gun lobby denied the connection between teen crime and firearms availability or dismissed the reproaches of worried citizens and legislators over gun violence as wrong minded. It focused more on what its constituents regarded as an immediate enemy—the agency for administering the federal gun regulations. For years the agency's task had been to collect taxes on alcoholic beverages. In 1951, as its jurisdiction expanded to include tobacco and supervision of the national gun laws, it became the Alcohol and Tobacco Tax Division of the Internal Revenue Service. Gun owners attributed to it an institutionalized determination to limit their shooting rights. They rose in wrath when in May 1957 they learned that officials had recommended several minor changes in the division's procedures for carrying out the nineteen-year-old Federal Firearms Act.

One revision called for manufacturers and importers of guns to stamp each weapon with a serial number and other identifying information. This recommendation accorded with the statute's prohibition on altered serial numbers as well as with what most American gunmakers were already doing. Another proposal would have required the buyer of a handgun, or of ammunition for it, to sign his or her name at the time of purchase. This plan accorded with the obligation of dealers to keep a record of their sales. A third modification would have compelled manufacturers and merchants to save their records for a given period of time, something the law specified but that the agency had not previously enforced.

Gun enthusiasts viewed the division officials as bureaucrats aligned with would-be firearms regulators who had become poised to accomplish through administrative maneuvering what they had been unable to do through legislation. To block the proposed changes, the National Rifle Association sent out danger signals that mobilized the gun community's constituent groups. Their lobbyists argued that through subterfuge and the bypassing of Congress, an agency of the executive branch intended to snuff out one by one the rights of private gun-keepers. The alerted owners poured thousands of letters into the offices of the Internal Revenue Service.

In August in two days of hearings crowded with gun aficionados, only four out of sixty-two witnesses spoke in favor of the changes. One prominent opponent, James H. Holton, representing the Veterans of Foreign Wars and the views of many other gun fans, declared as the conclusion of a long written statement, "We Believe That the Ultimate Defender of His Personal Liberty Is an Angry and Resolute Free Man, Armed with a Firearm."[22]

Even though in this era of nuclear armaments when the concept of a militia composed of ill-trained citizens had long become obsolete, the purveyors of sentiment such as Holton's prevailed. The alcohol and tobacco division's new regulations, adopted on January 18, 1958, contained the original plan but in a version watered down sufficiently to satisfy the gun community. The new procedures did, however, retain the requirement for manufacturers to stamp serial numbers on most firearms.

Despite the NRA's political activism in this episode as in others, its officials denied that it lobbied. It classified itself a nonprofit, private, nonpolitical organization, a status that exempted it from paying taxes on its substantial income. Its leaders took care not to lose that privilege. They maintained they merely informed or educated their members and the public on issues the association considered important to all of them rather than trying to influence them or legislators. This stance fooled few because the association officers' lobbying, for example, against the alcohol and tobacco agency proposals, had been obvious and well orchestrated.

Even though the gun fanciers had succeeded cooperatively in opposing the administrative changes, they split over a concurrent effort to impose a minor restriction on the sale of handguns. Small-arms makers were unhappy with the government's program of selling surplus guns cheaply through the rifle association and even more dissatisfied with the foreign weapons that for more than a decade had flooded the country. In 1958 the sales of American-made guns slumped badly. So, in April, Representative Albert P. Morano from Connecticut and Senator John F. Kennedy from Massachusetts, the two states that then housed most gun manufacturers, introduced similar measures in the House and Senate to bar the importing of foreign military firearms. Both legislators described these guns as spoiling the domestic industry and contributing to unemployment. In addition, Morano sought to elicit support by describing the weapons as posing "a definite safety hazard to American sportsmen" because they tended "to blow up in the shooter's face."[23]

Despite these arguments, progun members of Congress beholden or sympathetic to the gun lobby scuttled the bills. In their place, on June 23, Congress passed a bill sponsored by Robert L. F. Sikes of Florida, a hunter, an avid gun defender, and a director of the National Rifle Association. It prohibited only the return to the United States of those military arms it had sent abroad under its foreign assistance program.

The course of this legislation reflected the lack of focused concern in these cold-war years, in government and elsewhere, for checking gun violence. At this time, though, crime had started rising at an annual rate of 44 percent as estimated by the FBI, and the number of youths arrested for carrying guns rose 46 percent.[24] This jump in gun violence led a journalist to ask President Eisenhower if he personally believed in the need for more restrictions on the civilian use of firearms "at the Federal, State, or local level" to fight crime. The question seemed to startle the president. I need more data on this matter, he replied, "but my own instant reaction would be well, if there weren't so many of these weapons around, why, maybe you could be a little more peaceful."[25] Neither he nor others in his administration pursued the issue much beyond these words.

Nonetheless, as youth crime spiraled upward for the tenth straight year, the opposition of urban leaders and police to the free circulation of handguns rose. A survey in 1957 revealed that sixty-three of sixty-nine city chiefs of police queried favored more federal regulation of firearms entering their jurisdictions. Their professional association of some fifty-five hundred members wanted "existing controls of the sales of firearms" strengthened in the public interest.[26]

These data persuaded Thomas C. Hennings Jr.—one of the chairmen of the Senate Subcommittee on Juvenile Delinquency, which had been functioning for five years, and who had a record of interest in gun control—to decide to look into the possible connection between available guns and teenage crime. Hearings on this subject began on September 23, 1958, in New York City where

Mayor Robert F. Wagner and Governor Nelson Rockefeller discussed how easily guns, bought or stolen, were reaching more and more youths. Hennings commented that he had sponsored a number of bills calling for tougher gun controls that attracted no real backing. He reminded those who testified that speeches and pious words calling for gun control were fine but without votes in Congress nothing would happen. Even so, his committee held hearings in cities across the country.

Despite Hennings's pessimism, with the launching of these hearings gun keepers began sensing the possible end of an era of failed efforts to place additional selective restraints on guns. The *American Rifleman*'s editorialist warned that "there is a growing prejudice against firearms." Year after year, he pointed out, gun enthusiasts have to oppose "some sort of ill-advised" firearms legislation, frequently "the same stupid proposal." The time has come, he wrote, to make a nationwide effort to overcome the ignorance, "prejudice and fear and opposition to guns and shooting. . . . *Let's take the offensive.*"[27] Another writer urged readers to act "before it's too late" against antigun agitators who would usurp their rights.[28]

This fear of possible new gun regulation on the federal level increased on the heels of the publication in August 1959 of the results of a Gallup poll. This first survey of the gun problem in twenty years revealed that roughly half of America's homes had firearms. Even so, three out of four of those queried believed that anyone wishing to purchase a gun should be required to obtain a police permit. Fifty-nine percent wanted private ownership of handguns outlawed.[29] The NRA moved to counteract such reports.

At the end of the year, as part of its anticontrol offensive, the *Rifleman* came out with a new column, the "Armed Citizen." It listed instances in which a heroic, law-abiding American with a gun thwarted criminals. Two years later *Field and Stream* magazine beefed up the progun propaganda by sponsoring a conference that gave birth to the National Shooting Sports Foundation. This umbrella organization, headed by the president of the Colt firearms company, represented about one hundred firms dealing in guns, sporting publications, and various shooting groups. The foundation underwrote a campaign to emphasize the positive aspects of shooting as sport.[30]

The opponents of the free use of firearms, who now spoke out in greater numbers than in the previous decade, saw no social benefit in recreational shooting. They decried the large number of fatal accidents connected with it. With Americans firing guns in record numbers, often without adequate training in their use, the mishaps escalated. The quick-draw faddists, or neogunslingers who insisted on using live ammunition, shot themselves so often that doctors spoke of a new epidemic—gunshot wounds of the lower extremity, or the fast-draw syndrome.

Hunting, where millions of novices manned rifles, produced a greater number of firearms casualties. Even gun enthusiasts who rarely criticized their brethren-in-arms, for years had periodically complained about hunters' recklessness. They warned that those who could not handle a gun with proper care had no business in the field. A later hunter commented, "So-called sportsmen who stagger into the woods, shoot anything that moves," are "more deadly than grizzlies." Another critic observed that "the countryside is full of incompetent gunners and their human victims." He called the unregulated granting of hunting privileges "idiotic."[31]

Rifle association monitors became so concerned over the rate of injuries that they took to compiling statistics on hunting accidents and introduced courses on hunting safety. Still, the numbers of the wounded and dead mounted. So did the aversion to hunting, much of it now coming from ecologists and animal rights groups. They questioned the moral aspects of sport hunting, condemning its brutality. They suggested that people who engaged in it did so because they liked to kill.[32] Regardless, according to gunmakers and their lobbyists, those who shot for pleasure exceeded the number of participants in any other sport.

Meanwhile, the civil rights movement, with its exposure of deeply rooted racial wrongs, had shaken millions of Americans out of their seeming complacency toward social issues. It gained national prominence when Rosa Parks, a black, forty-three-year-old seamstress in Montgomery, Alabama, on December 1, 1955, refused to move to the back of a segregated bus to make room for a white passenger. Following her arrest, African Americans boycotted the bus system. Elsewhere they took to defying Jim Crow laws. In Greensboro, North Carolina, on February 1, 1960, black students staged a sit-in at the whites-only lunch counter of a variety store. As the rights movement spread, so did gun violence. Once again, as during the Reconstruction era, communities in the South came to resemble armed camps.

During this turmoil, gun organizations backed by manufacturers and sportsmen thrived. In the next year, the magazine *Shooting Times* reported that the foundation had taken as its mission "to educate the American public—to get across the *facts* about guns and shooting, and counter the Red-inspired propaganda 'scare' articles such as appeared recently in two women's magazines."[33]

All the while the National Rifle Association continued to thrive as a prestigious national institution. It attracted as life members luminaries such as Eisenhower, Richard M. Nixon, and John F. Kennedy. In 1963 its rolls showed a membership of more than five hundred thousand. Its impressive continuing growth over fifteen years came from aggressive recruiting, the expanding population, the continuing sale of cheap surplus arms to those who joined, and particularly from the popular interest in all that had to do with firearms.

For years, gunmakers had consistently recruited young boys as shooters in advertisements that claimed guns promoted "close companionship . . . between father and son" and agility in sports. As one advertisement stated it, "The boy who can put nine out of ten shots into the bull's eye learns the accuracy that makes a perfect 'forward pass' in football, or makes for victory at basketball, tennis or baseball."[34]

This fascination with arms existed alongside robberies, a suicide rate with firearms the highest in the world, and a continuing public concern with crime. The crime aspect persuaded the new attorney general, Robert F. Kennedy, the brother of President John F. Kennedy, to launch an assault on organized crime without showing overtly a concern over private gun-keeping. Even so, the obvious gun violence enlivened the gun-control movement especially in urban areas. For instance, the toy-gun craze among children alarmed citizens and health and law-enforcement officials in New York City. To counter the fad, municipal authorities prohibited the sale or possession of lifelike toy pistols in black, blue, silver, or aluminum colors. The ban hardly dented the craze.[35]

Elsewhere, too, the enthusiasm for guns of both children and adults remained high. Aware of this sentiment, Congress and the executive branch could largely ignore the gun-control movement. The firearms community could thwart the movement but could not ignore it because it had grown. Even in the previous decade during its seeming hibernation, the movement's dedicated supporters in Congress had introduced more than thirty-five regulatory bills. The gun lobby had blocked all of them.

In its struggle against gun violence, the movement had a long way to go in overcoming the power of the lobby because constituents benefited from the national security hysteria of the time. One gun defender, the popular novelist Robert Ruark, as others had done for years linked patriotism and gun keeping but with a new twist. "I wonder," he wrote, "how many people realize that federal and state registration of all firearms has long been a worked-for ideal of the Communist party in America. No doubt they stole this from the Nazis and Fascists."[36] As this far-fetched commentary indicated, patriotism, anticommunism, and gun keeping in these cold-war years lived in harmony. At the same time, public opposition to such thinking, along with the desire for more federal gun control, had risen.

The interest in regulation could be seen in the continuing investigations of the Senate Subcommittee on Juvenile Delinquency under Thomas J. Dodd of Connecticut, a former FBI agent, who after the death of Hennings in September 1960 took over as chairman. Some writers have depicted him as a gun-control crusader whereas others have portrayed him as an opportunist. In any case, in March 1961 as a consequence of a boom in the mail-order sale of guns, Dodd's committee revived the probe of juvenile access to firearms.

In hearings that followed, Dodd focused on a narrow aspect of gun control—the mail-order sale of cheap, imported, snub-nosed pistols. In three decades, their distribution, often to teenagers, had proliferated. These disparaged and easily concealed weapons had become infamous as Saturday night specials, a name originated by the Detroit police who associated the pistols with the gun violence on that night in their city. Foreign-made specials often entered the country dismantled and labeled as parts or as junk. Dealers then reassembled them and sold them through magazines for a few dollars each to anyone who ordered them. To avoid violating federal law, the suppliers shipped the guns to buyers through private parcel companies. Thus, the State Department, which licensed arms imports, and the Treasury Department's agency in charge of enforcing federal firearms regulation did nothing to stop the flow of these guns.

Although Congress purportedly had designed the federal gun laws to aid the states with their own control measures, only seven states required permits to purchase firearms. Even in the permit states, exporters could ship arms to federally licensed dealers. Almost anyone who filled out a form and paid a dollar could secure a dealer's license. In the public hearings Dodd emphasized, "We do not intend to tamper with the constitutionally guaranteed right of a free people to keep and bear arms," but instead will direct attention "to the sources of the 'criminal' gun."[37]

In another hearing, a Treasury official estimated that only half of the sixty thousand individuals with licenses were bona fide dealers. Despite Dodd's anti-weapons rhetoric, gun-club officials and gunmakers went along with him because he catered to them. Domestic arms-producers, however, complained that the imports really hurt them. They wanted the legislators to distinguish between good quality arms of reputable manufacturers and the cheap imports. Dodd then adopted the manufacturers' cause.

From the hearings, from data assembled over several years, and from the advice of gun lobbyists who promised support, Dodd prepared a bill. It proposed to tighten the dealer licensing system, raise the merchants' registration fee to ten dollars, and require them to be twenty-one years or older. On August 2, 1963, along with four other sponsors, he introduced the measure to the Senate as an amendment to the Federal Firearms Act. In keeping with Senate practice, the bill went to the commerce committee headed by Warren D. Magnuson of Washington, a legislator sensitive to the interests of his progun constituents.

In November the *Christian Science Monitor* ran a series of articles on the gun trade. It expressed concern over the "alarming rate at which the United States is being flooded with cheap foreign-made guns," which it described as "the hottest items in the mail-order gun business."[38] On November 19 in an editorial, "Murder by Mail Order," it announced support for the Dodd bill, which it characterized as "minimum legislation" and as "not tough enough to suit many."[39] For the gun lobby, though, it seemed too tough. Consequently, it languished in Magnuson's committee for three and a half months until another tragedy brought national attention to the gun issue.

12

Control Act of 1968

O n November 22, 1963, in Dallas, Texas, when the self-styled Marxist Lee Harvey Oswald assassinated President John F. Kennedy, he used an Italian Mannlicher-Carcano carbine fitted with a four-power telescopic sight. This gun was one of the hot mail-order items and one of about one hundred thousand of its kind that had entered the American market. Oswald had purchased it for $19.95 under a fictitious name from a mail-order house in Chicago with a coupon clipped from the *American Rifleman*.

This murder marked the beginning of a new era in the struggle over gun violence. As no assassination, attempted assassination, or firearms episode had before then, this shooting, captured on film and shown repeatedly on television, sensitized much of the public to the issues of gun keeping. It also galvanized the control movement into a stepped-up political activism. A river of mail calling for strong curbs on gun access poured into Congress. Within a few weeks, federal legislators introduced 17 gun-control bills while lawmakers in the states proposed more than 170 such bills. Most of the proposals aimed at banning all mail-order sales of firearms, not just of pistols.

The next week Senator Thomas Dodd amended his bill twice to include rifles and shotguns and to require dealers to have their licenses authenticated by senior law-enforcement officials. "What more do we need than the death of a beloved President," he asked, "to arouse us to place some regulation on the traffic in guns for crime?"[1] As did many within the administration of the new president, antigun activists wanted a stronger bill. At this point, Lyndon B. Johnson himself did not place stricter gun control high on his political agenda, but he quickly backed the measure.

Polls indicated broad public support for meaningful federal regulation. Organizations such as the National Committee for the Control of Weapons called for legislation requiring registration of rifles and shotguns as well as handguns, and for other restraints. Legislators linked to the NRA tried to avoid any positive connection with control proposals.

For instance, on December 13 when the Senate commerce committee began hearings on the various control bills, Senator Warren Magnuson chose not to preside. For the record, though, he stated that neither the present proposals nor any other federal legislation would provide effective firearms control. The public's demands, he said, "should be directed to their State legislatures. This is where the responsibility belongs . . . and the only place where there can be effective and meaningful control." He warned also against action "born of ignorance" in an atmosphere of "hysteria" against responsible citizens who "have the right to possess firearms."[2]

Iowa's Bourke B. Hickenlooper, a senator who belonged to and spoke for the National Rifle Association, claimed that with the federal legislation "we would, in effect, be establishing a police state."[3] Representative John D. Dingell of Michigan warned, "There is a growing prejudice against firearms in many segments of our society," and Congressman Robert Sikes of Florida stated "that a crime committed by one man [Oswald] should not cause 35 million gun owners to be persecuted."[4] These sentiments set the tone for the hearings and for a battle over controls that echoed across the nation.

The rifle association, whose membership now approached one million, or about one out of every forty gun owners, immediately sprang into action by mobilizing its devoted constituency and ample financial resources. Its leaders felt they had to move decisively because, as the *American Rifleman* acknowledged, "never before has there been such a wave of anti-firearm feeling or such vocal and almost universal demand for tighter controls over the mail-order sales of guns." Although characterizing much of this reaction as emotional, the official organ warned that "it has had its impact upon the U.S. Congress."[5]

Single-minded, grassroots gun devotees responded quickly to their lobby's SOS, even though thousands of them, one spokesman admitted, "didn't know what was in the bill."[6] On their own initiative four NRA members drove night and day from Phoenix, Arizona, to Washington, D.C.—a distance of twenty-five hundred miles—to plead with the Senate committee to preserve what one of them called their "God-given right" to keep arms. Another claimed that "the gun is the standard of freedom in the United States of America," and still others asked the legislators not to disarm honest citizens.[7] The bill had nothing in it about disarming.

In countertestimony, control advocates, well outnumbered by the progun representatives, pointed out this and other inconsistencies in the gun lobby's arguments. One control supporter, Representative John V. Lindsay of New York, had framed a gun bill stronger than Dodd's. To bring attention to his position, he brought a Carcano rifle to the hearings. Senator Ralph Yarborough of Texas, who at that point presided, asked him please to observe the NRA rules of safe gun-handling. Knowing the senator belonged to the association, Lindsay replied he could not do otherwise because the NRA ran the show.

Lindsay's views epitomized the position of moderate Republicans and other believers in the constitutional right of "responsible people" to own guns but who wished also to banish the use of "notoriously dangerous" guns. He perceived the Second Amendment right as subject to reasonable regulation in the same fashion as the right of free speech. The gun-keeping right, he wrote, "is not so absolute that it permits infringement of other rights of other people."[8]

This constitutional perspective did not have the impact on the public that moderate control advocates desired largely because the organized gun buffs opposed it. To this opposition Dodd responded, "I do not propose to let this legislation fade away."[9] It did fade because the civil rights violence and the turmoil over the Vietnam War overshadowed his committee hearings.

The war, the agitation against it, and the antiestablishment activities of militant blacks such as Stokely Carmichael and Malcolm X captured most of the headlines. In fiery rhetoric, these agitators rejected the nonviolence of Martin Luther King Jr., who had become the nation's foremost civil rights leader. King deplored what he called "raging torrents of violence," including gun violence. After Kennedy's murder he had stated that by "our readiness to allow arms to be purchased at will and fired at whim; by allowing our movie and television screens to teach our children that the hero is one who masters the art of shooting and the technique of killing . . . we have created an atmosphere in which violence and hatred have become popular pastimes."[10]

As had militant blacks since Reconstruction, Malcolm X argued differently. When "the government has proven itself unwilling or unable to defend the lives and the property of Negroes," he advised an audience in Cleveland, "it's time for Negroes to defend themselves. Article number two of the constitutional amendments provides you and me the right to own a rifle or a shotgun." He added, "If the white man doesn't want the black man buying rifles and shotguns, then let the government do its job. That's all."[11] He had brought up a problem that faced blacks constantly, especially in the South. They could not rely on police for protection. He also touched on an old fear widespread among whites—that of angry, armed blacks.

This apprehension dovetailed with the desire of most Americans, as well as of the president, that domestic gun violence, whether white or black, be checked. Even though the nation had been experiencing a long-term decline in such behavior, at this time this violence began to rise again.[12] As polls indicated, much of the public wished also to curb at least some homicides with tighter but not comprehensive federal gun control. Knowing this, members of the progun fraternity in the commerce committee hearings and elsewhere depicted themselves as belonging to an embattled minority shielded by the Constitution. As always, its spokesmen played on the public's reverence for that document, citing Second Amendment rights. As always, they also hammered away with the slogan "Guns don't kill people, people kill people." Typically, critics disparaged the statement as mindless because people could not kill as readily without guns as with them.

Other control advocates reminded opponents that the handgun "is really designed as an efficient instrument for one purpose: the killing and wounding of humans."[13] Even a progun witness in the hearings, which had resumed on March 26, 1964, admitted that whenever people have guns they will shoot somebody. This, he contended, is "part of the price of freedom that we are going to have to pay in order to have freedom."[14] Others of similar persuasion denounced gun control with traditional conspiracy theory. They depicted it as a plot to disarm law-abiding citizens. With these views repeated often in testimony before the commerce committee, sentiment ran overwhelmingly against the Dodd bill. On August 11 the committee buried the bill simply by doing nothing with it.

During this phase of the control struggle, the army and the National Board for the Promotion of Rifle Practice continued to sell surplus firearms at bargain prices to civilians and to give them millions of rounds of free ammunition. As in the past, numerous government officials in the program and elsewhere operated as allies of the gun community. Their activities reflected the rift within the executive branch between progun military men and procontrol civilian leaders.

As for the president, despite his relentless concentration on the war in Vietnam, he remained committed to working for some kind of additional federal gun regulation. His goal appeared attainable because in a landslide victory in November 1964 he won the presidency in his own right. The electorate also chose a liberal Congress. Immediately, the national debate on guns heated up again. In this atmosphere, on January 6, 1965, Dodd reintroduced his bill to ban mail-order guns as part of what he called a war on the firearms lobby. Now, though, the control struggle had widened to swirl around various aspects of gun violence.

Two months later in a special message, the president urged Congress to do something meaningful about crime. As a significant factor in its prevalence, he cited what had long been evident—"the ease with which any person can acquire firearms." At a minimum, he desired increased "federal control over interstate shipment of firearms" and limits on the importation of "surplus military weapons and other used firearms."[15] On March 22 Dodd presented the administration's bill and amended his own to reflect the president's wishes and to make it stronger. The two measures then differed only slightly.

At this point national attention became fixed on the war as well as on the civil rights movement, especially on Selma, Alabama, where segregationists murdered two blacks as they protested racial discrimination. Local authorities attacked demonstrators with clubs, whips, and tear gas. In response, King organized a civil rights march from Selma to Montgomery. On March 25, a Ku Klux Klansman gunned down Viola Gregg Liuzzo, a white participant from Detroit, as she rode in a car with a black youth. Again, gun violence outraged many but it did not stop. Both whites and blacks scurried for more firearms.

In the course of these racial confrontations, the gun lobby stepped up its campaign to demolish the firearms control bills. Thousands of progun letters streamed into Congress. During this struggle the NRA still presented itself as a quasigovernmental institution whose activities benefited society as well as gun owners. Its marksmanship and surplus arms distribution programs, still subsidized by Washington, continued to attract new members. This favorable relationship with the government did not in itself explain the association's continuing effectiveness in eviscerating gun-control legislation. Its leaders demonstrated impressive skill as coordinators of progun forces. With a signal, they could in a few days inundate Congress with thousands of progun telegrams or letters.

The NRA and other firearms organizations placed full-page advertisements in newspapers that mobilized constituents to battle for the gun lobby's cause as their cause. For example, the American Sportsmen's Foundation, Inc., exhorted shooters to write letters of protest to all members of Dodd's committee. "Our Goal—"it announced, "1,000,000 Letters to Protect Our Sport and Our Hobby."[16] This activism had a grassroots character that made it appear to arise spontaneously.

Firearms people reacted passionately to calls of alarm because they perceived the control movement in intensely personal terms. Many regarded themselves as belonging to a persecuted minority and hence viewed the control issue as so important to their lives that it guided their votes at election time. On May 19, 1965, after Dodd's subcommittee had again resumed hearings, this persecution attitude came out clearly. Gordon Allott, a Colorado senator and opponent of the bills, complained that " 'guns' is not a four-letter, Anglo-Saxon word with dirty connotations as some seem to think."[17]

The testimony of Attorney General Nicholas Katzenbach especially riled gun people by pointing out that in addition to handguns being widely used in crime, "it remains a fact that fully 30 percent of all murders committed by firearms involve rifles and shotguns." He also upset them by stating the Second Amendment did not protect the right of individuals to keep firearms.[18]

Five days later, Robert F. Kennedy, who had become a senator from New York, also spoke of the thousands killed each year by guns. "The great majority of these deaths," he said, "would not have occurred if firearms had not been readily available. For the evidence is clear that the availability of firearms is itself a major factor in these deaths." He urged legislative action, because "it is past time we wipe this stain of violence from our land."[19] In July as the hearings ended, the president established the Commission on Law Enforcement and Administration of Justice. Composed of jurists, law-enforcement officials, and scholars, it investigated the causes and cost of crime.

Less than a month later, one of the nation's worst race riots broke out in California. On the hot, smoggy night of August 11 near Watts, the sprawling black district of Los Angeles, a white California Highway Patrol motorcycle officer stopped Marquette Frye, a twenty-one-year-old black high-school dropout, for reckless driving. Frye failed a roadside sobriety test. When police officers arrived to cart him to jail, a crowd of blacks gathered and became unruly. An officer unsheathed his gun, the blacks stoned police cars, and rioting erupted.

Guns in private hands and in those of law officers quickly came into play. A teenage girl shouted at news reporters, "The next time you see us we'll be carrying guns. It's too late, white man. You had your chance. Now it's our turn."[20] Looters broke into gun shops and war surplus stores for firearms. Whites bought up guns throughout the city. In one day they bought four thousand guns. Snipers from rooftops shot at police and firefighters. Snipers also fired at police helicopters, as one observer reported, "in emulation of the South Vietnamese liberation army." They also shot at passenger planes landing at the nearby Los Angeles International Airport, causing disruptions in air traffic.[21]

Authorities set up checkpoints. They took guns away from blacks and whites, some of whom sold weapons out of their cars to whomever would buy. Whites described the six days of shooting, looting, and torching of businesses as rioting. Blacks, and even some police, termed the violence guerrilla warfare, an uprising, or a revolt. Police and National Guard troops numbering sixteen thousand gunned down looters and rioters. The upheaval left thirty-five people dead, most of them black, more than one thousand injured, some four thousand arrested, $200 million in property damage, and Watts's central business district in ashes. To deal with future urban guerrilla tactics with more than just police cars, the Los Angeles department acquired military equipment such as armored personnel carriers and helicopters.

In addition to shocking the nation, the civilian and police use of firearms delivered a mixed message. Control proponents read it as calling for much stronger federal firearms regulation whereas others perceived it as demonstrating the need for more guns in private hands for self-defense.

Elsewhere, right-wing paramilitary organizations such as the Minutemen of America, founded in 1960 by Missouri businessman and extremist Robert Bolivar de Pugh to counter "the international Communist conspiracy," flaunted guns. Minutemen practiced military tactics with rifles and other firearms, hid caches of weapons for use against a possible communist invasion, and supported the National Rifle Association. Like it, they opposed "laws which regulate the private ownership of firearms or which detract from the individual's ability to defend his family and personal property."[22]

Radical-left groups and militant blacks also continued to denounce firearms regulation, or what their spokespeople called antiweapon propaganda and legislation. They argued that when guns are outlawed, only pigs will have guns. This rhetoric, along with bloodletting as in Los Angeles, whipped up more demands for stricter federal firearms control. Even so, progun legislators kept the Dodd and administration bills bottled up in committee.

At the same time, as a favor to an arms manufacturer, Congress passed legislation easing access to guns. Under existing federal law, convicted felons automatically lost the privilege of owning firearms. The Olin Mathieson corporation pleaded guilty to felony counts involving kickbacks on pharmaceutical sales to Vietnamese and Cambodian importers. This conviction blocked the company's Winchester arms division from shipping its guns in interstate commerce. The new measure exempted Winchester from penalties under the umbrella statute but specifically excluded persons convicted of firearms crimes from the benefit. Through this broad interpretation of the exemption's wording, however, the firearms agency allowed convicted felons "once again" to acquire guns legally.[23]

Despite this end run around the existing law by the government's own enforcement agents, the president, in a special message on crime in March 1966, again asked for legislation "to regulate and control interstate traffic in dangerous firearms." With some care, he attempted also not to alienate most gun owners. He told them he saw "no need to curtail the right of citizens to keep arms for such traditional pastimes as hunting and marksmanship."[24] This overture failed to appease gun keepers. They viewed the message as confirming their conviction that virtually any control measure aimed ultimately to deprive them of firearms.

Two days later, Emanuel Celler of New York, chairman of the House Judiciary Committee, took up the president's crime bill. Shortly after, so did a Senate committee. Promptly, the gun lobby organized opposition to the measure. Pro-gun committee members employed various tactics to block consideration of the bill by the whole Congress.

While Congress stalled, gun violence, mingling at times with civil rights protests and the antics of right-wing extremist organizations, continued to capture headlines. A police roundup of New England Minutemen found them hoarding one million rounds of rifle and small-arms ammunition, more than one hundred rifles, numerous pistols and machine guns, and a mass of other arms. William E. Thorensen III, son of the president of the Great Western Steel Corporation, a thief, and an assault-and-battery specialist, owned an arsenal of seventy tons of weapons. At his arrest the next year for an attempted murder, a United States attorney quipped, "The guy has so many munitions, I don't know whether the government should prosecute him or negotiate with him."[25] When authorities in Illinois apprehended Rick Lauchli, a founding member of the Minutemen, they discovered another cache of more than one thousand firearms, primarily Thompson submachine guns.

In January 1967, during this firearms turmoil, the president's commission on law enforcement submitted its report. It concluded that crime and fear of it had eroded the quality of life of many Americans. It recommended that "each state should require the registration of all handguns, rifles, and shotguns." If, after five years, the states had not acted, the commission advised a federal control law stricter than what the administration had urged.[26]

Johnson adopted most of the recommendations. The next month he again implored Congress to place firearms legislation "high on its agenda in this session" and to enact the safe streets bill he favored.[27] As before, the legislators balked. In April they did pass the Civil Disobedience Act, which prohibited paramilitary instruction of civilians aimed at fomenting civil disorders and interstate travel with the intent to riot. Other countries, which at this time also were experiencing escalating gun violence associated usually with crime, enacted tougher measures.

An episode in Sacramento, California, appeared to demonstrate the need for the civil disobedience law. Since the incident involved race as well as guns, it received widespread publicity. On May 2 two dozen or more African American militants, calling themselves Black Panthers and armed with pistols, rifles, and at least one sawed-off shotgun, invaded the state's assembly chamber. They had come to the capitol to protest a bill prohibiting the carrying of loaded firearms openly in cities. They contended that their organization required each member "to acquire a gun and become familiar with its care and use." Panther chiefs preached that "the gun was a tool of black liberation."[28] When state police disarmed and arrested the Panthers, one leader, Bobby Seale, insisted they had a right to defend themselves. Quite a few gun proponents agreed.

In another instance that linked guns and civil rights, black activist Rap Brown urged ideological leftists to help him promote the racial uprising. "If you can't see yourself in the context of being John Brown, then bring me the guns," he urged. "If you can't give a gun, then give a dollar to somebody who can buy a gun."[29]

That summer the dread such words aroused among whites appeared to turn into reality. Race riots erupted in cities across the country. In most instances, they pitted black communities against police. The confrontation involved a greater dispersal of firearms and a much more intense use of firepower than in comparable past situations.

The first upheaval struck Newark, New Jersey, on July 12, and eleven days later the second hit Detroit. In Detroit the looting and arson escalated into one of the country's worst internal upheavals thus far. Rioters stole more than three thousand guns, few of which police tracked down. Again snipers targeted firefighters and police. "This is more than a riot," a police officer declared in alluding to the shooting. "This is war."[30] Clamoring for a means of protection, whole classes of people bought guns and hoarded them. The week of hell, with forty-three deaths, more than one thousand people injured, and millions of dollars in property damage, ended only after Washington dispatched federal troops to aid local and state enforcement units. Analysts concluded that "the sheer availability of weapons . . . tended to escalate racial conflict."[31]

Two days before the riots had erupted, Dodd's committee had resumed hearings on the gun-control bills before Congress. As usual, proponents and opponents remained far apart. For example, Neal Knox, editor of *Gun Week*, a firearms newspaper, explained that the "individual members of the gun fraternity are deeply concerned about the legislation before this committee." They regarded the bills as prohibition, not regulation and as "unreasonable and unnecessary," whereas Richard J. Hughes, New Jersey's governor, called for immediate "enactment of a strong and meaningful interstate gun control bill." He added, "Why must we make it so easy for everyone to purchase firearms of every kind with absolutely no questions asked?"[32] On August 1 the hearings adjourned with both sides still sparring.

On that same day another act of gratuitous gun violence shifted some attention away from the congressional deliberations and from the riots. At the University of Texas at Austin, Charles J. Whitman, an unbalanced twenty-five-year-old student, hauled a footlocker filled with guns to the observation ramp of a tower 307 feet above the campus. With a Remington rifle equipped with a telescopic lens, he indiscriminately picked off students below. Before police killed him, he murdered sixteen people, including his mother and wife, and wounded thirty-three.

This massacre again raised the question as to what state and national governments would do to curb the civilian gun carnage. The president denounced the killings and the next day pleaded once more with Congress to pass his gun-control bill. Within weeks a number of legislators came up with proposals to enhance federal authority in dealing with random shootings, as well as with urban riots, as a matter of public safety. Uncompromising weapons fanciers attacked the mild controls proposed in the president's bill. *Guns & Ammo* editors, for instance, denounced those who supported the bill as "criminal coddling do-gooders, borderline psychotics as well as Communists and leftists who want to lead us into the one world welfare state."[33]

This name-calling bothered antigun activists far less than did the situation in Congress. Despite Johnson's pleas for action, legislators beholden to the gun lobby still blocked consideration of the firearms measure. Gun-control leaders blamed it and specifically the National Rifle Association for throttling what they believed most Americans desired. To a degree, as polls indicated, the activists had assumed correctly, but the association did not regard itself as thwarting popular will.

Even though critics of the NRA may have been harsh, zealots frequently did push it into combative, hard-hitting campaigns in defense of guns. In turn, opponents picketed its headquarters, dissected its finances, challenged its tax-exempt status, and demanded that it register as a lobby according to the Federal Lobbying Act of 1946. Control activists also assailed the rifle association's marksmanship program, compelling the Department of Defense in 1967 to withdraw support from the national shooting matches. The next year when another trimmed budget terminated the pistol program and cut off or limited free ammunition, it almost killed the civilian marksmanship program.[34] Antigun lobbyists in the states, as in Connecticut, Illinois, New Jersey, and New York, also scored successes with regulatory legislation. Cities such as Chicago, Philadelphia, and New York adopted new, though still selective, gun-control measures.

At the same time, as though trying to deflect the wrath of gun keepers, Johnson announced he "did not propose that the Federal Government take over the job of dealing with crime in American streets" from local authorities. Later, he repeated that the federal government "must never assume the role of the Nation's policeman."[35]

In January 1968 the president renewed his appeal to Congress for action on his crime bill. He noted that in the previous year Americans with firearms had committed 7,700 murders, 55,000 aggravated assaults, and more than 71,000 robberies, a record of gun crime purportedly exceeding that in any other country. "There is no more urgent business before this Congress," he announced, "than to pass the Safe Streets Act this year that I proposed last year."[36] In the next few months, he reiterated his conviction several times.

Without blinking, the association's officials still pretended that it educated rather than lobbied. "All this talk about the gun lobby is baloney," its president, Harold W. Glassen, asserted. "We have yet to spend a single dollar on lobbying; we never hired a lobbyist. We don't tell anyone to write his Congressman."[37] The association's educating could not be distinguished from lobbying. Educating included tracking every proposed piece of federal or state legislation, carefully preparing critiques of the proposals, and promptly disseminating the materials to the membership to arouse pressure on pertinent legislators.

Despite the control ferment, the structure of American democracy as well as gun fans' militancy helped them derail significant new federal firearms legislation. On their side, the progun people had a Congress positioned to the right of the populace on matters affecting firearms. Many of the legislators shared the perspective of the weapons fraternity, belonged to it, or received funding from it. Gun money corrupted even Dodd. As aides disclosed, he accepted both "personal financial gifts and campaign contributions from officials of the arms industry" who opposed the meaningful gun controls he professed to desire.[38] He thus damaged the control movement he claimed to help.

Legislators from all parts of the country incurred obligations to the gun lobby but members of the House less so than senators. The House had the strongest control impulse because of heavy representation from the urban areas where the antigun movement had most of its followers. A larger proportion of the Senate came from the South and West, where constituents viewed gun control as anathema. Furthermore at this time, senators from these regions wielded crucial power because through seniority they usually dominated committees where most of the gun bills lodged. Therefore, the Senate tended to look askance at control proposals. In all, on the gun issue the legislators preferred to do little or nothing. They used obstructing techniques that casual voters usually forgave rather than giving support to regulation that would surely offend the potent and unforgiving gun minority.

Even presidents and presidential hopefuls of liberal persuasion took care not to go too far in antagonizing the organized progun forces. For instance, even though Johnson sided with control advocates, he had always to weigh the gun lobby's influence. It affected other policies he considered vital to his presidency, such as his conduct of the war in Vietnam. The rifle association wholeheartedly supported that conflict, citing it "as ample vindication for the marksmanship programs" it sponsored.[39] Although this stance pleased Johnson, it did not, outwardly at least, lessen his commitment to tighter federal gun control.

Ironically, in waging war in Vietnam against an enemy that millions of Americans viewed as posing no danger to their well-being, the pro–gun control president drafted youths by the thousands, placed guns in their hands, and taught them how to shoot to kill. Conscription permitted Johnson and his hawkish advisers to fight cheaply for five years. It also aroused intense opposition among conscripts, their families, friends, and others.

By fall 1967 both Republicans and liberal Democrats had challenged the legitimacy of the draft as well as of the war. Few perceived compulsory military duty as necessary or patriotic in an unwanted war. Massive dissent, greater than the antidraft opposition during the Civil War, compelled Johnson on March 31, 1968, to announce withdrawal of his bid for reelection. With this decision he appeared to lose some of his ability to influence the outcome of the gun-violence struggle. Shortly after, two more assassinations counterbalanced his assumed weakness as a lame duck. They energized his fight for more federal authority over civilian gun-keeping and catalyzed the antigun sentiment sufficiently to break the logjam blocking consideration of the control measures before Congress.

On April 4 James Earl Ray, a convict who had escaped from prison, shot Martin Luther King Jr. as he stood outside his motel room in Memphis, Tennessee.

The murder touched off more racial rioting, this time in 211 cities, to make it collectively the largest civil disorder in the nation's recent past. Various governmental entities deployed 21,000 regular army troops, 34,000 National Guardsmen, uncounted numbers of police, sheriff forces, and 22,000 other army troops on standby. This amounted to the biggest assembly of armed force to cope with internal violence since the Civil War.[40]

During this turmoil, the president again pleaded for modest gun control, writing, "Now, it is the time to stand up and show we are not a Government by lobby but a Government of law."[41] On June 5, less than a month later in Los Angeles in full view of a nationwide television audience, gun tragedy struck again. Right after Robert Kennedy had delivered a speech in his campaign for the Democratic presidential nomination, Sirhan Bishara Sirhan, a Jordanian immigrant and Arab nationalist, murdered him with a cheap .22-caliber pistol.

As had the King killing, the second Kennedy assassination prompted various bitter comments on gun keeping. Senator Joseph D. Tydings of Maryland asserted, "It is just tragic that in all Western Civilization the United States is the one country with an insane gun policy." The distinguished economist Gunnar Myrdal announced that if the Constitution allowed indiscriminate ownership of guns, "then to hell with the Constitution."[42] *Time* magazine characterized the United States as an arsenal. It editorialized that abroad "the country is regarded as a blood-drenched, continent-wide shooting range where toddlers blast off with real rifles, housewives pack pearl-handled revolvers, and political assassins stalk their victims at will."[43]

Meanwhile, on the day Kennedy died, pickets paraded before the rifle association's headquarters in Washington with placards reading, "NRA: Your Arms Have Bloody Hands," "The Air Is Alive with the Sound of Bullets," "Stop Violence, Stop the NRA," "When Will We Learn; Abolish the NRA," and "Ready, Aim, Love." Fear of bombs emptied the building twice and the association's president received death threats.[44]

The next day on national television, Johnson announced, "Today the nation cries out to the conscience of the Congress. Criminal violence from the muzzle of a gun has once again brought heartbreak to America." He also renewed his plea for broader control legislation than Dodd had shaped. He viewed the measures the senator had incorporated in the crime bill as inadequate. "The hour has come," Johnson told legislators, "for Congress to enact a strong and effective gun control law governing the full range of lethal weapons." He reminded them he had "fought for such a law through all the days of my presidency."[45]

That same day Congress passed the president's bill as the Omnibus Crime Control and Safe Streets Act of 1968.

Three days later, the president named another special investigatory body, the National Commission on the Causes and Prevention of Violence. Then he turned his attention to the omnibus act's Title IV, the gun-control section. Unlike the twenty-one-year-old Miller act, it banned the shipment by any means of pistols and revolvers across state lines to individuals. It also forbade the purchase of handguns in stores in a state where the buyer did not reside. Johnson called it a halfway step and a victory for the gun lobby because it excluded from regulation other firearms such as shotguns and rifles. But it did enhance the federal government's authority to exercise a police power at the local level. So, despite the measure's flaws, on June 19 he reluctantly signed it into law, declaring that the good in it outweighed the bad. In addition, once more he urged Congress to take immediate action on his own wider-ranging control bill.

In an effort to stimulate broad support for the latter measure, Attorney General Ramsay Clark had asked the National Council for a Responsible Firearms Policy, a special-interest organization concerned with informing the public about the dangers of unrestrained gun use, to help him. Previously, as a small, underfunded lobby, the council had been ineffectual. This time, however, it brought together representatives from thirty-eight groups that advocated comprehensive federal gun control. They included labor unions, the American Bar Association, and the American Civil Liberties Union. On the day of Johnson's speech, Clark met with the delegates. They established the Emergency Committee for Gun Control, a spin-off from the council.

The founders chose John Glenn, the former astronaut and close friend of the Kennedy family, as the committee's national chairperson. He announced that this first antigun political action committee aimed "to stir into action the overwhelming majority of the American people . . . who favor strong gun controls." He wanted those "tens of millions of Americans" to speak up, because "if there is ever to be strong and effective gun control, the time is now." His committee launched a nationwide write-in campaign for the president's bill.[46]

As Glenn's words indicated, unlike the national council with its long-term goals his organization had immediate objectives. It worked for registration of all guns and a ban on their interstate and mail-order sale. With a letter-writing program, newspaper ads, and television commercials it sought to persuade legislators to support its program. The committee leaders also favored a stronger measure than the one the administration proposed, but they deferred to the president's agenda. The control activists at the organization's helm thought this effort could succeed because the King and Kennedy assassinations had stimulated interest in gun regulation and that they could convey their message nationally. They also perceived, incorrectly, a splintering of the powerful gun lobby. Instead, the lobby proved itself solid and as effective as ever. The emergency committee had difficulty even in buying television time to make its case.[47]

Under these conditions, Johnson proceeded with his proposal for additional legislation dealing specifically with the gun-violence issue. In a televised presentation, he pointed out that "registration and licensing have long been an accepted part of daily life in America." Since we register automobiles, boats, bicycles, and even dogs, and require licenses to fish, to hunt, and to drive, he explained, "no less should be required for the possession of lethal weapons that have caused so much heartbreak and horror in this country." He appealed to Congress "in the name of sanity . . . in the name of safety and in the name of an aroused nation to give America the gun control law it needs."[48] As in past pleas, he also assured hunters and sport shooters he did not seek ultimately to confiscate privately owned guns.

Promptly, Dodd presented Johnson's bill to the Senate while Celler introduced it in the House. As with other control measures, it spurred resistance from the gun buffs and their organizations such as Gun Owners of America. In another Senate committee hearing, the NRA's Glassen attacked proponents of the bill as seeking "complete abolition of civilian ownership of firearms. The situation demands immediate action by every law abiding firearms owner in the United States."[49] On the Senate floor, Dodd accused the association of "blackmail, intimidation and unscrupulous propaganda."[50]

Polls indicated the public approved of registering all firearms as the best way of curbing gun violence.[51] The concerned gun lobby responded by exerting some of its most intense pressure to prevent any kind of registration. Glassen sent a letter to the NRA's one million or so members urging them to counter the rising pressure for stricter controls with a barrage of protests to Congress.[52] Gun devotees responded vigorously. In the state of Washington, for instance, they turned against Senator Warren Magnuson, who had a change of heart and now supported stricter controls. Majority leader Mike Mansfield of Montana, a state where gun toters had clout, reported that "mail on this subject is the heaviest to reach my office in 26 years as a Member of the Congress. . . . The division is overwhelmingly against control legislation."[53]

As various committees scrutinized the bill, congressional allies of the gun

lobby excised its two key provisions, those calling for the registering of all firearms and the licensing of all gun owners. This amputating frustrated control
advocates to the point that prompted Senator Tydings to threaten to take the
"fight for a sane gun law to the floor of the Senate." Others, such as a Washington *Post* editorial writer, denounced the "gun peddlers' lobby" as a "monstrous
fraud—without any valid claim to the exemption it enjoys from taxation and
from registration as a lobbying agent."[54]

The NRA continued to whip up the emotions of constituents under headlines that warned they were faced with "stiff controls" and that the "administration's aim [was] now total gun registration and owner licensing."[55] Leaders
of the gun community also felt so secure about their power that they no longer
minced words about their lobbying. "We don't give a darn under what banner
any candidate chooses to run," one of their leading journals explained. "We
care about one thing only—what is his—or her—attitude on gun laws, gun restrictions." Every candidate is asked, "Are you for or against us?"[56]

Although this strategy failed to deter the control activists, it succeeded at
this time in castrating the meaningful legislation they desired. After the House
and Senate ironed out their differences and after the majority overrode the die-
hard opposition of Southern and Western legislators, Congress passed the
weakened control bill. On October 22 Johnson reluctantly signed it into law
as the Gun Control Act of 1968 because he could obtain nothing better from
Congress. Along with the omnibus crime law, this legislation replaced the
thirty-year-old Federal Firearms Act with more comprehensive measures intended to help state and local law-enforcement agents, as well as federal officials, fight crime.

This new law tightened the dealer system by limiting the foreign and interstate traffic in arms primarily to bona fide importers, manufacturers, and merchandisers and by raising the dealer license fee to ten dollars.[57] It forbade the
importing of military rifles and Saturday night specials, and prohibited the sale
of rifles and shotguns to anyone under eighteen and of pistols to anyone less
than twenty-one years old. It placed restrictions but not prohibitions on the
marketing of bazookas, antitank guns, mortars, and other destructive devices.
Other provisions blocked the interstate transfer of firearms as well as their sale
to criminals and the mentally impaired. Lastly, it established a separate penalty
for anyone who used a gun in the commission of a federal felony. Johnson attributed the law's lack of an effective ban on all Saturday night specials, as well
as the defeat of his core features, to the power of the gun lobby.

In contrast, numerous firearms enthusiasts grumbled that, in this instance, their lobby had failed them. They perceived the administration as coercing patriotic gun-keepers into accepting restrictions they abhorred with the hackneyed threat of hammering out more stringent legislation. The rifle association called the act "the most sweeping Federal legislation ever imposed on U.S. firearms owners." It pointed out that Johnson wanted a tighter law and had taken "a backhand slap" at the association as a lobby.[58] The more ardent gun-keepers, then and later, denounced the law as part of "the fetish against guns." They linked its passage to "a dearth of old fashioned masculinity" in the United States, arguing in the words of one buff, "Our female-dominated, spastic, society has been working overtime for a generation or more to discredit manhood." Real men "still like blood sports, and practice the old skills, and have a hard-core contempt for softness and excessive emotionalism. They prefer to kill their own snakes."[59]

Despite the gun minority's bitterness toward the statute, in comparison to firearms regulations in other industrialized countries the new law was pallid. Various surveys found that most European countries, and others such as Argentina, Canada, and New Zealand, restricted the ownership of handguns and required their registration and/or a license to own or carry one. Britain, for instance, in 1962 had expanded its ban on ownership of small arms to include shotguns and in 1965, 1967, and 1968 had increased restrictions on obtaining firearms and penalties for possessing them with intent to endanger life or resist arrest.[60] Italy and France enforced similarly stringent laws. French gun enthusiasts complained that they lived "under the heavy heel of a law which makes even the liking for guns itself inherently suspect." Furthermore, the government assiduously discouraged "public interest in firearms and the shooting sports."[61] In Greece, where the state had long controlled guns, few citizens questioned its right to do so. Embattled Israel, with a high gun density for military purposes, imposed strict rules for private gun-permits, with harsh penalties for their infringement. Switzerland, with a high percentage of its population owning firearms, had the most permissive gun laws in Europe. Nonetheless, it required individuals who bought guns from dealers to have a license and to submit to a background check.

Even though Japan had a tradition of violence marked by assassinations of political figures, riots, and a cult of the sword, it had laws going back to 1872 that controlled the possession of guns and ammunition. Except for a few individuals who participated in international shooting exhibitions, legislation passed in 1946 and 1958 forbade private ownership of firearms. As a result, Japan's gun-control legislation came to be "among the toughest in the world," and its people's use of firearms in crimes was negligible. Mistakenly attributing this accomplishment to the postwar American occupation regime, a journalist, Yasushi Hara, commented, "we cannot quite comprehend that Americans cannot do for themselves what they did for us."[62] Exacting gun controls did not, however, cut down Japan's suicide rate, which stood as high or higher than that of the United States. Nor did the stringent laws prevent gangsters from acquiring pistols.[63]

In the United States, the investigations of select commissions, the concern over crime, and the fear engendered by rioting kept the gun-violence problem before the public as never before. For instance, one commission reported on the nation's glut of guns. In the past twenty-two years, it noted, domestic gun industries poured approximately forty-five million small arms, or as many as they had sold in the previous fifty years, onto the civilian market. Foreign producers still sold as many as ten million guns annually to American civilians, many of whom also purchased surplus government guns. Even so, as critics of the Gun Control Act of 1968 charged, "The gun control issue remained a relatively unimportant one for Congress."[64] Others who expressed disappointment with the statute characterized the title as its most imposing feature. As had the president, advocates of meaningful federal control moaned they had lost again to the NRA, widely regarded by friend and foe as the nation's most effective single-issue special-interest group. The more militant controllers portrayed the organization as Satan.

Those in the control cause overplayed their loss. Even though they had not obtained the stringent regulation they desired, they had registered notable gains, one of them being the law itself. With its authority resting on the federal government's power to regulate interstate commerce, it marked a significant step toward a national gun-control policy. In practice, the effectiveness of the law would depend on the disposition of the gun lobby to abide by it, proper enforcement by police and judges, and the willingness of Americans to embrace it as part of Washington's expanding role in social matters—as in health, the environment, welfare, and education.

13
Control Groups on the Rise

T he contending perspectives on the federal role in combating gun violence, the furor over the series of assassinations, the racial riots, and the framing of the national control law expanded the public debate over firearms regulation. Procontrol activists spoke up publicly with increasing frequency for tougher demands and with direct attacks on the gun lobby. "Put simply," in the words of one critic, "private citizens should be disarmed" and face stiff penalties for violating control laws.[1]

A religious editorialist wrote that the gun lobby wanted to solve the problem of killing and maiming with firearms "by turning a violent nation into an armed camp." He added that the "hazardousness of such an approach is exceeded only by its stupidity."[2] In response to such aroused emotion, politicians in 1968 for the first time placed differing attitudes toward the gun-control issue squarely in party platforms.

Richard M. Nixon, the Republican presidential nominee, ran on a platform that called for controls covering the "indiscriminate availability of firearms." It maintained that the primary responsibility for their regulation should remain with the states, which would establish as well safeguards for "the right of responsible citizens to collect, own and use firearms for legitimate purposes." The Democratic platform of nominee Hubert H. Humphrey praised the party's leadership in gaining enactment of the "new gun control law as a step toward putting the weapons of wanton violence beyond the reach of criminal and irresponsible hands."[3] In the campaign, however, Humphrey backed away from the platform, acting as "the hard-nosed old Nimrod, with rifle or shotgun under his arm," stalking game and NRA votes at the risk of alienating the majority of voters in favor of controls.[4]

These platforms laid out the fundamental positions of the major parties on the gun-violence struggle, usually in a crime-fighting context, for years to come. With occasional variation, Republicans would oppose federal controls and support private gun-ownership free of government regulation, except in the case of criminals. With similar consistency, Democrats would favor federal controls on gun keeping as well as regulations at the state and local level. Henceforth, clashes over what to do about guns in civilian hands and their use would become features of American politics at all levels of government and in all regions.

One such dispute started on November 6, just a few days after Nixon won the election. The Alcohol and Tobacco Tax Division of the Treasury Department revealed rules that it proposed to follow in its task of implementing the new federal gun-control act. Immediately, progun activists charged the agency with making the standard for enforcement "as tough as it is possible to make it." An academic analyst thought differently. He maintained that many of the gun proponents' charges, particularly as laid out in their magazines, "were patently false or misleading."[5] Nonetheless, with an awareness that a more conservative administration on firearms matters would soon take over, the tax division caved in and made its rules conform to the suggestions offered by the gun lobbyists.

This lobby clout bothered Lyndon Johnson even as he prepared to leave office. He confessed that "one of the great disappointments" of his presidency was the apparent unwillingness of the American people to accept "a gun registration law."[6] Ramsay Clark, who had managed much of Johnson's struggle for firearms control, viewed gun violence as "a national catastrophe." But he retained faith in regulation. "We must control guns," he wrote, "or continue to suffer the violence they generate, the crime they cause and the injury they inflict." He believed that past control efforts had not gone far enough or had failed not because of deficiency of will in government but "because history and habit are more powerful influences on human conduct than reason and recent experience."[7]

Although many people and organizations had been involved in the struggle over gun violence on a national scale, no individual did more to intensify it and bring about the strongest federal control up to this time than Johnson. Critics maintained that initially he had sponsored control legislation reluctantly but few of them could deny that later he backed it tenaciously. Often in the past, even legislators not beholden to the gun lobby had refused to embrace gun control because doing so would have brought them few votes and many headaches from gun-loving constituents. Even in the battles for the existing federal controls, without pressure from the White House most lawmakers would have settled for the status quo as the gun lobby desired.

While Johnson did not change this fence-sitting attitude, his efforts at least modified it. More even than Franklin D. Roosevelt, he used presidential clout to goad Congress and to place gun control center stage in American life. After Johnson left office, he lamented that "the issue faded away" because his successor and Congress made no serious effort to enforce the gun-control legislation he had obtained. He was wrong. Even though later executives and legislators would try to reverse the progress he had made, or attempt to brush aside the problem of civilian gun violence, it would not go away.

For years Congress had also steered away from the related issue of American participation in the international arms commerce. American firms had long profited from this trade but not without having at times to cope with attacks from investigative journalists or probing politicians. For instance, in the thirties congressional and other critics had denounced those who allegedly dominated the munitions trade as merchants of death. This agitation prompted the federal government to regulate some of this trafficking. During the Second World War when Allied belligerents pleaded for arms of all kinds and the United States produced them, these modest restraints languished. Restrictions remained dormant also during the early cold-war years.

To advance their national interests, the United States, Great Britain, and the Soviet Union gave away or sold at bargain-basement prices surplus firearms to allies or potential allies in various parts of the world. Later, in the sixties, the American government began selling arms abroad for profit on its own. It did so because newly independent nations boosted the demand for weapons and they and other countries could now pay for them. Washington wanted the money, in part to help fund the Vietnam War.

With both the government and private merchants immersed in the international arms trade, the United States became the world's leading supplier of guns and other conventional arms. The government operated the business subject to no designated controls, national or international.[8] Toward the end of the decade, when sales rose to several billion dollars annually, a number of legislators concluded that this marketing of arms abroad, as with the sales at home, needed regulation. Their efforts to bring this about, as had the domestic gun-control movement, met stiff resistance from the arms industry and the executive branch.

Nixon, a cold warrior who as a presidential candidate had spoken of a secret peace plan he never produced, was determined to win the Vietnam War with massive force. So, as president he offered no hope for regulating the trade in arms to foreign countries. He wanted no restraints on his ability to use weapons as a tool in international politics. Even though he had made law and order one of the major issues in his election campaign, he also opposed gun control at home.

At first Nixon appeared ready to continue his predecessor's assault on civilian bloodletting by extending on May 13, 1969, the life of the Johnson-appointed Commission on the Causes and Prevention of Violence. As had other commissions dealing with related problems, this one issued a report later in the year that called for more federal restrictions on the possession of firearms. It explained the obvious—that guns themselves did not cause the suicides, crime, and accidental deaths it analyzed. But it demonstrated that they did stand out as the common ingredient in the civilian mayhem.

With other substantial research, the report supported more common knowledge. It showed the doubtful utility of a gun to potential victims of crime. "Firearms, particularly handguns," it stressed, "facilitate the commission and increase the danger of the most violent crimes—assassination, murder, robbery and assault." Moreover, "the widespread availability of guns" contributed to civil disorder. Simply put, the more firearms, the more fatalities.[9]

Despite the piling of such data and the limitations of the federal gun-control statute, opponents of regulation either ignored the report or strove to counter it. Also, virtually from the day of the new federal control law's enactment, they had launched a campaign to eviscerate it. In November, they partially succeeded. They persuaded Congress to repeal the statute's provision requiring the sellers of shotgun and rifle ammunition to register the names and addresses of purchasers.

Such activity led humorist Art Buchwald to satirize the NRA's program to overturn or delete federal firearms law. "Unless everyone in America owns a handgun there will never be peace in this country [for] no country in the world offers its citizens a greater choice of guns than the United States," he wrote. "We are blessed because anyone in America can have the gun of his choice at a price he can afford. For those who are on relief and unemployed the government could supply surplus weapons from the armed forces at the same time they give out food stamps and unemployment checks. There is absolutely no reason why everyone in this country could not be armed by 1973."[10]

This humor pleased control advocates but did little for them in dealing with Congress. Friendly legislators offered a number of bills designed to close the federal control statute's loopholes and to stiffen it. Only one of the bills called for drastic change, such as outlawing the private possession of handguns. Opponents either killed these proposals or refused to report them out of the committees supposedly considering them.

The gun lobby continued likewise to thwart effective enforcement of what remained of the federal gun law. Ironically, the lobby acquired as a quasi-ally the Alcohol, Tobacco, and Firearms agency. The firearms statute had given it enlarged responsibility over weapons but the agency did little actual regulating, largely because of the gun lobby's influence and the administration's progun orientation. This Treasury division still functioned mainly to issue licenses to firearms dealers and to oversee record keeping. On July 1, 1972, to advance his war on crime and to facilitate direct control over the agency, Nixon removed the division from the immediate jurisdiction of the Internal Revenue Service. He elevated it from the status of a division to that of a bureau, or a specialized administrative unit such as the FBI, within the Treasury Department.

Technically, this change gave the Bureau of Alcohol, Tobacco, and Firearms more independence than its predecessor had enjoyed. Soon, a few of the bureau's officers attempted cautiously to exercise this paper authority by enforcing the control law as its provisions required. Immediately, gun groups saw this activity as a betrayal of an understanding with the administration that enforcement would be modest or lax. They accused the bureau of instituting arbitrary procedures to harass legitimate gun-owners and dealers. The president, who had promised the rifle association he would not increase efforts to stop the gun traffic, then placed wraps on the bureau.

Critics charged Nixon with having made his bargain with the firearms community because he believed his "political strength lies where the guns are," or basically with the Western and Southern conservative core of his constituency.[11] Those backers appreciated him. "I like Nixon," a writer for *Guns & Ammo* magazine wrote. "When a man supports the law abiding citizens' right to keep and bear arms it is likely other virtues naturally accrue to him." That journal designated him "The Shooter's Man for '72."[12]

Earlier, Congress had passed legislation that in November 1967 created the National Commission on Product Safety. For more than two years it identified products, including guns, which might present serious risks to consumers. Nixon endorsed the commission's work, praising in December 1971 a bill based on its recommendations as fully satisfying the public need for protection against hazardous products. It empowered the commission to test and regulate the marketing of thousands of commodities to determine if they might endanger the health and well being of consumers. Leaders of the still amorphous gun control movement did not share the president's perspective because in the next year when the bill became law as the Consumer Product Safety Act, only firearms had been excluded from its provisions.[13]

Many Americans, among them Justice William O. Douglas of the Supreme Court, saw the collective power of the gun owners as the source of a serious social dilemma. He summarized his position while dissenting in the decision in *Adams v. Williams* (1972) that extended the authority of police to stop and frisk suspects. He regarded the policing problem as acute "because of the ease with which anyone can acquire a pistol. A powerful lobby dins into the ears of our citizenry that these gun purchases are constitutional rights. . . . There is no reason why all pistols should not be barred to everyone except the police."[14]

Sentiment of this nature, the inadequacy of the four-year-old gun-control act, and an attempted assassination of Governor George Wallace of Alabama stirred concerned congressmen to hold hearings on a number of proposed regulatory bills. One of them, introduced by Emanuel Celler and titled the Gun Control, Registration and Licensing Act of 1971, received considerable attention.

Senator Edward M. Kennedy of Massachusetts called it "a model of the most comprehensive and logical way to begin curbing the widespread violence caused by the abuse and misuse of guns." Various religious, law enforcement, and civic groups testified in support of the proposed legislation. The Union of American Hebrew Congregations, which had opposed what it tagged as the gun lobby's repeated thwarting of effective control legislation, contended that the gun violence "has now become intolerable."[15] As usual in such instances, the NRA opposed the bills. Its spokesmen argued that "the very term 'gun control' is a misnomer. What we should be talking about is 'crime control.' "[16] The hearings produced no control legislation.

The hearings, as well as the enlivened public interest in gun violence, did lead journalists to query the president if he had changed his views on the need for additional firearms regulation. "I have always felt there should be a Federal law for the control of handguns," Nixon responded. "The problem there is to write the law . . . in such a way that it is precise and deals with that kind of handgun [the Saturday night special] which ought to be controlled." If Congress should pass such a law, he added, "I will sign it."[17] As though to compensate for their frustration over the administration's position, the more flippant controllers sarcastically disparaged firearms owners as "gun nuts" who "think their weapons are extensions of their penises."[18]

Nonetheless, within ten months the president repeated his position on gun violence, stating, "I have never hunted in my life. I have no interest in guns. . . . I am not interested in the National Rifle Association or anything from a personal standpoint." What is needed, he added, is "a precise definition which will keep the guns out of the hands of the criminals and not one that will impinge on the rights of others to have them for their own purposes in a legitimate way." He indicated an interest in a formula "that can get through Congress" but he never pursued the matter. As a critic pointed out, "It has been exactly those 'precise definitions' which . . . gun lobby senators have used to gun down restrictive legislation."[19]

Even though Nixon had given only lip service to mild regulation, in focusing on the Saturday night special he had touched on one of the least effective features of the federal law. Dealers had quickly circumvented the ban on cheap foreign handguns in two ways. First, much as they had done before the law, they imported parts, assembled them in the United States, and sold the reassembled guns as American weapons. Second, as the imports dropped, domestic manufacturers stepped up their own production of these guns. Indeed, in the seventies, sales by American gunmakers exploded. These manufacturers delivered 5.7 million small firearms to distributors.[20] In addition, as the flow of foreign rifles fell, shotgun imports increased. In all, small arms remained as available as ever, gun violence increased, and death by handguns continued to rise.

In other countries, too, the availability of inexpensive firearms contributed to violence, much of it criminal. In Nigeria, for one, when civil war ended in January 1970 guns became readily accessible to civilians throughout the country on an unprecedented scale. Armed robbery rose dramatically. To stop it, the government took draconian measures. It decreed that anyone found guilty of robbery with a firearm would suffer death before a firing squad. The robberies decreased considerably but possibly for reasons other than the decree, such as improvements in the economy. Although this approach to gun violence certainly did not deserve emulation, it did indicate the sense of desperation unfettered gun-keeping could produce.

At about the same time in the Philippines, lax or nonenforcement of colonial gun-control regulations into the era of independence, along with a proliferation of firearms, produced what outsiders called a reign of terror. Filipinos carried firearms everywhere, using them in crime, rebellion, and personal vendettas. "Macho trippers" swaggered around with guns "as if they had just stepped out of American-made Western and gangster movies."[21] This disorder, or what some termed "gun pollution," prompted, or provided the excuse, for President Ferdinand E. Marcos on September 1, 1972, to declare martial law and impose a dictatorship on the country. The gun violence abated in part because of his enforcing existing control legislation. Gun advocates claimed that the stepped-up effectiveness of regulation came at the cost of destroying civil liberties.

Other countries also had gun lobbies but they usually organized for a specific purpose as, for example, in Italy. There, despite tight firearms laws, hunters reputedly constituted "a powerful, well-heeled force" backed by a civilian hunting federation and merchants of hunting gear, rifles, and ammunition. In newspapers, the federation regularly placed advertisements showing brawny males holding firearms along with an invitation to "join the ranks of men."[22] This macho approach to shooting hardly differed from that in the United States. In political influence, however, the Italian and other foreign firearms organizations did not match America's National Rifle Association. Nor did Italy's gun crime compare in severity with that of the United States.

For 1972 the Federal Bureau of Investigation reported that murders had increased by 5 percent over the previous year while crime as a whole had decreased by 2 percent. Since 1967, however, violent crimes had jumped by 67 percent. As for years, the gun predominated as the weapon most favored in homicides. Of the 18,250 murders committed, 54 percent of the killers used handguns and another 12 percent used other firearms.[23] A third of the homicides occurred within families or between estranged lovers, whereas more than 40 percent erupted out of quarrels, mostly between people who knew each other. Criminals accounted for about 28 percent of the murders. Private investigators estimated that every two minutes someone committed a crime with a gun.[24]

Dismal statistics of this nature did little to stop, or even slow down, the gun lobby's efforts to uphold the alleged right to shoot. But the data did alarm numerous other Americans. One critic of the lobby, in a piece of admittedly sensationalist journalism, claimed that "next to the Mafia the National Rifle Association surely ranks as the most dangerously irresponsible organization in the country."[25] The more moderate opponents of the shooters, connected loosely in the gun-control movement, followed a different path. They advocated dealing with firearms violence by countering the rifle association's clout with coordinated national tactics similar to those the NRA used.

All the while, the NRA's liking for Nixon included its support of the continuing war in Vietnam. When he had campaigned for the presidency in 1968, he had capitalized on the popular opposition to the draft. He had said he would replace it with an all-volunteer army. On reaching the White House, he qualified the commitment, explaining he considered the movement to end the draft in the midst of war unwise. So he, too, extended conscription and counted on draftees to carry on the conflict in Southeast Asia. Predominantly for this reason, during his first administration student protests against the war continued, swelled, and intensified.

This dissent persuaded the president and other politicians that conscription had become an albatross. So in December 1972 he ended draft levies. When Nixon resigned the presidency in August 1974 an all-volunteer armed force had replaced the conscription army. What the nation's founders had dreaded had at last become a prominent feature of American life—a large standing army made up of professional soldiers instead of one with a core of regulars and mostly disadvantaged draftees. Few, except extreme gun activists, now spouted rhetoric about preserving what had long been patriotic myth—the concept of the self-armed citizen-soldier—even as a reason for civilian gun-keeping.

Conventional accounts tell us that just as the Vietnam War led to the creation of a professional army, that conflict, the riots, the dissent at home, and the rise in violent crime laid the groundwork for the emergence in 1974 of national gun-control organizations. Actually, as we have seen, control activists with at least hopes for national effect had been active since the beginning of the century. In the thirties, the National Anti-Weapons Society had national aspirations. In 1968 so did John Glenn's Emergency Committee for Gun Control and the National Council for a Responsible Firearms Policy.[26] Four years later the Americans for Democratic Action assembled a coalition of labor, religious, and other organizations for common action in combating gun violence. These groups diminished in importance or disappeared when the battle over a specific issue ended.

From this sketch, we can see that the precise origins of a nationwide effort to counter the affiliation of gun clubs are hazy. We do know that in 1974 control promoters moved more decisively than in the past toward a coordinated national antigun network. They succeeded in establishing one and with changes it has survived into the twenty-first century.

The new coordinating effort began when representatives of more than thirty religious, educational, and social institutions, such as the United Methodist Church, Common Cause, the American Jewish Committee, and the National Women's Political Caucus, came together. With the backing of prominent intellectuals and civic and political leaders, they formed the National Coalition to Ban Handguns and employed a young student of diplomacy, Michael K. Beard, as its executive director. It became a permanent lobby for outlawing the production and circulation of handguns, whether cheap or expensive, imported or produced domestically. As an umbrella organization, it sought to aid groups across the country that were dedicated to combating gun violence. Initially, this striving had a limited impact nationally for various reasons but mainly because the coalition was underfinanced.

What would become the most prominent of the coalition's member groups originated in the humiliation of Mark Borinsky, a graduate student at the University of Chicago. In 1973 thugs had robbed him at gunpoint, had threatened to shoot him, and had traumatized him. This experience led him, in the next year when he moved to Washington, D.C., to found with like-minded people the National Council to Control Handguns.

Meanwhile, several months after the Borinsky robbery, members of a black Muslim group known as the Zebra Killers, who declared whites so evil they must be destroyed, brought death and fear to San Francisco. One of them murdered Nick Shields, the twenty-three-year-old son of Nelson T. "Pete" Shields, a conservative Republican and a Du Pont company marketing executive. This violence turned Shields, too, into an antigun crusader. In May 1975 he left his job, joined the national council, helped energize it, and, in the next year, became its executive director.

Outwardly, the gun-control coalition seemed in tune with discernible popular sentiment. As had the opinion survey conducted sixteen years earlier, polls in June indicated that about half of all Americans favored a ban on the private ownership of handguns and 67 percent supported the idea of registering firearms. Although the National Rifle Association questioned the validity of the surveys, it took them into account in its political strategy and later countered them with surveys of its own. Those polls placed the "weight of public thinking" on its side of the gun issue.[27]

Within two years, the Council to Control Handguns reassessed its readings of the polls and its position vis-à-vis the gun lobby. Then it decided to face what it perceived as "political reality." It took as a working premise that the American public would not at this time accept "an outright ban on handguns," or as Shields put it, a ban that would be "inconsistent with the feelings of Americans."[28] As a result, the council switched its goal from seeking to prohibit the keeping of handguns to promoting their tight control while accepting their private ownership for specified purposes. It also changed its name to Handgun Control Inc. but with Shields still at the helm of the coalition.

Unlike the umbrella organization, Handgun Control Inc. focused its lobbying on incremental, selective controls rather than on immediate sweeping measures. Both it and the coalition, as did most other control groups, still viewed gun violence primarily from the perspective of abating crime. Like their opponents, and as had selective controllers for several hundred years, both organizations sought to keep guns out of the wrong hands. With these limited, old-fashioned goals, and despite their differences, the two major antigun societies battled the gun lobby. Immediately, their diverse strategies faced a critical test in Massachusetts. Citizens in the control movement there had mounted the nation's first statewide antihandgun campaign.

The effort had started slowly several years earlier when control activists in Massachusetts conducted polls that indicated popular support for strict hand-gun regulation. Nonetheless, all attempts to push a control bill through the state legislature failed. So in March 1974 the advocates founded People vs. Handguns, a statewide organization dedicated to placing the control issue be-fore the public through the initiative process. In the Boston area a major news-paper, all three television network affiliates, and many radio stations backed the tight-control idea as did 79 percent of the people in a nonbinding referen-dum in five communities.

This antigun activity moved lawmakers to try to placate the controllers with some concession. In July the legislature enacted an amendment to a 1968 gun-control law, naming it after David Bartley, speaker of the state legislature, and J. John Fox, a former criminal court judge. The new statute, which went into effect on April 1, 1975, mandated a one-year prison sentence for anyone con-victed of carrying an unlicensed gun outside the home or place of business. Despite the Bartley-Fox law's narrow focus on crime rather than on direct fire-arms control, progun attorneys attacked it in state and federal courts as uncon-stitutional but failed to overturn it.[29]

As research later would indicate, the Bartley-Fox measure had mixed results, in part because police and the courts did not enforce it rigidly as against pre-sumed respectable violators. It did not produce a decrease in armed robberies, reduce the number of firearms in the state, or directly deter crime. It did con-tribute to diminished gun assaults and gun homicides. Even so, proponents of tougher legislation regarded it as inadequate.[30] In December these controllers succeeded in obtaining the necessary number of signatures on a petition to qualify their referendum on gun control for the ballot. It proposed a ban on the private ownership of handguns except for collectors, licensed pistol clubs, police, and security personnel.

Early in the referendum campaign, an alliance of sportsmen's clubs, calling itself the Gun Owners Action League, opposed the ban movement. The league gained the support of the National Rifle Association whose leadership viewed Massachusetts as "a pilot battleground in the national effort to halt the increas-ing threat of firearms control laws."[31] Gun manufacturers, such as Smith & Wesson, also contributed funds to the progun side or promoted advertising that supported it. The Democratic governor, Michael Dukakis, on the other hand, favored the referendum, said he would vote for it, and also urged the people to do so "if they were serious about controlling crime."[32] Despite all this procontrol activity, in the course of the campaigning public support for the referendum dwindled. On November 2, 1976, the voters defeated the measure by a margin of two to one.

Stunned control activists pondered why they had lost so decisively in one of the most liberal states in the nation. Diverse factors contributed to the defeat. First, opponents raised more money than proponents. With their ample dollars the gun people through advertising succeeded in labeling the referendum as "really nothing less than confiscation" and in convincing many voters that the gun ban "would leave the law-abiding citizen unprotected." Second, the gun-owner league persuaded voters the measure would be too expensive to enforce. Third, the opponents had a deeper concern with the issue than the control proponents who had spread their interest over other proposals on the ballot. Fourth and last, the controllers pursued a flawed strategy.

The gun fraternity's victory in this battle enhanced its reputation for skill in overcoming initial majority sentiment on firearms regulation while exposing the weaknesses in the control movement's coordinating effort. The movement still suffered from a splintered attitude within its constituent groups toward what goals they could or should pursue in common.

As for the gun lobby, its success in Massachusetts impressed friend and foe. Its handling of the control issue on the national level through its allies in Congress and in the White House, however, held greater significance. Gerald R. Ford, who had assumed the presidency in August 1974 when scandal forced Nixon to resign rather than face impeachment, followed his predecessor's policies where he could. For instance, in April of the next year Ford suspended draft registration and later terminated it. He also adopted Nixon's policy of opposition to gun control almost to the letter but defended it more forthrightly. When journalists asked Ford repeatedly if he would get behind effective control legislation, he responded as though NRA propagandists had programmed him.

The new president explained he had "very strong feelings" about gun control and that he had "long been an adamant opponent of the registration of guns or the registration of gun owners, period." He favored state and local prohibitions on the manufacture of Saturday night specials but not on other firearms because "it is the person who uses the gun that causes the trouble." He claimed that the "most effective way to combat the illicit use of handguns" was mandatory prison terms for those who employed them in a crime. Even with such punishment, he urged caution so as not to "infringe upon the rights of law abiding citizens" or "penalize the people who are collectors or individuals who properly use guns."[33]

Throughout his presidency Ford never departed from these views, even after surviving two efforts to assassinate him. Lynette Alice Fromme, a young member of a cult with a record of murder, made the first attempt on September 5, 1975, in Sacramento, California. From a distance of two feet she pointed a borrowed automatic .45-caliber pistol at the president as he walked from his hotel. Fortunately, a Secret Service agent disarmed her before she could fire.

The second attempted assault followed shortly, on October 22 in San Francisco. When Ford left the St. Francis Hotel, Sara Jane Moore, a maladjusted police informer, at a distance of forty feet attempted to fire at him with a .38-caliber Smith & Wesson revolver. As she aimed, a bystander grabbed her arm. She still fired one shot but it missed the president. The court found Fromme guilty of attempted assassination and sentenced her to life imprisonment. Moore pleaded guilty to the same charge and received the same sentence. These acts again linked the protection of presidents and other public figures with the gun-violence issue, placing it in headline news everywhere in the country.

As with the assassination attempts, the clamor for tighter curbs on firearms use did not noticeably affect the rifle association's lobbying. It continued to devote time and money on specific legislative races where tangible results came promptly. It claimed credit, for example, for the earlier close defeats, in 1970, of two gun-control proponents, Democratic senators Joseph Clark of Pennsylvania and Joseph Tydings of Maryland. Tydings had commented, "I suppose this will discourage others from taking on the gun lobby," and apparently it did.[34]

Buoyed by triumphs such as these, the association in 1975 reconstituted its lobbying activities by concentrating them in its Institute for Legislative Action formed two years earlier. The institute could do its own fund-raising and even act independently of the rest of the association. More intensively than had NRA activists in the past, the institute concentrated on mobilizing support among legislators and gun proponents everywhere so as to balk gun-control legislation in the states as well as in Washington. When in the summer congressional committees in both houses of Congress held hearings on possible gun-control measures, the NRA opposed them and the legislators' interest in the matter waned. Soon, the institute became the association's center of power. Its watchdog activities, along with the politicians' knowledge that gun owners made up one of the largest and most potent single-interest blocs of the voting population, had an impact on the 1976 presidential campaign.

14
Gun Lobby Glory Years

During the later cold-war years, the role of the United States as global gunmaster became a political issue. Even though President Gerald Ford defended the selling of weapons abroad, Congress responded to the mounting criticism of the program with restrictive legislation. In 1976 the legislators pulled together earlier piecemeal restraints on arms exports with some modest reforms and placed them in the International Security Assistance and Arms Export Control Act. Armaments industry lobbyists blocked most of the important initial reform features, such as an annual ceiling on arms shipments.

When Congress finally passed and Ford signed the legislation, it contained striking inconsistencies. In one section it called for disarmament and for reduced international arms races and in another for arming allied countries, as in NATO, as well as countries threatened with "international communism."[1] By requiring the executive branch to report its weapons sales to Congress, the legislation had at least one seemingly workable control over the dispersal of firearms. It allowed Congress to exercise a limited veto over the sale of military arms to other countries.

In the matter of firearms in civilian hands at home, Congress still used its power to block or weaken controls but the courts continued to side with the controllers, as in the case of *United States v. Warin*, 530 F. 2d 103 (1976). Francis J. Warin, an engineer and designer of firearms, had made and kept a 9mm submachine gun without paying a transfer tax or registering it as required by federal law. When brought to court in December 1975 he claimed the right, as a member of a vague entity he called the "sedentary militia" of Ohio, and as protected by the Second Amendment, to possess the weapon unencumbered.

On February 4, 1976, the federal Court of Appeals for the Sixth Circuit dismissed Warin's contentions. It held he had "no private right to keep and bear arms under the Second Amendment" that would bar his prosecution and conviction. The court also rejected the *amicus curiae* brief that the Second Amendment Foundation had filed. It said the foundation's arguments were "based on the erroneous supposition that the Second Amendment is concerned with the rights of individuals." It also stated, "There can be no question that an organized society which fails to regulate the importation, manufacture and transfer of highly sophisticated lethal weapons in existence today does so at its peril." Warin appealed his conviction to the Supreme Court. In June 1976 it affirmed the lower court's decision.[2]

This and similar judicial rulings, as well as majority public sentiment in favor of regulation, contributed to making gun control a significant issue in the 1976 presidential campaign.[3] Ford continued wooing domestic gun-owners, promising that if elected he would "oppose any attempt to deprive law-abiding citizens of their traditional freedom to own firearms." To curry favor with the NRA, he even retreated from his earlier stand on Saturday night specials. He went along fully with his party's platform, which defended "the inviolability of the right to keep and bear arms," and in line with NRA lobbying called for the repeal of the Gun Control Act of 1968. As he told the editor of the *American Rifleman*, he believed "in punishing only those who commit crimes, not gun owners."[4] The pleased rifle association almost anointed him with an endorsement.

Ford's Democratic opponent, Jimmy Carter, ran on a platform calling for unspecified federal gun controls. Ironically, at times he sounded like Ford, stating he believed in protecting the rights of the "vast majority of hunters and other gun sportsmen [who] use their arms respectfully and responsibly." They "should not be penalized," Carter added, "because criminals use firearms, particularly handguns, to commit crimes." He also announced, "I favor registration of handguns, a ban on the sale of cheap handguns, reasonable licensing provisions including a waiting period and prohibition of ownership by anyone convicted of a crime involving a gun and by those not mentally competent."[5]

In addition, Carter made an issue of arms sales abroad. The United States cannot, he declared, be "both the world's leading champion of peace and the world's leading supplier of weapons of war."[6] He scorned Nixon's and Ford's efforts to "justify this unsavory business on the cynical ground that by rationing out the means of violence we can somehow control the world's violence."[7] Carter promised that if elected he would promote additional regulation of the sale of conventional arms, foreign as well as domestic.

Still, during a televised national debate when Ford repeated his views on gun control, Carter did not challenge him and even seemed to agree with him. Carter stated, "I have been a hunter all my life and happen to own both shotguns and rifles." He went on, saying the only purpose in the "registering of handguns and not long guns of any kind would be to prohibit the ownership of those guns by those who have used them in the commission of a crime or who have been mentally incompetent to own a gun." At this point, he favored "a limited approach" to the gun-control question.[8]

Despite Carter's inconsistencies, after winning the election he appeared determined to seek stronger firearms controls, especially over the marketing of handguns. His chief political adviser, W. Hamilton Jordan, announced in a newspaper interview in December that "Carter will really go on gun control and really be tough. We're going to get those bastards [the progun activists]."[9] Once in the White House, Carter made plans to address the issue of gun violence. His attorney general, Griffin Bell, told the Senate Judiciary Committee, "It is past time for handgun control," and the Department of Justice proceeded to draft comprehensive regulatory legislation.[10]

Developments in the government's backyard appeared to indicate the time was ripe for more regulation. During the election campaign, District of Columbia authorities had enacted a firearms control measure that because of litigation did not go firmly into effect until February 1977. Researchers reported that "the law reduced gun-related suicides and homicides substantially and abruptly," or by about 25 percent.[11]

Meantime, trouble had burst to the surface among leaders of the National Rifle Association. It had started during the debate over the 1968 gun control bill when Franklin Orth, a former major general and the association's executive vice president, stated that "any sane American" could not object to placing in the bill "the instrument which killed" President John Kennedy.[12] Hard-liners, who comprised a majority of the life, or voting, members, did object. They and the old guard also clashed over plans for the future of the association. On May 21, 1977, when members gathered at their convention in Cincinnati, Ohio, the hard-liners rebelled, removed the old guard, and placed Harlon B. Carter, a hunter, a target shooter, a lifetime United States border patrolman, and quintessentially one of their own, in charge.

In common with their predecessors, the hard-liners assumed that even minor measures would open the door to a flood of legislation designed to deprive gun owners of all claimed rights. Both old-timers and the inflexible new leaders wanted to repeal existing federal controls and block all antigun proposals. They differed in that the militants refused to compromise on virtually any controls.

They girded for battle against the control movement and the government in Washington as though they were battling Lucifer. As another of their leaders, Neal Knox, put it, "We are now taking the fight to our foes, forcing them to spend their strengths, their energies and their money."[13] This tough posture soon began weakening the longtime close relationship the NRA had enjoyed with numerous law-enforcement agencies.

At this point President Carter focused attention more on foreign arms-sales than on gun-control issues at home. He did so in keeping with his campaign rhetoric that had deplored the nation's role as arms salesman. He spoke on this foreign gun problem often, lamenting the nation's status as "the major arms supplier to the world." He added, though, "We have been working with our own allies to cut down this traffic." In May 1977 he announced that henceforth his administration would "view arms transfers as an exceptional foreign policy implement."[14] In July, as part of his policy to promote human rights worldwide, he held up sales of police firearms to Argentina, Uruguay, El Salvador, and other countries because they might be employed to suppress human rights.[15] Still, his government continued to merchandise guns to other countries.

The next year a State Department official rationalized why. "We became the world's largest seller of arms not because we were irresponsible masters of the hard sell," she explained, "but because we were fully convinced that a larger allied role in their own defense was in our national interest and that it was equally in our interest to sell them the required arms." Consequently, whereas Carter imposed a number of specific controls on the sale of arms abroad, he never did freeze or reduce those sales.[16]

The related problems of terrorism and the illegal flow of guns across frontiers, however, prompted other countries to seek enforceable controls on an international level. On January 28, 1978, at Strasbourg, the states of the Council of Europe adopted a special Convention on the Control of the Acquisition and Possession of Firearms by Individuals. It directed the contracting countries to assist each other in suppressing the illegal traffic in firearms and in tracing their movement across frontiers. It also urged strict national controls that would correspond with its rules. This effort did not stop either terrorism or gun trafficking but it spotlighted the connection between national and international gun violence.

Many in the Carter administration recognized the linkage. Those in the Justice Department who did so had consulted with gun-control leaders and drafted a bill for additional domestic firearms regulation. It called for national registration of firearms and a ban on many models of handguns. In June 1977, after completing the bill, they sent it to the president. Suddenly a wave of political trepidation, or what some called a failure of nerve, struck the administration. It feared massive grassroots opposition orchestrated by the gun lobby hard-liners. The president, therefore, chose to appease organized firearm owners by not introducing the bill on Capitol Hill.

In a plan announced in March of the next year, however, Carter did seek to improve the ability of the Bureau of Alcohol, Tobacco, and Firearms (BATF) to trace guns involved in crimes. The changes in the regulations he proposed called for individual identification of every new gun by manufacturer, model, caliber, and number; quarterly reports by dealers on their sales; and reports within twenty-four hours on all stolen guns. Mail to Congress condemning the proposal as "the first step toward gun control" outnumbered that of gun opponents by a margin of eighteen to one.[17] In response to this pressure, the House of Representatives removed $4.5 million from the budget for administering the program and hence killed it.

Carter's control agenda suffered also from opposition within agencies of the federal government. For example, he wanted to abolish the subsidy for the civilian marksmanship program and to destroy surplus M-1 rifles rather than sell seven hundred thousand of them to rifle association shooters as the National Board for the Promotion of Rifle Practice had proposed.[18] The army as well as the gun lobby fought him. Congress retained the program and the army continued to sell thousands of the surplus guns and ammunition to civilians at low prices, still through the NRA and its affiliates.

Meanwhile, NRA officers persisted in slamming the administration's efforts to enforce BATF regulations, which they labeled a form of gun registration, an interpretation of gun registration that the bureau's head denied.[19] As well, they attacked Carter for denying tax-exempt status to one of the organization's affiliates. The gun lobby obtained the exemption anyway, from Congress. In addition, the Senate voted to cut $3.8 million from the Treasury Department's budget to make sure the BATF would not establish a computerized tracking system.[20]

These skirmishes over control enforcement led shooters to denounce Carter for instituting what they perceived as "anti-gun, anti-hunting policies" and accused him of allowing the firearms bureau to harass, abuse, and persecute gun owners for mere "technical violations." In its campaign to block the president's gun measures, the rifle association spent more than $13.8 million. One of its editorial writers complained that "the litany of Jimmy Carter's affront on our

Second Amendment rights and upon hunting is endless." Despite his posturing as a hunter, "a good old boy, one of us," they said, "he is not."[21]

In 1978 also, through the National Institute of Justice the administration funded a review of the literature on guns to be carried out by the Social and Demographic Research Center of the University of Massachusetts. The completed study ended with a negative evaluation of the corpus of gun-control literature.[22]

The concern, and even confusion, over gun control expressed in various studies stemmed often from methodology but also from excessive attention to firearms laws and crime statistics. Laws became effective mainly when enforced with consistency. In the United States local, state, and legislative bodies passed numerous control laws but rarely carried them out meaningfully. For example, both New York City and Chicago at this time had on the books gun-control laws considered as among the strictest in the nation. Yet in New York a state senator, Ralph J. Marino, complained that "courts and prosecutors have effectively repealed the state's gun-control laws." While in Chicago Stephen A. Schiller, director of a crime commission, commented that "unlawful use of weapons charges evidently aren't considered important by the court, or the prosecutor, or the police. . . . The prosecutors blow these cases like popcorn."[23]

A survey of convictions for violations of gun laws showed "a pattern of low and steadily declining enforcement of gun control laws." Moreover, punishment for violations appeared as lenient as the conviction rate was low. A conservative estimate in 1979 indicated that "a violator of gun laws has only a .17 percent chance of being fined or going to jail."[24]

As for the administration's lack of progress on controls, the president blamed the legislators' subservience to the gun lobby. He explained, "Although I do favor increased safety of the American people, I think to pursue it aggressively in the Congress would be a mistake."[25] In addition, the power of the weapons lobby persuaded him that just the effort to improve the existing modest gun regulations would jeopardize his political base among conservatives in the South. His wavering policy on gun violence alienated both sides in the struggle to contain it.

Despite Carter's retreat on the controls issue when only presidential goading would produce any kind of action in Congress, the activities of the antigun groups showed some results in court. One case began when Geoffrey S. Gavett, on his own as a citizen, sought to buy a surplus rifle from the army. It turned him down because he did not belong to the rifle association. In November 1978, with the backing of the National Coalition to Ban Handguns, which wanted to end the shooters' government subsidy, he sued. The controllers' attorneys argued that the seventy-year-old statute granting association members the exclusive right to the guns was unconstitutional. A federal court agreed, striking down the law's requirement that restricted purchases to association members.

Control advocates rejoiced in this small victory over the gun lobby for its rarity. They welcomed it also because hate groups such as the revived Ku Klux Klan and the Minutemen had been obtaining many of the government weapons. Now, with the court ruling most civilians found the acquiring of surplus guns more difficult, particularly because buyers still had to belong to a government marksmanship club. Those clubs remained affiliated with the rifle association. Moreover, the government continued to subsidize national shooting matches conducted mainly by NRA members. It also allowed them to use federal shooting ranges free of charge and to construct their own ranges on public property. Understandably, the controllers' sense of victory at court had a short life.

The gun-control movement also suffered from internal friction. Despite its growth and efforts to coordinate constituent groups, the largest organizations within it vied for influence and still differed in objectives. The National Council to Control Handguns, which later changed its name to the Coalition to Stop Gun Violence, sought to ban all handguns except for police and for the military. It achieved a number of low-level successes, as in the Gavett case.

Handgun Control Inc. continued to fight for limited controls such as gun licensing and registration. It soon became the foremost control organization in the country. Within a few years it recruited what it called a citizen army of 750,000 members. Like the progun clubs it opposed, it lobbied Congress and state and local governments, aided gun-control groups throughout the country, endorsed and contributed money to politicians who agreed with its objectives, and sought to defeat those who did not. At this time, though, all the control activity had less effect on legislators than did the influence of the gun lobby.

What did attract the attention of previously disinterested legislators to the control movement was pervasive crime. In these years, crime rose in virtually every society that kept and made available reliable statistics. In the United States crime, as defined by government researchers, moved toward an all-time peak.[26] Crime increased even in Japan, England, and Canada—countries with notably stringent controls on the private possession of firearms. In Britain, where robbery appeared to account for the growth in felonies, the government sought to tighten gun-control legislation. In Japan the escalation in crime seemed connected to the temptations of affluence.

Even with their crime surges, these countries experienced much less gun violence than did the United States. There were still "over four times as many serious crimes per person in the United States as crimes of any sort per person in Japan." Homicides in the most violent American cities, usually with guns, exceeded even Jamaica's "extremely high" rate. There authorities tried to overcome the firearms violence with the Gun Court Act of 1974, a tough firearms control measure. They had difficulty doing so because of opposition from a "vociferous gun lobby."[27]

Analysts could not explain the precise reasons for these differences in national crime rates. As in previous studies, the considerable data they compiled did point to a connection between the high incidence of crime in the United States and the easy availability of guns. New surveys on the subject showed also that Americans used guns in about two-thirds of all homicides and suicides. Investigators concluded that "for any population group, the availability and lethality of firearms are major determinants in such death rates." Their information, which indicated that in moments of rage people grabbed the most readily accessible weapon, supported this judgment. Since Americans used the gun more than any other weapon, the statistics connoted a "strong correlation between the presence of firearms in the home and firearm injury and death."[28]

Psychological experiments also suggested that the presence of a gun in itself often stimulated deadly violence.[29] This research and the judgments drawn from it convinced doctors, social scientists, and others that guns cheapened life and menaced public health. They advocated that government should control firearms much as it did noxious substances, food packaging, and potentially dangerous medicines. Through the research of the professional scientists and the publicity it elicited, the availability concept gained wide acceptance.

Progun writers constantly disputed this linkage between guns and killing. They usually cited Switzerland as an example of a country with widespread firearms ownership but also with low homicide and crime rates. Research revealed flaws in the shooters' assumptions. It showed private ownership of guns in Switzerland as no greater "than in neighboring countries." It indicated also, as the investigator reported, that the Swiss had "remarkably high rates of homicides and suicides committed with guns" but of course not as high as those in the United States.[30]

Nonetheless, gun defenders argued that controls, wherever instituted, had not reduced crime primarily because firearms remained "readily available on the criminal black market." Some of them admitted, however, that controls worked elsewhere, as in Canada after the passage in August 1977 of stringent

federal gun legislation that called for prison terms for violators. There the people had "no *prima facie* right . . . to own handguns," and police had wide powers
to search for and seize private firearms. A Canadian police officer speculated
that his country's control system succeeded because, unlike the United States,
"we don't have the tradition here of people believing it's an inherent right to
carry a gun."[31]

True enough, in the United States many citizens still passionately defended
that assumed right and still perceived the gun in mythical terms as a symbol
of a unique freedom. Frequently they gave firearms greater significance in their
lives than even a job. "Mark this well," Harlon Carter, the NRA's spokesman
for this attitude, wrote at the time, "without a single exception in the history
of all peoples, those who are oppressed never—repeat, *never*—have arms." On
another occasion he stated with equal hyperbole, "Gun prohibition is the inevi-
table harbinger of oppression."[32]

Other NRA leaders of this persuasion and their supporters in Congress
claimed at this time to represent fifty million gun owners. This figure fluctu-
ated up and down even among spokespersons for the association.[33] Regardless
of the number represented, defenders of gun keeping still felt abused by the
Bureau of Alcohol, Tobacco, and Firearms. They accused it of violating their
constitutional and civil rights with various tactics. For one, they claimed, it
lured "honest, loyal citizens into violating the law through entrapment procedures" because honest gun-keepers were easier targets than "wily hardened
criminals."[34]

Gun lobbyists consequently prevailed on a Senate judiciary subcommittee
to investigate the complaints. The committee heard mostly from NRA representatives or supporters who testified that BATF agents pursued "law-abiding
individuals, seeking to inveigle them into unintentional and technical violations" while "almost totally ignoring the real criminal."[35] The director of the
BATF, G. R. Dickerson, denied the accusation, stating that "there has never
been an instance in which an employee of ATF has been prosecuted successfully for such an offense" and that he "would not tolerate such behavior."[36]
This defense did not deflect the accusations of the aggressive gun-keepers and
legislators.

During this controversy, control advocates derived consolation from the decision in *Lewis v. United States*, 496 U.S. 334 (1980). In this case the Supreme
Court rejected an appeal from a felon who had been convicted of violating the
crime control act of 1968. He contended he had a Second Amendment right
to possess a firearm. The Court ruled the amendment did not confer a right

on individuals that made them immune to regulation. This decision followed the principle, now well established among federal jurists, that "legislative restrictions on the use of firearms do not trench upon any constitutionally protected liberties." The Court commented also that the practice of medicine and even of holding office in a labor union were "activities far more fundamental than the possession of a firearm" and they were subject to regulation.[37]

This decision and the Democratic Party platform for the presidential campaign of 1980 also pleased gun controllers. The platform again urged a ban on Saturday night specials and recommended additional but limited federal firearms control legislation. The gun lobby, which found the Court's line of reasoning as well as the Democratic platform detestable, countered by denouncing both. Gun defenders liked the Republican platform, which called for preserving the right of private citizens to bear arms and for reversing the feeble national gun controls.[38] The gun lobby spent its money and exerted its considerable politicking influence to back mostly Republican officeholders and candidates beholden to it.

As the presidential campaign moved into high gear, at the instigation of cold-war militarists Carter revived the possibility of conscription, a firearms-related issue that for different reasons riled elements in both the Republican and Democratic camps. Liberal Democrats who usually favored firearms control also tended to oppose putting guns involuntarily into the hands of America's youth. They felt abandoned when Congress voted for a revival of youth registration for conscription. Although the professional armed forces had ample resources to handle most international crises, hawks portrayed draft registration as a necessary preparation for a possible showdown with the Soviet Union over its recent invasion of Afghanistan. Despite the opposition of the antidraft and pro-gun-control segments in his own party, Carter in July resumed the registration.

Many Republicans, among them Carter's opponent, the former movie star Ronald Reagan, viewed the peacetime draft as an infringement on personal liberty much as they did firearms control. In the perspective of organized gunowners, Reagan's equating guns with civil liberty as well as his record on arms keeping made him the Republican Party's ideal standard-bearer. As a lifetime member of the National Rifle Association and as governor of California, he had received from that state's affiliate its top honor, the outstanding public service award.

Reagan spoke openly of his admiration for guns, stating he liked shooting animals for sport. "Trophy hunting," he told *Field and Stream* magazine in echoing what hunters touted as gospel, "is a form of harvesting." He went on, "I like to shoot, and have done my share of varmint shooting on the ranch. I am not much of a hunter, but I believe I would enjoy it more if I were going to use the meat." Shooters relished hearing such talk because many believed hunting preserved "healthy, sustainable wildlife populations" and "is a legacy that should be passed along."[39] They liked the Californian so much that the NRA for the first time endorsed a presidential contender—him.

When Reagan trounced Carter to capture the presidency, gun-lobby constituents rejoiced that again their strategy of pouring money into political campaigns and courting influence in Washington had worked. *Washington Reports*, an NRA publication, boasted that "the political clout of the nation's gun owners and sportsmen was clearly evident in the final outcome of the November election."[40] The firearms fraternity claimed credit, too, for helping progun candidates in Senate and House races ride into office on Reagan's coattails.

In January 1981, a few days before inauguration, President-elect Reagan paid a goodwill visit to Ciudad Juarez, Mexico, across the border from El Paso, Texas. There he presented his host, President José López Portillo, with a Remington rifle, as though to reaffirm his own identification with firearms. This gesture went over well with admiring gun devotees while also boosting Reagan's image for macho showmanship. Carter, on the other hand, as he prepared to bid farewell to the presidency, lamented the power over Congress and the public of single-issue and special-interest organizations, labeling them a disturbing factor in American political life.

This concern had no impact on Reagan. Even though other presidents had been beholden to single-issue groups, he quickly became the first one to assume openly what appeared to many as the role of popular spokesman for such an organization. He boasted of his ties to the National Rifle Association. The closeness of this relationship became evident when the gun lobby stepped up its campaign against the Bureau of Alcohol, Tobacco, and Firearms, dubbing it derisively the bureau of "Whiskey, Cigarettes, and Pistols."

As before, gun-club officials blasted the BATF as irresponsible because, they alleged, it "persecutes ordinary citizens—people who have never been a party to crime." They claimed the bureau's agents "behave like street thugs" and charged it with "creating phony gun law violations to justify its existence."[41] A film the NRA produced at this time, *It Can Happen Here*, portrayed those agents as "Nazi Gestapos" and "jack-booted fascists." Representative John Dingell of Michigan, now a rifle association board member, castigated them as "knaves and rogues," asserting, "I would love to put them in jail. I would dearly love it."[42]

This animosity intensified when the bureau, in line with its legal mandate though not in accord with the president's position, announced renewed plans to computerize its records to facilitate gun tracing. As before, shooters immediately flooded Congress and the Treasury Department with letters denouncing the "gun police." Reminiscent of the tactic used against Carter, Congress denied the bureau the $4.2 million appropriation necessary to implement the computerizing program.

In addition, Reagan's staffers worked out a plan to dissolve the BATF, return its tax collection duties to the Internal Revenue Service, and transfer its enforcement authority of the firearm laws to the Secret Service. Many in Congress and numerous law officials opposed the scheme. Then, when gun-lobby strategists pondered its possible effect, they realized that Secret Service enforcement would be tougher and more difficult to counter than that of the bureau. They therefore halted their assault. As the lobbyists desired, the president agreed to an artful compromise. He accepted the budget cuts as meeting his objective of crippling the BATF but allowed it to survive as the weakened arm of gun-law enforcement.

This emasculating did not significantly affect the gun-violence struggle because control upholders had long viewed the BATF as a toothless watchdog. In large part, its weakness stemmed from gun-lobby might, from congressional and even executive hostility, and from a chronic insufficiency of personnel and other resources. Consequently, it relied heavily on voluntary compliance with many of the laws it had the responsibility of enforcing. Bureau officials admitted that in expending limited resources they assigned low priority to monitoring gun-law violations. They also did little to abate firearms smuggling. This laxity contributed to the status of the United States as the major source of illegal as well as legal guns shipped to nations everywhere.

Reagan liked the idea of selling arms. Soon after taking office, he not only reversed Carter's already weak effort to cut down on foreign arms-sales but also took steps to boost the merchandising of small arms. Reagan's administration justified such arms transfers as "a vital and constructive instrument of our foreign policy" and "an increasingly important component of our global security posture."[43] Firearms sales soared to new heights.

Domestically, the loose enforcement of weak controls continued to assure Americans of freer access to guns than other peoples in industrially advanced countries. This freedom made it easier for disgruntled Americans to shoot at their presidents more often than did dissidents in other countries at their rulers and to kill or maim others seemingly at will. Hard-core gun defenders dismissed this record of violence as having little to do with the availability of firearms. Some of them even blamed the victims, mouthing platitudes such as violent crime is feasible only if its victims are cowards.

This banality could hardly apply to Reagan's behavior when on March 30, 1981, John W. Hinckley Jr., a mentally disturbed young man who considered himself something of a warrior, stalked him. Armed with a Saturday night special, or Rohm RG-14 .22-caliber revolver made in Germany and purchased at a Dallas, Texas, pawnshop for twenty-nine dollars, he shot the president just below the heart as he stood outside the Washington Hilton Hotel. Hinckley also seriously wounded a police officer and a Secret Service agent, and lodged an exploding bullet in the head of James Brady, the forty-year-old White House press secretary, paralyzing him for life. Hinckley thus continued a sad tradition. Like every assassin or would-be assassin of presidents, he used a gun because he knew it as the most deadly concealable weapon at hand. Fortunately for Reagan that gun did not damage him irreparably.

Hinckley tried to kill out of an obsession for a young actress, Jodie Foster, then a student at Yale University. He wanted to impress her by committing a "historical deed" with a gun. After buying the weapon, he wrote a poem, "Guns Are Fun!" It reads, in part:

See that living legend over there?
With one little squeeze of the trigger
I can put that person at my feet moaning and groaning and pleading with God.
This gun gives me pornographic power.
If I wish, the President will fall and the world will look at me in disbelief
All because I own an inexpensive gun.[44]

For a time, the assault on the president appeared to give a boost to the gun-control movement. Then, to the astonishment of much of the public but to the admiration of gun enthusiasts, when Reagan recovered from his suffering he refused to change his position on guns. In his first news conference following the assault, he expressed concern "that focusing on gun control as an answer to the crime problem" would divert attention from "really" trying "to solve the crime problem." Shortly after, he also dismissed control laws as "virtually unenforceable."[45]

In a full-page tribute, *Pistolero*, a magazine that existed "for Americans who

believe that God, Guns & Guts Made US Great," stated, "THANK GOD FOR PRES-
IDENT REAGAN, a man who, even after being shot, realizes that more gun controls are not the solution to our crime problem." It added, "Here's a man of
guts, common sense and vision. May he live to be 120!" Similarly, Bill Ruger,
an executive of one of the nation's largest gun manufacturers, wrote, "Shooters,
generally—at least, handgunners—are fortunate that we have the President we
have."[46] The NRA named Reagan its Man of the Year.

Meanwhile, shortly after the assassination attempt, Geoffrey LaGioia, a resident of Morton Grove, Illinois, a Chicago suburb, applied to the local authorities for a permit to open a firearms store near the community's junior high
school. Most residents who "didn't want the kids looking in the window dream-
ing of guns" opposed the dealership but could find no legal grounds to block
it other than by prohibiting the sale and private possession of handguns. So, on
June 8, 1981, the town's trustees passed an ordinance requiring owners, except
mainly gunsmiths and licensed firearms collectors, to surrender their handguns
or be subject to a five-hundred-dollar fine. These trustees then voted to make
copies of the ordinance available to other municipalities and to urge Congress
to pass a similar antigun law.

As the nation's first community to ban most handguns, Morton Grove immediately became the center of extensive press and television coverage. Despite
the ordinance's focus on just handguns and its loopholes that permitted considerable firearms ownership, control advocates praised the measure. Opponents,
on the other hand, denounced it as vile, Nazi and communist inspired, and the
most dangerous attack ever staged against the right to keep and bear arms.

Four handgun owners in the village, including Victor D. Quilici, immediately
filed suit in a state court to block enforcement of the ordinance. The suits were
consolidated into one, and the litigation as *Quilici v. Village of Morton Grove*,
695 F. 2d 261, 270 (7th Cir. 1982), moved to a federal district court. The National Rifle Association and the Second Amendment Foundation financed the
plaintiffs, and the National Coalition to Ban Handguns paid the village's legal
fees. As usual in gun cases, the plaintiffs argued that the ordinance violated
the Second Amendment. Since for over a decade the Illinois constitution had
included a right-to-bear-arms provision, the gun litigants contended the Morton Grove law also breached the state constitution. Rejecting these contentions, the district court on December 29, 1982, ruled that the village had
exercised a valid police power to protect public health and safety and had not
deprived the plaintiffs of rights under federal or state constitutions.[47]

The Morton Grove ordinance did not, as gun-control advocates had assumed, stimulate local handgun bans across the country. Indeed, in the next year as though to rebut it, officials in Kennesaw, Georgia, a town of seven thousand near Atlanta, passed an ordinance requiring its citizens to keep guns in their homes. This legislation changed little except to bring notoriety to the town because 90 percent of its inhabitants already owned guns. In a few other small towns, banks tried to increase profit by offering depositors guns in lieu of money interest. The rush of new customers to the bank in Findlay, Illinois, astonished its executives. One of them explained it in terms of the town's conservatism expressed as belief in God, country, and guns.

Meanwhile, as the rifle association appealed the Morton Grove decision, it launched a nationwide campaign for preemption laws forbidding communities to pass gun ordinances stronger than state regulations. This endeavor had significant effects. For example, in 1982 after a gun wielder murdered the mayor of San Francisco along with a supervisor, the board of supervisors passed a limited ban on handguns in the city. Before the ordinance could go into effect, a California appellate court invalidated it on the preemption principle. In the next decade, as other communities passed ordinances regulating firearms, dealer and rifle association attorneys raised the preemption issue. With the courts ruling in favor of these state preemptions and with the president and Congress on the side of the gun lobby, its glory years rolled on.[48]

15

A Wholly Owned
NRA Subsidiary?

In the eighties a phase of the gun-violence struggle that generated a noteworthy legislative battle began when the arms industry developed armor-piercing bullets. Ostensibly they were designed to provide police with sufficient concentrated firepower to pierce engine blocks and stop cars involved in criminal activity. When law-enforcement officers began using the ammunition in their duties, they found they could not control its flight. Furthermore, in addition to penetrating cars and bouncing off walls and sidewalks and placing anyone nearby in peril, the bullets pierced the body armor worn mainly by police. Officers therefore categorized these bullets as potential cop-killers, declaring they had no legitimate use in or out of law enforcement.

As we noted earlier, this position differed from that of the NRA, whose tough-minded leadership had alienated various police and sheriff agencies. Early in 1982 the fissure widened. At that time at the behest of police organizations, Mario Biaggi, a former New York policeman, joined by New York's Democratic senator Daniel Patrick Moynihan, introduced legislation that would prohibit the manufacture, importation, sale, and use of armor-piercing bullets. Immediately, gun lobbyists opposed it as well as similar legislation proposed in states and cities. As Neal Knox, then the NRA's chief lobbyist, put it, "There's no such thing as a good bullet or a bad bullet."[1]

Vigilant rifle association monitors, via telegrams, alerted hundreds of firearms enthusiasts to protest vociferously while progun legislators stalled the Biaggi-Moynihan bill in committee. Law-enforcement groups across the country reacted in outrage. Handgun Control Inc. exploited the rift between the old allies by running an advertisement in police trade magazines with the headline "HELP STOP THE COP-KILLERS." Michael Beard, the director of the National Coalition to Ban Handguns, told the press he was astounded that the NRA, "which claims to be a friend of law enforcement officers, wants to stop a bill aimed at saving lives of those who protect our own."[2]

In this clash with the gun lobby, control advocates turned also to other new strategies, one of them being product liability suits. Tort law held manufacturers and dealers accountable for their faulty or unreasonably dangerous products that caused injury to consumers. On this basis, litigants had successfully sued the General Motors and Ford corporations for defects in their Corvair and Pinto cars. Thereafter, most courts recognized that producers bore some responsibility for the lethal quality of their goods.

Handgun suppliers, however, enjoyed virtual immunity from liability for deaths or wounds resulting from use of their products. In February 1982 when a jury in Washington, D.C., had awarded two million dollars to the family of a man shot and killed with a pistol stolen from the rifle association's headquarters, that exemption appeared to end. The following July, though, a federal district court set the award aside, ruling that the association could not be held legally responsible for the murder.

Nonetheless, control advocates continued their product liability strategy. They asked, as the core of their argument, "can concealable handguns, with generally ineffective warnings and instructions, be safely marketed to the general public?"[3] On this basis, James Brady pursued the product liability course by filing a twenty-million-dollar claim against R. G. Industries of Florida, the supplier of the gun John Hinckley had used against him. Meanwhile, victims of gun violence had filed an estimated one hundred lawsuits seeking to hold handgun manufacturers liable for murders and felonious injuries committed with their weapons. These suits came as the boom in gun sales fizzled, firearms glutted the market, and manufacturers became mired in a depression.[4]

For a time, the courts "nearly uniformly rejected these lawsuits," primarily on the ground that handguns differed from other dangerous products such as asbestos and pesticides because their manufacturers did not intend to include harmful ingredients. These jurists pointed out that handguns inflicted injury just as their producers intended them to do. Therefore, their reasoning went, gunmakers should not be penalized "for providing the consumer with exactly what he wanted," or the manufacturer could not be held negligible and liable for how someone used its products.[5] Ultimately, federal courts in Washington dismissed Brady's suit as well as that of Thomas K. Delahanty, the police officer Hinckley had also shot.[6]

While various other product liability suits made their way through the courts, Ronald Reagan reversed the position he had taken during the election campaign on compulsory draft registration. In opposing conscription, he had placed himself in a bind because he had also promised to build a stronger military establishment. This took precedence over concerns for individual liberty, except for gun keeping because he and his conservative advisers felt strongly that individuals should not flout the authority of the federal government, especially when pacifists, college students, and liberal Democrats remained conspicuous in the antidraft movement. So in 1982 his administration continued the draft registration and prosecuted the young men who refused to register.

In that year also, gun-control advocates in California formed Citizens Against Street Crime and Concealable Weapons, a political action group. Supported by national antigun organizations, film stars, and other prominent citizens, it secured more than six hundred thousand signatures on petitions that placed before the voters a referendum titled the Handgun Initiative but widely known as Proposition 15. It called for the registration of handguns, a ban on their mail-order sale, new sales only to law-enforcement officers, and a jail term of six months for anyone found carrying an unlicensed, concealable firearm.

With more than four million privately owned handguns in this bellwether state with the largest NRA membership in the nation, this measure seemingly provided a proper stage for what many observers perceived as a showdown in the gun-violence struggle. As in the battle over the referendum in Massachusetts five years earlier, pro- and antigun lobbies from within California and out of state jumped into the campaign. The measure's backers built a campaign chest of just over two million dollars and lined up celebrities and movie stars behind it.

Opponents of the proposition, organized as a coalition of gun groups titled Citizens Against the Gun Initiative, raised and spent more than six million dollars. They, too, drew support from distinguished individuals, such as George Deukmejian, the Republican attorney general running for governor, and various celebrities. One of them, cowboy film star Roy Rogers, declared, "They'll have to kill me first to take my gun."[7]

Early polls indicated strong public support for the measure, or that 64 percent of Californians against 30 percent favored it. Consequently, a spokesman for the rifle association called the proposition the most serious threat that had so far been mounted against firearms, a menace more dire than the concurrent Morton Grove case. The Los Angeles *Times*, which gave its "unqualified support" to the proposition, predicted that if passed it "would have a nationwide effect," and specifically on Congress.[8]

On November 2, the California voters rejected the proposition by a margin of 63 to 37 percent, thereby handing the gun lobby another impressive victory. On that same day, gun-control proposals failed also in New Hampshire and Nevada. Alan M. Gottlieb, the progun guru who founded the Citizens Committee for the Right to Keep and Bear Firearms, declared, "These votes clearly show that the antigun forces have been misrepresenting their polls and statistics for years. Where is their much proclaimed majority of Americans in favor of gun control? If they're out there, they certainly don't vote. . . . Why don't they [the antigun activists] listen to the will of the majority and just leave everybody alone?"[9]

Procontrol groups such as Handgun Control Inc. acknowledged that despite the heavy sentiment for their movement as shown by polls, public opinion on the issue of tough controls, where it counted, remained divided. Specifically, they attributed their failure in this instance to the superior financial muscle of the opposition. Doubtless, money helped the progun coalition but its power came more from the solidarity, discipline, and dedication of firearms owners to their cause. Controllers took some solace from elections in other parts of the country where candidates they supported came out winners.

The gun lobby had reason for greater satisfaction. It had never been stronger. Membership in its constituent organizations outnumbered the combined members of the antigun organizations. With a leadership leaning far to the right politically, the gun clubs wielded impressive influence in Congress, in the executive branch, in state legislatures, and in communities throughout the nation. All this aided the National Rifle Association, the Second Amendment Association, and the Citizens Committee for the Right to Keep and Bear Arms to uphold as gospel the belief that control promoters were gun grabbers who wanted to confiscate firearms from a patriotic citizenry. With such dedicated followers, the gun lobby could and did frighten legislators with its ability to motivate voters who could punish them in local as well as national elections.

Not only in California but also nationwide, firearms militants outspent the antigun lobbyists. For instance, in the election year 1982, the NRA financed a budget of $36 million to advance its agenda whereas Handgun Control Inc. raised $2.3 million for its politicking. Indeed, the rifle association expended more money on getting its message across to members, affiliates, and others to influence their voting than did any other well-known special-interest organization in the nation.

Harlon Carter told members, "We can reasonably and rightfully . . . aspire to a time when few politicians, mindful of their futures, will oppose us." Then he warned, "Don't trust a politician who won't trust you with a gun." In addi-

tion, the lobby had ready access to the corridors of power because more legislators than ever belonged to the rifle association or its affiliates. Critics who
described Congress as a wholly owned subsidiary of the NRA exaggerated, but
their main point hit close to the mark.

The president's behavior, too, contributed to the gun lobby's confidence. He
unequivocally cooperated with the NRA in pushing its agenda to weaken the
1968 gun-control statute. Reagan made his position clear while approving
amendments that eliminated the record-keeping requirement for sales of .22
rifle ammunition. "We are," he announced, "committed to the idea that it is
the criminal who is responsible for violence, not the law abiding firearms owner.
Accordingly, my administration has sought to remove restrictions that operate
only to burden the law abiding."[10]

Even at this peak of power, in the courts the gun fraternity showed some
vulnerability. On March 7, 1983, in the Morton Grove case the Seventh Circuit
Court of Appeals, 464 U.S. 863 (1983), in Chicago refused to apply the Second
Amendment against the village or against the state of Illinois. In upholding the
town's gun ban as legal, the jurists reaffirmed the numerous other decisions
that deemed the amendment's intent on gun keeping as collective, not individual as gun-lobby lawyers contended. Ignoring judicial history, NRA officials
called the ruling a day of darkness for both the courts and the Constitution.
Soon, as though in compensation, the gun community received another upbeat
message from on high.

In May, Reagan addressed the rifle association's annual convention in Phoenix, Arizona—the first sitting president to appear before such a gathering. "You
know," he said, "I've always felt a special bond with members of your group."
He praised the NRA for its growth to more than 2.5 million members. He
lauded as well its role in the defeat of California's Proposition 15 as evidence
of the organization's strength and contributions to society. He stressed support
for its civilian marksmanship program, pointing out that his administration had
"increased significantly" the sales of surplus M-1 rifles to participants and in-
structors.[11] He stated also he wanted to improve the government's role in the
shooting program.

As journalists and others noted, this anticontrol speech before an adoring
audience of legal gun owners had an ironic twist. To assure the president's
safety, the association imposed a form of gun control it claimed to detest. It
prohibited members from bringing firearms into the hall and had each entrant
checked with a metal detector. In addition, the president wore a bulletproof
vest and was surrounded by Secret Service agents and local police. Regardless

of these measures that ran counter to the creed of anticontrol militants, this convention marked a high point in their status.

Along with this expanding influence of the gun lobby came a rising public concern over firearms violence reflected on a small scale in the activities of anti-gun lobbies such as Handgun Control Inc. It pointed out ceaselessly that half of the nation's gun violence was accidental or emotional, not criminal. In 1983, therefore, it established the Center to Prevent Handgun Violence, a research, advocacy, and educational affiliate, to send this message to the public.

The problem of accidental gun deaths also continued to attract the attention of physicians and physical science researchers. Most of them, as did those at the Centers for Disease Control, declared gun wielding a significant public health hazard. Fresh evidence based on comparative statistics appeared to support this conclusion. It showed that the rate of homicide by guns in the United States exceeded that of Germany, Denmark, and Great Britain by a ratio of thirty-five to one, of Canada and France by seven to one. Other data connoted that localities with the lowest crime rates had the toughest gun laws, or that solidly enforced controls worked.[12]

Japan's experience with the most stringent controls in the democratic world illustrated this correlation. Even progun writers admitted it had "virtually nonexistent" gun crime but attempted to rationalize this by contending the Japanese lived in a police state that violated human rights. They also asserted incorrectly that the government possessed "the inherent authority to do what ever it wishes."[13]

The question of gun controls in other countries had only slight, if any, impact on American public opinion. As polls had indicated for decades, by a margin of at least 59 percent Americans still desired strict federal regulation. The samplings reported that unlike the president and much of Congress, a majority believed handgun controls would substantially lower the crime rate, reduce deaths stemming from family arguments, and cut down accidental casualties.[14]

In light of such sentiment a journalist asked the president, "Why are the public opinion polls a valid argument for the school prayer amendment, which you favor, and not a valid argument for [handgun control,] which you do not?" Reagan showed patience at having his inconsistency exposed publicly but could only say he always "preferred a different method with regard to handguns." He continued the evasion with resort to irrelevant anecdote, one of his trademarks.[15]

Meanwhile, rifle association attorneys had kept the Morton Grove case alive by filing a petition with the Illinois Supreme Court requesting it to overturn the earlier decisions on constitutional grounds. In October in *Kalodimos v. Vil-*

lage of Morton Grove the court upheld the previous judgments. It concluded that the town's "ordinance is a proper exercise of the police power authority."[16] This ruling disappointed gun owners, but buoyed by their high status in a popular conservative administration, their leaders decided to challenge it.

Gun-lobby attorneys asked the Supreme Court to rule whether or not the Second and Fourteenth Amendments prohibited state and local governments from enacting gun bans. They hoped to elicit from a presumed friendly judiciary an opinion upholding the NRA's interpretation of the Second Amendment. Instead, the high court dismissed the petition by declining to rule on the Illinois court's opinion. This action stands out as a rare setback for the gun lobby in the Reagan years. The lobby's basic political and financial power, however, remained undiminished.

As in the recent past, during these glory years for shooters gun violence played well in hundreds of movies and television productions. *Dirty Harry* (1971), *Death Wish* (1974), *First Blood* (1982), *The Terminator* (1984), *Top Gun* (1986), and several *Lethal Weapon* and *Rambo* films with a swaggering gun-toter as hero became box-office hits. When the films reappeared on television they attracted more millions of viewers. Early in the seventies the federal department concerned with health, education, and welfare had sponsored research on media violence and its effect on the public. The investigators concluded that televised gunplay induced "aggressive behavior," markedly so in adolescents. A decade later similar projects reaffirmed the findings, leading to renewed public debate on the problem of gun brutality.[17]

Few refuted this research but some media commentators pointed out that movies produced in other countries carried as much violence as those made in the United States. Yet several of these societies had lower gun-crime rates than the United States. Furthermore, for more than a decade many of the world's ultraviolent films featuring martial brutality and gunfire had come out of Hong Kong, not Hollywood. Indeed, analysts claimed the Asian genre influenced a generation of American filmmakers.

The visual media appeared to have a deeper impact on behavior in the United States because more often than elsewhere it starred guns as well as the macho heroes who used them. In addition, American productions dominated the field. Later, NRA officials would argue that the violence in films and television stimulated more gratuitous firearms rampages than did the easy availability of guns.

Meanwhile, handgun sales in the United States had slumped, apparently because the traditional male market had become saturated. So, in the mid-eighties the firearms industry worked to develop new customers "with primary focus on women," who represented a hitherto largely untapped market. Traditionally, women have been less interested in guns than men and have been more willing to endorse strict controls. According to critics of the new merchandising plan, the arms industry and the gun lobby "recognized that if enough women were brought into America's gun culture they could act as an effective bulwark against . . . control efforts." Gun sellers and shooters cooperated, therefore, "to both scare and entice women into buying handguns."[18]

While in itself not diabolical as some antigun activists implied, this strategy, with sensational advertising, did exploit women's fears of rape and other male-dominated crimes. To the dismay of controllers, it suggested the gun as the proper antidote for these apprehensions. Firearms producers claimed that sales to women increased as much as 53 percent. Taking this figure as fact, much of the media reported a "gender revolution" and a boom in females' purchase of handguns. In reality, the rush to guns never occurred and the gender gap in their ownership remained the same.[19]

Meanwhile, a spate of murders by unbalanced gun-toters captured headlines. On July 19, 1984, one of them, James Oliver Huberty, a forty-one-year-old fire-arms collector, gathered his Uzi 9mm carbine, Winchester 12-gauge shotgun, Browning automatic 9mm pistol, and a sack of ammunition magazines to go "hunting humans." He strode into a McDonald's hamburger outlet near his home in San Ysidro, California, and fired 140 rounds at the mostly Hispanic patrons. He slaughtered twenty-one and wounded nineteen before a police sniper downed him.

Although this massacre did not stimulate gun-control legislation, it did lead the Republicans in power to demonstrate their toughness in dealing with crime while placating the NRA. With the Comprehensive Crime Control legislation of 1984, they declared war on an image that frightened numerous Americans, that of the incorrigible criminal preying on the public after hasty release from prison.

As part of this legislative package, in the Armed Career Criminal Act Congress decreed that a person with three convictions for robbery or burglary or both when apprehended in another crime while carrying a gun would have his, or her, minimum sentence extended from ten years to not less than fifteen years' imprisonment. The maximum would be lifetime incarceration without eligibility for parole. The next Congress widened punishable legal violations to include any violent felony or serious drug offense.[20] This three-strikes legislation for a time seemed to have reassured the public of the seriousness of the

Reagan government's war on crime. It did not do much to placate the control advocates immersed in the gun-violence struggle.

Another act of gun violence on December 22, 1984, brought more national attention to the struggle. It started when Bernhard H. Goetz, a thirty-seven-year-old white electronics specialist, took a seat on a Manhattan subway car next to four boisterous black youths, later revealed to have criminal records. One of them asked for five dollars and repeated, "Give me five dollars." Instead of proffering the money or moving to the rear of the car or to another car for safety as had other passengers, Goetz pulled a .38-caliber Smith & Wesson pistol from a concealed in-belt holster and shot all four, severing the spinal cord of one of them, Darrell Cabey, and paralyzing him for life.

Goetz said he perceived himself menaced and hence fired in self-defense. His behavior, though, suggested he had armed himself and had fired as though seeking vengeance for having been mugged three times. He became a media celebrity where some termed him the subway vigilante. Three years later a lower-middle-class jury of whites and blacks found Goetz not guilty of attempted murder and all other charges except one—illegal possession of his gun.

This decision upholding deadly force in self-defense and much else in this episode fitted NRA slogans. For instance, at one point Goetz urged "distribution of an additional 25,000 guns to properly trained private citizens." His acquittal of the attempted murder charge reflected the prevailing climate of opinion, that shooting in alleged self-defense even when dubious, as indicated in polls taken shortly after the shootings and the trial, was proper.[21]

Meanwhile, the gun lobby's campaign to overturn the still-valid provisions of the 1968 federal gun-control act moved ahead with renewed vigor. Early on, NRA leaders had persuaded two legislative allies, Republican senator James A. McClure of Idaho, representing a committed progun constituency, and Democrat Harold L. Volkmer of Missouri, a lifelong hunter, to lead the attack. They contended that legitimate gun-owners needed additional changes in the statute to protect them against BATF harassment. After launching several failed efforts to gut the law with a bill they called initially the Gun Decontrol Act, they received a boost from Reagan's election and from the Republican majority in the Senate.

On December 8, 1981, a Senate Judiciary Committee weighted in favor of McClure and Volkmer's bill began hearings on the proposal to remove the limited federal controls on private firearms use. The acting chairman, Charles E. Grassley, opened the proceedings by announcing "it is time that we decided whether this society exists for the benefit of the law-abiding individual or for the benefit of the criminal." The mostly gun-lobby witnesses continued their bashing of the 1968 control act and of the BATF. One of them, John M. Snyder, stated for instance that without the act there would have been no BATF. Therefore, he said, "the real culprit . . . is the law itself and therefore it should be changed, if not totally repealed."[22] In contrast, Pete Shields expressed dismay that so soon after Reagan's shooting the committee "is even considering weakening our firearms laws."[23]

Two years later, on January 23, 1985, with Republicans in control of the Senate and with the backing of NRA lobbyists, McClure reintroduced his bill. In an unusual procedure, Robert J. Dole, the majority leader, allowed the bill to bypass the judiciary, skip a preliminary public hearing, and go directly onto the Senate's legislative calendar. After several days of considerable political maneuvering wherein opponents agreed not to filibuster if proponents accepted certain amendments, they struck a deal. Dole, a wounded war veteran, commented that "experience over the years has amply demonstrated that the subject of gun control is one of the most emotionally charged and explosive issues of our time."[24] He contended that with the amendments the bill would restrict "abuses of authority." It reached the floor of the Senate on July 9 where with a vote of seventy-nine to fifteen it passed.

The bill still had to make its way through the House where Democrats held a majority. Peter W. Rodino, the House Judiciary Committee chairman, commented "that the bill will be dead on arrival."[25] He explained later that he meant simply he could not imagine the House would consider a measure to weaken an already frail control law. He was wrong.

The NRA rallied its members, urging them to pressure their representatives to vote for the bill. "It's time now for your Congressman to fight for your gun and hunting rights," it warned them. "Don't let your Congressman 'take a walk.' . . . THIS IS THE LITMUS TEST." Control groups, of course, opposed the measure but so did various police organizations. One of them wrote Reagan that the legislation would "pose an immediate and unwarranted threat to the law enforcement community and to the citizens we are sworn to protect." Baltimore's police chief said, "No person out there facing guns supports this bill."[26]

This agitation for the McClure-Volkmer measure also incensed Sarah Brady, the wife of Jim Brady, daughter of a federal law-enforcement agent, and a Republican activist who had been busy caring for her injured husband and their young son. In summer 1984, out of indignation she had become an advocate of handgun regulation and joined Handgun Control Inc. In October of the next year, she gained a seat on the organization's board and began speaking in public against the gun-owner bill.

While picking up considerable public attention, this kind of opposition could not overcome the intense lobbying for the bill. In plugging it, the NRA with an expenditure of $1.6 million outspent Handgun Control Inc., which opposed the bill, by more than six to one. Individual supporters showered legislators with far more letters and phone calls than did their opponents. Their contributions and direct pressure on legislators made a difference. As researchers later substantiated, the gun keepers' lobbying reached 80 percent of those who voted for the bill.[27]

As for Reagan, despite his claim of being tough on crime, he endorsed the bill. This prompted a reporter to ask, why do you "support virtually no limits" on gun use at this point? The president responded with his usual NRA rhetoric, "that as long as there are guns, the individual that wants a gun for a crime is going to get it."[28]

After further parliamentary juggling, on April 10, 1986, its sponsors overcame stiff opposition in the House to gain approval by a vote of 292–130. Robert Torricelli, a Democratic congressman from New Jersey, denounced the outcome as "a genuine disgrace. It's a classic example of the power of big money and a well-orchestrated campaign by a narrow interest."[29] Gun lobbyists agreed with him but from a different perspective.

Wayne R. LaPierre, speaking for the rifle association, boasted that it had "won almost everything it had sought." Progun legislators perceived the victory in terms of safeguarding the "civil liberties" of gun owners. Journalists and others noted that the association's lobbying had remained "as effective as ever."[30] Jubilant NRA officials such as Executive Vice President G. Ray Arnett had looked beyond the legislation for a rosy future for gun keeping. "I think our objective primarily is to get constitutional amendments in all 50 states" upholding the right to bear arms, he stated. The amendments would ensure "that Morton Groves can't pop up in every city and county" in the country.[31] In keeping with such sentiment and his commitment to diminish the existing federal controls, Reagan signed the McClure-Volkmer bill into law as the Firearms Owners' Protection Act.

NRA gun-rights advocates who wrote the act maintained that it sought to block unnecessary federal restrictions or burdens on law-abiding citizens who used firearms in hunting, trapping, target shooting, personal protection, or any other lawful activity. The statute itself allowed interstate commerce in rifles and shotguns as long as the buyers' and sellers' states regarded the sales as legal.

It eliminated record-keeping requirements for ammunition dealers, eased restrictions on sales of guns by unlicensed individuals, and permitted dealers and individuals to do business at gun shows without federal licenses. These shows, held every weekend in communities across the country, would often become swap meets for stolen or otherwise illegal firearms. The statute also prohibited the Bureau of Alcohol, Tobacco, and Firearms from requiring gun dealers to maintain centralized records. In sum, the act gutted the already feeble federal firearms regulation. As a token to controllers, the legislation banned future possession or transfer of machine guns and retained most restrictions on handguns.[32]

This decontrol act overruled a number of Supreme Court decisions, negated about a third of the case law on the control act of 1968, and crippled a considerable portion of state firearms regulation. Although a defeat for proponents of gun control, it also marked a kind of political coming of age for Handgun Control Inc. It became more militant in battling for its kind of federal gun controls. At the same time, somewhat to pacify the law-enforcement agencies that had opposed the McClure-Volkmer measure, Congress passed a separate bill that tightened licensing, record keeping, and interstate transport requirements for guns. On July 8, 1986, it became law.

However, the gun lobby gained another, though partial, success in its four-year battle against the Biaggi-Moynihan bill. Police groups continued to stand behind it. Finally, when the lobby concluded it needed police support for other pet legislation, it worked out a compromise. It agreed to the bill after friendly legislators had narrowed its prohibitions to specific categories of armor-piercing bullets that left hundreds of others with similar capacity on the market. Then in both houses of Congress the legislation passed by wide margins. On August 28 Reagan signed it into law.

Gun aficionados also displayed their influence at the state level. In one of the nation's oldest forms of firearms control, most states prohibited the carrying of concealed weapons. In addition, for years a number of states granted law-enforcement officials authority to issue permits to individuals to carry concealed guns at their discretion, or on a "may issue" basis. At this time the NRA, as part of its effort to boost gun ownership, lobbied state governments to change their laws to a "shall issue" basis. To attain this goal, the rifle association explicitly accepted what it had previously opposed—compulsory licensing of firearms. Lobbyists persuaded Florida's legislators to mandate that on October 1, 1987, county authorities had to issue a permit to anyone, other than those with criminal records or other specified disabilities, who wished to carry a concealed handgun.

Soon, a batch of other state legislatures friendly to the NRA enacted similar "shall issue" concealed-handgun laws. They justified this reversal of a form of control backed by several hundred years of practical experience with the old self-defense argument, or that police did not provide sufficient protection against criminal violence. They thus voted no confidence in their own law-enforcement institutions while giving up a simple and effective means of preventing a considerable number of firearms deaths. They also set off another debate between progun and antigun writers.[33]

Studies by progun researchers claimed that "defensive gun use is very common in the U.S." Most other research showed that criminals faced inconsequential deterrence from concealed-gun carrying or that the progun researchers produced no evidence of "significant impact for any type of crime."[34] In Florida, for instance, within the next five years violent crime rose 17.8 percent. For years thereafter, that state had the nation's highest rate of violent crime.[35] The firearms industry and the NRA liked the concealed-carry laws because they helped sell handguns or, as a trade-journal headline later put it, "More Gun Permits Equal More Gun Sales."[36]

Back in Washington, the gun lobby balked at a broad-based control bill that Senator Edward Kennedy and Representative Peter Rodino had long cosponsored. It proposed banning the domestic manufacture of cheap handguns as well as the importing of parts used in assembling them. With letter writing, phone calling, and fund-raising campaigns, the leading national antigun organizations lobbied for the bill. This offensive produced no tangible result because few in Congress would support the measure. Even though discouraged, the control lobbyists refused to give up. They did, however, switch strategy.

The shift involved rallying behind Handgun Control Inc. and funneling resources in support of a cut-down version of the Kennedy-Rodino proposal, which, because of Sarah Brady's role in promoting it, came to be called the Brady bill. It aimed mainly to plug one of the loopholes in the 1968 statute that allowed convicted felons to circumvent the law by lying about their past when buying a gun.

Most law-enforcement officials believed the proposed legislation could block this evasion if it included a waiting period that gave them time to run background checks on buyers. On February 4, 1987, two Democrats from Ohio, Representative Edward F. Feighan and Senator Howard M. Metzenbaum, introduced the revised bill in Congress as an amendment to the Omnibus Drug Initiative Act, the centerpiece in the Reagan administration's battle against narcotics.

Previously in the Uniform Firearms Act of the twenties, the rifle association had promoted background checks, but later as it turned increasingly militant it reversed this position and denounced the idea. The NRA remained consistent, though, in its fundamental endeavor of battling virtually any new gun-control measure. In September 1988 the firearms lobby's opposition, combined with progun parliamentary maneuvering, defeated the Brady bill.[37] The rifle association contributed an estimated average of $1,964.00 to each House member who voted against the bill.[38] The well-financed shooters had won again.

A similar struggle swirled around the marketing of a new type of pistol made largely of plastic that could pass undetected through most airport security systems. Police organizations quickly called for a federal ban on these plastic guns. In 1987 sympathetic legislators introduced a bill in Congress that would outlaw them. As with other minor control efforts, the firearms groups opposed it. Using standard, gun-lobby rhetoric, their spokespersons warned that the bill would open the door to other restrictive laws and would lead incrementally to the confiscation of all guns in private hands. The lobby succeeded in blocking passage of the legislation at this time. It could not, however, kill the bill, which its sponsors reintroduced in the next Congress, or stop other challenges to its own power.[39] One of the measures gun keepers considered most menacing came out of Maryland.

That state's struggle to contain gun violence had begun three years earlier when a robber with an inexpensive handgun, a Rohm revolver model GR-38S, shot Olen J. Kelley, an employee in a Bethesda Safeway market, in the chest. Kelley filed a product liability suit, *Kelley v. R. G. Industries*, 497 A. 2d 1143 (1985), against R. G. Industries of Florida and its parent company, Rohm Gesellschaft of Germany, the manufacturer of the weapon. He contended the maker should have known that the low-quality gun had mainly criminal use.

In contrast to decisions in past suits of this nature, in 1985 Maryland's highest court ruled in Kelley's favor. It characterized the gun as "unreasonably dangerous." As a result, R. G. Industries could not obtain liability insurance. The parent company then took its American subsidiary out of the business of supplying cheap handguns. Thereafter in product liability cases the courts decided more often in favor of the plaintiffs.[40]

In the next two years, Maryland gun owners tried to overturn the Kelley decision but most settled for a compromise law that banned future sales of Saturday night specials. Diehards, who refused to compromise, organized the Maryland Committee Against the Gun Ban and then sought to overturn the law in a referendum battle. As in California earlier in the decade, the contest drew in outside money. The rifle association pumped in $6.1 million and other progun sources provided another half million dollars, whereas the proponents raised $752,000. The organized shooters feared that the law, if upheld, would become a model for similar legislation in other states. To attract the African American vote thought to be crucial, the progun campaigners charged that the ban on cheap guns would merely deprive the poor inner-city dwellers of a means of self-defense readily available to affluent whites. This tactic failed. On November 8, 1988, by a margin of 58 percent to 42 percent the voters retained the ban, making Maryland the first state in the nation to outlaw a particular category of handguns. Barbara Lautman, a spokeswoman for Handgun Control Inc., commented that the vote "proves you can stand up to the gun lobby despite the millions of dollars they've spent."[41]

Obviously, the NRA's first loss in a statewide referendum, even though it had outspent the antigun forces by more than ten to one, jolted gun keepers. Contrary to what both sides had predicted and what Lautman maintained, this defeat did not cripple the association or throttle civilian possession of handguns. Most Marylanders who wanted the weapons continued to obtain them without much difficulty, usually by crossing state lines. Even so, the control people regarded the political victory significant because it demonstrated that on occasion the gun lobby, even at its peak of power with its well-honed tactics and deep pockets, could lose.

16

The Struggle Nationalized

A s we have seen, in the Reagan years the gun community had fared well in national as well as state and local politics. Hence it approached the 1988 campaign period with confidence. Even so, toward Vice President George Herbert Walker Bush, who sought the Republican nomination, gun owners had an ambivalent attitude. He owned an arsenal of firearms and belonged to the community but two decades earlier while a member of Congress from Texas he had reluctantly voted for the Gun Control Act of 1968. At the time and thereafter he also made clear that he opposed the "federal registration and licensing of firearms." Then, when running for a Senate seat, he supported some form of firearms regulation. This advocacy alienated gun keepers and conservative voters and he lost. The defeat contributed to the solidifying of his opposition to gun control through "federal legislation."[1]

Despite this progun commitment, as a presidential candidate stumping for votes in New Hampshire Bush surprisingly spoke in favor of the stalled plastic-gun bill. Thus, he again alarmed the firearms buffs in his party, but his action did not amount to apostasy. Even Ronald Reagan at this time admitted that "maybe there could be some restrictions" on guns, a sentiment he repeated several months later.[2]

When Bush won the Republican nomination, his fellow gun-keepers remembered his spotty record on controls and were wary of him. However, they detested his Democratic opponent, Michael Dukakis. They recalled that as governor of Massachusetts he had backed the failed campaign to ban handguns in the state. For this reason and because Republicans in their platform came out squarely for the alleged constitutional right to own a gun and denounced liberals for being against it, leaders of the gun organizations willingly or unwillingly backed Bush.

Gratefully, Bush moved swiftly to overcome what remained of the gun own-ers' grumbling over the plastic-gun flap. "As a military veteran, hunter and a Life Member of the National Rifle Association," he informed its constituents, "I've owned, used and respected firearms for most of my life. . . . You can sup-port my opponent and give up the rights you cherish, or you can support me and maintain your right to keep and bear arms." The association responded by pumping through its political action committee more than $1.5 million into his campaign. It also named him its Person of the Year for 1988, praising him as the "one candidate [who] would stand up for the rights of millions of Ameri-can gun owners."[3] Dukakis lost for a number of reasons, among them the gun lobby's politicking against him and Bush's progun position.

During the campaign, Ronald Reagan had hammered out a compromise on the plastic-gun issue that banned firearms impervious to detection by the usual security systems. It pleased neither the gun lobby nor the police organizations. Nonetheless, the Undetectable Firearms Act easily passed both the House and Senate and on November 11 it became law.

For the gun community, the plastics issue amounted to a minor setback. It suffered more from the judiciary's continued denial of its interpretations of the Second Amendment. For instance, the Federal Court of Appeals for the Eighth Circuit in *United States v. Nelson*, 859 F. 2d 1318 (1988), stated that courts "have analyzed the Second Amendment purely in terms of protecting state mi-litias, rather than individual rights." Its ruling added another link to the chain of decisions going back nearly a half century that declared the amendment did not protect any individual right to bear arms or any right to use guns for sport or self-defense.[4]

Regardless of these legal losses, the gun lobby continued to function with its usual confidence and sense of power. Constituents such as John M. Snyder, the chief lobbyist for the Citizens Committee for the Right to Keep and Bear Arms, contended that guns benefited humanity.[5] On this basis, he petitioned the pa-pacy to designate a nineteenth-century saint, Gabriel Possenti, the "Patron of Handgunners."[6] Possenti, whom Snyder called "sort of a holy John Wayne," purportedly had saved an Italian village from bandits merely by brandishing a pair of pistols. The saint thus symbolized crime-deterrent theory in action, a theory with wide appeal to American shooters.

At the same time, the NRA launched its Eddie Eagle program to bolster its image with the public at large rather than just with gun keepers. As the program expanded into a curriculum accompanied by appealing colored cartoon figures and an animated video, "Learn Gun Safety with Eddie Eagle," it claimed to teach children in preschool through the sixth grade firearm precautions. As the program evolved, critics maintained that instead of truly safeguarding children it functioned to block child-safety gun-control legislation. It became an instrument designed to advance "the interests of the NRA and the firearms industry by increasing the acceptance of guns by children and youth."[7]

Shortly, as had happened often, on January 17, 1989, three days before Bush entered the White House, children became victims of random gun violence, this time highly publicized. Patrick E. Purdy, a twenty-four-year-old white supremacist with a criminal record, used guns to commit crime, not deter it. He walked onto the playground of an elementary school in Stockton, California, with a semiautomatic AK-47 assault rifle and a pistol. With the rifle he sprayed more than one hundred rounds into the crowded yard, slaughtering five students and wounding thirty-three plus one teacher. Then he killed himself. Although senseless shootings had happened throughout the century, this one, along with another rampage at a school in Virginia Beach, Virginia, a month earlier, marked the beginning of more than a decade of them, frequently at schools. One analyst maintained that the "institutions and mores" of a gun culture helped make them commonplace in America.[8]

The Stockton massacre also denoted a marked change in the public reaction to civilian gun violence. Except for murders or attempted murders of presidents and other prominent Americans, previously the public took such outrage virtually for granted. Control advocates agitated for government action but did not get far. Now, though, newspapers and television instantly highlighted the shootings. Gun-control groups demanded of Washington some form of action to stop the bloodshed. Polls showed that some three-quarters of the public desired a federal ban on semiautomatic rifles and cheap handguns.[9]

After every highly publicized shooting, reporters quizzed the president for his reaction and asked where Congress stood. His involvement, the publicity, a public sensitized to gun violence, and the growing clout of the control movement placed the gun organizations and their lawyers on virtually constant alert. They had to be ready to counterattack any movement toward placing restraints on private gun-owning. In this ambiance of media glare and confrontation, America's movement to contain gun violence, as never before, had become scrutinized, politicized, and nationalized.

In this climate the Purdy shooting stimulated renewed demands for bans on assault weapons. Reputable data indicated that increasingly terrorists, criminals, and others bought or stole them. Moreover, other countries were outlawing such guns. In the previous year Britain, for instance, significantly expanded its tough firearms laws to prohibit private ownership of most semiautomatic rifles and other technologically advanced firearms. Ironically, the People's Republic of China, which prohibited most of its citizens from possessing a gun of any kind, at this time had begun swamping the United States with inexpensive military-style assault weapons and handguns.[10]

Barbara Bush, the new first lady, shared public concern over the spread of these dangerous weapons among civilians. Unlike her husband, she acknowledged, "I have always been for gun control." Like numerous other Americans, she had assumed that assault weapons were already banned. When she learned differently, she said they should be, "absolutely." Even Reagan agreed. "I don't believe in taking away the right of the citizen to own a gun for sports, hunting, or their own personal defense," he declared. "But I do not believe that an AK-47, a machine gun, is a sporting weapon."[11]

On February 8 legislators in the Senate and on March 1 in the House introduced bills to restrict the importation of several types of semiautomatic guns. Since the NRA opposed the bills, journalists queried Bush on where he stood in this matter. "I would strongly go after the criminals who use these guns," he responded. "But I'm not about to suggest that a semi-automated hunting rifle be banned. Absolutely not." Five days later he announced, "I want to be the President that protects the rights of people to have arms."[12]

When public pressure for action on regulating those firearms mounted, the president drew back from his rigid anticontrol stance. He said he wished "to find a solution to the so-called AK-47 assault weapon problem."[13] Then, following the recommendation of William J. Bennett, the czar of his antidrug campaign, Bush reversed his original position. Through an executive order, he temporarily suspended the importing of the AK-47 and several other models of assault weapons. The ban would remain in place for several months, or until the Bureau of Alcohol, Tobacco, and Firearms could review the situation. The suspension kept perhaps 80 percent of the foreign-made assault rifles, which previously had been allowed in the United States, out of the country.

A week after the order, while again answering questions on control of automated firearms, Bush stated, "The White House has a role; the President has a key role. But it's got to be a shared responsibility, with all the people in this country." Privately, he explained that his commitment "to the rights" of legitimate gun owners remained firm but he would do "anything within reason" to keep assault weapons "out of the hands of criminals."[14] On April 5 he expanded the temporary ban to exclude from importation the other 20 percent of the foreign weapons that had been coming on the American market. He had addressed only a part of the problem because 66 percent or more of the estimated three million assault guns already in the country were domestically manufactured. He had no intention of restricting them.

Six days later Arizona Senator Dennis DeConcini, a Democrat who, as a staunch supporter of the rifle association, had been an opponent of control legislation, changed his mind. He introduced a bill that would place tight restrictions on the ownership and use of semiautomatic guns, domestic as well as imported. As a result, gun enthusiasts in Arizona considered him a traitor and later initiated a recall petition against him.

Two weeks after DeConcini presented his bill, the director of the firearms bureau announced the results of its study on assault weapons. The report persuaded the president to concede that the increasingly sophisticated guns in the hands of a new class of criminals and unstable persons required at least minimal regulation. Accordingly, he made the ban on imported semiautomatic guns firm in his term. Gun dealers who thereby lost their import permits challenged his action in court but lost.

Out in California in the wake of the Stockton massacre, two legislators, David A. Roberti and Michael Roos, had initiated a bill that would ban the sale, transfer, and importation of assault weapons within the state. The state's gun community opposed the bill, making its fate a hotly contested issue. Finally, on March 13, 1989, the legislature approved a diluted version of the Roberti-Roos Assault Weapons Control Act. It outlawed only a number of specifically listed guns. On May 24 the governor signed it into law, making California the first state to ban at least some assault weapons.

Shortly, the Colt Manufacturing Company filed a suit challenging the constitutionality of the law. Colt lost but its lawyers appealed. As happened often with control laws, enforcement became a problem. Official foot-dragging, technicalities, and legal loopholes made the legislation seem hollow. Finally, nine years later, an appellate court delivered what appeared to be the coup de grâce. It declared a key provision of the law dealing with copycat automated guns unconstitutional.[15] Again, the gun lobby had worked effectively to reverse what had been a striking defeat, but the triumph did not last long. Two years later the California Supreme Court overturned the lower court's decision. A gun-lobby lawyer said gun owners would continue to challenge the law.[16]

Bush, meanwhile, had brought up the control issue again when he announced a national program to combat crime. It included enhanced penalties for violation of firearms laws, such as for the theft of a gun. "The right to own a gun," he told peace officers, "is not a license to harm others." He asked Congress to do for dangerous firearms what it had done for dangerous drugs—enact "stiff penalties for the use of semiautomatic weapons."[17] With this move toward limited control of a specific type of firearm, along with his earlier ban, Bush further damaged his alliance with the NRA. Some members initiated a movement to expel him, even though he sided with them on most gun issues.

Furthermore, on opposition to more extensive controls the president remained adamant. He refused to budge even when confronted with continued civilian gun carnage, as in the case of Joseph T. Wesbecker, a disgruntled employee of a printing plant in Louisville, Kentucky, with an obsession for guns. On September 14 he entered company offices with an AK-47 and fired for thirty minutes, murdering seven coworkers and wounding thirteen before killing himself. He had purchased his guns legally.

The next day a broadcast journalist asked the president, "Why do we allow people to get hold of these weapons and massacre other people?" Bush expressed horror over the slaughter but explained defensively, "I don't think banning guns is going to be the ultimate answer, or could ever safeguard against that kind of tragedy."[18] There the matter rested.

As in the past, other countries experienced similar shooting incidents but treated them and the problems of gun violence differently than did the United States. In Britain in a quiet suburb in May 1989 a gunman shot down passersby indiscriminately, raising a cry for tighter gun control. "Indeed, it is good," an editorialist wrote, "that such incidents are still rare enough in Britain to provoke horror and shock."[19] Nonetheless, shooters objected to the "sledgehammer of yet more law." Their still-potent "shooting and hunting lobby" blocked efforts in Parliament for stronger legislation, as against shotguns.[20] It could not, however, defeat control legislation such as a government-financed buy-back of outlawed firearms.

On the other side of the world the Philippine government had to contend with an epidemic of gun violence that followed the collapse of Ferdinand Marcos's dictatorial regime. So, in October 1989 the new president, Corazon C. Aquino, launched a campaign for a "gunless society." The following year she banned gun carrying. Shooters, firearms dealers, and clubs such as the Philippine Practical Shooting Association organized a lobby to counter the program. The authorities reported a drastic drop in crime but the gun lobby questioned their statistics. Unlike the American shooters' success in diluting the 1968 statute, the Filipino lobby failed to enfeeble the tough national law. Although the Filipino controls worked, the government did have a problem with enforcement in specific instances.

Back in the United States, despite Bush's progun policy the control movement lurched ahead with its own program. Its most impressive gains followed Sarah Brady's assumption of the presidency of Handgun Control Inc. She stimulated fund-raising, kept the organization focused on what she saw as the need for more effective federal gun regulation, and initiated fresh, aggressive tactics against the gun lobby.

Under Brady's leadership, Handgun Control Inc. attracted an impressive number of new members. With headquarters in Washington, D.C., and offices in New York, Chicago, San Francisco, Los Angeles, and San Diego, it raised funds across the nation but mostly in urban areas. It lobbied Congress with increasing efficacy while its affiliated groups battled the NRA and other gun lobbyists in state and local politics. This politicking and Brady's knack for publicity energized the whole control movement.

With this new prominence and its still circumscribed goal, Handgun Control Inc. picked up more and more boosters for the Brady bill. Brady urged new members to contribute because, she said, it's "your first real chance to tell the National Rifle Association to go to hell."[21] As for the president, having pronounced repeatedly he would stand firm on the gun issue, he threatened to veto the revived bill. "I don't want to go for more Federal gun control," he declared, "I'm not going to do it."[22]

Nonetheless, with hopes high because of rising public sentiment for more federal gun regulation, supporters pushed ahead their revised version of the bill. On July 24, 1990, the House Judiciary Committee approved the measure but opponents blocked further consideration in this session of Congress. This stalling upset James Brady. Explaining, "Me and my boss really didn't see eye to eye" on gun control, he now also spoke up. "Ever since I was shot," he stated for an advertisement, "I have watched from my wheelchair as the gun lobby blocked one sane handgun control bill after another. But I'm not just watching anymore. I'm calling on Congress to pass a common-sense law—the Brady bill."[23] Only psychopaths, criminals, drug dealers, and madmen, he added, are against it.

This characterization not only treated opponents of the legislation unfairly but also underestimated them. Proponents also overestimated the potential of the Brady bill. It could not on its own resolve the gun-violence problem. Regardless of its flaws, it offered the possibility of paving the way for more effective federal firearms regulation than at any previous time.

That possibility intensified the gun lobby's fight against the measure. Contending as usual that even a minor restriction on guns would pave the way for

stronger controls, groups such as the National Rifle Association and Gun Owners of America mouthed the old arguments that it would not prevent criminals
from obtaining guns but would punish, or at least inconvenience, those entitled
to them. The gun enthusiasts perceived as most menacing the bill's provision
requiring a waiting period for a purchaser before he could take possession of a
gun. They denounced it as laying "the groundwork for a massive government
intrusion into the lives of ordinary, decent Americans."[24]

All the while Bush promoted his own crime-control bill, which mirrored the
shooters' attitude. The bill emphasized punishment of felons who used guns
rather than control of the weapons. Nonetheless, in March 1991 when he trans-
mitted it to Congress, the legislators refused to pass it. That month a Gallup
poll indicated that more than 80 percent of the public supported registration
of all handguns and 43 percent favored a complete ban.[25] As though somewhat
responsive to such sentiment, Bush again retreated a bit from his antiregulation
position with a willingness to sign a bill restricting possession of automatic
firearms. He would sign such a bill, he explained "even though the National
Rifle Association disapproves. We need to crack down a little bit on that."[26]

Meanwhile the Bradys had persuaded former presidents Nixon, Ford, and
Carter to endorse the gun-control bill. Even Reagan, influenced by his wife
Nancy who favored limited controls, broke with the gun lobby's position on this
issue. At George Washington University in Washington, D.C., after announcing support for the Brady bill, Reagan urged Congress to enact it without further delay. Citing data from states that already had waiting periods for
purchases, he predicted, "this bill—on a nationwide scale—can't help but stop
thousands of illegal handgun purchases."[27] Astonished gun lobbyists charged
their hero figuratively with stabbing them in the back.

The bipartisan backing appeared to help the reintroduced Brady bill. On May
8, 1991, the House approved it and on June 6 Joseph Biden, a Democrat from
Delaware, presented it to the Senate as part of the larger omnibus anticrime
bill. Gun supporters in the Senate blocked passage of the measure with a filibuster. In September Handgun Control Inc. launched "Free the Brady Bill," a
national campaign aimed at forcing Congress to vote on the measure. The effort failed.[28]

In this battle against what the rifle association termed incremental federal
gun control, it spent about ten million dollars, much of it on its legislative alert
program and mass mailings. This strategy paid off with the defeat of the Brady
bill and with triumphs for the association and its affiliates on a wide front. The
DeConcini bill that had languished in Congress for almost two years also took

a beating. In addition, gun devotees came out ahead in places such as Nebraska where the legislature amended the state's constitution to guarantee the inalienable right to bear arms for all persons.

Gun lobbyists gloated over their victories, expressing satisfaction with their well-honed tactics. They also commented on their battle against a tide of popular control sentiment, which for awhile appeared to roll against them, with clichés such as "It's never over until it's over." Antigun proponents found some consolation from a vote in Congress in November that ended the government subsidy for shooting practice under the Director of Civilian Marksmanship. The legislators at last perceived the programs as having little value for military preparedness.

Gun groups easily shrugged off this defeat because their lobbyists now routinely concentrated on assumed civilian needs. They portrayed gun keepers as law-abiding citizens who used their weapons only for legitimate purposes in everyday living. Lobbyists also depicted controls as unnecessary because of a dip in crime with guns from a peak in 1981.[29] In addition, the national homicide rate had dropped by 4 percent in the past year, the first recorded decline since 1984.[30] They attributed this drop to improved techniques in gun training, claiming shooters would be safer in the field hunting than in their bathtubs, in their swimming pools, or at their dining tables. Justice Department statistics also showed, however, that in 31 percent of all murders, robberies, and aggravated assaults the perpetrators used firearms. These data represented an increase in the past year of violent crimes with guns.[31]

Procontrol lobbyists, too, noted the decrease in criminal violence but questioned most of the gun fraternity's explanations for it. Controllers dismissed programs designed for safe firearms use as failures because those who framed them overlooked a fundamental characteristic of people who used guns against people—they intend to inflict harm. These advocates noted also that in some segments of the population the toll in gun deaths and injuries still remained exceptionally high. They cited the escalating juvenile homicides, primarily by males in inner cities, as prime contributors to the civilian bloodshed. These youths boasted they could get a gun with no trouble at all.

National crime surveys indicated that handgun crime victimized youngsters sixteen to nineteen years of age at a higher rate than people in other age groups. For a decade these youths had killed and had been killed in numbers exceeding those at any other time in the century. Teenagers claimed to carry guns not only for self-protection but also for macho swagger on the misguided supposition it earned them respect from peers. Whatever the motivation for boys toting guns, the reality of easy gun availability "transformed youth violence and in particular made it more lethal" than in the past.[32]

Physicians, epidemiologists, and others who studied firearms injuries agreed with control advocates on the youth crime problem but went further. They condemned the addiction to guns as a national affliction, a public-health menace that society should treat with as much urgency as any deadly disease. Government statistics compiled and analyzed since 1983 supported this theory. They showed that killings, as in rape, robbery, or burglary, made up only a small category of firearms deaths, or about 10 percent. Suicide rated number one as the cause for gun-related deaths. Gun violence by citizens in all walks of life but without felony connections cost society numerous deaths, mutilations, and millions of dollars annually.

Researchers ascribed the cause of the gun violence to the "virtually unregulated distribution of a hazardous consumer product, a problem that cannot be solved until the product is taken off the market."[33] Obviously, the 90 percent toll in firearms violence not directly related to crime provided a better reason for solid federal control than just the focus on crime narrowly defined.

The research of those concerned with gun violence as a social disease, along with their data, impressed an active minority within the control movement. For years control advocates, law-enforcement officials, legislators, and presidents basically had followed the lead of the firearms community in identifying gun bloodletting primarily with crime. Now control activists succeeded in enlarging the boundaries of the gun-violence debate to include the statistically established relationship of guns to public health. They attracted publicity in medical and scholarly journals that helped them in recruiting numerous new believers in their cause. The activists failed, though, in achieving their goal of steering politicians and the public away from perceiving gun control as primarily a means of putting down crime.

Meanwhile, the menace of automatic guns became striking in what the Los Angeles *Times* termed "the worst riots of the century." On April 29, 1992, in Simi Valley, California, a largely middle-class, white jury acquitted four white Los Angeles police officers of all but one count in the beating of Rodney King, a black motorist. The verdict astounded African Americans because a witness had videotaped the bashing and television stations nationwide repeatedly played an edited version of the tape that showed police brutality in action.

The verdict infuriated blacks and many whites too. For instance, as soon as a twelve-year-old black boy heard the verdict, he said, "I feel like going to get a gun." Within hours rioting erupted in Los Angeles, with guns appearing to pop up everywhere, as during the Watts riot, in the hands of rioters, merchants, looters, and police. Gunmen, sometimes cheered by rioters shouting "Kill 'em! Shoot 'em!" fired semiautomatic weapons at police cars. Veteran officers described the scene as "an absolute war zone."[34]

Frightened Angelenos purchased twenty thousand guns. After five days of mayhem—with fifty-four people killed, twenty-four hundred injured, and more than a billion dollars in property damage—police, National Guard, and federal forces restored order. Throughout the city the fear of more violence lingered as did the gun hoarding.

Researchers commented that "a plague of youth violence seems to be sweeping the country" and that gun violence or the fear of it pervaded life in the inner city. High-quality small arms, such as revolvers and automatic and semiautomatic pistols, had become abundant among the nation's youth.[35] These weapons had also become so lethal and the struggle over gun violence so much a part of the national scene that politicians could not, as after past riots, readily ignore demands to do more about it. As could be expected from such pressure in this election year, lobbies on both sides of the gun-control issue tried to influence the congressional and presidential races.

Bush ran for reelection on a platform that defended "the constitutional right to keep and bear arms." Still incensed by his stance on assault guns, the rifle association refused to contribute to his campaign or to endorse him again. It took this position even though the Democrats and their candidate, William Jefferson Clinton, the governor of Arkansas, posed a greater danger to the association's doctrines. The Democratic Party's platform declared the time had come "to shut down the weapons bazaars." It endorsed a waiting period for handgun purchases, called for a ban on "the most deadly assault weapons," and demanded swift punishment for those committing crimes with handguns. It also promised a crackdown on the black market in firearms and stiff penalties for sellers of guns to children. However, it opposed restrictions on hunting and sport guns.

As did Bush, Clinton announced support for "the right to keep and bear arms" but wanted "to have some way of checking handguns before they're sold." For this reason, he embraced the stalled Brady bill. He also favored "restrictions on assault weapons, whose only purpose is to kill." Bush repeated his standard lines for disapproving gun control in such statements as "Go after the criminal and not after the gun owner." He opposed the Brady bill because he viewed it as not being tough enough on the criminal.[36]

Under pressure from control advocates and the public, however, the president once more offended his gun constituency. He signed an appropriation bill that cut off funding for a program in the BATF that aided convicted felons who sought to regain the privilege of owning firearms. Even though Bush's action in this matter had little to do with boosting gun regulation, it angered NRA leaders because they regarded it as a form of gun control. To the embarrassment of all, it also again spotlighted the weakness of the BATF as a regulator of the gun traffic and the firearms industry.

Regardless, neither this ruckus nor Bush's stance on guns accounted for his narrow election loss in November. Clinton's win did indicate, though, that more and more politicians had become willing to incur the wrath of the gun lobby by endorsing some form of regulation. The election also confirmed a trend that had been evident since Franklin Roosevelt's time but now had become firm. On the gun issue, contenders for office split largely along party lines. Most Republicans opposed further gun controls whereas Democrats usually promoted them in some form.

While standing against strong federal gun-control at home, the Bush administration had favored controls for gun use in other parts of the world, for example for the peoples of sub-Saharan Africa. For years the United States and its communist rivals had flooded the region, as well as parts of Asia, with small arms—pistols, machine guns, rocket launchers, antipersonnel grenades, and assault rifles. When the cold war ended, the Soviet Union dissolved, and most of the ideological conflicts in those regions folded, but the weapons remained. Afghanistan and Pakistan, for instance, brimmed with guns. Throughout the world, more than five hundred million military-style firearms fell into the hands of criminals, vigilantes, private armies, and various civilians.[37]

These weapons streaming from Russia and other former Communist countries in Eastern Europe fueled the ethnic bloodletting and crime that threatened the stability of governments throughout the Third World. The availability of small firearms at low prices often charted the course of such violence. In South Africa, criminals and gun owners, blacks and whites, bought these guns in an internal arms race that local authorities could not halt. As observers noted, stabbings decreased and shootings increased. The gun replaced the panga, a broad-bladed knife, as the favored killing tool.

In the early nineties South Africa's homicide rate rose to ten times that of the United States. Its whites came to be "rated amongst the most heavily armed groups in the world." In subsequent years in cities such as Johannesburg, blood from shoot-outs flowed in the streets, contributing to the nation's reputation as one of "the most dangerous places on Earth."[38] In one instance, bandits armed with AK-47 rifles killed at least thirty-five guards while they hauled cash on a highway. To combat the criminal gangs, Cape Town citizens, among others, organized gun-toting vigilante groups. They compounded the firearm homicides.

Most of the former Communist countries in Eastern Europe also experienced a sharp rise in civilian gun violence. Before its breakup, the Soviet Union had strict gun-control laws and a homicide rate of about 40 percent less than that of the United States. In 1992 the government permitted Russian civilians to obtain guns for "self-defense" purposes—"a tacit recognition," a foremost analyst wrote, "that the state could no longer protect its citizens in the most fundamental matters of life and death." He maintained that no single factor did more "to transform the landscape of the former Soviet Union than the easy access to guns."[39]

The murder rate in the new Russian state began climbing to one of the world's highest. In 1993 it rose to double that in the United States. Gun violence became so rampant that entrepreneurs turned to armed private security guards for protection. Authorities could not cope with the illegal trafficking in firearms because the huge amounts of cash it generated attracted an army of traders.[40]

Bundles of the Russian guns also reached Western European countries, often through illegal channels, contributing to dramatic rises in crime even in Britain and Germany, despite their strict firearms controls. To the east, Czechoslovakia while under Communist rule had a well-enforced law that required permits for private ownership of guns. With freedom from puppet status, its people developed a flourishing trade in black-market weapons accompanied by a steep surge in robberies and murder.

Latin American nations, too, experienced raging domestic gun-violence, particularly Mexico, Brazil, and Colombia. Mexico had a crime rate of more than four times that of the United States. As individuals, Mexicans had clearer gun-owning privileges than their North American neighbors. Mexico's constitutions of 1857 and 1917 specified that every person had a right to possess and carry arms for legitimate defense. Various court decisions upheld this "fundamental right."[41] Governmental corruption, firearms smuggling from the United States, and ethnic antagonisms accounted for much of Mexico's rampant gun violence.

Brazil's gun brandishing outstripped Mexico's. A Gallup poll indicated that in the nineties 34 percent of all Brazilian families experienced crime of some kind whereas in the United States 13 percent did so. A journalist reported from Rio de Janeiro, "There is so much crime here, and so much toting of weapons, that news of violence just doesn't generate much excitement anymore." Ostensibly, Brazilians tolerated gun toting because as did North Americans, in rural areas they had a strong hunting tradition. Crime surveys designated Brazil the second most violent country in the world. In the nineties, in proportion to population, it had the highest rate of murders by gun in the world.

In 1997 in São Paulo hundreds died violently, 90 percent of them by gun. This situation led the state of Rio de Janeiro to prohibit the sale of guns and ammunition to anyone except police and security companies. As the next step, the president, Fernando Henrique Cardoso, introduced legislation that would ban personal possession of firearms throughout the nation but rampant crime and gun violence continued into the twenty-first century.[42]

For similar reasons, Colombia outranked all other countries with its crime and gun violence. In 1993 it had a murder rate well over five times that of the United States. A few years later, to counter the firepower of drug dealers and revolutionary guerrillas, the government handed out machine guns to untrained private individuals to defend themselves. That only increased the gun violence. In contrast, to the north, Canada had one of the world's lowest homicide rates—2.2 per 100,000 of its population. This rate ranked lower than those of Denmark, Finland, Sweden, and other lands with recent peaceful histories. The domestic gun violence in other countries—whether high or low, whether emanating from crime or other causes—did not have a direct impact on the problem in the United States. For control advocates, though, that record had an indirect cautionary value. It indicated that the internal gun-control struggle had an international dimension often overlooked. In addition, the mounting recognition by scholars and others of the relationship between domestic and international traffic in small arms aroused concern that out-of-control foreign gun-violence would step up pressure for more domestic firearms controls.[43]

17

The Brady Act

Most Americans who looked closely at the struggle to contain gun violence had usually focused on Congress or the judiciary. They seldom had paid serious attention to the part played by the executive branch. In the past, this indifference toward the presidency's role had a logic to it. Except for Franklin Roosevelt, Lyndon Johnson, and Jimmy Carter, presidents either had ignored agitation for federal controls or had opposed it.

When William Jefferson Clinton took office, the president's part changed dramatically. From the start, he assumed the leading role in the battle to reduce gun proliferation and violence, which in the previous year had risen by 5 percent.[1] Where he had the authority, he moved quickly to make up the losses the control movement had experienced during the Reagan era. For instance, through executive order Clinton increased the fee for a gun dealer's license from ten dollars to two hundred dollars, leading to a drop of more than two-thirds in the number of federally licensed gun merchants. On February 10, 1993, he declared the need "to stop all these people that go to legal gun stores and buy guns and then turn around and give them to kids like they're going out of style." A week later he told Congress, "I will make you this bargain: If you will pass the Brady bill, I'll sure sign it."[2]

Three days later, Charles E. Schumer, a Democratic congressman from New York, and Ohio's Howard M. Metzenbaum reintroduced the Brady bill in the House and Senate. A Gallup poll indicated that 88 percent of the public, or nearly nine out of ten Americans, desired its passage. At this time also, 77 percent of those polled, including 57 percent of the gun owners who responded, favored stricter gun laws.[3]

Even with this popular backing, Clinton found the gun lobby's opposition formidable. So he tried to placate firearm owners by saying he strongly supported "the rights of ordinary Americans to legitimately own handguns and rifles." He added that we must also think "about the reality . . . that millions of Americans face streets that are unsafe, under conditions that no other nation—no other nations—has permitted to exist." He also praised the National Rifle Association for having put out "valuable information about hunting and marksmanship and safe use of guns."[4]

In April when the president announced his anticrime program modeled in part on the stymied Bush plan, he spoke as did most politicians. He persisted in identifying the gun problem primarily with crime. Through executive action he continued suspending the import of specified foreign assault guns, pointing out they had become the weapons of choice for gangs and drug dealers. Through the firearms bureau he also limited the number of licensed gun-dealers, tightened standards for their compliance with existing federal controls, and ordered firmer enforcement of gun regulations.[5] The president appeared in step with public opinion.

On July 1 another grievance killer—or person who uses firearms to unleash his wrath on people indiscriminately—bolstered this antigun sentiment. Gian Luigi Ferri, a disgruntled mortgage broker, toted two Intratec TEC-DC-9 assault pistols to a law office in San Francisco, murdered eight people, wounded six, and then shot himself. This slaughter appalled Americans but neither it nor the Gallup survey prevented progun federal legislators from stalling the Brady bill.

Despite this congressional attitude and the continued potency of the gun lobby, it could no longer easily frighten legislators collectively to the point of quashing debate on a bill. The political influence of control organizations emboldened antigun members of Congress to speak out more often and more openly than in the past. For example, in September in a public hearing Schumer stated that "the Brady bill will save lives that are being wasted in an epidemic of handgun violence from Brooklyn to Florida and all across America. And that is not theory, that is fact." He added, "The day has passed when the NRA can bully the U.S. Congress."[6]

Representative Lamar S. Smith of Texas countered with similar hyperbole, declaring that the bill "fails the truth in packaging test. It is so marginal in its benefits and the claims of its supporters are so excessive that Congress would do well to relegate the bill to a permanent waiting period."[7] Smith parroted a standard gun-advocate strategy.

Ultimately, after seven years of struggle, intensive lobbying by organizations such as Handgun Control Inc., and mounting resentment against the tactics of the gun lobby, control proponents cracked the opposition to the Brady bill. Steady pressure from the White House persuaded a crucial number of Republican legislators in both houses of Congress to join Democrats in voting for the measure and overcome a last-ditch filibuster by progun senators.[8] On November 30 Clinton signed the Brady Handgun Violence Prevention Act into law, saying "grassroots America . . . demanded that this Congress not leave here without doing something about this [gun control]." He insisted that "this bill will make a difference" and also called it a "good beginning" for more firearms legislation.[9]

Control advocates had designed the Brady statute's key provisions to keep the notorious Saturday night specials out of the hands of convicted felons, drug users, mentally unbalanced persons, and illegal aliens. A prime condition subjected those who wished to purchase a handgun to a waiting period of five business days. During this time, as an interim measure until an instant check system could become operational, the statute called for the local "chief law enforcement officer" to make a "reasonable effort" to ascertain whether or not the applicant met the legal requirements to complete the purchase. Since on its face the law did not make the background checks mandatory, the federal government could not prosecute local police who did not conduct them.[10] The statute also increased fees for firearms licenses, made it a federal crime to steal weapons from licensed dealers, and required vendors to report multiple-handgun sales to state and local police.

This new step in federal regulation hardly compensated for the control losses in the McClure-Volkmer Act. In addition, in comparison to foreign legislation such as Britain's Criminal Justice and Public Order Act of 1994, which increased already-substantial penalties for firearms offenses, the Brady law was modest.[11] Several critics who analyzed its weaknesses called it "a sop to the widespread fear of crime and to the feeling that 'something has to be done' about guns."[12]

Among constituents of the gun lobby, the legislation created a furor. From the start, gunmakers had not liked it but had gone along with it because they realized that public sentiment viewed direct lobbying by their industry with hostility. Then in the battle to rescind or modify the new law many manufacturers remained outwardly passive. They preferred to leave the public grappling to the NRA—and grapple it did.

Playing on the power of well-anchored myth and some truth, NRA leaders described the law to members as "a gun-grabbing scheme" that initiated "the most dangerous, sweeping attack on your Second Amendment freedoms ever

undertaken in the history of the United States."[13] With a dues-paying membership that had climbed to over three million the association had pumped its
annual budget to more than seven million dollars. With these resources, it targeted for retribution in forthcoming elections the legislators who voted for the
Brady law.

Several months later, a television network news program, 60 *Minutes*, ran a
feature on another aspect of gun violence. It examined the exemption of guns
from the purview of the Consumer Product Safety Commission. In the drafting
stage of the Consumer Product Safety Act of 1972, this federal regulatory
agency had been given authority to apply and enforce restrictions on the marketing of firearms as well as on other inherently dangerous products such as
drugs, pesticides, alcohol, and even toys. In exchange for votes to pass the measure, progun legislators forced backers to exclude firearms from scrutiny.

As usual, the gun groups contended that firearms makers voluntarily held
themselves to higher standards than other manufacturers, hence further over-
seeing was unnecessary. They argued also that education, not regulation, would
protect users of their products against accidental shootings. This contention
ran counter to research on the subject showing that stringently enforced gun
laws, as in New Jersey, reduced accidental firearm deaths.[14]

Two years after passage of the product safety law, a gun-control organization
in Chicago asked the new consumer agency to exercise its authority over hazardous goods by prohibiting the sale of handgun ammunition to civilians.
Alerted progun groups flooded the commission and Congress with protests.
The commission then ruled that bullets, too, did not fall within its jurisdiction.
The Chicago controllers sued in a federal court, persuading the judge to over-
rule the commission and make way for reconsideration of the matter. Promptly,
Congress blocked that possibility by passing a law specifically barring the com-
mission from controlling bullets.

As a result, no governmental or other agency could offer assurance that guns
and bullets when produced and marketed were safe for intended use. This gave
firearms makers a privileged status among those who marketed potentially dangerous products. As one critic put it, Congress had placed Americans "in the
indefensible position of having stronger consumer protection standards for toy
guns—and teddy bears—than real guns."[15]

In the next two decades accidental shootings accounted for more than thirty
thousand deaths and nearly three hundred thousand injuries. Television investigators publicized the problem, stressing the contribution of defectively manufactured guns to this bloody toll. This adverse publicity on the safety record of

guns, as well as polls that continued to indicate the public wanted stiffer gun controls, did not keep Congress from refusing to deal with the problem.[16] Early in 1994 the gun fraternity, while less intimidating than in the past, through its lobby could still demonstrate it had power sufficiently awesome to manipulate Congress on crucial firearms issues.

For example, for years Senator Metzenbaum had tried to eliminate the firearms producers' privileged treatment by sponsoring a bill to incorporate guns in the safety commission's inspection program. When a television journalist asked why his bill went nowhere, he replied, "The NRA's position is consistent." It is "opposed to any legislation that has the word 'gun' in it." While responding to another question, he added that if the lobby dropped its opposition, "we would pass the bill overnight."[17]

The senator had exaggerated but not by much. Following Robert Kennedy's murder, the NRA had supported a ban on Saturday night specials because they were shoddily manufactured and unsafe even for shooters. Numerous members, however, wanted no limitation. They feared that safety standards as imposed on other consumer products could lead to outlawing all handguns. The association leadership embraced this tough position. It could not, though, block the persisting legislative and executive assault on shoddy handguns.

Control promoters who continued to push for firearms inspection also called attention to the need to tighten reins on gun merchants. In April a probing journalist reported that Colombian narcotics lords, Japanese gangsters, Croatian nationalists, Irish gunrunners, Argentine and Filipino rebels, and Mexican drug gangs obtained their small firearms largely from loosely regulated American dealers. As had preceding regimes, the Clinton administration encouraged and subsidized military arms sales to developing countries in Latin America, Asia, Africa, and the Middle East. It did so to retain the position of the United States as the world's foremost arms merchant.

Later, though, the president tried to curb aspects of the international trafficking in firearms. As Secretary of State Madeleine Albright reported, "We have tightened our laws to prevent Americans from facilitating arms deals abroad that would be illegal at home."[18] All the while Clinton also never stopped promoting stiffer domestic gun-controls as antidotes to crime.

At this point, Clinton sought to achieve his regulatory goal with a bipartisan strategy. He sponsored a get-tough-with-criminals bill he thought Republicans would accept. His program also included firearms restrictions, as on assault guns, that he believed would appeal to liberal Democrats. Many of the Republican legislators now came from the South, as well as from the rural West. They brought with them attitudes on social issues, such as abortion and gun control, that were more conservative than those of colleagues from the Northeast, Midwest, and big cities. Reflecting the party's changed composition, the national committee threatened to withhold campaign funds from any Republican in Congress who voted for the gun-control provision, the most controversial part of the crime bill.

Undeterred, the president pressed for passage of the bill, emphasizing that assault weapons were designed for war and had no place on American streets. With some hyperbole, he asserted that "one of the reasons we've got the highest murder rate is that we have more guns in the hands of criminals" and individuals likely to act on impulse. Nowhere else in the world, he said, are there "people walking in the streets better armed than the police. It's not right, and we've got to do something about it."[19]

The Senate bill called for a ban on assault weapons, so members of the House called for a similar proscription. Schumer perceived the semiautomatic guns as posing a special problem. "These machines are killing innocent people all over America," he pointed out. "Assault weapons are 18 times more likely to kill a cop than conventional firearms. They are 19 times more likely to be traced to crimes than conventional guns." They "are the weapon of choice of drug traffickers, violent youth gangs, and the seriously deranged bent on revenge through mass murders."[20]

In addition to using this scare tactic, administration leaders tried to pick up votes for the crime bill by buttonholing legislators. The usual conservatives resisted this or other legislation that would expand national jurisdiction over homicides and other violent firearms felonies. Jack Brooks, a Democrat who chaired the House Judiciary Committee, couched this opposition in traditional NRA rhetoric. He stated the proposed legislation would violate "the right of individual Americans" to keep arms as "protected by the Second Amendment . . . a stark fact of constitutional life."[21]

Chief Justice William H. Rehnquist agreed with the revived resistance to federalized police power from another perspective. He warned, as he had three years earlier, that Congress should not sweep "many newly created crimes, such as those involving juveniles and handgun murders, into a federal court system that is ill-equipped to deal with those problems." He maintained that "providing Federal jurisdiction over offenses traditionally reserved for state prosecution is not a wise use of our scarce Federal resources." If virtually every crime committed with a gun that crossed a state line were placed under federal jurisdiction the courts would be swamped.[22]

Others concerned about the firearms problem, such as C. Everett Koop, a former surgeon general of the United States, backed a program named Steps to Prevent Firearm Injury but known usually by its acronym STOP. It had much more modest goals than did scientific researchers and control activists. "The main message of the STOP program is simple," a spokesman explained. "A gun in the home is a danger to your family. Parents need to know that the safest thing to do is to remove the gun from your home."[23]

NRA officials applauded such innocuous approaches as proper means of dealing with gun violence. They also denounced the president and the media for seeking "to dispose of constitutional rights and replace them with government granted privileges." They asserted that with his crime bill Clinton had declared "war against lawful gun owners."[24] On August 9, 1994, the Republican National Committee threatened to condemn and deny campaign funds to any party representatives who voted for the ban on assault weapons. Two days later the Republican majority in the House killed the bill. Once again, the NRA had won. Still, voter surveys continued to report progressively rising sentiment for more stringent federal controls, especially for a handgun ban.[25]

The day following the House vote, Clinton castigated the legislators for participating "in a procedural trick orchestrated by the National Rifle Association and intensely promoted by the Republican congressional leadership." He called it "the same old Washington game; just stick it to ordinary Americans because special interests can beat you because they're organized and they have money and they can confuse God-fearing, hard-working ordinary Americans." In that vote, he added, "I'd much rather be on the losing side than on the winning side."[26] The president's counterattack worked. Congress reconsidered the crime bill.

On August 21, forty-six Republican representatives and six senators broke ranks with their party colleagues to vote with the Democrats to pass the president's Violent Crime Control and Law Enforcement Act. Senate majority leader George D. Mitchell noted the length of the fight to overcome gun-lobby and Republican stalling tactics, commenting that "six years is long enough to consider any bill." His colleague, Joseph R. Biden, perceived the crucial issue in the struggle for the law as "guns, guns, guns, guns and guns."[27]

On September 13, when Clinton signed the measure into law, he called it "the toughest, smartest crime bill in our nation's history." He said also that "to get this bill" was one of the reasons he sought his office.[28] The statute's gun-control section made juvenile ownership of handguns illegal and outlawed for ten years the manufacture, sale, and possession of nineteen specified semiautomatic guns and copycat weapons but exempted 650 sporting rifles. It also gave Congress the power to review the ban and to include within it additional weapons.

Twice now Clinton had bucked the gun lobby and twice he had won. The NRA's attacks against him appeared to have backfired and bolstered the control movement. Also, the gun lobby's assumed invincibility once again appeared to have been damaged but not irreparably. Its constituents viewed the assault-weapons ban as leading to the confiscation of other firearms, so they and the lobby vowed to fight it. One of them even predicted "that gun owners will resist the law in massive numbers."[29]

Shortly, another shooting episode raised questions about felons having access to banned weapons and the efficacy of piecemeal gun laws. On September 30 Francisco Martin Duran, a twenty-six-year-old from Colorado with a felony record, sprayed the north face of the White House with bullets from a semiautomatic rifle. Two months later when an unknown shooter fired six shots at the White House, the doubts about feeble gun-control laws came up again but with no meaningful answers.

The possibility of any kind of additional control measures dimmed after the November 1994 congressional elections. During the elections, the NRA had spent some seventy million dollars on political action, much of it to defeat Democrats who had supported the Brady Act and other gun-control measures. About twenty such Democrats lost their seats apparently because of this targeting. This special-issue politicking also helped Republicans gain majorities in both houses of Congress. Newt Gingrich, the Republican Speaker of the House, then promised the NRA he would block all gun-control legislation during his term. He and other new Republican leaders said they would work to repeal the limited assault-weapons ban, which rifle association moguls regarded as a prime goal, as well as the Brady law.[30]

Despite the Democratic losses, Clinton defended his own tough politicking for the crime bill as "one of the things I'm most proud of that has happened since I have been President." If to prevent the repeal of the assault ban, he announced, "I have to give up the White House for it, I'll do it. It will be over my dead body if they do it." At another time, he would explain that "sooner or later the Federal Government had to take on" the gun keepers. In doing so, he surmised, their power "alone may have cost us the House in '94."[31]

That power showed up quietly in another way. In 1995 Congress privatized the nation's old rifle practice board. Now dubbed the Corporation for the Promotion of Rifle Practice, it supposedly had to scrounge for its own funding.

Nonetheless, the next year Congress gave the corporation surplus government rifles, ammunition, and other goods valued at $76 million to start the shooting program up again. When Senator Frank Lautenburg, a New Jersey Democrat, tried to amend the bill to strip the funding, he lost by a vote of 29–71.[32]

Another effort to stop funding had a different outcome. Three years earlier the federal government had formally established the National Center for Injury Prevention and Control and brought within it a unit for Disease Control and Prevention that long had been conducting research on gun violence. About $2.4 million of the unit's budget went to research on firearms injuries and deaths. Gun lobbyists urged Congress to eliminate the money for gun researchers in the Center for Disease Prevention.

"We would like to see the programme disbanded, defunded, and taken completely apart," Joe Phillips, an NRA official, told a British journalist. "There is nothing important about their research, nothing objective about their analyses, and their mission is to distort issues relating to firearms." Another critic, Edgar Suter, a California physician and shooter, called the center "a cesspool of junk science" controlled by the "anti-defense lobby." The shooting promoters wanted government and its research groups to continue to treat gun violence as a criminal-justice issue, not as a public-health problem. In 1997 the gun lobby succeeded in persuading friendly legislators to attach to appropriations for the disease center a proviso that none of the funding could be used "to advocate or promote gun control."[33]

All the while, fear of crime and of more controls sent numerous Americans on a gun-buying spree. The nation's firearms industry set "all-time sales records."[34] Indeed, in states with firearms manufacturers and aggressive gun clubs, neither the Brady law nor the selective assault-weapons ban had a significant, verifiable effect on curtailing shooters. Precise results for these laws were difficult to obtain because no one knew how many operable guns Americans possessed. Most surveys indicated that civilians possessed two hundred million or more small firearms, that the number of households with guns had declined from 50 to about 35 percent, that their defensive use was rare, that most owners used guns for recreation, and that with increasing urbanization overall possession was declining.[35]

Within the gun-owning population, as earlier with vigilantes and in the seventies with the Posse Comitatus, Aryan Nations, and similar groups, extremists argued that the federal government had no authority at the state and local level. They expressed openly the determination to resist federal regulation, as with firearms. This attitude contributed to several well-publicized clashes with national authority as represented by agents of the Bureau of Alcohol, Tobacco, and Firearms.

The first major confrontation began in northern Idaho, near the town of Naples. The government charged Randall Weaver, a former Green Beret soldier and self-described white supremacist, with unlawfully selling two sawed-off shotguns to a BATF agent. Weaver defied an order to appear in court for trial and threatened to shoot anyone who came within three hundred yards of his remote mountain cabin at Ruby Ridge.[36] On August 21, 1992, six armed deputy federal marshals placed the cabin, with Weaver's family in it, under surveillance. In two shoot-outs that followed, the Weavers killed two deputy marshals and marshals killed Randy's fourteen-year-old son, Samuel, and his wife, Vicki.

The FBI then took command of the siege and an eleven-day standoff followed. When Weaver surrendered, authorities found a small arsenal in his cabin—rifles, shotguns, handguns, and thousands of rounds of ammunition. During Weaver's trial for the murder of one of the marshals, testimony revealed that the FBI had tampered with evidence. An Idaho jury held that in Weaver's selling of the shotguns government agents had entrapped him. It came to this verdict even though evidence showed he had agreed to sell more firearms. Declaring him not guilty of murder, the jury convicted him only on minor charges relating to his earlier refusal to appear in court. Later, in a settlement growing out of a civil suit, Weaver won $3.1 million in compensation for the deaths of his wife and son. Among his gun-owning neighbors and antigovernment extremists, he emerged as a gun-toting David fighting Goliath.

Seven months after the Ruby Ridge bloodshed, federal agents again clashed with gun traffickers, this time at Mt. Carmel, a religious compound near Waco, Texas. The occupants, known as Branch Davidians, belonged to a cult that had spun off from Seventh-Day Adventists. Officials of the BATF suspected the group of hoarding an arsenal of illegal firearms, including semiautomatic rifles. When the Davidians defied a search warrant, seventy-six bureau agents sought to arrest their leader, Vernon Wayne Howell, a militant, self-appointed prophet who had assumed the name David Koresh and who perceived himself a paramilitary warrior.

When an informant tipped off Koresh about the planned raid, he laid "a deadly ambush."[37] On February 28, 1993, when the agents arrived to apprehend him, the Davidians fired on them with guns and threw hand grenades at them, killing four and wounding twenty. The gun battle raged for nearly ninety minutes before the BATF officials could retreat without further losses.

A gun aficionado who bought and sold numerous firearms at gun shows, Koresh explained why he used them against law officers. "I don't care who they are. Nobody is going to come to my home, with my babies around, shaking guns around, without a gun back in their face. That's just the American way." He also viewed the firearms bureau as an "evil agency that threatened the liberty of U.S. citizens."[38]

Seven weeks of siege by BATF and FBI agents followed. When the besiegers could not with peaceful tactics overcome Koresh's determination to resist, they lost patience. On April 19 they fired incendiary canisters at a concrete bunker and broke into the wooden residential structure with armored vehicles. During the confrontation, the building burst into flames. Some cult members shot themselves and others perished in the fire. In all, seventy-six men, women, and children, including Koresh, died. When law officers entered the charred remains of the compound they found about three hundred machine guns, assault rifles, and pistols.

The Brady law, Ruby Ridge, and Waco galvanized the rise of armed, private paramilitary organizations known often in popular parlance as militias. They differed markedly from the enrolled citizen-soldier groups of the past. People in this new movement commonly believed that government as leviathan had intruded in their lives to regulate them beyond reason, as in their use of firearms. "Gun Control is for only one thing," they would repeat often as a kind of slogan, "people control."[39]

To counter federal authority, militia members asserted a Second Amendment right to bear arms and conduct paramilitary training without hindrance. They embraced the individual-rights concept as gospel, denounced control measures as violating this assumed right, and depicted themselves as carrying on traditional militia practice of combating centralized tyranny. They were convinced that the government would first confiscate everyone's gun and then take away other liberties. They exhibited hostility toward all federal enforcement agencies but tangled most with the BATF and FBI.

The first prominent, active paramilitary group, the Militia of Montana, exploited this antigovernment animosity, particularly as it pertained to guns, to attract recruits. Its leaders revived the legend that civilian gun-owners, as theoretically had militias of the colonial era and the early Republic, constituted the core of the nation's defense of individual freedom. At no time since independence, they claimed, have we "needed a network of active militias across America to protect us from the monster we have allowed our federal government to become." They also peddled T-shirts picturing an eighteenth-century

militia man along with the slogan, "The Second Amendment isn't about hunting and shooting. It's about FREEDOM!"[40]

This simplistic reasoning appealed to Timothy J. McVeigh, a decorated veteran of the war in the Persian Gulf who had used firearms since childhood and
traded them at gun shows. He and his friend, Terry L. Nichols, another govern-
ment-hating army veteran, shared the outlook of militia militants and had connections with them. The Waco conflagration in particular infuriated McVeigh.
In apparent retaliation, on April 19, 1995, he exploded a truck filled with am-
monium nitrate and fuel oil at a federal building in Oklahoma City. It killed
168 people and injured more than 500.

This worst deed of individual domestic terrorism in the nation's history
placed the militia movement on front pages across America. That publicity,
regardless of how negative, helped boost militia membership. In June, civil
rights activists noted that 224 militias and their support groups toted guns in
thirty-nine states. Yet polls indicated that Americans, by large majorities, disapproved of the armed militias as a threat to society.[41]

During the furor over the Oklahoma terrorism, Wayne R. LaPierre, now the
NRA's executive vice president, circulated a fund-raising letter that compared
federal agents enforcing gun laws to Nazi storm troopers. Repeating a charge
that outraged many, he characterized the agents as "jack-booted government
thugs" who sought to "harass, intimidate, even murder, law-abiding citizens."
This language persuaded even staunch progun members such as George Bush
that the association had become too extreme in its politics. He called the letter
"a vicious slander on good people."[42] In May, when the NRA refused to repudi-
ate the document, he and several other prominent individuals resigned their
membership in a glare of publicity.

Earlier, during Bush's presidency, in a number of militias even children bran-
dished guns. At times elsewhere, juveniles even brought firearms to school.
Viewing the "easy availability of firearms to children" as a national problem
affecting "public health and safety," Congress in 1990 had passed the Gun-
Free School Zones Act that banned guns within one thousand feet of a school.[43]
Since the legislators had wedged the measure into a comprehensive crime-control package he valued, Bush reluctantly had signed it into law. Two years later,
Alfonso Lopez Jr., a senior at Edison High School in San Antonio, Texas,
brought a concealed .38-caliber handgun and five bullets to school. Texas authorities arrested him but instead of prosecuting him for violating a one-hun-
dred-plus-year-old state statute that barred the toting of a gun on school
premises, they deferred to a federal grand jury that indicted him under the

Gun-Free statute. Lopez's attorneys called the federal law "unconstitutional as it is beyond the power of Congress to legislate control over public schools."[44]

A lower court convicted Lopez. Then, after drawn-out appeals, the case reached the Supreme Court as *U.S. v. Lopez*, 115 S.Ct. 1624 (1995). As had been the practice in much civil-rights litigation since the sixties, the federal prosecutors invoked the commerce clause of the Constitution as the source of Congress's power to pass the school act. On April 26, 1995, in a five to four decision, the high court knocked down the statute. It ruled that the law exceeded Congress's authority in the "states under the commerce clause." The possession of a gun in a school zone did not constitute an economic activity that affected interstate commerce.[45] The Lopez lawyers had not challenged federal statute as violating the Second Amendment and the Court had not expressed any concern over its gun-control aspects.

As had other decisions of the Rehnquist court, this one reflected a conservative view of federalism, or that the central government had usurped too much of the power that constitutionally under the Tenth Amendment belonged to the states. This attitude, the tendency of jurists to view a firearm as private property, and the litigant's focus on gun possession made the case significant. It demonstrated that legal concerns involving states' rights and intrusive federal police power still had to be taken into account in the widening control struggle.

Still, the problem of juvenile gun violence remained a concern for much of the public. From 1985 to 1995 the number of youths who died in gunfire rose by 150 percent.[46] Clinton therefore pressed Congress for new federal legislation similar to the quashed school law but that would meet judicial requirements. Opponents argued that the problem did not require "a Federal solution" but should be handled, "as it has traditionally been handled, on a State and local level."[47] The president prevailed. On October 16 he signed the Gun-Free Schools Act that called on education districts to expel for at least one year any student who carried a firearm to school. States that failed to comply would forfeit federal education assistance.

A month later Jamie Rouse, a seventeen-year-old student at Richland School in Lynville, Tennessee, with a Remington Viper .22-caliber rifle shot and killed a teacher and a student and seriously wounded another teacher. Jamie owned the gun and knew how to use it effectively. He had practiced with it shooting at targets and squirrels.

Three months later, lethal violence in another school confounded Great Britain and made headlines internationally. On March 13, 1996, Thomas Hamilton, a disturbed member of a local gun club who had legal access to firearms, walked into a primary school in Dunblane, Scotland, with four handguns and more than seven hundred rounds of ammunition. With a hail of fire from a 9mm Browning semiautomatic pistol he slaughtered sixteen children and a teacher and wounded twelve children and two teachers. He then took his own life. Enraged parents of the victims campaigned to extend the nation's firearms laws into a total ban of privately owned handguns.

In October the government moved to enact such legislation. Philip, the Duke of Edinburgh, the queen's consort, an avid hunter, and a man often called the "king of the gaffe" for his blunders, objected. On December 19 he told a radio interviewer, "There's no evidence that people who use weapons for sport are any more dangerous than people who use golf clubs or tennis racquets or cricket bats. If a cricketer, for instance, suddenly decided to go into a school and batter a lot of people to death with a cricket bat, which he could do very easily, I mean are you going to ban cricket bats?"[48] He also called the firearms bill under consideration in Parliament "unreasonable" and ineffective.

His remarks infuriated numerous Britons as insensitive. The mother of one of the children in the school retorted, "How many people can you kill in three and a half minutes with a cricket bat? It is not the same as an automatic gun." The nation's gun lobby and the conservative press welcomed Philip's words. Michael Yardley, who spoke for the Sportsman's Association of Great Britain and Northern Ireland, said he was delighted Philip "had the courage to make his statement."[49] Such support did not help the duke. He apologized for the distress his comments had caused but did not soften his views on guns. The following June Parliament overwhelmingly approved the bill outlawing handguns, signaling the end of their ownership in Britain, even for target shooting.

The Dunblane tragedy appeared to have some impact on the gun-violence struggle in the United States. The Republican ideologues eager to carry out their pledge to repeal recent gun-control measures finally overcame Democratic opposition. They sent to the floor of the House a bill entitled the Gun Crime Enforcement and Second Amendment Restoration Act. The debate opened on March 22, 1996, nine days after the Dunblane massacre. The horror of its bloodletting remained fresh in the minds of at least some of the legislators. When the bill came to a vote, 239 members supported it, 179 voted no, and 19 abstained. The balloting indicated that on this issue Republicans had split so deeply that their leadership in the Senate refused to take up the measure.[50] The episode also suggested another previously undetected weakness in the gun lobby's political clout.

Shortly, the American obsession with guns had repercussions in Australia.

On April 28 in the resort town of Port Arthur in Tasmania, Martin Bryant, an unemployed loner, went on a rampage in a diner. With an American-made assault rifle he slaughtered thirty-five men, women, and children, wounded nineteen, and then withstood police for sixteen hours before being captured.

Shocked Australians, especially those in the National Coalition for Gun Control, immediately demanded new nationwide legislation to supplement the strict handgun controls that had been in effect through provincial law since the twenties and thirties.[51] Within twelve days the state and territorial governments agreed on a uniform gun-control law. Australia's powerful gun lobby, which the NRA aided with money and political strategy, protested. The lobby filled Melbourne's streets with seventy thousand gun enthusiasts who contended the legislation would neither reduce crime nor prevent another massacre. Many of the demonstrators vowed to defy any effort to take their guns.[52]

As for the control supporters, their most "effective line" in amassing popular support came from Prime Minister John Howard. "I don't want Australia to go down the American path," he stated, of lax gun laws and high homicide rates.[53] Although Australia had a high rate of firearms casualties, it was lower than that of the United States.

As implemented by Australia's states and territories, the uniform legislation banned the keeping of semiautomatic and pump-action weapons, imposed new restrictions on civilian possession of all firearms, and subjected violators to fines as high as twelve thousand dollars and to two year prison terms. To make these controls reasonably palatable to the gun community, authorities set a period of fifteen months for owners to give up their outlawed weapons and receive payment for them. The federal government reimbursed the state and territorial treasuries for these expenditures. Shooting organizations could not block the controls in part because Australia had no fundamental law or firearms history they could cite as supporting the right to bear arms. The buy-back plan succeeded in destroying more than six hundred thousand guns and apparently in reducing firearms deaths.

The Australian regulations left the United States as the last major democratic nation to permit private citizens to possess guns with few meaningful restraints. Upset by this dubious exceptionalism, control lobbyists viewed the Australian program as a possible model because the two countries had frontier traditions, state and federal problems, and gun-owning passions in common. Nothing came of this idea, and in the United States the gun violence continued without truly significant hindrance.

18

School Shootings
and Gun Shows

To emphasize the gravity of America's gun-violence problem, President Bill Clinton invited Sarah Brady to address the Democratic National Convention meeting in August 1996 in Chicago. Every year, she reported, nearly forty thousand Americans kill someone with a firearm, and every two hours a child is killed with a gun. "This," she pleaded, "must stop."[1] Accordingly, the president fought for more, but not drastic, restrictions on firearms use. For example, he urged Congress to extend the Brady law to ban cop-killer bullets and to deny guns to persons who beat up spouses and children. His entreaty partially succeeded. On September 30 he signed legislation prohibiting anyone with a record of domestic violence from possessing a gun.

Meanwhile, the courts continued to rule against the personal-rights interpretation of the Second Amendment, notably in the case of *Hickman v. Block*, 81 F. 3d (98 Cir. 1996). Douglas Ray Hickman, a federally licensed firearms dealer in San Fernando, California, had applied a number of times for a permit to carry a concealed handgun. As allowed by law, the Los Angeles county sheriff turned him down. Hickman first appealed the decision in 1988 and four years later filed suit claiming the denial violated his Second Amendment right to bear arms. On April 5, 1996, after more appeals backed by NRA attorneys, the ninth circuit court in Pasadena declared, "We follow our sister circuits in holding that the Second Amendment is a right held by the states, and does not protect the possession of a weapon by a private citizen." It added bluntly, the amendment "creates a right, not a duty. It does not oblige the states to keep an armed militia."[2] The Supreme Court refused to review the decision.

This ruling, as with those in other Second Amendment cases, had little impact on progun legislators but the issue of gun violence figured with some prominence in the president's reelection campaign. In a nationally televised debate, the moderator asked Robert Dole, the Republican candidate, if elected would he repeal the Brady and assault-weapons laws. The statutes had been so ineffective, Dole responded, that he had devised a better plan that would "keep guns out of the hands of criminals."[3] In contrast, Clinton declared the Brady law a success and attacked Dole as fronting for the National Rifle Association.

In November, despite heavy shooter opposition, Clinton won reelection. In addition, in races for the House, among those targeted by control lobbyists eight progun representatives, including the ten-term spokesman for the NRA, Harold Volkmer, lost. These victories bolstered the administration's commitment to the control program.

At the start of his second term Clinton again pointed out that in various communities, criminals had become more heavily armed than law-enforcement officers. Quickly, he had another example. On February 28, 1997, two gunmen with convictions for illegal gun possession robbed a bank in North Hollywood, California. They wore masks, bulletproof vests, and carried an AK-47 assault weapon and an M-16 rifle with a 100-round magazine. As one observer commented, "These guys were ready for war." In fleeing, the robbers engaged Los Angeles police in a furious gun battle—captured live on national television— that terrorized a neighborhood and injured eleven officers and six bystanders. The shooting ended when police killed the bandits.

This firefight raised demands once more for stronger gun laws. "I can't think of a more graphic, visual reason," municipal official Laura Chick commented, "for the public of the United States of America to all get on board in advocating for rational, reasonable and sensible gun control."[4] Others called for arming the police with more powerful weapons so as to close the gap with well-armed criminals.[5] Already, in a number of American cities authorities had upped the firepower of their police until they had become more heavily armed than those in any other Western democracy.

Among others, Willie L. Williams, chief of the Los Angeles Police Department, urged restraint. "You can't equip our general patrol officer with an AK-47," he said. "We're supposed to live in somewhat of a civilized society." Another officer warned, "If you put [semiautomatic] rifles in everybody's vehicle, we're going to have more mishaps than positive results."[6] Despite the chief's concerns, officers clamored for more powerful weapons. Soon the police department acquired six hundred military surplus M-16 automatic rifles augmented later by the governor's donating four hundred M-16 assault rifles to help boost its firepower.

This internal arms race, the gun violence, and the rise of the paramilitary cultists alarmed numerous mainstream Americans. A national survey conducted at Johns Hopkins University showed overwhelming public support for an array of gun-control measures. For instance, 81 percent of those queried desired stricter regulation of gun sales, firearms registration, and the licensing of owners.[7]

This sentiment did not deter the gun lobbyists. They continued to attack virtually any kind of meaningful restriction on firearms possession, but their political influence seemed increasingly vulnerable. More than in the past, jurists, legislators, and other Americans viewed the Second Amendment as an anachronism. As evidence of diminishing lobby power, critics cited passage of the Brady measure as well as the reinvigorated opposition from control advocates.

Even the NRA felt the heat. In a two-year period its membership dropped about 20 percent to 2.8 million and assets fell from $80 million to $49 million.[8] For several years, because of the organization's heavy political spending, it had operated in the red. Nonetheless, it refused to retreat from its aggressive programs and even expanded them to overseas ventures. In 1997 it joined with firearms producers and gun organizations in eleven countries to combat international gun-control efforts. It also lobbied the United Nations to block a resolution that called for curbs on the illicit trafficking of firearms.[9] It and its allies campaigned against measures that would involve the United Nations in any kind of gun-control commitment.

Meanwhile, the NRA's sustained strength domestically became apparent again in its assault on the Brady law. Because the federal courts had consistently rejected suits based on the interpretation of the Second Amendment as guaranteeing a personal right to keep arms, the NRA changed tactics. Rather than continue fighting head-on for its version of the amendment and probably losing, its attorneys attacked one major provision of the Brady Act.

Soon after the law had gone into effect, the gun lobby had encouraged rural sheriffs to file suits against the act on the premise that its federal police power intruded on long-standing state authority guaranteed under the Tenth Amendment rather than under the Second. Richard Mack, a progun, promilitia sheriff of Graham County, Arizona, and Jay Printz, a long-standing member of the rifle association and sheriff of Ravalli County, Montana, filed such suits. NRA attorneys for the plaintiffs argued that in requiring local law-enforcement officials to divert scarce resources from other tasks to perform background checks on gun buyers the federal government breached the Constitution. Locally based federal judges agreed but a circuit court reversed their ruling. The Supreme Court then accepted the case consolidated as *Printz v. United States*.

On June 27, 1997, in a five to four decision the high court sided with the plaintiffs. As in the Lopez case, its conservative majority, focusing more on states' rights than on the gun-control issue, ruled that the federal government could not "conscript" state and local officers to enforce its regulatory programs. Whereas the executive branch had characterized the Brady law's check system as discretionary, the Court viewed it as mandatory. It held, therefore, that the system violated the Tenth Amendment's protection of state prerogatives under the doctrine of dual sovereignty that strictly limited federal jurisdiction. Despite this voiding of the background checks, the rest of the Brady Act survived.[10] Moreover, the decision affected only twenty-three states because the others scrutinized backgrounds under the authority of their own laws.

Tanya Metaksa, the rifle association's chief lobbyist, lauded the decision as "a strong and very desirable signal that local law enforcement serves only one master—not politicians in Washington, D.C., but the local community." In contrast, Congressman Charles Schumer predicted the ruling "will cost more lives than any decision they've rendered in the last 50 years."[11]

Viewing the Brady law as the crown jewel in his legislative record, the president had boasted repeatedly that it had barred 250,000 felons from buying handguns. He reacted to the Court's decision by announcing, "No state should become a safe haven for criminals who want to buy handguns." He also urged local law-enforcement agencies to conduct the checks on their own until the end of the following year when the federal government expected to have its computerized check system in order.[12]

Although frustrated by the *Printz* decision and the gun lobby's continued effectiveness, organizations within the control movement, such as Women Against Gun Violence, turned to pressuring cities and counties to pass and enforce ordinances limiting civilian access to guns. These advocates hoped that in time their efforts would carry over into the national struggle to generate similar controls in Washington. Affiliates of the NRA countered with lawsuits against communities that passed such laws. In many instances this tactic worked because fiscally constrained communities could not afford involvement in high-priced litigation.

Meanwhile, even though crime continued to drop, figures on gun violence remained high. In some areas fatal shootings even rose. The president reminded Americans of the still-significant juvenile criminality. "Over the past decades," he announced, "the number of gun murders by juveniles has skyrocketed by 300%. This is simply unacceptable."[13] Law-enforcement officers and control activists also expressed concern over the sievelike qualities of state and federal laws, particularly as related to assault firearms. They cited gun-industry guile, reluctant enforcement, and political opportunism as at least partially responsible for the inadequacies in the existing regulations.

In California, for instance, gun merchandisers bypassed the state's Roberti-Roos Act. Attorney General Dan Lungren, a shooter who found the feel of an assault weapon "pretty powerful," virtually ignored the law's requirements. Critics charged that he "sided with the National Rifle Assn. and against the state's police chiefs and sheriffs." In December 1997, Handgun Control Inc. filed suit against Lungren for not enforcing the Roberti-Roos registration provision. Six months later a judge in San Francisco ruled he had violated the law.[14]

Even though various communities banned specific makes of semiautomatic weapons, nationally gun sales flourished. Manufacturers flooded the country with copycat models that differed only cosmetically from restricted firearms. California's senior senator, Dianne Feinstein, expressed disgust with the arms industry and the gun community. "The biggest and most arrogant lobby back there [in Washington]," she said, "is 'Big Gun.' They pack a clout, particularly in the House, that I have never seen in my entire life."[15]

As we have noted, for decades gun advocates had made that clout possible by voting their representatives, state or federal, out of office if they embraced even mild controls. These citizens also backed all kinds of profirearms laws. In Louisiana, for instance, by law citizens could keep guns in their homes or cars. A "shoot the burglar" law also permitted them to use deadly force against a home invader. Another statute authorized residents, if they had no criminal record, to carry concealed weapons. In June, the legislature passed a "shoot the carjacker" law, the first of its kind in the nation. It empowered motorists who feared for their lives to kill carjackers.

Gun devotees of the Louisiana type provided the core constituency for a counterattack on the control movement. For some time NRA leaders had recognized that their version of the Second Amendment right, or "the one right that protects all the others" and "that allows 'rights' to exist at all," was in "grave peril." To meet the challenge, the association's first vice president, the right-wing movie actor Charlton Heston, pledged to lead a three-year, $100 million crusade aimed at restoring the amendment to its "rightful . . . place as America's first freedom." The association intended to bolster this commitment by working to elect a progun president and Congress and by teaching youngsters that the right to bear arms must "come first again."[16]

Heston also attacked Clinton personally. Alluding to sex scandals clouding the president's reputation, he announced, "We did not trust you with our 21-

year-old daughters, and we sure, Lord, don't trust you with our guns." On June 8, 1998, the association chose Heston as its president. He promised to bring the NRA "back into the mainstream" of the nation's political life.

Meanwhile, control proponents stepped up attacks against the highlighting of gun violence on television and in movies. Most studies maintained that these media had a "staggering" influence on children, teaching them "that guns and violence solve problems." Investigators also claimed that heavy exposure to televised brutality, "committed mostly by fists and guns," contributed to aggressive behavior and crime.[17]

A rough survey of adults across the United States in September 1997 suggested that most Americans, too, believed the home screen delivered too much gunplay and that the entertainment industry should clean up its act. In May the second volume of the National Television Violence Study substantiated this popular perception. It also reported that, despite the correlation of broadcast violence with "aggressive antisocial behavior," such programming had not changed.[18]

During these years, parent groups, too, expressed concern over video games portraying "death-defying, machine-gun-toting Rambos." As prices for these videos plummeted, children snapped them up for playing and replaying on their personal computers. Psychologists worried that the "violence in games further desensitizes youngsters already accustomed to violence on TV" because of "the accuracy of the simulations—the carnage, the blood, the guts." Producers, however, marketed ever bloodier games to ever younger audiences because as in films, they said, "violence sells." It sold not just in the United States but across global borders largely because it stimulated the players, made adrenaline flow, and gave the players a sense of power. Britain produced some of the most violent games.[19]

At the same time, the visual media also helped the gun-control cause. When the Supreme Court ruled on the Brady law, public television ran a documentary, "Hot Guns," that focused negatively on California manufacturers, who produced 80 percent of the nation's cheap handguns. Despite such agitation for tough firearms control, the gun lobby once more demonstrated its power. On September 26 Pete Wilson, California's Republican governor and a former Marine expert marksman, vetoed a hard-fought bill that would have banned the manufacture and sale of the junk handguns. As though by rote, he repeated gun-lobby arguments that the measure would deprive the poor of the opportunity to buy cheap guns for self-defense while not keeping them out of the hands of criminals. The following year, with the same strained reasoning that editorialists rated as another F in logic, Wilson vetoed several other weaker control bills. Since Democrats favored the measures and Republicans opposed them, the vetoes kept gun violence alive as a hot-button issue in California.

Nationally, too, the control question aroused deeper emotions than in the past, and proponents devised new ways to deal with it. Since the Olen Kelley case in Maryland in the previous decade, the antigun strategy of the product liability suit had worked effectively against domestic makers of Saturday night specials. Control activists had filed these suits with the intent of driving manufacturers out of business and of breaking the hold of the gun lobby on Congress. Firearms manufacturers and gun-keeper organizations had counterattacked by lobbying Congress with intensified determination. In spring 1995, shortly after winning control of Congress, Republican legislators had responded with bills to restrict product liability suits, essentially to limit their scope and make them virtually ineffective in gun cases. Deceptively, those in the Senate called their bill the Product Liability Fairness Act. Clinton's opposition prevented the legislation from becoming law and the suits continued unimpaired.

In one case in California in September 1997 an appeals court ordered Bryco Arms, a major manufacturer of such weapons, to pay a plaintiff $350,000 because one of its pistols exploded, causing him serious injury. In October, Lorcin Engineering, another large producer of cheap handguns, filed for bankruptcy protection because it faced liability suits of more than $18 million based on the malfunctioning of its weapons. It spent nearly twice as much on liability insurance for its products as it did to make them, and potentially even more in the litigation.[20]

The NRA offset these setbacks somewhat by triumphing in a head-on clash with control forces in the state of Washington. The controllers there placed before the electorate a measure calling for stringent restrictions on the use of handguns. Both sides poured heavy money into the campaign. Once again, with a fund of $2 million, the rifle association outspent its opponents and mobilized its supporters with more energy. On November 4 the voters defeated the proposal by a hefty margin.

Concurrently, control adherents had to fight the usual gun-lobby pressure in the nation's capital. In Congress in the previous month, Senator Feinstein and twenty-nine colleagues had petitioned the president to block the influx of foreign-made semiautomatics modified to slip through loopholes in the federal gun law. Soon after, these legislators learned that the BATF had approved entry of six hundred thousand foreign assault weapons. The White House attributed this to a rogue operation in the agency.

Still, the bureau did not crack down on firearms importers. Investigation indicated that BATF officials had aided importers in circumventing the law. Yet, just two years earlier, the rifle association had continued its standardized bashing of the bureau for allegedly "harassing, intimidating and hurting honest citizens."[21] The president admonished the agency but lax enforcement of gun laws persisted. On November 14 he ordered a temporary ban on the importation of modified assault-type rifles and a four-month suspension of the six hundred thousand guns already approved for entry.

This small measure helped but did not keep guns out of the reach even of children, whose shooting sprees continued to make headlines. On October 1, 1997, in Pearl, Mississippi, a sixteen-year-old boy, Luke Woodham, killed his mother then brought to school a rifle and shot nine students, two of whom died. On December 1 Michael Carneal, a fourteen-year-old living in West Paducah, Kentucky, went to his Heath High School carrying two semiautomatic rifles, two shotguns, and a handgun, all of which he had stolen. He fired into a crowd of praying students, killed three and injured several. No one had perceived Carneal as a threat. Schoolmates characterized him as sometimes odd but "a good kid."

On March 24, 1998, the grounds of the Westside Middle School near Jonesboro, Arkansas, became another shooting gallery. Andrew Golden, age thirteen, and Mitchell Johnson, age eleven, dressed in hunter's camouflage attire, fired handguns and rifles twenty-seven times at the school from a wooded area. They murdered four students and a teacher and wounded thirteen students and a teacher.

Andrew had learned marksmanship from his father, Dennis, the registered representative for a local gun club, the Jonesboro Practical Pistol Shooters Association. The boys stole the guns they used from Andrew's grandfather, who, like many Jonesboro residents, possessed a number of firearms. The youngsters' behavior corresponded with research showing that troubled youths usually borrowed or stole guns from family and friends when they went berserk.[22]

Journalists reported that Jonesboro folks loved three things above all others—God, each other, and guns. Still, the bloodletting puzzled many of them. "I know this is hunting country," one parent commented. "But these were little kids, children. How do two kids get away with running around on their own on a school day with a bunch of guns?"[23]

In response to the widespread concern arising from the Jonesboro killings, Clinton, by executive order on April 6, blocked the importation of 1.6 million military-style rifles, mostly variations of the AK-47 and Uzi semiautomatics banned earlier. He said, "As everyone knows, you don't need an Uzi to go deer hunting. . . . These are military weapons of war." The NRA immediately promised to overturn the ban in Congress. Its Tanya Metaksa announced, "We believe the people who have responsibility for writing gun laws are the Congress, not the president."[24]

Shortly the federal Centers for Disease Control and Prevention released data on firearm-related deaths, showing that in the past year only motor vehicle incidents exceeded them. Nonetheless, consistent with the drop in violent crime, it reported that for the past five years firearms injuries had declined but that gun violence remained a "serious public health concern."[25] Gun lobbyists rejected the study as another antigun propaganda stunt.

The lobbyists could not, however, so readily dismiss the stepped-up lethality in juvenile gun violence. On April 24 Andrew Wurst, a fourteen-year-old student at Parker Middle School in Edinboro, Pennsylvania, attended a graduation dance with a .25-caliber handgun. He shot a science teacher to death and wounded another teacher and two students. Wurst killed to make the occasion memorable.

Not long after, a like tragedy struck Thurston High School in Springfield, Oregon. On May 23 Kipland P. Kinkel, a slight fifteen-year-old freshman, shot his parents to death. Then at school, carrying a .22 rifle, a 9mm Glock semiautomatic handgun, and a .22 Ruger semiautomatic, he sprayed the crowded cafeteria with bullets, killing one student and injuring twenty-two others. He had learned to shoot at an early age, frequently had gone hunting with his father and uncles, and had long been fascinated with firearms and violence.

Again Clinton placed some blame for the school massacres on the entertainment industry. "When mindless killing becomes a staple of family entertainment, when over and over children see cinematic conflicts resolved not with words but with weapons, we shouldn't be surprised when children, from impulse or design, follow suit."[26] Hoping the shootings would provide new impetus for legislative action, he urged the Republican-controlled Congress to pass his juvenile crime bill. This legislation would permit authorities to treat young lawbreakers as adults, prohibit gun sales to anyone who as a youth had committed a violent crime, and require child-safety locks on handguns.

The school shootings also stimulated a fresh response from organized religion. For three decades a number of Protestant, Roman Catholic, and Jewish organizations had been calling for uncompromising restrictions on handguns and assault weapons. Finally, on June 19, the policymaking body of the Presbyterian Church, tired of waiting for government action, passed a resolution asking its 2.6 million members to remove handguns and assault weapons from their homes. This problem of civilian gun terror also produced, for the first time, limited international cooperation. On July 14 in Oslo the United States and twenty other nations adopted measures designed to control sales of small arms, both illicit and legal, in much of the world.

Three days later mayhem erupted before legislators' eyes in Washington's crowded Capitol. Russell Eugene Weston Jr., who had a grudge against Clinton and the government, pushed his way past sightseers while carrying a .38-caliber Smith & Wesson handgun. He killed two federal guards and seriously wounded a tourist before other guards shot him. Editorialists across the country hoped this episode and the school shootings would shake lawmakers into listening more to their control constituents than to the gun lobby. Control groups did benefit from the public outrage by gaining new members and from a rise in opinion favoring firearms regulation.[27] This sentiment did not pressure politicians into backing more controls, however. At the same time the gun lobby again flaunted its power. The Senate overwhelmingly rejected a simple bill requiring trigger locks on guns.

NRA and affiliates also succeeded in persuading thirty-one state legislatures to enact laws compelling local authorities to issue a permit to anyone without a criminal record to carry a hidden gun. As foreign observers commented, "In many places in America it is now easier to carry a concealed weapon in public than it is to smoke a cigarette."[28]

In October, New Orleans and in November, Chicago, and later other cities filed suits against gunmakers. The municipalities charged the manufacturers with some responsibility for the firearms violence just as sick smokers blamed the tobacco industry for their woes. The Chicago suit accused thirty-eight firearms manufacturers, distributors, and dealers of illegally inundating the city with guns they knew would be used in gang killings and other crimes. New Orleans sued under product liability law. Shortly after, gun enthusiast Alan M. Gottlieb announced firearms organizations would countersue cities that filed frivolous suits against gunmakers.

All the while, Clinton continued to press his piecemeal attack against civilian gun violence. In November, he signed into law legislation that increased prison sentences for felons who committed crimes while carrying a gun. At the end of the month, as the Brady law required, the instant background check went into effect. For four years, the purchasers of rifles and shotguns had been exempt from such investigation. Now in another incremental expansion of the federal government's authority over firearms sales, the checks applied to them.

Bit by bit some states and cities also placed restraints on gun wielders. In December, a California appeals court upheld the right of cities to ban the sale of cheap handguns despite the state government's contention it had exclusive jurisdiction over such sales. The ruling rested on the public health postulate that local governments have the power to protect the well-being of their citizens.

About three months later San Francisco and Los Angeles joined other cities in the effort to use the courts as a tool for gun control. They sued gunmakers for broad social reasons, not in the pattern of product liability suits. They sought monetary damages for costs they incurred for police deployment, medical treatments, and other expenditures stemming from gun crimes and accidents. Controllers estimated that defense against the lawsuits "could cost the gun manufacturers as much as a million dollars a day."[29]

The gun lobby and concerned legal critics, too, denounced all the suits as legislation by judiciary. Gun promoters repeated a charge they had made often, that in seeking to destroy the arms industry the plaintiffs wanted to disarm America. Controllers defended the suits as necessary end-runs around a Congress incapable of enacting effective regulation of a social menace because it could not escape the NRA's stranglehold. Association leaders viewed the suits ominously because they struck at its economic base. Without money from arms and ammunition manufacturers who contributed to anticontrol campaigns and who advertised heavily in weapons magazines, the gun lobby could not intimidate or buy state and federal legislators.

As the community suits against the firearms industry proliferated, they attracted the attention of minority advocate groups such as the National Association for the Advancement of Colored People (NAACP). Its leaders pointed out that deaths by gun struck blacks at high rates. Indeed, African American males suffered more from lethal violence, most of it by gun, than men in any other major population group. "We represent a significant constituency that is disproportionately affected by gun violence," the association's president, Kweisi Mfume, announced. "The time has come for us to look at the proliferation of handguns."[30] Following this announcement, the NAACP joined numerous cities and counties in their suits against firearms producers. The expanding controllers' offensive in the courts, along with the huge costs involved, heightened the alarm of the gun clubs over how to cope with the litigation.[31]

Meanwhile, mostly white, suburban America experienced more juvenile gun violence. On April 20, 1999, two students, Eric D. Harris, eighteen, and Dylan B. Klebold, seventeen, entered the grounds of Columbine High School in Littleton, Colorado, a suburb of Denver. They carried a semiautomatic carbine, two sawed-off shotguns, an Intratec AB-10 semiautomatic handgun, and dozens of homemade bombs. They killed fifteen people, tore the bodies of twenty others with bullets, and left a horrified nation asking again about kids with guns, "Why?" In many ways these shooters seemed normal. They came from comfortable middle-class families and participated in the usual teenage rituals such as baseball and video games, and had a fascination for guns.

Like other student massacres, this one immediately boosted gun-control activism all over the country. Abroad, once more it raised questions about the morbidity of "American gun culture." Coincidentally, the foremost supporter of that culture, the NRA, had scheduled its annual meeting in Denver just ten days after the Littleton carnage. In a rare instance of retreat over public reaction to its activities, the association abandoned the usual festivities accompanying annual gatherings, such as a gun show. Not even intense public pressure, however, could compel it to cancel the meeting itself.[32] As a result, thousands of opponents circled the hotel where the delegates met, some waving signs that read, "Shame on the NRA" and "NRA, Pusher of Child Killer Machines."

Again, Charlton Heston rose in defense of gun bearing. Referring to the Second Amendment, he said, "We cannot, we must not let tragedy lay waste to the most rare, hard-won right in history."[33] Later, though, he campaigned to end the sale of semiautomatic small arms and armor-piercing bullets and to keep guns out of the hands of criminals, children, and other wrong people.

The public wrath of the moment also helped derail three NRA-sponsored bills in the progun Colorado state legislature. In other states, too, gun rights proponents pulled back, at least for a while, from similarly proposed legislation. Some analysts claimed prematurely that the Columbine murders marked a watershed in the control struggle, one favorable to the controllers. Polls indicated that women in particular responded favorably to the calls for tougher federal gun-control measures. Ironically, polls also showed that half the public still held the NRA in high esteem, higher than four years earlier.[34]

For a time, the public reaction to the shootings placed both the progun forces and the media on the defensive. Once more, the president criticized the media as a part of a "culture of violence." Parents, he said, "should turn off the television, pay attention to what's on the computer screen, and refuse to buy products that glorify violence."[35]

Clinton, control organizations, and much of the public again called for more stringent federal restrictions on gun ownership. On April 27 he urged legislation that would tighten access to guns, impose penalties on parents and other adults who allowed children access to guns, and require for the first time a background check for anyone who sought to purchase a weapon at a gun show. This latter request ripped aside whatever defensiveness over the shootings the gun community had recently experienced.

Individuals had always been able to sell firearms privately without a license or other significant restraint. They did so at the more than four thousand gun shows held annually. Sales at these shows accounted for a substantial share of the nation's firearms business. Vendors there sold for cash, often to felons, asking no questions, and making healthy profits. According to researched estimates, 45 percent of the 4.5 million gun sales each year were made at these shows or by private sellers.[36] These data ran counter to the gun keepers' contention that criminals stole most of their guns. It indicated that felons obtained about 30 percent of their firearms from the underground market, a market that operated steadily at gun shows.[37]

Even federal licensing as under the Brady law did little to prevent felons and others from acquiring guns at the shows. Dealers there often masqueraded as private sellers. In other instances, individuals with criminal records used relatives, friends, or third parties called straw purchasers to buy guns for them from licensed dealers. As critics pointed out, at the shows the licensing and other restraints on sales often amounted to little more than smoke and mirrors. Even so, firearms buffs perceived the extension of background investigations to all gun-show purchasers, whether they bought from merchants or private individuals, as a prelude to registering all gun owners. They regarded such a requirement as anathema and were determined to fight it.

The most bitter opponents of checks and licensing, the NRA and other gun clubs, sounded an alarm heard across the country. It immediately brought a massive response as well as a rise in their membership rolls. As a recruiter explained, the antigun sentiment frightened gun owners who believed their Second Amendment rights were in jeopardy. The NRA called also for help from its mostly Republican supporters. They quickly fell into line. Leaders such as former vice president Dan Quayle, who sought the party's presidential nomination, hoped "we don't use this [the Columbine tragedy] as an excuse to go and take away guns. Let's focus on behavior."[38]

On May 10, while the gun constituency mobilized, the president held a three-hour summit in Washington aimed at addressing the problem of juvenile gun violence. About fifty people spoke. "So many factors were identified—the Internet, movies, parental responsibility, domestic violence, lack of religious faith, a coarsening of the culture—" an observer reported, "that guns were lost in the shuffle." Another commentator called the gathering "a feel good forum, lots of talk and not much action."[39] Exasperated skeptics consequently demanded more. Stop the carnage at its most deadly point, they urged, where guns are made readily available to the public.

One aroused critic asked, "Is anyone really surprised about another deadly school shooting in the U.S.? I am not! We have a president who thinks that only with violence can we solve our problems. Examples, bombings of Afghanistan, Sudan, Iraq, Somalia, Bosnia, and now Serbia." Another skeptic queried, "Why does a nation persist in celebrating violence as an honorable expression of disapproval," as in Yugoslavia, Iraq, and elsewhere? "Why do we believe guns and bombs are the answer?"[40]

In fund-raising speeches in mid-May, Clinton also linked the school shootings and ethnic cleansing in the Balkans but from a different perspective. Both tragedies, he claimed, stemmed from "darkness of the heart, the fear of the other." That is why, he explained vaguely, he waged war against Serbia while also crusading for handgun controls and against civilian violence at home. He claimed also that the crime-busting legislation he pushed accounted for the decline in crime for the seventh straight year.

Meanwhile, two days after the conference on violence, the Senate voted unanimously for a federal investigation of the entertainment industry as a purveyor of violent products. The legislators rejected a stiff proposal to keep children and criminals from obtaining firearms at gun shows. Instead, on May 19, the Senate passed a juvenile justice bill crafted by NRA lawyers without such a curb. Attorney General Janet Reno remarked, "I am stunned that less than one month after the worst school shooting in our nation's history, the Senate has decided to make it easier for felons, fugitives and other prohibited purchasers to buy guns."[41]

The public backlash became so intense that on the next day a crucial number of Republicans reversed themselves. They joined Democrats in passing, with the tie-breaking vote of the vice president, a juvenile crime bill to make a background check mandatory with a three-day waiting period, as under the Brady law, for anyone attempting to buy a weapon at a gun show. It also included a ban on importing high-capacity ammunition clips and required safety devices on handguns. It was the first gun-control measure the Senate enacted since 1994.

As in the past with such measures, supporters hailed the legislation as a sign of weakness in the gun lobby. This rejoicing was premature because the measure required approval in the House, where the gun lobby had greater influence. There, NRA power stalled action on the matter until public rage over Littleton had time to cool.

Polls showed not only an increase in public demand for stronger gun control but also a significant new element in such support—Republican women. Almost three out of four of them now regarded increasing restrictions on guns more important than protecting the rights of Americans to own them.[42] Women also rejected the gunmaker pitch that they needed firearms for protection against rape and other violent crimes. As touched upon previously, research in the nineties indicated that women with guns were fewer than firearms makers and the media claimed. Less than 12 percent owned one and about half that number possessed handguns. Married women in rural areas owned more guns than city dwellers, mostly for hunting. Few possessed them for protection against crime.[43] All the while gun-lobby pressure on the Republican Congress outweighed the sentiment of women and other Americans for stiffer controls over firearms at gun shows and elsewhere.

19

Clinton v. the NRA

On May 20, 1999, the day the Senate by a bare majority passed President Bill Clinton's juvenile crime bill, another school shooting made headlines. Fifteen-year-old Thomas J. Solomon, a sophomore at Heritage High School in Conyers, Georgia, broke into his parents' gun cabinet, grabbed a .22-caliber rifle and a .357 Magnum revolver, smuggled them into the school, and shot and injured six students. As had happened in similar rampages, friends and school officials described Solomon as the kind of student incapable of such violence.

Two days later, the president urged the House of Representatives to pass his juvenile bill. On that day too, he unleashed massive bombing of Serbia. "What were students to think?" a critic asked. "Non-violence and new gun controls in the U.S., but violent bombing over Belgrade, same as usual?"[1]

On May 25, another national gun-control organization, the Bell Campaign, debuted. Mary Leigh Blek, who with her husband Charles headed the western regional office in Long Beach, California, explained, "The bell represents freedom in our country, and we want to be free from gun trauma." Founders characterized the group as a grassroots opponent of the National Rifle Association. As had earlier control organizations, Bell sought a national ban on assault weapons and Saturday night specials, more federal oversight of firearms producers, and community monitoring of local gun-markets.

What immediately distinguished Bell from other control groups was its start-up money. It received a $4.3 million grant from the Richard and Rhoda Goldman Fund, a philanthropy based in San Francisco. Blek assumed that the passion of families of gun victims would outmatch the strong feelings of gun owners. "Things are going to change; we have reached critical mass," she said. "We love our kids more than the gun lobby loves their guns."[2]

A week later Clinton shifted attention from the gun lobby by ordering a federal inquiry into the entertainment industry's marketing of violent movies, music, and video games to children. The move startled Hollywood. "We can no longer ignore the well-documented connection between violence in the media and the effects it has on children's behavior," he said, citing about three hundred studies stretched over thirty years. Yet violent American films had huge audiences abroad, where they did not appear linked to youth gun violence.[3]

In the United States, despite outrage over the media and continued grievance gun killings, the gun lobby had defeated efforts to hold small-arms manufacturers responsible for criminal and other lethal use of their products. Now though, in a case in Brooklyn, New York, *Hamilton v. Accu-Tek*, control advocates made progress. The litigation began when the relatives of six persons that gun wielders had killed and one injured survivor, Steven Fox, sued twenty-five manufacturers for negligence. Fox's agony had begun in November 1994 at age sixteen in Queens when a friend shot him in the head. The bullet remained lodged in his brain, thereby disabling him.

After a four-week trial in January 1999, a jury found fifteen of the manufacturers guilty. Jurors concluded that the "criminal misuse of handguns was a reasonably foreseeable result of defendants' negligent marketing and distribution; that easy access to illegal guns increases gun violence and homicide."[4] On June 3 the New York eastern district court awarded more than five hundred thousand dollars to Fox and his mother. Gun-control activists hailed the verdict as a huge victory but it did not much impair deaths by bullet.

All the while, cities and counties pursued their suits against the gun industry for the costs of responding to gun violence. The gunmakers contended they were not responsible for criminal use of their products. A court of appeals in San Francisco in a case against Navegar Inc. of Florida, which manufactured the gun Gian Luigi Ferri used in the 1993 high-rise shooting, believed differently. It cited evidence that Navegar "deliberately targeted the marketing" of its semiautomatic weapons to "persons attracted to or associated with violence." The company advertised the weapons in magazines such as *Soldier of Fortune, Combat, Handguns, Guns, Firepower*, and *Heavy Metal Weapons*, claiming they had "excellent resistance to fingerprints." On September 29 the panel ruled that gunmakers could be sued for promoting their products to people who used them in crimes such as murder.[5]

Three months later, California's Supreme Court decided to review the case. In seeking to overthrow the panel's decision, Navegar pointed out that sixteen other courts had rejected claims similar to those of the plaintiffs in the Ferri case.[6] In Ohio, for instance, Judge Robert Ruehlman had tossed out Cincinnati's case. Echoing the contention of gun-industry lawyers, he ruled the suit an "improper attempt" to use courts to legislate firearms controls. He declared also that the city could not obtain damages for injuries to third parties, for police work, or for other ordinary service it had a duty to provide.[7]

Still, society continued to pay dearly for gun violence. On September 14 a gunman shot to death three people in the West Anaheim Medical Center in southern California. Two days later a Los Angeles *Times* editorialist commented, "Hospital violence, aggravated by the flood of guns in our midst, has become a grim fact of life in the big cities. Los Angeles and other urban centers have been forced to respond by installing metal detectors and other security measures. . . . The evidence is clear: too many firearms are too easily available to those with grievances."[8] Investigators found that in the late nineties the cost of treating gunshot victims amounted to $2.3 billion, a sum equal to the spending on guns. Much of this money came from taxpayers through the funding of Medicare and Medicaid.

On another judicial front, the gun lobby had found comfort from the ruling of a Texas judge, Sam Cummings, who maintained the Second Amendment conferred on individuals a sweeping right to keep firearms, including bazookas and other military hardware. That opinion moved up on appeal to the fifth circuit court. The lobby sought a similar opinion from the Supreme Court's conservative wing. In two cases it asked the Court to rule that the Second Amendment gave carte blanche for unregulated gun ownership. As with similar past appeals, the Court refused to hear the cases.[9]

In November, the Second Amendment Foundation entered the legal fray, filing suit in the federal district court in Washington, D.C., against the United States Conference of Mayors and the mayors of twenty-three cities. It accused them of violating the rights of gun consumers by trying to drive manufacturers out of business. Its head, Alan Gottlieb, described the suit as "basically a civil rights action on behalf of consumers."[10]

A week later the federal government announced it would join negotiations between twenty-nine cities and counties and the gun industry aimed at limiting the flow of handguns to children and criminals. The Clinton administration hoped, thereby, to persuade gunmakers to accept controls over their production and marketing.[11]

For British-owned Smith & Wesson, the largest firearms concern in the United States, the pressure made life uncomfortable. Faced with a series of lawsuits, the owners placed the firm up for sale and broke their relationship with the gun lobby. The company negotiated with the federal government, mainly through Andrew Cuomo, the secretary of the Department of Housing and Urban Development. It also entered discussions with more than a dozen cities over numerous safety and marketing restrictions, such as child-safety trigger locks and hidden serial numbers, on its guns. In return for the company's acceptance of these conditions, the plaintiffs would drop their suits. In addition, federal, state, and local governments would give preference to Smith & Wesson and other firms that accepted the government code when buying guns for law enforcement.

Other gun producers refused to admit administration officials to their negotiations with the litigating communities. In turn, municipal representatives balked at resuming talks by themselves. Robert Delfay, president of the National Shooting Sports Foundation, which represented eighteen hundred gunmakers, distributors, and retailers and who spoke for them in the talks, vowed not to "allow the most anti-gun administration in history to bully our industry." He prodded foundation members to support and contribute to a new political action committee that would soon become involved in the upcoming elections. "The stakes could not be higher," he added. "The next president could appoint up to five Supreme Court justices who could decide the future of the 2nd Amendment. A Democratic House and Senate would blaze through a myriad of gun-control measures that have been stymied to date."[12]

Then, on February 27, 2000, seven major gunmakers, including Glock, Colt, and Browning, accused Cuomo and sixteen state and local officials of conspiring against them. The gun companies wanted to block preferential treatment for arms producers who adopted the government's standard in the design and sale of firearms by filing suit in a federal court in Atlanta. The manufacturers alleged that the preferential buying program infringed on Congress's power to regulate interstate commerce. A San Francisco official commented that his city was simply doing what any consumer could do: "We certainly have a right as a market participant to choose who we're going to do business with."[13]

The next month, when 411 communities signed on to the arrangement with the federal government and Smith & Wesson, Cuomo commented, "It would be near lunacy to patronize a company more likely to be providing criminals with guns when you are in the business of hiring police officers to fight the criminals."[14] Observers called this agreement, to be monitored by BATF officials, "the first big concession by the industry to the mounting public and political pressure for stronger gun controls" and "a crushing defeat for the National

Rifle Association."[15] The administration threatened legal action against the manufacturers who refused to negotiate safety standards for their guns, as all of them but Smith & Wesson did.

Promptly, Orrin G. Hatch of Utah, chairman of the Senate Judiciary Committee and a longtime ally of the NRA, introduced legislation to block federal legal proceedings. He said his bill would call a halt to "frivolous and burdensome lawsuits against law-abiding manufacturers, dealers and firearms owners." It would also require "the immediate destruction of background check records."[16] A few months later, the Republican majority in the House of Representatives voted to prohibit the housing department from proceeding with its gun program. Cuomo commented that "gun lobby extremists" had again prevailed.[17]

Two months later, a Republican congressman, John N. Hostettler of Indiana, sponsored legislation to prevent the housing department from working with the Communities for Safer Guns Coalition. This organization represented a group of municipalities that had agreed to give preference to Smith & Wesson when buying guns. The House narrowly approved. Hostettler also introduced an amendment to a spending bill designed to bar the Justice Department from enforcing the federal government's agreement with Smith & Wesson. He wanted to destroy the arrangement because, he stated, "this is backdoor gun control through coercion and through threat of litigation." By a vote of 201–196 the House barely defeated the measure. Still, the city and county liability lawsuits against the firearms industry for gun-connected violence made little real headway in the courts.[18] As the litigation faltered, the NRA and its Republican allies sponsored legislation that would permit trial of gun cases in federal courts rather than as usual in state and local jurisdictions. They contended that punishment for a gun violation would be prompter and more severe in federal cases. A state court might penalize a gun offender with probation or a few months in jail whereas a federal court would impose a sentence of five years in jail. Earlier, as we have seen, organized gun-keepers had opposed most expansion of federal law enforcement as leading to a police state. They had denounced federal enforcers of gun laws as gestapo agents who sought to entrap gun owners. In several instances they had also persuaded Congress to deny enforcement funds to the BATF. Astonished Democrats accepted the NRA's argument and proposed to incorporate it in gun-control legislation.[19]

Meanwhile, despite the school shootings and numerous antigun measures proposed in federal and state legislatures in the wake of the Columbine tragedy, few laws of significance to curb gun violence emerged. Some states even took action favoring gun promoters. Thirteen mostly rural states across the South and Mountain West, as well as Alaska, passed NRA-sponsored legislation prohibiting municipal lawsuits against manufacturers.[20]

In Colorado, polarization on controls increased. Voters in Larimer County voted Sheriff Richard Shockley out of office because progun groups such as Rocky Mountain Gun Owners targeted him as an enemy. They also harassed locals who demonstrated for stricter gun laws. Ray Hickman, Colorado coordinator of the Gun Owners, explained their concern. "We are profoundly against the registration and licensing of handguns for the simple reason," he said, "that it will be used for the confiscation of all firearms in the event of the wrong people getting into government."[21] The state legislature rejected three out of five gun-control bills while favoring two toothless measures the NRA sponsored.

This activity and gun-lobby tactics in the House prompted Clinton to assail Republican gun proposals "as plainly ghostwritten by the NRA. . . . I think it is wrong," he added, "to let the NRA call the shots on this issue." He labeled this "a classic horrible example of how Washington is out of touch with the rest of America." James Jay Baker, the NRA's chief lobbyist, admitted that the organization had spent huge sums in pushing for legislation it desired.[22]

Then, on June 17, 1999, House Republicans voted for watered-down regulations for gun shows. They also passed an amendment declaring that states had the authority to display the Ten Commandments in public places. Democrats, the media, and much of the public lampooned this measure as the do-nothing response to the Littleton massacre and the gun-control fever arising from it.

Referring to the balloting taken at midnight to avoid immediate extensive scrutiny, the president commented, the House had "voted in the dark of night to let criminals keep buying guns at gun shows. This vote will not stand the light of day."[23] He indicated he would not sign the bill if it reached his desk. The NRA employed tactics, which except for the modern-day use of computers, had proved successful for more than a half century. It mobilized its membership with the Internet, direct mail, and newspaper advertisements, running up a lobbying tab of more than $1.5 million to achieve this latest victory. The lobby dispelled the notion that public sentiment had turned so decisively against the gun minority that it would not tolerate such politicking.[24]

The next day, in another vote, the House killed what appeared to be a last chance in the twentieth century to pass even a modest gun measure. Mostly Republican legislators rejected an amendment to the control bill that called for trigger locks on handguns and looser restrictions on firearms sales, such as a one-day waiting period for background checks on purchasers at gun shows. "I hope in my lifetime that the marriage between my party and the NRA ends in a divorce," a disappointed Christopher Shays, a Republican representative from Connecticut, commented.[25]

Thus, the demand for significant controls that had started with the Columbine slayings at this point looked like another failure in the continuing struggle to control gun violence. This time, though, the NRA victory came after a bitter battle and some significant losses.

One of the notable setbacks for the gun community occurred in California, where a Democratic legislature and a Democratic governor, Gray Davis, adopted what some viewed as "the toughest gun control package of legislation in America." It restricted individuals to the purchase of one gun in a month, a ban on the sale of unsafe handguns, a requirement for trigger locks on a gun when sold, and tighter controls over sales at gun shows.[26]

The next year Massachusetts's attorney general, Scott Harshbarger, using consumer protection rules, relying on his power to regulate consumer products, and with approval of the state's high court, also imposed stringent regulations on guns. They banned Saturday night specials, required childproof locks on any gun sold in the state, safety warnings with each gun, tamper-resistant serial numbers, and a device on semiautomatic handguns that would indicate if the chamber contained a bullet. The spokesman for the state's Gun Owners' Action League, Kevin Sowyrda, accused Harshbarger of exploiting the firearms issue to increase his popularity. "This is," he said, "an assault on veterans and an assault on gun owners."[27] At about the same time, Maryland's legislature required built-in locks for all new guns sold in the state.

In line with the local legislation, liberal Democratic legislators in Congress with urban constituencies had become bolder in favoring a ban on all civilian firearms. One party chieftain even asked, "Why don't we just collect all the damn things and melt them down?"[28]

Clinton stuck to his incremental approach in dealing with gun violence. He maintained that with the Brady law "we've got the lowest crime rate in 15 years, and the American people are safer, and honest hunters and sportsmen haven't been hurt a bit."[29] Again, the president had skimmed the real problem, that despite piecemeal controls Americans of all kinds still had ready access to guns. As for the juvenile killings, they had a discernible common denominator, the shooters' familiarity with guns and their ease of access to them. The bloodletting occurred in small communities as well as in big cities, and in states that promoted gun use for recreation such as hunting and for personal protection.

Hate-mongers still easily bought guns and continued to kill with them, as did Benjamin N. Smith, a twenty-one-year-old university student from Illinois. Because he belonged to a white-supremacist organization called the World Church of the Creator, when he tried to buy guns from a licensed dealer he failed to pass a background check. So he purchased a Bryco .38-caliber semiautomatic handgun and a Sturm Ruger .22-caliber pistol from an illegal street vendor. With them, on the weekend of July 4, 1999, he targeted blacks, Asians, and Jews, slaughtering two people and injuring nine before killing himself to avoid capture. Antigun activists contended that this rampage, like others, demonstrated the need for tighter controls, as over gun shows, street dealers, and the Internet.

Within a week another episode of hate-generated gun violence erupted. On July 10 Buford Oneal Furrow, a thirty-seven-year-old mentally disturbed mechanic and anti-Semite who belonged to the racist Aryan Nations, blasted the Jewish Community Center in Granada Hills, Los Angeles, with semiautomatic gunfire. He also murdered Joseph Ileto, a Filipino American mail carrier, because of his race. Furrow had in his car an arsenal of five assault weapons, two handguns, and seven thousand rounds of ammunition.[30]

Particularized controls did not deter Furrow. He acquired his arsenal legally. His guns came originally from the police department in Cosmopolis, Washington, which had sold them as surplus to dealers, one of whom resold several to Furrow—a common practice. For years police departments nationwide sold or traded guns they no longer needed to licensed dealers who in turn recirculated them for profit. In 1998 the BATF had traced 1,100 former police guns out of 193,203 used in crimes.[31]

Even cities that filed suits against gun manufacturers placed their used police guns on the civilian market. New Orleans, notorious for its gun crime, acknowledged that its police agreed to trade ten thousand used and confiscated guns to Glock Inc. for new weapons. Company officials explained that in good years they traded twenty-five thousand firearms to police agencies. Finally, in 1998 the International Association of Police Chiefs had endorsed the obvious. It called for the destruction of unnecessary firearms because the costs of gun violence far outweighed the revenue gained from reselling them. The practice of federal, state, and local agencies, such as the army and police forces, of selling firearms while other branches of government battled to enact weak controls never made sense except for shooters who wanted cheap guns.

The publicity over the inconsistencies in the gun selling and in the controlling policies of government entities led to an effort to ameliorate the problem.

On September 10 the president announced the federal government would subsidize local agencies in their efforts to buy back guns from civilian owners. To
receive funding, municipal officials had to agree to destroy the firearms they
bought. Clinton avoided a fight with gun proponents in Congress over the
funding by using $15 million already at his disposal for the program. Unaccom-
panied by well-enforced control legislation, as had been the case in Australia,
this plan did not curb gun violence much. Nonetheless, it underscored the administration's commitment to its bit-by-bit policy of trying to reduce the number of wrong people with guns.

Clinton used the program to boast again about the control measures he had
sponsored, claiming they had stopped thousands of criminals from purchasing
guns.[32] Critics pointed out he could not substantiate the claim and that his
government had rarely prosecuted violators of the Brady law. Indeed, in 1999,
of the more than twenty-three thousand cases the FBI had referred to the firearms bureau for possible prosecution, the BATF arrested only sixty-five people.
The administration backtracked, explaining it had to be selective and thus had
concentrated on big violators and big crime to conserve limited resources and
staff. It contended with good cause, as had critics of federal enforcement of
controls, that if the BATF prosecuted every minor gun-law violation it would
inundate the federal courts.

Since the federal government and state and local police did not devote significant resources to enforcing existing gun laws, skeptics retorted why pass
laws if government agencies will not or cannot enforce them? As one control
proponent commented, without vigorous enforcement "gun laws are nothing
more than ink on paper."[33] The NRA's Wayne LaPierre blamed the increasing
gun violence on the Clinton administration rather than on guns. Repeating
standard gun-lobby rhetoric, he called its record on gun prosecutions a "national disgrace." Instead of seeking to pass more gun-control laws, he said, the
administration should enforce those already on the books.[34]

Clinton responded by proposing a $280 million program to crack down on
illegal firearms and improve handgun safety. He called for five hundred more
BATF agents and inspectors to police gun dealers, and one thousand more federal and state attorneys to prosecute violators of gun laws. In his State of the
Union address he said, "Now, we have all seen what happens when guns fall
into the wrong hands." Then he announced, "We must strengthen our gun
laws and enforce those already on the books better." We must give prosecutors
of bad-apple gun traffickers and BATF agents "the tools they need, tools to
trace every gun and every bullet used in every gun crime in the United States."

He also asked Congress "to fund research in smart-gun technology."[35] The NRA and most Republicans welcomed the approach, claiming he had adopted their position.

At the same time, the Department of Justice released figures showing that in 1999 federal gun prosecutions had increased. Attorney General Janet Reno pointed out that federal prosecutors "all over the country are vigorously enforcing firearms laws" and collaborating with state and local officials. The Washington-based Coalition to Stop Gun Violence joined its conservative opponents in calling the president's proposals "a huge step in the right direction."[36]

In February, Clinton invoked executive authority to crack down on merchants who provided the majority of weapons used in crimes. He ordered federal agents to target 1,020 gun dealers in what he termed the "most aggressive effort ever undertaken to ensure responsible behavior by gun dealers." When twelve children die "every day in America because of gun violence . . . we can't wait for congressional action." NRA lobbyists dismissed the announcement as an "election-year stunt" designed to harass gun dealers. It did serve the Democratic strategy of keeping gun control a hot-button issue so the party could take control of Congress and retain the presidency.[37]

Meanwhile, corrupt dealers thwarted control laws by falsifying records so as to conceal transfers of thousands of firearms. At the peak in the early nineties the United States had 285,000 licensed dealers, or more than it had gas stations. Tighter requirements and higher fees whittled the total to 183,000. Limited manpower, loopholes in gun laws, and sentencing guides that punished convicted felons severely for owning a gun but treated arms trafficking as a relatively minor offense, hamstrung BATF and federal prosecutors in dealing with lawless gun peddlers.

As for the BATF, largely because of gun-lobby opposition to its expansion, it had not grown in thirty years. Into the year 2000 it had twenty-four hundred inspectors and agents and only two hundred in the field to monitor dealers. By law, they could conduct surprise inspections of dealers only once a year. The bureau could not impose fines, suspend licenses, or crack down on problem dealers. It could revoke licenses but it rarely used this power. Clinton asked Congress to invigorate the BATF, strengthen its regulatory authority, and provide funding for five hundred more agents and one thousand more prosecutors. Congress did not respond.[38]

Despite these control problems, during these years of ferment over gun violence FBI figures showed that since 1993, or for eight years in a row, serious crime in the United States with guns had dropped steadily. Never since the beginning of reasonably reliable record-keeping had there been so long a stretch of decline.[39] At the same time, though, suicide with guns had risen. Researchers, pundits, and government officials perceived tougher gun-control laws, a booming economy, better police work, and gun-safety courses as causes for the drop in crime. They also held "guns, not just criminals," responsible for large numbers of American deaths.[40]

The Milton S. Eisenhower Foundation, a nonprofit research group, disputed the decline statistics. It reported crime more prevalent than thirty years ago. It placed the cause, in part, on the doubling of firearms in private hands to two hundred million. Many were high-powered easily concealed models "with no other logical function than to kill humans." Regardless of control laws or receding crime, the United States still retained its unenvied status as the most gun-violent industrialized country in the world.[41] Shortly, moreover, crime in many parts of the nation began rising again. No one could explain convincingly why. In New York City and Los Angeles, even while crime had dropped nationally in 1999, homicides had jumped 6 percent and 8 percent respectively in the first six months of 2000.[42]

Meanwhile, another spate of juvenile shootings riled the country. In one instance at Buell Elementary School in working-class Mount Morris Township, Michigan, a six-year-old boy quarreled with another first-grade, six-year-old classmate, Kayla Rolland. At his uncle's house, where he lived, he removed a loaded .32-caliber gun from under the blankets in a bedroom. When he returned to school he pointed the gun at Kayla, pulled the trigger, and killed her.[43]

In the wake of this shooting, Clinton pleaded with Congress to end the stalemate over additional gun-control legislation. "I know the gun lobby is cranking up pressure on Congress again," he said. "But when first graders shoot first graders, it's time for Congress to do what's right for America's families."[44] He now called for legislation to hold adults accountable when they allowed deadly guns to fall into the hands of children.

This White House pressure along with personalized gun-lobby attacks on the president gave the struggle to contain gun violence the appearance of a war between Clinton and the NRA. The association produced thirteen television commercials condemning the president and promoting gun owners' alleged rights. All featured Charlton Heston. In one advertisement he stated, "Mr. President, when what you say is wrong, that's a mistake. When you know it's wrong, that's a lie." In another appearance, he accused Clinton of slurring lawful gun-owners as savage murderers. Despite this insult, NRA lobbyists, as though representing a state within a state, wanted the president to debate Heston.

Shortly, in an interview with Clinton on ABC's television program *This Week*, commentator Sam Donaldson stated he could not recall an occasion when someone so publicly called the president of the United States a liar. He asked Clinton how he felt about that. The president responded, "It's the way they've [NRA officers] treated me for more than a decade." Donaldson also asked, "Why aren't you for gun registration?" The president replied, "I think I can make a strong argument for it . . . [but] look, I can't even pass a bill closing the gun show loophole through this Congress."[45]

On a later appearance on the same program LaPierre accused Clinton of exploiting gun deaths for political purposes. "I've come to believe he needs a certain level of violence in this country," LaPierre said. "He's willing to accept a certain level of killing to further his political agenda and his vice president too."[46]

The vice president, Albert A. Gore Jr., called on LaPierre to apologize. A Los Angeles *Times* editorial commented that "instead of keeping silent, the gun lobby insists on turning every tragedy into another display of insensitivity." It pointed out that more than one gun spokesman insisted, with a straight face, that the real lesson of Littleton was that high schoolers should be able to bring guns onto campus so they can defend themselves. It called the NRA "obstructionist, hysterical and dangerous."[47] A New York *Times* editorial stated, "The fact that this nation is awash in guns has been a key factor in making rampage killings possible." It later conducted a survey of gun killings over fifty years that supported this judgment. The survey also showed little evidence that video games, movies, or television encouraged many of the attacks.[48]

Even George W. Bush, then the foremost Republican candidate for president and an ally of the NRA, admitted it had gone too far in its attacks on Clinton. "What they said about the president," he stated, "I don't think is right. I thought they were wrong in saying the president condones killing."[49]

This controversy between Clinton and the NRA suggested that, for the first time, gun violence and how to control it might become an issue early in a presidential campaign. Assuming a backlash against gun keeping, Democrats came out for tougher federal controls, and Republicans hedged or opposed them. A poll by the CBS news network indicated that 56 percent of the men and 73 percent of the women quizzed wanted stricter gun laws. Even among Republican women, support for gun control had within seven years increased 24 percent. Among Democratic women, 75 percent wanted stronger controls.

Gore, the Democrats' candidate for president, while a senator from Tennessee had opposed gun controls but as vice president had become a convert to federal regulation. He appealed to women to vote for him because he would continue Clinton's crusade against gun violence. He and various pundits may have overestimated the potency of backlash against gun keeping because surveys consistently placed Bush ahead of him, even when pollsters asked Americans which candidate they trusted more to handle the gun issue.[50]

As governor, Bush had liberalized gun keeping by signing into law a measure permitting Texans, for the first time in 125 years, to carry concealed guns and another forbidding Texas cities to sue gun manufacturers. He blamed a "wave of evil passing through America," not firearms, as the problem in gun violence.[51] Similarly, conservative church groups did not alter their traditional opposition to gun control. Franklin Graham, a prominent evangelical clergyman, maintained the true problem lies in our sinful nature. "Cain," he said, "didn't use a gun."[52]

The NRA did abandon a traditional stance. For decades, in efforts to influence gun legislation it had made a point of donating to candidates of both major parties. Now, on the assumption that gun control had risen to the level of a key issue in the elections, the association shifted strategy. It decided to concentrate on electing Republican candidates nationwide. Its political arm raised $25 million for that program. It donated more than $550,000 to Republican committees, putting it for the first time among the party's top five givers of unregulated soft money. By April 2000 the NRA's contributions ranged six times greater than its soft-money donations for the whole previous presidential campaign.

Grover Nordquist, president of Americans for Tax Reform and a key mover in the Republican Party's right wing, explained that the donations reflected the NRA's apprehension over the growing momentum for gun control, especially among Democrats. This worry attracted new members for the NRA, a membership its leaders claimed had now risen to 3.4 million.[53]

Control groups also received unprecedented funds for politicking. Joe Sudbay, the director of state legislation for Handgun Control Inc., pointed out that in the past couple of elections "we spent about $200,000 from our political action committee. This year we're going to spend $2 million." Despite the deep divide between the two major parties over gun-violence control, it had not yet become a straight line partisan issue. Some forty Democrats in Congress remained NRA loyalists whereas a number of congressional Republicans favored controls.

Regardless, the NRA counted heavily on a Republican victory. Its vice president, Kayne Robinson, at a closed meeting of three hundred members in Los Angeles had boasted that if Bush won in November "we'll have . . . a president where we work out of his office." He added that the NRA enjoyed "incredibly friendly relations with the Texas governor." Lobbyist Baker commented, "Bush is very supportive of the rights of law-abiding gun owners, and he's followed his words with deeds." Bush denied such a close relationship but Handgun Control Inc., in a nationwide television campaign, emphasized the intimate connection with a broadcast of Robinson's taped remarks.[54]

In the course of this politicking, the gun-control movement's effort to keep public attention focused on firearms violence received some nationwide support. It began when Donna Dees-Thomases, a New Jersey mother of two, a former publicist for CBS News, and a friend of the Clintons, became upset with the shooting at the Jewish Community Center in San Fernando Valley. With the help of mothers and control groups, she organized a Million Mom March to be held in Washington, D.C., to challenge the power of the NRA over Congress and to protest the congressional deadlock over new control legislation. Carolyn McCarthy, the congresswoman from New York whose husband had died at the hands of gunman on a Long Island commuter train seven years earlier, explained the rationale simply: "The Moms of this country have had it."[55]

The Bell Campaign coordinated plans for the march. Donations from the Funders Collaborative for Gun Violence Prevention set up by billionaire George Soros, and other wealthy donors, helped finance it. As these plans progressed, receiving massive publicity from the media, progun groups organized gun-owning women in a new society, Second Amendment Sisters, to mount a counterdemonstration.

As planned, on Mother's Day, May 15, 2000, an estimated 750,000 mothers and others marched in Washington, D.C. Some of them pushed strollers with children and others carried signs with slogans such as "Melt the Guns" and "Be Mad about Guns." The television personality and outspoken foe of private gun-keeping, Rosie O'Donnell, mastered the ceremonies that included an array of prominent procontrol speakers, among them Sarah Brady. She told the marchers, "We must either change the minds of the lawmakers on these issues or, for God's sake, this November, let's change the lawmakers."[56] Mothers held similar demonstrations in seventy other cities, from Atlanta to Los Angeles, to make the whole affair the largest gun-control rally in the nation's history.[57]

In Washington, a few blocks away from the marching moms, about one thousand supporters of the Second Amendment Sisters carried signs that read, "Registration, Then Confiscation." LaPierre called the mothers' march agenda "a controlled burn of the Second Amendment" and "out of step with moms" and "the American public."[58]

From the control movement's perspective, the mothers had helped stigmatize private arms-keeping as a vice similar to smoking cigarettes and drinking alcohol. Its leaders saw it also as stimulating fund-raising, highlighting gun vio lence as a priority voting issue, and aiding in the recruiting of supporters who would work to get out the vote for procontrol candidates. The rallies' impact on Congress appeared mixed. They stimulated friendly senators to praise the march and to vote 50–49 for a nonbinding resolution calling for immediate passage of stalled control measures. Republicans countered by voting a resolu- tion reaffirming faith in their interpretation of the Second Amendment and accusing the administration of not enforcing existing firearms laws aggressively.

The mothers' rallies, the support they attracted, and the coming elections appear to have persuaded the NRA to announce plans for a massive, multime- dia retail store and dining and entertainment center in Times Square in New York City. The association envisaged it as a shrine to sport shooting and a vehi- cle for maintaining support for private arms-keeping. At its convention in Char- lotte, North Carolina, the association also premiered a new magazine, titled *America's First Freedom*. It sported a cover image combining the features of Clinton and Gore with the caption, "The face of gun hatred in America."[59]

At the meeting, Heston brandished a gold-plated musket, declaring the only way the government would take it away was "from my cold, dead hands." Lead- ers announced they planned to spend fifteen million dollars in the November elections, an increase of nearly 30 percent over their peak in past elections. Kayne Robinson warned that if Gore were elected the Second Amendment would face eight more years of attacks. "It cannot survive." LaPierre accused Gore and Clinton of lying about guns "to scare America's moms and run against the Second Amendment."[60]

The platforms of the two major parties carried what had become standard- ized planks. Republicans promised to "defend the constitutional right to keep and bear arms" because, they asserted, "self-defense is a basic human right." Democrats stressed "the need to keep guns away from those who shouldn't have them—in ways that respect the rights of hunters, sportsmen, and legiti- mate gun owners."[61] What differed from the parties' time-worn stances on gun violence was a deeper divide between them on the issue.

At the Democratic National Convention in Los Angeles speakers hammered away at the problem. In their convention in Philadelphia, Republicans hardly alluded to the gun-violence issue. Seemingly they allowed the NRA to speak for them. On the opening day of the Democratic convention, the NRA sponsored a full-page newspaper advertisement that asked in a bold headline, "DO DEMO-CRATS WANT TO DESTROY THE SECOND AMENDMENT?" The NRA alleged that "honest gunmakers are being sued out of business by the Clinton-Gore admin-istration and twenty-six big-city mayors who are all, but three, Democrats. Their trial lawyers are almost all Democrats. The anti-gun lobbies are com-posed of almost all Democrats."[62]

Despite the NRA's partisan stance, it did not formally endorse Bush because it did not want to risk a backlash among swing voters that would injure his campaign. Moreover, in the presidential campaigning the issue did not occupy center stage. Fearing that by taking a strong stand for or against controls they would alienate key voting blocs in a close race, both candidates sought to avoid addressing the issue, as during their nationally televised debates. Nonetheless, the moderator did bring it up in the third debate in St. Louis.

Bush defended gun keeping, repeated NRA dogma on enforcing existing laws, and said "I believe that we ought to keep guns out of the hands of people who shouldn't have them." Gore, who had retreated from his earlier gun-vio-lence agenda, called for more cosmetic restrictions on firearms possession but ended virtually on the same note as his opponent. Gore stated he wanted "to make sure that criminals and people who really shouldn't have guns don't get them." The caution of both men appeared justified because in states such as Michigan, Ohio, Illinois, and Florida, with avid hunters and anticontrol gun-keepers as well as with large cities with procontrol majorities, the gun-violence issue in the close contest could determine the outcome. As anticipated, Bush carried virtually all the states across the South, the Midwest, and the Far West with rural progun populations and Gore won in the western and other states with procontrol majorities. In addition, once more single-issue passion, backed by NRA money and political strategy, influenced the electorate.[63]

All the while, stories of crime, shootings at schools, and slaughter by gun elsewhere cropped up in the media so often that many Americans appeared hardened to gun violence. Nonetheless, with every fresh, bloody episode even jaded neutrals in the struggle to curb gun violence reacted with horror. A mounting number of knowledgeable citizens raised demands for more federal regulation of firearms. They knew that civilian gunfire had become increasingly lethal. They understood, as research and statistical data indicated, that in the past decade gun violence had receded but in some areas had started rising again. They realized also that federal and state laws, such as the Brady Act, had had some successes but in total had failed to control gun violence effectively.[64]

Still, Americans could not reach a consensus on what to do about the gun violence that remained much too pervasive, an attitude reflected in the differences among lawmakers in Washington. Hence, the outlook for far-reaching federal controls looked dim. So, as had been the case for more than a century, in the matter of containing gun violence the United States still remained out of step with the world's socially advanced countries.

20
Summing Up

A s we have seen, in most developed societies in the struggle to contain private gun-violence control advocates won. Governments restricted civilian possession of firearms or, with a few exceptions, banned their use. In the United States the shooting fraternity dominated the control struggle. Occasionally the gun lobby grudgingly accepted feeble federal regulations or lost battles in state and local jurisdictions. On the big control issues it usually triumphed. When the lobby lost, it fought again and often nullified laws it disliked.

Conventional lore explains this record with a variety of reasons, such as the assumption that gun keeping has been, and still is, a unique aspect of American culture. As a gun-rights advocate explains, "From the gun culture's viewpoint, restrictions on the right to 'keep and bear arms' amount to the systematic destruction of a valued way of life and are thus a form of cultural suicide."[1] In this perspective, civilian gun-keepers stand as defenders of a national heritage that gun controllers would tear apart.

This heritage-belief relates well with the passion hypothesis that contends Americans inherited a special love of firearms from their Anglo-Saxon forebears and cherished it. No one can substantiate this assumption or explain why the British and non-Anglo peoples who became equally avid gun users have accepted workable controls. Gun devotees give high standing also to the birthright theory, expressed often as the God-given right to keep and bear arms. They argue that "unlike either Europe or Asia, the right to purchase, possess and use firearms for traditionally legitimate purposes has a profoundly unique symbolism among Americans and constitutes a part of their birthright. It is only natural and proper that this should be so."[2] This concept presents numerous problems, especially that of rights being conferred by deities, a ritual impossible to confirm.

Scores of progun writers see arms keeping as inherited from "three hundred years of Indian wars" and the nation's revolutionary origin.[3] This misreading of the past goes well with the frontier hypothesis of sharpshooting Westerners expanding an empire of liberty. Supposedly, this idea has had such a grip on patriotic legislators they would not defile it with restrictions on the weapons that made the country great. Other peoples, such as Australians, have frontier traditions but in time they agreed to workable gun controls without betraying their past. Furthermore, few of America's professional criminals who made gun violence a feature of life in big cities could identify with frontier practices, real or imagined.

Another theory holds that Americans have rejected substantive gun regulation because they perceive it as an enemy to individual liberty. This perspective depicts controls as conferring on government an arbitrary power to decide who can or cannot possess a gun. Officialdom would lull citizens into accepting "expanded police powers and abuses" and impair their ability to defend themselves if they spoke out against oppressive government.[4] This idea of guns as instruments for countering tyranny misses the mark because in the hands of tyrants firearms have been more effective in suppressing popular will than in the hands of its defenders.

A similar defect applies to the related contention that solid firearms-regulation would come at high cost to democracy. The experience of other countries indicates that stringent controls and collective liberties are compatible. Britain, France, Italy, Germany, and Japan have enforced such controls while retaining representative government. In these societies even those who loved their guns accepted, often grudgingly, regulation desired by the majority. The British, for instance, value their freedoms as much as do Americans but have banned private possession of guns with little or no impairment of domestic order. Moreover, the democratic countries with tough controls have not enforced them with unusually large police forces.

Most often, gun keepers maintain that Americans need firearms to protect themselves, mainly against other armed Americans. This argument perceives society much as did philosopher James Harrington—a jungle with everyone a prey. By dismissing police as incapable of upholding their social contract to preserve order, defend citizens against criminals, and prevent crime, this theory conveys a distrust of popular government that gun owners have claimed they wish to defend.

Proponents of the self-defense theory claim that contemporary Americans have used firearms more than 2.5 million times a year for personal protection. Some promoters of this assumption even maintain that the mere brandishing of a gun deters crime. Whether a person carries a visible or concealed firearm, they contend, the result has been the same—"more guns, less crime." Most studies show that guns in private hands, regardless of how carried, have not stopped crime with any significance capable of measurement. Attempts to use a gun against an armed assailant usually have been more deadly for the victim than for the attacker.[5]

Critics view the statistics used by progun writers as flawed and also dangerous because they have influenced public opinion.[6] Still, legislators favorable to the gun lobby have liked the idea of citizens carrying concealed firearms so much that they have desired to extend the practice throughout the country with a national concealed-weapons standard.[7] Violence surveys have shown that in the course of quarrels friends and relatives have committed more gun homicides than have criminal gun toters. These data have revealed also that firearms stored in the home increase the risk of death at the hands of family members far more than they provide protection against intruders.[8] Still, millions of Americans accept the protection hypothesis because many of them feel an intangible sense of power in having a firearm near at hand.

At times control advocates muddy the gun-violence issue with arguments as fanciful as those of the firearms supporters, as, for instance, in espousing the machismo explanation. It portrays the gun as a "man thing," an instrument of virility. Allegedly, macho owners view the loss of their guns as the equivalent of castration and hence will never give them up. Significantly, in other societies where men exuded as much or more machismo as American males, they have given up private ownership of guns without damaging masculinity

Moreover, when American women took up shooting in large numbers they often explained their fascination with guns as enthusiastically as did men. "People just love to shoot," Martha Beasley, a champion small-bore rifle shooter opined, "and they really should get the chance." A freelance writer spoke of the appeal of firearms virtually in macho terms. What "I like about guns is the sense of power, and the real power, they give me," she said. "That's the attraction."[9] Nonetheless, fewer women have been involved in gun violence than men and, according to polls, they have consistently outnumbered men in favoring legislation to curtail gun violence.

The contention of control activists that the American glorification of guns in popular fiction, comics, movies, and television is distinctive also merits questioning. Considerable research does indicate that media exploitation of violence handicaps the control movement but media violence is not singularly American. Other peoples make films and video games or publish stories of comparable brutality. Other peoples view violent American films by the millions while acquiescing in their government's firearms controls. Other peoples also have gun lobbies.

What most other peoples do not have is an enigmatic gun "right" embedded in a Constitution and vaunted as a civil liberty. Until the Civil War, most state constitutions accepted the individual-rights theory of gun ownership, except of course, for the wrong people.[10] After that conflict when federal courts heard gun cases, they rejected the individual-right assumption but upheld the authority of states to protect or restrict civilian use of firearms.

These decisions, and the reality of the Second Amendment referring to a nonexisting well-regulated national militia rather than to an armed civilian population, had no discernible impact on the convictions of the gun fraternity. Its lawyers and friendly criminologists insisted that the Constitution protected gun keeping as a personal right. They spoke of an "almost unanimous scholarly endorsement" of their self-proclaimed "Standard Model" interpretation, a unanimity that did not exist. Often in their use of the past to support their arguments they quoted each other's opinions, or cited views congenial to their position, as though fact. They tended also to discount historical scholarship inconsistent with their perspective or advanced unwarranted claims such as that widespread civilian gun ownership benefited society.[11]

Progun lawyers usually ignored the reality that few state courts have accepted the individual-rights theory and no federal court has done so. Nonetheless, these attorneys wanted Congress to set a national standard for the right to bear arms. They called for passage of a "Second Amendment Restoration Act" that would declare clearly the keeping of arms an individual right "guaranteed against abrogation by the States, as well as the federal government."[12]

Numerous shooting organizations have promoted and continue to promote the privilege of gun keeping as though immune to curtailment. Presidents, legislators, and other office seekers have accepted this concept largely because many of them owned firearms or knew that defense of their use brought political benefits. Federal executives or legislators could not, however, support this stance with credible historical or legal documentation.

As we have noted, for more than a century federal courts have ruled that the Constitution does not stand in the way of "gun regulation in the interest of public safety."[13] In brief, then, the Second Amendment should not pose an insurmountable barrier to solid federal gun control.[14] Even progun writers or those who view the amendment as the only justification for private gun-keeping, point out that as with "the freedoms of speech and press" the right or privilege to keep firearms is "not absolute."[15]

Democratic societies confer rights primarily to benefit the citizenry. If harm from rights or privileges comes to outweigh benefits, then society can modify or rescind what it granted. On this basis, Congress, state legislatures, and municipal lawmakers have restricted freedom of religion and of speech, have outlawed polygamy and solicitation for murder, and have intruded on personal freedoms by requiring motorists to wear seat belts, and in California to equip their cars with antismog devices. Legislators enacted these restrictions to advance the general welfare. Logically, for the same concerns they could by law subject gun keeping to comparable controls.

The Second Amendment has fierce defenders for various reasons but especially because most people find guns, like alcohol, tobacco, and drugs, so attractive that virtually all societies have had difficulty coping with their indiscriminate use. Accordingly, since the beginning of the nation, contrary to the frontier and other myths, Americans have kept guns more for pleasure, as in sport shooting and hunting, than for protection.

In this perspective, the American struggle over gun violence pits those who defend a pleasure as a right against those who recognize private gun-keeping as a high-cost menace to society. The number of individuals owning guns has been shrinking steadily while the number of guns in civilian hands has been increasing. Fewer and fewer Americans own more and more guns.[16] Why, controllers ask, should the will of a minority, many of whom within it view shooting as just fun, continue to prevail at the expense of injury to society? Why should government not control guns as carefully as it does other individual practices harmful to society? Why should shooters be able to invoke the Second Amendment to justify the alleged right of every American to own his or her own assault gun?

Gun devotees have thwarted solid control because they give higher priority to protecting their pleasure than do their opponents in crusading against a social hazard. Prohibition failed in good measure for a roughly comparable reason, or because millions of Americans valued the pleasure derived from alcohol more than their obligation to obey federal law. The historian of Prohibition perceived another reason. It failed for lack of efficient central control. In other words, the American federal system made enforcement difficult if not impossible.

Some analysts apply this kind of reasoning to America's failure to contain gun violence but it does not fit the case. Other nations with federal systems, such as Australia, have enforced firearms control through regional governments.[17] In the United States an aroused public supported by state legislation led to the banishing of dueling. Similar sentiment produced federal action that outlawed polygamy. Experience thus demonstrates that laws with broadly based public support can abate, if not cure, what society perceives as a social ill.

Effective gun control in the United States has never attained such backing because gun keepers, working within the political system, built and maintained one of the most powerful special-interest organizations in the nation's history. Since its rise, the National Rifle Association, along with other firearms clubs, has battled practically all efforts to control gun violence. It has deeply influenced, if not dominated, Congress and most presidents.

In recent years the NRA has extended its reach globally, particularly as the United Nations has focused on containing gun violence worldwide. That effort aroused resistance from the NRA and other gun groups. Gun Owners of America, for instance, described the United Nations as "a tourniquet that is slowly being drawn around gun owners' necks" and a front for domestic gun control.[18] They perceived that organization as building momentum for global gun control and hence they called for America's withdrawal from it, a desire that neither Congress nor the president considered.

In the matter of domestic controls, however, as we have seen, Congress has consistently kept chief executives on a short leash. Congress and dubious precedent have permitted presidents to exercise the power to wage war unilaterally. Congress has not, except for mostly Band-Aid laws since 1933, allowed chief executives comparable authority to combat domestic gun-violence. This failure stands out because so far in all the big battles for federal firearms control, presidential leadership has been vital.

Ardent activists believe that with executive leadership they could take a big step toward comprehensive federal gun regulation. Another step would be simply to repeal the Second Amendment. Fifty-two percent of the respondents to a recent poll favored modifying or eliminating it.[19] This procedure has precedent. Originally the Constitution sanctioned slavery and barred women from voting. As sentiment against human bondage and gender discrimination shifted, the Thirteenth Amendment altered fundamental law by abolishing slavery. The Nineteenth Amendment changed the Constitution by granting women suffrage. Similarly, in keeping with transformed public sentiment, the Twenty-first Amendment repealed national Prohibition.

Even though jurists such as onetime Chief Justice Warren Burger have de-nounced the Second Amendment's use by gun advocates as a fraud "on the American public," so far the repeal strategy has failed.[20] It has foundered be-cause, as polls indicate, numerous Americans remain swayed more by argu-ments in support of shooting than by public-safety concerns. Furthermore, gun zealots have repeatedly countered both Second Amendment repeal and control sentiments by focusing on the fate of guns as a single issue.

We can see how this narrow interest-group dedication works in the attitude of Frank Church, a senator from Idaho for more than twenty years and a liberal on most causes except firearms regulation. He "always opposed all forms of federal gun control" because he could not survive politically without doing so. "Gun controls," he wrote, "are anathema to the people I represent."[21] In Idaho, Texas, and other states with powerful shooting fraternities, for a politician to take a procontrol stance amounted to instant death for his or her career. This concentrated pressure on politicians contributed substantially to the gun com-munity's ability to block most control legislation.

Gun-lobby tactics frighten vulnerable members of Congress, so they dance to its tune. Numerous other legislators often fudge when dealing with control issues. They attempt piecemeal to ban junk guns and specific assault weapons, to call for safety locks, or to limit gun sales to individuals to one per month. Few of these measures pass. Those that do rarely have a significant impact on gun violence. Consequently, despite the spreading influence of control advo-cates, they still do not have enough of it in comparison to the organized gun defenders.

Control lobbies appear weak also because the public fear of crime continues to hobble their cause. This apprehension persists even though accidental and emotional shootings and firearm suicides account for more deaths and injuries than do guns in the hands of felons.[22] Medical researchers maintain the best way to deal with this problem would be as a public-health issue and through strong gun control compatible with American federalism as long advocated by leaders such as Franklin D. Roosevelt. This strategy would block the practice of traffickers of moving guns from states with effective controls to those with weak laws or inadequate enforcement.

Centralized gun control would, of course, bring more federal intrusion in daily living. It could also, as critics maintain, clog courts and overwhelm federal enforcement agencies. However, nothing in the American experience indicates that regulation sponsored by the federal government as a standard would erode the principle of state and local responsibility for most law enforcement to any extent greater than have other federal laws.

The FBI and the BATF already exercise specialized police powers. They could collaborate with state and local agencies, which would do most of the enforcing in the field. The federal agencies could work much as they do in carrying out laws applying to narcotics smuggling, tax collecting, or kidnapping. Enforcement in these areas has not required a vast federal police force nor has it curtailed personal rights to any greater extent than most government regulation or local policing already does.

This concept of tight regulation goes unheeded in large measure because America's majority does not appreciate the public-health, economic, and other benefits that would derive from it. According to polls, Americans desire specific federal regulation of handguns as one means of handling crime. They do not, however, want to control other firearms as stringently as do most other peoples. A substantial majority would like to stop, deter, or at least diminish the domestic bloodletting by gun but only a minority of about 20 percent favors the most effective form of regulation, the prohibiting of private gun-ownership.[23]

As gun lobbyists argue, probably even an efficiently enforced ban on private possession would not prevent determined criminals and militia fanatics from acquiring guns or eliminate homicides, suicides, and impulsive shooting. This reasoning does not contradict the considerable data showing that deaths from accidental or emotional shooting diminish when controls apply to all types of firearms and to all civilians.[24]

In Japan suicides, with or without guns, have been high, but other forms of gun violence have been low. In all, there we can see how domestic disarmament works. When the government prohibited private ownership of firearms, criminals did obtain them illegally but the ban cut down gun casualties overall. This experience fits the simple logic that the easy availability of firearms fuels their use in violent crimes, accidents, and suicides—or, more guns, more deaths.[25]

In the United States the limited goals of most gun-control organizations also stand as obstacles to comprehensive regulation. Most control activists remain dedicated to denying firearms mainly to "high risk groups" rather than to a comprehensive ban. Handgun Control Inc., for instance, fights to keep specific weapons away from unsuitable persons but not from all civilians. As Sarah Brady put it to shooters, "Look, nobody is trying to take your guns away, or your right to have one for protection, as long as you know how to use it, how to store it, and how to take care of it."[26]

Even with such care, responsible people have long used guns with lethal results. No one can draw a clear line separating reputable citizens from those having characteristics designated as inappropriate for gun keeping or predict who will misuse guns. Consequently, virtually all control laws remain selective, aimed primarily at handguns and assault weapons. None of the national or state statutes prohibit private gun-ownership and no president has advocated a sweeping ban.

In California, Audie Bock, the legislature's most liberal member, in 1999 voted against several gun-control bills. She explained, "These well-intentioned fragments of what we charitably call gun control do not get rid of guns. . . . I want real legislation, not phony 'write another gun law, get reelected' business." Similarly, Josh Sugarmann, executive director of the Violence Policy Center, urged Congress to skip "incremental legislation that won't control handgun violence" and immediately "pass far-reaching industry regulation that would effectively ban handguns."[27]

Nonetheless, in the Clinton era control activists have come to view the future with an unaccustomed optimism. They note that in recent decades several presidents have thrust their power behind limited federal regulation. Other elected officials also have become more willing than at any time in the past to enact restraints on civilian possession of firearms. Opinion sampling indicates an ebbing in the power of the gun lobby. An alarmed spokesman commented, "The anti-gun movement clearly is emboldened under the Clinton administration and is on the march under a public health banner."[28] Membership in gun clubs slipped as did the number of licensed firearms dealers. Households with guns decreased to less than 30 percent.[29]

Control advocates also see in the antismoking campaign a harbinger of change in the attitude of the American public toward federal regulation. For years, physicians, public-health officials, and others had attacked the use of tobacco as an affliction harmful to society. Their call for government-backed monitoring of the marketing for cigarettes met resistance from millions of smokers who claimed a right to puff as they pleased, from a lobby of tobacco growers, from well-financed manufacturers, and from legislators beholden to this constituency. Slowly, public sentiment turned against the tobacco industry, forcing it to acknowledge that its products injured national health and even to admit fraudulent conduct in marketing them. Mounting legislation restricted the right of individuals to smoke, of tobacco companies to promote smoking, and of tobacco growers to obtain subsidies.

These proregulation developments as well as the increased public wariness of the toll that gun violence exacts in blood and dollars also appeared to bode

ill for Republican officeholders. For more than three decades they had benefited from opposing even mild controls because gun owners formed one of their
key constituencies. As bitter control partisans put it, "The gun nuts are the
tail that wags the Republican dog." In urban America especially, Republican
legislators often find themselves on the defensive.

Democrats sponsored the three major federal gun-control laws. Some Republicans also favored controls but no regulatory legislation of consequence
passed in Congress during Republican administrations. As more and more
Democratic politicians with urban constituencies perceive the gun issue as a
vote getter, they campaign openly for tighter controls. Perhaps, as Lyndon
Johnson prophesied, "the Congress will not continue forever to ignore the will
of the majority."[30]

Nonetheless, given the financial strength, disciplined organization, and ardor
of gun keepers, along with the public ambiguity toward controls, a comprehensive federal firearms ban still appears unrealistic. In many areas the NRA, which
retains its status as the most powerful long-term special-interest group in the
nation, can punish federal and state legislators for espousing, or merely flirting
with, firearms regulation. It continues to exert a political clout powerful enough
in most instances to derail significant federal and state efforts to contain firearms violence.

Moreover, during the 2000 election campaign, when gun proponents perceived their interests imperiled, NRA membership shot up again. In time of
perceived crisis, some gun defenders even resorted to the threat of violence. "If
the federal government actually attempted to disarm Americans," two private
militias warned, "not only would many Americans likely fight back, but the
number of those who would do so could conceivably be in the millions."[31]

Blame for the failure to contain gun violence cannot be placed solely on the
NRA. That failure derives also from a history of associating gun keeping with
personal protection, anachronistic rural values in one of the world's most urbanized nations, impractical militia theory, states' rights, and myth.[32] Gun-
lobby attorneys who have interpreted data to suit the outlook of their clients
have perpetuated firearms legends, especially the idea that gun control violates
the civil rights of shooters. Fearful authorities, therefore, remain wedded to
selective restrictions on gun keeping for the wrong people.

As suicides by gun, schoolyard shootings, and rampage gunfire indicate,
allowing all citizens except the perceived wrong people to possess firearms has
not worked. That concept has, instead, been a key element in the nation's un-
enviable distinction of having the highest homicide rate among the world's in-

dustrial societies.[33] The fine-tuning of narrowly focused federal, state, and municipal gun laws also has not curbed gun violence much. The tinkering has brought small gains, no fundamental change, and public skepticism toward such regulation.[34] What has worked elsewhere is the practical application of the contrary principle of denying guns even to the right people, except for compelling cause.

Proper reasons for owning a gun could be for law enforcement or for personal protection in isolated areas where no police are readily available. Individuals who liked to shoot for recreation could have access to guns in their clubs where the weapons remained under lock and key except when in use. The same restraints would apply to hunters, whom state and local authorities would register and certify as qualified to kill for approved social purposes.

This practice would place the burden of proving need for a gun on each shooter. It would fit with data indicating that if society limits civilian possession of firearms, as mainly to the military and the police as its servants, gun violence diminishes. Such a federal ban would go a long way toward reversing America's history of failure in handling domestic gun-violence as capably as have most peoples of comparable wealth, education, and self-government.

.

Epilogue

S ince completion of the first edition of this book, the pros and cons of gun control have continued to provoke passionate controversy. The firearms lobby reacquired considerable power in the federal government, while the control movement suffered a number of setbacks. In this new epilogue, I examine these developments in keeping with the book's original purpose, to place America's gun violence in its long-term context. Even the recounting of that history arouses deep emotions, as can be seen in the case of Michael A. Bellesiles and his book *Arming America.*

Bellesiles devoted twelve years or so to the research and writing that went into the volume and into the several articles he wrote on the place of firearms in early Anglo America. In 1996 the Organization of American Historians, the foremost professional society in its field, commended him with an award for the scholarship of one of the articles. When his book appeared, prominent historians and others showered it with praise. In April 2001 Columbia University honored him with the Bancroft Prize for history in recognition of what professional peers regarded as a pathbreaking work. Bellesiles became something of a celebrity. Since his interpretations challenged the conventional perspective that pictured Americans as having always loved firearms and having always used them in abundance, gun keepers and the hierarchy of the National Rifle Association understandably dissented. In addition, they attacked the book and the integrity of the author.

Soon a number of academic reviewers, historians, political scientists, law professors, and others not associated with progun organizations also criticized the book. They tagged it as marred by questionable research methods, as selective or deceptive in its use of sources, as driven by ideological bias, and as fabricating a vision of early America as relatively gunless.[1] The harshest critics called on

Emory University at Atlanta, where Bellesiles served as professor of history, to dismiss him. They also urged those organizations that had awarded him prizes to rescind them. In February 2002 Emory responded by appointing a committee of local scholars to investigate the allegations of misconduct in research. In May the university deemed further investigation warranted and turned the task over to a small, secret committee of scholars from outside the university.

Bellesiles admitted errors, particularly in his manipulation of probate records and statistics, but defended his book as fundamentally sound. In July, in a forty-page report, the external committee stated it found no evidence of intentional fabrication or falsification in the volume and declared the footnotes, in most instances, extensive and accurate. Still, it too criticized the work as slanted ideologically, careless in the use of archival records, and sloppy in quantitative analysis—in other words, it condemned its scholarship as flawed. Bellesiles refuted the negative appraisal, pointing out that the committee had uncovered errors in only 5 of 1,347 of his footnotes. Nonetheless, in October he resigned his professorship, effective at the end of the year.[2]

I did not use Bellesiles's book for my study because I had completed my research and writing before it appeared, but I had read his earlier articles. I found their scholarship sufficiently persuasive to incorporate some of his interpretations in my own work. When I read his book, it too impressed me. I regarded his thesis of limited firearms ownership as a compelling challenge to the widespread but unproven belief that early American society brimmed with guns. Moreover, even though we have no reliable data on how many Americans actually owned and used firearms in the pre–Civil War era, his larger speculations on this subject corresponded with my own assessment, which I based on literature on both sides of the issue. His defenders take a similar stance.[3]

As critics noted, though, Bellesiles unduly minimized the extent of firearms possession and exaggerated the concept of a gun culture as emerging only after the Civil War. Nonetheless, these are the kinds of interpretations historians often advance in broad studies that properly stimulate intellectual exchanges. In this instance, the theorizing generated scholarly debate and an intense scrutiny of Bellesiles's evidence. Scholars pro and con rightly subjected it to standards higher than those applied to popular discourse on the subject. In addition, the book proved unique in provoking vehement protests from ideologues and special-interest groups sensitive to studies that could possibly impair contemporary gun keeping.

Another hotly disputed issue in the gun-control struggle swirled around the interpretation of the Second Amendment, which two new books address. Both volumes challenge the theory of an individual having a constitutional right to own firearms that is espoused by gun keepers and organizations such as the National Rifle Association.

In a symposium, "The Second Amendment in Law and History," a number of leading constitutional historians and legal scholars aimed to correct what they regarded as misinformation peddled in progun studies, many of them published as articles in law journals with inadequate peer review standards. In one way or another, all the contributors to the symposium made the case for the collective interpretation of gun keeping under the Second Amendment. Robert J. Spitzer, one of the symposium essayists, elaborated on this theme in *The Right to Bear Arms*. With authoritative narrative, selected documents, summaries of court cases, a chronology, and an up-to-date bibliography, it offers a readable introduction to the Second Amendment controversy as well as to important elements of the debate over gun keeping and gun control.

At the same time, progun writers produced books and tracts touting their perspective and attacking the scholarly studies they disliked. Among them, Joyce Lee Malcolm's *Guns and Violence* repeats some of her earlier writing but does approach the subject with a concern for historical scholarship. Another prominent progun book, Wayne LaPierre and James Jay Baker's *Shooting Straight*, offers unabashed endorsement of propaganda initiated by the National Rifle Association of America.

Studies such as those on the Second Amendment and on gun keeping in the colonial era and the early republic not only shed light on the past but also offer sound scholarship important for understanding the struggle to control gun violence in its contemporary milieu. Lobbyists, jurists, and politicians on both sides of the control issue, however, often overlook or ignore such scholarship. In their efforts to advance gun-control legislation or oppose it, they continue to cite primarily the literature favorable to their perspectives. Rarely has this clashing of concepts on how to manage America's gun violence been as intense as it is at present.

When the National Rifle Association and other profirearms organizations went all out in campaigning for George W. Bush in the 2000 election, they expected rewards if he won. Once he took over the presidency, he did not disappoint them. As expected, he filled major posts in his administration with foes of gun control. He acted in keeping with his strong support for individual gun rights, his suspicious view of control measures Bill Clinton had sponsored, and the conviction that the National Rifle Association and gun owners had been a critical force in his narrow victory. For attorney general he chose John D. Ashcroft, a former governor of Missouri who had backed measures allowing people in his state to carry concealed guns, a former senator, and a lifetime member of the National Rifle Association.

In the congressional elections accompanying Bush's win, however, six pro-firearms senators, including Ashcroft, although backed by huge amounts of gun-lobby money and politicking, had lost their seats. Opinion polls also indicated a clear majority of Americans still favored effective gun control. Nonetheless, even many Democrats believed Albert Gore's support for controls had contributed to his defeat. With this sentiment and largely passive behavior, Democratic lawmakers went along with the administration's progun program. This attitude became evident in their reaction to two more highly publicized school shootings.

On March 5, 2001, a fifteen-year-old boy at Santee High School in a San Diego suburb shot and killed two students and injured thirteen people. During that week an eighth-grade girl also shot and wounded a classmate at Bishop Neumann High School near Williamsport, Pennsylvania. In the aftermath of this juvenile violence, neither the president nor the Democrats in Congress called for stronger gun regulation. Even groups dedicated to firearms control seemed subdued. Carolyn McCarthy, the New York Democrat and a prominent supporter of the Million Mom March organization, remarked, "Until we're as organized as the NRA, we're not going to get anything done."

For a brief time, control advocates had assumed the initial enthusiasm behind the Million Mom March would provide fund-raising power, attract recruits to its cause, and counter the clout of the NRA. That did not happen, but not because the Moms lacked effort. They tried to generate political power by turning their organization into a national lobby patterned after the successful grass-roots MADD, or Mothers Against Drunk Driving. The Moms called their organization the Million Mom March Foundation and based it in San Francisco in affiliation with the Bell Campaign.

Focusing on state legislatures, the foundation opened 230 chapters in 46 states but could not raise the large amounts of money necessary to finance its scattered efforts. On March 9, 2002, it laid off most of its employees. In October it combined with the old Handgun Control Inc., which earlier in the year had changed its name to the Brady Center to Prevent Gun Violence. Control advocates claimed the merger brought strength to their whole movement, although the NRA and other gun societies labeled the Million Mom effort a failure. These firearms associations thrived on their recent successes. Analysts regarded them collectively as "the most motivated single issue group in the country."[4]

Meanwhile, more than two hundred organizations opposed Ashcroft's nomination, many because of his extreme views on guns. He deflected these concerns by promising that regardless of his personal convictions, he would vigorously defend federal firearms control laws. The Senate then confirmed him. Soon the attitude he had taken in the Senate hearings appeared to change. On April 10 James Jay Baker, now the NRA's executive director, wrote to Ashcroft, requesting his "view and that of the current Department of Justice" on the Second Amendment. On May 17, one day before the NRA opened its national convention in Kansas City, the new attorney general responded.

"Let me state unequivocally my view," Ashcroft said, "that . . . the Second Amendment [protects] the right of individuals to keep and bear arms." This belief, he added, "comports with the all but unanimous understanding of the Founding Fathers."[5] He rejected the interpretation of most well-versed scholars and jurists that it "guarantees only a 'collective' right of the State to maintain militias."[6] Henceforth, he added, the Justice Department would act to uphold the version he had advanced. The Violence Policy Center described Ashcroft's letter as "a shoddy piece of legal and historical research."[7]

Such critics pointed out that the justification for the change in firearms policy came from the kind of sources progun publicists, NRA officials, and lawyers they hired or others congenial to the gun cause had long used and misused. They discounted or twisted historical scholarship to spin their interpretations of constitutional issues pertaining to gun keeping. As a close student of this problem put it, "These authors have succeeded in finding legitimacy for a variety of erroneous and even nonsensical arguments concerning the meaning of the Second Amendment" and the "imagined" rights they claimed it protected.[8]

Ashcroft tried to bolster his position by citing these slanted writings, mostly from law journals and irrelevant court cases. He also disregarded historical data as well as court decisions that ran counter to his convictions. To give more weight to his policy, he directed lawyers in the Office of Legal Council to draft an opinion that would support his views.

As part of this new policy, Ashcroft in June announced the Justice Department would slash the time enforcement agencies would retain the records of background checks for gun buyers to 90 days instead of the 180 the Brady law required. Then, as the NRA desired, authorities would hold the records for just one business day before destroying them. He justified the change as giving proper priority to protecting the "privacy of legitimate gun purchasers."[9] Control activists protested that the twenty-four-hour policy made it impossible for police to review records satisfactorily to ascertain fraud and abuse in firearms sales.

Progun groups gained additional vitality after foreign terrorists on September 11, 2001, crashed two passenger planes into the twin towers of the World Trade Center in New York City and the Pentagon outside Washington, D.C., killing about three thousand people. The president immediately declared what he called a "war on terrorism," hysteria swept across the nation, and gun and ammunition sales rose sharply.[10] The Federal Bureau of Investigation then reviewed Brady law records to determine if persons detained as terrorist suspects had recently bought firearms. In December Ashcroft stopped such investigation because he perceived it as violating private gun rights.

With such actions, Ashcroft's standing with the gun community zoomed. This popularity stood out at the NRA's annual convention, held late in April 2002 in Reno, Nevada. According to association estimates, it swarmed with some 40,000 visitors. Speakers who addressed the 4,500 delegates praised the attorney general and referred constantly to the September 11 terror. Some of them vilified gun-control activists as the equivalent of terrorists. Executive vice-president Wayne R. LaPierre characterized the control advocates as "a sort of Taliban, an intolerant coalition of fanatics."[11] Another speaker, Lee Greenwood, said, "The connection between the NRA and 9/11 is that America has to remain strong and the NRA is one of the strengths of America."[12]

Gun keepers had more reason for celebrating when Ashcroft intervened in *United States v. Emerson.* The case had begun in 1999 when authorities in Texas had charged Timothy Joe Emerson, a physician, with violating a five-year-old federal law, the Violence Against Women Act, which bars any person subject to a restraining order from possessing firearms. Emerson had defied the order, which prohibited him from stalking or threatening his estranged wife, by brandishing a Beretta pistol in her presence and that of their child. His attorney challenged the law on several counts, including one that contended the restraining order denied Emerson his Second Amendment rights.

As I noted in the first edition, the district judge, Sam R. Cummings, maintained surprisingly that the amendment protected an individual right to bear arms. He ruled, therefore, that the portion of the restraining order preventing Emerson from having a gun violated his constitutional rights. Cummings supported his decision mainly with historically inaccurate data from law review articles by progun writers who advanced the individual rights perspective.[13]

Critics denounced the ruling as elevating Emerson's alleged right to own a gun above the safety of his estranged wife and child.

After hearing an appeal, the Fifth Circuit court, based in New Orleans, on October 16, 2001, ruled that Emerson's claimed gun rights could be curtailed because he had menaced his wife. It also maintained the Second Amendment gave individuals the right to "privately possess and bear their own arms," the first time an appeals court took that position. Judge William Garwood, a Republican whom Ronald Reagan had placed on the court, wrote, "We find that the history of the 2nd Amendment reinforces the plain meaning of its text, namely that it protects individual Americans in their right to keep and bear arms whether or not they are a member of a select militia." A second judge, whom George H. W. Bush had selected, agreed but the third, a Clinton appointee, dissented.

The gun fraternity hailed the latter part of the ruling as a gain for its cause. James Jay Baker called it "the most important and favorable Second Amendment judicial decision in American history."[14] Control advocates, such as Matthew Nosanchuk, an attorney for the Violence Policy Center, claimed, "This ultimately is a victory for us because domestic abusers don't have a right to have guns."[15]

On November 9 Ashcroft expressed a contrary perspective. "In my view," he wrote "the Emerson opinion, and the balance it strikes, generally reflect the correct understanding of the Second Amendment." He also instructed all United States Attorneys' offices to advise headquarters in Washington promptly "of all cases in which Second Amendment issues are raised."[16] The NRA's *American Rifleman* magazine called Ashcroft "a breath of fresh air to freedom-loving gun owners."[17] In contrast, Michael D. Barnes, the president of the Brady Center to Prevent Gun Violence, commented, "This action is proof positive that the worst fears about Attorney General Ashcroft have come true— his extreme ideology on guns has now become government policy."[18] In the broad perspective, the ruling and the Bush administration's support for it benefited gun keepers much more than it did the control movement.

The lesser-known case of *Haney v. United States* revolved around John Lee Haney, a gun zealot who on August 25, 1999, showed up at a police station in western Oklahoma boasting he owned unlicensed semiautomatic and automatic firearms and that the federal government lacked authority to require licensing. In searching his car and house, police found two automatic weapons. They arrested him for defying gun legislation. In court he contended they had breached his Second Amendment rights, but a jury convicted him of possessing firearms in violation of federal law and the court sentenced him to thirty-three months in prison. On October 30, 2001, the appeals court in Oklahoma upheld the conviction. In January and February 2002 both Emerson and Haney petitioned the Supreme Court to reverse the rulings of the appellate courts.

On May 6, on behalf of the Bush administration, Solicitor General Theodore B. Olson filed two briefs asking the high court not to review the cases. Repeating Ashcroft's views, he announced that the Fifth Circuit court's decision in the Emerson case "reflects a sounder understanding of the scope and purpose of the Second Amendment than does the court of appeals' decision." Thus, for the first time in formal papers, the federal government argued that the Second Amendment granted the individual right to possess firearms. As Olson requested, on June 10 the Supreme Court refused to review either the Emerson or the Haney case.[19]

This power of right-wing Republicans and the resurgence of gun-rights advocacy appeared to reinforce the conviction of conservative and centrist Democrats that their support for gun control had hurt them in recent elections. So later in the year, in the campaigning for the midterm elections, most Democratic candidates said little about the struggle to contain firearms violence. Mark Pertschuk, the legislative director for the Coalition to Stop Gun Violence, commented, "In Washington it's absolute religious faith now that being for gun control is dangerous and bad for Democrats." In September LaPierre stated, "Democrats are running away from gun control like the plague."[20] Both men exaggerated, but gun owners and their various organizations exuded a confidence that grew out of their enhanced status.

In two years membership in the National Rifle Association had climbed to about 4.3 million, up to this point the highest in its history. In listing the nation's most effective lobbies, *Fortune* magazine had named it number one. No gun-control lobby even made the list.[21] In Congress, gun-rights Republicans rode high, introducing various firearms protection bills. For example, in 2001 Cliff Stearns of Florida, an extreme gun advocate, had crafted a preemption bill, cosponsored by 231 members of the House of Representatives, which would confer special immunity on the firearms industry from litigation over the use of its products. Firearms manufacturers regarded the bill as important because by 2002 more than thirty cities and counties had filed lawsuits that would hold them responsible for harm inflicted by shooters who used their weapons.

Despite loss of influence in the federal government, the gun-control movement had retained potency on the state and local levels, particularly in urban areas, where new advocacy groups came into being while gun killings neither ceased nor diminished significantly. This concern with firearms became evident again when another outbreak of gun violence began making headlines in newspapers and on prime-time television newscasts across the nation. A roving sniper in the vicinity of Washington, D.C., shot, wounded, and killed people at random, including a thirteen-year-old boy in Bowie, Maryland, as he stood outside the doors of his middle school on October 7.

John Conyers, the top Democrat on the House Judiciary Committee, called for an investigation of the marketing of sniper rifles. "There is no legitimate purpose for a military rifle other than to make war," he said. "There is no reason these rifles should be marketed to civilians."[22]

Other critics assailed the gun lobby and the administration for blocking legislation for creating a national system of ballistic fingerprinting of firearms, which could help trace bullets to the weapon that discharged them. Bush and the NRA opposed use of this technology, arguing "it isn't foolproof." They also saw no need, as a response to the sniper crisis, for any new gun control laws. Nonetheless, the Republican-controlled House canceled a vote on the Stearns bill to shield firearms manufacturers from lawsuits resulting from gun violence. Also, in the first control measure to come before it in more than a year, the House passed a bill to improve the database used to check the backgrounds of gun buyers. Noting the bill's weaknesses, control advocates labeled it a placebo.[23]

Finally, on October 22, after the sniper had murdered ten people and wounded three in a three-week shooting spree, Maryland authorities arrested two suspects, John Allen Muhammad, a drifter and Gulf War veteran, and his traveling companion, seventeen-year-old Lee Boyd Malvo, an illegal immigrant from Jamaica. They possessed two Bushmaster XM-15 .223-caliber assault rifles, copies of military weapons, which Muhammad had purchased secondhand, or stolen, at gun shops. Since a court had placed Muhammad under a restraining order for domestic violence, by law in the state of Washington, where he had obtained the guns, he should not have been able to buy the rifles or any other firearms. The Bushmasters were manufactured in Windham, Maine, and equipped with telescopes for long-range, accurate sniping; the shooters used bullets designed to spin and rip apart human innards.[24] Critics called their sale to civilians insane, but some gun keepers still defended the opportunity to acquire the weapons as a right.

On October 28, within a week of the sniper arrests, at the University of Arizona in Tucson, before a classroom with twenty classmates taking an examination, a student with a failing academic record shot and killed three of his nursing professors. He then committed suicide. In the shooter's backpack police found five handguns and at least three hundred rounds of ammunition. Two days later the National Rifle Association sponsored a get-out-the-vote rally in Tucson, at which Charlton Heston spoke.[25]

Despite the public concerns over the sniper murders and the Arizona killings, except for the governor's race in Maryland, gun control rarely emerged as an important issue for the whole electorate during the campaigning for the midterm congressional elections. More even than during the Reagan era, Republican candidates profited from the NRA's financial backing as well as from carefully organized, grassroots, gun-keeper politicking. The NRA contributed 92 percent of its money allotted for electioneering to Republicans. It backed no Democrats. Its activism had more effect on the outcome than had the gun violence.[26] On November 5 voters handed Republicans a victory that brought them control of the three branches of the federal government. With some justification, the gun lobby claimed to have contributed substantively to that triumph.

Various analysts regarded the gun keepers and their allies, such as firearms manufacturers, as representing the most significant financial and voter mobilizing force within the Republican Party and the dominant lobby for the conservative movement. Some observers described the NRA as having become a subsidiary of the Republican Party, while others viewed the party as now a subsidiary of the NRA.

Regardless of such conflicting views once more the NRA, as it often had in the past, demonstrated it could deliver conservative votes in crucial contests. "This may be the most historic election in history," Robert Morris, a Miami gun company executive said. "Now we will see a law that prohibits suing an industry for the actions of an individual."[27]

NRA leaders exulted that when gun controllers tangled with gun owners head-on over issues such as concealed-weapon carry laws, the control lobby "lost election after election."[28] Yet in a number of state contests, progun proposals and progun candidates went down in defeat. In California, for example, in 2002 the NRA lobby failed consistently in efforts to block control legislation. The Democratic legislature passed and the Democratic governor, Gray Davis, signed more major gun-control legislation than all other governors in the nation combined. For instance, on January 1, 2003, California became the first state to repeal legislation granting firearms manufacturers unique immunity against lawsuits for product liability. Moreover, opinion polls indicated a majority of the state's heavily urban population favored even tighter control laws.[29]

In the ambience of this control struggle, gun enthusiasts never ceased in their efforts to spread their gospel seemingly everywhere, including academia and corporate America. One of them even proposed that a prominent retirement fund for professors with more than two million participants cease "investing in companies that publicly support gun control efforts."[30] As justification, he cited the usual gun-keeper clichés such as "control laws impede the ability of the public to defend itself" and such misinformation as that control laws destroy constitutional rights. At their annual meeting on November 7 the shareholders voted down the proposal.

Concurrently, the control organizations' lawsuits against manufacturers and sellers continued. One example is the case of a thirteen-year-old boy at the Lake Worth middle school in Florida. Two years earlier, with a Saturday night special, in this instance a .25-caliber Raven handgun, he had shot and killed his teacher, Barry Grunow. Represented by attorneys from the Brady Center to Prevent Gun Violence, Grunow's widow, Pamela, sued the manufacturer for his death because of the gun's design. It had no safety lock. On November 14, 2002, a jury in West Palm Beach awarded her a total of $24 million. It placed 95 percent of the blame on the Palm Beach County School Board and 5 percent on the Valor Corporation, the weapon's distributor. It ordered these defendants to pay accordingly but spared the manufacturer of any liability. Still, the gun-control attorneys considered the verdict a significant victory for safe guns because for the first time a court had found a firearms distributor guilty and liable in part for damages in a shooting death.[31]

Gun manufacturers, however, remained exempt from the usual rules of product liability, which in most instances still hold industries liable for the foreseeable harm their goods or their use causes. In theory, the liability laws compensate people injured by the dangerous products and deter their manufacture. As we have noted, control advocates wanted to hold gun makers to these standards, but without legislative support they have tried to do so, as in the Florida case, through lawsuits.

All the while, Chicago's ongoing suit against the firearms industry encountered opposition from the Bush administration. The city contended the industry had sabotaged its ban on the sale of new handguns. For help in the litigation, Chicago attorneys and antigun activists asked the federal government to make public its tracking of guns used in crimes, as it did data in other crime records. The Bureau of Alcohol, Tobacco and Firearms agreed to open records dealing with gun crimes in Chicago but refused to release national information. The city then challenged the decision in a federal court under the Freedom of Information Act.

The Justice Department's Olson and the NRA contended the records should remain closed because opening them would invade the privacy of gun sellers and buyers. The lower court sided with Chicago but the administration appealed to the Supreme Court, which in November agreed to hear the case.

Another prominent case evolved out of the assault weapons ban the California legislature had enacted in July 1999, which went into effect in January 2000. The next month, as has happened often after state and local control laws are enacted, gun keepers challenged the legislation as violating their Second Amendment rights. A federal district court ruled against them. The plaintiffs then appealed. On December 5, 2002, the Ninth Circuit Court of Appeals in San Francisco unanimously upheld the lower court's decision. Also, because of the hot debate over the Second Amendment, the three-judge panel, in a ruling covering eighty-six pages, examined the issue in detail.

Writing for the court, a liberal judge, Stephen Reinhardt, stated, "The historical record makes it plain that the Amendment was not adopted in order to afford rights to individuals with respect to private gun ownership or possession."[32] He thus directly contradicted Ashcroft's and Olson's claims and rebuked the administration for its gun policy. Control advocates praised the opinion as the most thorough yet on the subject, while gun defenders denounced it.

The gun-control movement fared well in this case. Usually, though, in this era, when its attorneys and lobbyists went up against the federal government, they lost. They came up short mainly because they had no voice in the Bush administration. The small gains they made came through the promotion of narrow local control laws. For example, the movement had been effective in the passage of legislation in California that set up a database for tracking convicted felons, spouse abusers, and others barred from owning guns and for feeding the information to local police forces. This first-in-the-nation-program provided investigators with an important tool for apprehending illegal possessors of firearms.[33] Some of these guns fell into the hands of gang members, who at this time had sent Los Angeles' murder rate soaring. On the big national issues, however, the gun control movement, made up of unconnected or loosely linked groups such as the Brady Center to Prevent Gun Violence, the Violence Policy Center, and Doctors Against Handgun Injury, continued to suffer because of fragmentation.

The inability of these groups to influence the federal government at this time became evident in the gun lobby's campaign to shield weapons manufacturers from civil lawsuits filed by victims of crimes with firearms. The lobby had launched its effort within Congress early in the Bush administration with a bill titled the Protection of Lawful Commerce in Arms Act. The National Rifle Association dubbed it, "the Reckless Lawsuit Protection Act." Its sponsors had scheduled it for a vote in the fall of 2002, but tabled it because of the public furor over the sniper shootings in the Washington, D.C., area.

Six months later, at a time of renewed public tolerance for firearms and for those who made and sold them as a consequence of the patriotic fervor during the war on Iraq, the bill's sponsors reintroduced it. The administration backed it as part of the Republican Party's agenda, stating, "The manufacturer or seller of a legal, nondefective product should not be liable for the criminal or unlawful misuse of that product by others."

In the debate in the House of Representatives, the bill's backers denounced the lawsuits as frivolous. They argued that if not checked, the litigations would shrink the supply of firearms, and hence violate gun owners' claimed Second Amendment rights. Opponents criticized the bill as an egregious form of special-interest lawmaking that would close the courts to victims of gun violence, cripple the gun control movement, and halt the trend of making guns safer for civilian use.

As usual within this Congress, the gun lobby prevailed. On Aril 9, 2003, by a vote of 285 to 140, the House approved the bill. Proponents in the Senate, which had a companion measure before it, announced they already had a majority for the bill's passage.

Still, polls continued to indicate that the public favored firearms controllers over the gun keepers but Congress's balloting did not reflect that support. So far, only when the struggle to control gun violence had Democratic presidential leadership behind it, had it made headway in the federal government. Without such political support, without a steady stream of funding such as gun makers provided to the NRA and to the Republican Party, and without a grassroots passion comparable to that of the gun keepers, the activists stumbled. The constant localized gun violence—another fatal shooting in a New Orleans high school in which teenage assailants fired an AK-47 rifle and a handgun, occurred five days after the House passed the arms protection bill—seemed to have little impact on either the public or lawmakers. Ostensibly, the cause made gains in the polls only when big shooting binges captured headlines and aroused emotions across the country. Without the staying power to match that of the gun lobby, the movement's leaders could seldom translate the public sentiment into federal legislation.

For this and other reasons, the control movement has not been able to act as an effective, one-issue pressure group in the manner of the NRA. The movement could, though, use some of the techniques of its adversary, such as building a money-raising affiliate and working closely with local gun-control groups that have been effective in states, counties, and cities. In these areas the movement had the advantage of numbers and could energize constituents to politick and raise money the year round, as some of the small control organizations try to do. The leading control-movement organizations could also recognize political reality and attach themselves openly to the Democratic Party, as have gun societies to the Republican Party, at least until the gun struggle becomes clearly bipartisan politically.

Alexander DeConde, January 1, 2003

Notes

Introduction

1   In Harold F. Williamson, *Winchester: The Gun That Won the West* (New York, 1952), 3.
2   The quotations come from William Weir, *A Well Regulated Militia* (North Haven, Conn., 1997), 157; Lee B. Kennett and James L. Anderson, *The Gun in America* (Westport, Conn., 1975), 249; and Robert Sherrill, *The Saturday Night Special* (New York, 1973), 5.
3   Carroll C. Holloway, *Texas Gun Lore* (San Antonio, Tex., 1951), 179–80.
4   For the quotation, see Franklin E. Zimring and Gordon Hawkins, *The Citizen's Guide to Gun Control* (New York, 1987), xi, 5–6. See also Michael A. Bellesiles, "The Origins of Gun Culture in the United States, 1760–1865," *Journal of American History* 83 (Sept. 1996): 425–6, and Michael Renner, *Small Arms, Big Impacts* (Washington, D.C., 1997).
5   Statistics should be viewed cautiously because until the twentieth century, reliable data on guns manufactured, on their use by civilians, on homicides, on crime however defined, and on public sentiment are scarce. In the twentieth century, especially in the United States after 1933, the numbers are profuse but often marked by flawed methodology and subject to widely varying interpretation.
6   Richard Hofstadter, "America as a Gun Culture," *American Heritage* 21 (Oct. 1970): 4.
7   The quotation comes from B. Bruce Biggs, "The Great American Gun War," *Public Interest* 45 (fall 1976): 37.
8   Garry Wills, "To Keep and Bear Arms," *New York Review of Books* 42 (Sept. 21, 1995), 62. For the claim, see Glenn Harlan Reynolds, "A Critical Guide to the Second Amendment," *Tennessee Law Review* 62 (spring 1995): 463. For a thorough critique, see Saul Cornell, "Common Place or Anachronism: The Standard Model, the Second Amendment, and the Problem of History in Contemporary Constitutional Theory," *Constitutional Commentary* 16 (summer 1999): 221–46.
9   See, for instance, Colin Greenwood, *Firearms Control* (London, 1972), 3.
10 For statistics, see Franklin E. Zimring and Gordon Hawkins, *Crime Is Not the Problem* (New York, 1997), 9, 12, 18, 106.

Chapter 1

1   For the quotations, see John U. Nef, *War and Human Progress* (Cambridge, Mass., 1950), 43, and Robert L. O'Connell, *Of Arms and Men* (New York, 1989), 114.
2   The quotations come from David Ayalon, *Gunpowder and Firearms in the Mamluk Kingdom*, 2d ed. (London, 1978), 88, 93.
3   See Walter E. Oberer, "The Deadly Weapon Doctrine—Common Law Origin," *Harvard Law Review* 75 (June 1962): 1573.

4   For contrasting perspectives, see Charles P. Chenevix Trench, A History of Marksmanship (London, 1972), 110, and Vernon Foley, "Leonardo and the Invention of the Wheellock," Scientific American 278 (Jan. 1998): 100, the source of the quotation.

5   See Niccolò Machiavelli, The Art of War, in Machiavelli: The Chief Works and Others, vol. 2, trans. Allan Gilbert, 3 vols. (Durham, N.C., 1965), 577, 581, 585, and John G. A. Pocock, The Machiavellian Moment (Princeton, 1975), 176–7.

6   Library of Congress, Gun Control Laws in Foreign Countries (Washington, D.C., 1981), 47.

7   Joyce Lee Malcolm, To Keep and Bear Arms (Cambridge, Mass., 1994), 10.

8   Kennett and Anderson, The Gun in America, 15.

9   Library of Congress, Gun Control Laws, 47.

10   Quoted from Noel Perrin, Giving Up the Gun (Boston, 1979), 26.

11   Quoted in Delmer M. Brown, "The Impact of Firearms on Japanese Warfare, 1543–98," Far Eastern Quarterly 7 (May 1948): 241.

12   For details on the fyrd, see C. Warren Hollister, Anglo-Saxon Military Institutions (Oxford, Eng., 1962), 2, 25–37.

13   Lois C. Schwoerer, "No Standing Armies!" (Baltimore, 1974), 3, 51.

14   John R. Western, Monarchy and Revolution (Totowa, N.J., 1972), 144.

15   Quoted in Earl R. Kruschke, The Right to Keep and Bear Arms (Springfield, Ill., 1985), 33.

16   Quoted in Roy S. Wolper, "The Rhetoric of Gunpowder and the Idea of Progress," Journal of the History of Ideas 31 (Oct.–Dec. 1970): 594.

17   Marcelle Thiébaux, "The Mediaeval Hunt," Speculum 42 (April 1967): 261.

18   See P. B. Munsche, Gentlemen and Poachers: The English Game Laws, 1671–1831 (Cambridge, Eng., 1981), 15, 79, 82, and Ian Gilmour, Riot, Risings and Revolution (London, 1992), 196.

19   Speech to Parliament, Nov. 9, 1685, quoted in John Childs, The Army, James II, and the Glorious Revolution (Manchester, Eng., 1980), 11.

20   Bill of Rights, 1689, printed in Bernard Schwartz, ed., The Bill of Rights, 2 vols. (New York, 1971), i, 43. See also John K. Rowland, "Origins of the Second Amendment: The Creation of the Constitutional Rights of Militia and of Keeping and Bearing Arms" (Ph.D. diss., Ohio State University, 1978), 51.

21   Malcolm, To Keep and Bear Arms, 115, 130, 134, 142.

22   See Lois G. Schwoerer, The Declaration of Rights, 1689 (Baltimore, 1981), 74–8, and Michael A. Bellesiles, "Gun Laws in Early America: The Regulation of Firearms Ownership, 1607–1794," Law and History Review 16 (fall 1998): 571.

23   Kennett and Anderson, The Gun in America, 21.

24   Quoted from John Trenchard, An Argument, Shewing that a Standing Army Is Inconsistent with a Free Government and Absolutely Destructive to the Constitution of the English Monarchy (London, 1697), 3–4, 29.

25   See Chester Kirby, "The English Game Law System," American Historical Review 38 (July 1933): 249, 254.

Chapter 2

1   Quoted from John Shy, Toward Lexington (Princeton, 1965), 1.

2   Terry G. Jordan and Matti Kaups, The American Backwoods Frontier (Baltimore, 1989), 221.

3   Darrett B. Rutman, "A Militant New World, 1607–1640" (Ph.D. diss., University of Virginia, 1959), 117.

4   Adam J. Hirsch, "The Collision of Military Cultures in Seventeenth-Century New England," Journal of American History 74 (March 1988): 1188–9, 1194.

5   Rutman, "New World," 330, 524.

6   Daniel J. Boorstin, The Americans: The Colonial Experience (New York, 1958), 355.

7   See William L. Shea, The Virginia Militia in the Seventeenth Century (Baton Rouge, La., 1983), 53, 75, 92.

8   See Shy, *Toward Lexington*, 17, and Allan R. Millet, "The Constitution and the Citizen-Soldier," in Richard H. Kohn, ed., *The United States Military under the Constitution of the United States, 1789–1989* (New York, 1991), 99.

9   See Patrick M. Malone, *The Skulking Way of War* (Lanham, Md., 1991), 42–3, and for later trafficking see Frank R. Secoy, *Changing Military Patterns of the Great Plains Indians* (Lincoln, Nebr., 1992), 66.

10 Quoted in Carl P. Russell, *Guns on the Early Frontiers* (Berkeley, 1957), 40–2.

11 Allen W. Trelease, *Indian Affairs in Colonial New York* (Ithaca, N.Y., 1960), 95.

12 Ibid., 89.

13 Quoted in Malone, *Skulking Way of War*, 47.

14 William Waller Hening, *The Statutes at Large: Being a Collection of All the Laws of Colonial Virginia*, vol. 1 (1809–23; reprint, Wilmington, Del., 1978). March 8–9, 1657, p. 441.

15 Ibid., March 9–10, 1658, p. 525.

16 Wilcomb E. Washburn, *The Governor and the Rebel* (Chapel Hill, N.C., 1957), 27–8.

17 The quotation and statistics on prices of trading goods, 1716–18, come from Verner W. Crane, *The Southern Frontier, 1670–1732* (Durham, N.C., 1928), 46, 332–3.

18 Hening, *Statutes at Large*, 579.

19 The quotation, July 18, 1715, comes from Benjamin Quarles, "The Colonial Militias and Negro Manpower," *Mississippi Valley Historical Review* 45 (March 1959): 644.

20 The statistics are in Lyle D. Brundage, "The Organization, Administration, and Training of the United States Ordinary and Volunteer Militia, 1792–1861" (Ph.D. diss., University of Michigan, 1958), 3.

21 Rowland, "Origins of the Second Amendment," 95, and Adam J. Hirsch, "The Collision of Military Cultures in Seventeenth-Century New England," *Journal of American History* 74 (March 1988): 1188.

22 Bellesiles, "Gun Laws in Early America," 574.

23 See Jack D. Marietta and G. S. Rowe, "Violent Crime, Victims, and Society in Pennsylvania, 1682–1800," *Pennsylvania History* 24 (Supplemental issue, 1999): 26, and Douglas Greenberg, "Crime, Law Enforcement, and Social Control in Colonial America," *American Journal of Legal History* 26 (Oct. 1982): 293–325.

24 Rachel N. Klein, "Ordering the Backcountry: The South Carolina Regulation," *William and Mary Quarterly* 38 (Oct. 1981): 668.

25 The quotation and statistic come from Richard M. Brown, *The South Carolina Regulators* (Cambridge, Mass., 1963), 38–9.

26 For a discussion of the regulatory pattern, see William J. Novak, *The People's Welfare* (Chapel Hill, N.C., 1996), 14–15.

27 See Carl Bridenbaugh, *The Colonial Craftsmen* (Chicago, 1961), 117–19, and Richard G. Stone Jr., *A Brittle Sword* (Lexington, Ken., 1977), 14.

28 David H. Fischer, *Albion's Seed* (New York, 1989), 189, 697, 766. For details on maintaining colonial law and order, see Carl Bridenbaugh, *Cities in the Wilderness*, 2d ed. (New York, 1964), 64–8, 215–20, 278–9.

29 See Malcolm, *To Keep and Bear Arms*, 143, and William Blackstone, *Commentaries on the Laws of England* (1765–69; reprint, Philadelphia, 1856). Book 1, 104 and Book 4, 110.

30 Rowland, "Origins of the Second Amendment," 204–5, and Bellesiles, "Gun Laws in Early America," 570, 586.

31 Malcolm, *To Keep and Bear Arms*, 20–21, 83.

32 For data on arms scarcity, see Alan McFarlane, *The Justice and the Mare's Ale* (Oxford, Eng., 1981), 191. The quotation comes from Lindsay Boynton, *The Elizabethan Militia, 1558–1638* (London, 1967), 67.

33 For the quotations, see Edmund S. Morgan, *American Slavery, American Freedom* (New York, 1975), 239–40, and for other data, Kennett and Anderson, *The Gun in America*, 28, 42–4.

34 Bellesiles, "Gun Laws in Early America," 571.

Chapter 3

1   The quotations come from David E. Young, ed., *The Origin of the Second Amendment*, 2d ed. (Ontonagon, Mich., 1995), xxv, and John R. Galvin, *The Minute Men* (New York, 1967), 14, 255.

2   Quoted from Malcolm, *To Keep and Bear Arms*, 134.

3   Bellesiles, "Gun Laws in Early America," 581.

4   To John Hancock, New York, Sept. 2, 1776, *The Papers of George Washington*, Revolutionary Series, ed. Dorothy Twohig (Charlottesville, Va., 1994), VI: 199. The second quotation comes from John Shy, *A People Numerous and Armed* (New York, 1976), 217. For details on the failings of militia, see Don Higginbotham, *War and Society in Revolutionary America* (Columbia, S.C., 1988), 116–17.

5   Merrill Jensen, ed. *The Documentary History of the Ratification of the Constitution*, vol. 1 (Madison, Wis., 1976), 88.

6   To James Warren, a former militia general, Nov. 20, 1780, quoted in Charles A. Royster, *A Revolutionary People at War* (Chapel Hill, N.C., 1979), 37.

7   Philip B. Sharpe, *The Rifle in America* (New York, 1938), vii, 4.

8   Washington, "Circular to the States," Newburgh, N.Y., June 8, 1783, in *The Writings of George Washington*, ed. John C. Fitzpatrick. 39 vols. (Washington, D.C., 1931–44), xxvi, 494.

9   Report of a committee on a military peace arrangement, Oct. 23, 1783, *Journals of the Continental Congress, 1774–1789*, ed. Gaillard Hunt. Vol. 25 (Washington, D.C., 1922), 741.

10 To Harry Lee Jr., Mount Vernon, Oct. 31, 1786, *The Papers of George Washington*, Confederation Series, ed. W. W. Abbot and Dorothy Twohig (Charlottesville, Va., 1995), IV: 319.

11 David P. Szatmary, *Shays' Rebellion* (Amherst, Mass., 1980), 111.

12 To David Humphreys, Mount Vernon, Dec. 16, 1786, *Papers of Washington*, Confederation Series, IV: 476.

13 For the quotations, see Aug. 23, 1787, in Max Farrand, ed., *The Records of the Federal Convention of 1787*, 3 vols. (New Haven, 1911), II: 388, and *The Federalist*, ed. Jacob E. Cooke (Middletown, Conn., 1961), No. 46, Jan. 29, 1788, p. 321.

14 Oct. 1, 1787, and June 16, 1788, in *The Papers of James Mason, 1725–1792*, 3 vols. (Chapel Hill, N.C., 1970), I: 997, 1084.

15 Jack N. Rakove, *Original Meanings* (New York, 1996), 288.

16 Quoted in ibid., 318.

17 For Madison's comments, see *The Federalist*, June 29 and Aug. 23, 1787, and *The Federalist*, No. 41, Jan. 19, 1788; *The Papers of James Madison*, vol. 10, ed. Robert A. Rutland (Chicago, 1977), 87, 156, 392–3, 394–5.

18 Quoted in Rowland, "Origins of the Second Amendment," 410.

19 "Impartial Examiner," Feb. 27, 1788, quoted in Jackson Turner Main, *The Antifederalists* (Chapel Hill, N.C., 1961), 147. See also Don Higginbotham, "The Federalized Militia Debate: A Neglected Aspect of Second Amendment Scholarship," *William and Mary Quarterly* 55 (Jan. 1998), 46.

20 June 5, 1788, in Schwartz, ed., *The Bill of Rights*, II: 773.

21 June 14, 1788, in Farrand, ed., *Records of Federal Convention*, III: 319.

22 For other details, see Stuart Leibiger, "James Madison and Amendments to the Constitution, 1787–1789: 'Parchment Barriers,' " *Journal of Southern History* 59 (Aug. 1993): 441, 446, 467; Lance Banning, *The Sacred Fire of Liberty* (Ithaca, N.Y., 1995), 270, 280–81; and Gordon S. Wood, *The Creation of the American Republic, 1776–1787* (Chapel Hill, N.C., 1969), 536–43.

23 Aug. 17, 1789, *Annals of the Congress, 1789–1824*, 42 vols. (Washington, D.C., 1834–56), I: 749–50.

24 See *Creating the Bill of Rights*, ed. Helen E. Veit, Kenneth R. Bowling, and Charlene B. Bickford (Baltimore, 1991), 183, 198, 260–1.

25 John Randolph to St. George Tucker, Sept. 11, 1789, ibid., 293.

26   Malcolm, *To Keep and Bear Arms*, 161. See also Stephen P. Halbrook, "The Original Under-
     standing of the Second Amendment," in *The Bill of Rights*, ed. Eugene W. Hickok Jr. (Char-
     lottesville, Va., 1991), 126.

27   Malcolm, *To Keep and Bear Arms*, 162.

28   Quoted from Brannon P. Denning, "Gun Shy: The Second Amendment as an 'Underenforced
     Constitutional Norm,'" *Harvard Journal of Law and Public Policy* 21 (summer 1998): 739.
     See also Academics for the Second Amendment, "An Open Letter on the Second Amend-
     ment," *Journal of Higher Education* 41 (Aug. 11, 1995), A23.

29   Carl T. Bogus, "The Hidden History of the Second Amendment," *U. C. Davis Law Review*
     31 (winter 1998): 366, 369.

30   See Bellesiles, "Gun Laws in Early America," 588.

31   A considerable literature deals with this controversy. For convenient summaries of opposing
     views, see Bogus, "Hidden History," 408; Gregg Lee Carter, *The Gun Control Movement* (New
     York, 1997), 33–5; Bellesiles, "Origins of Gun Culture," 425–55; Robert E. Shalope, "The
     Ideological Origins of the Second Amendment," *Journal of American History* 69 (Dec. 1982):
     599–614; Lawrence D. Cress, "An Armed Community: The Origins and Meaning of the Right
     to Bear Arms," ibid. 71 (June 1984): 22–42; Cress and Shalhope, "The Second Amendment
     and the Right to Bear Arms: An Exchange," ibid. (Dec. 1984): 587–93; Irving Brant, *The Bill
     of Rights* (Indianapolis, 1965), 486; and Leonard W. Levy, *Origins of the Bill of Rights* (New
     Haven, 1999), 133–4.

Chapter 4

1   *Journal of William Maclay*, ed. Edgar S. Maclay (New York, 1890), entry of April 16, 1790, p.
     2421.

2   To the Senate, Dec. 14, 1793, *American State Papers*, Class V, *Military Affairs*. 7 vols. (Wash-
     ington, D.C., 1832–61), I: 44.

3   Ibid., 60. For comparative analysis of the arms statistics, see Bellesiles, "Origins of Gun Cul-
     ture," 431.

4   *U.S. Statutes at Large*, I: 352.

5   Quoted in Thomas P. Slaughter, *The Whiskey Rebellion* (New York, 1986), 213.

6   To House of Representatives, Dec. 10, 1794, *American State Papers, Military Affairs*, I: 69, and
     Richard H. Kohn, *Eagle and Sword* (New York, 1975), 135.

7   Quoted in Alexander DeConde, *The Quasi-War* (New York, 1966), 198.

8   Quoted in David B. Kopel, "The Second Amendment in the Nineteenth Century," *Brigham
     Young University Law Review* 51 (1998): 1377.

9   Merritt Roe Smith, "Military Entrepreneurship," in *Yankee Enterprise*, ed. Otto Mayr and
     Robert C. Post (Washington, D.C., 1981), 76.

10   For details, see Reginald Horsman, *The War of 1812* (New York, 1969), 19–20, 30–31, 167–8,
     211, and for the quotations, Akhil Reed Amar, *The Bill of Rights* (New Haven, 1998), 57–8.

11   To George W. Caldwell, Nov. 29, 1812, and to Brig. Gen. John Adair, April 2, 1815, *Correspon-
     dence of Andrew Jackson*, ed. John S. Bassett, 7 vols. (Washington, D.C., 1926–33), I: 244, II:
     200–201.

12   G. W. Gooch, March 7, 1818, quoted in Kenneth O. McCreedy, "Palladium of Liberty: The
     American Militia System, 1815–1861" (Ph.D. diss., University of California, Berkeley, 1991),
     74.

13   Robert Baldick, *The Duel* (London, 1965), 42.

14   See Bertram Wyatt-Brown, *Southern Honor* (New York, 1982), 351, 356, and W. J. Rorabaugh,
     "The Political Duel in the Early Republic: Burr v. Hamilton," *Journal of the Early Republic*
     15 (spring 1995): 14.

15   Ibid., 72.

16   See V. G. Kiernan, *The Duel in European History* (Oxford, Eng., 1988), 310, and Dickson D.
     Bruce Jr., *Violence and Culture in the Antebellum South* (Austin, Tex., 1979), 27.

17 Quoted in William Weir, *Written With Lead* (Hamden, Conn., 1992), 30.

18 Lyman Beecher, "The Remedy for Duelling," *Lyman Beecher and the Reform of Society: Four Sermons, 1804–1828*, ed. Edwin S. Gaustad (New York, 1972), iii, 24–5, 37, 40.

19 The quotations come from Robert V. Remini, *Andrew Jackson and the Course of American Empire, 1767–1821* (New York, 1977), 143.

20 Quoted from Kiernan, *Duel in Europe*, 308.

21 Quoted in John Hope Franklin, *The Militant South, 1800–1861* (Cambridge, Mass., 1956), 49.

22 Daniel W. Howe, *The Political Culture of the American Whigs* (Chicago, 1979), 127.

23 Russell I. Fries, "A Comparative Study of the British and American Arms Industries, 1790–1890" (Ph.D. diss., Johns Hopkins University, 1972), 28.

24 *Yankee Enterprise: The Rise of the American System of Manufactures*, ed. Otto Mayr and Robert C. Post (Washington, D.C., 1981), Introduction, xii.

25 See Bellesiles, "Origins of Gun Culture," 426, 428, 443.

26 Secretary of War John H. Eaton to the chairman of the House Committee on the Militia, Feb. 23, 1830, *American State Papers, Military Affairs*, IV: 310 (table).

27 Joseph Story, *Commentaries on the Constitution of the United States*, 3 vols. (1833; reprint, Boston, 1970), III: 746.

28 Eighth Annual Message, Washington, D.C., Dec. 5, 1836, in *State of the Union Messages of the Presidents, 1790–1966*, ed. Fred L. Israel, 3 vols. (New York, 1966), I: 464.

29 Munsche, *Gentlemen and Poachers*, 36.

30 Bellesiles, "Origins of Gun Culture," 447.

31 For pertinent statistics, see Carole Shammas, *The Pre-Industrial Consumer in England and America* (Oxford, Eng., 1990), 206, 208.

32 See Ora B. Peake, *A History of the United States Indian Factory System, 1795–1822* (Denver, 1954), 63, 74.

33 See Elliott West, *The Contested Plains* (Lawrence, Kans., 1998), 48–9, 55, 71, and Wilbur R. Jacobs, *Dispossessing the American Indian* (New York, 1972), 53, 64, 195 n. 17.

34 Act of June 30, 1834, *U.S. Statutes at Large*, IV: 730.

35 Joseph Jablow, *The Cheyenne in Plains Indian Trade Relations, 1795–1840* (New York, 1950), 18, 36, 52, 79.

36 Everett Dick, *The Dixie Frontier* (1948; reprint, New York, 1964), 40, 142–3.

37 Richard Slotkin, *Regeneration Through Violence* (Middletown, Conn., 1973), 464, 508, who quotes William G. Simms.

38 Quoted from Benjamin L. Oliver, *The Rights of an American Citizen* (1832; reprint, Boston, 1970), 177–8.

39 Bellesilles, "Gun Laws in Early America," 87, and Kopel, "Second Amendment in Nineteenth Century," 1416–17.

Chapter 5

1 Sidney I. Pomerantz, *New York: An American City, 1783–1803* (1938; reprint, New York, 1965), 321.

2 Richard C. Wade, *The Urban Frontier* (Cambridge, Mass., 1959), 88.

3 Dennis C. Rousey, *Policing the Southern City* (Baton Rouge, La., 1996), 13–14, 19, 24.

4 Charles Christian, *A Brief Treatise on the Police of the City of New York* (New York, 1812), 4.

5 Quoted in David Ascoli, *The Queen's Peace* (London, 1979), 1.

6 Novak, *The People's Welfare*, 54–5, 57, 62–3, 66.

7 See Roger Lane, "Crime and Criminal Statistics in Nineteenth-Century Massachusetts," *Journal of Social History* 2 (winter 1968): 157; Fred P. Graham, "A Contemporary History of American Crime," in Graham and Gurr, eds., *Violence in America*, 490; and for the colonial era, Carl Bridenbaugh, *Cities in Revolt* (New York, 1965), 299–334.

8 *Louisiana Advertiser* (New Orleans), Feb. 17, 1834, quoted in Rousey, *Policing Southern City*, 33.

9   John C. Schneider, "Mob Violence and Public Order in the American City, 1830–1865" (Ph.D. diss., University of Minnesota, 1971), 68, 75.
10 Bellesiles, "Origins of Gun Culture," 439.
11 Kopel, "Second Amendment in Nineteenth Century," 1422–24, 1428–29.
12 The quotations come from Sydney G. Fisher, *A Philadelphia Perspective: The Diary of Sidney George Fisher Covering the Years 1834–1871*, ed. Nicholas B. Wainwright (1967), entry of May 15, 1844, pp. 167–68.
13 Ibid., entry of July 24, 1844, pp. 172–3. For other data, see Michael Feldberg, *The Philadelphia Riots of 1844* (Westport, Conn., 1975), 4, 10.
14 *Philadelphia Public Ledger*, Nov. 29, 1844, quoted in David R. Johnson, *Policing the Urban Underworld* (Philadelphia, 1979), 137.
15 *New York Herald*, Oct. 1, 1844, in ibid.
16 Sean Wilentz, *Chants Democratic* (New York, 1984), 332, and Raymond B. Fosdick, *American Police Systems* (New York, 1921), 66.
17 Merritt Roe Smith, *Harper's Ferry Armory and the New Technology* (Ithaca, N.Y., 1977), 281.
18 *A Compilation of the Messages and Papers of the Presidents, 1789–1897*, comp. James D. Richardson, 19 vols. (1896–97; reprint, Washington, D.C., 1922), vol. 5, Dec. 2, 1845, p. 2263 and Dec. 29, 1846, p. 2358.
19 David A. Hounshell, *From the American System to Mass Production, 1800–1932* (Baltimore, 1984), 47.
20 Quoted in Fries, "British and American Arms Industries," 121.
21 *Niles Register* 70 (July 25, 1846): 326 as cited in Jack K. Bauer, *The Mexican War, 1846–1848* (New York, 1974), 83.
22 Winfield Scott, *Memoirs of Lieut.-General Winfield Scott, LL.D.* (New York, 1864), 392.
23 Fourth Annual Message, Dec. 5, 1848, Richardson, ed., *Messages of Presidents*, VI: 2481.
24 James O'Meara, "Concealed Weapons and Crime," *Overland Monthly* 2 (1890): 12.
25 Emerson Hough, "The American Six-Shooter," *Outing Magazine* 54 (Nov. 1909): 503.
26 For the quotations, see Walter P. Webb, "The Story of the Six-Shooter," in *The Old West in Fact*, ed. Irwin R. Blacker (New York, 1962), 306, and Robert Easton, "Guns of the American West" in *Book of the American West*, ed. Jay Monaghan (New York, 1963), 408.
27 Fries, "British and American Arms Industries," 98–99.
28 William Hosley, *Colt: The Making of an American Legend* (Amherst, Mass., 1996), 55.
29 Bellesiles, "Origins of Gun Culture," 450.
30 The statistics come from Edward K. Spann, *The New Metropolis* (New York, 1981), 238.
31 Russell S. Gilmore, "Crackshots and Patriots: The National Rifle Association and America's Military-Sporting Tradition, 1871–1929" (Ph.D. diss., University of Wisconsin, 1974), 7.
32 Robert Reinders, "Militia and Public Order in Nineteenth-Century America," *Journal of American Studies* 2 (April 1977): 88.
33 Spann, *New Metropolis*, 325.
34 Schneider, "Mob Violence," 128.
35 Entry of Feb. 1, 1857, *The Diary of George Templeton Strong*, ed. Allan Nevins and Milton H. Thomas, 4 vols. (New York, 1952), II: 320.
36 *New York Times*, Nov. 7, 1857, p. 4.
37 Ibid., Nov. 12, 1858, p. 8, and "Police with Pistols," Nov. 15, p. 4:2.
38 Thomas H. Gladstone, *The Englishman in Kansas* (New York, 1857), 7.
39 Ibid., 57.
40 Halford Ryan, *Henry Ward Beecher* (New York, 1990), 33.
41 Charles Sumner, "The Crime Against Kansas," *New York Tribune*, May 23, 1856, p. 23.
42 Republican Platform of 1856 in *National Party Platforms, 1840–1976*, comp. Donald B. Johnson, rev. ed., 2 vols. (Urbana, Ill., 1978), I: 27.
43 See Mark E. Neely Jr., *The Fate of Liberty* (New York, 1991), 52, 69.
44 Robert A. Howard, "Interchangeable Parts Reexamined: The Private Sector of the American

Arms Industry on the Eve of the Civil War," *Technology and Culture* 19 (Oct. 1978): 634, 642.

45   William B. Edwards, *Civil War Guns* (Harrisburg, Pa., 1962), Prologue, n.p.

46   Russell F. Weigley, *History of the United States Army*, enlarged ed. (Bloomington, Ind., 1984), 235.

47   Democratic Platform of 1864 in Johnson, comp., *National Party Platforms*, I: 34.

48   Schneider, "Mob Violence," 156.

49   The statistics come from Iver Bernstein, *The New York City Draft Riots* (New York, 1990), 5, 288–9n. For the police role, see James F. Richardson, *The New York Police* (New York, 1970), 129.

50   Stewart M. Brooks, *Our Murdered Presidents* (New York, 1966), 23.

51   *The United States Army and Navy Journal and Gazette of the Regular and Volunteer Forces* 2 (June 10, 1865): 664.

52   Bellesiles, "Origins of Gun Culture," 452.

Chapter 6

1   Eric H. Monkkonen, "Diverging Homicide Rates: England and the United States," in Gurr, ed., *Violence in America*, I: 93.

2   O'Meara, "Concealed Weapons and Crime," 13.

3   Edith Abbott, "Crime and the War," *Journal of the American Institute of Criminal Law and Criminology* 9 (1918–19): 41, 44.

4   Herman Belz, *Reconstructing the Union* (Ithaca, N.Y., 1969), 282.

5   Martin Delany, quoted in Dan T. Carter, *When the War Was Over* (Baton Rouge, La., 1985), 197.

6   *Congressional Globe*, 39th Cong., 1st Sess., Part 2, March 8, 1866, H.R., p. 1266.

7   Quoted in Noah Andre Trudeau, *Out of the Storm* (Boston, 1994), 390.

8   The numbers come from Rousey, *Policing Southern City*, 118–19.

9   For details, see James G. Randall and David Donald, *The Civil War and Reconstruction*, 2d ed. (Boston, 1961), 595.

10   The quotation and statistics are in Allen W. Trelease, *White Terror* (New York, 1971), 119, 156.

11   Quoted in Ted Tunnell, *Crucible of Reconstruction* (Baton Rouge, La., 1984), 157.

12   Ibid.

13   The quotation and details come from Eric Foner, *Reconstruction* (New York, 1988), 555.

14   Report of Lieut. T. W. Morrison, Jan. 29, 1872, in *Documentary History of Reconstruction*, ed. Walter L. Fleming, 2 vols. (1909; reprint, New York, 1966), II: 76–7.

15   Tunnell, *Crucible of Reconstruction*, 192.

16   Otis A. Singletary, *Negro Militia and Reconstruction* (Austin, Tex., 1957), 75–8.

17   Michael K. Curtis, *No State Shall Abridge* (Durham, N.C., 1986), viii, 1.

18   Richard N. Current, *Those Terrible Carpetbaggers* (New York, 1988), 354.

19   Herbert Shapiro, *White Violence and Black Response* (Amherst, Mass., 1988), 21.

20   For speculation on Southern violence, see Edward L. Ayers, *Vengeance and Justice* (New York, 1984), 269–70, and for the quotation, Singletary, *Negro Militia*, 3.

21   Quoted from Allen W. Trelease, *Reconstruction* (New York, 1971), 23.

22   See Jo Dixon and Alan J. Lizotte, "Gun Ownership and the 'Southern Subculture of Violence,'" *American Journal of Sociology* 93 (Sept. 2, 1987): 383, 299, 401, and Howard S. Erlanger, "Is There a 'Subculture of Violence' in the South?" *Journal of Criminal Law and Criminology* 66 (Dec. 1975): 483–90.

23   Ayers, *Vengeance and Justice*, 232–3.

24   See Bellesiles, "Origins of Gun Culture," 52–3; and for the crime statistics, Graham, "American Crime," 490.

25   Report of the Executive Committee of the Prison Association of New York, quoted in Edith

Abbott, "The Civil War and the Crime Wave of 1865–70," *Social Service Review* 1 (1927): 224.

26 New York *Times*, Aug. 16, 1866, cited in Frank T. Morn, "Firearms Use and the Police: A Historic Evolution of American Values," in *Firearms and Violence*, ed. Don B. Kates Jr. (San Francisco, 1984), 502.

27 Reinders, "Militia and Public Order," 82, 91.

28 *Army and Navy Journal*, April 13, 1867, quoted in Gilmore, "Crackshots and Patriots," 21.

29 See, for example, Williamson, *Winchester*, 72–3, 119.

30 Felicia J. Deyrup, *Arms Makers of the Connecticut Valley* (Northampton, Mass., 1948), 7, 202, and Eric Mottram, " 'The Persuasive Lips': Men and Guns in America, the West," *Journal of American Studies* 10 (April 1976): 64.

31 Joe B. Frantz, "The Frontier Tradition: An Invitation to Violence," in *Violence in America*, ed. Graham and Gurr, 51–2.

32 *Congressional Globe*, 30th Cong., 2d Sess., Senate, Feb. 22, 1849, p. 580.

33 Diary entry of May 22, 1849, in J. S. Holliday, *The World Rushed In* (New York, 1981), 52–3, 123, 138, 230, 365.

34 Quoted in John P. Reid, *Law for the Elephant* (San Marino, Calif., 1980), 5–6.

35 The quotations come from Robert M. Senkewicz, *Vigilantes in Gold Rush San Francisco* (Stanford, Calif., 1985), 171, 194.

36 For details on fact and legend, see Philip D. Jordan, "The Pistol Packin' Cowboy: From Bullet to Burial," *Red River Valley Historical Review* 2 (Sept. 1975): 75, 82–3, 87, 91; Donald Curtis Brown, "The Great Gun-Toting Controversy, 1865–1910" (Ph.D. diss., Tulane University, 1983), 89, 91; and David T. Courtwright, *Violent Land* (Cambridge, Mass., 1996), 88, 91, 103–4.

37 *Daily Colorado Tribune* (Denver), Aug. 12, 1869, cited in Brown, "Gun-Toting Controversy," 108.

38 Roger D. McGrath, *Gunfighters, Highwaymen, and Vigilantes* (Berkeley, 1984), 79.

39 Philip D. Jordan, "The Town Marshal and the Police," in *People of the Plains and Mountains*, ed. Ray Allen Billington (Westport, Conn., 1973), 104.

40 Mottram, "Persuasive Lips," 60.

41 The data on Hickok come from the Abilene *Chronicle*, June 8, 1871, and on Masterson from the Dodge City *Times*, April 23, 1878, reproduced in Nyle H. Miller and Joseph W. Snell, *Great Gunfighters of the Kansas Cowtowns, 1867–1886* (Lincoln, Nebr., 1963), 130, 182.

42 Quoted from Reid, *Law for the Elephant*, 359. For conflicting views on this point, see Courtwright, *Violent Land*, 101–2; Clare V. McKanna Jr., *Homicide, Race, and Justice in the American West, 1880–1920* (Tucson, Ariz., 1997); Richard M. Brown, "Historiography of Violence in the American West," in *Historians and the American West*, ed. Malone, 234–69; Brown, *No Duty to Retreat* (New York, 1991), 39–40; Frank R. Prassel, *The Western Peace Officer* (Norman, Okla., 1972); Robert R. Dykstra, *The Cattle Towns* (New York, 1968); and Richard White, *"It's Your Misfortune and None of My Own"* (Norman, Okla., 1991).

43 See, for example, David J. Bodenhamer, "Law and Disorder on the Early Frontier: Marion County, Indiana, 1823–1850," and Lynn I. Perrigo, "Law and Order in Early Colorado Mining Camps," in *Crime and Justice in American History*, ed. Eric H. Monkkonen, vol. 4: 23, 33, 269–70; and Jeremy W. Kilar, "Great Lakes Lumber Towns and Frontier Violence: A Contemporary Study," *Journal of Forest History* 31 (April 1987): 83–4.

44 For the statistics, see Ann P. Baenziger, "The Texas State Police During Reconstruction: A Reexamination," *Southwestern Historical Quarterly* 72 (April 1969): 473.

45 Quoted in Brown, "Gun-Toting Controversy," 33. For a different version of events, see Walter Prescott Webb, *The Texas Rangers*, 2d ed. (Austin, Tex., 1965), 225–6.

46 Brown, "Gun-Toting Controversy," 214, 311.

47 See, for example, McKanna, *Homicide, Race, and Justice*, 11, 14, 24.

48 Roger D. McGrath, "Violence and Lawlessness on the Western Frontier," in Gurr, ed., *Violence in America*, I: 123, 136.

49   Dykstra, *Cattle Towns*, 123, 125, 144, 148; White, *"It's Your Misfortune,"* 329–30; and Graham, "American Crime," 504.

50   *Western Independent* (Fort Smith, Ark.), Aug. 28, 1873, as quoted in Glenn H. Shirley, *Law West of Fort Smith* (New York, 1957), 23.

51   Brown, "Gun-Toting Controversy," 298.

52   Henry S. Drago, *The Great Range Wars* (New York, 1970), 51.

53   Quoted from Robert M. Utley, *Billy the Kid* (Lincoln, Nebr., 1989), 32.

54   *Texas Livestock Journal* (Fort Worth), Feb. 1882, quoted in *Trailing the Cowboy*, ed. Clifford P. Westermeier (Caldwell, Idaho, 1955), 112.

55   Brown, "Gun-Toting Controversy," 108, and 131, 134, 141, quoting from the *Texas Livestock Journal*, Dec. 29, 1882; Feb. 3, 1883; and *El Paso Lone Star*, Feb. 25, 1884. For earlier opposition to the carrying of concealed weapons, see Redfield, *Homicide, North and South*, 193–207.

56   Edward C. Abbott and Helena H. Smith, *We Pointed Them North* (New York, 1939), 250.

57   Kenneth M. Stampp, *America in 1857* (New York, 1990), 207.

58   Quoted in Richard S. Van Wagoner, *Mormon Polygamy* (Salt Lake City, 1986), 105–6. For Morrill's position, see Coy F. Cross II, *Justin Smith Morrill* (East Lansing, Mich., 1999), 34–7.

59   Howard R. Lamar, *The Far Southwest, 1846–1912* (New Haven, 1966), 398.

Chapter 7

1   Quoted from Edward F. Leddy, *Magnum Force Lobby* (Lanham, Md., 1987), 287.

2   Quoted in *Americans and Their Guns*, ed. James B. Trefthen and James E. Serven (Harrisburg, Pa., 1967), 88.

3   Quoted in Gilmore, "Crackshots and Patriots," 71.

4   Chicago *Tribune*, Aug. 4, 1877, p. 8, cited in Kennett and Anderson, *The Gun in America*, 147. For details, see Paul A. Gilje, *Rioting in America* (Bloomington, Ind., 1996), 118–19.

5   Robert M. Fogelson, *America's Armories* (Cambridge, Mass., 1989), 28.

6   Jerry Cooper, *The Rise of the National Guard* (Lincoln, Nebr., 1997), 46.

7   David E. Engdahl, "Soldiers, Riots, and Revolution: The Law and History of Military Troops in Civil Disorders," *Iowa Law Review* 57 (Oct. 1971): 62–3.

8   Greenback Party Platform of 1880 in Johnson, comp., *National Party Platforms*, I: 58.

9   See Roger Lane, *Violent Death in the City*, 2d ed. (Columbus, Ohio, 1999), 116.

10   Guiteau's words are quoted from *American Violence*, ed. Richard Hofstadter and Michael Wallace (New York, 1970), 413.

11   "Shooting in Sport," New York *Times*, Aug. 22, 1881, p. 6.

12   Roger Lane, *Policing the City: Boston, 1822–1885* (Cambridge, Mass., 1967), 203.

13   Courtwright, *Violent Land*, 102.

14   "The Progress of the Revolver," *Saturday Review* (London) 59 (Feb. 14, 1885): 198.

15   Colin Greenwood, *Firearms Control* (London, 1972), 20.

16   George H. Paul to John C. McMynn, Jan. 7, 1888, quoted in Gilmore, "Crackshots and Patriots," 75.

17   The quotations come from O'Meara, "Concealed Weapons and Crimes," 2, 15.

18   New York *Daily Tribune*, Sept. 12, 1892, p. 4, cited in Kennett and Anderson, *The Gun in America*, 101.

19   See Charles Fairman and Stanley Morrison, *The Fourteenth Amendment and the Bill of Rights* (New York, 1970), xii, iv, 218–19.

20   Richard C. Cortner, *The Supreme Court and the Second Bill of Rights* (Madison, Wis., 1981), 11, and Curtis, *No State Shall Abridge*, 113, 203.

21   Robert Dowlut, "The Right to Arms: Does the Constitution or the Predilection of Judges Reign?" *Oklahoma Law Review* 36 (1983): 100.

22   Akhil Read Amar, "The Bill of Rights and the Fourteenth Amendment," *Yale Law Journal* 101 (April 1992): 1284.

23   See Osgood Hardy, "The *Itata* Incident," *Hispanic American Historical Review* 5 (May 1922): 195–226.
24   Fogelson, *America's Armories*, 45.
25   Quoted in Cooper, *Rise of National Guard*, 58.
26   "Civis" in *Journal of the Knights of Labor*, Aug. 16, 1894, quoted in Reinders, "Militia and Public Order," 99.
27   Message to the Texas legislature, Austin, Jan. 12, 1893, in *Addresses and State Papers of James Stephen Hogg*, ed. Robert C. Cotner (Austin, Tex., 1951), 322–3.
28   *Texas Baptist Standard* (Waco), Dec. 9, 1897, cited in Brown, "Gun-Toting Controversy," 253.
29   Quoted in James W. Clarke, *American Assassins* (Princeton, 1982), 39.
30   Brown, "Gun-Toting Controversy," 240.
31   To Anna Roosevelt, Wyoming, Sept. 20, 1884, in Theodore Roosevelt, *The Letters of Theodore Roosevelt*, ed. Elting E. Morison, 8 vols. (Cambridge, Mass., 1951–54), I: 82.
32   For Roosevelt's affection for guns, see Williamson, *Winchester*, 189–200.
33   Walter I. Trattner, *Crusade for the Children* (Chicago, 1970), 46.
34   First annual message, Dec. 3, 1901, in Richardson, ed., *Messages of Presidents*, XIV: 6672.
35   Second annual message, Dec. 2, 1902, in ibid., XIV: 6721.
36   Quoted in Walter Millis, *Arms and Men* (New York, 1956), 177.
37   Leddy, *Magnum Force Lobby*, 65.
38   May 4, 1903, Columbus, Ohio, in Elihu Root, *The Military and Colonial Policy of the United States: Addresses and Reports*, ed. Robert Bacon and James B. Scott (1916; reprint, Cambridge, Mass., 1970), 142.
39   Kopel, "Second Amendment in Nineteenth Century," 1510–11.
40   Feb. 25, 1907, quoted in Trefthen and Serven, eds., *Americans and Guns*, 142.
41   See Millet, "Constitution and Citizen Soldier," 108–9.

Chapter 8

1   New York *Tribune*, June 21, 1903, Sec. 2, p. 1, cited in Kennett and Anderson, *The Gun in America*, 179.
2   Andrew Phelan, "Men and Arms," *The Law Journal* 110 (Feb. 26, 1960): 131.
3   *Nation* 85 (July 15, 1907): 68.
4   T. C. Dabney, Clarksdale, Miss., Aug. 5, 1907, to the editor in ibid. (Aug. 22): 161–2.
5   *Enid Weekly Eagle* (Oklahoma), Aug. 27, 1908, cited in Brown, "Gun-Toting Controversy," 417–18.
6   Kennett and Anderson, *The Gun in America*, 172.
7   October 1910, quoted in Charles E. Van Loan, "Disarming New York," *Munsey's Magazine* 46 (Feb. 1912): 687.
8   Quoted in Kennett and Anderson, *The Gun in America*, 175.
9   Owen R. Lovejoy, *Better Child Labor Laws* (New York, Sept. 1911), 2.
10   Quoted from Jac Weller, "The Sullivan Law," *American Rifleman* 110 (April 1962): 34.
11   See, for example, Alan S. Krug, *Does Firearms Registration Work?* (Riverside, Conn., 1968), 5.
12   William G. McAdoo, *When the Court Takes a Recess* (New York, 1924), 96.
13   Quoted in Osha Gray Davidson, *Under Fire* (New York, 1998), 29.
14   New York *Times*, March 14, 1912, p. 1:5, and March 15, p. 2:6.
15   For the Roosevelt quotations, Oct. 12, 1912, and to John St. Loe Strachey, Dec. 16, see Roosevelt, *Letters*, VII: 629, 677.
16   Quoted in James B. Whisker, "The Second Amendment: The Right to Keep and Bear Arms" (Ph.D. diss., University of Maryland, 1969), 91–2.
17   George S. McGovern, *The Great Coalfield War* (Boston, 1972), 141.
18   To Elias Milton Ammons, April 28, 1914, *The Papers of Woodrow Wilson*, ed. Arthur S. Link, 69 vols. (Princeton, 1966–94), 29: 528–9.

19   For the statistics, see McKanna, *Homicide, Race, and Justice*, 107–8, and Gilje, *Rioting in America*, 120.
20   Lucilius A. Emery, "The Constitutional Right to Bear Arms," *Harvard Law Review* 28 (March 1915): 473, 476, 477.
21   Quoted in John P. Finnegan, "Military Preparedness in the Progressive Era, 1911–1917" (Ph.D. diss., University of Wisconsin, 1969), 38–9.
22   Quoted in Millis, *Arms and Men*, 215.
23   *Current Opinion* 58 (April 1915): 224.
24   Quoted in John P. Finnegan, *Against the Specter of the Dragon* (Westport, Conn., 1974), 73.
25   Quoted in Cooper, *Rise of National Guard*, 163.
26   Weigley, *History of Army*, 349.
27   Gilmore, "Crackshots and Patriots," 191.
28   Edwin Pugsley, quoted in Williamson, *Winchester*, 236.
29   Quoted in John W. Chambers II, *To Raise an Army* (New York, 1987), 170.
30   Ibid., 182.
31   Augustine Lonergan, from Connecticut, 1918, quoted in Anne Garner and Michael Clancy, *Firearms Statutes in the United States* (Washington, D.C., 1979), 27.
32   Manny Molina, *Guns and the Filipino Right to Arms* (Quezon City, Philippines, 1993), 27–8.
33   *U.S. Statutes at Large* 41: 759–87.
34   See Betty B. Rosenbaum, "The Relationship between War and Crime in the United States," *Journal of the American Institute of Criminal Law and Criminology* 30 (1939–40): 730–33, and Roger Lane, "On the Social Meaning of Homicide Trends in America," in *Violence in America*, ed. Gurr, I: 70.

Chapter 9

1   David B. Kopel, *The Samurai, the Mountie, and the Cowboy* (Buffalo, N.Y., 1992), 74.
2   For the quotation, see Fred L. Holmes, "Making Criminals Out of Soldiers," *Nation* 121 (July 22, 1925): 14, and for the statistics, see Margaret A. Zahn, "Homicide in the Twentieth Century: Trends, Types, and Causes," in *Violence in America*, ed. Gurr, I: 220.
3   Andrew Sinclair, *Prohibition* (Boston, 1962), 178, and Lawrence M. Friedman, *Crime and Punishment in American History* (New York, 1993), 266.
4   Association Against the Prohibition Amendment, *Reforming America With a Shotgun* (Washington, D.C., Nov. 1929), 33, 37.
5   Kennett and Anderson, *The Gun in America*, 189.
6   From Chicago *Tribune*, Feb. 6, 1922, p. 1, quoted in ibid., 190.
7   William B. Swaney and others, "For a Better Enforcement of the Law," *American Bar Association Journal* 8 (Sept. 1922): 591.
8   Quoted in Stephen P. Halbrook, "Congress Interprets the Second Amendment: Declarations by a Co-Equal Branch on the Individual Right to Keep and Bear Arms," *Tennessee Law Review* 62 (spring 1995): 601.
9   Kennett and Anderson, *The Gun in America*, 194.
10   Ibid., 195–6.
11   *Pacific Reporter* (Oct. 30, 1924), vol. 231 (St. Paul, Minn., 1925), 601–2.
12   Kennett and Anderson, *The Gun in America*, 191.
13   Colin Loftin, David McDowall, and James Boudouris, "Economic Change and Homicide in Detroit, 1926–1979," in Gurr, ed., *Violence in America*, I: 167.
14   *Congressional Record*, U.S. Congress, House, 68th Cong., 2d Sess., Dec. 17, 1924, vol. 66, p. 727.
15   Ibid., 727–8.
16   Virgil W. Peterson, *Barbarians in Our Midst* (Boston, 1952), 110.
17   Mark H. Haller, "Bootlegging: The Business and Politics of Violence," in Gurr, ed., *Violence in America*, I: 151.

18 Quoted in Frederick L. Hoffman, *The Homicide Problem* (Newark, N.J., 1925), 31.

19 Ibid., 4.

20 The quotations come from the *Toledo City Journal*, Aug. 26, 1925, reprinted in *Outlawing the Pistol*, ed. Lamar T. Beman (New York, 1926), 30, and Kennett and Anderson, *The Gun in America*, 191.

21 Editorial, *Christian Science Monitor*, Oct. 12, 1925, reprinted in Gurr, ed., *Violence in America*, I: 53.

22 As paraphrased in the New York *Times*, Oct. 14, 1925, p. 1:7.

23 William J. Helmer, *The Gun That Made the Twenties Roar* (New York, 1969), 72, 78.

24 Owen P. White, quoted in ibid., ix, 120.

25 Peterson, *Barbarians in Our Midst*, 133–4.

26 James F. Richardson, *Urban Police in the United States* (Port Washington, N.Y., 1974), 91.

27 *Carrying of Pistols, Revolvers, and Other Firearms Capable of Being Concealed on the Person in the Mails* (hearings before a subcommittee of the Committee on the Post Office Post Roads), 69th Cong., 1st Sess. (Feb. 17, 1926), 9.

28 Ibid., 3.

29 William G. McAdoo, "Crime and Punishment: Causes and Mechanisms of Prevalent Crimes," *Scientific Monthly* 24 (May 1927): 418.

30 H. C. Brearley, *Homicide in the United States* (Chapel Hill, N.C., 1932), 76.

31 Edward H. Bierstadt, "Our Permanent Crime," *Harper's* 156 (Dec. 1927): 65–6.

32 Homicide rates increased markedly in 1929. Zahn, "Homicide in Twentieth Century," 221.

33 *Firearms* (hearing before a subcommittee of the Committee on Interstate and Foreign Commerce), House of Representatives, 71st Cong., 2d Sess. (April 11, 1930), 14, 16.

34 Ibid., 27–9.

35 Virgil W. Peterson, *Crime Commissions in the United States* (Chicago, 1945), 11.

36 The press and Hoover, Dec. 6, 1930, are quoted in Richard G. Powers, *G-Men* (Carbondale, Ill., 1983), 24.

37 New York *Times*, Sept. 7, 1931, p. 4:3.

38 Speech of Jan. 8, 1932, in *Congressional Record*, U.S. Congress, Senate, 72d Cong., 1st Sess. (Jan. 15, 1932), vol. 75, p. 1999.

39 Statement on Lindbergh Kidnapping, May 13, 1932, *Public Papers of the Presidents of the United States: Herbert Hoover, 1932–33* (Washington, D.C., 1977), 215.

40 Speech, Madison, Wis., Nov. 5, 1932, in ibid., 742. Mitchell, Nov. 1932, is quoted in Max Lowenthal, *The Federal Bureau of Investigation* (New York, 1950), 402.

41 New York *Times*, Sept. 3, 1931, p. 1:7 and Sept. 6, p. 1:8.

42 Ibid., March 25, 1932, p. 4:2; March 29, p. 4:2 for the veto and quotation, and p. 18:5 for the editorial.

43 Quoted in Arthur M. Schlesinger Jr., *The Crisis of the Old Order, 1919–1933* (Boston, 1957), 465.

44 Quoted by J. Weston Allen in U.S. Attorney General, *Proceedings of the Attorney General's Conference on Crime . . . 1934* (Washington, D.C., 1936), 258.

Chapter 10

1 Radio address, June 10, 1933, *Selected Papers of Homer Cummings*, ed. Carl B. Swisher (New York, 1939), 28.

2 Quoted in Sanford J. Ungar, *FBI* (Boston, 1976), 39.

3 Louis McH. Howe, "Uncle Sam Starts After Crime," *Saturday Evening Post* 206 (July 29, 1933): 71.

4 Homicides rose again in 1933. "Homicide in the Twentieth Century: Trends, Types, and Causes" in *Violence in America*, I, *The History of Crime*, ed. Ted R. Gurr (Newbury Park, Calif., 1989), 220.

5 Howe, "Uncle Sam Starts After Crime," 6.

6 H. C. Engelbrecht, *"One Hell of a Business"* (New York, 1934), 24.

7 Millet, "The Constitution and the Citizen-Soldier," 111.

8 Quoted in Ungar, *FBI*, 75.

9 May 18, 1934, *The Public Papers and Addresses of Franklin D. Roosevelt*, ed. Samuel I. Rosenman, 13 vols. (New York, 1938–50), III: 242.

10 Powers, *G-Men*, 65.

11 See David R. Johnson, *American Law Enforcement* (St. Louis, 1981), 173–4.

12 William E. Leuchtenburg, *Franklin D. Roosevelt and the New Deal, 1932–1940* (New York, 1963), 333.

13 Quoted in Carl Bakal, *The Right to Bear Arms* (New York, 1966), 169–70.

14 The quotations come from the *National Firearms Act Hearings* before the Committee on Ways and Means. House of Representatives, 73d Cong., 2d Sess. (April 14, 15, and 16, 1934), 36–7, 43.

15 Quoted in Bakal, *Right to Bear Arms*, 172.

16 *National Firearms Act Hearings*, Senate, 1934, as quoted in Kennett and Anderson, *The Gun in America*, 208.

17 Quoted in Carol S. Leff and Mark H. Leff, "The Politics of Ineffectiveness: Federal Gun Legislation, 1919–1938," *Annals of The American Academy of Political and Social Science* 455 (May 1981): 61.

18 See *U.S. Statutes at Large*, vol. 48, pp. 1236–40.

19 Sept. 23, 1934, quoted in Ernest K. Alix, *Ransom Kidnapping in America, 1874–1974* (Carbondale, Ill., 1978), 107.

20 Dec. 10, 1934, Roosevelt, *Papers*, III: 493.

21 The quotations come from U.S. Attorney General, *Proceedings*, 255, 297.

22 Bob Nichols and Mr. and Mrs. Robert E. Simon, "Should a Boy Have a Gun? A Symposium," *Parents' Magazine* 9 (Oct. 1934): 75.

23 U.S. Department of the Interior, *Restoring America's Wildlife* (pamphlet), rev. ed. (Washington, D.C., 1995), 3.

24 Roosevelt to Milton A. Reckord, Feb. 4, 1938, in Trefthen and Serven, eds., *Americans and Guns*, 294.

25 Address to chiefs of police, Oct. 5, 1937. Cummings, *Select Papers*, 89.

26 U.S. Congress, Senate, *To Regulate Commerce of Firearms* (hearing before the Committee on Commerce), 74th Cong., 1st Sess., April 16, 1935 (Washington, D.C., 1935), 6–7, 43.

27 Ibid., 19, 21.

28 U.S. Congress, House of Representatives, *To Regulate Commerce in Firearms* (hearing before a subcommittee of the Committee on Interstate and Foreign Commerce), 75th Cong., 1st Sess., June 23, 1937 (Washington, D.C., 1937), 17, 18.

29 Interviews conducted April 1–6, 1938, *The Gallup Poll*, 3 vols. (New York, 1972), I: 99.

30 New York *Times* (May 7, 1938), p. 2:8.

31 Phelan, "Men and Arms," 131–2.

32 Franklin E. Zimring, "Firearms and Federal Law: The Gun Control Act of 1968," *Journal of Legal Studies* 4 (Jan. 1975): 143.

33 For details, see Deborah L. Madsen, *American Exceptionalism* (Jackson, Miss., 1998), 131–44.

34 See Andrew D. Herz, "Gun Crazy: Constitutional False Consciousness and Dereliction of Dialogic Responsibility," *Boston University Law Review* 75 (spring 1995): 689.

35 For the advertisement, see Shooting Industry, *The World of Guns*, ed. E. B. Mann (Skokie, Ill., 1964), 21.

36 Address of Aug. 17, 1940, quoted in Mark L. Chadwin, *The Hawks of World War II* (Chapel Hill, N.C., 1968), 93.

37 Robert E. Sherwood, *Roosevelt and Hopkins*, rev. ed. (New York, 1950), 157, 162.

38 Quoted in J. Garry Clifford and Samuel R. Spencer Jr., *The First Peacetime Draft* (Lawrence, Kans., 1986), 212.

39 Quoted from Sherwood, *Roosevelt and Hopkins*, 190.

40 Marvin A. Kreidberg and Merton G. Henry, *History of Military Mobilization in the United States Army, 1775–1945* (Washinton, D.C., 1955), 579–80, 592–3.

41 Jackson to William B. Bankhead, Speaker of the House, May 29, 1940, quoted in Warren Freedman, *The Privilege to Keep and Bear Arms* (New York, 1989), 61–2.

42 *American Rifleman* 89 (Feb. 1941): 2, italics in the original, and March 1941, p. 4.

43 The quotations from the House Committee on Military Affairs' explanation, and Chandler's remarks, are in Halbrook, "Congress Interprets the Second Amendment," 624, 625.

44 H. DeWitt Erk, "Are You a Gun-Shy Parent?" *Parents' Magazine* 27 (Aug. 1942): 64.

45 The quotations are in Stephen P. Halbrook, *That Every Man Be Armed* (Albuquerque, N.M., 1984), 188–9, and *United States v. Tot*, 131 F. 2d 261 (3d Cir. 1942), as cited in Denning, "Gun Shy," 740.

Chapter 11

1   The Eisenhower and Bradley statements are in U.S. Congress, Senate, Committee on the Judiciary, *Federal Firearms Act* (hearings before the Subcommittee to Investigate Juvenile Delinquency of the Committee on the Judiciary), 90th Cong., 1st Sess., S. Res. 35 (July, Aug., 1967), 485.

2   Truman to C. B. Lister of the National Rifle Association, Nov. 14, 1945, in ibid., 484.

3   Quoted from James B. Whisker, *The Rise and Decline of the American Militia System* (Selinsgrove, 1999), 18.

4   New York *Times* (report for 1946), Aug. 3, 1947, p. 3:1.

5   Bakal, *Right to Bear Arms*, 180.

6   New York *Times*, Sept. 19, 1947, p. 35:3.

7   Kennett and Anderson, *The Gun in America*, 218.

8   The details and quotations come from the New York *Times*, Jan. 16, 1949, p. 59:3; April 6, p. 1:2, 35:8; Oct. 25, 21:5.

9   Howard Whitman, *Terror in the Streets* (New York, 1951), 9.

10 U.S. Congress, Senate, 82d Cong., 1st Sess., *Third Interim Report of the Special Committee to Investigate Organized Crime in Interstate Commerce* (Washington, D.C., 1951), 3, 8.

11 Estes Kefauver, *Crime in America* (Garden City, N.Y., 1951), 321.

12 See Arthur Krock's commentary, New York *Times*, Nov. 2, 1950, p. 30:1, 5 and Nov. 5, IV, p. 3.1.

13 Quoted in David McCullough, *Truman* (New York, 1992), 501.

14 For details, see George Q. Flynn, *The Draft, 1940–1973* (Lawrence, Kans., 1993), 113–14, 14.

15 Aug. 1, 1950, to Congress and address to the nation, Dec. 15, *Public Papers of the Presidents of the United States: Harry S. Truman, 1950* (Washington, D.C., 1965), 565, 743.

16 Dwight D. Eisenhower, *The White House Years, 1953–1956: Mandate for Change* (New York, 1963), 451–2.

17 New York *Times*, March 2, 1954, 1:8 and March 3, 14:5.

18 The statistics on the Cassidy films are in Marshall W. Fishwick, "The Cowboy: America's Contribution to the World's Mythology," *Western Folklore* 11 (1952): 89.

19 "Films Go Gun-Happy and a Great Fighter Offers Some Advice," *Life* 51 (July 2, 1956): 28.

20 Richard Slotkin, *Gunfighter Nation* (New York, 1993), 383.

21 For the murder rate, see Margaret A. Zahn and Patricia L. McCall, "Trends and Patterns of Homicide in the 20th Century United States," in *Homicide*, ed. M. Dwayne Smith and Zahn (Thousand Oaks, Calif., 1999), 17, 21, and for other data, William C. Kvaraceus, *The Community and the Delinquent* (Yonkers-on-Hudson, N.Y., 1954), 2–3.

22 Quoted in Bakal, *Right to Bear Arms*, 185.

23 *Congressional Record*, 80th Cong., 2d Sess. (April 15, 1958), vol. 104, p. 6471.

24 Bakal, *Right to Bear Arms*, 30, 32.

25 News Conf., Aug. 20, 1958, *Public Papers of the Presidents of the United States: Dwight D. Eisenhower, 1958* (Washington, D.C., 1959), 625–6.

26 Bakal, *Right to Bear Arms*, 96–7.
27 Editorial, *American Rifleman* 106 (Sept. 1958): 40.
28 John H. Soubler in ibid., 41.
29 Aug. 30, 1959, *The Gallup Poll*, 3 vols. (New York, 1972), III: 1625–6.
30 Kennett and Anderson, *The Gun in America*, 226.
31 Quoted from Paul Schubert, "A Hunter's Greatest Peril," *Saturday Evening Post* 25 (Oct. 25, 1958): 37, and Donald E. Feltz, "Speaking Out: Boobs in the Woods," ibid., 235 (Oct. 13, 1962): 8.
32 Kennett and Anderson, *The Gun in America*, 224.
33 Bakal, *Right to Bear Arms*, 120–21.
34 Quoted in *The World of Guns*, ed. E. B. Mann (Skokie, Ill., 1964), 69, 73.
35 Dorothy Barclay, "Behind All the Bang-Bang," *New York Times Magazine* (July 22, 1962): 47.
36 Quoted in *World of Guns*, 37.
37 U.S. Congress, Senate, *Interstate Traffic in Mail-Order Firearms* (hearings before the Subcommittee to Investigate Juvenile Delinquency of the Committee on the Judiciary), 88th Cong., 1st Sess. (Jan. 29–30, March 7, and May 1–2, 1963), 3185, 3186.
38 *Christian Science Monitor* (Nov. 2, 1963): 3:2.
39 Ibid. (Nov. 19, 1963): 16:1.

Chapter 12

1 Quoted in Bakal, *Right to Bear Arms*, 194. For a discussion of the assassination in an international context, see Weir, *A Well Regulated Militia*, 83–4.
2 Jan. 22, 1964, U.S. Congress, Senate, *Interstate Shipment of Firearms* (hearings before the Committee on Commerce), 88th Cong., 1st and 2d Sess. (Dec. 13, 18; Jan. 23, 24, 30; March 4, 1964), 9.
3 Ibid., 38. See also Richard Harris, "Annals of Legislation: If You Love Your Guns," *New Yorker*, April 20, 1968, 63.
4 *Interstate Shipment of Firearms*, 59, 92.
5 Editorial, "Realistic Firearms Controls," *American Rifleman* 112 (Jan. 1964): 14.
6 Statement of Ben Avery, gun club representative, *Interstate Shipment of Firearms*, 205.
7 Thurman B. Gibson and William G. Gibson from Bagdad, Ariz., ibid., 250, 253.
8 Lindsay's testimony and his bills are in ibid., 229–34, and the quotations and argumentation are in John V. Lindsay, "Speaking Out: Too Many People Have Guns," *Saturday Evening Post* 237 (Feb. 1, 1964): 12.
9 *Christian Science Monitor* (Feb. 14, 1964): 1:4.
10 In Lerone Bennett Jr., *What Manner of Man*, 4th ed. (Chicago, 1976), 166.
11 Speech, "The Ballot or the Bullet," Cleveland, April 3, 1964, in Malcolm X, *Malcolm X Speaks*, 2d ed. (New York, 1969), 43.
12 Zahn, "Homicide in the Twentieth Century," 220.
13 Senator Philip Hart quoted in Robert J. Riley, "Shooting to Kill the Handgun: Time to Martyr Another American 'Hero,'" *Journal of Urban Law* 51 (Feb. 1972): 506.
14 Burr D. Marley, in Kennett and Anderson, *The Gun in America*, 234.
15 Special message, March 8, 1965, *Public Papers of the Presidents of the United States: Lyndon B. Johnson, 1965* (Washington, D.C., 1966), I: 267.
16 *The Shotgun News*, Columbus, Nebr., May 15, 1965, reprinted in U.S. Congress, Senate, Committee on the Judiciary, *Federal Firearms Act* (hearings before the Subcommittee to Investigate Juvenile Delinquency of the Committee on the Judiciary), 89th Cong., 1st Sess. (Washington, D.C., 1965), 35.
17 Ibid., 247.
18 Ibid., 37, 41.
19 Ibid., 87–9, and Robert F. Kennedy, *RFK: Collected Speeches*, ed. Edwin O. Guthman and C. Richard Allen (New York, 1993), 214–5.

20   Quoted in Gerald Horne, *Fire This Time* (Charlottesville, Va., 1995), 75.
21   Ibid., 66.
22   Quoted from David H. Bennett, *The Party of Fear* (Chapel Hill, N.C., 1988), 325.
23   See Violence Policy Center, *Putting Guns Back Into Criminals' Hands* (Washington, D.C., May 1992), 1.
24   March 9, 1966, *Papers of Presidents: Lyndon B. Johnson, 1966*, I: 296.
25   Mottram, "Persuasive Lips," 54.
26   U.S. President's Commission on Law Enforcement and Administration of Justice, *The Challenge of Crime in a Free Society* (Washington, D.C., 1967), 242.
27   Feb. 6, 1967, *Papers of Presidents: Lyndon B. Johnson, 1967*, I. 142.
28   Quoted from G. Louis Heath, *Off the Pigs!* (Metuchen, N.J., 1976), 2, 39.
29   Quoted in Garry Wills, *The Second Civil War* (New York, 1968), 125.
30   Quoted in Sidney Fine, *Violence in the Model City* (Ann Arbor, Mich., 1989), 300.
31   Quoted from Morris Janowitz, "Patterns of Collective Racial Violence," in *Violence in America*, ed. Graham and Gurr, 421–22.
32   U.S. Congress, Senate, Committee on the Judiciary, *Federal Firearms Act* (hearings before the Subcommittee to Investigate Juvenile Delinquency of the Committee on the Judiciary), 90th Cong., 1st Sess., S. Res. 35 (July, Aug., 1967), 668, 997.
33   Quoted in "Glory of Guns: Gun Magazines Campaign Against Legal Control of Gun Sales," *Time*, Aug. 25, 1967, 63.
34   See "New DCM Cuts Hit Senior Clubs Most," *American Rifleman* 116 (Aug. 1968): 40.
35   Remarks to police chiefs, Kansas City, Mo., Sept. 14, 1967, *Papers of Presidents: Lyndon B. Johnson, 1967*, II: 832–33 and special message, Feb. 7, 1968, ibid., 1968, I: 185.
36   Annual message to Congress, Jan. 17, 1968, ibid., *1968–69*, I: 30.
37   Quoted in "The Gun Under Fire," *Time*, June 21, 1968, 15.
38   Quoted from James Boyd, *Above the Law* (New York, 1968), 264.
39   Donald G. Le Fave, "The Will to Arm. The National Rifle Association in American Society, 1871–1970" (Ph.D. diss., University of Colorado, 1970), 283.
40   For the statistics, see Sherrill, *Saturday Night Special*, 289.
41   To majority leader of the Senate, May 9, 1968, *Papers of Presidents: Lyndon B. Johnson, 1968–69*, I: 586
42   Hofstadter, "America as a Gun Culture," 4, and Kennett and Anderson, *The Gun in America*, 255.
43   Quoted in "Gun Under Fire," *Time*, 13.
44   Quoted in Don S. Cupps, "Bullets, Ballots, and Politics: The National Rifle Association Fights Gun Control" (Ph.D. diss., Princeton University, 1969), 150.
45   Letter to Senate, June 6, 1968, *Papers of Presidents: Lyndon B. Johnson, 1968–69*, I: 694.
46   ECGC news release, June 24, 1968, quoted in Cupps, "Bullets, Ballots," 169.
47   June 29, 1968, New York *Times*, p. A11, and Maurine Christopher, "Guns, Congress, and the Networks," *Nation* 207 (Aug. 19, 1968): 115.
48   June 24, 1968, *Papers of Presidents: Lyndon B. Johnson, 1968–69*, I: 739.
49   U.S. Congress, Senate, Committee on the Judiciary, *Federal Firearms Legislation* (hearings before the Subcommittee to Investigate Juvenile Delinquency of the Committee on the Judiciary), 90th Cong., 2d Sess., S. Res. 240 (June, July, 1968), 413.
50   Quoted in Robert J. Spitzer, *The Politics of Gun Control* (Chatham, N.J., 1995), 145.
51   Aug. 27, 1967, *Gallup Poll*, III: 2077, and New York *Times*, June 9, 1968, p. 68:3.
52   New York *Times*, June 15, 1968, p. 1:2.
53   July 3, 1968, quoted in Cupps, "Bullets, Ballots," 187.
54   For the quotations, see the Washington *Post*, July 12, 1968, pp. A6, A20.
55   *American Rifleman* 116 (Aug. 1968): 41.
56   *Guns and Ammo* (Sept. 1968): 6, quoted in Cupps, "Bullets, Ballots," 206.
57   Zimring, "Firearms and Federal Law," 133.
58   "New U.S. Law Limits All Gun Sales," *American Rifleman* 116 (Dec. 1968): 17.

59 Bill R. Davidson, *To Keep and Bear Arms* (New Rochelle, N.Y., 1969), 254.

60 See tables in David Windlesham, *Responses to Crime*, 3 vols. (Oxford, Eng., 1987–96), II: 2–3; III: 164–5.

61 *Journal Officiel*, January 23, 1969, quoted in Michel H. Josserand and Jan A. Stevenson, *Pistols, Revolvers, and Ammunition* (New York, 1972), 292–3.

62 See Library of Congress, *Gun Control Laws*, 136; David H. Bayley, *Forces of Order*, 2d ed. (Berkeley, 1991), 172–3; and Pete Shields, *Guns Don't Die—People Do* (New York, 1981), 65.

63 For pertinent statistics, see William Gifford, *Crime in Japan* (Lexington, Mass., 1976), 122.

64 The statistics come from George D. Newton Jr. and Franklin E. Zimring, *Firearms and Violence in American Life* (Washington, D.C., 1969), 172–3, and the quotation comes from Zimring, "Control Act of 1968," 147.

Chapter 13

1   James Ridgeway, "The Kind of Gun Control We Need," *New Republic*, June 22, 1968, 11.

2   "Gun Control: Melodrama, Farce and Tragedy," *Christian Century* 85 (June 26, 1968): 832.

3   See Johnson, comp., *National Party Platforms*, II: 751, 722.

4   "The Crawfisher," *Nation* 211 (Oct. 26, 1970): 387–88.

5   Don S. Cupps, "Evading Gun Control," *New Republic* 160 (May 3, 1969): 17.

6   Press conf., Jan. 17, 1969, *Papers of Presidents: Lyndon B. Johnson, 1968–69*, II: 1358.

7   Ramsay Clark, *Crime in America* (New York, 1970), 102–3.

8   George Thayer, *The War Business* (New York, 1969), 364.

9   U.S. National Commission on the Causes and Prevention of Violence, *To Establish Justice, To Insure Domestic Tranquility, Final Report* (1969; reprint, Washington, D.C., 1970), 145.

10 Art Buchwald, *Washington Post*, May 23, 1972, p. 1B:1.

11 See Carl Bakal, "The Failure of Federal Gun Control," *Saturday Review* 54 (July 3, 1971): 49, and William J. Vizzard, *In the Crossfire* (Boulder, Colo., 1997), 11–12.

12 Quoted in John G. Mitchell, " 'God, Guns, and Guts Made America Free': The National Rifle Association and the Constitutional Right to Bear Arms," *American Heritage* 29 (Feb./March 1978): 11.

13 For details see Tom Diaz, *Making a Killing in America* (New York, 1999), 13–16.

14 Quoted in Josh Sugarmann, *National Rifle Association* (Washington, D.C., 1992), 267.

15 U.S. Congress, House of Representatives, *Gun Control Legislation* (hearings before Subcommittee No. 5 of the Committee on the Judiciary), 92d Cong., 2d Sess., June 27–29, 1972 (Washington, D.C., 1972), 94, 144.

16 From statement of Maxwell E. Rich, executive vice president of the NRA, in ibid., 272.

17 News conf., June 29, 1972, *Papers of Presidents: Richard Nixon, 1972*, 715–6.

18 New York Police Commissioner John M. Murphy, quoted in Paul Good, "Blam! Blam! Blam! Not Gun Nuts But Pistol Enthusiasts," *New York Times Magazine* (Sept. 17, 1972): 28.

19 The first quotation comes from press conf., Jan. 31, 1973, *Papers of Presidents: Richard Nixon, 1973*, pp. 59–60, and the second quotation from "Handgun Violence," *New Republic*, Feb. 17, 1973, 9.

20 Christopher Geehern, "Arms and the Man," *New England Business* 12 (Aug. 1990): 26.

21 Molina, *Filipino Right to Arms*, iii.

22 Sherrill, *Saturday Night Special*, 80–1.

23 U.S. Department of Justice, Uniform Crime Reports, *Crime in the United States, 1972* (Washington, D.C., 1973), 1–3, 6.

24 Mottram, "Persuasive Lips," 55–6.

25 Paul J. Weber, "The National Rifle Association: Public Enemy No. 2," *Christian Century* 91 (Oct. 16, 1974): 958.

26 New York *Times*, June 25, 1968, p. 24:1.

27 See *Gallup Opinion Index*, No. 123 (June 1975), 8, and James D. Wright, "Public Opinion

and Gun Control: A Comparison of Results from Two Recent National Surveys," *Annals of the American Academy of Political and Social Science* 455 (May 1981): 25.

28   Carter, *Gun Control Movement*, 75–6, and Roger M. Williams, "The Gun Fighters," *Foundation News* 31 (March–Apr. 1990): 38.

29   For the court cases, see Harvard Law School, Gun Law Project, "And Nobody Can Get Out," unpublished manuscript (Cambridge, Mass., July 14, 1976), 10–13.

30   See Glenn L. Pierce and William J. Bowers, "The Bartley-Fox Gun Law's Short-Term Impact on Crime in Boston," *Annals of the American Academy of Political and Social Science* 455 (May 1981): 123, 131, 134, 136; Stewart J. Deutch and Francis B. Alt, "The Effect of Massachusetts' Gun Control Law on Gun-Related Crimes in the City of Boston," *Evaluation Quarterly* 1 (Nov. 1977): 567; and James A. Beha II, " 'And Nobody Can Get You Out': The Impact of a Mandatory Prison Sentence for the Illegal Carrying of a Firearm on the Use of Firearms and on the Administration of Criminal Justice in Boston," *Boston University Law Review* 57 (Jan. 1997), Part II, 314–19.

31   See Judith V. Holmberg and Michael Clancy, *People vs Handguns* (Washington, D.C., 1977), 29.

32   Ibid., 66.

33   The quotations come from various news conferences and speeches. See *Papers of Presidents: Gerald R. Ford, 1975*, May 6, 1975, I: 651; June 19, II: 848; Oct. 7, 10, pp. 1616, 1659; and *1976–77*, April 2, 1976, I: 924.

34   Quoted in Michael J. Harrington, "The Politics of Gun Control," *Nation*, Jan. 12, 1974, 43.

Chapter 14

1   Archibald S. Alexander, "Arms Transfers by the United States: Merchant of Death or Arsenal of Democracy," *Vanderbilt Journal of Transnational Law* 10 (spring 1977): 255.

2   The quotations come from *Lexis-Nexus*, Academic Universe document No. 75-1734 [7 pp.] App. Lexis 13001; 37 A.L.R.

3   See editorial, New York *Times*, April 6, 1976, p. 34:1.

4   See Johnson, comp., *National Party Platforms*, II: 948, and Davidson, *Under Fire*, 40.

5   Quoted in Shields, *Guns Don't Die—People Do*, 107.

6   Quoted in Jo L. Husbands, "The Arms Connection: Jimmy Carter and the Politics of Military Exports," in *The Gun Merchants*, ed. Cindy Cannizzo (New York, 1980), 25.

7   June 23, 1976, quoted in Michael T. Klare, *American Arms Supermarket* (Austin, Tex., 1984), 3.

8   Presidential campaign debate, Oct. 22, 1976, *Papers of Presidents: Gerald R. Ford, 1976–77*, III: 2639.

9   Quoted in Alan Gottlieb, *The Gun Grabbers* (Bellevue, Wash., 1986), 8.

10   Quoted in Charles J. Orasin, "Handgun Control and the Politics of Fear," *USA Today* 108 (Jan. 1980), reprinted in *The Issue of Gun Control*, ed. Thomas Draper (New York, 1981), 98.

11   Colin Loftin and others, "Effects of Restrictive Licensing of Handguns on Homicides and Suicide in the District of Columbia," *New England Journal of Medicine* 325 (No. 23, Dec. 5, 1991): 1615, 1620.

12   Weir, *Well-Regulated Militia*, 91. For details, see also Davidson, *Under Fire*, 30–36.

13   Jim Oliver, "Washington Report," *Guns & Ammo* 23 (May 1979), quoted in *The Issue of Gun Control*, ed. Thomas Draper (New York, 1981), 115.

14   March 5, 24, and May 19, 22, 1977, *Papers of Presidents: Jimmy Carter, 1977*, I: 289, 496, 931, 960.

15   New York *Times*, July 18, 1977, p. 3:3.

16   The quotation, from Undersecretary of State Lucy W. Benson, is in Husbands, "The Arms Connection," 20. For details, see Klare, *American Arms Supermarket*, 43, 48–9.

17   Quoted in Wilbur Edel, *Gun Control* (Westport, Conn., 1995), 108.

18   New York *Times*, March 18, 1978, p. 8:6.

19   Ibid., April 15, 1978, p. 18:6 and editorial, April 30, p. 18:1.

20 Ibid., June 28, 1978, p. 13:2.
21 For the statistics and quotation, see "Four Years of the Carter Administration: An Affront to the Rights of Gun Owners," *American Rifleman* 128 (Oct. 1980): 59.
22 Don B. Kates Jr., "Firearms and Violence: Old Premises and Current Evidence," in *Violence in America*, ed. Gurr, I: 197.
23 Quoted in Paul Bendis and Steven Balkin, "A Look at Gun Control Enforcement," *Journal of Police Science and Administration* 7 (No. 4, 1979): 441.
24 Ibid., 442, 444, 447.
25 News conf., April 10, 1979, *Papers of Presidents: Carter, 1979*, 652.
26 In 1980 the homicide rate reached a point higher than any time in the past. Zahn, "Homicide in Twentieth Century," 220.
27 For the quotations, see David H. Bayley, "Learning About Crime—The Japanese Experience," *The Public Interest* 44 (summer 1976): 55; Paul Gendreau and C. Thomas Surridge, "Controlling Gun Crimes: The Jamaican Experience," *International Journal of Criminology and Penology* 6 (Feb. 1978): 57; and Kopel, *Samurai and Mountie*, 259, 431.
28 Anthony J. Mahler and Jonathan E. Fielding, "Firearms and Gun Control: A Public Health Concern," *New England Journal of Medicine* 297 (Sept. 8, 1977): 557.
29 For the quotation and statistical data, see Susan Baker, "Without Guns, Do People Kill People?" *American Journal of Public Health* 75 (June 1975): 587; Leonard Berkowitz, "Impulse, Aggression and the Gun," *Psychology Today* 2 (Sept. 1968): 19–22; Berkowitz, "How Guns Control Us," *Psychology Today* 15 (June 1981): 11–12; and Charles H. Browning, "Suicide, Firearms, and Public Health," *American Journal of Public Health* 64 (April 1974): 315.
30 The quotations come from Martin Killias, "Gun Ownership and Violent Crime: The Swiss Experience in International Perspective," *Security Journal* 1 (No. 3, 1990): 170, 174.
31 The quotations come from Library of Congress, *Gun Control Laws in Foreign Countries* 25, 30, and Kopel, *Samurai and Mountie*, 164.
32 Davidson, *Under Fire*, 46.
33 Philip J. Cook and Mark H. Moore, "Guns, Gun Control, and Homicide: A Review of Research and Public Policy," in *Homicide*, ed. Smith and Zahn, 278–9.
34 David T. Hardy, *The BATF's War on Civil Liberties* (Bellevue, Wash., 1979), 4, iii.
35 Neal Knox in U.S. Congress, Senate, Committee on the Judiciary, *Gun Control and Constitutional Rights* (hearings before the Subcommittee on the Constitution), 96th Cong., 2d Sess. (Sept. 15, 1980), 333.
36 Ibid., 155.
37 Josh Sugarmann and Kristen Rand, *Cease Fire* (Washington, D.C., 1994), 69.
38 See Johnson, comp., *National Party Platforms*, 66, 189.
39 Ted Kerasote, *Bloodties* (New York, 1993), ix.
40 The quotations come from Jervis Anderson, *Guns in American Life* (New York, 1984), 4–5.
41 Wayne R. LaPierre Jr., *Guns, Crime, and Freedom* (Washington, D.C., 1994), 177–8, 197.
42 Sugarmann, *National Rifle Association*, 124–5.
43 Klare, *American Arms Supermarket*, 27, 48.
44 Anderson, *Guns in American Life*, 6–7.
45 April 22 and June 16, 1981, *Papers of Presidents: Ronald Reagan, 1981* (Washington, D.C., 1982), 373, 522.
46 Quoted in Anderson, *Guns in American Life*, 10.
47 See Eric S. Freibrun, "Banning Handguns: *Quilici v. Village of Morton Grove* and the Second Amendment," *Washington University Law Quarterly* 60 (fall 1982): 1103, 1107–10.
48 For the courts' actions, see Laura Linden, "Grassroots Gun Control," *California Lawyer* 27 (July 1997): 25–8.

Chapter 15

1 Weir, *Well-Regulated Militia*, 103.
2 Davidson, *Under Fire*, 89.

3   Windle Turley and Cliff Harrison, "Strict Tort Liability of Handgun Suppliers," *Hamline Law Review* 6 (1983): 299–300.

4   Geehern, "Arms and the Man," 26.

5   Carl Bogus, "Pistols, Politics and Products Liability," *Cincinnati Law Review* 59 (spring 1991): 1104, 1111, and "Handguns and Products Liability," *Harvard Law Review* 97 (June 1984): 1928.

6   See Washington *Post*, April 23, 1986, p. A14:1, and New York *Times*, April 18, 1987, p. A26:6.

7   Quoted in Anderson, *Guns in American Life*, 121.

8   The statistics come from *The California Poll*, April 30, 1982, release no. 1165, and Oct. 15, release no. 1192, which showed a decline in public support. The quotations come from an editorial in the Los Angeles *Times*, Nov. 1, 1982, p. E4.

9   Anderson, *Guns in American Life*, 122.

10   Jan. 23, 1983, *Papers of Presidents: Ronald Reagan, 1983*, I: 126.

11   May 6, 1983, ibid., 660, 662.

12   See, for instance, Catherine F. Sproule and Deborah J. Kennett, "Killing with Guns in the USA and Canada, 1977–1983: Further Evidence for the Effectiveness of Gun Control," *Canadian Journal of Criminology* 31 (July 1989): 249–50.

13   Kopel, *Samurai and Mountie*, 20–1, 26–7.

14   "Handguns: Majority Supports Stiffer Handgun Laws," *The Gallup Report*, No. 215 (Aug. 1983), 3–4.

15   News conf., April 4, 1984, *Papers of Presidents: Reagan, 1984*, I: 465.

16   *Kalodimos v. Village of Morton Grove*, Oct. 19, 1984, reprinted in *Gun Control and the Constitution*, ed. Robert J. Cottrol, 4 vols. (New York, 1993–94), I: 138, 151.

17   U.S. Department of Health, Education and Welfare, *Television and Social Behavior: Reports and Papers*, 5 vols. (Washington, D.C., 1972), III: 32, and U.S. Department of Health, Education and Welfare, *Television and Behavior*, 2 vols. (Washington, D.C., 1982), II: 38.

18   For the quotations, see Susan Glick, *Female Persuasion* (Washington, D.C., 1994), 1, 6, 21.

19   Tom W. Smith and Robert J. Smith, "Changes in Firearms Ownership Among Women, 1980–1994," *Journal of Criminal Law and Criminology* 86 (fall 1995): 136, 143.

20   See David Windlesham, *Politics, Punishment, and Populism* (New York, 1998), 24–6.

21   For the quotation and public reaction to the verdict, see George P. Fletcher, *A Crime of Self-Defense* (New York, 1988), 5, 199, and *Gallup Report*, Nos. 232–3 (Jan.–Feb. 1985), 12.

22   U.S. Congress, Committee on the Judiciary, *The Firearms Owner Protection Act* (hearings before the Committee on the Judiciary), 97th Cong., 1st and 2d Sess., S. 1030 (Dec. 9, 11, 1981, and Feb. 8, 1982), 1, 121.

23   Ibid., 98th Cong., 1st Sess., S. 914 (Oct. 4, 1983), 98.

24   Speech, June 25, 1985, printed in *Gun Control*, ed. Robert E. Long (New York, 1989), 116.

25   Weir, *Well-Regulated Militia*, 96.

26   The quotations come from Richard Corrigan, "NRA, Using Members, Ads and Money, Hits Police Line in Lobbying Drive," *National Journal* 18 (Jan. 4, 1986): 8.

27   See Laura I. Langbein and Mark A. Lotwis, "The Political Efficacy of Lobbying and Money: Gun Control in the U.S. House, 1986," *Legislative Studies Quarterly* 15 (Aug. 1990): 423, 430–1.

28   Interview with New York *Times* reporters, March 21, 1986, *Papers of Presidents: Reagan, 1986*, I: 388.

29   Quoted in Long, ed., *Gun Control*, 145–6.

30   Linda Greenhouse, New York *Times*, April 11, 1986, p. A19, and April 13, 1986, p. E5.

31   Quoted in Corrigan, "NRA, Ads and Money," 14.

32   U.S. *Statutes at Large* (Washington, D.C., 1989), 100: 449–61.

33   See Gordon Witkin, "The Great Debate: Should You Own a Gun?" *U.S. News and World Report* 117 (Aug. 15, 1996): 24–36, and Handgun Control Inc., *Carrying Concealed Weapons: Questions and Answers* (Washington, D.C., 1995), 2.

34   For statistics from a progun perspective, see Gary Kleck and Mark Gertz, "Armed Resistance

to Crime: The Prevalence and Nature of Self-Defense with a Gun," *Journal of Criminal Law and Criminology* 86 (fall 1995): 180, and John R. Lott Jr. and David B. Mustard, "Crime, Deterrence, and Right-to-Carry Concealed Handguns," *Journal of Legal Studies* 26 (Jan. 1997): 1–68. For refutations, see David McDowell and Brian Wiersma, "The Incidence of Defensive Firearms Use by US Crime Victims, 1987 through 1990," *American Journal of Public Health* 84 (Dec. 1994): 84; David Hemenway, "Survey Research and Self-Defense Gun Use: An Explanation of Extreme Overestimates," *Journal of Criminal Law and Criminology* 87 (summer 1997): 1430–45; and Dan A. Black and Daniel S. Nagin, "Do 'Right-To-Carry Laws' Deter Violent Crime?" *Journal of Legal Studies* 27 (Jan. 1998): 209.

35   David McDowell, Colin Loftin, and Brian Wiersma, "Easing Concealed Firearms Laws: Effects on Homicide Rates in Three States," *Journal of Criminal Law and Criminology* 86 (fall 1995): 193, 204. See also Susan Glick, *Concealing the Risk* (Washington, D.C., 1996), 1–2.

36   Tom Diaz, *Making a Killing in America* (New York, 1999), 168–9.

37   Richard M. Aborn, "The Battle Over the Brady Bill and the Future of Gun Control Advocacy," *Fordham Urban Law Journal* 22 (1995): 420.

38   Freedman, *Privilege to Bear Arms*, 76.

39   Bill offered on Jan. 4, 1989, Aborn, "Brady Bill," 420.

40   See Patrick S. Davies, "Saturday Night Specials: A 'Special' Exception in Strict Liability Laws," *Notre Dame Law Review* 61 (June 1986): 482–3, 491–4.

41   Washington *Post*, Nov. 9, 1988, pp. A1:1–2, A43:1.

Chapter 16

1   For the quotations and details, see Bush to Stephen Melinder, Houston, June 4, 1970, in George Bush, *All the Best* (New York, 1999), 125–6, and Herbert S. Parmet, *George Bush* (New York, 1997), 142–213.

2   June 21, and Nov. 14, 1988, *Papers of Presidents: Ronald Reagan, 1988–89*, I: 808 and II: 1506.

3   For the quotations, see Davidson, *Under Fire*, 142, and Sugarmann, *National Rifle Association*, 207.

4   See Windlesham, *Politics, Punishment*, 45.

5   For elaboration of this thesis, see David Kopel, "Guns in the Right Hands Make Society Safer," in *Guns and Crime*, ed. Roleff, 13–18.

6   New York *Times*, July 21, 1987, p. A18, and Freedman, *Privilege to Bear Arms*, 20–21.

7   Susan Glick and Josh Sugarmann, *Joe Camel With Feathers* (Washington, D.C., Nov. 1997), 4.

8   Erik Larson, "The Story of a Gun," *Atlantic* 271 (Jan. 1993): 48.

9   *Gallup Report*, Nos. 282–3 (March–Apr. 1989), 2–3.

10   Diaz, *Making a Killing*, 72–3.

11   For the quotations, see Donnie Radcliffe, *Simply Barbara Bush* (New York, 1989), 59, 62, and Davidson, *Under Fire*, 201.

12   News confs., Feb. 16 and 21, 1989, *Papers of Presidents: George Bush, 1989*, I: 105, 116.

13   Remarks in Houston, March 16, 1989, ibid., 247.

14   March 28, 1989, Vienna, Va., ibid., 322, and March 28, Washington, D.C., to Mrs. Sarah Brady, Bush, *All the Best*, 419.

15   Los Angeles *Times*, March 5, 1998, pp. A3, A21.

16   Ibid., June 30, 2000, pp. A1, A34, and editorial, July 5, 2000, p. B6.

17   May 15, 1989, *Papers of Presidents: Bush, 1989*, I: 558.

18   Dialogue with journalists and broadcasters, Sept. 15, 1989, ibid., II: 1198.

19   "Firearms and the Law," London *Times*, May 2, 1989, p. 17a.

20   Ibid., May 1 and 3, 1989, pp. 3a, 17d.

21   Feb. 1989, letter to new members quoted in James W. Gibson, *Warrior Dreams* (New York, 1994), 249–50.

22   News conf., Jan. 24, 1990, *Papers of Presidents: Bush, 1990*, I: 79.

23 Quoted in Wayne King, "Target: The Gun Lobby," *New York Times Magazine* (Dec. 9, 1990): 45, 76.

24 LaPierre, *Guns, Crime, and Freedom*, 41.

25 *Gallup Poll Monthly*, No. 306 (March 1991): 49.

26 Bush diaries, March 13, 1991, quoted in Parmet, *George Bush*, 486.

27 Ronald Reagan, "Why I'm For the Brady Bill," New York *Times*, March 29, 1991, p. A21:3, and related article, p. A1:3.

28 Aborn, "Brady Bill," 424.

29 See Michael R. Rand, "Guns and Crime," in *Crime Data Brief* (Justice Dept., Washington, D.C., April 1994).

30 U.S. Department of Justice, Uniform Crime Reports, *Crime in the United States, 1992* (Washington, D.C., 1993), 6.

31 Ibid., 11

32 For the quotations and statistics, see Joseph F. Sheley and James D. Wright, *In the Line of Fire* (New York, 1995), 6, 46, and Philip J. Cook, "Foreword," in "Kids, Guns, and Public Policy," ed. Cook, *Law and Contemporary Problems* 59 (winter 1996): 1, 2.

33 For the quotation and related data, see Sugarmann, *National Rifle Association*, 263; American Medical Association Council on Scientific Affairs, "Firearms Injuries and Deaths: A Critical Public Health Issue," *Public Health Reports* (March–Apr. 1989). 111; Marsha F. Goldsmith, "Epidemiologists Aim at New Target: Health Risk of Handgun Proliferation," *Journal of the American Medical Association* 261 (Feb. 3, 1989). 675–6; and Mark L. Rosenberg, Patrick W. O'Connor, and Kenneth E. Powell, "Let's Be Clear: Violence Is a Public Health Problem," ibid. 247 (June 10, 1992): 3071.

34 The quotations come from Los Angeles *Times* Staff, *Understanding the Riots* (Los Angeles, 1992), 46, 59, and Lou Cannon, *Official Negligence* (New York, 1997), 312.

35 James D. Wright, Joseph F. Sheley, and M. Dwayne Smith, "Kids, Guns, and Killing Fields," *Society* 30 (Nov.–Dec. 1992): 84, 89.

36 The quotations come from presidential debates, Oct. 15, 1992, Richmond, Va., and Bush, speech, Billings, Mont., Oct. 25, 1992, *Papers of Presidents: Bush, 1992–93*, II: 1029, 1820, 1895.

37 The quotation comes from Jacklyn Cock, *Towards a Sociological Account of Light Weapons Proliferation in Southern Africa* (Johannesburg, 1995), 9, and the figures come from World Watch as reported in the Santa Barbara *News Press*, Oct. 26, 1997, p. A3.

38 See Weir, *Well-Regulated Militia*, 225; Dean E. Murphy, "Highway Robberies Terrorize S. Africans," Los Angeles *Times*, Feb. 7, 1998, p. A2, and ibid., June 8, 1998, p. A1.

39 Stephen Handelman, *Comrade Criminal* (New Haven, 1995), 207–8.

40 United Nations Institute for Disarmament Research, *Small Arms Management and Peacekeeping in Southern Africa* (New York and Geneva, 1996), 11–12.

41 Library of Congress, *Gun Control Laws in Foreign Countries*, 139–40.

42 The quotation and statistics come from Weir, *Well-Regulated Militia*, 224–5, and statistics and other data from the Santa Barbara *News-Press*, June 13, 1999, p. A8, and July 7, 2000, p. A8.

43 Natalie J. Goldring, "The NRA Goes Global," *The Bulletin of the Atomic Scientists* 55 (Jan.–Feb. 1999): 63.

Chapter 17

1 For the statistics, see Windlesham, *Responses to Crime*, II: 178.

2 Feb. 10 and 17, 1993, *Papers of Presidents: William J. Clinton, 1993*, I: 76, 117.

3 Leslie MacAneny, "Americans Tell Congress: Pass Brady Bill, Other Tough Gun Laws," *Gallup Poll Monthly*, No. 330 (March 1993): 2. See also, *The Field Poll*, Feb. 1, 1994, release #1699, and Robert J. Spitzer, *The Politics of Gun Control* (New York, 1998), 96.

4 March 1, 1993, *Papers of Presidents: Clinton, 1993*, I: 223.

348   Notes to Pages 250–257

5   Aborn, "Brady Bill," 429.
6   U.S. Congress, House of Representatives, *Brady Handgun Violence Prevention Act* (hearing before the Subcommittee on Crime and Criminal Justice of the Committee on the Judiciary), 103d Congress, 1st Sess., Sept. 30, 1993, 1–2.
7   Ibid., 32.
8   See Aborn, "Brady Bill," 426–7.
9   *Papers of Presidents: Clinton, 1993*, II: 2080.
10 See Carol J. DeFrances and Steven K. Smith, "Federal-State Relations in Gun Control: The 1993 Brady Handgun Violence Prevention Act," *Publius* 24 (summer 1994): 76.
11 See Windlesham, *Responses to Crime*, II: 164–5.
12 James B. Jacobs and Kimberly A. Potter, "Keeping Guns Out of the 'Wrong' Hands: The Brady Law and the Limits of Regulation," *Journal of Criminal Law and Criminology* 86 (fall 1995): 119.
13 "The Threat: *Next* Time Is *This* Time," *American Rifleman* 142 (Jan. 1994): 32.
14 See Martin S. Geisel, Richard Roll, and Stanton Wettick Jr., "The Effectiveness of State and Local Regulation of Handguns: A Statistical Analysis," *Duke Law Journal* 1969 (Aug. 1969): 647, 664–5.
15 David Hemenway, "Regulation of Firearms," *New England Journal of Medicine* 339 (Sept. 17, 1998): 844.
16 David W. Moore and Frank Newport, "Public Strongly Favors Stricter Gun Control Laws," *Gallup Poll Monthly* 340 (Jan. 1994): 2.
17 March 20, 1994, quoted in Spitzer, *Politics of Gun Control*, 111.
18 Remarks of Nov. 12, 1998, in Lora Lumpe, "The Leader of the Pack," *Bulletin of the Atomic Scientists* 55 (Jan.–Feb. 1999): 31.
19 News conf., April 19, 1994, *Papers of Presidents: Clinton, 1994*, I: 716.
20 U.S. Congress, House of Representatives, Committee on the Judiciary, *Public Safety and Recreational Firearms Use Protection Act* (hearing before the Subcommittee on Crime and Criminal Justice), 103d Cong., 2d Sess., H.R. 3527 (April 25, 1994), 1–2.
21 May 5, 1994, quoted in Windlesham, *Politics, Punishment*, 84.
22 The comments of John F. Gerry of the Judicial Conference of the United States, and of Rehnquist, its presiding officer, come from the *Congressional Record*, May 19, 1994, Senate, 6090.
23 Dr. George Cohen, June 22, 1994, quoted in Weir, *Well-Regulated Militia*, 199.
24 Wayne R. LaPierre Jr., "The Final War Has Begun," *American Rifleman* 142 (June 1994): 52.
25 David W. Moore, "Public Wants Crime Bill," *Gallup Poll Monthly*, No. 347 (Aug. 1994): 11.
26 To conference of police chiefs, Minneapolis, Aug. 12, 1994, *Papers of Presidents: Clinton, 1994*, II: 1464–5. See also Martin Walker, *The President We Deserve* (New York, 1996), 325.
27 Mitchell and Biden's remarks are in Washington *Post*, Aug. 26, 1994, p. A14:1–2.
28 *Papers of Presidents: Clinton, 1994*, II: 1539.
29 The quotation comes from Bryan R. Johnson, "Concealed Weapons: Congress Can Pass a Law Banning an Arbitrary List of Firearms, But It Can't Make Americans Obey It," *National Review* 46 (Sept. 26, 1994): 56.
30 For the statistics and other data, see Robert Dreyfuss, "Political Snipers: How the NRA Exploited Loopholes and Waged a Stealth Campaign against the Democrats," *American Prospect* 23 (fall 1995): 28–9, and Elizabeth Drew, *Showdown* (New York, 1996), 100–101.
31 Feb. 28 and June 22, 1995, *Papers of Presidents: Clinton, 1995*, I: 272, 925. For the later remarks to the Democratic National Committee Dinner, Oct. 8, 1997, see *Weekly Compilation of Presidential Documents* 33 (1997): 1530.
32 Charles Lewis and the Center for Public Integrity, *The Buying of the Congress* (New York, 1998), 133. On the use of federal tax dollars to subsidize shooting, see Susan Glick and Josh Sugarmann, "Why Johnny Can Shoot," *Mother Jones* 20 (Jan.–Feb. 1995): 15, and Spitzer, *Politics of Gun Control*, 70–3.
33 The quotations come from Julie Rovner, "US Gun Lobby Takes Aim at CDC Injury Centre," *The Lancet* 346 (Aug. 26, 1995): 563, and Windlesham, *Politics, Punishment*, 116.

34   David B. Kopel, ed., *Guns: Who Should Have Them?* (Amherst, N.Y., 1995), 11.
35   Philip J. Cook and Jens Ludwig, *Guns in America* (National Institute of Justice, Washington, D.C., 1977), 1–2, 5, 8.
36   U.S. Congress, Senate, *The Federal Raid on Ruby Ridge, ID* (hearings before the Subcommittee on Terrorism, Technology, and Government Information of the Committee of the Judiciary), 101st Cong., 1st Sess., Sept. 1–26, Oct. 13–19, 1995 (Washington, D.C., 1997), 3. A transcript of the firearms sale is printed on 116–21.
37   U.S. Department of the Treasury, *Report on the Bureau of Alcohol, Tobacco and Firearms Investigation of Vernon Wayne Howell also Known as David Koresh* (Washington, D.C., 1993), 11.
38   Quoted in James D. Tabor and Eugene V. Gallagher, *Why Waco?* (Berkeley, 1995), 64, and Edward M. Gaffney Jr., "The Waco Tragedy: Constitutional Concerns and Policy Perspectives," in Wright, ed., *Armageddon in Waco*, 335.
39   Kenneth S. Stern, *A Force Upon the Plain* (New York, 1996), 14, 72.
40   From a newsletter of Oct. 1994, cited in Daniel Junas, "Angry White Guys with Guns: Rise of the Militias," *Covert Action Quarterly* 52 (spring 1995): 25, and a catalogue of Nov. 21, 1994, cited in David C. Williams, "The Militia Movement and Second Amendment Revolutions: Conjuring with the People," *Cornell Law Review* 81 (May 1996): 886.
41   See, for example, Mark DeCamillo and Mervyn Field, *The Field Poll*, May 31, 1995, release #1754.
42   For the letter and its defense, see Marjolijn Bijlefeld, ed., *The Gun Control Debate* (Westport, Conn., 1997), 56–8. Bush is quoted in Jack Anderson, *Inside the NRA* (Beverly Hills, Calif., 1996), 118.
43   The quotation comes from U.S. Congress, *Children and Guns* (hearing before the Select Committee on Children, Youth, and Families), 101st Cong., 1st Sess., June 15, 1989 (Washington, D.C., 1989), 3.
44   Quoted in Louis H. Pollak, Foreword, in a "Symposium: Reflections on United States v. Lopez," *Michigan Law Review* 94 (Dec. 1995): 542.
45   *United States Supreme Court Reporter*, Lawyers' edition, 2d series, 131 (Rochester, N.Y., 1997): 626.
46   Alfred Blumenstein, U.S. Department of Justice, National Institute of Justice, *Youth Violence, Guns, and Illicit Drug Markets* (Washington, D.C., 1996), 1–2, and "America Under the Gun," *Time*, July 6, 1998, 34.
47   U.S. Congress, Senate, *Guns in Schools: A Federal Role?* (hearings before the Subcommittee on Youth Violence of the Committee on the Judiciary), 104th Cong., 1st Sess., July 18, 1995 (Washington, D.C., 1997), 1.
48   *Times* (London), Dec. 20, 1966, via Lexis-Nexis, *Academic Universe*.
49   Quoted in the *Daily Telegraph* (London), Dec. 19, 1996, via Lexis-Nexis, *Academic Universe*.
50   See Windlesham, *Politics, Punishment*, 188–90, and Spitzer, *Politics of Gun Control*, 110–9.
51   Richard Harding, *Firearms and Violence in Australian Life* (Nedlands, Australia, 1981), 1–2.
52   See Stephen Cordiner and Kathy Ettershank, "Gun Toting Australians Take Aim at New Weapons Control Law," *The Lancet* 347 (June 8, 1996): 1616.
53   Quoted from Jeff Brazil and Steve Berry, "Outgunned: The Holes in America's Assault Weapons Laws," Los Angeles *Times*, Aug. 27, 1997, p. A16.

Chapter 18

1   New York *Times*, August 27, 1996, p. A14.
2   *Federal Reporter* 8, 3d series (St. Paul, Minn., 1996): 101.
3   Presidential debate, Hartford, Conn., Oct. 6, 1996, *Weekly Compilation of Presidential Documents 1996* (Washington, D.C., 1996), 1983.
4   Los Angeles *Times*, March 1, 1997, p. A19.
5   For a critique of the concept of the increasing deadliness of small arms, see David Grossman, *On Killing* (Boston, 1995), 347, n. 2.

6   Los Angeles *Times*, March 2, 1997, p. A1.
7   Johns Hopkins Center for Gun Policy and Research, *1996 National Gun Policy Survey* (Baltimore, March 1977), ii–iii.
8   Los Angeles *Times*, June 4, 1997, p. A3.
9   Spitzer, *Politics of Gun Control*, 2d ed. (New York, 1998), 76–8.
10 Santa Barbara *News Press*, June 28, 1997, p. A1.
11 Los Angeles *Times*, June 28, 1997, p. A23.
12 Ibid.
13 Radio addresses, July 19 and 28, 1997, *Weekly Compilation of Presidential Documents 1997* (Washington, D.C., 1997), 1107, 1145.
14 The suit was filed on Dec. 16, 1997, in San Francisco. See Los Angeles *Times*, Dec. 17, 1997, pp. A3, A38, and July 23, 1998, p. A3.
15 The quotations come from Brazil and Berry, "Outgunned," Los Angeles *Times*, Aug. 24, 1997, pp. A1, A17, and Aug. 25, p. A10.
16 From a full-page advertisement in Los Angeles *Times*, Sept. 17, 1997, p. A12.
17 See George Comstock, "Juvenile Crime," in *TV and Teens*, ed. Meg Schwarz, 188–9; Newton N. Minow and Craig L. LaMay, *Abandoned in the Wasteland* (New York, 1995), 7–8; and *National Television Violence Study*, Vol. 1 (Thousand Oaks, Calif., 1997), 8–10, 302.
18 See Brandon S. Centerwall, "Television Violence: The Scale of the Problem and Where to Go from Here," *Journal of the American Medical Association* 267 (Feb. 10, 1992): 3060; Los Angeles *Times*, Sept. 21, 1997, p. A41; *National Television Violence Study*, Vol. 2, pp. 1, 5; and Sissela Bok, *Mayhem* (Reading, Mass., 1998), 47, 57.
19 For the quotations, see Leslie Helm, "Making a Killing," Los Angeles *Times*, Jan. 26, 1998, pp. D1–2; Dave Grossman and Gloria DeGaetano, *Stop Teaching Our Kids to Kill* (New York, 1999), 66; and for other data, Bok, *Mayhem*, 59–60.
20 See Los Angeles *Times*, Oct. 19, 1997, p. M14, and Dec. 17, pp. A1, A14.
21 "Time for Congress to Rein in the BATF," *American Rifleman* 142 (April 1995): 38.
22 See Joseph F. Sheley and James D. Wright, *High School Youths, Weapons, and Violence: A National Survey* (U.S. Dept. of Justice, Washington, D.C., Oct. 1998), 2.
23 Quoted in the Los Angeles *Times*, March 25, 1998, p. A10.
24 For the quotations, see April 6, 1998, *Weekly Compilation of Presidential Documents* 34 (April 13, 1998): 582, and Los Angeles *Times*, April 7, 1998, p. A14.
25 "Nonfatal and Fatal Firearms-Related Injuries—United States, 1993–1997," *Journal of the American Medical Association* 203 (Jan. 5, 2000): 47–8.
26 Radio address, June 13, 1998, *Weekly Compilation of Presidential Documents* 34 (June 29, 1998): 1119–20.
27 Stephen P. Teret and others, "Support for New Policies to Regulate Firearms: Results of Two National Surveys," *New England Journal of Medicine* 339, No. 12 (Sept. 17, 1998): 817.
28 *The Economist*, Nov. 21, 1998, p. 17.
29 Peter J. Boyer, "Big Guns," *New Yorker*, May 17, 1999, p. 61.
30 The statistics come from Zimring and Hawkins, *Crime Is Not the Problem*, 87, and the quotation from the Santa Barbara *News-Press*, February 21, 1999, p. A3.
31 Wendy Max and Dorothy P. Rice, "Shooting in the Dark: Estimating the Cost of Firearms Injuries," *Health Affairs* 12 (winter 1993): 171, estimated on the low side that in 1990 firearms injuries cost Americans $20.4 billion.
32 Lance Morrow, "Coming to Clarity About Guns," *Time*, May 3, 1999, p. 46.
33 Santa Barbara *News-Press*, May 2, 1999, p. A3.
34 Frank Newport, "Gun Control Support Increases Modestly in Wake of Littleton Tragedy," *Gallup Poll Monthly*, No. 404 (May 1999): 5.
35 Radio address, April 24, 1999, *Weekly Compilation of Presidential Documents* 35 (May 3, 1999): 718.
36 Los Angeles *Times*, June 18, 1999, p. A29.
37 James K. Hahn, city attorney of Los Angeles, ibid., May 22, 1999, p. B5.

38   Quoted in Santa Barbara *News-Press*, April 29, 1999, p. A15.
39   Katharine Q. Seelye, of the New York *Times*, reported in the Santa Barbara *News-Press*, June 11, 1999, p. A3.
40   Boba Shaw, to the editor, Los Angeles *Times*, April 23, 1999, p. B6, and Barbara Kingsolver, May 2, p. M5.
41   Ibid., May 14, 1999, p. A9.
42   Ibid., May 21, 1999, p. A21.
43   Smith and Smith, "Changes in Firearms Ownership Among Women," 145.

Chapter 19

1   Faith Berry, "War Games and Lessons of Columbine," Santa Barbara *News-Press*, June 7, 1999, p. A9.
2   The quotations come from the Los Angeles *Times*, May 25, 1999, p. A21.
3   Ibid., June 2, 1999, p. A1, and Robert W. Welkos, "A Few New Tricks of the Hollywood Trade," *Calendar*, in Los Angeles *Times*, Aug. 8, 1999, p. 9.
4   *Freddie Hamilton et al. v. Accu-Tek et al.*, Lexis-Nexis, *Academic Universe*, 1999, p. 37.
5   Los Angeles *Times*, Sept. 30, 1999, p. A1.
6   Ibid., Jan. 21, 2000, p. A3.
7   Ibid., Oct. 8, 1999, pp. A1, A15.
8   Ibid., Sept. 19, 1999, p. B8.
9   Santa Barbara *News-Press*, Oct. 19, 1999, p. A11.
10   Ibid., Dec. 1, 1999, p. C3.
11   Los Angeles *Times*, Dec. 8, 1999, p. A1.
12   Ibid., Jan. 19, 2000, pp. C1, C4.
13   Ibid., Feb. 27, 2000, p. A17.
14   Ibid., March 19, 2000, p. A17.
15   As reported in the Santa Barbara *News-Press*, March 23, 2000, p. A4.
16   Ibid.
17   Ibid., April 1, 2000, p. A9, and June 22, p. A13.
18   Los Angeles *Times*, June 27, 2000, p. A16, and Robert L. Jackson, "Communities' Liability Suits Against Gun Makers Falter," ibid., Oct. 25, 2000, p. A5.
19   Ibid., March 24, 2000, p. A13.
20   Ibid., June 14, 1999, p. A5, also July 16.
21   Ibid., March 7, 2000, p. A12.
22   The quotation comes from *Weekly Compilation of Presidential Documents* 35 (June 9, 1999): 1065, and the statistics come from the Santa Barbara *News-Press*, June 9, 1999, p. A7.
23   *Weekly Compilation of Presidential Documents* 35 (June 18, 1999): 1135–6.
24   See Mark Gillespie, "New Gun Control Efforts Draw Mixed Support," *Gallup Poll Monthly* 406 (July 1999): 21–3.
25   Los Angeles *Times*, June 19, 1999, p. A19.
26   Ibid., July 20, 1999, p. A3, and Aug. 29, p. B1, and Santa Barbara *News-Press*, Jan. 1, 2000, p. A26.
27   Los Angeles *Times*, April 4, 2000, p. A15.
28   Quoted by George Skelton, ibid., Aug. 23, 1999, p. A3. For a larger perspective, see Roger Rosenblatt, "Get Rid of the Damned Things," *Time*, Aug. 9, 1999, pp. 38–9.
29   Los Angeles *Times*, June 20, 1999, p. A8.
30   For a listing of the weapons, see ibid., Aug. 14, 1999, p. A16.
31   Santa Barbara *News-Press*, Aug. 30, 1998, p. A14.
32   For more of Clinton's touting of the Brady law, see Los Angeles *Times*, Dec. 1, 1999.
33   The statistics come from Santa Barbara *News-Press*, Sept. 7, 1999, pp. A1–2, and the quotation of Los Angeles Councilman Mike Feuer from the Los Angeles *Times*, Aug. 29, 1999, p. A1.
34   Los Angeles *Times*, Sept. 18, 1999, p. B4.

35 State of the Union message, Jan. 27, 2000, *Weekly Compilation of Presidential Documents* 36 (Jan. 31, 2000): 165–6.

36 Los Angeles *Times*, Jan. 19, 2000, p. A8.

37 Ibid., Feb. 5, 2000, p. A14.

38 Ibid., June 1, 2000, pp. A1, A22.

39 For statistics on the dropping crime rate, see U.S. Department of Justice, Uniform Crime Reports, *Crime in the United States 1998* (Washington, D.C., Oct. 1999), 11; Los Angeles *Times*, Oct. 18, 1999, p. A1, Nov. 22, 1999, p. A1, B7, Oct. 16, 2000, p. A10; and Santa Barbara *News-Press*, Nov. 19, 1999, p. A8.

40 For the suicides, see Everett S. Lee and Jiafeng Chen, "The Toll of Guns," in U.S. Department of Justice, National Institute of Justice, *Lethal Violence: Proceedings of the 1995 Meeting of the Homicide Working Group* (Washington, D.C., 1997), 70–71.

41 Violence Policy Center, *Unsafe in Any Hands* (Washington, D.C., 2000), 1, and Los Angeles *Times*, Dec. 6, 1999, p. A22.

42 Los Angeles *Times*, June 5, 2000, pp. A1, A22.

43 Ibid., March 1, 2000, p. A1.

44 Remarks Following a Meeting With Congressional Leaders, March 7, 2000, *Weekly Compilation of Presidential Documents* 36 (March 13, 2000): 477.

45 The quotations come from an interview with Sam Donaldson, March 10, 2000, in ibid. (March 20, 2000): 521–24. See also Los Angeles *Times*, March 14, 2000, p. A5.

46 Los Angeles *Times*, March 13, 2000, p. A12.

47 Ibid., March 15, 2000, p. B6.

48 Santa Barbara *News-Press*, April 17, 2000, p. A9, and April 9, 2000, pp. A1, A2.

49 Ibid., March 16, 2000, p. A3.

50 See ibid., March 26, 2000, p. A3; Lydia Saad, "Columbine Could Cast a Long Shadow Over 2000 Election," *Gallup Poll Monthly* 405 (June 1999): 37; Erik Larson, "Squeezing Out the Bad Guys," *Time*, Aug. 9, 1999, pp. 28–36; and Los Angeles *Times*, May 11, 2000, p. A1.

51 Los Angeles *Times*, Sept. 17, 1999, p. A17. Details on the Texas concealed-gun law are in the *Times*, Oct. 3, 2000, pp. A1, A16–17, and Nov. 2, 2000, p. A5.

52 Quoted in David Van Biema, "Terror in the Sanctuary," *Time*, Sept. 27, 1999, p. 43.

53 Los Angeles *Times*, April 5, 2000, p. A1.

54 The Los Angeles meeting took place on Feb. 17, 2000. See Los Angeles *Times*, May 4, 2000, p. A26.

55 Ibid., May 3, 2000, p. E1.

56 Santa Barbara *News-Press*, May 15, 2000, p. A2.

57 Los Angeles *Times*, May 15, 2000, p. A1.

58 Ibid., p. A10.

59 Ibid., May 20, 2000, pp. A1, A16.

60 Ibid., May 21, 2000, p. A28.

61 Republican and Democratic platforms, 2000, the Internet, www.cnn.com.

62 Los Angeles *Times*, Aug. 14, 2000, p. U12.

63 The debate quotations, Oct. 17, 2000, come from ibid., Oct. 18, 2000, p. A23:1. For other data on conflicted gun-control loyalties, see ibid., Oct. 22, 2000, pp. A1, A16, and "Gun Issues Staying Off the Firing Line," Santa Barbara *News-Press*, Oct. 26, 2000, p. A3.

64 For statistics on gun crime and conflicting views on their significance, see Los Angeles *Times*, Aug. 2, 2000, p. A10, and Aug. 28, 2000, pp. A10, B1.

Chapter 20

1 James D. Wright, "Ten Essential Observations on Guns in America," *Society* 32 (March–April 1995): 67.

2 Robert J. Kukla, *Gun Control* (Harrisburg, Penn., 1973), 444.

3 See Weir, *Written with Lead*, viii, x.

4 Raymond G. Kessler, "Gun Control and Political Power," *Law and Policy Quarterly* 5 (July 1983): 383, 384.

5 See John R. Lott Jr., *More Guns, Less Crime* (Chicago, 1998), 3, 5, 19, 51; Franklin E. Zimring and Gordon Hawkins, "The Research on Concealed Weapons Laws Is Flawed," in Roleff, ed., *Guns and Crime*, 33–44; and "America Under the Gun," *Time*, 48.

6 Philip J. Cook, Jens Ludwig, and David Hemenway, "The Gun Debate's New Mythical Number: How Many Defensive Gun Uses Per Year?" *Journal of Policy Analysis and Management* 16 (summer 1997): 463, 466.

7 U.S. Congress, *Interstate Carrying of Concealed Firearms by Law Enforcement Officials* (hearing before the Subcommittee on Crime of the Committee on the Judiciary), 105th Cong., 1st Sess., H.R. 218 and H.R. 339 (July 22, 1997), 1.

8 See Marcus Nieto, *Concealed Handgun Laws and Public Safety* (Sacramento, Calif., Nov. 1997), 15–16; Robert L. Young, David McDowell, and Colin Loftin, "Collective Security and the Ownership of Firearms for Protection," *Criminology* 25 (Feb. 1987): 47; Gary S. Green, "Citizen Gun Ownership and Criminal Deterrence: Theory, Research, and Policy," ibid., p. 63; Arthur L. Kellermann and others, "Gun Ownership as a Risk Factor for Homicide in the Home," *New England Journal of Medicine* 329 (Oct. 7, 1993): 1084, 1087, 1090; and Jerome P. Kassirer, "Guns in the Household," ibid., pp. 1117–18. For the progun perspective, see Gary Kleck and Karen McElrath, "The Effects of Weaponry on Human Violence," *Social Forces* 69 (March 1991): 669, 675.

9 Quoted in Patrick Carr and George W. Gardner, *Gun People* (Garden City, N.Y., 1985), 32, 68.

10 For a listing of state laws, see Bijlefeld, ed., *The Gun Debate*, 249–53. See also Bellesiles, "Gun Laws in Early America," 58–9.

11 Don B. Kates Jr., "Shot Down," *National Review* 47 (March 6, 1995): 50.

12 Denning, "Gun Shy," 730, 777–8.

13 Dennis A. Henigan, E. Bruce Nicholson, and David Hemenway, *Guns and the Constitution* (Northampton, Mass., 1995), 12.

14 See, for example, Peter B. Feller and Karl L. Gotting, "The Second Amendment: A Second Look," *Northwestern University Law Review* 61 (March–April 1966): 46, 70; Keith A. Ehrman and Dennis A. Henigan, "The Second Amendment in the Twentieth Century: Have You Seen Your Militia Lately?" *University of Dayton Law Review* 15 (1989): 7; and Antonin Scalia, *A Matter of Interpretation: Federal Courts and the Law* (Princeton, 1997), 43, 136–7n.

15 William W. Van Alstyne, "The Second Amendment and the Personal Right to Arms," *Duke Law Journal* 43 (April 1994): 1250, 1254. For a critique of Second Amendment myths and individual gun possession, see Garry Wills, *A Necessary Evil* (New York, 1999), 255–9.

16 Diaz, *Making a Killing*, 11, 92–3.

17 See Sinclair, *Prohibition*, 193, and United Nations, *International Study on Firearm Regulation* (New York, 1998), 11.

18 Quoted in Natalie J. Goldring, "The NRA Goes Global," *Bulletin of the Atomic Scientists* 55 (Jan.–Feb. 1999): 65.

19 Gregg Easterbrook, "America's Poll," *USA Weekend*, July 2–4, 1999, p. 7.

20 "Perspectives," *Newsweek*, Dec. 30, 1991, p. 11.

21 Quoted in Don B. Kates Jr., ed., *Restricting Handguns* (Croton-on-Hudson, N.Y., 1979), xi.

22 Garen J. Wintemute and others, "Mortality Among Recent Purchasers of Handguns," *New England Journal of Medicine* 341 (Nov. 18, 1999): 1583.

23 See Dennis A. Gilbert, *Compendium of American Public Opinion* (New York, 1988), 47–8; Moore and Newport, "Public Opinion," *Gallup Poll Monthly*, 18; and Steven T. Seitz, "Firearms, Homicides, and Gun Control Effectiveness," *Law and Society Review* 6 (May 1972): 609. For the progun contention, see Don B. Kates and Gary Kleck, eds., *The Great American Gun Debate* (San Francisco, 1997), 34.

24 See Douglas R. Murray, "Handguns, Gun Control Laws, and Firearms Violence," *Social Problems* 23 (Oct. 1975): 81, 89, and Bayley, *Forces of Order*, 173.

25 Martin Killias, "International Correlations between Gun Ownership and Rates of Homicide and Suicide," *Canadian Medical Association Journal* 168 (May 15, 1993): 1721; Zimring and Hawkins, *Citizen's Guide,* 53, 58, 62–3. See also U.S. Comptroller General's Report to Congress, "Handgun Control: Effectiveness and Cost" (Washington, D.C., Feb. 6, 1978), 1, and Massachusetts Council on Crime Correction, Inc., *A Shooting Gallery Called America* (Boston, 1974), 2. For the progun perspective on this matter, see James D. Wright and others, *Weapons, Crime and Violence in America* (Washington, D.C., 1981), i.

26 Quoted in Mollie Dickenson, *Thumbs Up* (New York, 1987), 522.

27 For the quotations, see Los Angeles *Times,* Oct. 10, 1999, p. M6, and Santa Barbara *News-Press,* Nov. 13, 1999, p. A1.

28 James J. Baker, "Gun Control Is Bad Medicine," *American Rifleman* 142 (Feb. 1994): 76.

29 Los Angeles *Times,* Oct. 3, 1998, p. A3.

30 The "wag" comment comes from George Skelton, Los Angeles *Times,* Oct. 1, 1998, p. A3. Johnson's words come from his "Agenda for the Future: A Presidential Perspective," *Britannica Book of the Year 1969* (Chicago, 1969), 44.

31 David B. Kopel and Christopher C. Little, "Communitarians, Neorepublicans, and Guns: Assessing the Case for Firearms Prohibition," *Maryland Law Review* 56 (1997): 462–3.

32 Richard Maxwell Brown explains America's high rates of gun violence and homicide with the concept that a person faced with menace has no duty to retreat. Instead, legally he can stand his ground and "kill in self-defense." See his *No Duty to Retreat,* 4–6.

33 For further analysis and details, see Franklin E. Zimring, "Firearms, Violence, and Public Policy," *Scientific American,* Nov. 1991, pp. 48, 52–3, and Roger Lane, *Murder in America* (Columbus, Ohio, 1997), 214, 237–8, 341, 343, 348.

34 A Field poll in California reported the skepticism, Santa Barbara *News-Press,* July 13, 2000, p. A4.

Epilogue

1 For examples of the criticisms, see James Lindgren, "Fall from Grace: *Arming America* and the Bellesiles Scandal," *Yale Law Journal* 111, no. 8 (2002): 2195–2249; Robert H. Churchill, "Guns and the Politics of History," *Reviews in American History* 29 (Sept. 2001): 329–37; and *Forum:* "Guns and History," *William and Mary Quarterly,* 3d Series, 59 (Jan. 2002), 203–68, which also contains a defense of the book by Bellesiles.

2 The *History News Network* (http://HNN.us) chronicles the controversy. It also contains the texts of the investigating committee's report and Bellesiles's rebuttal.

3 See, for example, Jon Wiener, "Fire at Will," *Nation* 275 (Nov. 4, 2002): 28–32.

4 The quotations and other data come from James Dao, "Over a Barrell: New Gun-Control Politics: A Whimper, Not a Bang," *New York Times,* March 11, 2001, sec. 4, p. 1.

5 *Weekley Standard* (June 25, 2001) and *Washington Times,* (May 23, 2001), via LexisNexis, *Academic Universe.*

6 *Legal Times* (July 29, 2002) via LexisNexis.

7 "Shot Full of Holes: Deconstructing John Ashcroft's Second Amendment," *U.S. Newswire, Inc.,* Aug. 3, 2001, via LexisNexis.

8 Robert J. Spitzer, "Saving the Constitution from Lawyers," in *Politics and Constitutionalism,* ed. Spitzer (Albany, N.Y., 2000), 192–93.

9 *Washington Post,* June 29, 2001, p. A2.

10 New York *Times,* Dec. 16, 2001, sec 1A, p. 1.

11 Quoted in Dick Dahl, "The NRA Sees Room to Grow as Faithful Adjunct to the GOP," *Nation* 275 (Nov. 4, 2002): 18.

12 *Christian Science Monitor,* April 29, 2002, p. 4.

13 Robert J. Spitzer, *The Right to Bear Arms* (Santa Barbara, Calif., 2001), 112–14.

14 Baker, "Federal Appeals Court Upholds Second Amendment as Individual Right," *American Rifleman* 149 (Dec. 2001), 64.

15   The quotations come from the David G. Savage article in the Los Angeles *Times*, Oct. 17, 2002, p. A22.
16   *Findlaw*, Google search, Internet.
17   The quotations come from Linda Greenhouse, New York *Times*, May 8, 2002, sec. A, p. 1.
18   Quoted by Anne Gearan, Associated Press (May 7, 2002), via LexisNexis.
19   The quotation and other data come from *Findlaw* and the *Legal Times* (July 22, 2002), via LexisNexis.
20   Dahl, "NRA Sees Room," p. 18.
21   *American Rifleman* 149 (Aug. 2001): 90.
22   Santa Barbara *News-Press*, Oct. 11, 2002, p. B5.
23   Los Angeles *Times*, Oct. 16, 2002, p. A15.
24   Much of this data comes form the Los Angeles *Times*, Oct. 26, 2002, pp. A1, A20, A23.
25   Los Angeles *Times*, Oct. 29, 2002, pp. A1, A16, and Oct. 30, 2002, p. E5.
26   The statistics and other data come from Dahl, "NRA Sees Room," p. 17–18.
27   Santa Barbara *News-Press*, Nov. 15, 2002, p. A10.
28   Wayne LaPierre and James J. Baker, *Shooting Straight* (Washington, D.C., 2002), 175.
29   George Skelton, Los Angeles *Times*, Dec. 12, 2002, p. B5.
30   David I. Caplan in *Notice of Annual Meeting*, College Retirement Equities Fund, New York, Oct. 7, 2002, p. 17.
31   Los Angeles *Times*, Nov. 14, 2002, p. A30.
32   Ibid., p. A29.
33   Los Angeles *Times*, Nov. 19, 2002, p. B7.
34   Ibid., Apr. 10, 2003, p. A34.

Bibliography

Abbott, Edith. "The Civil War and the Crime Wave of 1865–70." *Social Service Review* 1 (1927): 212–34.

———. "Crime and the War." *Journal of the American Institute of Criminal Law and Criminology* 9 (1918–1919): 31–45.

Abbott, Edward C., and Helena H. Smith. *We Pointed Them North: Recollections of a Cowpuncher.* New York, 1939.

Aborn, Richard M. "The Battle Over the Brady Bill and the Future of Gun Control Advocacy." *Fordham Urban Law Journal* 22 (1995): 417–39.

Abrams, Daniel. "Ending the Other Arms Race: An Argument for a Ban on Assault Weapons." *Yale Law and Policy Review* 10, No. 2 (1992): 488–519.

Academics for the Second Amendment. "An Open Letter on the Second Amendment." *Journal of Higher Education* 41 (Aug. 11, 1995): A23.

Adams, John. *A Defence of the Constitutions of Government of the United States of America.* 3 vols. London, 1787.

———. *The Works of John Adams.* Ed. Charles F. Adams. 10 vols. Boston, 1850–1856.

Adams, Lynn G. "Adequate and Proper Restriction on Sale and Ownership of Firearms." *Annals of the American Academy of Political and Social Science* 125 (May 1926): 153–7.

Aho, James A. *This Thing of Darkness: A Sociology of the Enemy.* Seattle, 1994.

Alexander, Archibald S. "Arms Transfers by the United States: Merchant of Death or Arsenal of Democracy." *Vanderbilt Journal of Transnational Law* 10 (spring 1977): 249–67.

Alix, Ernest K. *Ransom Kidnapping in America, 1874–1974: The Creation of a Capital Crime.* Carbondale, Ill., 1978.

Allen, Durward L. "The Growing Antagonism to Hunting." *Field & Stream* 68 (Sept. 1963): 12–16.

Allen, Harry C. *Bush and Backwoods: A Comparison of the Frontier in Australia and the United States.* Sydney, 1959.

Alviani, Joseph D., and William R. Drake. *Handgun Control: Issues and Alternatives.* Rev. ed. Chicago, 1984.

Amar, Akhil Reed. "The Bill of Rights as a Constitution." *Yale Law Journal* 100 (March 1991): 1131–1210.

———. *The Bill of Rights: Creation and Reconstruction.* New Haven, 1998.

———. "The Bill of Rights and the Fourteenth Amendment." *Yale Law Journal* 101 (Apr. 1992): 1193–1284.

"America Under the Gun." *Time,* July 6, 1998, pp. 34–62.

American Medical Association Council on Scientific Affairs. "Firearms Injuries and Deaths: A Critical Public Health Issue." *Public Health Reports* 104 (March–Apr. 1989): 112–20.

Anderson, Fred. *A People's Army: Massachusetts Soldiers and Society in the Seven Years' War*. Chapel Hill, N.C., 1984.

Anderson, George M. "Gun Control: New Approaches." *America* 172 (March 11, 1995): 26–9.

Anderson, Jack. *Inside the NRA: Armed and Dangerous: An Exposé*. Beverly Hills, Calif., 1996.

———. "Where Johnny Gets His Gun." *Reader's Digest* 83 (July 1963): 138–40.

Anderson, Jervis. *Guns in American Life*. New York, 1984.

Anderson, Thornton. *Creating the Constitution: The Convention of 1787 and the First Congress*. University Park, Pa., 1993.

Angelucci, Angelo. *Documenti inediti per la storia delle armi da fuoco italiane* (pamphlet). Turin, It., 1869.

Anti-Defamation League. *Armed and Dangerous: Militias Take Aim at the Federal Government*. New York, 1994.

"Anti-Gun Lawsuits." *The Economist*, Nov. 21–27, 1998, pp. 28–29.

Archer, Dane, and Rosemary Gartner. *Violence and Crime in Cross-National Perspective*. New Haven, 1984.

Army and Navy Chronicle 66 (1838).

Asbury, Charles J. "The Right to Keep and Bear Arms in America: The Origins and Application of the Second Amendment to the Constitution." Ph.D. diss., University of Michigan, 1974.

Ascoli, David. *The Queen's Peace: The Origins and Development of the Metropolitan Police, 1829–1979*. London, 1979.

Ash, Peter, Arthur L. Kellermann, Dwana Fuqua-Whitley, and Amri Johnson. "Gun Acquisition and Use by Juvenile Offenders." *Journal of the American Medical Association* 275 (June 12, 1996): 1754–8.

Askins, Charles. *Texas, Guns, and History*. New York, 1970.

Association Against the Prohibition Amendment. *Reforming America With a Shotgun: A Study of Prohibition Killings*. Washington, D.C., Nov. 1929.

Astor, Gerald. *The New York Cops: An Informal History*. New York, 1971.

Athearn, Robert G. *The Mythic West in Twentieth-Century America*. Lawrence, Kans., 1986.

Ayalon, David. *Gunpowder and Firearms in the Mamluk Kingdom: A Challenge to a Mediaeval Society*. 2d ed. London, 1978.

Ayers, Edward L. *Vengeance and Justice: Crime and Punishment in the Nineteenth-Century South*. New York, 1984.

Baenziger, Ann P. "The Texas State Police During Reconstruction: A Reexamination." *Southwestern Historical Quarterly* 72 (1969): 470–91.

Bailyn, Bernard. *The Ideological Origins of the American Revolution*. Cambridge, Mass., 1967.

Baird, Bruce C. "The Social Origins of Dueling in Virginia." In Bellesiles, ed. *Lethal Imagination*, 87–114.

Bakal, Carl. "Failure of Federal Gun Control." *Saturday Review*, July 3, 1971, pp. 12–15, 49–50.

———. *The Right to Bear Arms*. New York, 1966.

———. "This Very Day a Gun May Kill You." *McCall's*, July 1959, pp. 50–51, 84, 86–90.

Baker, James J. "Gun Control Is Bad Medicine." *American Rifleman* 142 (Feb. 1994): 40–41, 76–9.

Baker, Susan. "Without Guns, Do People Kill People?" *American Journal of Public Health* 75 (June 1985): 587–88.

Baldick, Robert. *The Duel: A History of Duelling*. London, 1965.

Balk, Alfred. "The Firearms Theater of the Absurd." *Saturday Review*, July 22, 1967, pp. 28, 52.

Banning, Lance. *The Sacred Fire of Liberty: James Madison and the Founding of the Federal Republic*. Ithaca, N.Y., 1995.

Barclay, Dorothy. "Behind All the Bang-Bang." *New York Times Magazine*, July 22, 1962, p. 47.

Barnett, Randy E. "Foreword: Guns, Militias, and Oklahoma City." *Tennessee Law Review* 62 (spring 1995): 443–59.

Barnett, Randy E., and Don B. Kates. "Under Fire: The New Consensus on the Second Amendment." *Emory Law Journal* 45 (summer 1996): 1139–1259.

Barr, Ronald J. *The Progressive Army: US Army Command and Administration, 1870–1914.* New York, 1998.

Bartlett, William C. *Gun Control Legislation in Canada, the United Kingdom, and the United States.* Ottawa, Feb. 1990.

Batey, Robert. "Strict Construction of Firearms Offenses: The Supreme Court and the Gun Control Act of 1968." *Law and Contemporary Problems* 49 (winter 1986): 163–98.

"The Battle Over Gun Control: The Black Community Has the Greatest Stake in the Outcome of the Gun Control Debate." *Black Enterprise* 23 (July 1993): 27.

Bauer, Jack K. *The Mexican War, 1846–1848.* New York, 1974.

Bayley, David H. *Forces of Order: Policing Modern Japan.* 2d ed. Berkeley, 1991.

———. "Learning About Crime—The Japanese Experience." *The Public Interest* 44 (summer 1976): 55–68.

Beard, Michael K., and Kristin M. Rand. "The Handgun Battle." *Bill of Rights Journal* 10 (1987): 13–15.

Beccaria, Cesare. *On Crimes and Punishments.* Trans. Henry Paolucci. Indianapolis, 1963.

Beecher, Lyman. *Lyman Beecher and the Reform of Society: Four Sermons, 1804–1828.* Ed. Edwin S. Gaustad. New York, 1972.

Beeman, Richard, and others, eds. *Beyond Confederation: Origins of the Constitution and American National Identity.* Chapel Hill, N.C., 1987.

Beha, James A., II. " 'And Nobody Can Get You Out': The Impact of a Mandatory Prison Sentence for the Illegal Carrying of a Firearm on the Use of Firearms and on the Administration of Criminal Justice in Boston." *Boston University Law Review* 57 (Jan. 1997): Part I, 96–146; Part II, 289–333.

Behr, Edward. *Prohibition: Thirteen Years That Changed America.* New York, 1996.

Bellamy, John G. *Criminal Law and Society in Late Medieval and Tudor England.* Gloucester, Eng., 1984.

Bellesiles, Michael A. *Arming America: The Origins of a National Gun Culture.* New York, 2000.

———. "Gun Laws in Early America: The Regulation of Firearms Ownership, 1607–1794." *Law and History Review* 16 (fall 1998): 567–89.

———. "The Origins of Gun Culture in the United States, 1760–1865." *Journal of American History* 83 (Sept. 1996): 425–55.

———. "Suicide Pact: New Readings of the Second Amendment." *Constitutional Commentary* 16 (summer 1999): 247–61.

———, ed. *Lethal Imagination: Violence and Brutality in American History.* New York, 1999.

Belz, Herman. *Reconstructing the Union: Theory and Policy during the Civil War.* Ithaca, N.Y., 1969.

Beman, Lamar T., ed. *Outlawing the Pistol.* New York, 1926.

Bendis, Paul, and Steven Balkin. "A Look at Gun Control Enforcement." *Journal of Police Science and Administration* 7, No. 4 (1979): 439–48.

Benedict, Michael Les. *A Compromise of Principle: Congressional Republicans and Reconstruction, 1863–1869.* New York, 1974.

Bennett, David H. *The Party of Fear: From Nativist Movements to the New Right in American History.* Chapel Hill, N.C., 1988.

Bennett, James V. "The Gun and How to Control It." *New York Times Magazine*, Sept. 25, 1966, pp. 34–5, 133–40.

Bennett, Lerone, Jr. *What Manner of Man: A Biography of Martin Luther King, Jr.* 4th ed. Chicago, 1976.

Berger, Raoul. *Fourteenth Amendment and the Bill of Rights.* Norman, Okla., 1989.

———. *Government by the Judiciary: The Transformation of the Fourteenth Amendment.* Cambridge, Mass., 1977.

Berger, Warren. "Perspectives." *Newsweek*, Dec. 30, 1991, p. 11.

Berkowitz, Leonard. "Guns and Youth." In Eron, ed. *Reason to Hope*, 251–79.

———. "How Guns Control Us." *Psychology Today* 15 (June 1981): 11–12.

———. "Impulse, Aggression and the Gun." *Psychology Today* 2 (Sept. 1968): 19–22.

Berkowitz, Leonard, and Anthony LePage. "Weapons as Aggression-Eliciting Stimuli." *Journal of Personality and Social Psychology* 7 (Oct. 1967): 202–207.

Bernstein, Iver. *The New York City Draft Riots: Their Significance for American Society and Politics in the Age of the Civil War*. New York, 1990.

Berry, Jeffrey M. *Lobbying for the People: The Political Behavior of Public Interest Groups*. Princeton, 1977.

Beschle, Donald. "Reconsidering the Second Amendment: Constitutional Protection for a Right of Security." *Hamline Law Review* 9 (1986): 69–104.

Biendon, Robert J., John T. Young, and David Hemenway. *Journal of the American Medical Association* 275 (June 12, 1996): 1719–22.

Bierstadt, Edward H. "Our Permanent Crime." *Harper's* 156 (Dec. 1927): 61–70.

Bijlefeld, Marjolijn, ed. *The Gun Conrol Debate: A Documentary History*. Westport, Conn., 1997.

———. *People For and Against Gun Control: A Biographical Reference*. Westport, Conn., 1999.

Billias, George A. *Elbridge Gerry: Founding Father and Republican Statesman*. New York, 1976.

Billington, Ray Allen. *The Protestant Crusade, 1800–1860: A Study of the Origins of American Nativism*. New York, 1938.

———, ed. *People of the Plains and Mountains*. Westport, Conn., 1973.

Birnbaum, Jeffrey H. *The Lobbyists: How Influence Peddlers Get Their Way in Washington*. New York, 1992.

Bjerregaard, Beth, and Alan J. Lizotte. "Gun Ownership and Gang Membership." *Journal of Criminal Law and Criminology* 86 (fall 1995): 37–58.

Black, Dan A., and Daniel S. Nagin. "Do 'Right-To-Carry Laws' Deter Violent Crime?" *Journal of Legal Studies* 27 (Jan. 1998): 209–20.

Black, Jack. "What's Wrong With the Right People?" *Harper's* 159 (June 1929): 75–82.

Blacker, Irwin R., ed. *The Old West in Fact*. New York, 1962.

Blackman, Paul H. "A Critique of the Epidemiological Study of Firearms and Homicide." *Homicide Studies* 1 (May 1997): 169–89.

Blackmore, Howard L. *Guns and Rifles of the World*. London, 1965.

Blackstone, William. *Commentaries on the Laws of England*. 2 vols. 1765–1769. Reprint, Philadelphia, 1856.

Blakely, Mary Kay. "Would You Feel Safer Carrying a Gun?" *Ms* 10 (May 1982): 16–18.

Blitzer, Charles. *An Immortal Commonwealth: The Political Thought of James Harrington*. New Haven, 1960.

Bodenhamer, David J. "Law and Disorder on the Early Frontier: Marion County, Indiana, 1823–1850." *Western Historical Quarterly* 10 (July 1979): 323–36. Reprinted in Monkkonen, ed. *Crime and Justice in American History*. Vol. 4: 20–33.

Bodenhamer, David J., and James W. Ely Jr., eds. *The Bill of Rights in Modern America: After 200 Years*. Bloomington, Ind., 1993.

Bogus, Carl T. "The Hidden History of the Second Amendment." *U.C. Davis Law Review* 31 (winter 1998): 309–408.

———. "How Not to Be the NRA." *Tikkun* 9 (Jan.–Feb. 1994): 19–81.

———. "Pistols, Politics and Products Liability." *Cincinnati Law Review* 59 (spring 1991): 1103–64.

———. "The Strong Case for Gun Control." *The American Prospect* 10 (summer 1992): 19–28.

———, ed. *The Second Amendment in Law and History: Historians and Constitutional Scholars on the Right to Bear Arms*. New York, 2002.

Bok, Sissela. *Mayhem: Violence as Public Entertainment*. Reading, Mass., 1998.

Boorstin, Daniel J. *The Americans: The Colonial Experience*. New York, 1958.

Boothroyd, Geoffrey. *Guns Through the Ages*. New York, 1961.

———. *The Handgun*. New York, 1970.

Bopp, William J., and Donald O. Schultz. *A Short History of American Law Enforcement*. Springfield, Ill., 1972.

Borden, Morton, ed. *Antifederalist Papers*. East Lansing, Mich., 1965.

Bork, Robert H. *The Tempting of America: The Political Seduction of the Law.* New York, 1990.
Borland, John. "The Arming of California." *California Journal* 26 (Oct. 1995): 36–41.
Boutwell, Jeffrey, and Michael T. Klare. *Light Weapons and Civil Conflict: Controlling the Tools of Violence.* Lanham, Md., 1999.
Bowling for Columbine. A film written, produced, and directed by Michael Moor. 2002.
Bowling, Kenneth R. " 'A Tub to the Whale': The Founding Fathers and Adoption of the Federal Bill of Rights." *Journal of the Early Republic* 8 (fall 1988): 223–51.
Boyd, James. *Above the Law.* New York, 1968.
Boyer, Peter J. "Big Guns." *New Yorker,* May 17, 1999, pp. 54–67.
Boynton, Lindsay. *The Elizabethan Militia, 1558–1638.* London, 1967.
Brady, Sarah. *A Good Fight.* New York, 2002.
Brander, Michael. *Hunting and Shooting: From Earliest Times to the Present Day.* New York, 1971.
———. *The Hunting Instinct: The Development of Field Sports over the Ages.* Edinburgh, 1964.
Brant, Irving. *The Bill of Rights: Its Origin and Meaning.* Indianapolis, 1965.
Brearley, H. C. *Homicide in the United States.* Chapel Hill, N.C., 1932.
Breen, David H. *The Canadian Prairie West and the Ranching Frontier, 1874–1924.* Toronto, 1983.
Bridenbaugh, Carl. *Cities in Revolt: Urban Life in America, 1743–1776.* New York, 1965.
———. *Cities in the Wilderness: The First Century of Urban Life in America, 1625–1742.* 2d ed. New York, 1964.
———. *The Colonial Craftsmen.* Chicago, 1961.
Brill, Steven. *Firearms Abuse: A Research and Policy Report.* Washington, D.C., 1977.
Britt, Chester L., Gary Kleck, and David J. Bordua. "A Reassessment of the D.C. Gun Law: Some Cautionary Notes on the Use of Interrupted Time Series Designs for Policy Impact Assessment." *Law and Society Review* 30, No. 2 (1996): 361–80, 381–97.
Brodie, Bernard, and Fawn Brodie. *From Crossbow to H-Bomb.* Rev. ed. Bloomington, Ind., 1973.
Bronars, Stephen G., and John R. Lott Jr. "Criminal Deterrence, Geographic Spillovers, and the Right to Carry Concealed Handguns." *American Economic Review* 88 (May 1988): 475–9.
Brooks, Stewart M. *Our Murdered Presidents: The Medical Story.* New York, 1966.
Brown, Delmer M. "The Impact of Firearms on Japanese Warfare, 1543–98." *Far Eastern Quarterly* 7 (May 1948): 236–53.
Brown, Donald Curtis. "The Great Gun-Toting Controversy, 1865–1910: The Old West Gun Culture and Public Shootings." Ph.D. diss., Tulane University, 1983.
Brown, M. L. *Firearms in Colonial America: The Impact on History and Technology, 1492–1792.* Washington, D.C., 1980.
Brown, Richard M. "The American Vigilante Tradition." In Graham and Gurr, eds. *Violence in America,* 154–226.
———. "Historical Patterns of Violence in America." In Graham and Gurr, eds. *Violence in America,* 45–84.
———. "Historiography of Violence in the American West." In Malone, ed. *Historians and the American West,* 234–69.
———. *No Duty to Retreat: Violence and Values in American History and Society.* New York, 1991.
———. *The South Carolina Regulators.* Cambridge, Mass., 1963.
———. *Strain of Violence: Historical Studies of American Violence and Vigilantism.* New York, 1975.
Brown, Wendy. "Guns, Cowboys, Philadelphia Mayors, and Civic Republicanism: On Sanford Levinson's 'The Embarrassing Second Amendment.' " *Yale Law Journal* 99 (Dec. 1989): 661–67.
Browning, Charles H. "Suicide, Firearms and Public Health." *American Journal of Public Health* 64 (April 1974): 313–17.
Brownmiller, Susan. *Against Our Will: Men, Women and Rape.* New York, 1975.
Bruce, Dickson D., Jr. *Violence and Culture in the Antebellum South.* Austin, Tex., 1979.
Bruce, John M., and Clyde Cox, eds. *The Changing Politics of Gun Control.* Lanham, Md., 1998.
Bruce, Robert V. *1877: Year of Violence.* Indianapolis, 1959.
———. *Lincoln and the Tools of War.* New York, 1956.

Bruce-Briggs, B. "The Great American Gun War." *The Public Interest* 45 (fall 1976): 37–62.

Brundage, Lyle D. "The Organization, Administration, and Training of the United States Ordinary and Volunteer Militia, 1792–1861." Ph.D. diss., University of Michigan, 1958.

Buckley, William F., Jr. "The Great American Gun War." *National Review*, Feb. 18, 1977, p. 223.

Burger, Warren E. "The Right to Bear Arms." *Parade*, Jan. 14, 1990, pp. 4–6.

Burlingame, Roger. *March of the Iron Men: A Social History of Union Through Invention.* New York, 1943.

Burnett, Edmund C. *The Continental Congress.* New York, 1941.

Burrows, William E. *Vigilante!* New York, 1976.

Bush, George H. W. *All the Best, George Bush: My Life in Letters and Other Writings.* New York, 1999.

Caetano, Donald F. "The Domestic Arms Race." *Journal of Communication* 29 (spring 1979): 39–46.

Cairncross, John. *After Polygamy Was Made a Sin: The Social History of Christian Polygamy.* London, 1974.

Califano, Joseph A., Jr. *The Triumph and Tragedy of Lyndon Johnson: The White House Years.* New York, 1991.

California Department of Justice. *California Firearms Laws.* Sacramento, Calif., 2000.

Canada, Geoffrey. *Fist, Stick, Knife, Gun: A Personal History of Violence in America.* Boston, 1995.

Cannizzo, Cindy, ed. *The Gun Merchants: Politics and Policies of the Major Arms Suppliers.* New York, 1980.

Cannon, Lou. *Official Negligence: How Rodney King and the Riots Changed Los Angeles and the LAPD.* New York, 1997.

Caplan, David I. "Restoring the Balance: The Second Amendment Revisited." *Fordham Urban Law Journal* 5 (1976): 31–53.

Caras, Roger A. *Death as a Way of Life.* Boston, 1970.

Carey, A. Merwyn. *American Firearms Makers . . . From the Colonial Period to the End of the Nineteenth Century.* New York, 1953.

Carman, W. Y. *A History of Firearms: From Earliest Times to 1914.* London, 1955.

Carr, Patrick, and George W. Gardner. *Gun People.* Garden City, N.Y., 1985.

Carter, Dan T. *When the War Was Over: The Failure of Self-Reconstruction in the South, 1865–1867.* Baton Rouge, La., 1985.

Carter, Gregg Lee. *The Gun Control Movement.* New York, 1997.

Carter-Yamauchi, Charlotte A. *A Clash of Arms: The Great American Gun Debate.* Honolulu, 1991.

Cary, Lucian. *Lucian Cary on Guns.* New York, 1960.

Casey, Verna. *Gun Control: A Selected Bibliography.* Monticello, Ill., April 1988.

Cawelti, John G. *The Second Amendment Myth and Meaning.* Washington, D.C., 2000.

———. *The Six-Gun Mystique.* 2d ed. Bowling Green, Ohio, 1984.

Centerwall, Brandon S. "Television Violence: The Scale of the Problem and Where to Go from Here." *Journal of the American Medical Association* 267 (Feb. 10, 1992): 3059–63.

Chadwin, Mark L. *The Hawks of World War II.* Chapel Hill, N.C., 1968.

Chambers, John W., II. *To Raise an Army: The Draft Comes to Modern America.* New York, 1987.

Chapel, Charles E. *Guns of the Old West.* New York, 1961.

Chenevix Trench, Charles P. *A History of Marksmanship.* London, 1972.

Childs, John. *The Army, James II, and the Glorious Revolution.* Manchester, Eng., 1980.

Christian, Charles. *A Brief Treatise on the Police of the City of New York.* New York, 1812.

Christoffel, Katherine K. "As American as Apple Pie: Guns in the Lives of US Children and Youth." *Pediatrician* 12 (1983–1985): 46–51.

Christoffel, Tom. "A Ban on Handguns: They Tried It and They Liked It." *Journal of Public Health Policy* 7, No. 3 (1986): 296–99.

Christoffel, Tom, and Stephen P. Teret. *Protecting the Public: Legal Issues in Injury Prevention.* New York, 1993.

Christopher, Maurine. "Guns, Congress, and the Networks." *The Nation*, Aug. 19, 1968, pp. 115–16.

Cigler, Allan J., and Burdett A. Loomis, eds. *Interest Group Politics*. 5th ed. Washington, D.C., 1998.

Cipolla, Carlo M. *Guns, Sails and Empires: Technological Innovation and the Early Phases of European Expansion, 1400–1700*. New York, 1965.

Clark, Ramsay. *Crime in America: Observations on Its Nature, Causes, and Control*. New York, 1970.

Clarke, James W. *American Assassins: The Darker Side of Politics*. Princeton, 1982.

Clifford, J. Garry, and Samuel R. Spencer Jr. *The First Peacetime Draft*. Lawrence, Kans., 1986.

Clifford, William. *Crime Control in Japan*. Lexington, Mass., 1976.

Coakley, Robert W. *The Role of Federal Military Forces in Domestic Disorders, 1789–1878*. Washington, D.C., 1988.

Coalition to Stop Gun Violence, Web site. <http://www.gunfree.org>.

Coates, James. *Armed and Dangerous: The Rise of the Survivalist Right*. New York, 1987.

Cochran, Hamilton. *Noted American Duels and Hostile Encounters*. Philadelphia, 1963.

Cock, Jacklyn. *Towards a Sociological Account of Light Weapons Proliferation in Southern Africa*. Johannesburg, 1995.

Cogan, Neil H. *The Complete Bill of Rights: The Drafts, Debates, Sources, and Origins*. New York, 1997.

Colvard, Karen. "Crime Is Down? Don't Confuse Us With the Facts." *HFG Review* 2 (fall 1997): 19–26.

"The Combat Zone: Once More into the Breach of Gun Control." *Playboy* 41 (May 1994): 43–46.

The Control of Firearms in Great Britain: A Consultative Document. Command 5297. Her Majesty's Stationery Office. London, May 1973.

Cook, Adrian. *The Armies of the Streets: The New York Draft Riots of 1863*. Lexington, Ken., 1974.

Cook, Philip J. "The Effect of Gun Availability on Violent Crime Patterns." *Annals of the Academy of Political and Social Science* 455 (May 1981): 63–79.

———, ed. "Gun Control," Special Edition. *Annals of the Academy of Political and Social Science* 455 (May 1981).

———. *Kids, Guns, and Public Policy*. Durham, N.C., 1996.

———. "Kids, Guns, and Public Policy." Symposium, *Law and Contemporary Problems* 59 (winter 1996).

Cook, Philip J., and Thomas B. Cole. "Strategic Thinking About Gun Markets and Violence." *Journal of the American Medical Association* 276 (June 12, 1996): 1765–7.

Cook, Philip J., and Jens Ludwig. *Guns in America: National Survey on Private Ownership and Use of Firearms*. National Institute of Justice. Washington, D.C., 1997.

Cook, Philip J., Jens Ludwig, and David Hemenway. "The Gun Debate's New Mythical Number: How Many Defensive Gun Uses Per Year?" *Journal of Policy Analysis and Management* 16 (summer 1997): 463–69.

Cook, Philip J., Stephanie Molliconi, and Thomas B. Cole. "Regulating Gun Markets." *Journal of Criminal Law and Criminology* 86 (fall 1995): 59–92.

Cook, Philip J., and Mark H. Moore. "Guns, Gun Control, and Homicide: A Review of Research and Public Policy." In Smith and Zahn, eds. *Homicide*, 277–96.

Cook, Philip J., and Daniel Nagin. *Does the Weapon Matter?* Washington, D.C., 1979.

Cooper, Cynthia A. *Violence on Television: Congressional Inquiry, Public Criticism and Industry Response*. Lanham, Md., 1996.

Cooper, Jerry. *The Rise of the National Guard: The Evolution of the American Militia, 1865–1920*. Lincoln, Nebr., 1997.

Cooper, Marc. "The N.R.A. Takes Cover in the G.O.P." *The Nation*, June 19, 1995, pp. 877–82.

Corcoran, James. *Bitter Harvest: Gordon Kahl and the Posse Comitatus: Murder in the Heartland*. New York, 1990.

Cordiner, Stephen, and Kathy Ettershank. "Gun Toting Australians Take Aim at New Weapons Control Law." *The Lancet*, June 8, 1996, p. 1616.

————. "Landmark Australian Gun Laws Finally Get Go-Ahead." *The Lancet*, Aug. 3, 1996, p. 327.

Cornell, Saul. "Aristocracy Assailed: The Ideology of Back Country Anti-Federalism." *Journal of American History* 76 (March 1990): 1148–72.

————. "Common Place or Anachronism: The Standard Model, the Second Amendment, and the Problem of History in Contemporary Constitutional Theory." *Constitutional Commentary* 16 (summer 1999): 221–46.

————. *The Other Founders: Anti-Federalism and the Dissenting Tradition in America, 1788–1828.* Chapel Hill, N.C., 1999.

Cornell, Saul, ed. *Whose Right to Bear Arms Did the Second Amendment Protect?* Boston, 2000.

Corrigan, Richard. "NRA, Using Members, Ads and Money, Hits Police Line in Lobbying Drive." *National Journal* 18 (Jan. 4, 1986): 8–14.

Cortner, Richard C. *The Supreme Court and the Second Bill of Rights: The Fourteenth Amendment and the Nationalization of Civil Liberties.* Madison, Wis., 1981.

Cottrol, Robert J. "The Second Amendment: Toward an Afro-Americanist Reconsideration." *Georgetown Law Journal* 80 (Dec. 1991): 309–61.

————, ed. *Gun Control and the Constitution: Sources and Explorations on the Second Amendment.* 4 vols. New York, 1993–1994.

Cottrol, Robert J., and Raymond T. Diamond. "Public Safety and the Right to Bear Arms." In Bodenhamer, ed. *Bill of Rights*, 72–86.

Courtwright, David T. *Violent Land: Single Men and Social Disorder from the Frontier to the Inner City.* Cambridge, Mass., 1996.

Covey, Preston K. "The 'Sporting Purpose' Issue in Gun-Control Policy." *Journal on Firearms and Public Policy* 6 (fall 1994): 55–67.

Cozic, Charles P., and Carol Wekesser, eds. *Gun Control.* San Diego, 1992.

Cramer, Clayton E. *Concealed Weapon Laws of the Early Republic: Dueling, Southern Violence, and Moral Reform.* Westport, Conn., 1999.

————. *For the Defense of Themselves and the State: Original Intent and Judicial Interpretation of the Right to Keep and Bear Arms.* Westport, Conn., 1994.

Cramer, Clayton E., and David B. Kopel. " 'Shall Issue': The New Wave of Concealed Handgun Permit Laws." *Tennessee Law Review* 62 (spring 1995): 679–757.

Crane, Robert C. "Can We Stop the Anti-Gun Cranks?" *Field and Stream* 64 (Jan. 1960): 25, 73–5, 95.

Crane, Verner W. *The Southern Frontier, 1670–1732.* Durham, N.C., 1928.

"The Crawfisher" (editorial). *The Nation*, Oct. 26, 1970, pp. 387–88.

Cress, Lawrence D. "An Armed Community: The Origins and Meaning of the Right to Bear Arms." *Journal of American History* 71 (June 1984): 22–42.

————. *Citizens in Arms: The Army and the Militia in American Society to the War of 1812.* Chapel Hill, N.C., 1982.

————. "A Well-Regulated Militia: The Origins and Meaning of the Second Amendment." In Kukla, ed. *Bill of Rights*, 55–66.

Cress, Lawrence D., and Robert E. Shalhope. "The Second Amendment and the Right to Bear Arms: An Exchange." *Journal of American History* 71 (Dec. 1984): 587–93.

Critchley, T. A. *The Conquest of Violence: Order and Liberty in Britain.* London, York, 1970.

————. *A History of Police in England and Wales, 900–1966.* London, 1967.

Cross, Coy F., II. *Justin Smith Morrill: Father of the Land-Grant Colleges.* East Lansing, Mich., 1999.

Crunden, Robert M. *Ministers of Reform: The Progressives' Achievement in American Civilization, 1899–1920.* New York, 1982.

Culberson, William C. *Vigilantism: Political History of Private Power in America.* New York, 1990.

Cummings, Homer S. *Selected Papers of Homer Cummings, Attorney General of the United States, 1933–1939.* Ed. Carl B. Swisher. New York, 1939.

Cunliffe, Marcus. *Soldiers and Civilians: The Martial Spirit in America, 1775–1865.* Boston, 1968.

Cunningham, Eugene. *Triggernometry: A Gallery of Gunfighters.* Caldwell, Idaho, 1941.

Cupps, Don S. "Bullets, Ballots, and Politics: The National Rifle Association Fights Gun Control." Ph.D. diss., Princeton University, 1969.

———. "Evading Gun Control." *New Republic*, May 3, 1969, pp. 16–18.

Current, Richard N. *Those Terrible Carpetbaggers*. New York, 1988.

Curtis, Lynn A., ed. *American Violence and Public Policy: An Update of the National Commission on the Causes and Prevention of Violence*. New Haven, 1985.

Curtis, Michael K. *No State Shall Abridge: The Fourteenth Amendment and the Bill of Rights*. Durham, N.C., 1986.

Dabney, T. G. "Carrying Pistols." *Nation*, Aug. 22, 1907, pp. 161–62.

Dahl, Dick "The NRA Sees Room to Grow as Faithful Adjunct to the GOP." *Nation*, Nov. 4, 2002: pp. 16–19.

Dallek, Robert. *Flawed Giant: Lyndon Johnson and His Times, 1961–1973*. New York, 1988.

Daly, Martin, and Margo Wilson. "The Biology of Violence." *New Yorker*, March 13, 1995, pp. 68–77.

Davidson, Bill R. *To Keep and Bear Arms*. New Rochelle, N.Y., 1969.

Davidson, Osha Gray. *Under Fire: The NRA and the Battle for Gun Control*. Rev. ed. New York, 1998.

Davies, Patrick S. "Saturday Night Specials: A 'Special' Exception in Strict Liability Laws." *Notre Dame Law Review* 61 (June 1986): 478–94.

Davis, William W. H. *The Fries Rebellion, 1798–99*. 1899. Reprint, Doylestown, Pa., 1969.

Deakin, James. *The Lobbyists*. Washington, D.C., 1966.

DeConde, Alexander. *The Quasi-War: The Politics and Diplomacy of the Undeclared War with France, 1797–1801*. New York, 1966.

Dees, Morris, and James Corcoran. *Gathering Storm: America's Militia Threat*. New York, 1996.

Defensor, H. Charles. *Gun Registration Now—Confiscation Later?* New York, 1970.

DeFrances, Carol J., and Steven K. Smith. "Federal-State Relations in Gun Control: The 1993 Brady Handgun Violence Prevention Act." *Publius* 24 (summer 1994): 69–82.

Denning, Brannon P. "Gun Shy: The Second Amendment as an 'Underenforced Constitutional Norm.'" *Harvard Journal of Law and Public Policy* 21 (summer 1998): 719–91.

Dennis, Anthony J. "Clearing the Smoke from the Right to Bear Arms and the Second Amendment." *Akron Law Review* 29 (summer 1995): 57–92.

Derthick, Martha. *The National Guard in Politics*. Cambridge, Mass., 1965.

Deutch, Stewart J., and Francis B. Alt. "The Effect of Massachusetts' Gun Control Law on Gun-Related Crimes in the City of Boston." *Evaluation Quarterly* 1 (Nov. 1977): 543–69.

Deyrup, Felicia J. *Arms Makers of the Connecticut Valley: A Regional Study of the Economic Development of the Small Arms Industry, 1789–1870*. Northampton, Mass., 1948.

DeZee, Matthew R. "Gun Control Legislation: Impact and Ideology." *Law and Policy Quarterly* 5 (July 1983): 367–79.

Dezhbakhsh, Hashem, and Paul H. Rubin. "Lives Saved or Lives Lost: The Effects of Concealed Handgun Laws on Crime." *American Economic Review* 88 (May 1988): 468–73.

Dhanapala, Jayantha, and others, eds. *Small Arms Control: Old Weapons, New Issues*. Aldershot, Eng., 1999.

Diamond, Jared. *Guns, Germs, and Steel: The Fates of Human Societies*. New York, 1988.

Diaz, Tom. *Making a Killing in America: The Business of Guns in America*. New York, 1999.

DiCanio, Margaret. *The Encyclopedia of Violence: Origins, Attitudes, Consequences*. New York, 1993.

Dick, Everett. *The Dixie Frontier: A Social History of the Southern Frontier from the First Transmontane Beginnings to the Civil War*. New York, 1948.

Dickenson, Mollie. *Thumbs Up: The Life and Courageous Comeback of White House Press Secretary Jim Brady*. New York, 1987.

Diener, Edward, and Kenneth W. Kerber. "Personality Characteristics of American Gun Owners." *Journal of Social Psychology* 107 (April 1979): 227–38.

Dixon, Jo, and Alan J. Lizotte. "Gun Ownership and the 'Southern Subculture of Violence.' " *American Journal of Sociology* 93 (Sept. 2, 1987): 383–405.

Dizard, Jan E., Robert M. Muth, and Stephen P. Andrews Jr., eds. *Guns in America: A Reader.* New York, 1999.

Dolan, Edward F., and Margaret M. Scariano. *Guns in the United States.* New York, 1994.

Dolan, Paul. "The Rise of Crime in the Period 1830–1860." *Journal of Criminal Law and Criminology* 30 (May–June 1939): 857–64.

Dolmén, Lars, ed. *Crime Trends in Sweden 1988.* Stockholm, 1990.

Donnerstein, Edward. "Mass Media Violence: Thoughts on the Debate." *Hofstra Law Review* 22 (1994): 827–32.

Dowlut, Robert. "The Right to Arms: Does the Constitution or the Predilection of Judges Reign?" *Oklahoma Law Review* 36 (1983): 65–105.

Drago, Harry S. *The Great Range Wars: Violence on the Grasslands.* New York, 1970.

Draper, Thomas, ed. *The Issue of Gun Control.* New York, 1981.

Drew, Elizabeth. *Showdown: The Struggle Between the Gingrich Congress and the Clinton White House.* New York, 1996.

———. *Whatever It Takes: The Real Struggle for Political Power in America.* New York, 1997.

Dreyfuss, Robert. "Good Morning Gun Lobby!" *Mother Jones* 21 (July/Aug. 1996): 38–47.

———. "Political Snipers: How the NRA Exploited Loopholes and Waged a Stealth Campaign against the Democrats." *American Prospect* 23 (fall 1995): 28–36.

Drinan, Robert F. "Gun Control: The Good Outweighs the Evil." *Civil Liberties Review* 3 (Aug.–Sept. 1976): 44–59.

Dumbauld, Edward. *The Bill of Rights: And What It Means Today.* Norman, Okla., 1957.

Dunlap, Charles J., Jr. "Revolt of the Masses: Armed Civilians and the Insurrectionary Theory of the Second Amendment." *Tennessee Law Review* 62 (spring 1995): 643–77.

Dupuy, R. Ernest. *The National Guard: A Compact History.* New York, 1971.

Dupuy, Trevor N. *The Evolution of Weapons and Warfare.* Indianapolis, 1980.

Dykstra, Robert R. *The Cattle Towns.* New York, 1968.

———. "The Last Days of 'Texan' Abilene: A Study in Community Conflict on the Farmer's Frontier." *Agricultural History* 34 (Oct. 1960): 107–19.

Easterbrook, Gregg. "America's Poll." *USA Weekend,* July 2–4, 1999, pp. 6–8.

Easton, Robert. "Guns of the American West." In Monaghan, ed. *Book of West,* 377–426.

Edel, Wilbur. *Gun Control: Threat to Liberty or Defense Against Anarchy?* Westport, Conn., 1995.

Edwards, James E. *Myths About Guns.* Coral Springs, Fla., 1978.

Edwards, William B. *Civil War Guns: The Complete Story of Federal and Confederate Small Arms. . . .* Harrisburg, Pa., 1962.

———. *The Story of Colt's Revolver: The Biography of Col. Samuel Colt.* Harrisburg, Pa., 1953.

Ehrenreich, Barbara. *Blood Rites: Origins and History of the Passions of War.* New York, 1997.

Ehrman, Keith A., and Dennis A. Henigan. "The Second Amendment in the Twentieth Century: Have You Seen Your Militia Lately?" *University of Dayton Law Review* 15 (1989): 5–58.

Eisenhower, Dwight D. *The White House Years, 1953–1956: Mandate for Change.* New York, 1963.

Ekirch, Arthur A. *The Civilian and the Military.* New York, 1965.

———. *Progressivism in America: A Study of the Era from Theodore Roosevelt to Woodrow Wilson.* New York, 1974.

Elliot, Jonathan, ed. *Debates in the Several State Conventions on the Adoption of the Federal Constitution.* 5 vols. 2d ed. 1888. Reprint, Washington, D.C., 1965.

Ellis, Edward R., and George N. Allen. *Traitor Within: Our Suicide Problem.* Garden City, N.Y., 1961.

Ellis, John. *The Social History of the Machine Gun.* New York, 1975.

Elman, Robert. *Badmen of the West.* Secaucus, N.J., 1974.

———. *Fired in Anger: The Personal Handguns of American Heroes and Villains.* New York, 1968.

Emery, Lucilius A. "The Constitutional Right to Bear Arms." *Harvard Law Review* 28 (March 1915): 473–77.

Emsley, Clive. *The English Police: A Political and Social History*. 2d ed. London, 1996.

Engdahl, David E. "Soldiers, Riots, and Revolution: The Law and History of Military Troops in Civil Disorders." *Iowa Law Review* 57 (Oct. 1971): 1–73.

Engelbrecht, Helmuth C. *"One Hell of a Business."* New York, 1934.

Engelbrecht, Helmuth C., and F. C. Hanighen. *Merchants of Death: A Study of the International Armament Industry*. New York, 1934.

Epstein, Fred. "California Sticks to Its Guns." *Rolling Stone*, Feb. 17, 1983, pp. 19–21.

Epstein, Julian. "Evolving Spheres of Federalism after *U.S. v. Lopez* and Other Cases." *Harvard Journal on Legislation* 34 (summer 1997): 525–55.

Erk, H. DeWitt. "Are You a Gun-Shy Parent?" *Parents' Magazine* 27 (Aug. 1942): 31, 64.

Erlanger, Howard S. "Is There a 'Subculture of Violence' in the South?" *Journal of Criminal Law and Criminology* 66 (Dec. 1975): 483–90.

Eron, Leonard D., and others. *Reason to Hope: A Psychosocial Perspective on Violence and Youth*. Washington, D.C., 1994.

Erskine, Hazel. "The Polls: Gun Control." *Public Opinion Quarterly* 36 (fall 1972): 455–69.

Esler, Gavin. *The United States of Anger: The People and the American Dream*. London, 1997.

Ethington, Philip J. "Vigilantes and the Police: The Creation of a Professional Police Bureaucracy in San Francisco, 1847–1900." *Journal of Social History* 21 (winter 1987): 197–227.

Etzioni, Amitai. "Gun Control: A Vanilla Agenda." *Responsive Community* 1 (summer 1991): 6–10.

———, ed. *Rights and the Common Good: The Communitarian Perspective*. New York, 1995.

Euloge, Georges-André. *Histoire de la Police et de la Gendarmerie: Des Origines à 1940*. Paris, 1985.

Fairchild, Erika. *Comparative Criminal Justice Systems*. Belmont, Calif., 1993.

Fairman, Charles, and Stanley Morrison. *The Fourteenth Amendment and the Bill of Rights: The Incorporation Theory*. New York, 1970. Reprint of 1949 articles in the *Stanford Law Review*.

Farnham, Alan. "Inside the U.S. Gun Business." *Fortune*, June 3, 1991, pp. 191–4.

Farrand, Max. *The Framing of the Constitution of the United States*. New Haven, 1913.

———, ed. *The Records of the Federal Convention of 1787*. 3 vols. New Haven, 1911.

Faulk, Odie B. *Dodge City: The Most Western Town of All*. New York, 1977.

Feldberg, Michael. *The Philadelphia Riots of 1844: A Study of Ethnic Conflict*. Westport, Conn., 1975.

Feller, Peter B., and Karl L. Gotting. "The Second Amendment: A Second Look." *Northwestern University Law Review* 61 (March–Apr. 1966): 46–70.

Feltz, Donald E. "Speaking Out: Boobs in the Woods." *Saturday Evening Post*, Oct. 13, 1962, pp. 8–11.

Field, Mervin D. *The Field Poll* [formerly the *California Poll*]. San Francisco, 1947–2000, selected vols.

Filler, Louis. *Muckraking and Progressivism in the American Tradition*. New Brunswick, N.J., 1996.

"Films Go Gun-Happy and a Great Fighter Offers Some Advice." *Life*, July 2, 1956, pp. 28–9.

Fine, J. David. *Firearms Laws in Australia*. North Ryde, Australia, 1985.

Finkelman, Paul. "James Madison and the Bill of Rights: A Reluctant Paternity." *The Supreme Court Review 1990* (Chicago, 1991), 301–47.

Finnegan, John P. *Against the Specter of the Dragon: The Campaign for American Military Preparedness, 1914–1917*. Westport, Conn., 1974.

———. "Military Preparedness in the Progressive Era, 1911–1917." Ph.D. diss., University of Wisconsin, 1969.

Fischer, David H. *Albion's Seed: Four British Folkways in America*. New York, 1989.

Fisher, Jim. *The Lindbergh Case*. New Brunswick, N.J., 1987.

Fisher, Sydney G. *A Philadelphia Perspective: The Diary of Sidney George Fisher Covering the Years 1834–1871*. Ed. Nicholas B. Wainwright. Philadelphia, 1967.

Fisher, Vardis, and Opal L. Holmes. *Gold Rushes and Mining Camps of the Early American West*. Caldwell, Ida., 1968.

Fishwick, Marshall W. "The Cowboy: America's Contribution to the World's Mythology." *Western Folklore* 11 (1952): 77–92.

Fleming, Walter L., ed. *Documentary History of Reconstruction: Political, Military, Social, Educational, and Industrial, 1865 to 1906.* 2 vols. 1906–7. Reprint, New York, 1966.

Fletcher, George P. *A Crime of Self-Defense: Bernhard Goetz and the Law on Trial.* New York, 1988.

Flynn, George Q. *The Draft, 1940–1973.* Lawrence, Kans., 1993.

Fogelson, Robert M. *America's Armories: Architecture, Society, and Public Order.* Cambridge, Mass., 1989.

———. *Big-City Police.* Cambridge, Mass., 1977.

Foley, Vernon. "Leonardo and the Invention of the Wheellock." *Scientific American* 278 (Jan. 1998): 96–101.

Foner, Eric. *Reconstruction: America's Unfinished Revolution, 1863–1877.* New York, 1988.

———. *The Story of American Freedom.* New York, 1998.

Forrest, Earle R. *Arizona's Dark and Bloody Ground.* Tucson, Ariz., 1979.

Fosdick, Raymond B. *American Police Systems.* New York, 1921.

"Four Years of the Carter Administration: An Affront to the Rights of Gun Owners" (editorial). *American Rifleman* 128 (Oct. 1980): 59.

Frankfurter, Felix. "Memorandum on 'Incorporation' of the Bill of Rights into the Due Process Clause of the Fourteenth Amendment." *Harvard Law Review* 78 (Feb. 1965): 746–83.

Franklin, John Hope. *The Militant South, 1800–1861.* Cambridge, Mass., 1956.

Frantz, Joe B. "The Frontier Tradition: An Invitation to Violence." In Graham and Gurr, eds. *Violence in America,* 127–54.

Frantz, Joe B., and Julian E. Choate Jr. *The American Cowboy, the Myth, and the Reality.* Norman, Okla., 1955.

Freedman, Warren. *The Privilege to Keep and Bear Arms: The Second Amendment and Its Interpretation.* New York, 1989.

Freibrun, Eric S. "Banning Handguns: *Quilici v. Village of Morton Grove* and the Second Amendment." *Washington University Law Quarterly* 60 (fall 1982): 1087–1118.

Frevert, Ute. *Men of Honour: A Social and Cultural History of the Duel.* Trans. from German by Anthony Williams. Cambridge, Eng., 1995.

Friedman, Lawrence M. *Crime and Punishment in American History.* New York, 1993.

Fries, Russell I. "British Response to the American System: The Case of the Small Arms Industry After 1850." *Technology and Culture* 16 (July 1975): 377–403.

———. "A Comparative Study of the British and American Arms Industries, 1790–1890." Ph.D. diss., Johns Hopkins University, 1972.

Fuller, Claud E., and Richard D. Steuart. *Firearms of the Confederacy: The Shoulder Arms, Pistols and Revolvers of the Confederate Soldier.* Huntington, W.Va., 1944.

Gaffney, Edward M., Jr. "The Waco Tragedy: Constitutional Concerns and Policy Perspectives." In Wright, ed. *Armageddon in Waco,* 323–58.

Gallup, George H. *The Gallup Poll: Public Opinion 1935–1971.* 3 vols. New York, 1972, and selected volumes of subsequent polls.

Galvin, John R. *The Minute Men: A Compact History of the Defenders of the American Colonies, 1645–1775.* New York, 1967.

Gamba, Virginia. *Society Under Siege: Licit Responses to Illicit Arms.* Midrand, S. Africa, 1998.

Gard, Wayne. *Frontier Justice.* Norman, Okla., 1949.

Garner, Anne, and Michael Clancy. *Firearms Statutes in the United States.* Washington, D.C., 1979.

Gazori, James K. *Firearms in America: The Costs and Benefits Associated with the Private Citizen Ownership of Firearms.* Washington, D.C., 1987, n.p.

Geary, James W. *We Need Men: The Union Draft in the Civil War.* DeKalb, Ill., 1991.

Geehern, Christopher. "Arms and the Man." *New England Business* 12 (Aug. 1990): 24–9, 63.

Geisel, Martin S., Richard Roll, and Stanton Wettick Jr. "The Effectiveness of State and Local Regulation of Handguns: A Statistical Analysis." *Duke Law Journal* Vol. 1969 (Aug. 1969): 647–76.

Gendreau, Paul, and C. Thomas Surridge. "Controlling Gun Crimes: The Jamaican Experience." *International Journal of Criminology and Penology* 6 (Feb. 1978): 43–60.

Gettleman, Marvin E. *The Dorr Rebellion: A Study in American Radicalism: 1833–1849.* New York, 1973.

Gibbs, Nancy. "The Littleton Massacre." *Time,* May 3, 1999, pp. 25–36.

Gibson, James W. *Warrior Dreams: Paramilitary Culture in Post-Vietnam America.* New York, 1994.

Gilbert, Dennis A. *Compendium of American Public Opinion.* New York, 1988.

Gilje, Paul A. *Rioting in America.* Bloomington, Ind., 1996.

———. *The Road to Mobocracy: Popular Disorder in New York City, 1763–1834.* Chapel Hill, N.C., 1987.

Gilligan, James. *Violence: Our Deadly Epidemic and Its Causes.* New York, 1997.

Gilmore, Russell S. "Crackshots and Patriots: The National Rifle Association and America's Military-Sporting Tradition, 1871–1929." Ph.D. diss., University of Wisconsin, 1974.

Gilmour, Ian. *Riot, Risings and Revolution: Governance and Violence in Eighteenth-Century England.* London, 1992.

Gladstone, Thomas H. *The Englishman in Kansas: Or Squatter Life and Border Warfare.* New York, 1857.

Glaeser, Edward, and Spencer Glendon. "Who Owns Guns? Criminals, Victims, and the Culture of Violence." *American Economic Review* 88 (May 1988): 458–67.

Glick, Susan. *Concealing the Risk: Real-World Effects of Lax Concealed Weapons Laws.* Washington, D.C., 1996.

———. *Female Persuasion. A Study of How the Firearms Industry Markets to Women and the Reality of Women and Guns.* Washington, D.C., 1994.

Glick, Susan, and Josh Sugarmann. *Joe Camel With Feathers: How the NRA with Gun and Tobacco Industry Dollars Uses Its Eddie Eagle Program to Market Guns to Kids.* Washington, D.C., Nov. 1997.

———. "Why Johnny Can Shoot." *Mother Jones* 20 (Jan.–Feb. 1995): 15.

"Glory of Guns: Gun Magazines Campaign Against Legal Control of Gun Sales." *Time,* Aug. 25, 1967, pp. 62–3.

Gluckman, Arcadi. *United States Martial Pistols and Revolvers.* Harrisburg, Pa., 1956.

Goldfarb, Ronald. "Domestic Disarmament: It's Time to Take a Second Look at the Second Amendment." *Washington Post,* Nov. 21, 1993, p. C3.

Goldring, Natalie J. "The NRA Goes Global." *Bulletin of the Atomic Scientists* 55 (Jan.–Feb. 1999): 61–5.

Goldsmith, Marsha F. "Epidemiologists Aim at New Target: Health Risk of Handgun Proliferation." *Journal of the American Medical Association* 261 (Feb. 3, 1989): 675–6.

Good, Paul. "Blam! Blam! Blam! Not Gun Nuts But Pistol Enthusiasts." *New York Times Magazine,* Sept. 17, 1972, pp. 28–9, 32–43, 46–9.

Gorn, Elliott J. " 'Good-Bye Boys, I Die a True American': Homicide, Nativism, and Working-Class Culture in Antebellum New York City." *Journal of American History* 74 (Sept. 1987): 388–410.

Gottlieb, Alan M. *The Gun Grabbers.* Bellevue, Wash., 1986.

———. *The Gun Owner's Political Action Manual.* Ottawa, Ill., 1976.

——— *The Rights of Gun Owners.* Aurora, Ill., 1981.

Graham, Fred P. "A Contemporary History of American Crime." In Graham and Gurr, eds. *Violence in America,* 485–504.

Graham, Hugh D., and Ted R. Gurr, eds. *The History of Violence in America: Historical and Comparative Perspectives* (report submitted to the National Commission on the Causes and Prevention of Violence). New York, 1969.

Green, Gary S. "Citizen Gun Ownership and Criminal Deterrence: Theory, Research, and Policy." *Criminology* 25 (Feb. 1987): 63–81.

Greenberg, Douglas. "Crime, Law Enforcement, and Social Control in Colonial America." *American Journal of Legal History* 26 (Oct. 1982): 293–325.

Greener, William W. *The Gun and Its Development.* London, 1881.

Greenfeld, Lawrence A., and Marianne W. Zawitz. *Weapons Offenses and Offenders: Firearms, Crime, and Criminal Justice.* U.S. Dept. of Justice. Washington, D.C., Nov. 1996.

Greenwood, Colin. *Firearms Control: A Study of Armed Crime and Firearms Control in England and Wales.* London, 1972.

Grey, Hugh, and Ross McCluskey, eds. *Field and Stream Treasury.* New York, 1955.

Grimstead, David. "Rioting in Its Jacksonian Setting." *American Historical Review* 77 (Apr. 1972): 361–97.

Gross, Robert A., ed. *In Debt to Shays: The Bicentennial of an Agrarian Rebellion.* Charlottesville, Va., 1993.

Grossman, David. *On Killing: The Psychological Cost of Learning to Kill in War and Society.* Boston, 1995.

Grossman, David, and Gloria DeGaetano. *Stop Teaching Our Kids to Kill: A Call to Action Against TV, Movie, and Video Game Violence.* New York, 1999.

"Gun Control," Special Issue. *Law and Contemporary Problems* 40 (winter 1968).

"Gun Control: Melodrama, Farce and Tragedy" (editorial). *Christian Century,* June 26, 1968, pp. 831–2.

"The Gun Law, A Step Toward Sanity." *Life,* May 10, 1968, p. 4.

"The Gun Under Fire." *Time,* June 21, 1968, pp. 13–18.

Guns and Ammo magazine staff. *Guns and Gunfighters.* New York, 1982.

Gurr, Ted R., ed. *Violence in America.* 2 vols. Newbury Park, Calif., 1989.

Gurr, Ted R., and others. *Rogues, Rebels, and Reformers: A Political History of Urban Crime and Conflict.* Beverly Hills, 1976.

Guthman, William H. *March to Massacre: A History of the First Seven Years of the United States Army, 1784–1791.* New York, 1975.

Hackney, Sheldon. "Southern Violence." *American Historical Review* 74 (Feb. 1969): 906–25.

Halbrook, Stephen P. "Congress Interprets the Second Amendment: Declarations by a Co-Equal Branch on the Individual Right to Keep and Bear Arms." *Tennessee Law Review* 62 (spring 1995): 597–641.

———. *Freedmen, the Fourteenth Amendment, and the Right to Bear Arms, 1866–1876.* Westport, Conn., 1998.

———. *A Right to Bear Arms: State and Federal Bills of Rights and Constitutional Guarantees.* New York, 1989.

———. *That Every Man Be Armed: The Evolution of a Constitutional Right.* Albuquerque, N.M., 1984.

———. "Tort Liability for the Manufacture, Sale, and Ownership of Handguns?" *Hamline Law Review* 6 (July 1983): 351–80.

———. "What the Framers Intended: A Linguistic Analysis of the Right to 'Bear Arms.' " *Law and Contemporary Problems* 49 (1983): 151–62.

Haller, Mark H. "Bootlegging: The Business and Politics of Violence." In Gurr, ed. *Violence in America* I: 146–62.

Halpern, Thomas, and Brian Levin. *The Limits of Dissent: The Constitutional Status of Armed Civilian Militias.* Amherst, Mass., 1996.

Halsey, Ashley, Jr. "Murder Weapons for Sale." *Saturday Evening Post,* Feb. 8, 1958, pp. 17, 100.

Hamilton, Alexander, James Madison, and John Jay. *The Federalist.* Ed. Jacob E. Cooke. Middletown, Conn., 1961.

Handelman, Stephen. *Comrade Criminal: Russia's New Mafiya.* New Haven, 1995.

Handgun Control Inc., Web site. <http://www.handguncontrol.org>.

Handgun Control Inc. *Carrying Concealed Weapons: Questions and Answers.* Washington, D.C., 1995.

"Handgun Violence." *New Republic,* Feb. 17, 1973, p. 9.

"Handguns: Majority Supports Stiffer Handgun Laws." *The Gallup Report* 215 (Aug. 1983): 3–12.

"Handguns and Products Liability." *Harvard Law Review* 97 (June 1984): 1912–28.

Hands Without Guns, Web site. <http://www.handswithoutguns.org>.

Harding, Richard. *Firearms and Violence in Australian Life: An Examination of Gun Ownership and Use in Australia*. Nedlands, Australia, 1981.

Hardy, David T. *The BATF's War on Civil Liberties: The Assault on Gun Owners*. Bellevue, Wash., 1979.

———. *Origins and Development of the Second Amendment*. Southport, Conn., 1986.

———. "The Second Amendment and the Historiography of the Bill of Rights." *Journal of Law and Politics* 4 (1987): 1–62.

Hardy, Osgood. "The *Itata* Incident." *Hispanic American Historical Review* 5 (May 1922): 195–226.

Harrington, Michael J. "The Politics of Gun Control." *The Nation*, Jan. 12, 1974, pp. 41–5.

Louis Harris and Associates, Inc. *The Harris Survey Yearbook of Public Opinion: A Compendium of American Attitudes*. 4 vols. New York, 1971–1976.

Harris, Richard. "Annals of Legislation: If You Love Your Guns." *New Yorker*, April 20, 1968, pp. 56–155.

Harvard Law School, Gun Law Project. " 'And Nobody Can Get Out': The Impact of a Mandatory Prison Sentence for the Illegal Carrying of a Firearm on the Use of Firearms and on the Administration of Criminal Justice in Boston." Cambridge, Mass., July 14, 1976, n.p.

Hatch, Alden. *Remington Arms in American History*. New York, 1956.

Haven, Charles T., and Frank A. Belden. *A History of the Colt Revolver and Other Arms Made by Colt's Patent Firearms Manufacturing Company from 1836 to 1940*. New York, 1940.

Hay, Douglas. "Crime and Justice in Eighteenth- and Nineteenth-Century England." In *Crime and Justice*, ed. Norval Morris and Michael Tonry II, 45–84. Chicago, 1980.

Hays, Stuart R. "The Right to Bear Arms: A Study in Judicial Misinterpretation." *William and Mary Law Review* 2 (1959–1960): 381–406.

Heath, G. Louis. *Off the Pigs! The History and Literature of the Black Panther Party*. Metuchen, N.J., 1976.

Heim, David. "American Mayhem." *Christian Century*, June 13, 1998, pp. 563–4.

Heller, Scott. "The Right to Bear Arms: Some Prominent Legal Scholars Are Taking a New Look at the Second Amendment." *Chronicle of Higher Education*, July 21, 1995, pp. A8, A12.

Helm, Leslie. "Making a Killing." *Los Angeles Times*, Jan. 26, 1998, pp. D1–2.

Helmer, William J. *The Gun That Made the Twenties Roar*. New York, 1969.

Hemenway, David R. "Regulation of Firearms." *New England Journal of Medicine* 339 (Sept. 17, 1998): 843–45.

———. "Survey Research and Self-Defense Gun Use: An Explanation of Extreme Overestimates." *The Journal of Criminal Law and Criminology* 87 (summer 1997): 1430–45.

Hemenway, David, Sara J. Solnick, and Deborah R. Azrael. "Firearms and Community Feelings of Safety." *Journal of Criminal Law and Criminology* 86 (fall 1995): 121–32.

Henderson, Harry. *Gun Control*. New York, 2000.

Henigan, Dennis A. "Arms, Anarchy, and the Second Amendment." *Valparaiso University Law Review* 26 (1991): 107–29.

———. "Gun Manufacturers Should Be Held Responsible for Illegal Use of Guns." In Roleff, ed. *Guns and Crime*, 82–92.

Henigan, Dennis A., E. Bruce Nicholson, and David Hemenway. *Guns and the Constitution: The Myth of the Second Amendment Protection for Firearms in America*. Northampton, Mass., 1995.

Hening, William Waller. *The Statutes at Large: Being a Collection of All the Laws of Colonial Virginia*. Vols. 1 and 2. 1809–1823. Reprint, Wilmington, Del., 1978.

Herz, Andrew D. "Gun Crazy: Constitutional False Consciousness and Dereliction of Dialogic Responsibility." *Boston University Law Review* 75 (spring 1995): 57–153.

Hickey, Donald R. *The War of 1812: A Forgotten Conflict*. Chicago, 1989.

Hickok, Eugene W., Jr., ed. *The Bill of Rights: Original Meaning and Current Understanding*. Charlottesville, Va., 1991.

Higginbotham, Don. "The Federalized Militia Debate: A Neglected Aspect of Second Amendment Scholarship." *William and Mary Quarterly* 55 (Jan. 1998): 39–58.

————. "The Second Amendment in Historical Context." *Constitutional Commentary* 16 (summer 1999): 263–8.

————. *War and Society in Revolutionary America: The Wider Dimension of Conflict.* Columbia, S.C., 1988.

Hill, Jim Dan. *The Minute Man in Peace and War: A History of the National Guard.* Harrisburg, Pa., 1964.

Hirsch, Adam J. "The Collision of Military Cultures in Seventeenth-Century New England." *Journal of American History* 74 (March 1988): 1187–1212.

History of the Gun. Narr. Cliff Robertson. 4 vols. History Channel, 1996. Videocassette.

Hoffman, Frederick L. *The Homicide Problem.* Newark, N.J., 1925.

Hoffman, Ronald, and Peter J. Albert, eds. *Arms and Independence: The Military Character of the American Revolution.* Charlottesville, Va., 1984.

————. *The Bill of Rights: Government Proscribed.* Charlottesville, Va., 1997.

Hofstadter, Richard. "America as a Gun Culture." *American Heritage* 21 (Oct. 1970): 4–11, 82–85.

Hofstadter, Richard, and Michael Wallace, eds. *American Violence: A Documentary History.* New York, 1970.

Hogg, James S. *Addresses and State Papers of James Stephen Hogg.* Ed. Robert C. Cotner. Austin, Tex., 1951.

Holland, Barbara. "Bang! Bang! You're Dead." *Smithsonian* 27 (Oct. 1997): 122–33.

Holliday, J. S. *The World Rushed In: The California Gold Rush Experience.* New York, 1981.

Hollister, C. Warren. *Anglo-Saxon Military Institutions on the Eve of the Norman Conquest.* Oxford, Eng., 1962.

Hollon, W. Eugene. *Frontier Violence: Another Look.* New York, 1974.

Holloway, Carroll C. *Texas Gun Lore.* San Antonio, Tex., 1951.

Holmberg, Judith V., and Michael Clancy. *People vs Handguns: The Campaign to Ban Handguns in Massachusetts.* Washington, D.C., 1977.

Holmes, Fred L. "Making Criminals Out of Soldiers." *The Nation*, July 22, 1925, pp. 114–16.

Holmes, Joseph J. "The Decline of the Pennsylvania Militia, 1815–1870." *Western Pennsylvania Historical Magazine* 57 (Apr. 1974): 199–217.

Horan, James D. *The Authentic Wild West.* 3 vols. New York, 1976–1980.

Horne, Gerald. *Fire This Time: The Watts Uprising and the 1960s.* Charlottesville, Va., 1995.

Horsman, Reginald. *The War of 1812.* New York, 1969.

Hosley, William. *Colt: The Making of an American Legend.* Amherst, Mass., 1996.

Hough, Emerson. "The American Six-Shooter." *Outing Magazine* 54 (Nov. 1909): 503–10.

Hounshell, David A. *From the American System to Mass Production, 1800–1932: The Development of Manufacturing Technology in the United States.* Baltimore, 1984.

Howard, Robert A. "Interchangeable Parts Reexamined: The Private Sector of the American Arms Industry on the Eve of the Civil War." *Technology and Culture* 19 (Oct. 1978): 633–49.

Howe, Daniel W. *The Political Culture of the American Whigs.* Chicago, 1979.

Howe, Louis M. "Uncle Sam Starts After Crime." *Saturday Evening Post*, July 29, 1933, pp. 5–6, 71–2.

Howe, Walter J. *NRA Firearms and Ammunition Fact Book.* Washington, D.C., 1964.

Howison, Robert R. "Dueling in Virginia." *William and Mary Quarterly* 4 (Oct. 1924): 217–44.

Huesmann, L. Rowell, and Leonard D. Eron, eds. *Television and the Aggressive Child: A Cross-National Comparison.* Chicago, 1986.

Hunter, George. *How to Defend Yourself, Your Family, and Your Home: A Complete Guide to Self-Protection.* New York, 1967.

Imlay, Charles V. "The Uniform Firearms Act." *American Bar Association Journal* 12 (Dec. 1926): 767–9.

————. "Uniform Firearms Act Reaffirmed." *American Bar Association Journal* 17 (Dec. 1930): 799–801.

"Is the Pistol Responsible for Crime?" *Journal of the American Institute of Criminal Law and Criminology* 1 (May 1910–March 1911): 793–4.

"Is There a Right to Shoot?" (editorial). *Saturday Evening Post,* July 27, 1968, p. 8.

Jablow, Joseph. *The Cheyenne in Plains Indian Trade Relations, 1795–1840.* New York, 1950.

Jackson, Andrew. *Correspondence of Andrew Jackson.* Ed. John S. Bassett. 7 vols. Washington, D.C., 1926–1933.

Jackson, Maynard Holbrook, Jr. "Handgun Control: Constitutional and Critically Needed." *North Carolina Central Law Journal* 8 (1977): 189–98.

Jackson, Theron T. "Gun Control Programs—Past and Present." LL.M. thesis, University of Wisconsin Law School, 1997.

Jacobs, James B. *Can Gun Control Work?* New York, 2002.

———. "Exceptions to a General Prohibition on Handgun Possession: Do They Swallow Up the Rule?" *Law and Contemporary Problems* 49 (winter 1986): 5–34.

Jacobs, James B., and Kimberly A. Potter. "Keeping Guns Out of the 'Wrong' Hands: The Brady Law and the Limits of Regulation." *Journal of Criminal Law and Criminology* 86 (fall 1995): 93–120.

Jacobs, Wilbur R. *Dispossessing the American Indian: Indians and Whites on the Colonial Frontier.* New York, 1972.

Jensen, Merrill, ed. *The Documentary History of the Ratification of the Constitution.* Vol. 1. Madison, Wis., 1976.

Johannsen, Robert W. *To the Halls of the Montezumas: The Mexican War in the American Imagination.* New York, 1985.

Johns Hopkins Center for Gun Policy and Research. *1996 National Gun Policy Survey: Questionnaire with Weighted Frequencies.* Baltimore, 1997.

Johnson, David R. *American Law Enforcement: A History.* St. Louis, 1981.

———. *Policing the Urban Underworld: The Impact of Crime on the Development of the American Police, 1800–1887.* Philadelphia, 1979.

Johnson, Donald B., comp. *National Party Platforms, 1840–1976.* Rev. ed. 2 vols. Urbana, Ill., 1978.

———. *National Party Platforms of 1980.* Urbana, Ill., 1982.

Johnson, Eric A., and Eric H. Monkkonen, eds. *The Civilization of Crime: Violence in Town and Country since the Middle Ages.* Urbana, Ill., 1996.

Johnson, Lyndon B. "Agenda for the Future: A Presidential Perspective." *Britannica Book of the Year 1969.* Chicago, 1969, pp. 17–48.

Jones, Edward, III. "The District of Columbia's 'Firearms Control Regulations Act of 1975': The Toughest Handgun Control Law in the United States—Or Is It?" *Annals of the American Academy of Political and Social Science* 455 (May 1981): 138–49.

Jordan, Philip D. *Frontier Law and Order: Ten Essays.* Lincoln, Nebr., 1970.

———. "The Pistol Packin' Cowboy: From Bullet to Burial." *Red River Valley Historical Review* 2 (Sept. 1975): 65–91.

———. "The Town Marshal and the Police." In Billington, ed. *People of the Plains,* 101–19.

Jordan, Terry G. *North American Cattle-Ranching Frontiers.* Albuquerque, N.M., 1993.

Jordan, Terry G., and Matti Kaups. *The American Backwoods Frontier: An Ethnic and Ecological Interpretation.* Baltimore, 1989.

Josephy, Alvin M., Jr. *On the Hill: A History of the American Congress.* New York, 1979.

Josscrand, Michel H., and Jan A. Stevenson. *Pistols, Revolvers, and Ammunition.* New York, 1972.

Junas, Daniel. "Angry White Guys with Guns: Rise of the Militias." *Covert Action Quarterly* 52 (spring 1995): 20–25.

J. W. G. "Is the Pistol Responsible for Crime?" *Journal of the American Institute of Criminal Law and Criminology* 1 (Jan. 1911): 793–4.

Kachur, S. Patrick, and others. "School-Associated Violent Deaths in the United States, 1992 to 1994." *Journal of the American Medical Association* 276 (June 12, 1996): 1729–33.

Kalman, Laura. "Border Patrol: Reflections on the Turn to History in Legal Scholarship." *Fordham Law Review* 66 (Oct. 1997): 87–124.

———. *The Strange Career of Legal Liberalism.* New Haven, 1996.

Kane, Harnett T. *Gentlemen, Swords, and Pistols.* New York, 1951.

Kaplan, John. "The Wisdom of Gun Prohibition." *Annals of the American Academy of Political and Social Science* 455 (May 1981): 11–21.

Kaplan, Michael. "New York City Tavern Violence and the Creation of a Working-Class Male Identity." *Journal of the Early Republic* 15 (fall 1995): 591–617.

Kaplan, Robert D. "The Coming Anarchy: How Scarcity, Crime, Overpopulation, Tribalism, and Disease Are Rapidly Destroying the Social Fabric of Our Planet." *Atlantic Monthly* 273 (Feb. 1994): 44–76.

Kassirer, Jerome P. "Guns in the Household." *New England Journal of Medicine* 329 (Oct. 7, 1993): 1117–19.

Kates, Don B., Jr. "Firearms and Violence: Old Premises and Current Evidence." In Gurr, ed. *Violence in America* I: 197–215.

———. *Guns, Murders, and the Constitution: A Realistic Assessment of Gun Control*. San Francisco, 1990.

———. "Handgun Prohibition and the Original Meaning of the Second Amendment." *Michigan Law Review* 82 (1983): 204–73.

———. "The Second Amendment: A Dialogue." *Law and Contemporary Problems* 40 (1986): 143–50.

———. "The Second Amendment and the Ideology of Self-Preservation." *Constitutional Commentary* 9 (winter 1992): 87–104.

———. "The Second Amendment and States' Rights: A Thought Experiment." *William and Mary Law Review* 36 (Aug. 1995): 1737–67.

———. "Shot Down." *National Review*, March 6, 1995, pp. 49–54.

Kates, Don B., Jr., ed. *Firearms and Violence: Issues of Public Policy*. San Francisco, 1984.

———. *Restricting Handguns: The Liberal Skeptics Speak Out*. Croton-on-Hudson, N.Y., 1979.

Kates, Don B., Jr., and Gary Kleck, eds. *The Great American Gun Debate: Essays on Firearms and Violence*. San Francisco, 1997.

Kates, Don B., Jr., and others. "Guns and Public Health: Epidemic of Violence or Pandemic of Propaganda?" *Tennessee Law Review* 62 (spring 1995): 513–96.

Kauffman, Henry J. *The Pennsylvania-Kentucky Rifle*. New York, 1968.

Kawashima, Yasuhide. *Puritan Justice and the Indian: White Man's Law in Massachusetts, 1630–1763*. Middletown, Conn., 1986.

Kefauver, Estes. *Crime in America*. Garden City, N.Y., 1951.

Kellerman, Arthur L., and Donald T. Reay. "Protection or Peril? An Analysis of Firearm-Related Deaths in the Home." *New England Journal of Medicine* 329 (June 12, 1986): 1557–60.

Kellermann, Arthur L., and others. "The Epidemiological Basis for the Prevention of Firearm Injuries." *Annual Review of Public Health* 12 (Palo Alto, Calif., 1991): 17–40.

———. "Gun Ownership as a Risk Factor for Homicide in the Home." *New England Journal of Medicine* 329 (Oct. 7, 1993): 1084–91.

Kellerman, Arthur L., and Philip J. Cook. "Armed and Dangerous: Guns in American Homes." In Bellesiles, ed. *Lethal Imagination*, 424–39.

Kennedy, Robert F. *RFK: Collected Speeches*. Ed. Edwin O. Guthman and C. Richard Allen. New York, 1993.

Kennett, Lee B., and James L. Anderson. *The Gun in America: The Origins of a National Dilemma*. Westport, Conn., 1975.

Kerasote, Ted. *Bloodties: Nature, Culture, and the Hunt*. New York, 1993.

Kessler, Raymond G. "Gun Control and Political Power." *Law and Policy Quarterly* 5 (July 1983): 381–400.

Kiernan, V. G. *The Duel in European History: Honour and the Reign of Aristocracy*. Oxford, Eng., 1988.

Kilar, Jeremy W. "Great Lakes Lumber Towns and Frontier Violence: A Contemporary Study." *Journal of Forest History* 31 (April 1987): 71–85.

Killias, Martin. "Gun Ownership and Violent Crime: The Swiss Experience in International Perspective." *Security Journal* 1, No. 3 (1990): 169–74.

————. "International Correlations between Gun Ownership and Rates of Homicide and Suicide." *Canadian Medical Association Journal* 148 (May 15, 1993): 1721–25.

King, Wayne. "Target: The Gun Lobby." *New York Times Magazine*, Dec. 9, 1990, pp. 43–5, 76–84.

Kipling, Rudyard. *American Notes.* New York, n.d.

Kirby, Chester. "The English Game Law System." *American Historical Review* 38 (July 1933): 240–62.

Kirkham, James F., Sheldon G. Levy, and William J. Crotty. *Assassination and Political Violence: A Report to the National Commission on the Causes and Prevention of Violence.* New York, 1970.

Klare, Michael T. *American Arms Supermarket.* Austin, Tex., 1984.

————. "The Kalashnikov Age." *Bulletin of the Atomic Scientists* 55 (Jan.–Feb. 1999): 18–22.

Kleck, Gary. "Crime Control Through the Private Use of Armed Force." *Social Problems* 35 (Feb. 1988): 1–21.

————. *Point Blank: Guns and Violence in America.* New York, 1991.

————. *Targeting Guns: Firearms and Their Control.* New York, 1997, a revision of *Point Blank.*

Kleck, Gary, and Mark Gertz. "Armed Resistance to Crime: The Prevalence and Nature of Self-Defense with a Gun." *Journal of Criminal Law and Criminology* 86 (fall 1995): 150–87.

Kleck, Gary, and Don B. Kates. *Armed: New Perspectives on Gun Control.* Amherst, N.Y., 2001.

Kleck, Gary, and Karen McElrath. "The Effects of Weaponry on Human Violence." *Social Forces* 69 (March 1991): 669–92.

Klein, Rachel N. "Ordering the Backcountry: The South Carolina Regulation." *William and Mary Quarterly* 38 (Oct. 1981): 661–80.

Kluger, Richard. *Ashes to Ashes: America's Hundred-Year Cigarette War, the Public Health, and the Unabashed Triumph of Philip Morris.* New York, 1966.

Kohn, Richard H. *Eagle and Sword: The Federalists and the Creation of the Military Establishment in America, 1783–1802.* New York, 1975.

————, ed. *The United States Military under the Constitution of the United States, 1789–1989.* New York, 1991.

Kohn, Stephen M. *Jailed for Peace: The History of American Draft Law Violators, 1658–1985.* Westport, Conn., 1986.

Kopel, David B. *Gun Control in Great Britain: Saving Lives or Constricting Liberty?* Chicago, 1992.

———— "Guns in the Right Hands Make Society Safer." In Roleff, ed. *Guns and Crime,* 13–18.

————. *The Samurai, the Mountie, and the Cowboy: Should America Adopt the Gun Controls of Other Democracies?* Buffalo, N.Y. 1992.

————. "The Second Amendment in the Nineteenth Century." *Brigham Young University Law Review* 51 (1998): 1359–1545.

————, ed. *Guns: Who Should Have Them?* Amherst, N.Y., 1995.

Kopel, David B., and Paul H. Blackman. *No More Wacos: What's Wrong with Federal Law Enforcement and How to Fix It.* Amherst, N.Y., 1997.

Kopel, David B., and Christopher C. Little. "Communitarians, Neorepublicans, and Guns: Assessing the Case for Firearms Prohibition." *Maryland Law Review* 56 (1997): 438–554.

Kreidberg, Marvin A., and Merton G. Henry. *History of Military Mobilization in the United States Army, 1775–1945.* Washington, D.C., 1955.

Kriegel, Leonard. "A Loaded Question: What Is It About Americans and Guns?" *Harper's* 284 (May 1992): 45–51.

Kroes, Rob, ed. *The American West: As Seen by Europeans and Americans.* Amsterdam, 1989.

Krug, Alan S. *Does Firearms Registration Work? A Statistical Analysis of New York State and New York City Crime Data.* Riverside, Conn., 1968.

Krug, E. G., K. E. Powell, and L. L. Dahlberg. "Firearm-Related Deaths in the United States and 35 Other High- and Upper-Middle Income Countries." *International Journal of Epidemiology* 27, No. 2 (1998): 214–21.

Kruschke, Earl R. *Gun Control: A Reference Handbook.* Santa Barbara, Calif., 1995.

————. *The Right to Keep and Bear Arms: A Continuing American Dilemma.* Springfield, Ill., 1985.

Kukla, John, ed. *The Bill of Rights: A Lively Heritage.* Richmond, Va., 1987.

Kukla, Robert J. *Gun Control*. Harrisburg, Pa., 1973.

Kurtz, Lester, ed. *Encyclopedia of Violence, Peace, and Conflict*. 3 vols. San Diego, Calif., 1999.

Kvaraceus, William C. *The Community and the Delinquent*. Yonkers-on-Hudson, N.Y., 1954.

Lacey, Michael J., and Knud Haakonssen, eds. *A Culture of Rights: The Bill of Rights in Philosophy, Politics, and Law—1791 and 1991*. New York, 1991.

Lake, Peter A. "Shooting to Kill." *Esquire* 95 (Feb. 1981): 70–75.

Lamar, Howard R. *The Far Southwest, 1846–1912: A Territorial History*. New Haven, 1966.

Landau, Elaine. *Armed America: The Status of Gun Control*. Englewood Cliffs, N.J., 1991.

Lane, Roger. "Crime and Criminal Statistics in Nineteenth-Century Massachusetts." *Journal of Social History* 2 (winter 1968): 156–63.

———. *Murder in America: A History*. Columbus, Ohio, 1997.

———. "On the Social Meaning of Homicide Trends in America." In Gurr, ed. *Violence in America* I: 55–79.

———. *Policing the City: Boston, 1822–1885*. Cambridge, Mass., 1967.

———. "Urban Police and Crime in Nineteenth-Century America." In *Crime and Justice*, ed. Norval Morris and Michael Tonry, vol. 2: 1–43. Chicago, 1980.

———. *Violent Death in the City: Suicide, Accident, and Murder in Nineteenth-Century Philadelphia*. 2d ed. Columbus, Ohio, 1999.

Langbein, Laura I., and Mark A. Lotwis. "The Political Efficacy of Lobbying and Money: Gun Control in the U.S. House, 1986." *Legislative Studies Quarterly* 15 (Aug. 1990): 413–40.

LaPierre, Wayne R., Jr. *Guns, Crime, and Freedom*. Washington, D.C., 1994.

———. "The Final War Has Begun." *American Rifleman* 142 (June 1994): 51–9.

LaPierre, Wayne, and James Jay Baker. *Shooting Straight: Telling the Truth About Guns in America*. Washington, D.C., 2002.

Laqueur, Walter. *The New Terrorism: Fanaticism and the Arms of Mass-Destruction*. New York, 1999.

Larson, Erik. "The Story of a Gun." *Atlantic* 271 (Jan. 1993): 48–78.

———. "Squeezing Out the Bad Guys." *Time*, Aug. 9, 1999, pp. 32–6.

Larson, Gustive O. *The "Americanization" of Utah for Statehood*. San Marino, Calif., 1971.

Leddy, Edward F. *Magnum Force Lobby: The National Rifle Association Fights Gun Control*. Lanham, Md., 1987.

Le Fave, Donald G. "The Will to Arm: The National Rifle Association in American Society, 1871–1970." Ph.D. diss., University of Colorado, 1970.

Leff, Carol S., and Mark H. Leff. "The Politics of Ineffectiveness: Federal Gun Legislation, 1919–1938." *Annals of the American Academy of Political and Social Science* 455 (May 1981): 48–62.

Leibiger, Stuart. "James Madison and Amendments to the Constitution, 1787–1789: 'Parchment Barriers.'" *Journal of Southern History* 59 (Aug. 1993): 441–68.

Lenihan, John H. *Showdown: Confronting Modern America in the Western Film*. Urbana, Ill., 1980.

Leo, John. "The Coming Shootout Over Guns." *U.S. News and World Report*, Jan. 25, 1993, p. 27.

Leonard, John. *Smoke and Mirrors: Violence, Television, and Other American Cultures*. New York, 1997.

Leppard, David. *Fire and Blood: The True Story of David Koresh and the Waco Siege*. London, 1993.

Lessing, Lawrence. "Translating Federalism: United States v. Lopez." *Supreme Court Review* 5 (Chicago, 1995): 125–215.

Lester, David. *Gun Control: Issues and Answers*. Springfield, Ill., 1984.

Lester, David, and Mary Murrell. "The Influence of Gun Control Laws on Suicidal Behavior." *American Journal of Psychiatry* 137 (Jan. 1980): 121.

"Let's Take the Offensive" (editorial). *American Rifleman* 106 (Sept. 1958): 16.

Leuchtenburg, William E. *Franklin D. Roosevelt and the New Deal, 1932–1940*. New York, 1963.

Levin, Jack, and James A. Fox. *Mass Murder: America's Growing Menace*. New York, 1985.

Levin, John. "The Right to Bear Arms: The Development of the American Experience." *Chicago-Kent Law Review* 148 (1971): 148–67.

Levine, Peter. "The Fries Rebellion: Social Violence and the Politics of the New Nation." *Pennsylvania History* 15 (1973): 241–58.

Levine, Ronald B., and David B. Saxe. "The Second Amendment: The Right to Bear Arms." *Houston Law Review* 7 (Sept. 1969): 1–19.

Levinson, Sanford. "The Embarrassing Second Amendment." *Yale Law Review* 99 (Dec. 1989): 637–59.

Levinson, Sanford, and others. "To Keep and Bear Arms: An Exchange." *New York Review of Books*, Nov. 16, 1995, pp. 61–4.

Lévi-Strauss, Claude. *Myth and Meaning: Cracking the Code of Culture.* New York, 1995.

Levy, Leonard W. *Origins of the Bill of Rights.* New Haven, 1999.

Lewis, Charles, and the Center for Public Integrity. *The Buying of the Congress: How the Special Interests Have Stolen Your Right to Life, Liberty, and the Pursuit of Happiness.* New York, 1998.
———. *The Buying of the President.* New York, 1996.

Lexis-Nexis. *Academic Universe.* Selected documents on pertinent law cases.

Library of Congress. *Federal Regulation of Firearms: A Report.* Prepared for the use of the Committee on the Judiciary, U.S. Senate. Washington, D.C., 1982.
———. *Firearms Regulations in Various Foreign Countries.* Washington, D.C., 1990.
———. *Gun Control Laws in Foreign Countries.* Washington, D.C., 1981.

Lichtenberger, J. P., ed. "Modern Crime: Its Prevention and Punishment," Special Edition. *Annals of the Academy of Political and Social Science* 125 (May 1926).

Limerick, Patricia N. *The Legacy of Conquest: The Unbroken Past of the American West.* New York, 1987.

Limerick, Patricia N., Clyde A. Milner II, and Charles E. Rankin, eds. *Trails: Toward a New Western History.* Lawrence, Kans., 1991.

Linden, Laura. "Grassroots Gun Control." *California Lawyer* 17 (July 1997): 25–8.

Lindsay, John V. "Speaking Out: Too Many People Have Guns." *Saturday Evening Post*, Feb. 1, 1964, pp. 12–14.

Lindsay, Merrill. *The New England Gun: The First Hundred Years.* New Haven, 1975.
———. *One Hundred Great Guns: An Illustrated History of Firearms.* New York, 1967.

Link, Mary. "Candidates on the Issues: Gun Control." *Congressional Quarterly Weekly Report* 34 (April 3, 1976): 791.

Lipset, Seymour M. *American Exceptionalism: A Double-Edged Sword.* New York, 1996.

Little, Craig B., and Christopher P. Sheffield. "Frontiers and Criminal Justice: English Private Prosecution Societies and American Vigilantism in the Eighteenth and Nineteenth Centuries." *American Sociological Review* 48 (Dec. 1883): 796–808.

Lofgren, Charles A. "Compulsory Military Service under the Constitution: The Original Understanding." *William and Mary Quarterly* 33 (Jan. 1976): 61–88.

Loftin, Colin, and David McDowell. "The Deterrent Effects of the Florida Felony Firearm Law." *Journal of Criminal Law and Criminology* 75 (spring 1984): 250–59.

Loftin, Colin, David McDowell, and James Boudouris. "Economic Change and Homicide in Detroit, 1926–1979." In Gurr, ed. *Violence in America* I: 163–77.

Loftin, Colin, and others. "Effects of Restrictive Licensing of Handguns on Homicides and Suicide in the District of Columbia." *New England Journal of Medicine* 325, No. 23 (Dec. 5, 1991): 1615–20.

Long, Robert E., ed. *Gun Control.* New York, 1989.

Los Angeles *Times* Staff. *Understanding the Riots.* Los Angeles, 1992.

Lott, John R., Jr. *More Guns, Less Crime: Understanding Crime and Gun-Control Laws.* Chicago, 1998.

Lott, John R., Jr., and David B. Mustard. "Crime, Deterrence, and Right-to-Carry Concealed Handguns." *Journal of Legal Studies* 26 (Jan. 1997): 1–68.

Lovejoy, Owen R. *Better Child Labor Laws* (pamphlet). New York, Sept. 1911.

Loving, Nancy, and others. *Organizing for Handgun Control: A Citizen's Manual.* Washington, D.C., 1977.

Lowenthal, Max. *The Federal Bureau of Investigation.* New York, 1950.

Luke, Brian. "The Second Amendment, Political Liberty, and the Right to Self-Preservation." *Alabama Law Review* 39 (1987): 103–30.

———. "Violent Love: Hunting, Heterosexuality, and the Erotics of Men's Predation." *Feminist Studies* 24 (fall 1998): 627–55.

Lumpe, Lora. "The Leader of the Pack." *Bulletin of the Atomic Scientists* 55 (Jan.–Feb. 1999): 27–33.

———, ed. *Running Guns: The Global Black Market in Small Arms.* London, 2000.

Lutz, Donald S. "The State Constitutional Pedigree of the U.S. Bill of Rights." *Publius: The Journal of Federalism* 22 (spring 1992): 19–45.

Lyon, Peter. *The Wild, Wild West.* New York, 1969.

McAdoo, William G. "Crime and Punishment: Causes and Mechanisms of Prevalent Crimes." *Scientific Monthly* 24 (May 1927): 415–20.

———. *When the Court Takes a Recess.* New York, 1924.

McAfee, Thomas B., and Michael J. Quinlan. "Bringing Forward the Right to Keep and Bear Arms: Do Text, History, or Precedent Stand in the Way?" *North Carolina Law Review* 75 (March 1997): 781–899.

McAneny, Leslie. "Americans Tell Congress: Pass Brady Bill, Other Tough Gun Laws." *Gallup Poll Monthly* 330 (March 1993): 2–5.

McClurg, Andrew J. "The Rhetoric of Gun Control." *American University Law Review* 42 (fall 1992): 53–113.

McCreedy, Kenneth O. "Palladium of Liberty: The American Militia System, 1815–1861." Ph.D. diss., University of California, Berkeley, 1991.

McCullough, David. *Truman.* New York, 1992.

McDonald, Forrest. *Novus Ordo Seclorum: The Intellectual Origins of the Constitution.* Lawrence, Kans., 1995.

McDowell, David, Colin Loftin, and Brian Wiersma. "Easing Concealed Firearms Laws: Effects on Homicide Rates in Three States." *Journal of Criminal Law and Criminology* 86 (fall 1995): 193–206.

McDowell, David, and Brian Wiersma. "The Incidence of Defensive Firearms Use by US Crime Victims, 1987 through 1990." *American Journal of Public Health* 84 (Dec. 1994): 182–4.

———. "Additional Discussion About Easing Concealed Firearms Laws." *American Journal of Public Health* 84 (Dec. 1994): 221–26.

McFarlane, Alan. *The Justice and the Mare's Ale: Law and Disorder in Seventeenth-Century England.* Oxford, Eng., 1981.

McGovern, George S. *The Great Coalfield War.* Boston, 1972.

McGrath, Roger D. *Gunfighters, Highwaymen, and Vigilantes: Violence on the Frontier.* Berkeley, 1984.

———. "Violence and Lawlessness on the Western Frontier." In Gurr, ed. *Violence in America* I: 122–45.

Machiavelli, Niccolò. *Machiavelli: The Chief Works and Others.* Trans. Allan Gilbert. 3 vols. Durham, N.C., 1965.

McKanna, Clare V., Jr. *Homicide, Race, and Justice in the American West, 1880–1920.* Tucson, Ariz., 1997.

McKelvey, Blake. *The Urbanization of America, 1860–1915.* New Brunswick, N.J., 1963.

McKenna, David J. "The Right to Keep and Bear Arms." *Marquette Law Review* 12 (Feb. 1928): 138–49.

McKinley, James. *Assassination in America.* New York, 1977.

Maclay, William. *Journal of William Maclay.* Ed. Edgar S. Maclay. New York, 1890.

Madison, James. *The Papers of James Madison.* Ed. William T. D. Hutchinson and others. 17 vols. Chicago and Charlottesville, Va., 1962–1991.

Madsen, Deborah L. *American Exceptionalism.* Jackson, Miss., 1998.

Maestro, Marcello. *Cesare Beccaria and the Origins of Penal Reform.* Philadelphia, 1973.

Mahler, Anthony J., and Jonathan E. Fielding. "Firearms and Gun Control: A Public Health Concern." *New England Journal of Medicine* 297 (Sept. 8, 1977): 556–8.

Mahon, John K. *The American Militia: Decade of Decisions, 1789–1800*. Gainesville, Fla., 1960.

———. *History of the Militia and the National Guard*. New York, 1983.

Maier, Pauline. "Popular Uprisings and Civil Authority in Eighteenth Century America." *William and Mary Quarterly* 27 (Jan. 1970): 3–35.

Main, Jackson Turner. *The Antifederalists: Critics of the Constitution, 1781–1788*. Chapel Hill, N.C., 1961.

Malcolm, Joyce Lee. "Gun Control and the Constitution: Sources and Explorations of the Second Amendment." *Tennessee Law Review* 62 (spring 1995): 813–21.

———. *Guns and Violence: The English Experience*. Cambridge, Mass., 2002.

———. *To Keep and Bear Arms: The Origins of an Anglo-American Right*. Cambridge, Mass., 1994.

———. "The Right of the People to Keep and Bear Arms: The Common Law Tradition." *Hastings Constitutional Law Quarterly* 10 (1983): 285–314.

Malcolm, Joyce Lee, and Michael A. Bellesiles. "Exchange: On the History of the Right to Bear Arms." *Law and History Review* 15 (fall 1997): 339–45.

Malcolm X. *Malcolm X Speaks: Selected Speeches and Statements*. 2d ed. New York, 1989.

Malone, Michael P., ed. *Historians and the American West*. Lincoln, Nebr., 1983.

Malone, Patrick M. *The Skulking Way of War: Technology and Tactics among the New England Indians*. Lanham, Md., 1991.

Manning, Roger B. *Hunters and Poachers: A Social and Cultural History of Unlawful Hunting in England, 1485–1640*. Oxford, Eng., 1993.

Marchiafava, Louis J. "The Houston Police." *Rice University Studies* 63 (1977).

Marietta, Jack D., and G. S. Rowe. "Violent Crime, Victims, and Society in Pennsylvania, 1682–1800." *Pennsylvania History* 24 (Supplemental issue, 1999): 24–54.

Marine, Gene. *The Black Panthers*. New York, 1969.

Markusen, Ann, Peter Hall, Scott Campbell, and Sabina Deitrick. *The Rise of the Gunbelt: The Military Remapping of Industrial America*. New York, 1991.

Marshall, S. L. A. *Crimsoned Prairie: The Indian Wars on the Great Plains*. New York, 1972.

Martin, James K., and Mark E. Lender. *A Respectable Army: The Military Origins of the Republic, 1763–1789*. Arlington Heights, Ill., 1982.

Massachusetts Council on Crime Correction, Inc. *A Shooting Gallery Called America*. Boston, 1974.

Mason, George. *The Papers of George Mason, 1725–1792*. Ed. Robert A. Rutland. 3 vols. Chapel Hill, N.C., 1970.

Mauser, Gary A. "Gun Control Is Not Crime Control." *Critical Issues Bulletin*. Vancouver, Canada, 1987.

Max, Wendy, and Dorothy P. Rice. "Shooting in the Dark: Estimating the Cost of Firearms Injuries." *Health Affairs* 12 (winter 1993): 171–85.

Mayr, Otto, and Robert C. Post, eds. *Yankee Enterprise: The Rise of the American System of Manufactures*. Washington, D.C., 1981.

Miller, John. "The Militia and the Army in the Reign of James II." *Historical Journal* 26 (Dec. 1973): 659–79.

Miller, John C. *The First Frontier: Life in Colonial America*. New York, 1966.

Miller, Maryann. *Working Together Against Gun Violence*. Rev. ed. New York, 1997.

Miller, Nyle H., and Joseph W. Snell. *Great Gunfighters of the Kansas Cowtowns, 1867–1886*. Lincoln, Nebr., 1963.

Miller, Wilbur R. *Cops and Bobbies: Police Authority in New York and London, 1830–1870*. Chicago, 1977.

Millet, Allan R. "The Constitution and the Citizen-Soldier." In Kohn, ed. *The United States Military under the Constitution*, 97–119.

Millis, Walter. *Arms and Men: A Study in American Military History*. New York, 1956.

Minow, Newton N., and Craig L. LaMay. *Abandoned in the Wasteland: Children, Television, and the First Amendment*. New York, 1995.

Mitchell, John G. " 'God, Guns, and Guts Made America Free': The National Rifle Association and the Constitutional Right to Bear Arms." *American Heritage* 29 (Feb./March 1978): 4–17.

Molina, Manny. *Guns and the Filipino Right to Arms.* Quezon City, Philippines, 1993.

Monaghan, Jay, ed. *The Book of the American West.* New York, 1963.

Monkkonen, Eric H. *America Becomes Urban: The Development of U.S. Cities and Towns, 1780–1980.* Berkeley, 1988.

———. "Diverging Homicide Rates: England and the United States." In Gurr, ed. *Violence in America* I: 80–101.

———. *Police in Urban America, 1860–1920.* Cambridge, Eng., 1981.

———, ed. *Crime and Justice in American History: Historical Articles on the Origins and Evolution of American Criminal Justice.* 11 vols. Westport, Conn., 1991–1992.

Moore, David W., and Frank Newport. "Public Opinion Strongly Favors Stricter Gun Control Laws." *Gallup Poll Monthly* 340 (Jan. 1994): 18–24.

Moore, James. *Very Special Agents: The Inside Story of America's Most Controversial Law Enforcement Agency—The Bureau of Alcohol, Tobacco, and Firearms.* New York, 1997.

Moore, Warren. *Weapons of the American Revolution . . . and Accoutrements.* New York, 1967.

Morgan, Edmund S. *American Slavery, American Freedom: The Ordeal of Colonial Virginia.* New York, 1975.

———. *Inventing the People: The Rise of Popular Sovereignty in England and America.* New York, 1988.

Morrow, Lance. "Coming to Clarity About Guns." *Time,* May 3, 1999, p. 46.

Mortenson, C. David. *Violence and Communication: Public Reactions to an Attempted Presidential Assassination.* Lanham, Md., 1987.

Mosse, George L., ed. *Police Forces in History.* London, 1975.

Mottram, Eric. " 'The Persuasive Lips': Men and Guns in America, the West." *Journal of American Studies* 10 (April 1976): 53–84.

Mowry, George E. *Theodore Roosevelt and the Progressive Movement.* New York, 1946.

Mundt, Robert J. "Gun Control and Rates of Firearms Violence in Canada and the United States." *Canadian Journal of Criminology* 33 (Jan. 1990): 137–54.

Munsche, P. B. *Gentlemen and Poachers: The English Game Laws, 1671–1831.* Cambridge, Eng., 1981.

Murray, Douglas R. "Handguns, Gun Control Laws, and Firearms Violence." *Social Problems* 23 (Oct. 1975): 81–93.

Musicant, Ivan. *Empire by Default: The Spanish-American War and the Dawn of the American Century.* New York, 1998.

National Institute of Mental Health. *Television and Growing Up: The Impact of Televised Violence.* Washington, D.C., 1972.

National Rifle Association, Web site. <http://www.nra.org>.

National Television Violence Study. Center for Communication and Social Policy, University of California at Santa Barbara. 2 vols. Thousand Oaks, Calif., 1997–1998.

Neely, Mark E., Jr. *The Fate of Liberty: Abraham Lincoln and Civil Liberties.* New York, 1991.

Nef, John U. *War and Human Progress: An Essay on the Rise of Industrial Civilization.* Cambridge, Mass., 1950.

Nelson, Daniel L. "Damage Control." *Bulletin of the Atomic Scientists* 55 (Jan.–Feb. 1999): 55–7.

Nelson, David E., and others. "Population Estimates of Household Firearm Storage Practices and Firearm Carrying in Oregon." *Journal of the American Medical Association* 276 (June 12, 1996): 1744–8.

"New DCM Cuts Hit Senior Clubs Most." *American Rifleman* 116 (Aug. 1968): 40.

"New U.S. Law Limits All Gun Sales." *American Rifleman* 116 (Dec. 1968): 17–18.

Newman, Kim. *Wild West Movies or How the West Was Found, Won, Lost, Lied About, Filmed, and Forgotten.* London, 1990.

Newton, David E. *Gun Control: An Issue for the Nineties.* Hillside, N.J., 1992.

Newton, George D., Jr., and Franklin E. Zimring. *Firearms and Violence in American Life: A Staff*

Report Submitted to the National Commission on the Causes and Prevention of Violence. Washington, D.C., 1969.

Nichols, Bob, and Mr. and Mrs. Robert E. Simon. "Should a Boy Have a Gun? A Symposium." *Parents' Magazine* 9 (Oct. 1934): 26–7, 75–9.

Nieto, Marcus. *Concealed Handgun Laws and Public Safety.* Sacramento, Calif., Nov. 1997.

Nisbet, Lee, ed. *The Gun Control Debate: You Decide.* Buffalo, N.Y., 1990.

Nisbett, Richard E., and Dov Cohen. *Culture of Honor: The Psychology of Violence in the South.* Boulder, Colo., 1996.

"Nonfatal and Fatal Firearms-Related Injuries—United States, 1993–1997." *Journal of the American Medical Association* 203 (Jan. 5, 2000): 47–8.

North, S. N. D., and Ralph H. North. *Simeon North, First Official Pistol Maker of the United States: A Memoir.* Concord, N.H., 1913.

Novak, William J. *The People's Welfare: Law and Regulation in Nineteenth-Century America.* Chapel Hill, N.C., 1966.

———. *"Salus Populi*: The Roots of Regulation in America, 1787–1873." Ph.D. diss., Brandeis University, 1991.

Nugent, Ted. *God, Guns, & Rock 'n' Roll.* Washington, D.C., 2000.

Oberer, Walter E. "The Deadly Weapon Doctrine—Common Law Origin." *Harvard Law Review* 75 (June 1962): 1565–76.

O'Connell, Robert L. *Of Arms and Men: A History of War, Weapons, and Aggression.* New York, 1989.

Oliver, Benjamin L. *The Rights of an American Citizen.* 1832. Reprint, Boston, 1970.

Olsen, Jack. *Give a Boy a Gun: A True Story of Law and Disorder in the American West.* New York, 1985.

O'Meara, James. "Concealed Weapons and Crimes." *Overland Monthly* 2 (1890): 11–15.

Orasin, Charles J. "Handgun Control and the Politics of Fear." *USA Today*, Jan. 1980. Reprinted in *The Issue of Gun Control*, ed. Thomas Draper, 97–104. New York, 1981.

Orey, Michael. *Assuming the Risk: The Mavericks, the Lawyers, and the Whistle-Blowers Who Beat Big Tobacco.* Boston, 1999.

Osgood, Ernest S. *The Day of the Cattleman.* Chicago, 1957.

Pacific Reporter. Vols. 231–2. St. Paul, Minn., 1925.

Paludan, Phillip S. "The American Civil War Considered as a Crisis in Law and Order." *American Historical Review* 75 (Oct. 1972): 1013–34.

Parmet, Herbert S. *George Bush: The Life of a Lone Star Yankee.* New York, 1997.

Patterson, Kelly. "The Political Firepower of the National Rifle Association." In Cigler and Loomis, eds. *Interest Group Politics*, 119–42.

Peake, Ora B. *A History of the United States Indian Factory System, 1795–1822.* Denver, 1954.

Peek, Ralph L. "Lawlessness in Florida, 1868–1871." *Florida Historical Quarterly* 40 (Oct. 1964): 164–85.

Pelton, Robert Y. *Fielding's the World's Most Dangerous Places.* 3d ed. Redondo Beach, Calif., 1998.

Pencak, William. *War, Politics and Revolution in Provincial Massachusetts.* Boston, 1981.

Perrigo, Lynn I. "Law and Order in Early Colorado Mining Camps." *Mississippi Historical Review* 28 (June 1941): 41–62. Reprinted in Monkkonen, ed. *Crime and Justice in American History.* Vol. 4, 262–83.

Perrin, Noel. *Giving Up the Gun: Japan's Reversion to the Sword, 1543–1879.* Boston, 1979.

Peterson, Harold L. *Arms and Armor in Colonial America, 1526–1783.* Harrisburg, Pa., 1956.

———. *Pageant of the Gun: A Treasury of Stories of Firearms: Their Romance, and Lore, Development and Use through Ten Centuries.* Garden City, N.Y., 1967.

Peterson, Virgil W. *Barbarians in Our Midst: A History of Chicago Crime and Politics.* Boston, 1952.

———. *Crime Commissions in the United States.* Chicago, 1945.

Phelan, Andrew. "Men and Arms." *The Law Journal* 110 (Feb. 26, 1960): 131–2.

Pierce, Glenn L., and William J. Bowers. "The Bartley-Fox Gun Law's Short-Term Impact on Crime in Boston." *Annals of the American Academy of Political and Social Science* 455 (May 1981): 120–37.

"The Pistol in America." *Gentleman's Magazine* 23 (1879): 321.

Pitcavage, Mark. "An Equitable Burden: The Decline of the State Militias, 1783–1858." Ph.D. diss., Ohio State University, 1995.

———. "Ropes of Sand: Territorial Militias, 1801–1812." *Journal of the Early Republic* 13 (winter 1993): 482–500.

Pocock, John G. A. *The Machiavellian Moment: Florentine Political Thought and the Atlantic Republican Tradition*. Princeton, 1975.

Poe, Richard. *The Seven Myths of Gun Control: Reclaiming the Truth About Guns, Crime, and the Second Amendment*. Roseville, Calif., 2001.

Polesky, Joelle E. "The Rise of Private Militia: A First and Second Amendment Analysis of the Right to Organize and the Right to Train." *University of Pennsylvania Law Review* 144 (Apr. 1966): 1593–1642.

Pollak, Louis H., and others. "Symposium: Reflections on *United States v. Lopez*." *Michigan Law Review* 94 (Dec. 1995): 533–831.

Pollard, Hugh B. C. A *History of Firearms*. Boston, 1936.

Polsby, Daniel D. "The False Promise of Gun Control." *Atlantic Monthly* 273 (March 1994): 57–70.

———. "Firearms Costs, Firearms Benefits, and the Limits of Knowledge." *Journal of Criminal Law and Criminology* 86 (fall 1995): 207–20.

———. *Firearms and Crime*. Oakland, Calif., 1997.

Pomerantz, Sidney I. *New York: An American City, 1783–1803: A Study of Urban Life*. 1938. Reprint, New York, 1965.

Pontonne, S., ed. *Gun Control Issues*. Commack, N.Y., 1997.

Powe, L. A. "Guns, Words, and Constitutional Interpretation." *William and Mary Law Review* 38 (May 1997): 1311–1403.

Powers, Richard G. *G-Men: Hoover's FBI in American Popular Culture*. Carbondale, Ill., 1983.

Prassel, Frank R. *The Great American Outlaw: A Legacy of Fact and Fiction*. Norman, Okla., 1993.

———. *The Western Peace Officer: A Legacy of Law and Order*. Norman, Okla., 1972.

Prince Alfonso de Bourbon et Autriche-Este. "The Effort to Abolish the Duel." *North American Review* 175 (July 1902): 194–200.

Prince, Carl E. " 'The Great Riot Year': Jacksonian Democracy and Patterns of Violence in 1834." *Journal of the Early Republic* 5 (spring 1985): 1–19.

"The Progress of the Revolver." *Saturday Review*, Feb. 14, 1885, p. 198.

Public Papers of the Presidents of the United States. Vols. Herbert Hoover through William Clinton.

Quarles, Benjamin. "The Colonial Militias and Negro Manpower." *Mississippi Valley Historical Review* 45 (March 1959): 643–52.

Quigley, Paxton. *Armed and Female*. New York, 1989.

Raber, Michael S. "Conservative Innovators, Military Small Arms, and Industrial History at Springfield Armory, 1794–1918." *Journal of the Society for Industrial Archeology* 14, No. 1 (1988): 1–21.

Rable, George C. *But There Was No Peace: The Role of Violence in the Politics of Reconstruction*. Athens, Ga., 1984.

Radcliffe, Donnie. *Simply Barbara Bush: A Portrait of America's Candid First Lady*. New York, 1989.

Rakove, Jack N. *Declaring Rights: A Brief History with Documents*. Boston, 1998.

———. *Original Meanings: Politics and Ideas in the Making of the Constitution*. New York, 1996.

———, ed. *Interpreting the Constitution: The Debate Over Original Intent*. Boston, 1990.

Ramage, B. J. "Homicide in the Southern States." *Sewanee Review* 4 (1896): 2215–31.

Rana, Swadesh. *Small Arms and Intra-State Conflicts*. New York, 1995.

Rand, Kristen. *Gun Shows in America: Tupperware Parties for Criminals*. Washington, D.C., 1996.

———. *Lawyers, Guns, and Money: The Impact of Tort Restrictions on Firearms Safety and Gun Control*. Violence Policy Center, Washington, D.C., 1996.

Rand, Michael R. "Guns and Crime: Handgun Victimization, Firearm Self-Defense and Firearm Theft." In *Crime Data Brief*. U.S. Dept. of Justice, Washington, D.C., Apr. 1994.

Randall, James G., and David Donald. *The Civil War and Reconstruction*. 2d ed. Boston, 1961.

Reagan, Michael D. *The New Federalism*. New York, 1972.

Reagan, Nancy. *My Turn: The Memoirs of Nancy Reagan*. New York, 1989.

Reagan, Ronald. "Why I'm For the Brady Bill." New York *Times*, March 29, 1991.

"Realistic Firearms Controls" (editorial). *American Rifleman* 112 (Jan. 1964): 14.

Reavis, Dick J. *The Ashes of Waco: An Investigation*. New York, 1995.

Reed, John S. "To Live—and Die—in Dixie: A Contribution to the Study of Southern Violence." *Political Science Quarterly* 86 (Sept. 1971): 429–43.

Reichmann, Felix. "The Pennsylvania Rifle: A Social Interpretation of Changing Military Techniques." *Pennsylvania Magazine of Biography and History* 69 (Jan. 1945): 3–14.

Reid, John P. *In Defiance of the Law: The Standing Army Controversy, the Two Constitutions, and the Coming of the American Revolution*. Chapel Hill, N.C., 1981.

———. *Law for the Elephant: Property and Social Behavior on the Overland Trail*. San Marino, Calif., 1980.

Reinders, Robert. "Militia and Public Order in Nineteenth-Century America." *Journal of American Studies* 2 (Apr. 1977): 81–101.

Reiss, Albert J., Jr., and Jeffrey A. Roth, eds. *Understanding and Preventing Violence*. 4 vols. Washington, D.C., 1993–1994.

Remini, Robert V. *Andrew Jackson and the Course of American Democracy, 1833–1845*. New York, 1986.

———. *Andrew Jackson and the Course of American Empire, 1767–1821*. New York, 1977.

Renner, Michael. "Arms Control Orphans." *Bulletin of the Atomic Scientists* 55 (Jan.–Feb. 1999): 22–6.

———. *Small Arms, Big Impacts: The Next Challenge of Disarmament*. Washington, D.C., 1997.

Reynolds, Glenn Harlan. "A Critical Guide to the Second Amendment." *Tennessee Law Review* 62 (spring 1995): 461–512.

Rich, Bennett M. *The Presidents and Civil Disorder*. Washington, D.C., 1941.

Richards, Leonard L. *Gentlemen of Property and Standing: Anti-Abolition Mobs in Jacksonian America*. New York, 1970.

Richardson, James D., comp. *A Compilation of the Messages and Papers of the Presidents, 1789–1897*. 19 vols. 1896–1897. Reprint, Washington, D.C., 1922.

Richardson, James F. *The New York Police: Colonial Times to 1901*. New York, 1970.

———. *Urban Police in the United States*. Port Washington, N.Y., 1974.

Ridgeway, James. "The Kind of Gun Control We Need." *New Republic*, June 22, 1968, pp. 10–11.

The Right to Bear Arms in the Twentieth Century. Twentieth Century with Mike Wallace. CBS, 1997. Videocassette.

Riker, William. *Federalism: Origin, Operation, Significance*. Boston, 1964.

———. *Soldiers of the State: The Role of the National Guard in American Democracy*. Washington, D.C., 1957.

———, ed. *The Development of American Federalism*. Boston, 1987.

Riley, Robert J. "Shooting to Kill the Handgun: Time to Martyr Another American 'Hero.' " *Journal of Urban Law* 51 (Feb. 1972): 491–524.

Riling, Raymond L. J. *Guns and Shooting: A Selected Chronological Bibliography*. New York, 1951.

Rister, C. C. "Outlaws and Vigilantes on the Southern Plains." *Mississippi Valley Historical Review* 19 (March 1933): 537–54.

Robbins, Caroline. *The Eighteenth-Century Commonwealthman: Studies in the Transmission, Development, and Circumstance of English Liberal Thought from the Restoration of Charles II until the War with the Thirteen Colonies*. Cambridge, Mass., 1959.

Roberts, Gary L. "The West's Gunmen." *The American West*. Part 1 (Jan. 1971): 10, 15, 64, and Part 2 (March 1971): 18–23, 61–2. Reprinted in Monkkonen, ed. *Crime and Justice in American History*. Vol. 4, 321–50.

Robin, Gerald D. *Violent Crime and Gun Control*. Highland Heights, Ky., 1991.

Roe, Tangela G. *Gun Control: Selected References, 1980–1991*. Bethesda, Md., 1991.

Rogers, Alan. *Empire and Liberty: American Resistance to British Authority, 1755–1763*. Berkeley, 1974.

Roleff, Tamara L., ed. *Guns and Crime*. San Diego, Calif., 2000.

Rolph, C. H. "Guns and Violence." *New Statesman*, Jan. 15, 1965, pp. 71–2.

Roosevelt, Franklin D. *The Public Papers and Addresses of Franklin D. Roosevelt*. Ed. Samuel I. Rosenman. 13 vols. New York, 1938–1950.

Roosevelt, Theodore. *The Letters of Theodore Roosevelt*. Ed. Elting E. Morison. 8 vols. Cambridge, Mass., 1951–1954.

Root, Elihu. *The Military and Colonial Policy of the United States: Addresses and Reports*. Ed. Robert Bacon and James B. Scott. 1916. Reprint, Cambridge, Mass., 1970.

Rorabaugh, W. J. "The Political Duel in the Early Republic: Burr v. Hamilton." *Journal of the Early Republic* 15 (spring 1995): 1–23.

Rosa, Joseph G. *The Gunfighter: Man or Myth?* Norman, Okla., 1969.

Rosenbaum, Betty B. "The Relationship between War and Crime in the United States." *Journal of the American Institute of Criminal Law and Criminology* 30 (1939–1940): 722–40.

Rosenberg, Mark L., Patrick W. O'Connor, and Kenneth E. Powell. "Let's Be Clear: Violence Is a Public Health Problem." *Journal of the American Medical Association* 247 (June 10, 1992): 3071–2.

Rosenblatt, Roger. "Get Rid of the Damned Things." *Time*, Aug. 9, 1999, pp. 38–9.

Roth, Jeffrey A. *Firearms and Violence*. U.S. Dept. of Justice, Washington, D.C., Feb. 1994.

Rousey, Dennis C. *Policing the Southern City: New Orleans, 1805–1889*. Baton Rouge, La., 1996.

Rovner, Julie. "US Gun Lobby Takes Aim at CDC Injury Centres." *The Lancet*, Aug. 26, 1995, pp. 563–4.

Rowland, John K. "Origins of the Second Amendment: The Creation of the Constitutional Rights of Militia and of Keeping and Bearing Arms." Ph.D. diss., Ohio State University, 1978.

Royster, Charles A. *A Revolutionary People at War: The Continental Army and American Character, 1775–1778*. Chapel Hill, N.C., 1979.

Rubinstein, Jonathan. *City Police*. New York, 1973.

Rudé, George. *The Crowd in History: A Study of Popular Disturbances in France and England, 1730–1848*. New York, 1964.

Russell, Carl P. *Firearms, Traps, and Tools of the Mountain Men*. New York, 1967.

———. *Guns on the Early Frontiers: A History of Firearms from Colonial Times Through the Years of the Western Fur Trade*. Berkeley, 1957.

Russell, Todd. "The Ethics of Field Shooting." *Outing Magazine* 543 (Nov. 1908): 253–4.

Ruth, David E. *Inventing the Public Enemy: The Gangster in American Culture, 1918–1934*. Chicago, 1996.

Rutland, Robert A. *The Birth of the Bill of Rights, 1776–1791*. Chapel Hill, N.C., 1955.

Rutman, Darrett B. "A Militant New World, 1607–1640." Ph.D. diss., University of Virginia, 1959.

Ryan, Halford. *Henry Ward Beecher: Peripatetic Preacher*. New York, 1990.

Samora, Julian, Joe Bernal, and Albert Peña. *Gunpowder Justice: A Reassessment of the Texas Rangers*. Notre Dame, Ind., 1979.

Sandys-Winsch, Godfrey. *Gun Law in England and Wales*. 3d ed. London, 1979.

Scalia, Antonin. *A Matter of Interpretation: Federal Courts and the Law*. Princeton, 1997.

Scarry, Elaine. "War and the Social Contract: Nuclear Policy, Distribution, and the Right to Keep and Bear Arms." *University of Pennsylvania Law Review* 139 (May 1991): 1257–1316.

Schlesinger, Arthur M. *The Rise of the City, 1878–1898*. New York, 1933.

Schlesinger, Arthur M., Jr. *The Crisis of Confidence: Ideas, Power, and Violence in America*. Boston, 1969.

———. *The Crisis of the Old Order, 1919–1933*. Boston, 1957.

Schneider, John C. "Mob Violence and Public Order in the American City, 1830–1865." Ph.D. diss., University of Minnesota, 1971.

Schubert, Paul. "A Hunter's Greatest Peril." *Saturday Evening Post*, Oct. 25, 1958, pp. 37, 95–8.

Schulman, Joseph Neil. *Stopping Power: Why 70 Million Americans Own Guns*. Santa Monica, Calif., 1994.

Schuman, Howard, and Stanley Presser. "Attitude Measurement and the Gun Control Paradox." *Public Opinion Quarterly* 41 (winter 1977–1978): 427–38.

Schwartz, Bernard, ed. *The Bill of Rights: A Documentary History*. 2 vols. New York, 1971.

Schwarz, Meg, ed. *TV and Teens: Experts Look at the Issues*. Reading, Mass., 1982.

Schwoerer, Lois G. *The Declaration of Rights, 1689*. Baltimore, 1981.

———. *"No Standing Armies!" The Antiarmy Ideology in Seventeenth-Century England*. Baltimore, 1974.

Scott, Winfield. *Memoirs of Lieut.-General Winfield Scott, LL.D.* 2 vols. New York, 1864.

Second Amendment Foundation, Web site. <http://www.saf.org>.

"Second Amendment Symposium Issue." *Tennessee Law Review* 22 (spring 1995).

Secoy, Frank R. *Changing Military Patterns of the Great Plains Indians (17th Century through the Early 19th Century)*. 1953. Reprint, Lincoln, Nebr., 1992.

Segal, Charles M., and David C. Stineback. *Puritans, Indians, and Manifest Destiny*. New York, 1977.

Seitz, Steven T. "Firearms, Homicides, and Gun Control Effectiveness." *Law and Society Review* 6 (May 1972): 595–613.

Selesky, Harold E. *War and Society in Colonial Connecticut*. New Haven, 1990.

Senkewicz, Robert M. *Vigilantes in Gold Rush San Francisco*. Stanford, Calif., 1985.

Serven, James E. *Colt Firearms from 1836*. Santa Ana, Calif., 1954.

Shalhope, Robert E. "The Armed Citizen in the Early Republic." *Law and Contemporary Problems* 49 (winter 1986): 125–41.

———. "The Ideological Origins of the Second Amendment." *Journal of American History* 69 (Dec. 1982): 599–614.

———. "To Keep and Bear Arms in the Early Republic." *Constitutional Commentary* 16 (summer 1999): 269–81.

Shammas, Carole. *The Pre-Industrial Consumer in England and America*. Oxford, Eng., 1990.

Shapiro, Herbert. *White Violence and Black Response: From Reconstruction to Montgomery*. Amherst, Mass., 1988.

Sharpe, Philip B. *The Rifle in America*. New York, 1938.

Shea, William L. *The Virginia Militia in the Seventeenth Century*. Baton Rouge, La., 1983.

Sheley, Joseph F., and James D. Wright. *Gun Acquisition and Possession in Selected Juvenile Samples*. U.S. Dept. of Justice, Washington, D.C., Dec. 1994.

———. *High School Youths, Weapons, and Violence: A National Survey*. U.S. Dept. of Justice, Washington, D.C., 1998.

———. *In the Line of Fire: Youths, Guns, and Violence in Urban America*. New York, 1995.

Sherrill, Robert. *The Saturday Night Special*. New York, 1973.

Sherwood, Robert E. *Roosevelt and Hopkins: An Intimate History*. Rev. ed. New York, 1950.

Shields, Pete. *Guns Don't Die—People Do*. New York, 1981.

Shirley, Glenn H. *Law West of Fort Smith: A History of Justice in the Indian Territory, 1834–1896*. New York, 1957.

Shooting Industry. *The World of Guns*. Ed. E. B. Mann. Skokie, Ill., 1964.

Shy, John. *A People Numerous and Armed: Reflections on the Military Struggle for American Independence*. New York, 1976.

———. *Toward Lexington: The Role of the British Army in the Coming of the American Revolution*. Princeton, 1965.

Simkin, Jay, Aaron Zelman, and Alan M. Rice. *Lethal Laws*. Milwaukee, 1994.

Sinauer, Nancy, Joseph L. Annest, and James A. Mercy. "Unintentional, Nonfatal Firearm-Related Injuries: A Preventable Public Health Burden." *Journal of the American Medical Association* 276 (June 12, 1996): 1740–43.

Sinclair, Andrew. *Prohibition: The Era of Excess*. Boston, 1962.

Singletary, Otis A. *Negro Militia and Reconstruction*. Austin, Tex., 1957.

Sinha, Anil Kumar. *Use of Firearms and Their Control: A Critique (In Special Reference to Assam, 1975–85)*. New Delhi, 1991.

Skowronek, Stephen. *Building a New American State: The Expansion of National Administrative Capacities, 1877–1920*. Cambridge, Eng., 1982.

Slaughter, Thomas P. *The Whiskey Rebellion: Frontier Epilogue to the American Revolution*. New York, 1986.

Sloan, John Henry, and others. "Handgun Regulations, Crime, Assaults, and Homicide: A Tale of Two Cities." *New England Journal of Medicine* 309 (Nov. 10, 1988): 1256–62.

Slotkin, Richard. *The Fatal Environment: The Myth of the Frontier in the Industrial Age, 1800–1890*. New York, 1985.

———. *Gunfighter Nation: The Myth of the Frontier in Twentieth-Century America*. New York, 1993.

———. *Regeneration Through Violence: The Mythology of the American Frontier, 1600–1860*. Middletown, Conn., 1973.

"Small Arms, Big Problem," Special Issue. *Bulletin of the Atomic Scientists* 55 (Jan.–Feb. 1999).

Smith, Bruce, Jr. *Police Systems in the United States*. 2d ed. New York, 1960.

Smith, Craig R. *To Form a More Perfect Union: The Ratification of the Constitution and the Bill of Rights, 1787–1791*. Lanham, Md., 1993.

Smith, Douglas A., and Craig D. Uchida. "The Social Organization of Self Help: A Study of Defensive Weapon Ownership." *American Sociological Review* 53 (Feb. 1988): 94–102.

Smith, Henry Nash. *Virgin Land: The American West as Symbol and Myth*. Cambridge, Mass., 1950.

Smith, M. Dwayne, and Margaret A. Zahn, eds. *Homicide: A Source Book of Social Research*. Thousand Oaks, Calif., 1999.

Smith, Merritt Roe. *Harper's Ferry Armory and the New Technology: The Challenge of Change*. Ithaca, N.Y., 1977.

———. "Military Entrepreneurship." In Mayr and Post, eds. *Yankee Enterprise*, 68–102.

Smith, Tom W. *1996 National Gun Policy Survey: Research Findings*. Chicago, March 1997.

Smith, Tom W., and Robert J. Smith. "Changes in Firearms Ownership Among Women, 1980–1994." *Journal of Criminal Law and Criminology* 86 (fall 1995): 133–49.

Snyder, Jeffrey R. "Fighting Back: Crime, Self-Defense, and the Right to Carry a Handgun." Cato Institute, Washington, D.C. *Policy Analysis* 284 (Oct. 22, 1997): 64.

———. "A Nation of Cowards." *The Public Interest* 113 (fall 1993): 40–55.

Socolofsky, Homer E. *Arthur Capper: Publisher, Politician, and Philanthropist*. Lawrence, Kans., 1962.

Sorenson, Susan B., and Richard A. Berk. "Young Guns: An Empirical Study of Persons Who Use a Firearm in a Suicide or a Homicide." *Injury Prevention* 5 (Dec. 1999): 280–83.

Spann, Edward K. *The New Metropolis: New York City, 1840–1857*. New York, 1981.

Spiegler, Jeffrey H., and John J. Sweeney. *Gun Abuse in Ohio*. 2d ed. Cleveland, June 1976.

Spitzer, Robert J. *The Politics of Gun Control*. Chatham, N.J., 1995. 2d ed., 1998.

———. *The Presidency and Public Policy: The Four Arenas of Presidential Power*. University, Ala., 1983.

———. *The Right to Bear Arms: Rights and Liberties under the Law*. Santa Barbara, Calif., 2001.

———. "Saving the Constitution from Lawyers" in *Politics and Constitutionalism: The Louis Fisher Connection*. Ed. Spitzer (Albany, N.Y., 2000), 185–225.

Sprecher, Robert A. "The Lost Amendment." *American Bar Association Journal* 51 (June 1965): 554–7, (July 1965): 665–9.

Sproule, Catherine F., and Deborah J. Kennett. "Killing with Guns in the USA and Canada, 1977–1983: Further Evidence for the Effectiveness of Gun Control." *Canadian Journal of Criminology* 31 (July 1989): 245–51.

Squires, Peter. *Gun Culture or Gun Control? Firearms, Violence and Society*. London, 2000.

Stampp, Kenneth M. *America in 1857: A Nation on the Brink*. New York, 1990.

———. *The Era of Reconstruction: 1865–1877*. New York, 1965.

Stange, Mary Z., and Carol K. Oyster. *Gun Women: Firearms and Feminism in Contemporary America*. New York, 2000.

State of the Union Messages of the Presidents, 1790–1966. Ed. Fred L. Israel. 3 vols. New York, 1966.

Stead, Philip J. *The Police of France.* New York, 1983.

Steckmesser, Kent L. *The Western Hero in History and Legend.* Norman, Okla., 1965.

———. *Western Outlaws: The "Good Badman" in Fact, Film, and Folklore.* Claremont, Calif., 1983.

Stern, Kenneth S. *A Force Upon the Plain: The American Militia Movement and the Politics of Hate.* New York, 1996.

Stevens, William O. *Pistols at Ten Paces: The Story of the Code of Honor in America.* Boston, 1940.

Stinchcombe, Arthur L., and others. *Crime and Punishment—Changing Attitudes in America.* San Francisco, 1980.

Stone, Richard G., Jr. *A Brittle Sword: The Kentucky Militia, 1776–1912.* Lexington, Ken., 1977.

Story, Joseph. *Commentaries on the Constitution of the United States.* 3 vols. 1833. Reprint, Boston, 1970.

Strong, George T. *The Diary of George Templeton Strong.* Ed. Allan Nevins and Milton H. Thomas. 4 vols. New York, 1952.

Sugarmann, Josh. *Cease Fire: A Comprehensive Strategy to Reduce Firearms Violence.* Washington, D.C., 1994.

———. *Every Handgun Is Aimed at You: The Case for Banning Handguns.* New York, 2001.

———. *National Rifle Association: Money, Firepower and Fear.* Washington, D.C., 1992.

Sugarmann, Josh, and Kristen Rand. *Assault Weapons: Analysis, New Research, and Legislation.* Washington, D.C., 1989

Sumner, Charles. "The Crime Against Kansas" (pamphlet) *New York Tribune,* May 23, 1856.

Swaney, William B., and others. "For a Better Enforcement of the Law." *American Bar Association Journal* 8 (Sept. 1922): 588–91.

Szatmary, David P. *Shays' Rebellion: The Making of an Agrarian Insurrection.* Amherst, Mass., 1980.

Tabor, James D., and Eugene V. Gallagher. *Why Waco? Cults and the Battle for Religious Freedom in America.* Berkeley, 1995.

Tardiff, Kenneth, and others. "Homicide in New York City: Cocaine Use and Firearms." *Journal of the American Medical Association* 272 (July 1994): 43–6.

Teret, Stephen P., Gregg R. Alexander, and Linda A. Bailey. "The Passage of Maryland's Gun Law: Data and Advocacy for Injury Prevention." *Journal of Public Health Policy* 11, No. 2 (1990): 26–38.

Teret, Stephen P., and Garen J. Wintemute. "Hand Injuries: The Epidemiological Evidence for Assessing Legal Responsibility." *Hamline Law Review* 6 (July 1983): 341–50.

———. "Policies to Prevent Firearms Injuries." *Health Affairs* 12 (winter 1993): 96–108.

Teret, Stephen P., and others. "Support for New Policies to Regulate Firearms: Results of Two National Surveys." *New England Journal of Medicine* 339 (Sept. 17, 1998): 813–18.

"Texas Pistol Law." *The Nation,* July 25, 1907, p. 68.

Thayer, George. *The War Business: International Trade in Armaments.* New York, 1969.

Thiébaux, Marcelle. "The Mediaeval Hunt." *Speculum* 42 (April 1967): 260–74.

Thomas, Chauncey. "Frontier Firearms." *Colorado* 8 (1930): 102–109.

"The Threat: Next Time Is This Time." *American Rifleman* 142 (Jan. 1994): 32–4.

"Time for Congress to Rein in the BATF." *American Rifleman* 143 (Apr. 1995): 38.

Tirman, John. *Spoils of War: The Human Cost of America's Arms Trade.* New York, 1997.

Tompkins, Jane T. *West of Everything: The Inner Life of Westerns.* New York, 1992.

Tonry, Michael. *Malign Neglect—Race, Crime, and Punishment in America.* New York, 1995.

Tonso, William R. *Gun and Society: The Social and Existential Roots of the American Attachment to Firearms.* Washington, D.C., 1982.

———, ed. *The Gun Culture and Its Enemies.* Bellevue, Wash., 1990.

Torrance, Judy M. *Public Violence in Canada, 1867–1982.* Kingston, 1986.

Trachtman, Paul. *The Gunfighters.* New York, 1974.

Trattner, Walter I. *Crusade for the Children: A History of the National Child Labor Committee and Child Labor Reform in America.* Chicago, 1970.

Trefthen, James B., and James E. Serven, eds. *Americans and Their Guns: The National Rifle Association Story Through Nearly a Century of Service to the Nation*. Harrisburg, Pa., 1967.

Trelease, Allen W. *Indian Affairs in Colonial New York: The Seventeenth Century*. Ithaca, N.Y., 1960.

————. *Reconstruction: The Great Experiment*. New York, 1971.

————. *White Terror: The Ku Klux Klan Conspiracy and Southern Reconstruction*. New York, 1971.

Trenchard, John. *An Argument, Shewing that a Standing Army Is Inconsistent with a Free Government and Absolutely Destructive to the Constitution of the English Monarchy*. London, 1697.

Trudeau, Noah Andre. *Out of the Storm: The End of the Civil War, April–June, 1865*. Boston, 1994.

Truman, Ben C. *The Field of Honor: Being a Complete and Comprehensive History of Duelling in All Countries*. New York, 1884.

Tunnell, Ted. *Crucible of Reconstruction: War, Radicalism, and Race in Louisiana, 1862–1877*. Baton Rouge, La., 1984.

Turley, Windle, and Cliff Harrison. "Strict Tort Liability of Handgun Suppliers." *Hamline Law Review* 6 (1983): 285–310.

Ungar, Sanford J. *FBI*. Boston, 1976.

United Nations. *International Study on Firearm Regulation*. New York, 1998.

United Nations Institute for Disarmament Research. *Small Arms Management and Peacekeeping in Southern Africa*. New York and Geneva, 1996.

The United States Army and Navy Journal and Gazette of the Regular and Volunteer Forces. New York, 1962–1965.

United States Supreme Court Reports. Lawyers' edition. 2d series. Selected volumes.

U.S. Attorney General. *Proceedings of the Attorney General's Conference on Crime . . . 1934*. Washington, D.C., 1936.

U.S. Bureau of Alcohol, Tobacco, and Firearms. *State Laws and Published Ordinances—Firearms*. 19th ed. Washington, D.C., 1988.

————. *Your Guide to Firearms Regulation*. Washington, D.C., 1978, and subsequent revised editions.

U.S. Comptroller General's Report to Congress. "Handgun Control: Effectiveness and Cost." Washington, D.C., Feb. 6, 1978, n.p.

U.S. Congress. *American State Papers: Documents, Legislative and Executive, of the Congress of the United States*. 38 vols. Washington, D.C., 1832–1861.

————. *Congressional Globe*. 23d Congress to the 42d Congress, Dec. 2, 1833, to March 3, 1873. 43 vols. Washington, D.C., 1834–1873.

————. *Congressional Record*. Washington, D.C., 1873–2000.

————. *The Debates and Proceedings in the Congress of the United States . . . 1789–1824*. 42 vols. Washington, D.C., 1834–1856.

U.S. Congress, House of Representatives. *Brady Handgun Violence Prevention Act* (hearing before the Subcommittee on Crime and Criminal Justice of the Committee on the Judiciary). 103d Cong., 1st Sess., Sept. 30, 1993.

————. *Carrying of Pistols, Revolvers, and Other Firearms Capable of Being Concealed on the Person in the Mails* (hearings before a subcommittee of the Committee on the Post Office Post Roads). 69th Cong., 1st Sess., Feb. 17, 1926.

————. *Children and Guns* (hearing before the Select Committee on Children, Youth, and Families). 101st Cong., 1st Sess., June 15, 1989.

————. *Dismantling of the Bureau of Alcohol, Tobacco, and Firearms* (hearings before the subcommittee on crime of the Committee on the Judiciary). 97th Cong., 1st Sess., Apr. 30 and Dec. 16, 1981. Serial no. 127, Washington, D.C., 1983.

————. *Firearms* (hearing before a subcommittee of the Committee on Interstate and Foreign Commerce). 71st Cong., 2d Sess., Apr. 11, 1930.

————. *Gun Control Legislation* (hearings before Subcommittee No. 5 of the Committee on the Judiciary). 92d Cong., 2d Sess., June 27–29, 1972.

————. *Interstate Carrying of Concealed Firearms by Law Enforcement Officials . . .* (hearing before the Subcommittee on Crime of the Committee on the Judiciary). 105th Cong., 1st Sess., H.R. 218 and H.R. 339, July 22, 1997.

———. *National Firearms Act* (hearings before the Committee on Ways and Means). 73d Cong., 2d Sess., April 14, 15, and 16, 1934.

———. *Public Safety and Recreational Firearms Use Protection Act* (hearing before the Subcommittee on Crime and Criminal Justice). 103d Cong., 2d Sess., H.R. 3527, April 25, 1994.

———. *Public Statutes at Large of the United States of America . . . 1789 to March 3, 1845.* 8 vols. Boston, 1845.

———. *To Regulate Commerce in Firearms* (hearing before a subcommittee of the Committee on Interstate and Foreign Commerce). 75th Cong., 1st Sess., June 23, 1937.

U.S. Congress, Senate. *Gun Control and Constitutional Rights* (hearing before the Subcommittee on the Constitution of the Committee on the Judiciary). 96th Cong., 2d Sess., Sept. 15, 1980.

———. *Federal Firearms Act* (hearings before the Subcommittee to Investigate Juvenile Delinquency of the Committee on the Judiciary). 89th Cong., 1st Sess., S. Res. 52, May, June, and July 1965.

———. 90th Cong., 1st Sess., S. Res. 35, July and Aug. 1967.

———. *Federal Firearms Legislation.* 90th Cong., 2d Sess., S. Res. 240, June and July 1968.

———. 91st Cong., 1st Sess., S. Res 48, July 23, 24, and 29, 1969.

———. *The Federal Raid on Ruby Ridge, ID* (hearings before the Subcommittee on Terrorism, Technology, and Government Information of the Committee on the Judiciary). 101st Cong., 1st Sess., Sept. 1–26 and Oct. 13–19, 1995. Washington, D.C., 1997.

———. *The Firearms Owner Protection Act* (hearings before the Committee on the Judiciary). 97th Cong., 1st and 2d Sess., S. 1030, Dec. 9, 11, 1981, and Feb. 8, 1982.

———. 98th Cong., 1st Sess., S. 914, Oct. 4, 1983.

———. *Gun Control and Constitutional Rights* (hearing before the Subcommittee on the Constitution of the Committee on the Judiciary). 96th Cong., 2d Sess., Sept. 15, 1980. Washington, D.C., 1981.

———. *Guns in Schools: A Federal Role?* (hearings before the Subcommittee on Youth Violence of the Committee on the Judiciary). 104th Cong., 1st Sess., July 18, 1995. Washington D.C., 1997.

———. *Interstate Traffic in Mail-Order Firearms* (hearings before the Subcommittee to Investigate Juvenile Delinquency of the Committee on the Judiciary). 88th Cong., 1st Sess., Jan. 29–30, March 7, and May 1–2, 1963.

———, Senate. *Third Interim Report of the Special Committee to Investigate Organized Crime in Interstate Commerce.* 82d Cong., 1st Sess. Washington, D.C., 1951.

———. *To Regulate Commerce of Firearms* (hearing before the Subcommittee on Surface Transportation of the Committee on Commerce), 74th Cong. 1st Sess. April 16, 1935.

U.S. Continental Congress. *Journals of the Continental Congress, 1774–1789.* Ed. Gaillard Hunt. 34 vols. Washington, D.C., 1904–1937.

U.S. Department of Health, Education and Welfare. *Television and Behavior: Ten Years of Scientific Progress and Implications for the Eighties.* 2 vols. Washington, D.C., 1982.

———. *Television and Growing Up: The Impact of Televised Violence.* Washington, D.C., 1972.

———. *Television and Social Behavior: Reports and Papers.* 5 vols. Washington, D.C., 1972.

U.S. Department of the Interior. *Restoring America's Wildlife.* Rev. ed. Washington, D.C., 1995.

U.S. Department of Justice. Alfred Blumenstein, au. *Youth Violence, Guns, and Illicit Drug Markets.* Washington, D.C., 1996.

———. Bureau of Justice Statistics. *Guns and Crime: Handgun Victimization, Firearm Self-Defense, and Firearm Theft.* Washington, D.C., Apr. 1994.

———. *Criminal Justice Research Under the Crime Act—1995 to 1996.* Washington, D.C., Sept. 13, 1997.

———. *Lethal Violence: Proceedings of the 1995 Meeting of the Homicide Working Group.* Washington, D.C., 1997.

————. National Institute of Justice. *Arrestees and Guns: Monitoring the Illegal Firearms Market.* Washington, D.C., 1995.

————. Uniform Crime Reports. *Crime in the United States.* Washington, D.C., 1971–2000.

U.S. National Commission on the Causes and Prevention of Violence. *To Establish Justice, To Insure Domestic Tranquility, Final Report.* 1969. Reprint, Washington, D.C., 1970.

U.S. National Commission on Law Observance and Enforcement (Wickersham Commission). *Report on the Causes of Crime.* 2 vols. Washington, D.C., 1931.

U.S. President's Commission on Law Enforcement and Administration of Justice. *The Challenge of Crime in a Free Society.* Washington, D.C., 1967.

U.S. Treasury Department. *National Firearms Act and Federal Firearms Act.* Washington, D.C., 1966. Publication no. 364.

————. *Report on the Bureau of Alcohol, Tobacco, and Firearms Investigation of Vernon Wayne Howell also Known as David Koresh.* Washington, D.C., 1993.

Upton, Emory. *The Military Policy of the United States.* Washington, D.C., 1912.

Utley, Robert M. *Billy the Kid: A Short and Violent Life.* Lincoln, Nebr., 1989.

————. *High Noon in Lincoln: Violence on the Western Frontier.* Albuquerque, N.M., 1987.

————. *The Indian Frontier of the American West, 1846–1890.* Albuquerque, N.M., 1984.

Utter, Glenn H., ed. *Encyclopedia of Gun Control and Gun Rights.* Phoenix, Ariz., 2000.

Vagts, Alfred. *A History of Militarism: Civilian and Military.* Rev. ed. New York, 1959.

Van Alstyne, William W. "The Second Amendment and the Personal Right to Arms." *Duke Law Journal* 43 (Apr. 1994): 1236–55.

Van Biema, David. "Terror in the Sanctuary." *Time,* Sept. 27, 1999, pp. 42–3.

Vandal, Gilles. *The New Orleans Riot of 1866: Anatomy of a Tragedy.* Lafayette, La., 1983.

————. *Rethinking Southern Violence: Homicides in Post–Civil War Louisiana, 1866–1884.* Columbus, Ohio, 2000.

Vandercoy, David E. "The History of the Second Amendment." *Valparaiso Law Review* 28 (1994): 1007–39.

Van Loan, Charles E. "Disarming New York." *Munsey's Magazine* 46 (Feb. 1912): 687–92.

Van Wagoner, Richard S. *Mormon Polygamy: A History.* Salt Lake City, 1986.

Vassar, Mary J., and Kenneth W. Kizer. "Hospitalizations for Firearm-Related Injuries: A Population-Based Study of 9562 Patients." *Journal of the American Medical Association* 276 (June 12, 1996): 1734–9.

Veit, Helen E., Kenneth R. Bowling, and Charlene B. Bickford, eds. *Creating the Bill of Rights: The Documentary Record from the First Federal Congress.* Baltimore, 1991.

Vila, Bryan, and Cynthia Morris, eds. *The Role of Police in American Society.* Westport, Conn., 1999.

Villard, Oswald Garrison. "Official Lawlessness: The Third Degree and the Crime Wave." *Harper's* 155 (Oct. 1927): 605–14.

Violence Policy Center. *Kids Shooting Kids: Stories From Across the Nation of Unintentional Shootings Among Children and Youth.* Washington, D.C., March 1997.

————. *NRA with the Gun and Tobacco Industry Dollars Uses Its Eddie Eagle Program to Market Guns to Kids.* Washington, D.C., 1997.

————. *Putting Guns Back Into Criminals' Hands.* Washington, D.C., May 1992.

————. *The Second Amendment: No Right to Keep and Bear Arms.* Washington, D.C., 1998.

————. *Unsafe in Any Hands: Why America Needs to Ban Handguns.* Washington, D.C., 2000.

Violence Policy Center, Web site. <http://www.vpc.org>.

Vizzard, William J. *In the Crossfire: A Political History of the Bureau of Alcohol, Tobacco, and Firearms.* Boulder, Colo., 1997.

————. *Shots in the Dark: The Policy, Politics, and Symbolism of Gun Control.* Lanham, Md., 2000.

Volokh, Eugene. "The Amazing Vanishing Second Amendment." *New York University Law Review* 73 (June 1998): 831–40.

————. "The Commonplace Second Amendment." *New York University Law Review* 73 (June 1998): 793–821.

Wade, Richard C. *The Urban Frontier: The Rise of Western Cities, 1790–1830*. Cambridge, Mass., 1959.

Wade, Wyn Craig. *The Fiery Cross: The Ku Klux Klan in America*. New York, 1987.

Walker, Jack L., Jr. *Mobilizing Interest Groups in America: Patrons, Professions, and Social Movements*. Ann Arbor, Mich., 1991.

Walker, Martin. *The President We Deserve: Bill Clinton: His Rise, Falls, and Comebacks*. New York, 1996.

Walker, Samuel. *A Critical History of Police Reform: The Emergence of Professionalism*. Toronto, 1977.

Wallman, Joel. "Disarming Youth." *HFC Review* 2 (fall 1997). 3–9.

Warner, Sam Bass, Jr. *The Private City: Philadelphia in Three Periods of Its Growth*. Philadelphia, 1968.

Washburn, Wilcomb E. *The Governor and the Rebel: A History of Bacon's Rebellion in Virginia*. Chapel Hill, N.C., 1957.

Washington, George. *The Papers of George Washington*. Part IV, Confederation Series, ed. W. W. Abbot and Dorothy Twohig. Part VI, Revolutionary Series, ed. Dorothy Twohig. Charlottesville, Va., 1994, 1995.

———. *The Writings of George Washington . . . 1745–1799*. Ed. John C. Fitzpatrick. 39 vols. Washington, D.C., 1931–1944.

Waterman, Charles F. *Hunting in America*. New York, 1973.

Weatherup, Roy G. "Standing Armies and Armed Citizens: An Historical Analysis of the Second Amendment." *Hastings Constitutional Law Quarterly* 2 (fall 1975): 961–1001.

Webb, Walter P. "The Story of the Six-Shooter." In Blacker, ed. *Old West*, 303–12.

———. *The Texas Rangers: A Century of Frontier Defense*. 2d ed. Austin, Tex., 1965.

Weber, Paul J. "The National Rifle Association: Public Enemy No. 2." *Christian Century* 91 (Oct. 16, 1974): 958–60.

Webster, Donald B., Jr. *Suicide Specials*. Harrisburg, Pa., 1958.

Weigley, Russell F. *History of the United States Army*. Enlarged ed. Bloomington, Ind., 1984.

Weil, Douglas S., and Rebecca C. Knox. "Effects of Limiting Handgun Purchases on Interstate Transfer of Firearms." *Journal of the American Medical Association* 276 (June 12, 1996): 1759–61.

Weir, William. *A Well-Regulated Militia: The Battle Over Gun Control*. North Haven, Conn., 1997.

———. *Written with Lead: Legendary American Gunfights and Gunfighters*. Hamden, Conn., 1992.

Welkos, Robert W. "A Few New Tricks of the Hollywood Trade." *Calendar* In Los Angeles Times, Aug. 8, 1999, pp. 9, 24–6.

Weller, Jac. "The Sullivan Law." *American Rifleman* 110 (Apr. 1962): 33–6.

Weller, Sheila. "Sarah Brady." *Ms.* 17 (Jan.–Feb. 1989): 84–7.

West, Elliott. *The Contested Plains: Indians, Goldseekers, and the Rush to Colorado*. Lawrence, Kans., 1998.

West, Jenny. *Gunpowder, Government, and War in the Mid-Eighteenth Century*. Woodbridge, Eng., 1991.

Westermeier, Clifford P. "The Cowboy—Sinner or Saint!" *New Mexico Historical Review* 25 (Apr. 1950): 89–108.

———, ed. *Trailing the Cowboy: Life and Lore as Told by Frontier Journalists*. Caldwell, Ida., 1955.

Western, John R. *The English Militia in the Eighteenth Century: The Story of a Political Issue, 1660–1802*. London, 1965.

———. *Monarchy and Revolution: The English State in the 1680s*. Totowa, N.J., 1972.

"When Lawsuits Make Policy." *The Economist*, Nov. 21–27, 1998, pp. 17–18.

Whisker, James B. *Arms Makers of Colonial America*. Selinsgrove, Pa., 1992.

———. *The Citizen Soldier and United States Military Policy*. Croton-on-Hudson, N.Y., 1979.

———. *Our Vanishing Freedom: The Right to Keep and Bear Arms*. McLean, Va., 1972.

———. *The Rise and Decline of the American Militia System*. Selinsgrove, Pa., 1999.

———. "The Second Amendment: The Right to Keep and Bear Arms." Ph.D. diss., University of Maryland, 1969.

White, John T. "Standing Armies in Time of War: Republican Theory and Military Practice During the American Revolution." Ph.D. diss., George Washington University, 1978.

White, Richard. *"It's Your Misfortune and None of My Own": A History of the American West.* Norman, Okla., 1991.

———. "Outlaw Gangs of the Middle Border: American Social Bandits." *Western Historical Quarterly* 12 (Oct. 1981): 387–408.

Whitman, Howard. *Terror in the Streets.* New York, 1951.

Wiener, Frederick B. "The Militia Clause of the Constitution." *Harvard Law Review* 54 (Dec. 1940): 181–220.

Wikstrom, Per-Olof H. *Urban Crime, Criminals, and Victims: The Swedish Experience in an Anglo-American Comparative Perspective.* New York, 1991.

Wilentz, Sean. *Chants Democratic: New York City and the Rise of the American Working Class, 1788–1850.* New York, 1984.

Williams, David C. "Civic Republicanism and the Citizen Militia: The Terrifying Second Amendment." *Yale Law Review* 101 (Dec. 1991): 551–615.

———. "The Constitutional Right to 'Conservative' Revolution." *Harvard Civil Rights–Civil Liberties Law Review* 32 (summer 1997): 413–47.

———. "The Militia Movement and Second Amendment Revolutions: Conjuring with the People." *Cornell Law Review* 81 (May 1996): 879–952.

———. "The Unitary Second Amendment." *New York University Law Review* 73 (June 1998): 822–30.

Williams, J. Sherwood, and John H. McGrath. "Why People Own Guns." *Journal of Communication* 26 (autumn 1976): 22–30.

Williams, Roger M. "The Gun Fighters." *Foundation News* 32 (March–Apr. 1990): 37–41.

Williamson, Harold F. *Winchester: The Gun That Won the West.* New York, 1952.

Williamson, Joel. *The Crucible of Race: Black-White Relations in the American South Since Emancipation.* New York, 1984.

Williamson, Robert L. "The Muzzle-Loading Rifle: Frontier Tool." In *Essays on the American West,* ed. Harold M. Hollingsworth and Sandra L. Myres, 66–88. Austin, Tex., 1969.

Wills, Garry. *John Wayne's America: The Politics of Celebrity.* New York, 1997.

———. *A Necessary Evil: A History of American Distrust of Government.* New York, 1999.

———. "The New Revolutionaries." *New York Review of Books,* Aug. 10, 1995, pp. 50–55.

———. *The Second Civil War: Arming for Armageddon.* New York, 1968.

———. "To Keep and Bear Arms." *New York Review of Books,* Sept. 21, 1995, pp. 62–73.

Wilson, James Q. "Crime and American Culture." *The Public Interest* 70 (winter 1983): 22–48.

———. "Crime and Punishment in England." *The Public Interest* 43 (spring 1976): 3–25.

Wilson, John L. *The Code of Honor, or Rules for the Government of Principals and Seconds in Duelling.* Charleston, S.C., 1838.

Wilson, Theodore B. *The Black Codes of the South.* University, Ala., 1965.

Wilson, Woodrow. *The Papers of Woodrow Wilson.* Ed. Arthur S. Link. 69 vols. Princeton, 1966–1994.

Wiltz, John E. *In Search of Peace: The Senate Munitions Inquiry, 1934–36.* Baton Rouge, La., 1963.

Windlesham, David J. G. H. *Politics, Punishment, and Populism.* New York, 1998.

———. *Responses to Crime.* 3 vols. Oxford, Eng., 1987–1996.

Wintemute, Garen J. "The Relationship Between Firearm Design and Firearm Violence: Handguns in the 1990s." *Journal of the American Medical Association* 276 (June 12, 1996): 1749–53.

———. *Ring of Fire: The Handgun Makers of Southern California.* Violence Prevention Research Program, Sacramento, Calif., 1994.

Wintemute, Garen J., and others. "Mortality Among Recent Purchasers of Handguns." *New England Journal of Medicine* 341 (Nov. 18, 1999): 1583–89.

Wintemute, Garen J., and others. "Prior Misdemeanor Convictions as a Risk Factor for Later Violent and Firearm-Related Criminal Activity Among Authorized Purchasers of Handguns." *Journal of the American Medical Association* 280 (Dec. 23/30, 1998): 2083–93.

Witkin, Gordon. "The Great Debate: Should You Own a Gun?" *U.S. News and World Report*, Aug. 15, 1996, pp. 24–36.

Wolfe, Bruce C., and Bertram J. Levine. *Lobbying Congress: How the System Works*. 2d ed. Washington, D.C., 1996.

Wolfgang, Marvin E. *Patterns in Criminal Homicide*. Philadelphia, 1958.

Wolper, Roy S. "The Rhetoric of Gunpowder and the Idea of Progress." *Journal of the History of Ideas* 31 (Oct.–Dec. 1970): 589–98.

Wood, Gordon S. *The Creation of the American Republic, 1776–1787*. Chapel Hill, N.C., 1969.

Wright, James D. "Bad Guys, Bad Guns." *National Review*, March 6, 1995, pp. 51–2.

———. "Public Opinion and Gun Control: A Comparison of Results from Two Recent National Surveys." *Annals of the American Academy of Political and Social Science* 455 (May 1981): 24–39.

———. "Second Thoughts About Gun Control." *The Public Interest* 91 (spring 1988): 23–39.

———. "Ten Essential Observations on Guns in America." *Society* 32 (March–Apr. 1995): 63–8.

Wright, James D., and Kathleen Daly. *Under the Gun: Weapons, Crime, and Violence in America*. New York, 1983.

Wright, James D., and Linda Marston. "The Ownership of the Means of Destruction: Weapons in the United States." *Social Problems* 23 (Oct. 1975): 93–107.

Wright, James D., and Peter H. Rossi. *Armed and Considered Dangerous: A Survey of Felons and Their Firearms*. New York, 1986.

———. *Weapons, Crime, and Violence in America: Executive Summary*. Washington, D.C., 1981.

Wright, James D., Peter H. Rossi, Kathleen Daly, and Eleanor Weber-Burdin. *Weapons, Crime, and Violence in America: A Literature Review and Research Agenda*. Washington, D.C., 1981.

Wright, James D., Joseph F. Sheley, and M. Dwayne Smith. "Kids, Guns, and Killing Fields." *Society* 30 (Nov.–Dec. 1992): 84–9.

Wright, Robert K., Jr. *The Continental Army*. Washington, D.C., 1983.

Wright, Robert M. *Dodge City: Cowboy Capital and the Great Southwest*. Wichita, Kans., 1913.

Wright, Stuart A., ed. *Armageddon in Waco: Critical Perspectives on the Branch Davidian Conflict*. Chicago, 1995.

Wright, Will. *Six Guns and Society: A Structural Study of the Western*. Berkeley, 1975.

Wrobel, David M. *The End of American Exceptionalism: Frontier Anxiety from the Old West to the New Deal*. Lawrence, Kans., 1993.

Wyatt-Brown, Bertram. *Southern Honor: Ethics and Behavior in the Old South*. New York, 1982.

Yeager, Matthew G., Joseph D. Alviani, and Nancy Loving. *How Well Does the Handgun Protect You and Your Family?* Washington, D.C., 1976.

Young, David E., ed. *The Origin of the Second Amendment: A Documentary History of the Bill of Rights . . . 1787–1792*. 2d ed. Ontonagon, Mich., 1995.

Young, Robert L., David McDowell, and Colin Loftin. "Collective Security and the Ownership of Firearms for Protection." *Criminology* 25 (Feb. 1987): 47–62.

Zahn, Margaret A. "Homicide in the Twentieth Century: Trends, Types, and Causes." In Gurr, ed. *Violence in America* I: 216–34.

———. "Trends and Patterns of Homicide in the 20th-Century United States." In Smith and Zahn, eds. *Homicide*, 9–23.

Zehr, Howard. "The Modernization of Crime in Germany and France, 1803–1913." *Journal of Social History* 8 (summer 1975): 117–41.

Zimring, Franklin E. *American Youth Violence*. New York, 1996.

———. "Firearms and Federal Law: The Gun Control Act of 1968." *Journal of Legal Studies* 4 (Jan. 1975): 133–98.

———. "Firearms, Violence, and Public Policy." *Scientific American* 265 (Nov. 1991): 48–54.

———. "Games with Guns and Statistics." *Wisconsin Law Review* 4 (1968): 113–26.

———. "Gun Control." *National Institute of Justice: Crime File Study Guide*. Washington, D.C., 1988.

———. "Is Gun Control Likely to Reduce Violent Killings?" *University of Chicago Law Review* 35 (summer 1968): 721–37.

————. "Reflections on Firearms and the Criminal Law." *Journal of Criminal Law and Criminology* 86 (fall 1995): 1–9.

————. "Street Crimes and New Guns: Some Implications for Firearms Control." *Journal of Criminal Justice* 4 (summer 1976): 95–107.

Zimring, Franklin E., and Gordon Hawkins. *The Citizen's Guide to Gun Control.* New York, 1987.

————. *Crime Is Not the Problem: Lethal Violence in America.* New York, 1997.

————. "The Research on Concealed Weapons Laws Is Flawed." In Roleff, ed. *Guns and Crime,* 33–44.

Index

accidental gun deaths, 166, 224
accidental shootings, 252–53
Accu-Tek, 282
Act Preventing Negroes from Bearing Arms, An, 21
Adams, John, 32–33, 42
Adams, John Quincy, 46
Adams, Samuel, 29
Adams v. Williams, 194
advertising, 282
Afghanistan, 246
African Americans. *See* blacks
AK-47. *See* assault weapons
Albright, Madeleine, 253
Alcohol and Tobacco Tax Division, 162–63, 190
    (*see also* Bureau of Alcohol, Tobacco, and Fire-
    arms)
Allott, Gordon, 176
American Bar Association, 121, 184
American Civil Liberties Union, 184
American Committee for Defense of British
    Homes, 149–50
American Federation of Labor, 97–98
American Game Association, 142
American Legion, 146–47
American Rifleman magazine: about, 116; on anti-
    firearm sentiment, 172; "Armed Citizen" col-
    umn, 165; against legislation, 151, 165; military
    image of, 157; Oswald's rifle purchased through,
    171; on positive aspects of gun keeping, 161, 317
American Sportsmen's Foundation, 175
American Wildlife Institute, 145
Americans for Democratic Action, 197
America's First Freedom magazine, 295
anarchism, 100
Anderson, James L., 5
Andros, Edmund, 20
animal rights groups, 166

anti-Federalists, 31–34, 36
anticommunism, 166, 167
antismoking campaign parallel, 307
antitank guns, 186
Aquino, Corazon C., 240
Argentina, ownership restrictions, 187
Armed Career Criminal Act, 226
Arming America (Bellesiles), 5, 311–13
armor-piercing bullets, 219, 265, 276
Arms and the Man magazine, 116
arms industry: aggressive marketing by, 95; all-time
    sales records of, 257; during Civil War, 65–66,
    68; condemnation of, 127; conservation agenda
    of, 145–46; copycat weapons sales, 269; in Eu-
    rope, 95–96; expansion in WWII, 153; against
    foreign imports, 163–64, 168; lawsuits against,
    220, 232, 274–75, 282; in lean times, 117–18;
    manufacturing ban attempt, 121–22; mass
    handgun production by, 79–80; in Mexican
    War, 59; and NRA, 142; and popular interest in
    guns, 60; preferential treatment issue, 283–85;
    privileged treatment of, 253; record-keeping re-
    quirements on, 162–63; against regulation, 109;
    safety standards of, 96, 284–85; as stimulant for
    gun-control movement, 139; tariff protections
    for, 128; in WWI, 116
arms race, 203
arms trafficking embargoes, 97, 111
army: Civil War conscriptions, 65, 67–68; Congres-
    sional power to raise, 33; expanded federal con-
    trol of, 139; federal legislation of, 101; in
    Mexican War, 58; as official defense establish-
    ment, 160; professionalization of, 10–11, 13,
    197; quality of volunteers, 59; recruitment into,
    58; sentiments toward, 35, 68; Washington's re-
    quest for, 39
Arnett, G. Ray, 229

395

arsenals, 40, 42, 99
Arthur, Chester A., 87
Articles of Confederation, 29, 31
Asano Yoshinaga, 10
Ashcroft, John D., 313–15, 316, 317, 318, 322
assassination attempts: on Brady, 215; on Ford, 201; on Gaynor, 108; on Jackson, 50; on Reagan, 215–16; on F. D. Roosevelt, 134–35; on T. Roosevelt, 111–12; on Truman, 159; on Wallace, 194
assassinations: of Garfield, 92; of J. F. Kennedy, 171; of R. F. Kennedy, 183; of King, 182–83; of Lincoln, 68; of McKinley, 100
assault weapons: bans on, 237–40, 245; G. H. W. Bush on, 238–39, 242; imports of, 250, 271–73; legislation against, 254–56; police outgunned by, 266
Assault Weapons Control Act, California, 239, 269
Australia, 262–63, 304
automatic weapons. See assault weapons; machine guns
Aymette v. the State, 52

background checks, 232, 274, 276–77
Bacon, Nathaniel, Jr., 20
Baker, James Jay, 286, 294, 313, 315, 317
ballistic coding, 142
Barnes, Michael D., 317
Bartley, David, 199
BATF. See Bureau of Alcohol, Tobacco, and Firearms
bazookas, 186, 283
Beard, Michael K., 197, 219–20
Beasley, Martha, 301
Beecher, Henry Ward, 64
Beecher, Lyman, 45
Bell Campaign, 281, 294
Bell, Griffin, 205
Bellesiles, Michael A., 5, 61, 311–13
Bennett, William J., 238
Benton, Thomas Hart, 81
Berkeley, William, 20
Biaggi, Mario, 219
Biaggi-Moynihan bill, 219–20, 230
Biden, Joseph, 242, 255
Bill of Rights: approval of, 34; debate over, 32, 33–34; enactment of, 36; English model, 13–14, 24, 32, 35; in states, 36; states rights controversy, 77–78
Billy the Kid, 85
birthright theory, 299–300
Black Codes, 72
black militants, 173, 177, 179, 198
Black Panthers, 179
black-market weapons, 247
blacks: in armed conflict with whites, 76–77, 78; arming of, 72; citizen-soldiers against, 28; death

by guns, 275; denial of right to bear arms, 65, 75, 78; and doctrine of incorporation, 96; guns viewed as freedom symbol, 75; laws directed against, 21–22; murdered by segregationists, 175; against police, 179; under Reconstruction, 71–73; right to bear arms, 72–73; in Rodney King riots, 244–45; self-defense arming of, 56, 173, 175
Blackstone, William, 13, 24
Blanton, Thomas, 124
Blek, Mary Leigh, 281
Bliss v. Commonwealth, 52
Bock, Audie, 307
Boer War, 106
Bolivar de Pugh, Robert, 177
Bonaparte, Charles J., 138
Bonney, William H., 85
Boone, Daniel, 51
Booth, John Wilkes, 68
bootlegging, 120
"Border Ruffians," 64
Borinsky, Mark, 198
Boston Harbor rebellion, 27
Boy Scouts of America, 107
Boyd, William, 161
Bradley, Omar N., 155
Brady bill, 231–32, 241–42, 245, 249–51, 316
Brady Center to Prevent Gun Violence, 314, 317, 321, 322
Brady Handgun Violence Prevention Act: crime rate decline under, 287; failures of, 297; NRA against, 267–68; passage of, 251–52; as presidential campaign issue, 265–66; prosecution rates under, 289; Tenth Amendment challenge of, 267–68
Brady, James, 215, 220, 241, 242
Brady, Sarah: about, 228–29; at Democratic National Convention, 265; as Handgun Control president, 241; and Kennedy-Rodino proposal, 231; lobbying of, 242; at Million Mom March, 294; speaking to shooters, 306
Branch Davidians, 258–59
Brandegee, Frank, 122
Brazil, 247–48
breech-loading rifles, 43
Brisbane, Arthur, 108
Britain: bans on technologically advanced firearms, 238; control legislation, 240; Criminal Justice and Public Order Act, 251; early gun-control efforts, 11–13, 14; Firearms Act, 119; Firearms Amendment Act, 147; Game Licenses Act, 91; Gun Licenses Act, 91; gun violence, 240; handgun restrictions, 94; law enforcement, 54–55; low civilian demand for guns, 47; Metropolitan Police Bill, 54–55; Militia Ordinance, 11; ownership restrictions, 91, 187; Pistols Act, 106, 119;

rise in crime, 209; selective gun registration, 47–48; sporting privileges, 15; surplus arms sales, 191

Brooks, Jack, 254

Brown, Rap, 179

Bryant, Martin, 263

Bryco Arms, 271

Buchanan, James, 86

Buchwald, Art, 192

Buck, Ellsworth H., 158

bullets, under product safety law, 252

Buntline, Ned (Judson pseudonym), 61

Bureau of Alcohol, Tobacco, and Firearms: Clinton proposals for, 289–90; enforcement of Gun Control Act, 193; felon rehabilitation program of, 246; and Gun Decontrol Act, 227; gun-lobby bashing of, 228; gun tracing by, 207, 214, 321; NRA opposition to, 207, 211, 213–14; rogue operation within, 271–72; in Ruby Ridge siege, 258; safety standards monitoring by, 284; specialized police powers of, 306; in Waco siege, 258–59; weakness of, 214, 230, 246, 285, 290

Burger, Warren, 305

Burke-Wadsworth Act, 150

Burr, Aaron, 45

Bush, Barbara, 238

Bush, George H. W.: about, 235; on assault weapons, 238–39, 242; concessions to control advocates, 245–46; condemnation of NRA, 260; crime control program of, 239–40; election campaigns of, 235–36, 245, 246; gun control act signed by, 260; on plastic-gun bill, 235–36; on Wesbecker massacre, 240

Bush, George W., 292–93, 296, 313

Butler, Andrew P., 64

Cabey, Darrell, 227

California gold rush, 81

Calling Forth Act, 40

Camperlingo, Joseph, 124

Canada: gun-control effectiveness in, 210–11; homicide rate in, 248; ownership restrictions, 187; rise in crime, 209

Capone, Alphonse "Scarface Al," 127, 129

Capper, Arthur, 133

Cardoso, Fernando Henrique, 248

carjackers, 269

Carmichael, Stokely, 173

Carneal, Michael, 272

Carter, Harlon B., 205, 211, 222–23

Carter, Jimmy: BATF improvement proposals of, 207; Brady bill endorsement by, 242; denunciation by progun faction, 207–8; draft registration under, 212; in election debates, 205; for gun controls, 205; against international gun commerce, 203, 206; mentioned, 249; platform of, 204;

Reagan's defeat of, 213; for registration, 206–7; on subservience to gun lobby, 208

Cases v. United States, 152

Catholics: disarmed in England, 11, 13, 14; firearms denied to, 22–23; nativist attacks on, 57

Celler, Emanuel, 178, 185, 194

Centers for Disease Control and Prevention, 273

Center to Prevent Handgun Violence, 224

Cermak, Anton J., 135

Chandler, Albert B., 151–52

Charles I, King of England, 11

Charles II, King of England, 11

cheap handguns: availability of, 79–80, 90, 105, 195; legislation on, 206–7, 232–33, 287; media on, 169

Chicago: crime in, 120–22, 129; gangster activities in, 125; gun-control laws of, 208; St. Valentine's Day massacre, 129; submachine gun use in, 126–27

Chick, Laura, 266

childproof locks, 287

children, 237, 260 (*see also* juvenile gun violence; school shootings; youth crime)

Christian, Charles, 54

Christian Science Monitor, 169

Church, Frank, 305

Church of Jesus Christ of Latter-Day Saints, 86–87

church shooting ranges, 90

Church, William C., 89

cities, legislation by, 275

Citizens Against Gun Initiatives, 221

Citizens Against Street Crime and Concealed Weapons, 221

Citizens Committee for the Right to Keep and Bear Arms, 222

citizen-soldiers, 28–30, 48–49, 59–60

Civil Disobedience Act, 178–79

civil rights, 179

Civil Rights Act of 1866, 73, 76

civil rights movement, 166, 175, 178

Civil War, 65–68

Civil War acts, 66–67

Clark, Grenville, 150

Clark, Joseph, 201

Clark, Ramsay, 184, 190

Clark, Thomas C., 156

class restraints, 90, 107

Clay, Henry, 46

Clayton, Powell, 74

Cleveland, Grover, 98

Clinton, Bill: anticrime program of, 250, 253–54, 255–56; in BATF reinvigoration, 290; bipartisan strategy of, 253–54; Brady bill endorsed by, 245, 287; on criminal violence, 266; election campaigns of, 245, 246, 266; entertainment industry inquiry of, 282; gun buyback program of, 289;

Clinton, Bill (*cont.*)
  gun-control agenda of, 249–50; against gun dealers, 290; and Gun-Free Schools Act, 261; gun
  ownership legislation of, 276–77; illegal firearms
  crackdown of, 289; juvenile crime bill of, 281; on
  juvenile gun murders, 268, 273, 278, 291; NRA
  against, 255, 269–70, 291–92; prison sentence
  legislation of, 274; against Republican legislation, 271, 286; and Sarah Brady, 265; and Serbia
  bombing, 281; smart-gun technology research
  request of, 290
Coalition to Stop Gun Violence, 209, 318
cold-war era, 160–61
Coll, Vincent "Mad Dog," 131
Collazo, Oscar, 159
colleges, marksmanship taught in, 95
Colombia, 248
colonial America: crime and vigilantism, 23–24;
  gun production in, 24; gun keeping restrictions,
  17–24; rebellion in, 27–30
Colt company: about, 60; against assault weapon
  ban, 239; against federal license fees, 143; handgun mass production by, 79; lobbies against legislation, 122; on National Firearms Act
  amendment, 147; on preferential treatment,
  284; as sole machine gun manufacturer, 143
Colt, Samuel, 58, 59, 60–61
Columbine High School shootings, 275–76
commerce clause, 261
Commission on the Causes and Prevention of Violence, 184, 192
Commission on Law Enforcement and Administration of Justice, 176
Committee to Ban Teen-Age Weapons, 156
Communities for Safer Guns Coalition, 285
Comprehensive Crime Control legislation, 226
concealed weapons: crime linkage of, 98; legislation against, 51–52, 107, 121; licensing of, 109;
  in post–Civil War era, 80; sentiment against,
  106
concealed-carry laws, 230–31, 274
conscription: as Carter campaign issue, 212; in
  Civil War, 65; under Eisenhower, 160; end of,
  197; under L. B. Johnson, 182; under Nixon, 196;
  Reagan on, 220–21; resistance against, 67–68,
  182, 196; under Truman, 159; under Wilson,
  116–17; in WWII, 150–51
conservation movement, 145–46
conspiracy theory, 174
Constitution (*see also* specific amendments):
  amendment process, 34; commerce clause of,
  261; creation of, 31–33; doctrine of incorporation, 77, 93, 96–97
Consumer Product Safety Act, 193, 252
consumer protection laws, 287
Continental Army, 28–30

Continental Congresses, 27, 29
Convention on the Control of the Acquisition and
  Possession of Firearms by Individuals, 206
conviction rates, 208
Conyers, John, 319
Coolidge, Calvin, 126, 127
Cooper, James Fenimore, 51
cop-killer bullets, 219, 265, 276
Copeland, Royal S., 142, 143, 146
copycat weapons, 256, 269
Cornell, Alonzo B., 89
Corporation for the Promotion of Rifle Practice,
  256–57
Council to Control Handguns, 198, 209
cowboys, 85, 148
Crail, Joe, 129–30
crime: across state borders, 128–29; under Brady
  Handgun Violence Prevention Act, 287; Clinton
  anticrime program, 250, 253–54, 255–56; in
  cold-war era, 164; in colonial era, 23–24; commissions on, 176, 188, 192; concealed handgun
  linkage, 98; early police prevention efforts,
  54–55; federal programs against, 144–45; G. H.
  W. Bush anticrime program, 239–40, 242;
  media views of, 129; in New York City, 63, 131;
  in nineteenth century, 50, 55; organized crime,
  158, 167; police guns used in, 288; in post–Civil
  War era, 71; in postbellum North, 79; in Wild
  West, 83–85; worldwide rise in, 209–10; youth
  crime, 243–44, 245, 261
Crimean War, 61
Crockett, Davy, 161
Cromwell, Oliver, 11
Cruikshank, William J., 77
cults, 258–59
Cummings, Homer S., 137–39, 144, 146
Cummings, Sam R., 283, 316
Cuomo, Andrew, 284
Czechoslovakia, 247
Czolgosz, Leon F., 100

Davis, Gray, 287, 320
Davis, Jefferson, 44
dealers. *See* gun dealers
DeConcini, Dennis, 239
Dees-Thomases, Donna, 294
defense-of-liberty argument, 80
Delahanty, Thomas K., 220
Delfay, Robert, 284
democracy erosion theory, 300
Democrats: campaign platforms of, 212, 295; on
  conscription, 212; future considerations for,
  308; on gun control, 189–90, 246; for juvenile
  crime bill, 278; as minority in Congress, 256; for
  right to bear arms, 67
derringers, 80

Detroit riots, 179
Deukmejian, George, 221
Dick, Charles F., 101–2
Dickerson, C. R., 211
Dickinson, Charles, 45–46
Dillinger, John, 140, 141
Dingell, John D., 172, 213–14
District of Columbia, 133, 205
Doctors Against Handgun Injury, 322
doctrine of incorporation, 77, 93, 96–97
Dodd, Thomas J., 168–69, 171, 173–75, 179–81, 185
Dole, Robert J., 228, 266
domestic terrorism, 260
domestic violence offenders, 265
Donaldson, Sam, 292
Donovan, William J., 150
Douglas, William O., 194
draft evasion, in Civil War, 67
draft registration, 212, 221 (see also conscription)
Drain, James A., 103, 110–11
Dred Scott v. Sanford, 65
due process issues, 96, 112–13
dueling, 44–47
Dukakis, Michael, 199–200, 235–36
Dunblane, Scotland tragedy, 261–62
Duran, Francisco Martin, 256

Earp, Wyatt Berry Stapp, 82
Eastern Europe, 247
ecology groups, 166
economic depression, 120
Eddie Eagle program, 236–37
Edmunds-Tucker Act, 87
Edward VI, King of England, 9
Egypt, Mamluk military society, 8
Eighteenth Amendment, 120
Eisenhower, Dwight D., 155, 160, 164, 167
Eliot, Charles W., 95
Emergency Committee for Gun Control, 184–85, 197
Emerson, Timothy Joe, 316
Emery, Lucius, 113–14
Enfield rifles, 66
England. See Britain
entertainment industry, 278, 282 (see also film; television)
Europe: arms industry in, 95–96; Convention on the Control of the Acquisition and Possession of Firearms by Individuals, 206; early gun-control efforts, 8–10, 14–15; Eastern Europe gun violence, 247; firearms laws, 94–95; gun-control measures in, 48, 105–6; gun violence compared to America, 3–4; historical perspectives, 7–10; hunting privileges, 94; ownership restrictions, 91, 187

executive action, 249–50, 272–73, 290
extremists, 257–60

fast-draw syndrome, 166
FBI. See Federal Bureau of Investigation
Federal Aid in Wild Life Restoration Act, 145
Federal Bureau of Investigation: after 9/11, 316; alleviating fear of national police, 144; crime statistics of, 196; establishment of, 138; popularity of, 141; responsibilities of, 140–41; in Ruby Ridge siege, 258; specialized police powers of, 306; in Waco siege, 259
Federal Firearms Act, 147, 152, 162–63, 169, 186
federal government: anticrime program of, 144–45; criminal code of, 140; expanded authority of, 75–76; foreign arms sales by, 206, 214, 253; gun-regulation campaign of, 137–40, 142–49; and incorporation doctrine, 97; legitimacy of gun-control role, 148; negotiation with Smith & Wesson company, 283–85; and NRA, 102–3, 104, 131–32, 180–81; police power of, 140, 184; precedents for gun control, 76, 117, 120, 133–34; Prohibition enforcement performance, 128; shooting match subsidies by, 209; surplus firearms sold to NRA members, 131–32, 163–64, 174, 208–9, 223; weapons acquisition by, 99
Federal Lobbying Act, 180–81
federal systems, 303–4
Federalists, 32–34, 36
Feighan, Edward F., 231
Feinstein, Diane, 269, 271
felons: banned weapon access of, 256; Brady law effect on, 268; under Gun Control Act, 186; gun show access to weapons, 277; increased prison sentences for violations, 274
felony classification, 109
Ferri, Gian Luigi, 250, 282
Field and Stream magazine, 165
Fifteenth Amendment, 75
Fifth Amendment, 77
film: G-man movies, 141; gangster movies, 148; glorification of guns, 301–2; gun violence, 225, 270; marketing of violence, 282; Westerns, 148, 161
fines, 106, 107
fingerprinting, 144
firearms: under Consumer Product Safety Act, 252; identifying information requirements, 162–63; manufacturing improvements in, 47; military-style firearms, 246–48 (see also assault weapons); nationwide registration measures, 141; passions aroused by, 7–8, 12; portability of, 7; production in eighteenth century, 28; proliferation after WWII, 155–56; in Reconstruction South, 74–75; scholarly reasoning, 113–14;

firearms (*cont.*)
  sentiments after Civil War, 68–69; technological improvements in, 8, 10, 43, 58; theft as federal crime, 251; war's popularization of, 68
Firearms Act of 1938. *See* Federal Firearms Act
Firearms Owners' Protection Act, 229–30
Fish, Hamilton, Jr., 129
Fisher, Sidney George, 57
Floyd, Charles A. "Pretty Boy," 138, 141
Force Acts, 75–76
Ford, Gerald R.: assassination attempts on, 201; assumption of presidency, 200; Brady bill endorsement by, 242; in election debates, 204–5; on gun control, 200–201, 204; for international gun commerce, 203
Foster, Jodie, 215
founding fathers, 30, 31–32
Fourteenth Amendment, 73, 74, 75, 77, 96 (*see also* due process issues)
Fourth Amendment, 96
Fox, John J., 199
Fox, Steven, 282
Francis I, King of France, 9
Franklin, Benjamin, 44
Frederick, Karl T., 131–32, 134, 142, 146
Freedmen's Bureau, 71, 72–73
freedom, guns as symbol of, 211
Fries, John, 42
Fromme, Lynette Alice, 201
frontier (*see also* pioneers): and dueling, 46; myths of, 80, 148, 300; romantic portrayals of, 50–51, 98
Frye, Marquette, 176
Funders Collaborative for Gun Violence Prevention, 294
Furrow, Buford Oneal, 288

Gage, Thomas, 27–28
Gallagher, James, 108
gangsters: in films, 148; in Prohibition era, 125, 126–27; as stimulant for gun-control movement, 138–39, 140
Garfield, James A., 92
Garwood, William, 317
Gavett, Geoffrey S., 208–9
Gaynor, William J., 108
General Confederation of Women's Clubs, 143–44, 145
Gerry, Elbridge, 31–32, 34
Gingrich, Newt, 256
Glassen, Harold W., 181, 185
Glenn, John, 184, 197
Glock company, 284
Goetz, Bernhard H., 227
gold miners, 81
Golden, Andrew, 272

Golden, Dennis, 272
Goldman Fund, 281
Gompers, Samuel, 97
Gordon, Seth, 142
Gore, Albert A., Jr., 292, 293, 295, 296, 314
Gottlieb, Alan M., 222, 274, 283
Graham, Franklin, 293
Grant, Ulysses S., 68, 89
Grassley, Charles E., 227–28
Great Britain. *See* Britain
Greece, ownership restrictions, 187
Greenback Party, 92
Grey, Zane, 148
grievance killers, 250, 274
Guiteau, Charles J., 92
gun availability, in colonial era, 24
gun clubs, 98–99
gun collecting, 161
Gun Control Act (1968): attacks on, 204, 227–29; enforcement of, 190, 193; loopholes of, 192; passage of, 186–87, 188; repeal of provisions, 192
Gun Control, Registration and Licensing Act of 1971, 194
Gun Court Act (Jamaica), 210
Gun Crime Enforcement and Second Amendment Restoration Act, 262
gun culture, 61, 161
gun dealers: against assault-weapon ban, 239; Brady law requirements of, 251; control legislation on, 144, 186; falsification of records, 290; gun show masquerades as private sellers, 277; import laws circumvented by, 195; license fee increases on, 249; limits to number of, 250; lobbies against legislation, 142; restrictions eased on, 230; in school zones, 260
Gun Decontrol Act, 227
Gun Digest, 161
Gun in America, The (Kennett and Anderson), 5
gun lobby: against Brady bill, 241–43, 249–50; conclusions about, 299; confidence of, 222–24; contributions by, 181; against Control Act, 178; against Dodd bill, 175, 179–80; effectiveness of, 201; in foreign countries, 195–96; government allies of, 193, 208; and Gun Control Act, 193; and L. B. Johnson, 182, 190; membership in constituent organizations, 222; in Nixon era, 190; obligations to, 181–82; in product liability lawsuits, 271; spending power of, 200, 201, 222; vulnerability of, 267
gun merchants, 253
Gun Owners Action League, 199, 287
Gun Owners of America, 185, 304
gun production, in colonial era, 24
gun shows, 161, 277, 278, 286
gun tracing, 207, 214
Gun Week, 179–80

gun-buyback programs, 289
gun-control movement: activism of, 189, 190, 197–
    200; conclusions about, 305–7; crusades of,
    107–8; ignored by government, 167; internal dis-
    sent in, 209; after Kennedy assassination, 172–
    73, 174; lobbies for legislation, 143–44; local
    campaigns of, 123–24, 268; in Massachusetts,
    199–200; political influence of, 250; on recre-
    ational shooting, 165–66; revival in 1920s, 120;
    spending of, 281; state activity of, 181; stimu-
    lants for, 138–39, 140; support from national
    journals, 126; and television documentaries,
    270; on Watts riot, 177; in West, 85
gunfighter model, 81–83, 162
Gun-Free School Zones Act, 260–61
Gun-Free Schools Act, 261
gunpowder, policing of, 55
gunrunning, 97
Guns & Ammo, 180, 193
Guns and Violence, 313
Guzik, Jack, 129

Hall, John H., 43
Hamilton, Alexander, 30–31, 41, 45
Hamilton, Thomas, 261–62
Hamilton v. Accu-Tek, 282
Handgun Control, Inc.: about, 209; against armor-
    piercing bullets, 219; Assault Weapon Control
    Act lawsuit of, 269; and Brady bill, 231, 241, 242,
    250–51; Sarah Brady in, 228–29, 241; budget of,
    222; on G. W. Bush, 294; on divided public
    opinion, 222; foundation of, 198–99; member-
    ship of, 241; merge with MMMF, 314; militancy
    of, 230
Handgun Initiative, 221–22, 223
handguns: Colt's popularization of, 60; juvenile
    ownership of, 255, 261; mass production of,
    79–80; NRA defense of, 157; public opinion on,
    242; sales slumps of, 225–26; social criticism of,
    95; violent use of, 55–56
Haney, John Lee, 317
Haney v. United States, 317
Hanley-Fake firearms bill, 132, 134
Harmar, Josiah, 39
Harper's Ferry arsenal, 40, 66
Harrington, James, 11, 300
Harris, Eric D., 275–76
Harshbarger, Scott, 287
Hatch, Orrin G., 285
hate-mongers, 288
Hauptman, Bruno R., 144
Hayes, Rutherford B., 85
Hennings, Thomas C., Jr., 164–65, 168
Henry, Patrick, 33
Henry II, King of England, 10
Henry IV, King of England, 9

Henry VIII, King of England, 9
heritage-belief, 299–300
Heston, Charlton, 269–70, 276, 291–92, 295
Hickenlooper, Bourke B., 172
Hickman, Douglas Ray, 265
Hickman, Ray, 286
Hickman v. Block, 265
Hickock, James Butler "Wild Bill," 82
hidden serial numbers, 284
Hinckley, John W., Jr., 215, 220
historical perspective: colonial America, 3–5; on
    frontier gun violence, 85–86; revisionist views,
    25, 82–83; traditionalist views, 25
Hobbies magazine, 161
Hofstadter, Richard, 4
Hogg, James Stephen, 98
Holliday, John Henry "Doc," 82
Holt, George C., 108
Holton, James H., 163
homicide rates: in Canada, 248; comparison of
    countries, 224; drop in 1908s, 243; in South Af-
    rica, 246; in Soviet Union, 247
Hoover, Herbert C., 130, 134
Hoover, J. Edgar, 138–39, 141
Horbach v. State of Texas, 84
Hostettler, John N., 285
House of Representatives, gun attack in, 160
Howard, John, 263
Howe, Louis McHenry, 138–39
Howell, Vernon Wayne (aka Koresh), 258
Huberty, James Oliver, 226
Huddleston, George, 129
Hughes, Richard J., 180
human rights, 206
humane movement, 101
humor, 192
Humphrey, Hubert H., 189
hunting accidents, 166

Ileto, Joseph, 288
imports: of cheap guns, 155–56, 163–64, 168; cir-
    cumvention of laws, 195; of foreign weapons,
    163–64, 168, 250, 271–73; of military rifles, 186;
    restrictions on, 39, 42, 186; of Saturday night
    specials, 186; of semiautomatic guns, 238–39
incarceration rates, 208
incorporation, doctrine of, 77, 93, 96–97
Indian Intercourse Act, 50
Indians: citizen-soldiers against, 28; defense
    against, 17, 18; gun trafficking with, 18, 19–20,
    21, 50; militias against, 30; self-defense in West,
    84–85; tribal warfare among, 50
individual rights, 97, 300, 302
instant background checks, 274
Institute for Legislative Action, 201
interchangeable gun parts, 47, 58

Internal Revenue Service, 141, 162–63
international gun commerce, 191–92, 203–4, 206, 267, 274
International Security Assistance and Arms Export Control Act, 203
interstate commerce: attempted handgun ban, 122; L. B. Johnson's regulation proposals, 178; legislation to restrict, 129–30, 131; organized crime investigation, 158–59; regulatory proposals, 142; F. D. Roosevelt as proponent, 134
Israel, ownership restrictions, 187
Italy, macho approach to guns, 196

Jackson, Andrew, 44, 45–46, 48–49, 50
Jackson, Rachel, 45
Jackson, Robert H., 151
James, Frank, 82
James, Jesse, 82
James II, King of England, 13, 14
Japan: early gun-control efforts, 9–10; gun crime virtually nonexistent, 224; ownership restrictions, 187–88; rise in crime, 209; suicides in, 306
Jefferson, Thomas, 44
Jerome, William T., 107
Johnson, Andrew, 71, 72–74
Johnson, Lyndon B.: crime bill of, 175, 181, 183–84, 185; for Dodd legislation, 171, 174; federal controls of, 190–91; Gun Control Act signed by, 186; and gun lobby, 182, 190; interstate gun trafficking request of, 178, 180; mentioned, 249; NRA on, 187; prophesy of, 308; use of presidential clout, 191; and Vietnam War, 182
Johnson, Mitchell, 272
Jones, Albert S., 99
Jonesboro Practical Pistol Shooters Association, 272
Jordan, W. Hamilton, 205
Joseph Patsone v. Commonwealth, 112–13
journalists. See media
Judson, Edward Z. C., 61
juvenile delinquency, 162, 164–65, 168
juvenile gun violence, 261, 268–69, 277–78 (see also school shootings; youth crime)

Kalodimos v. Village of Morton Grove, 225
Kansas City massacre, 138
Katzenbach, Nicholas, 176
Keenan, Joseph B., 146
Kefauver, Estes, 158–59
Kelley, Olen J., 232, 271
Kelley v. R. G. Industries, 232
Kennedy, Edward M., 194, 231
Kennedy, John F., 160, 164, 167, 171, 205
Kennedy, Robert F., 167, 176, 183, 253
Kennesaw, Georgia ordinance, 217
Kennett, Lee, 5

kidnapping laws, 133–34, 139, 140
King, Martin Luther, Jr., 173, 175, 182–83
King, Rodney, 244–45
King, William A., 139–40
King Philip's War, 20
Kinkel, Kipland P., 273
Klebold, Dylan B., 275–76
Knights of the White Camelia, 73
Knox, Henry, 40, 41
Knox, Neal, 179–80, 206, 219
Koop, C. Everett, 255
Korean War, 160
Koresh, David, 258–59
Krag-Jorgenson rifle, 99
Ku Klux Klan, 73–75, 175, 209
Ku Klux Klan Act, 76

labor unions, 97–98, 184
LaGioia, Geoffrey, 216
LaPierre, Wayne R., 229, 260, 289, 292, 295, 313, 316, 318
Latin America, gun violence in, 247–48
Lauchli, Rick, 178
Lautenberg, Frank, 257
Lautman, Barbara, 233
Law and Order Leagues, 91
law enforcement (see also police): commissions on, 130, 176, 178, 184; by gunfighters, 82; local gun regulations, 91, 94, 100; professionalization of, 101; responsibility for, 53–56; in Wild West, 83–85
Lawrence, Richard, 50
Layton, Frank, 149
Lebrun, George P., 108–9, 110
Lee, Henry "Light Horse Harry," 41
Lee, Robert E., 68
left-wing radicals, 177
legislation (see also specific acts): against armor-piercing bullets, 219–20; and arms industry, 95, 142, 144, 148; against assault weapons, 237–40, 245, 254–56; against blacks, 21–22; California voter initiative, 221–22; colonial restrictions, 18, 19–20, 21–22; against concealed weapons, 51–52, 107, 121; against dueling, 46–47; easing gun access, 177; England's early restrictions, 11–13, 14; Europe's early restrictions, 14–15; expansion of federal government authority, 75–76; for federal trial of gun cases, 285; and gun lobby, 132, 167; on gun shows, 286; on handguns, 206–7, 232–33, 287; importation/exportation restrictions, 39, 42; under L. B. Johnson, 171–73, 174–76, 178–88; juvenile crime bill, 273, 278, 281; lobbies against, 142–43; municipality laws, 216–17; overruling Supreme Court decisions, 230; Parliamentary firearms embargo, 27–28; against polygamy, 86–87; presidential leader-

ship in, 304, 307; product safety law, 193, 252; with racist aims, 122; religious regulations, 22–23; Republican blockage of, 285; under F. D. Roosevelt, 138, 139–41, 142–49; "shall issue" laws, 230–31; "shoot the carjacker" law, 269; state laws, 75, 108–10, 122–23, 132, 199–200; against target-shooting clubs, 62; three-strikes law, 226–27; vetoes of gun-control measures, 270–71

legislation by judiciary, 275

Leisler, Jacob, 21

Leonardo da Vinci, 7

Lewis v. United States, 211–12

liberty, 42, 80

license fees, 251

Lincoln, Abraham, 65, 68, 71, 86–87

Lindbergh, Anne Morrow, 133

Lindbergh, Charles A., 133

Lindbergh law, 133–34, 139, 140

Lindsay, John V., 173

literature: cowboy novels, 148; fiction glorification of guns, 301–2; government study of gun literature, 208; research articles, 5–6; on Wild West, 81–82, 84

Liuzzo, Viola Gregg, 175

lobbying (*see also* gun lobby): of arms industry, 142, 148; by gun-control movement, 143–44; for handgun control, 198–99; on National Firearms Act, 146–47; of National Rifle Association, 143, 146; registration for, 180–81

Lopez, Alfonso, Jr., 260–61

López Portillo, José, 213

Lorcin Engineering, 271

Louis XIV, King of France, 10

Louis Philippe, King of France, 48

Lungren, Dan, 269

Lusitania, 115

McAdoo, William G., 110, 127

McCarthy, Carolyn, 294, 314

McClure, James A., 227–28

McClure-Volkmer bill, 227–30

Machiavelli, Niccolò, 9

machine guns: Colt as sole manufacturer, 143; control legislation on, 144; invention of, 126–27; Minutemen caches of, 178; ownership restrictions on, 145; registration proposals for, 141; in St. Valentine's Day massacre, 129; as stimulant for gun-control movement, 138–39

Mack, Richard, 267–68

McKinley, William, 100

Macready, William, 61

McVeigh, Timothy J., 260

Madison, James, 31, 32, 34, 36

magazines (*see also* specific magazines): on positive aspects of gun keeping, 161; propaganda of, 165, 166; pulp magazines, 82; weapon advertising in, 282

Magnuson, Warren D., 169, 172, 185

mail-order guns, 93, 124–26, 127, 168, 174–75

Malcom, Joyce Lee, 313

Malcolm X, 173

Malvo, Lee Boyd, 319

Mansfield, Mike, 185

Marcos, Ferdinand E., 195, 240

Marino, Ralph J., 208

marksmanship: American Legion support of, 146–47; church promotion of, 90; government support of, 89, 107, 115–16, 131–32, 207, 243; NRA promotion of, 89, 107, 116, 131–32, 155; Roosevelt's support of, 101; taught in educational institutions, 95

Maryland Committee Against the Gun Ban, 232–33

Mason, George, 31–32

Massachusetts Emigrant Aid Company, 64

Massachusetts, gun-control movement, 199–200

massacres (*see also* school shootings): in Dunblane, Scotland, 262–63; in Kansas City, 138; in Louisville, Kentucky, 240; in San Francisco, 250; in San Ysidro, California, 226; in West Anaheim, California, 283; by white supremacists, 288

Masterson, William Barclay "Bat," 82

mayors conference, 283

media: in antihandgun crusade, 121; on cheap handguns, 169; demand for regulation, 93; exploitation of violence, 301–2; on gun violence, 145, 252; on rise in crime, 129; taxes urged by, 105

mental impairment, 186

Metaska, Tanya, 268, 273

Metzenbaum, Howard M., 231, 249, 253

Mexican War, 58–60

Mexico, 247

Mfume, Kweisi, 275

militant blacks, 173, 177, 179, 198

militarists vs. pacifists, 114–15

military conscription. *See* conscription

military-style firearms, 246–48 (*see also* assault weapons)

militia act of 1862, 65

Militia of Montana, 259–60

militias (*see also* National Guard; paramilitary organizations): absent at Bill of Rights enactment, 36; arms shortages in, 41; in Article 1 of Constitution, 35; and blacks, 22, 75; under Calling Forth Act, 40; in colonial rebellion, 27–28; constitutional debate over, 32–37; declining rationale for, 49; early controversy over, 10–15, 20–21; evasion of service in, 62; fabled qualities of, 29–30; against Indians, 30; last vestiges of old system, 139; local law enforcement by, 53;

militias (*cont.*)
manpower shortages, 40–41; National Guard incorporation of, 90, 102; origins of, 17–19; poor performance in combat duty, 22, 29, 43; in post–Civil War era, 80; in Reconstruction South, 74–75; recruitment problems of, 43–44; against rioters, 57–58, 61; Supreme Court interpretation of, 149; under Uniform Militia Act, 39–40; unions against, 97–98; as upper-class social clubs, 48; in Whiskey Rebellion, 41

Miller, Franklin P., 96
Miller, Jack, 149
Miller, John F., 124, 127
Miller v. Texas, 96
Million Mom March, 294–95, 314
Milton S. Eisenhower Foundation, 291
minutemen, 28
Minutemen of America, 177, 178, 209
Mitchell, George D., 255
Mitchell, William D., 134
Montana Militia, 259–60
Montluc, Blaise de, 8
Moore, Sara Jane, 201
Moran, George "Bugs," 129
Morano, Albert P., 164
Mormons, 86–87
Morrill, Justin S., 86
mortars, 186
Morton Grove case, 216–17, 221, 223, 224–25
motion pictures. *See* film
movies. *See* film
Moynihan, Daniel Patrick, 219
Muhammad, John Allen, 319
Mutual Security Act, 160
Myrdal, Gunnar, 183

National Anti-Weapons Society, 133, 197
National Association for the Advancement of Colored People, 275
National Board for the Promotion of Rifle Practice, 102, 174, 207
National Center for Injury Prevention and Control, 257
National Coalition to Ban Handguns, 197, 208–9, 216
National Commission on Law Observance and Enforcement, 130
National Commission on Product Safety, 193
National Committee for the Control of Weapons, 156, 171–72
National Council for a Responsible Firearms Policy, 184, 197
National Crime Commission, 132, 134, 145
National Defense Act, 115, 117
National Firearms Act, 144, 145, 146–47, 149
National Guard: armories of, 90; authority to deploy abroad, 103; desertions from, 115; federalization of, 92, 101–2, 149; militias incorporated into, 62, 90, 102; under National Defense Act, 115; in NRA formation, 89; as organized component of army, 139; origin of, 43; poor training of, 113, 114; popular opposition to, 97; in race riots, 183; Southern states' use of, 91; in Spanish-American War, 99; against strikers, 97–98, 113; in Watts riot, 177; WWII training of, 150–51

National Guard Association, 90–91
National Institute of Justice, 208
National Prohibition Act, 120
National Rifle Association: allies of, 204, 213, 223; and arms industry, 142; against BATF, 207, 211, 213–14; boasts of, 229; budget of, 222, 229; California membership of, 221; conclusions about, 304; conflicting goals within, 123; conservation agenda of, 146; critics of, 180, 196; denial of lobbying activities, 163, 181; diversity of membership, 156–57; effectiveness of, 201; federal government cooperation with, 102–3, 104, 131–32; formation of, 89; future considerations for, 308; growth of, 99–100, 103, 172, 318; gun-control measures approved by, 276; handgun defense by, 157; internal dissent in, 205–6; against IRS, 163; in local control struggles, 110–11; membership claims of, 211, 293; membership loss of, 267; for military preparedness, 114; mobilization of membership, 286; on New Deal legislation, 141–42; nonmilitary image adopted by, 157; opponents of, 134, 255, 291–92; Person of the Year awards, 216, 236; picketing against, 183; political influence of, 107, 213, 222, 293, 320; position after Columbine tragedy, 276; position after Kennedy assassination, 172; praise for, 155; prominent members of, 100, 111, 166–67, 172, 212; publications of, 116; in *Quilici v. Village of Morton Grove*, 216; against registration, 156, 185–86; and "shall issue" laws, 230–31; slander of federal agents, 260; as special-interest group, 103, 132; surveys conducted by, 198; women admitted to, 103

National Shooting Sports Foundation, 165, 284
National Television Violence Study, 270
National Wildlife Federation, 145
Native Americans. *See* Indians
NATO, allies armed by, 203
Navegar, Inc., 282–83
Nelson, "Baby Face," 141
New Deal era, 137
New England Minutemen, 178
New York City: crime in, 63, 131; gun-control laws of, 208; gun ownership in, 105; restrictions in, 107–10; riots in, 57, 61, 67
New York City Federation of Women's Clubs, 147
New York state, weak legislation in, 132

New Zealand, ownership restrictions, 187
newspapers. *See* media
Nichols, Frank C., 143
Nichols, Terry L., 260
Nigeria, gun availability in, 195
Nineteenth Amendment, 304
Nixon, Richard M.: BATF moved to Treasury by, 193; Brady bill endorsement by, 242; controls platform of, 189–90; denial of gun lobby affiliation, 194–95; gun supporters for, 193; as NRA member, 167; NRA support of, 196; resignation of, 197, 200; on Saturday night specials, 194–95; Vietnam War plans of, 191–92
Nordquist, Grover, 293
North, Simeon, 42
Norwich Pistol Company, 90
NRA. *See* National Rifle Association

O'Donnell, Rosie, 294
Oklahoma City bombing, 260
Olin Mathieson Corporation, 177
Olson, Theodore B., 318, 322
Olympic rifle team, 103–4
Omnibus Crime Control and Safe Streets Act, 184
Omnibus Drug Initiative Act, 231
Orth, Franklin, 205
Oswald, Lee Harvey, 171
ownership restrictions, 91, 145, 187–88, 276

pacifists vs. militarists, 114–15
Paine, Thomas, 44
Pakistan, 246
paramilitary organizations, 259–60
Parents magazine, 145
Parks, Rosa, 166
patent-arms makers, 47
Patron Saint of Handgunners nomination, 236
Patsone, Joseph, 112
Peel, Robert, 54
People v. Camperlingo, 124
People vs. Handguns, 199
percussion-cap guns, 58
percussion powder, invention of, 42
Pershing, John J., 115
Pertschuk, Mark, 318
Philip, Duke of Edinburgh, 262
Philippine Practical Shooting Association, 240
Philippines: gun control in, 117; gunless society campaign, 240; martial law in, 195
Phillips, Joe, 257
pioneers, 51, 64 (*see also* frontier)
Pistolero magazine, 215–16
Pittman-Robertson Act, 145
plastic guns, 232, 235, 236
pocket pistols, 80
police: arming of, 53–54, 63–64, 93–94; attitudes toward, 62; against blacks, 179; British establishment of, 54–55; establishment of police forces, 56–58, 62–63, 67; expanded powers of, 109–10; fear of, 55; firepower increases for, 266; in national gun-regulation campaign, 138; in nineteenth-century California, 81; resistance to federalized power, 254; sale of used guns, 288; Supreme Court test of authority, 194; in Watts riot, 177
political contributions, 181, 293
political power, of guns, 75
political survival, 305
Polk, James K., 58
Polydore Virgil, 8
polygamy, 86–87
Porter, William T., 49
posse comitatus, 53
posse comitatus act, 92
Possenti, Gabriel, 236
presidential campaigns: Bush vs. Clinton, 245–46; Bush vs. Dukakis, 235–36; Carter vs. Ford, 204–5; Carter vs. Reagan, 212–13; Clinton vs. Dole, 265–66; Gore vs. Bush, 292–93, 294, 295–96, 308
Presser, Herman, 92–93
Presser v. Illinois, 92–93, 96
Printz, Jay, 267–68
Printz v. United States, 267–68
Product Liability Fairness Act, 271
product liability lawsuits, 220, 232–33, 271, 274–75
product safety law, 193, 252
profit, from gun making, 59
Progressive era politics, 100–101
Prohibition, 120, 303
Proposition 15, California, 221–22, 223
prosecution rates, 289, 290
Protection of Lawful Commerce in Arms Act, 323
public health, 244
public opinion: on acceptance of guns, 148; on Brady bill, 249; with Clinton, 250; conclusions about, 306; divided on tough controls, 222; on entertainment industry violence, 270; on federal legislation, 171–72, 174, 224, 253; first Gallup poll on gun control, 147; on gun-control measures, 267; on handgun bans, 242; during presidential campaign of 2000, 292; on private gun ownership, 165, 198; on registration, 185, 198, 242; on Second Amendment modification, 304; tolerance of civilian gun violence, 159; women's attitudes, 276, 279, 301
pulp magazines, 82
Purdy, Patrick E., 237

Quasi-War, 42
Quayle, Dan, 277

quick-draw faddists, 165–66
Quilici v. Village of Morton Grove, 216
Quilici, Victor D., 216

race riots, 73, 176–77, 179, 183
racial prejudice, 21
Radical Republicans, 74, 77
Randolph, Edmund, 33
Randolph, John, 46
ransom laws, 134
Ray, James Earl, 182–83
Raymond, Henry J., 72
Reagan, Nancy, 242
Reagan, Ronald: admiration for guns, 212–13; assassination attempt on, 215–16; BATF dissolution plans of, 214; Brady bill endorsement by,
    242; Carter's defeat by, 213; on conscription,
    220–21; cooperation with NRA, 223–24; endorsement of Firearms Owners' Protection Act,
    229; inconsistency of, 224; for international gun
    commerce, 214; as lifetime NRA member, 212,
    213; for limited gun restrictions, 235, 238;
    macho image of, 213; on plastic-gun issue, 236;
    praised by progun faction, 215–16
rebellion: in Boston Harbor, 27; in colonial
    America, 27–30; Fries against federal taxes, 42;
    Shays Rebellion, 30–31; Whiskey Rebellion,
    40–41
Reckord, Milton A., 141–42, 143
Reconstruction, 71–79
Reconstruction Act, 74
recreational shooting, 165–66
registration proposals, 141, 156, 185, 206–7
Regulators, 23, 30
Rehnquist, William H., 254
Reinhardt, Stephen, 322
religious organizations, call for restrictions, 273–74
religious regulations, 22–23
Remington company, 60, 79, 117–18, 153
Remington, Eliphalet, II, 59
Reno, Janet, 278, 290
repeating rifles, 66
Republicans: on assault weapon legislation, 255;
    backlash over Columbine shootings, 278; campaign platforms of, 212, 295; and Clinton, 253–
    54, 255; on conscription, 212; on constitutional
    rights, 173; future considerations for, 308; on
    gun control, 190, 246; for juvenile crime bill,
    278; legislation blocked by, 285; majority in
    Congress, 256; on Reconstruction, 71–72; repeal
    of gun-control measures, 262; for right to bear
    arms, 64–65; Second Amendment affirmation
    resolution of, 295; tough crime stance of,
    226–27
restrictions: in colonial America, 17–24; on manufacture of specified guns, 139; in New York City,

107–10; on ownership, 91, 145, 187–88, 276; religious organizations calling for, 273–74; on sales
    to criminals and mentally impaired, 186
Revolutionary War, 27–30
Reynolds v. United States, 87
R. G. Industries, 220, 232
Richard and Rhoda Goldman Fund, 281
rifle clubs, in Reconstruction South, 78
Right to Bear Arms, The, 313
right to bear arms: and Articles of Confederation,
    29; for blacks, 72–73; Democrats on, 67, 83; denied to blacks, 75; and disdain of militias, 92;
    and original Constitution, 33; as quintessentially individual right, 97; Republicans on, 64–
    65, 83; scholarly dispute over, 24–25; in
    Supreme Court, 77–78
right-wing radicals, 178
riots (*see also* race riots): in Chicago, 91; against
    conscription, 67–68; in Los Angeles, 244–45;
    militias against, 57–58, 61; in New York City, 57,
    61, 67; in Philadelphia, 56–57; in St. Louis, 63
Robbins and Lawrence company, 60
Roberti, David A., 239
Robert-Roos Assault Weapons Act, 239
Robinson, Kayne, 294, 295
Rockefeller, John D., Jr., 108
Rockefeller, Nelson, 165
Rodino, Peter W., 228, 231
Rogers, Roy, 221
Rohm Gesellschaft, 232
Rolland, Kayla, 291
Roos, Michael, 239
Roosevelt, Franklin D.: assassination attempt on,
    134–35; on conscription, 150–51; disengagement with gun control, 146; federalism of, 305;
    as gun-control advocate, 137–38, 148; on handguns, 157; mentioned, 249; and National Firearms Act, 144
Roosevelt, Theodore, 99, 100–101, 102, 104, 111–
    12, 114
Root, Elihu, 101, 102, 103
Rouse, Jamie, 261
Ruark, Robert, 167
Rubey, Thomas L., 127
Ruby Ridge siege, 258
Ruehlman, Robert, 283
Ruger, Bill, 216
Runyan, Joe, 158
Russia, 247

safety warnings, 287
St. Clair, Arthur, 39
St. Valentine's Day massacre, 129
Salina v. Blakesly, 102
Saturday night specials: about, 168; in Brady law,
    251; under consumer protection laws, 287; Ford

on, 200, 204; import restrictions on, 186; Maryland ban on, 232; Nixon on, 194–95; NRA support of ban, 253; in product liability lawsuits, 271

sawed-off shotguns, 144

scare tactics, 143, 254

Schiller, Stephen A., 208

school shootings: Conyers, Georgia, 281; Dunblane, Scotland, 261–62; Edinboro, Pennsylvania, 273; Jonesboro, Arkansas, 272; Littleton, Colorado, 275–76; Lynville, Tennessee, 261; Mount Morris Township, Michigan, 291; Pearl, Mississippi, 272; San Antonio, Texas, 260–61; Springfield, Oregon, 273; Stockton, California, 237; West Paducah, Kentucky, 272

schools, marksmanship taught in, 95

Schrank, John N., 111–12

Schumer, Charles E., 249, 250, 254, 268

Scott, Winfield, 46, 59

Seale, Bobby, 179

Sears and Roebuck Company, 125

Second Amendment: and blacks, 72–73, 78; in circuit courts, 223, 265; citations of, 64; conclusions about, 302–3; doctrine of incorporation, 77, 93, 96–97; in federal courts, 74, 152, 203–4, 216–17, 236; federal regulation barred by, 112; initial debate over, 34–35; interpretations of, 35–37, 265, 312–15; modification proposals for, 304–5; NRA defense of, 269; and paramilitary organizations, 259; perceptions of, 173, 176; public reverence for, 174; and Reconstruction South, 74–75; as regulation obstacle, 148; Republicans on, 295; standard model for interpretation, 5; in state courts, 102, 124, 224–25; Supreme Court interpretations of, 92–93, 96, 149, 204, 211–12

Second Amendment Foundation, 216, 222, 283

Second Amendment Sisters, 294–95

selective service, 150 (see also conscription)

Selective Service Act of 1917, 116

Selective Service Act of 1948, 159–60

Selective Training and Service Act, 150

self-defense theory, 84, 156, 177, 227, 300–301

semiautomatic rifles. See assault weapons

September 11, 2001, 317

serial numbers, 162, 284, 287

Seven Years' War, 22

Shays, Christopher, 287

Shays, Daniel, 30–31

Shays Rebellion, 30–31

Shields, John K., 122

Shields, Nelson T. "Pete," 198, 228

Shields, Nick, 198

Shockley, Richard, 286

shooting clubs, 49–50, 142–43

Shooting Straight, 313

Shooting Times magazine, 166

shotguns, 144

Sikes, Robert L., 164, 172

silencers, 152

Sirhan, Sirhan Bishara, 183

Skinner, John Stuart, 49

slavery controversy, and gun violence, 64–65

slaves, police surveillance of, 53–54

small-arms makers, against imports, 163–64

smart-gun technology, 290

Smith, Benjamin N., 288

Smith, Lamar S., 250

Smith & Wesson company, 60, 153, 199, 283–85

smoothbore muskets, 66

smuggling, 214

snipers, 180

Snyder, John M., 228, 236

social regulation, 109

Society for the Prevention of Cruelty to Animals, 101

Solomon, Thomas J., 281

Sonzinsky v. United States, 146

Soros, George, 294

South: National Guard used to quell violence, 91; popular perceptions of violence in, 78–79; during Reconstruction, 72–79; rejection of Fourteenth Amendment, 74

South Africa, 246–47

Soviet Union, 191, 247

Sowyrda, Kevin, 287

Spanish-American War, 99, 130

spending: against Brady bill, 232, 242; by gun-control movement, 281; by gun lobby, 200, 201, 202; against Handgun Control, Inc., 229; during presidential campaigns, 295; against product liability lawsuits, 233; on Second Amendment defense, 269

Spitzer, Robert J., 313

Sporborg, Mrs. William D., 145

sport: alliance of sportsmen's clubs, 199; dueling as, 45; enthusiasts on legislation, 142–43; National Shooting Sports Foundation, 165; shooting clubs, 49–50

sport shooting, criticism of, 92

Sporting Arms and Ammunition Manufacturers Association, 142

sporting guns, 80, 256

Springfield armory, 47

Springfield rifles, 66

state governments: frontier guns provided by, 84; gun-control movement lobbies of, 181; handgun regulations in, 126; inconsistent legislation of, 132; ineffectiveness of gun-control laws, 208; interstate law conflicts, 122–23; legislation by, 106–7, 149, 275; National Guard Association formation by, 90–91; NRA-sponsored legislation

state governments (*cont.*)
in, 286; with permits required, 168; regulations on sales and ownership, 107; repeals of firearms registration, 128; "shall issue" laws, 230–31; Sullivan law ripple effect on, 110–11; voter initiatives, 221–22

State v. Buzzard, 56

State v. Newsom, 56

states' rights, 77–78, 128, 130, 142, 261

statistics: American gun ownership, 105, 257; crime in Chicago, 121; crime in nineteenth century, 55; decline in crime rates, 290; by FBI on crime, 196; on firearms-related deaths, 273; gun crime in L. B. Johnson era, 181; homicide rates, 224; New York City gun ownership, 105

Stone, Harlan F., 146

STOP (Steps to Prevent Firearm Injury), 255

Story, Joseph, 48

strikers, in armed conflict, 91, 97–98, 113

Strong, George Templeton, 63

Stuyvesant, Peter, 19

submachine guns. *See* machine guns

Sudbay, Joe, 293

suffrage, for blacks, 71, 73

Sugarmann, Josh, 307

suicide, 244, 306

suicide rates, 167, 188

Sullivan, Timothy D. "Big Tim," 108–10

Sumner, Charles, 64

Sumners, Hatton W., 144

Supreme Court: commerce clause invoked in, 261; conservatism of Rehnquist court, 254; decisions overruled by legislation, 230; on due process clause, 112–13; on federal firearms laws, 146; in *Miller v. Texas*, 96; on National Firearms Act, 149; petitions dismissed by, 225, 283; on police authority, 194; under Rehnquist, 261; on right to bear arms, 77–78; Second Amendment interpretations of, 92–93, 149, 204, 211–12; Tenth Amendment decision of, 267–68; on validity of federal laws, 149

Suter, Edgar, 257

Swain, William, 81

Switzerland, gun regulation, 210

Taft, William H., 111

tamper-resistant serial numbers, 287

Taney, Roger B., 65

target-shooting clubs, 49, 61–62

taxation, 105, 106

Taylor, Zachary, 59

teenagers, and handgun crime, 243–44

television: glorification of guns, 301–2; gun violence, 161, 225, 270; and Kennedy assassination, 171; PBS documentary on gun violence, 270; on school shootings, 237

Tenth Amendment, 267–68

terrorism, 206

Third World firearms availability, 246–48

Thirteenth Amendment, 72, 304

Thompson, John R., 121

Thompson, John T., 126

Thompson, Uly O., 135

Thorensen, William E., III, 178

three-strikes law, 226–27

tobacco campaign parallel, 307

Tommy guns, 126–27 (*see also* machine guns)

Torresola, Griselio, 159

Torricelli, Robert, 229

Torrio, John, 125

tort law. *See* product liability lawsuits

Tot, Frank, 152

Touhy, Roger, 125

toy-gun craze, 167

Toyotomi Hideyoshi, 10

trap-shooting, 90

Treasury Department, in gun law enforcement, 117

Trenchard, John, 14–15

trigger locks, 284, 286–87

Truman, Harry S., 155, 159–60

Tucker, St. George, 42

Tumulty, Joseph, 115

Twenty-first Amendment, 304

Tydings, Joseph D., 183, 186, 201

ubiquity of guns: in colonial America, 17; vs. rarity, 25

underground markets, 277

Undetectable Firearms Act, 236

Uniform Firearms Act, 132, 137, 232

Uniform Militia Act, 39–40, 43

Uniform Pistol Act, 132

unions. *See* labor unions

United Mine Workers, 113

United Nations, 304

United States: editorial opinions, 183; gun ownership statistics, 95; gun violence compared to Europe, 3–4; highest crime rate in world, 210; historical perspective, 3–5; as homicide rate leader, 224; insurrection against, 30–31; as leader in gun manufacturing, 60; surplus arms sales by, 191; world arms supply by, 191, 203, 246, 253; in WWI, 116

United States Conference of Mayors, 283

United States Revolver Association, 122, 131

United States v. Cruikshank, 77, 93, 96

United States v. Emerson, 316

United States v. Lopez, 261

United States v. Miller, 149

United States v. Nelson, 236

United States v. Tot, 152

United States v. Warin, 203–4
Universal Military and Training Service Act, 160
universal military training, 114–15

Van Newkirk, Charles, 158
veterans, 80, 120, 155
video games, 270, 282
Vietnam War, 173, 182, 191–92, 196, 197
vigilantism: in colonial America, 23–24; Law and Order Leagues, 91; in nineteenth-century California, 81, in Reconstruction South, 78–79
violence: celebration of, 278; stimulated by guns, 210
Violence Against Women Act, 316
Violence Policy Center, The, 315, 317, 322
Violent Crime Control and Law Enforcement Act, 255–56
Virginia House of Burgesses, 18
virility, 7, 45, 301
Volkmer, Harold L., 227, 266
Volstead Act, 120

Waco siege, 258–59
Wagner, Robert F., 165
waiting periods, 132, 251, 287
Wallace, George, 194
Wannamaker, John, 108
"war on terrorism," 316
war revenue act of 1919, 117
Warin, Francis J., 203–4
Warner, Thomas, 58
Washington, George, 28–31, 32, 39, 41
Watts riot, 176–77
Weaver, Randall, 258
Weaver, Samuel, 258
Weaver, Vicki, 258
Webster, Daniel, 13
Weigley, Russell, 66
Weiss, Hymie, 127
Wesbecker, Joseph T., 240
West: arming of emigrants, 80–81; emigration to, 83; in literature, 81–82; revisionist history, 82–83
Weston, J. Allen, 144–45
Weston, Russell Eugene, Jr., 274
Whigs, 46–47, 56, 57

Whiskey Rebellion, 40–41
White House, shots fired at, 256
White League, 77
white supremacists, 73–75, 76–77, 258, 288
Whitman, Charles J., 180
Whitney, Eli, 42
Whitney, Eli, Jr., 59
Wickersham, George W., 130
Wigfall, Louis T., 46
Wild West, 80–86
Wildlife Management Institute, 145
wildlife organizations, 142–43
Wiley, Alexander, 156
William of Orange, 13, 14
Williams, Willie L., 266
Wills, Garry, 5
Wilson, John Lyde, 46
Wilson, Pete, 270–71
Wilson, Woodrow, 113, 114–15, 116–17, 120
Winchester company: after Mexican War, 60; exempted from federal penalties, 177; in lean times, 116, 117–18; political clout of, 131–32; record production by, 157
Wingate, George W., 89, 99–100
Wister, Owen, 148
women: for gun-control measures, 276, 279, 292, 301, market focus on, 225–26; in NRA, 103
Women Against Gun Violence, 268
Wood, Leonard, 114
Woodham, Luke, 272
World War I, 113–18
World War II: civilian gun registration plan, 151; conscription in U.S., 150–51; Europe's entry into, 149–50; U.S. entry into, 152
Wurst, Andrew, 273

xenophobia, 107

Yarborough, Ralph, 173
Yardley, Michael, 262
Yasushi Hara, 188
Young, Brigham, 86
youth crime, 243–44, 245, 261

Zangara, Giuseppe, 135
Zebra Killers, 198